#mylifeasawoman

Sponsored By

Confessions of the Professions

NOTETOSERVICES

Copyright © 2020 Confessions of the Professions NoteToServices, LLC.

ISBN: 978-0-578-75783-4

ASIN: B08GZK2MRG

The claims that any of the works within these collective stories are authentic and non-fiction have not been officially verified, unless stated otherwise. All stories were written from May 2020 – August 2020.

Copyright © 2020 Illustration Cover by Mr. Asfandyar

Copyright © 2020 Map Illustration by radhikayadav

Editing and proofreading with help from Sudipta Dey and Danna Joyce.

Spellcheck and grammar check by Microsoft Office 365 Pro Plus.

The collective works within this book are registered with the United States Copyright Office.

Albuquerque, New Mexico, USA.

https://confessionsoftheprofessions.com

https://mylifeasawomanproject.com

Disclaimer

The collection of works within this book are presented as non-fiction and contain real life events or stories that are based on the lives of real people. Names may or may not have been changed to protect the innocent or the guilty. Nothing in the collection of stories has been filtered. This book is a collection of literary stories by women from around the world with very few curse words and no erotic literature, but may contain passages describing ageism, discrimination, sexism, FGM, prostitution, sex work, and death among friends or family members.

Due to the nature of this book, it is deemed to be read by a mature audience, but most chapters are suitable for children of all ages who are of reading age. Stories containing certain words or actions that would suit a mature audience only, or violent or graphic content, may be denoted before the story is presented. When you proceed to read each story, you do so at your own risk, mentally and physically, and do not hold anyone accountable, especially the authors, for choosing to proceed with any content that may be disturbing or unsuitable for a non-mature audience. The women who presented their stories did so in good faith to share with the world and with readers of all ages in mind.

These stories were collected for a total of 115 days, written from May 5, 2020 to August 28, 2020 and are from women of all backgrounds. All stories are in English or were translated from another language to English, if they were written or spoken from another language. No persons were harmed or exploited to the best of the **source author's** knowledge when collecting these stories. The authenticity of several authors could not be verified due to submission by family, friends, or acquaintances. A good faith effort was made to treat every person who was part of this project with dignity and respect. Please enjoy this collection of works from women around the world.

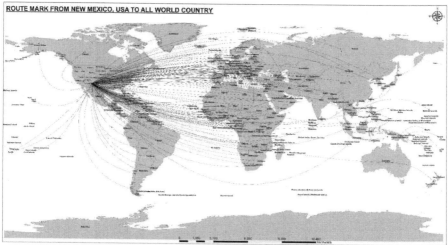

ROUTE MARK FROM NEW MEXICO, USA TO ALL WORLD COUNTRY

Visual Map Illustration

Contact From New Mexico, USA To The World

Created By radhikayadav

My Life As A Woman Project: Table of Contents

Barra Island (1^)

Great Cumbrae Island (1^)

Islay Island (1^)

Isle of Arran (1^)

Isle of Bute (1^)

Isle of Coll (1^)

Isle of Colonsay (1^)

Isle of Eigg (1^)

Isle of Jura (1^)

Isle of Lewis and Harris (1^)

Isle of Mull (1^)

Isle of Skye (1^)

Isle of Tiree (1^)

Orkney Islands (1^)

Shetland Islands (1^)

South Uist Island (1^)

^ = considered an unincorporated and organized territory of or a dependent state or territory of a specific country

✧ = an independent territory, independent republic, or sovereign state, not considered a country, which may or may not have associations with another country

§ = considered a disputed, unincorporated territory

My Life As A Woman Project: Prologue

Women Inspiring Women In 2020 And Beyond

During the month of May 2020 when we were still experiencing the harsh impact of the COVID-19 pandemic, I began a quarantine project. People were doing a variety of things, from being bored at home and doing nothing to being bored at home and starting their businesses, freelancing, and learning how to make money through the Internet. Some people may have even found the time while employed or unemployed to finally do things around the house that they had always wanted to do or take up hobbies that they never had time for before.

Since I could not take a physical vacation somewhere in the world, I would take a mental vacation around the world for this new quarantine project on the Internet. This project started out as a fun project simply to know what was going on in certain countries with the COVID-19 outbreak, particularly in China. However, I quickly realized the access I had to women around the world, who were mostly home under government restrictions of ensuring that everyone was quarantined in their homes. During this time, many people turned to the Internet for work and I had plenty of work to give after realizing that I could get more than just a COVID-19 story. My efforts for obtaining COVID-19 stories was switched to obtaining a story from a woman in at least 30 countries.

The first woman I reached out to about this project was a woman I had only hired once before, a year earlier, for some short article writing, so I was familiar with her work. I had no idea where this project would go, or even if she would understand it. She had the hardest job of all the women because I did not have any guidelines at all for her. I only asked her to tell me something about her life as a woman, not even knowing what she would return to me. Once she returned her story to me, I knew exactly where this project was going. That woman was Valerie from Nigeria, giving significance to this project because while I initiated it in New Mexico, USA, the very first story came from a woman in Africa.

Once I reached my 30 countries, I thought I would obtain just a few more remote countries, and once I got those countries, I just kept going because Fiverr made it easy to do, with its pool of so many countries, and women available. I set out to convince women that this project should happen and needed to happen. Facebook Groups and Instagram also played an essential role in finding women from around the world. No woman was forced to take part in this project, and all women who contributed their stories did so voluntarily of their own free will. Of course, offering a little compensation for their time and story definitely helped to convince them in sharing something about themselves.

While enjoying this Internet vacation, I ended up hiring women throughout the world, between the ages of about 17 to 90 years old from a total of 200 countries, and numerous territories and islands, to be a part of this project. What I wanted of this project was to understand what women were going through around the world, how they were treated in their countries, what they have suffered or struggled within their countries, what they are doing for work, and what has led to their successes, if any, and especially, what they love about being a woman. I wanted them to tell their stories about what life has been like for them growing up in their part of the world. More importantly, what inspiring message did they have for other women around the world? These women are also the country-representatives serving to show how their governments treat women. The responses from women all over the world were overwhelming, but the importance of having the voice of women from the world in their own writing is to show that women do exist, they are resilient, they are powerful, and they are strong.

Before I continue, let me take one paragraph to explain that this book, this project welcomes all genders, races, orientations, religions, cultures, countries, ages, and everything and everyone I missed. This project is not about gender bashing, gender diminishing, gender discrimination, misandry, or anti-patriarchal establishment or anything like that. Men are encouraged to read this book without feeling as if they are the reason for the cause of all women's suffering. Most women, especially the ones in this project, were very on board with me to understand that this project was to highlight their accomplishments and dealings in everyday life, and from what I could tell, no woman seemed bitter towards the male gender. All of them were very happy to speak to me or my male comrades without any issues at all. So I highly doubt any woman would fault you for being male, especially if you took the time to actually read this book. Rather, it is the policies and traditions in place that came long before

33

you. Most likely, the men who are going to read this book are the ones who actually appreciate women and respect and admire all they have accomplished. While there are certainly patterns of oppression and suppression by the patriarchal society or certain behaviors that men exhibit towards women, from what I read and from talking to these women, none of them seemed to hate men nor did they seem like misandrists at all. In fact, they speak highly of their fathers, brothers, uncles, sons, and even their male friends. So as a man, feel free to read on, this book was not intended to make you feel guilty at all. I felt no guilt or shame writing it, and you shouldn't feel any guilt or shame reading it, either. Kudos to you if you are reading it, and if you do enjoy it, don't hesitate to share it with the males and the females of your life. Women have a lot to teach us and there is a lot to learn.

Throughout history, women have been praised for the good they have done and without them, men would truly be nothing. Life would have no meaning. In fact, without women, the human race could not continue. Yet, throughout the history of humanity, women have been overlooked, disadvantaged, taken advantage of, and abused. And this still continues through 2020. They have remained, for the most part, silent. They have sat on the sidelines. They have cheered men on. They have listened to their fathers with obedience. They have grown up, usually in less favor, to their brothers. They have been married off as property for money and "the best interests of the family". They have stood behind their husbands. They have raised multiple children without complaint. They have even faked their own names to appear as if they were men, in order to make change happen, particularly in writing. This does not even account for all the women who will never be known and are long forgotten for their contributions to humanity. To this day, women still do not get the recognition they deserve, but that is certainly changing, and it is a much needed change, for the betterment of our world.

Within this project, despite my own realizations and my own efforts, the "powers that be" or "forces of nature" had continuously tried to silence me or delay this project from becoming a reality. Some are directly related to this project, while others are indirectly related. My Fiverr account was banned; my credit card payment accounts were frozen, including my PayPal account; I faced multiple illnesses from an allergic reaction to food I had eaten; there was a family member scare who got sick with COVID-19 – the test came back negative; on separate incidents, my wife lost a family member, not due to COVID-19, and I lost four elder family members, two were due to COVID-19; relationships were strained; I was nearly fired from my day job several times; I dealt with a malware virus that nearly took my website down, and eventually, the server where all of my websites were ended up crashing, and in a perfect storm, so did the backup server, and I lost a big part of my business, resulting in severe data loss, and the loss of all my clients and customers, including having to redo parts of this project; and I also faced some harsh criticism from several men and women who were more focused on whatever little revenue I was going to make from this book and convinced I had taken advantage of every woman who was part of this project despite ensuring those women compensation to the best of my ability, then they were on the fact that I could bring a project such as this to life. A project like this incurred its many fees, as I did have to compensate the women, the translators, the interviewers, and the additional assistants and help I required to complete this project. Deep in my being, I knew this project was always worth it, and I have no regrets.

I did not quite understand it myself, but if it is any consolation, it made me realize just what women may go through when facing the issues of the world, whether it be working for a company or starting their own businesses, trying to balance a life with children and still somehow find the time to go after their aspirations, and the struggles they may face which may keep them silent, ignored, or kept suppressed or oppressed by the same sex or opposite sex, because of a seemingly natural phenomenon that I, myself, cannot explain. It made me wonder about the possibility of the potential of women everywhere. If women suddenly spoke up, spoke out, and began to take control, what exactly would happen?

"For now she need not think of anybody. She could be herself, by herself. And that was what now she often felt the need of - to think; well not even to think. To be silent; to be alone. All the being and the doing, expansive, glittering, vocal, evaporated; and one shrunk, with a sense of solemnity, to being oneself, a wedge-shaped core of darkness, something invisible to others... and this self having shed its attachments was free for the strangest adventures."

As multiple women told me, they wrote without thinking about the money at all. I felt the same way when I spent a lot of time tracking women down from every country, island, and territory, pitching to them the idea about the project, and hiring them to write their stories, if they were interested, including hiring men to hire women where I had no social media platform or any means to reach them. I was investing into this project, but I was not thinking about money or fame while doing it nor the massive amount of debt I took on to complete this project. Very few people ever become famous for writing a book and I am sure I am no different nor am I the exception. I was actually thinking about the impact it might have on current and future generations of women as no one has ever done this type of project before. I was thinking about how it might be good for the historical records, if anyone is keeping them, as books usually do a good job of that, to at least track our progress on the treatment of women around the world. If the treatment is still the same a hundred years from now, or hundreds of years from now, as it has been for the past hundreds of years, with some improvements along the way, then we still have a very serious problem with humanity.

Before and even during the time I was engaged in this project, as I write this very sentence, I am just another nameless American with an entrepreneurial mindset and random ideas trying to find work, make money, and pay my bills. This was a vision project that I had in a dream, woke up, and realized, there was an opportunity to speak with so many women while they were at home in quarantine lockdown during the COVID-19 pandemic, with many of them also looking for work to do, which allowed me to employ them for their time to participate in this project.

I knew that no matter what happened, I had to keep this project going, even if it meant financial disaster or worse for me. I couldn't quite understand this myself, but having observed it and witnessed it, I can only write what happened without any scientific backing. Whether I brought this on myself, I am not quite sure. I thought this project would be a breeze for me, but it ended up being quite a challenge, especially considering that normally I'm a busy person, but during the COVID-19 quarantine, I somehow managed to be even busier than I ever was before. Had I started this project in June or July instead of May, then I probably would not have been as successful in completing it as I was. Everything seemed to fall into sync and worked out very well, including all the people who were a part of this project, as if I was being guided by unforeseen forces that wanted this project to happen. Fortunately, I did have people who loved the idea of the project and were there for moral support in the times I felt like giving up.

The education and empowerment of
women throughout the world
cannot fail to result in a more caring,
tolerant, just and peaceful life for all.

Aung San Suu Kyi

If the world is ever going to change, then women can no longer remain silent. Women can no longer suppress or ignore the powers that they know are hidden deep within all of them. It is a calling that they might not even know they have, a calling for a better world. A world that may still be ruled by men, but a world in which women are able to co-rule as well. There are only so many more war games that women are going to continue to tolerate and watch men play, until they finally have had enough of their sons, brothers, fathers, uncles, and husbands being sent off to fight and violently die in conflicts and wars that seem almost pointless and without end.

Aristophanes, a man and playwright of Ancient Greece, was certainly way ahead of his time when he wrote the comedy play of Lysistrata.

From the 2005 staging of Lysistrata produced in Central Park, courtesy of Wikipedia

If you are not familiar with the play, I suggest you read it. Patriarchy vs. Matriarchy. To give you a brief summary, it's a "comical" feminist and political masterpiece, in which the women of Greece are exhausted of the Peloponnesian War between the Greek city-states, wishing their men were home to be with them. One brave woman, Lysistrata, steps up with an extraordinary mission and idea to end the war. She persuades all of the women to take away what men want and desire of them most: sex. At first, it is very hard to do and the women are reluctant, but after a while, they begin to understand. Unfortunately, she also has to go to the wives of the political leaders and convince them to do the same. Eventually, they finally do so and it enrages a battle between the sexes, until the male leaders are forced to negotiate peace.

LYSISTRATA

There are a lot of things about us women

That sadden me, considering how men

See us as rascals.

CALONICE

37

As indeed we are!

Written in 411 BC, and as of 2020 AD, is there still any relevance to a 2,430 year old passage or the play itself? The point of the play is not that sex has to be used as a weapon against men in order to change them, although it is quite a powerful weapon. However, the themes of the play are to show the frustrations of women, from ageism to sexism to objectification to their opinions largely being ignored. The play shows the extremes that women must take, but in the process, the realization is that they do not have to remain silent or put up with "the way it is"; that women can and should have a large sense of social responsibility; and that women should be involved in how they shape our world and our politics.

There is nothing I can really say that could make you understand the reasons for why this project needed to happen, other than to read the stories of the women themselves in order to see why I had to bring this project to light. I am a graduate from Ocean County College with an associate degree in Social Science and Loyola University Chicago with a bachelor's degree of science in Psychology. I fell in love with psychology from a young age, in order to deal with my major depression, and I do some minor experimenting on the human race a few times a year, usually random projects that involved friends, family, or a few strangers, and are very minor and would never be headline-worthy. Most of my experiments would put me back in the 1940s, 1950s, 1960s, and 1970s, when psychology was really awesome. Psychological experiments during those times were quite a bit unethical but taught the world so much.

For this project, however, it was a very ethical social psychology experiment in its own right, with all women willingly participating and giving permission, to see what women around the world really had to say about their lives. Perhaps, it was to show if there were any collective thoughts from all of these women who do not know each other, have never spoken to each other, did not read each other's stories in advance, and had nothing but some light guidelines to go on. Or maybe I initiated this project just because I could do it. To put it simply, if not me, then who? Was anyone else willing to do something like this? To put it more complexly, many women already know what they are going to read.

Deep within all of them, there is some sort of collective consciousness going on that men may or may not know about or choose to ignore. Even many women still choose to ignore it. Some women will get it and some women won't get it. Some men will get it and some men won't get it. It is not really me who has to convince anyone at all to read this book. If you want to continue reading, great. If not, then you never are going to understand the reasons for such a massive project as this, or my own reasons for undertaking it, or really, why the world is the way it is. For those of you who think there is nothing wrong in the world, it is quite nice to live in a bubble, as most people do, but I'm not the one who is going to pop it for you. Ignorance is bliss and sometimes I do wish I could go back to living in my own bubble as well. So for my many reasons of engaging this project, I would say that I grew up around many strong women and have observed strong women throughout my life.

From my mother to my sister to my grandmother to my wonderful older or similar-age cousins to my wonderful younger cousin and aunt; to my Hillel director, to my biggest crush at university who inspired me and who I admire still so much to this day; and to my dear loving and protective wife with her own many ambitions and business ventures; to my female friends, to the community directors from the time I lived in Israel, with so many strong women there who I lived and worked with and everywhere; and every woman along the way who has displayed such potential and true leadership, and has shown that she is more than just a pretty smile or face, but that she has a personality that shines with the intelligence and desire to make everything she wants to happen in her life come true.

I wanted to see a project like this come to life, and although I am a man, the one and only man who spearheaded and funded this type of project, and brought it to life, does not change the fact that this book is for women, by women, to women, for all the world and for future generations to read, both male and female. I am only the messenger. These are the collections of stories that will no doubt have an impact on you, no matter who you are, that will change your life forever. Not only will you learn about the lives of these women, but they were asked to share something about their culture, including the foods, clothing, customs, festivals, etc., and many were very happy to express how great their cultures were, how fun and exciting it is to be a part of their country. These are real people, real women, real lives, real cultures, real experiences, and real stories. Immerse yourself and learn everything you can as every one of these women have something to teach you.

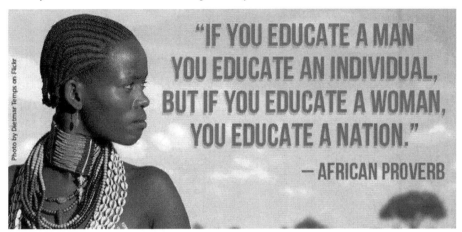

"IF YOU EDUCATE A MAN YOU EDUCATE AN INDIVIDUAL, BUT IF YOU EDUCATE A WOMAN, YOU EDUCATE A NATION."
— AFRICAN PROVERB

Photo by Dietmar Temps on Flickr

From women who had nothing to women who have everything: a very lovely real life Princess, the granddaughter of Princess Grace Kelly and Prince Rainier III; the Vice President of the Philippines; to women who are teachers, lawyers, doctors, nurses, authors, actresses, secretaries, entrepreneurial businessowners, freelance writers, and even – probably not by choice – sex workers and refugees. Let us not forget the many women who sacrificed so much when they became mothers and grandmothers to make sure they were raising a new generation under their wings.

This project was not about race, religion, preference, political background, or status, but to capture a snapshot of stories from women of all backgrounds, no matter their views. Because of this, there may be multiple perspectives on the views of a particular country. Sure, it was definitely about gender, as a woman is a woman, and the world, especially men, can learn a lot from women. Aside from all the women who were hired, some multiple times, a team of 34 great men who understood the mission were also hired to help put this project together, and without them, I would not have been able to accomplish what I've been able to do. Every walk of life of woman is in this book with her perspectives on her life. Women with and without children, from daughters to mothers to sisters to grandmothers and even great-grandmothers, cousins, aunts, godmothers, etc. There is even a mother and a daughter within this book, where mother was born in one country and daughter was born in another country; hint: both are in the region of the Caribbean islands and South America.

Whether she chose this life or this life was chosen for her, she did make the choice to share and be a part of this project for a reason, because she understood the meaning of it beyond even what I could understand. The women who believed in this project knew it was for more than just a story, more than just a read, they knew that this book would be passed on to future generations of women. It is for those without a voice, for those with a voice, and for those who know they are going to be the change in this world, just like all of these women, who took part in a project and decided to make their own changes in the world.

As you obtain a copy of these stories, whether on your Kindle, in an eBook, or a hard copy, you are ultimately holding generations upon generations of women's knowledge within your library. You will probably not finish this book overnight, but over time, as you read these stories and become intimate with these women, you will feel as if they are your family, your mothers, your sisters, your cousins, your daughters, your girlfriends, your friends, and your wives.

For every woman who said yes to being a part of this project, she had at least two counterparts who said no. Whether distrusting me and my team or just not wanting to share her story at all, it begs the question of why? Knowing all that women go through in the world, knowing everything they have been through and will continue to go through, why do the majority of women still choose to remain silent? This is not a question I, nor my team who helped me, are able to answer, but I do know that the ones who remain silent are the easiest ones to keep under control and rule.

Fortunately for you and me, there were enough women in the world, from every country on this Earth, who saw the significance and importance of such a project, and these are the brave and courageous women you will get to know, as I am very proud and honored to introduce every one of them to you. None of these women know each other nor were they given any examples to read from other women's stories. These women were given only some guidelines for writing which they could choose to follow, or they could write whatever they wished without the guidelines, if they chose to do so, as long as it pertained to a story about their lives. I do not remember all of their names, and there were many who participated on the condition that they could remain anonymous, but I do know their stories, and they will always know their stories. Some had given me their names at a later time, but I lost them because my website crashed with all their information on it and I did not have a latest backup. The reason I could not go back and retrieve any of this information is because I was banned from the platform where most of these women were hired to share their stories. But in a way, I do remember having a conversation with every one of them because not only did I lose the final-proofed stories once and had to redo this entire project, I had to proofread twice, check for grammar twice, and read every story twice. Thus, when I say I am familiar with many of these stories, I too, can only show my appreciation and gratitude for every word and every thought that these women contributed to this project.

Not every single woman who was a part of this project spoke English very well or even wrote it well, but she did her best. Some women were about to back out of this project because of their lack of English skills until I assured them to have confidence in what they were writing, and once they started writing from the heart, they would know exactly what they needed to say in English. Although I did have to take care of some spelling and grammar issues, for the most part, every woman wrote beautifully in English. Several of them wrote in their native tongues and then translated into English, with one woman even accidentally delivering her story to me in her own language, but the point of writing completely in English was because as of 2020, English currently serves as one of the most universal languages in the world. Kudos to every woman who gave it her best to be a part of this project and deliver her story in English.

Whether this anthology is meant to be informative, poetic, or historical, every woman has her story to tell and wrote it in her own poetic way, and this was her platform to do it. There are still several countries in the world where people, especially women, do not enjoy the rights of the First Amendment of the United States, or the right to the freedom of speech. Speaking out may result in accusations of blasphemy, ridicule, outright imprisonment, or even death. Many women who are hardly ever asked about their opinions on anything were ecstatic to take part in this project.

Fortunately for this project, a story from a woman in every country was obtained, regardless of the restrictions of her speech by her country, as she is taking part in writing for a book that was written in the United States, which currently still enjoys the highest level of freedom of speech. Even currently in the United States of America in 2020, however, where it seems everyone is offended by everything; especially for having a political ideology, it is getting harder to voice our opinions and thoughts without being suppressed or having to worry about getting fired from our jobs, outcast by our friends and family, banned from social media platforms; all of whom claim to protect free speech and supposedly encourage individuals to exercise their rights to use that freedom of speech, but somehow still suppress many individuals from speaking out. All women were encouraged not to filter anything they had to say, and as the Chief editor of this book, and an advocate of the right to free speech and free thought, nothing was filtered on my end.

To all the lovely ladies who were a part of this project, you are the leaders the world needs. You were all very different and fit for a project like this. You saw this project as something different from the norm as well and that is why you were so attracted to it. You were all different from the thousand plus women I spoke to who said no or were indifferent to having anything to do with this project. You are different from the women who don't care and don't mind the way things are. And as you ladies may or may have heard before, an amazing quote comes to mind for every one of you:

"Well-behaved women seldom make history."
− Professor Laurel Thatcher Ulrich

I could see it in your words and even your actions when we spoke and you joined the project. You are the seldom-behaved. You are what the world needs. You are the ones who choose and love to be different. You are the ones who see things the way they are and also see the opportunity and potential for change and improvement with everything you do. You push for the change; you embrace the change. You are the women that the present and future needs. Make sure the legacy carries on through your daughters and don't fail to educate your sons about the mighty power within all of you.

You are all amazing. You are all now part of this history, this story, part of a project called **My Life As A Woman**. This may have been my dream and vision, but it seems, I was not the only one, and I was far from alone, and you all made it into a reality and saw well beyond my dream and understood the absolute vision. Without you, this project could not and would not have been possible. I appreciate you placing your trust in me to bring this project to life. I love you all. I hope you will share this with your friends and families and networks across the Internet and the entire world, including the places I could never reach, and make it go as far as you can so that the world understands the message loud and clear:

Women Are Resilient. Women Are Strong. Women Are Powerful.

If there was anything good that came of 2020, let this be it. This is my gift, our gift to you, the world, a concept born out of the quarantine lockdown of the COVID-19 pandemic.

Matt Gates

These were just some quotes that stood out for the importance of this project and really encapsulates the grasp of women's well-being around the world.

"No nation can rise to the height of glory unless your women are side by side with you. We are victims of evil customs. It is a crime against humanity that our women are shut up within the four walls of the houses as prisoners. There is no sanction anywhere for the deplorable condition in which our women have to live." — **Muhammad Ali Jinnah**

"Her mother told her she could grow up to be anything she wanted to be, so she grew up to become the strongest of the strong, the strangest of the strange, the wildest of the wild, the wolf leading wolves." — **Nikita Gill**

"Women have sat indoors all these millions of years, so that by this time the very walls are permeated by their creative force, which has, indeed, so overcharged the capacity of bricks and mortar that it must needs harness itself to pens and brushes and business and politics." — **Virginia Woolf, A Room of One's Own**

"It is easier to live through someone else than to complete yourself. The freedom to lead and plan your own life is frightening if you have never faced it before. It is frightening when a woman finally realizes that there is no answer to the question 'who am I' except the voice inside herself." — **Betty Friedan**

"Do not let your fire go out, spark by irreplaceable spark in the hopeless swamps of the not-quite, the not-yet, and the not-at-all. Do not let the hero in your soul perish in lonely frustration for the life you deserved and have never been able to reach. The world you desire can be won. It exists.. it is real.. it is possible.. it's yours." — **Ayn Rand, Atlas Shrugged**

"If you ever find yourself in the wrong story, leave." — **Mo Willems**

"My silences had not protected me. Your silence will not protect you. But for every real word spoken, for every attempt I had ever made to speak those truths for which I am still seeking, I had made contact with other women while we examined the words to fit a world in which we all believed, bridging our differences." — **Audre Lorde, The Cancer Journals**

"If women want rights more than they got, why don't they just take them, and not be talking about it." — **Sojourner Truth**

"You deserve to be here. You deserve to exist. You deserve to take up space in this world of men." — **Mackenzi Lee, The Lady's Guide to Petticoats and Piracy**

"The fact that I was a girl never damaged my ambitions to be a pope or an emperor." — **Willa Cather**

"Everyone has inside of her a piece of good news. The good news is that you don't know how great you can be, how much you can love, what you can accomplish, and what your potential is." — **Anne Frank**

"The way in which we think of ourselves has everything to do with how our world sees us and how we see ourselves successfully acknowledged by the world." — **Arlene Rankin**

"Define success on your own terms, achieve it by your own rules, and build a life you're proud to live." — **Anne Sweeney**

"If you want something said, ask a man; if you want something done, ask a woman." — **Margaret Thatcher**

"Little girls with dreams become women with a vision." — Unknown

My Life As A Woman: Afghanistan Edition

I am Sehar from Afghanistan. I grew up in a small family in the Kunduz province of Afghanistan. My family is an open-minded family. In the very first years of my life, my family didn't allow me to study because it is a tradition in my country. When I graduated from school, I wanted to study abroad, but it didn't happen. However, I have always been very patient with my achievements.

I was upset that I could not study, but my patience paid off. My aunt was a very kind and very independent-minded woman, so she asked my dad if he would allow me to study and he agreed. I studied law at one of the best universities in Afghanistan. I was very interested in writing articles and so I started my own blog when I was 20 years old.

Our culture and traditions are very rich and old, but it doesn't give equal rights for women as it gives for men. One of the things that I don't like about our culture is that it doesn't allow women to work outside. One of the things that I like about my culture is that women are somewhat respected. because men are very sensitive about the fame and respect of their women.

As an Afghan woman, I have always struggled to do the things that I want. For example, I wanted to have my own business when I graduated from school, but it was not possible when I was younger. Today, I now work in an online store. There is always something that the people of my country struggle with. I can say that I am a successful woman. As a woman, working outside is not a very easy thing. But I made it happen and I say that it is a success. Being successful is not very easy. However, I think that if someone wants to do something, s/he should work hard to get it done.

There are lots of successful women in Afghanistan. You can call them, 'Heroes of cold war'. They have always been my inspiration, especially women who are members of parliament. They teach us that being a woman is a very good thing, but being a close-minded woman is a bad thing. I remember that once a woman said, 'Wait for sometimes, your dreams will come true one day if you want'.

Afghanistan and Afghan women have always been in news' headlines. Being a woman in Afghanistan is very hard. Yesterday, the Taliban attacked a hospital and killed 14 pregnant women. This is very frustrating for me. In our country, hearing sad news like this is a very ordinary thing, but I should say that living in Afghanistan has something more to it.

My message to all women right across the world is, 'Be strong and don't lose your temper. You will succeed in your life one day. I know that women are strong but allow men to help you as they need your help also. Don't allow others to make you weak. Instead, become stronger and stronger every day.

My Life As A Woman: Albania Edition #1

I am a woman who was born in Albania. Born at a time when communism was on the verge of collapse and the struggle for freedom had begun. I grew up in a time of transit, kidnapping, hunger, and corruption. I grew up feeling prejudiced because I was am a woman. I grew up feeling the weight of being a woman since I was a child.

I grew up fearing that I would never succeed because I was a woman and being a woman in my country is not easy. Over the years, I was able to see the position of the female gender in my life, in my social circle, at school or work, and I knew it would not be easy and I had to fight hard for it and keep in a world where masculinity had taken root for centuries.

I didn't realize that just being proud of being born a woman or supporting the female gender would often lead to a problem or a closed path in my life. I grew up in the capital city of Albania with a big dream; to help others by always focusing on the female gender. I have always wanted to be the voice of the obedient, violated, disrespected women, or even those who have not had the opportunity to be educated or to read more or what not, and for those who haven't discovered their feminine world.

My wish has always been that every woman, not only in Albania, but everywhere in the world, would be able to understand her values. Understand that she was born a woman before she became a friend, a sister, a girlfriend, a wife, or even a mother. A woman needs to know how much she is worth, how much she weighs, or what she deserves before being something else.

We, the women of Albania, understand that no matter how violated or disrespected we may be, we can make it if we have the support of another woman. And this is something I had to understand after many years of my life. I realized that a woman in Albania survives by the strength of her ancestors.

Today's women in Albania are the ashes of their ancestors. Their strength has helped us till today to seek the best in ourselves and to share it wherever we can or wherever it's needed. And this is something that here in Albania is very little understood or sometimes not at all.

We, the women of Albania, perhaps even unconsciously, choose to support every woman who is or feels like that. Women in Albania choose to inherit to their future generations the best they have, the most beautiful part of themselves that they have discovered through their lives which has not always been easy. Even my grandmother, just like every woman who is a friend, a sister, a wife, and a mother, she chose to inherit the essence of her fighting spirit.

Often in our conversations, her eyes were filled with memories which she uttered in such a melodious calm voice that in the most silent way the mantle of memories covered us. She spoke for herself, for women, for being a woman in times when everything was black and white, for those times when if you had a little, you had everything. For those times when you were somebody's woman before being a newborn female child.

She always used to say; being a woman in Albania means growing up in the dark but knowing how to give light. To grow in the middle of a war and to give peace. Growing up among illiteracy and writing as a romantic poet. To be broken through battles thousands of times and to fight without giving up. We, Albanian women, are like that thin line that separates joy from anger, love from hatred, or strength from weakness. We are the balance and we must never give up for ourselves, nor for the older generations, and above all, not for the generations to come.

Among everything else, this was my favorite, because this time-traveling with my grandmother, for me, was the thread that separated the surrender from the desire to move on. Every time I heard the painful stories of the female world during her lifetime in Albania, it hurt me, but the strength inherited from among generations didn't let me lose hope.

Thanks to her stories, I am here at this moment today, writing not only about the story of an Albanian woman but about every woman who believes the truth, her dreams, her voice, the unique essence of her soul. Being grateful and admiring my heritage culture, I choose to say that today I have gone through every challenge, every struggle of being a woman in a world with male dominance. From the grace of ancient women, I am today a fulfilled, listened, and respected woman. I am a confident woman who is not afraid to express or seek what she feels.

Today, as any woman here in Albania, I rely on the strength of my female friends, sisters, colleagues, and every woman around me. Among them, I have come to realize that every woman in the world can succeed if she fights for her voice, if she believes in her soul, as long as she believes in her path, if she does not give up even the most bitter trials. Today, my grandmother would be very content to see and hear that even the male gender is now fighting together with us, giving us everything that has been missing for generations.

This is how our ancestors have inherited their powerful soul not only to us, the females but also, to the males. We are the women born in Albania; a new powerful generation inspired from the past always wanting to fight for the future.

My Life As A Woman: Albania Edition #2

Through the years, the unequal status of Albanian women has been a constant presence. International Women's Day may be the only day the society and families honor women. The other three-hundred and sixty-four days, many Albanian women must live by an oppressive, devaluing, and antiquated code in a very male-dominated culture.

This is particularly evident in rustic territories, for example, Maliq where I was born and grew up. Maliq is a small town located near Korça in south east of Albania. Women there need to live by an abusive, degrading and obsolete code in a patriarchal society. Ladies are limited by their husband or fathers' authority and denied choosing themselves what to do and where to go.

I remember when I was 18 and wanted to move to the Capital for studies and my father was mad about it. He could not bear the fact of me living on my own, apart from our family in complete freedom. He, as well as other males, strongly disbelieved that young ladies could handle life alone.

My family still shared a home with my grandfathers at that time. Therefore, this was something they would never consider. Nobody understood that I was in need for a better life and I really tried hard to change that traditional attitude.

So, I decided to apply to the University of Tirana without anybody knowing. I waited for two months until I got a positive answer and then decided to give the big news. What I expected from my parents was completely beyond my belief. I was banned to proceed with the studies since it was far from home. They refused to do the financing and so on. I had nothing but my dreams, but this did not stop me following what I had started.

I borrowed some money from my cousins and left the town. The capital was indeed very different from what I had expected but I got used to things soon. I started a job, and, in a few months, I was able to pay my own bills. This was the first time I presented myself and showed everybody who did not believe I would make it. I realized how wonderful I felt by surprising my father.

Yet in 2020, after continuous awareness activities, women still struggle and mostly emphasize the importance of having a closer relationship with their family members. "This is much more important than our daily basic needs," the women repeated together in one voice on their Women's Day movement.

Quotes from Albanian women:

"Now I have a different life, I get out of my house in the morning and I have objectives for the day".

"I am learning new skills which are opening new opportunities for my life".

"I have a better time thanks to my friends with whom I work with".

My Life As A Woman: Algeria Edition

Being a woman means being a warrior for change because she is the source of changing everything, her life, thinking, shape, home, and her children. Whether she is a mother, daughter, or wife. Being a woman means you are half of society, while you have a special day to celebrate every year when everyone glorifies your value in society. but let's focus on one woman's life.

In a region in this whole world, I was born in Algeria, my country. I grew up in a very conservative family with my father, mother, and brothers. My father was an engineer working hard to provide us with food and clothes and maybe going out for a walk to the sea every summer, and my mom stayed at home taking care of us. My childhood was good because of our house that made me very happy. It was small and had a garden full of plants.

Suddenly my father decided to move to another big house and there I lived until now. It was the first time that I knew the meaning of sadness because it was not easy for me to leave that house. At the same time, that moment was the beginning of a new life, new friends, a new school and a new world, so I spent half of my childhood in our new house and while I was growing up, I realized that my childhood was influenced by one hugely powerful woman who is my MOM! She was the source of inspiration and always keen to educate me and take care of me.

My mother is a strong woman in the full sense of the word, despite her stay at home without any ambition, but her children were the project she worked on every day to achieve her desire to succeed and she did. I grew up and became an ambitious social girl, who loves life, and I set many goals when I was in high school. Until I went to university, I dreamt of becoming a teacher of the French language, so I chose this file from my deep heart, but here my struggles began, because I suffered from panic attacks that made everything hard. Just waking up every day and going to university was hard. My psychological suffering shattered my dreams and my aspirations. So, I became just a person seeking to finish his studies as soon as possible. Then I graduated from college and didn't give in to my fears, so I started looking for my passion, Asking myself: do I really want to be a teacher? Before that let me tell you a little bit about my community around me.

I grew up in a society that has a fossilized mindset against women, wherein their eyes, a woman is just a pleasant being who stays at home, cares for children, cooks, and cares for men. That's why my dreams as a woman were not that much so I looked for a job that would please me and my conservative community. In this way, I decided to become a recipe writer because I love everything about food, and I'm still working on it until I achieve success.

I want to tell every woman to remember that your emotion is the strength, your mood and your precarious thoughts are the power of change and know that your dreams will come true if you decide, neither society nor anyone else will prevent you and remember without you, society would not be complete.

My Life As A Woman: Andorra Edition

My name is Patricia. I am from Andorra. I grew up in La Vieja, the capital of Andorra. I work as a nurse in a hospital in Escaldes. I always wanted to be a nurse. I searched for job stability, which is not impacted by a recession. Working in a hospital is incredible. No day is the same. I like nursing because it's a profession that never stops giving. You learn new things every day, and the opportunity for growth is almost unlimited. I feel so good inside when I see improvement in my patients and when giving emotional support by holding hands of family members who have just experienced tragedy. My sister left Andorra to study in Spain and used to come back home every weekend. Andorra connects to both Spain and France by highways.

My mother always inspired me as a woman. She followed her dreams. She was always there for me whenever I asked her to do it. My father was a Hotel director. The country is primarily sustained by the tourism industry (more than 9 million people visit Andorra each year). I studied a Nursing degree which allowed me to work wherever I wanted. I worked in Spain for a while but then I realized I missed my country, the mountains, the people and my family. I decided to go back 7 years ago, and I am pleased I did it. Andorra's healthcare system has 3.6 physicians for every 1,000 residents. Many world-class medical services are offered locally but are also integrated into the neighboring healthcare systems in France and Spain.

Andorra is a beautiful and safe place to live. The safety of the streets in Andorra is yet another advantage of the welfare in this privileged state. With a virtually non-existent crime rate, Andorra is one of the safest countries in the world. The cost of living in Andorra is affordable compared to Spanish cities like Barcelona and Madrid. Especially for things like accommodation, transportation, food and utilities, Andorra's cost of living tends to be 30% below what you'd expect in major world cities.

The public health system is exceptional and enables via international agreements, benefitting from healthcare abroad. Abortion is illegal for women under all circumstances, forcing women to travel to Catalonia and France for the procedure. If you are offered employment in Andorra, your employer should sponsor you for a work permit.

You will ideally need to speak Catalan, Spanish or French, or all three languages: the first two are more critical and the official language is Catalan (bureaucracy will need to be conducted in that language). Catalan is the official language of Andorra. It is the first language of only about 10 million people worldwide, so it's likely that most newcomers to Andorra won't speak it already. However, being English-speaking is also an advantage, given the number of English-speaking visitors to Andorra. Once you get past the language barrier, Andorra is a particularly friendly and welcoming place. Most Andorrans speak French or Spanish as a second language. English is on the rise, but it's still most common in tourist areas. It is also started playing a more prominent role in Andorra's school system at international schools in Andorra.

Andorra has a well-established business network. With business schedules adapted to the needs of the tourism sector, Andorra is known for its highly competitive pricing strategy and its wide-ranging supply of products and services. Andorra is in the process of improving and redesigning its routes of communication to make it much more accessible by land and air. For Andorrans, the closest major airports are in Barcelona (2.5 hours away by car) and Toulouse (3 hours).

The Andorran Tax System is probably the most significant benefit of living in Andorra – you'll have to pay a maximum rate of 10% taxes of your income. Andorra is one of the smallest states in Europe, bordering Spain and France in the region of the Pyrenees. With a population of 80,000 people, my country is more often known as a ski and shopping destination.

My Life As A Woman: Angola Edition

I grew up in Angola, more precisely in Luanda, the capital of Angola, life was great and there was less and less social unrest and discrimination, my father was a soldier in wars and my mother was in trade.

I grew up with my mother and my two little brothers. My father, on the other hand, only came home about twice a year. I learned to live with my mother and life was good.

My studies

I studied in business school. With my comrades, we wanted to become an entrepreneur and provide work for us.

She inspired me

My entrepreneurial tent at the time and her life was great, she traveled to almost all continents. I liked her way of doing things and it was she who had inspired me to study business and be able to do the same thing she did one day.

What I love about my culture

What I like in my culture is the carnival. a practice that celebrates Angolan creativity, art and music. The carnival was a good deal for the groups participating in it. The winners could pocket up to $3,000 US dollars, but this practice is no longer celebrated as before.

My work

I traded a few years ago, my job is to order goods from other African countries (South Africa, Congo, etc.) and to resell them at home.

My successes as a woman

Being in a country like Angola, women are taken with equal esteem to man, which doesn't stop me from working the way I want. I got married and I have the coolest husband on the planet. He works 6 hours a day and he is available at home from time to time and he takes good care of me and our daughter. We often travel three with our daughter and life is good.

My difficulties as a woman

As you know, in the imperfect world in which we live, difficulties cannot be escaped. As a woman, taking care of my children and working at the same time was too difficult for me, and learning after my father died in wars and you couldn't even bury him.

Faced with all this, I only had to be strong and endure anything that could present itself as obstacles. I do not regret any moment of my life and I also wish it to all the women of Angola.

I would like to tell the women of Angola to stay firm and strong. No matter what you are going to do. Difficulties are like a shadow that appears when you are in front of a light, and that should not prevent you from living your life, even if you have family responsibilities, no matter if you are despised by confrontation. Keep going and don't trust other people's opinions. Having goals and reaching them will make you happy and fulfilled.

My Life As A Woman: Antigua And Barbuda Edition

Antigua and Barbuda are a small yet magnificent set of islands that are a part of the Caribbean. It is considered a "British Overseas Territory" country, located East of the Bahamas and the Dominican Republic. Antigua represents lands of 40 coral islands. There are tons of small and large islands that surround us that makes it a beautiful vacation destination. These islands are known for their natural beauty, fabulous beaches, and stunning scenery. They also have many other things to offer, such as fantastic restaurants, hotels, and resorts to enjoy with your family and friends. Growing up in the islands is a different experience than growing up in the United States.

My name is Sara Kufman, I am nineteen years old, and I grew up in the beautiful Antigua. Growing up as a woman comes with many expectations from everyone everywhere. As a woman, we are expected to be reliable, independent, and confident, while also being able to take care of the household, for example, cook, clean, and take on the necessary responsibilities to live day to day. It is also expected to have a good education and work hard for what you want.

I grew up without a father, so it was just me, my mother, and my five siblings. Growing up was challenging because my mother had to provide for herself, and all her children, and we weren't a fortunate family. My mom had to work two jobs to keep up with the bills and provide food on the table each night. Growing up, seeing how strong my mom was to do everything in her power to provide for us, inspired me to work hard and never give up.

Every day as a woman, I am reminded of the daily struggles and blessings in my life. I am blessed with many opportunities to grow and learn from my experiences. For example, I had the chance to go to a University to study nursing and push through the obstacles that have come along. I have learned to be grateful for everything in my life and not take anything for granted because that was how my mother raised me. The reason why I decided to major in nursing is that I love helping people. My mother always told me that if you want to help someone, you must do so yourself.

Growing up in Antigua is a unique experience, anyone would love to live here. I have been able to see the beauty of nature and its natural wonders from afar and up close. Whenever I decide to go to the beach, I don't have to plan because all I do is change, grab a towel, and drive to the beach. The environment here is relaxing, and the people are friendly. They operate on "island time," which means it is a low-key and slow-paced environment. I would highly recommend anyone to come to visit. In Antigua, women have made remarkable changes in areas such as education, success to health care, and social security. Women have made such significant contributions to the economy, and that shows strength, persistence, and capability. If you believe in something, follow your dreams until you have completed your goals.

My Life As A Woman: Argentina Edition

My name is Nadia Evangelina Carrizo and I have a degree in Curatorship and Criticism of Visual Arts. I was born and raised in a small neighborhood in Buenos Aires, capital of Argentina. Since my childhood, I have needed to express myself through art, be it through music, drawing or dance. I have always considered this concern to be innate, however, my home, even my neighborhood, has encouraged my approach to art. In general, Argentina is a country in which multiple cultures and ethnic groups coexist under a social-democratic and progressive thought that allows a wide development of culture.

I am a person of grandiloquent dreams. When I was a child, I fantasized about being a music star, later a writer, and today I like to imagine myself as a museum director. I still don't know what the future holds for me, but I intend to leave a mark. As a Latin American feminist woman, I want to raise my voice and represent the struggle of women to conquer more and more spaces that have been denied to them. From walking the streets without fear to the possibility of occupying positions of power that have always belonged to men. As well as this, I must confront the socio-economic inequalities and stereotypes of living in a "third world" country. From what I can contribute, I see culture as a propitious environment to express my thoughts.

I come from a lower-middle class but still, my family has supported me to study whatever I wanted because going to university was an important step for me. I was also able to study because education is public in my country. I know that many people cannot enjoy this right that I consider fundamental since it has given many, as in my case, the possibility of professional training. Thanks to my parents, I did not have to work while I was studying and so I was able to receive two degrees at the age of 23.

Buenos Aires was a key city to develop my interest in art since it presented a great diversity of artistic activity. I could say that it is a city where you can breathe culture wherever you go, you can always find a gallery or a cultural space. Argentine culture is promoted by the State since it assures its free access. Most of the museums are public and private spaces are also accessible. Free activities also include conferences, concerts, courses and theatre performances.

However, Argentina, like many South American countries, is going through a political-economic crisis since the last dictatorship in the 70s and this directly affects our decisions. The labor system has strong problems because it is unfair and prejudiced. Getting a job seems like an odyssey in which your studies are not relevant. Although the culture plays a very important role for Argentines, their budget is so low that the chances of being hired are minimal.

I believe that there is a great offer of university careers but that your job opportunities are almost non-existent. For this reason, since I started my studies until today, I had to face many challenges to be considered. But I have learned from all the internships I have done in museums, galleries and the media. Currently, I decided to create my work. Thanks to the freelance writing modality, I was able to apply my knowledge and connect with artists from all over the world, from the United States to Bangladesh, Hong Kong, Singapore, and Germany. Despite the freedom I have, it is a bold decision as it requires a lot of effort to maintain. I see in my mother and grandmother two role models; they never gave up in the face of adversity and knew how to make their way. I am growing up and have achieved many goals so far; however, I aspire to greater achievements. I do not intend to work all my life in front of a computer without leaving the confines of my room.

All cultural workers know that we choose this path only because we are passionate about what we do. It is not an easy path. As I also tell all women never to give up and to follow their wishes no matter what they are despite everything. I dream of a society where all people are equal, so I tell women everywhere to be patient that this future is getting closer.

My Life As A Woman: Armenia Edition

Armenia is not that popular and not everyone knows where it is and that people, especially women, live there. So, I would like to introduce my country, tell about my life and my experiences as a woman living and working in Armenia. I am a young female born and raised in Yerevan, capital of Armenia. This country is conservative, especially when we speak about women, their rules are limited like if you're married your destiny is to be an experienced housewife, but this is not my story.

I am a marketing specialist and a freelancer with great experience but let me tell you about the way I reached this. I grew up in a poor family with my mom and grandma, without any horizons for me and my future, and despite it all, my mom was dreaming that I could reach many heights and become a strong support for them both. With time our life improved and I got an opportunity to enter one of the best universities in Armenia and study one of the most required professions of these times – marketing.

I already got used to the idea that I was going to marry someone rich and become a mom of three children, but things changed when I thought about working and earning money, in which my grandma played a big role. I was 18 years old when she told me that she heard about an online platform where students earn money, in fact, not only students but also many people earn money through freelance platforms and become rich. She inspired me to start working and all the plans for my future collapsed. Every day I set goals for me and realized that my life became a game for me, and each level had its difficulties.

Many things have changed and now I see another image of women's roles in Armenia. Now they work harder than men, they earn more than their husbands or boyfriends, Armenian women become more confident, independent, and hard-working. They always were hard-working and smart, but as their lives were limited, they couldn't self-develop and improve themselves. Although they are busy, they did not forget about their families which are and will always be the priority for Armenian women. I always loved the Armenian culture, but some of them were annoying me like the one about men who do not let their women work.

As I have mentioned, I am a marketing specialist, and I work in the most famous Factories of Armenia, in Yerevan Brandy Company. I am a brand design manager, and I really love my job, I work with the coolest people and strive to develop every day I pass at my desktop. I understand that everything starts from small steps. Yesterday, I was a freelancer who was writing 3000 words for only $5 and now I am a freelancer who earns more than a few hundred dollars a month and I am that little girl who was dreaming about her own little business and now planning to open one. WOMEN! Do not be afraid of any changes, do not be afraid of the first day at work. Nothing is given so easily, you must invest all you have, to reach some heights and be proud of yourself. Now I am 22 years old, and I can surely say that I AM PROUD OF ME. Don't hesitate that something will not work for you, believe in you and you'll get everything you wish.

I hope my little story will help some of you to find confidence in yourselves and start something you were dreaming of for a long time. Always repeat a sentence in your mind 'I will get everything I want and reach everything I dreamt'. Good luck!

My Life As A Woman: Artsakh Edition

No doubt Karabakh is probably known as a center of many discussions between two neighboring countries, Armenia and Azerbaijan, but not all know that it is already an independent country with its President and political structure. Yes, the capital is Karabakh, Artsakh was and always will be in the center of attention, but thanks to our strong and supportive population, no one can conquer our country. Artsakh is really an interesting place, where you can admire beautiful nature, tasty food, and kind people. Karabakh and Armenia have a lot in common and that is why we have a strong connection and powerful friendship. What I love about my country is that people here are super neat, you will never see a little garbage on the ground, which is really a rare thing. I can't stop talking about our national dishes, and no comment about beautiful places, so it is worth visiting our country.

My name is Anna, I am already a grandmother with a rich life and experiences. I am a 71-year-old woman, I was born and grew up in a stepfamily, but received all the love from my step-parents. My father was my uncle, yes, it is an accepted tradition among Armenians to give your child to your brother or sister if they can't have them. And so, my mom gave me to her brother as she already had a lot of children. My uncle was very rich, and I grew up with no need of anything, he gave me everything he had, and I was a very happy child. I studied in a local school after I went to Yerevan, Armenia to study at a State University. In Yerevan, I met my future husband, I married him and stayed in Yerevan. Only in my 40 years, I knew that all this time I didn't know who I called father and mother. It was really hard to accept, to know that your cousins are your native sisters and brothers, but I always remembered how I grew up, in a peaceful and beautiful family and I was a mature and wise woman so everything was fine.

As an individual, I was always dreaming about my own business, about being self-established and confident, but Armenian women live in a different world when they marry someone. Every Armenian guy can approve it, that here in Karabakh, Armenia women will be modest, household and calm. And yes, that is what my life became. I had four children and my whole life I gave them. I can surely announce that I am the happiest mother, wife, and granny and I wish all the women in this world to find their halves, be happy, and enjoy life because it is given once, and we have to live our lives in the way we want. Also, I advise being strong because, believe me, life is not that easy, and many different bad and good situations will happen with each of us. Be strong, never give up, and be the way you want to be.

My Life As A Woman: Aruba Edition #1

I grew up on the island of Aruba, also known as the happiest island in the Caribbean. I am the youngest of four siblings but not really the most spoiled, like most people would think. My parents were both Dutch and strict with all of us, but that didn't stop me from having such an amazing life surrounded by the sea and sun every day. One of my favorite childhood memories is having the chance to go and swim in the ocean during my class break, and then go back to the classroom salty and ready to learn! I could spend hours in the sea just swimming and enjoying the weather with my friends, and to be honest, I am sure I spent more time barefoot than the time I spent wearing shoes.

My family on the island was small, just my parents, my siblings and me. My aunts and uncles lived in either the Netherlands or any other country nearby. Most of them married people from other countries, so you can imagine… whenever we are at family reunions, none of us look alike, but we all speak multiple languages so it's funny to talk to them. You can start the conversation in English and then answer in Dutch and go from there to Spanish in seconds.

My dream was to become a doctor just like my father. He was my biggest motivation and inspiration because he worked in the Red Cross during World War II, before moving to the island and meeting my mother. However, when it was time for me to choose a degree, I decided to study Tourism instead. The reason? To be a doctor, I had to go live in the Netherlands because the island didn't have a school for that. I wasn't very excited with the idea, so I stayed and studied for a couple of years and then got married, so I couldn't finish my studies. Not having a degree didn't stop me because I knew four languages: Papiamento (the native language on the island), Dutch, English and Spanish. The latter one I learned thanks to my husband, because it was the only way we could communicate.

Growing up I opened a few businesses with some friends that didn't last long, but we had a lot of fun and learned how to treat clients and deal with inventories. Later, in my career, I found a job in an embassy thanks to the many languages I spoke. That was by far one of the best work experiences I had. Although I didn't have much free time to spend with my kids, I had the chance to go to important events, get to know people, and work with employees from different parts of the world.

My advice to other women out there would be sometimes you have to stop and smell the roses. Not everything has to be about work, you also need to have free time to invest in yourself, and of course in your family as well. Sometimes we get too caught up with work that we forget we have lives outside of it. Also, don't be afraid if you don't have enough experience, there is always an opportunity to learn. Go out there and find something you enjoy doing!

My Life As A Woman: Aruba Edition #2

Where did you grow up?

I grew up on a tiny island in the Caribbean called Aruba, close to the coast of Venezuela. White sand and beautiful blue water where it's summer every day.

How did you grow up?

My parents got divorced when I was four and I was brought up by my mother, who is a dance teacher, together with my older sister, grandmother and grandfather.

Did you have anyone who inspired you?

My grandmother, for sure, has inspired me a lot in being a strong independent woman that I am today. She taught me that everyone can achieve whatever they want in life, ONLY if you are willing to sacrifice and work hard for what you really want.

I have my bachelor's degree for dance teacher and studied in Holland. My mom has her own dance school here in Aruba, Skol di Baile Diana Antonette and she is the first person on this island to get a scholarship for studying the art of Dance. So, I basically grew up taking dance classes almost every day in the dance school.

What you love about your culture?

Aruba has a lot of culture! We are also a multicultural island, people from all over the world live here, and we as Arubans can speak four languages first our native language Papiamento, English, Dutch and Spanish. We celebrate Carnival every year in the months of January and February where everyone will dance upon the streets in beautiful Carnival Costumes with the music of Steelpan, brass bands, and Road March music (Soca music).

We celebrate on the 18th of March, our national day with typical Aruban Food, which is Pan Bati (corn bread) with Carni Stoba (stewed beef/chicken) and lots of cultural dances like, the waltz, mazurka, tumba, polka, and the danza. All these dances came to Aruba from Europe a long time ago. In the beginning, we only had Indians living on the island, you can still see their paintings in the caves that we have here in Aruba.

What are you currently doing for work?

I work as a dance teacher in a high school and I also teach dance classes at my mother's dance school. I had breast cancer in 2015 and it was a very hard time for me, but I pulled through and survived. It wasn't easy for me, being then only 34 years old, healthy, and being super active getting a disease like cancer. It broke me physically but most of all mentally. It took time for me to fully get out of that dark period, but I think the support of family and close friends helped a lot.

After getting cancer, I felt I was reborn, giving a second chance to share my passion, knowledge and love that I have for the Art of Dance. I started at the end of 2016 with new dance styles on the island that nobody had given before and by organizing different dance workshops about dance as an empowerment medium for women. They feel more confident about themselves not only in my dance classes but also in their daily routines!

I became my own boss in creating things that I love and enjoy, and I get to share this with all the women in Aruba, the Caribbean and the rest of the world, through social media.

Advice that I have for women here in Aruba and for women across the world is; life is too short to doubt yourself. Live with passion and do what makes YOU happy! We only have one life, so LIVE IT!

My Life As A Woman: Australia Edition #1

Being a woman in Australia is a lot easier compared to the previous years and equality is all the rage, not just for same sex-marriage but equality in the workforce as well, which is good in my opinion. What I love about being Australian is the Australian food. Our culture is diverse and is not just one cuisine. Religions in Australia are also not pressed upon such as other countries due to having a diverse culture.

I grew up in Perth of the western side of Australia, being the eldest of 6 children who all were more diverse than the next, was difficult. Due to be the eldest, I also carried a lot of the responsibility in the family and was the one to make all the mistakes, so my siblings didn't have to, which sucked! But being the eldest has its perks because I never got hand-me-downs!

Growing up, the person I was truly inspired by the most was my mother, she influenced me to work hard at my hobbies which were cooking and roller-skating *spoiler alert* I earnt my certificates in Kitchen Operations and became a professional coach in roller-skating. After many years of hard work and winning, I had to leave the roller-skating industry due to moving to the countryside. From growing up at a young age (too early might I add), I made it my personal mission to one day follow my dreams to own my own business. By age 13, I was starting my first job at the local roller-skating rink and extra money on the side from coaching. By age 16, I made the decision to study Business Cert II and III and Kitchen operations Cert II in school. By 18, I moved myself into a rental and found I wanted to enhance my career in business, so I applied myself to move onto Cert IV. By 20, I moved back to my parents onto their farm and built my own tiny home. I think my real motive to choose this career path was to be my own boss.

I currently have a job working in the city as a materials handling operator, which isn't as glamorous as it sounds but it's a job and a good paying one for a woman my age. I'll soon have my dream job.

My struggles as a woman has been growing up in the spotlight to sexual abuse and all that good stuff, NOT! Don't worry ladies, you are never alone, it had pushed me to be a better person by shaping the woman I am today. Though I have achieved a lot of my goals in life, there will always be something missing which is to have grown up too fast. Another struggle I had was not being able to enhance my career development in the company I was working for; my ideas and processes were never recognised, as I was perceived as too young and a woman without experience.

My successes in life have been my greatest achievements. 108 gold, silver and bronze medals and 7 trophies from roller-skating, holding over 20 certificates, 5 of which are recognised worldwide and the rest from my current job and from roller-skating. I also set up my life's goals and bucket list that I am slowly working through such as travelling, owning my own house, gaining more experience, and qualifications to own my own business.

BUT that is enough about me. Australian women, my advice to you is we women stand together, live happy and on your own terms!

My Life As A Woman: Australia Edition #2

I didn't exactly have the most conventional upbringing. My parents had spent most of their lives living in Illinois suburbia and were desperate to explore the world, so I grew up with a very alternative, nomadic lifestyle. We had lived in different US states by the time I had turned 7, and then we packed up and permanently and relocated to Australia.

Their love of traveling intensified, so I was homeschooled for several years while we jetted around the globe. We would spend months at a time exploring different continents. They wanted their children to be exposed to the world, so they adopted a unique style of education by completely immersing us in different cultures.

When I eventually started attending a traditional school, it was incredibly difficult to fit in and interact with other students in a classroom setting. There wasn't anything inherently normal about me. I was the weird, homeschooled American kid with the hippie parents. In retrospect, I can understand how that may have been difficult for others to relate to.

I was dragging behind socially, so I switched my focus back to learning. I wanted to explore every interest I had. I studied Italian for six years, learned the violin, started writing, read every book I could get my hands on, and auditioned for every musical. Eventually, when I was wrapping up high school, it was evident that doing things the 'normal' way wasn't an option. I worked three jobs to save up money fast and then enrolled in University to complete my degree remotely so I could continue to travel while studying at the same time.

I chose to major in Journalism so I could be a storyteller. I had seen some incredible things early on in life and wanted to share them with others to inspire them to do things differently. But more importantly, I wanted to start a discussion about things that mattered and write the stories of people who may be unable to do so themselves.

I was studying a double course load and writing my undergrad thesis as I was traveling solo through Mexico and Guatemala. My goal was to finish my 4-year degree in 2 years - right before my 21st birthday. I was repeatedly told that I wouldn't be able to do it, that I wouldn't know how to keep myself safe, and that I was being unrealistic about my goals.

I ended up graduating just a couple days before my 21st birthday while I was volunteering on Lake Atitlan, Guatemala. I decided to ditch my flight back home and settle down in this beautiful country. Over the years, I had also been slowly taking classes in website creation, graphic design, and marketing strategy. I honed up those skills and began freelancing immediately. I wanted to work with small businesses that I adored and help them grow.

There were a few instances of me not being taken seriously as a young female freelancer. Despite building up an extensive portfolio of work and delivering consistent results, I would have clients refuse to speak to me and only communicate with my male partner because they made it abundantly clear that they thought I wouldn't understand.

I worked hard and was able to shatter a lot of people's assumptions about me. Now I run a marketing and design company dedicated to helping small businesses, and I am also in the process of creating my own online writing publication. I've been working from home for years and can absolutely attribute my success to my parents who encouraged me to think outside the box and strive for abnormality.

The truth is - many people fear being different. It can be confusing and at times, quite isolating. However, your individual quirks and unusual interests are the things that will drive your success throughout your life. Embrace your weirdness and don't shy away from the unknown. Open yourself up to new experiences, cultures, and opinions. But most importantly, believe in your own goals and ideas. I've always told people that you'll regret the things you didn't do far more than the ones you did - so take a risk and bet on yourself.

Perspective of an allodial Woppaburra Wise One

By Brisbane Black Community Elder, Activist/Journalist/Author, Warinkil (Crow-woman) Auntie Glenice Croft

Good-ar-moo-lee Ya-nga,

From a young age seeing and experiencing the injustice done to original first nation people, my political intuition was born. My sense of the importance of cultural knowledge, protocols/songlines, language and being educated in the colonial systems was my pathway. Culturally listening to elders like my grandfather Munquadum (Black Cockatoo), who was an initiated Woppaburra man that was removed from our island home, Woppa (Great Keppel Island) in 1902, at the age of 16. He was removed with less than twenty other Woppaburra descendants, who saw and experienced terrible atrocities.

He returned to his homeland many years later but could not stay as the memories hurt too much. My daughter Anunakiu (Shella) and I, as well as two other sisters of mine, two of their daughters, a Woppaburra Elder and friend incorporated a body called KILAC (Keppel Island Lifestyle Aboriginal Corporation). Of which we had the opportunity to take a group of our Elders and witheroos (young people) back to country, where we felt the spirit of our ancestors welcome us home in 1984. We organised for the return of our ancestors skeletal remains from museums and other places to have a cultural burial ceremony on our country.

In my pursuit of truth, I realised how the colonisers/invaders use their English words to confuse us and try to change our perception of who we are, for example the word "aboriginal", is a general word, not our identity. The word aboriginal is used all over the world and as we have many nations in the country it does not culturally refer to us, as our own identity is our bloodline, our land, our history, and our culture.

"I am Woppaburra, not Aboriginal, not Indigenous."

I refuse to be programmed with their English vocabulary. As I write this article, I speak proper Woppaburra way with respect for Elders and Ancestors of this land.

Standing up and speaking out about the injustice and racism and the importance of education and cultural knowledge comes easy to me, because of my life's experience in the Brisbane Black Community and being in black media. Having been part of a group of community people, who established a black radio station in Brisbane, a black community school, and young girl's shelter, this was a time of much activism in Brisbane in the 1980s, and the black community was in unity and our Elders were strong and respected. Also being involved in an organisation called Link Up, of which I was Chairperson in early 2000s and on the National Sorry Day Committee with Elder Auntie Doris Pilkington (now with ancestors), who wrote a book that was made into a movie called "Rabbit Proof Fence". Her book exemplifies the truth about our stolen generation. This organisation was setup by dedicated community people, throughout Australia, to help our stolen generation find their way home.

Today in this country, a new stolen generation is happening as our children are being taken away again. Our children as young as 10 years old are in Youth Detention and treated, in some cases, very badly. Youth suicides are another sadness for our mobs. As Elders within our own tribes, now is the TIME for us to bring back structural cultural protocols, so our mobs can feel and sense our living culture. As the representative/Elder on the Woppaburra Tribal Elders and a Keeper of Knowledge, passed down to me from my grandfather, I find it is important to offer advice to my mob and to be.

Perspective of an allodial Woppaburra Wise One part of the renewal of our young ones learning songlines, language and respecting Elders and men's' and women's business and cultural protocols.

As I walk in ancestors' footprints, visiting many other tribal nations with permission and observing our different ways, as myself being a salt water Inkl (woman). The sea and the winds are a special healing process for me. Other tribes have their Tribal Healing practices. Also to see how the three 'c's,

Colonialization, Capitalism and Christianity, have affected our mobs, our lands and our culture. Original First Nation People are survivors, having lived on this land for over 60+ thousand years. Our culture is everywhen. Our circle of life, yesterday, today and tomorrow is linked so our future cannot be lost.

Peace, love and healing.

At-ta Yani (I go) Kat-tu (the end)

Nha In'da Dhin'd-hinda'lum At-ta bun'dah' Bar-ra'gam (See you when I come back here).

My Life As A Woman: Australia Edition #4

I was born in Inverell and was rejected by my stepdad who was part of the KKK. He was okay with an Aboriginal male stepson, but I came into the world as a girl and was left at the Inverell for days. My grandmother, as a WW II nurse, took me from the hospital to raise me as her own. My pop was a WW II serviceman, and both were proud Aboriginal people. I was taught to stand strong and never give up no matter the cost.

My pop had died and my Nan was getting sick. My bio mother refused to accept her culture due to it being stolen. I was put through hell and abused by my stepfather as his opinion of Aboriginal was one of disrespect. That is putting it lightly and I was forced into a life of abuse. Nobody cared beside my strong Nan, my warrior. She tried very hard but couldn't, but nothing would stop me from living here.

At 11, I was put onto the street. I was alone, and being an Australian Aboriginal, racism was strong. I was at a place in the Armadale youth refuge in 1992. It was hell and I tried to take my life and I remember bleeding out in a bathtub. My mother refused to admit I was Aboriginal and convinced everyone my father was dead. I woke up and an adult was talking, and nothing made sense. After one medical team looked up and saw me awake to their shock, I was then placed in foster care. It was hell on earth.

In the evenings, I was locked in a room with an urn bowl and some food and the door was always kept locked until 6 am the next morning. I was 14 and then placed by DOCS (Department of Children Services) in the care of my stepfather, who convinced them he wasn't abusive, and he was a great man. I was placed back into his care until one day, I was called to the school reception. From there, I was rushed back to Armadale after being told DOCS failed me. I didn't know what that meant. I laid in youth refuge alone and every night was crying for my Nan. My Nan used to write or send money, and we did have a spiritual bond. Her totem was a Koloa and that was my thought every night. I was held in her arms like a little bear.

You mayn't know. Indigenous women have been to hell. My Nan used to cry herself to sleep every night crying for her brown-eyed babies. It seemed the system was ordered by the government to wipe our people out. I used to crawl into my Nan's arms every night as a little girl to comfort her. She had 9 children who were all taken away from her. It killed my Nan inside and my Pop dealt with the grief in another way. My Nan was always there to clean up the mess after my stepfather's madness. My bio mum believed she was an Australian Mexican that came about after she was stolen and put in a home.

My bio father was stolen and placed in the same home as my bio mum. That's how they met, and where I was conceived. They both fell into addiction and lost so much. My biological mother is still struggling with the demons, sadly. My father Harold found his soulmate and decided to continue the search for all of his children. This decision made his life complete and after that, he found happiness in his life. Sadly, cancer took his life away, but he left a legacy that nobody was going to take away his identity as a proud Aboriginal man. He was a very proud man when he finally discovered all his kids and was able to have them all together at once. Together, we could work as a family and finally found peace.

I remember contemplating a second time of suicide after his passing but sat down and stopped when I felt the words of my name run through me. I clearly heard the pros and cons. "This will lead you into the path that you should be going. You were brought up always weighing your pros and cons. Never be afraid of your spiritual connection and you are a strong black woman. Too deadly to give up."

So, I took this quote, "Today I didn't make it but there is always tomorrow." I weighed the odds in favor of my life. I made a formal decision to get an education no matter the cost. I knew this was going to be my future and I would not allow my past to define me, for it would lead to rejection of my future. I fought a battle so hard to learn and in 1994, I was given a gift to move to Brisbane to rebuild myself at Teen Challenge. At 15, I moved around the first 6 months. I found a spiritual grounding inside and it felt like my name was always with me. I refused to accept that I was a nobody and that I am a somebody. With my faith, I believe I was called to go to this private school. I saw my pastor David McDonald and explained my situation.

I asked for no pity and told him I would work to clean toilets, the grounds, whatever it took so I could get an excellent education like everybody else. David said I did not need to do that, just to attend to the exam and meet the Principal of the school and move forward from there. In 1995, I went to Christian outreach college Mansfield for year 11 and I learnt to be an independent strong black woman. The school gave me the grounding I needed to teach myself, nothing is impossible and always know your dreams are possible. Even though I may not ever had a stable home, home is to a point, I was making adult choices that helped me to grow into the person I needed to be.

In 1996 and year 12, I had the opportunity to go overseas on a missionary trip. I was very grateful I was living at home with a family through my church. The father of the house was an ex-police officer who found my bio mum. He had my biological mother sign the paperwork to release me away from her custody completely and outside of Australia, as I was still 17. I learnt what it meant to be free and I controlled my destiny. I went to Tonga, Western Samoa, and New Zealand. It was the best time to see that what I went through was nothing compared to what these islanders have gone through. They were happy and they could travel for four days just to get to worship or to be with the family. It was amazing to see they had nothing but that they were still happy. And that changed my life.

I graduated and finished my law degree. I married in 1998 to my husband and am still married to this day. We have three children and my faith has always got me through. In my journey of life, I had the blessing to find my father who I got to be with for many years before he died in 2015 with cancer. I may not have a great relationship with my biological mother, but I had a wonderful relationship with my Nan who sadly passed in 2006. I want to be encouraging for my Aboriginal community who have been disadvantaged in so many ways. Dream and don't let people tell you that you can't do something. No matter what your circumstances around you are, if you stay focused, you can become the person you want to become. Stand up for what you are and who you want to become stable too late to change who you are to become a better person.

My Life As A Woman: Australia Edition #5

I was born and brought up in Australia in a city known as Canberra. Life was hard since I lost my mother when I was still young. My father married another wife, who accelerated my situation. My stepmother was cruel because she told my father to stop schooling me. My father hated me and would sometimes beat me for no reason. Since I could not withstand the beatings, I decided to go to my grandmother who lived in the same city but a different street. My grandmother, who was an Aboriginal widow, was a good-hearted woman. She taught me to be reliable, no matter how difficult the situation was.

The teachings my grandmother gave me reminded me of what I should do to make my dream come true. My goal was to be a lawyer. This dream could only be realized if I was away from my father's house, which was under the influence of my stepmother. He did not value my education. I felt that my dream of becoming a lawyer wouldn't be realized since my grandmother had no money to help me continue with my studies. The society I lived in valued women as the most critical being, but to me, my future mattered a lot. Each day I would think of what would happen tomorrow considering the situation I was in.

Since my grandmother was unable to educate me, I dropped out of school and started hawking at 12 years of age. The struggle was so hard that I sometimes wished for death. I had to walk long distances to sell fruits and return home late in the evening. Sometimes customers would eat the fruits without paying or would pay half the price of the fruit. After a year of struggle, I met one middle-aged man who approached me as a customer. The man had seen one of the customers picking my fruits without paying. He asked me about my situation and decided to accompany me to my grandmother's home. Upon seeing our condition, he volunteered to sponsor my education. I felt happy since I knew I could accomplish what I had always dreamed.

That marked the end of my suffering and the beginning of my success. I finished my studies and graduated with good grades. I was employed as a lawyer, a career that most people in my community considered for men. I also joined a women's group that was to inspire young and older women of their struggle in life. Up to date, I am a lawyer advocating for voiceless women in society.

My journey to where I am has been a difficult one. It has been full of ups and downs. Despite the society valuing Aboriginal women, education and empowerment are still lacking for them. My advice to women in Australia is that they should be firm, and focused on achieving what they desire in life. Since challenges are inevitable, the best thing is to be determined and find positive alternatives as well as sharing problems with their fellow women.

My Life As A Woman: Christmas Island Edition

Living on a small remote island means family is important. You rely on them to be your role models on how to get through each day as an islander especially with limited places to go. Keeping yourself busy is a big thing especially when you have spent your whole life here with a population of only approximately 1,000 people.

Growing up on a small island means you need to get used to no malls, things taking forever to get here, slow internet, expensive groceries due to pricey shipping, but despite all these things, it makes you appreciate what you have. Living on Christmas Island has taught me what it feels like to be part of a tight community where everyone looks after each other and respects each other's differences and cultures. What I love about living here is that men and women are treated quite fairly. We are acknowledged all the time and we are recognised for our outstanding efforts to help bring this community together. Whether it be volunteering, working, playing sports, we as women come out to be just as good as men.

Things have changed as the years went by. Women are getting more involved. I have learnt a lot being part of our local Kung Fu club where we perform Lion Dance as part of our Chinese culture and beliefs. Over the years, more women have joined the club compared to when I first joined in 2010 where there were many more men than women. As the years passed, more women were encouraged to join in and overcome the stereotype where Lion Dance was for men only. Back then, no women got to perform Lion, only instruments. Nowadays we are seen to be performing in the costume on a more regular basis.

The hardest thing I had to overcome was losing my grandpa to cardiac arrest almost four years ago. It all felt unreal to witness him lying on the floor motionless. I admired his strength, especially during the years he was diagnosed with cancer and overcame it. He became deaf because of chemotherapy but that did not stop him from making the most of his life. We had an unbreakable grandpa and granddaughter connection and for that I am grateful. He taught me the importance of providing for your family and looking after your loved ones through his love for fishing. Providing for your family is a key skill you must have whether it be fishing or growing your own fruit and vegetables as it helps with the costs of pricy groceries.

Over the years, I became a strong talker mentally. My grandma is another great inspiration to me, and I admire her strength. She raised my mum and four other kids mostly on her own for a while back in Malaysia when my grandpa worked on Christmas Island. Years later, she worked tirelessly looking after her grandchildren from our childhood until now. She brought us home cooked lunch every day to school from kindergarten until we graduated. To this day, she still cooks dinner for my family and me. She is in her late 60s but is still getting actively involved in gardening and walking. She is a strong woman and I aspire to be just like her.

I currently work at our local supermarket as a cashier and help wherever I am needed. I also like to keep myself busy, so I have a second job as a volleyball umpire every Thursday night for our local competitions and occasionally, I also babysit. Living here and having multiple jobs really takes the pressure off your finances. I always try to take in as much advice as possible from the people around me as it really helped me grow as a person and makes me appreciate my loved ones while they are still around. Do not be afraid of trying new things as I always tell myself, if you believe, you have the power to succeed and you will go far in life.

My Life As A Woman: Cocos (Keeling) Islands Edition

Hi all, my name is Lauren Gloria, I grew up in Home Island, located in Cocos (Keeling) Island, a remote territory of Australia. Despite the remoteness of the island, children are raised just like any country other across the globe where they are taught values and traditions. As a young girl, my grandmother was my role model. We were so close that I learned plenty from her, such as her many recipes and secret ingredients. This knowledge essential as it allowed me to take a more active role in the celebrations on the island where both communities from West Island Home Island come together for a feast.

This part of the culture was amazing as I felt significant in helping out with the cooking, which was the woman's role while the men set up tents to hold the feast. Thus, I wanted to be a chef, but I studied until the secondary level. Despite this, I actively sought out opportunities in the major hotels and cottages on the island.

I got lucky and found a position as a kitchen porter as I did not have formal training. Despite gaining experience for ten years, I never got promoted to junior chef. My concern was that I had seen other individuals with less experience and the same level of education get promoted ahead of me. The only difference between them and I was the gender. At first, I believed that I was doing something wrong, and I asked my supervisor why I never got a promotion. There was never an answer, and I worked intending to save up some cash and open a small restaurant. This was a challenge as the pay was not great, but I finally managed to leave the restaurant. Despite the hardship of working in the restaurant, I had acquired plenty of knowledge of the operations.

I opened a small restaurant focused on selling traditional foods with recipes that I had acquired from my role model. This was a huge success, but I struggled with operations due to the amount of capital needed to run the restaurant. My friend advised me to apply for a loan as he had gotten approval on his first application while in a worse financial situation than mine. However, this also proved to be unfruitful as I had no collateral, unlike my other male siblings, who had inherited a piece of property when my dad passed away. The business did get off running thanks to a friend's loan but not without understanding the subtle challenges that women face daily. The society is structured in a manner that makes it difficult for women to access finance as they lack the collateral. My success in running the restaurant was a testament to the struggles women face in overcoming social challenges.

My advice for women in Cocos (Keeling) Island is to form women empowering groups that can allow women to influence changes in society and improve their lives. I have learned that trying to make it by yourself is challenging but very possible. However, having a large group of women in your community means that it is possible to point out the challenges and ensure that they are addressed as there is power in numbers. Women worldwide face a society designed to undermine their contribution, and not acknowledging these challenges is a way to ensure things remain the same.

My Life As A Woman: Norfolk Island Edition

My name is Anna. I was born and grew up in a town of Burnt pine in Norfolk Island. I was brought up in an impoverished family since my mother, who was the breadwinner, had lost her job. My mother lost her job due to lateness, as she spent a lot of time preparing my sister and I for school. My jobless father also relied on my mother. When my mother lost her job, my father left home and never came back. My mother ended up doing small chores like laundry in our neighbors. She could sometimes go to hotels to do the laundry and come back the following day. The town I grew up in was the best for women to live, though, women's safety was the primary concern.

I loved Norfolk Island because of the different cultures brought by different people. These people mostly share their culture through sports, like golf. The sport was for leisure and usually played by men, though I had a chance of playing, people especially, women looked astonished upon seeing me playing. I discovered from their reaction that most hindrances that women face are created by themselves. The stains my mother went through inspired my dream of becoming a manager. I went to a business school where I graduated with honors. Currently, I am a manager in one of the best hotels in Norfolk Island. I represent women who are discriminated against because of their gender. I am also the chair of women group formed to explore the struggles that women face like my mother.

My journey from childhood to where I am today has been full of strains and achievements. Ideally, Norfolk Island is one of the best places for women to stay. Though it is true, challenges like social class and gender inequality still exist. This is because when I joined golf, there was a mix of reactions concerning gender. If my father had been a rich man, my mother would not have struggled so much to take care of us. My mother could have still retained her job because they could have afforded the salary of a nanny.

I advise women of all ages in Norfolk Island that the towns they live in offer an excellent condition for them to achieve. However, some cultural beliefs are hard to endure. Therefore, the struggles they face should not discourage them but motivate them. Successful women across the globe did not look at their culture or rely on their society to be what they are today. They looked at their capabilities and skills to attain their objectives. Participating in small groups that have definite goals is essential. These groups may offer advice that may help solve problems that most women go through. Groups can also have project ideas that can help secure their future, since they will not depend on one job to get income. The society we live in may be useful in valuing women, but other issues like gender equality and social classes remain. Therefore, empowering women through education and groups will shape their future.

My Life As A Woman: Tasmania Edition

I was brought up in Tasmania, which is one of the States of Australia. In this State, I discovered many things that define a woman. Being a young kid, my parents were alcoholics and could not take good care of me. I had to migrate to my maternal Aunt, who had five children, to stay there. My Aunt being a divorcee, had to struggle hard to feed and educate her kids and me. Despite all the struggles she underwent, she was a great contributor to my teenage life. In Tasmania, women are highly recognized in society, but as a teenager, my worries were about my future life. Although the State had a good condition for women to live in, influences such as drug abuse were the major challenge. Therefore, women had to control their motion to endure the problem.

One thing I loved about Tasmania was the diversity of culture. It is a place for people from different backgrounds. These people come with their cultures, experiences, and traditions. Participating in various activities is possible, though, from a traditional perspective, there are certain activities such as certain sporting activities that women are not allowed to play. It made me realize that most barriers to women's success are not natural but human-generated. All the strains that my Aunt went through inspired me of becoming a businesswoman. I went to a school of business, where I completed my studies and graduated with good marks. Currently, I own a boutique shop and am the chair of the women's group formed to appreciate and motivate women like my Aunt for the struggles they encounter.

Strains and achievements have influenced my present situation. Tasmania is one of the States that recognizes women most but still has hidden facts. One of them is a social class that still exists. It is influenced by a lack of proper education and upbringing since not all young women get the opportunity of being educated. Some women fail in life due to poverty while others due to poor upbringing and negligence by parents due to substance abuse. After my graduation, I started as a volunteer counsellor to both single and married women. This motivated women that I decided to form a group consisting of women from different classes. My boutique shop has different ladies fashions and those of baby girls. Seeing women walking around the shop while picking their best attires encourages my goal of making them shine more.

I advise women of Tasmania that despite the recognition in society, poverty remains the biggest challenge. Fighting this challenge requires motivation and teamwork. It will empower women from all the social classes, both young and old. Therefore, the struggles they face should not be a barrier to their achievement but an inspiration to pave the way for future success. Success does not come from depending on society but self-reliance and a positive attitude towards life. Engaging in group formation not only helps share our problems but also enlightens us of what to do to become successful women. It also makes women busier that they do not indulge in drug and substance abuse due to idleness.

My Life As A Woman: Austria Edition

Hi! My name is Dorothea, and I am a 23-year-old English student from Austria. I grew up in a four-membered family and my upbringing was conventional. My parents were loving and took great care of me and my little brother. My mother's parents, originally from Montenegro, often visited and helped with household matters, especially when my parents would go on business trips. My brother and I were very lucky never to lack in anything, and we even enjoyed some privileges such as competitive tennis training, science camps, school vacations, and ski trips to the Alps.

My life revolved around tennis and school until I was about 14. My parents were entrepreneurs, but in the economic turbulence of 2008, they had lost almost all their assets which had an impact on their relationship and resulted in a divorce. As an aftermath, the new financial situation required us to cut on some non-essential things, so I quit playing competitive tennis and so did my brother. However, I could not let go of my love for tennis and I knew that, even if I would never play competitively again, I could at least someday become a coach.

English was my favorite subject in school, and I was always quite proficient at it. My knowledge of English helped me to research and enroll myself in a college program for young tennis players and I received multiple scholarship offers from Division I colleges to study and play competitive tennis in the US. However, I decided against it because I knew that, by staying in Austria, I could not only be close to my family, but also make an above-average income as a tennis coach. Soon after graduating from high school, I finished my coaching certificate and started working.

Even though working as a tennis coach enabled me to afford my apartment and car, I felt the desire to go to university. I enrolled in English and American Studies at the University of Vienna, continued coaching tennis and even decided to take up a degree in Sports Nutrition. The biggest struggle for me was balancing a private life with all the goals that I have set out for myself career-wise. I would often leave the house at six o'clock in the morning to make it to my lectures and come back at nine o'clock in the evening after spending most of the afternoon on the tennis court. That kind of a schedule can often harm personal relationships, so I would say that my biggest success was that I hadn't allowed that to happen. I am very proud of my strong family bonds, my relationship, and my friendships.

My advice to young women would be to try and define what happiness and success mean to them as early as possible. Decide on what you want to do and work towards it. Don't be afraid to adjust along the way but have a destination in mind. The path shows itself only to those who know where they are going.

My Life As A Woman: Azerbaijan Edition

I was born and raised in a small town in northern Azerbaijan. I won't divulge the name, but everyone knows that it is one of the strictest cities where tradition is respected, and people live in a patriarchal society. It's perfectly normal for men here to celebrate the birth of sons more than the birth of daughters. My father is one of those men. He always told me to obey my brother, even though he was seven years younger than me. My mother is a housewife who sees the meaning of life in marriage, and how best to get her daughter married. I never realized, does she really like to sit around and watch TV all the time? Doesn't she want to build a career, travel, or go out for a walk or go shopping whenever she wants?

She absolutely did not understand me when I told her with burning eyes how I wanted to travel the world, learn new languages, build a career. I had no friends with whom I could share this, but only a couple of neighboring girls who also did not understand me; they didn't even have a clue that there is another parallel world where girls, for example, can wear whatever they want or live as they want.

I wanted to enter the university in the capital city of Baku, become a linguist and learn many foreign languages, but of course, no one would let me. When I asked my father, he firmly refused me even when I tried to negotiate with him and explain that I do not want to marry a distant relative, as every girl here. I wanted to build my career, but this turned into a scandal, and my mother cried when she saw all this, and there was chaos at home. There were a couple of months left before the entrance exams, and I began to give up and already accepted that I could never realize my dream.

On Nowruz holiday, my grandmother came to us. I really love this holiday, because the whole family gets together, and we all have fun. I really like the process of preparing for the holiday. I always admired my grandmother when she talked about the stories of her youth.

My grandmother ran away from home with her beloved, that is, with my grandfather when she was 17, because they wanted to force her to marry a man whom she had never seen, simply because her father decided so. My grandfather began his career as a military man, and in Soviet times, he was sent to a military city in Germany, before the destruction of the Berlin wall. As a result, he took my grandmother with him, and so my young grandfather and grandmother went to a completely foreign country, not knowing the language. I was delighted that my grandmother, being a girl from the village, was able to find her place in the German city, get a job at a local factory in Weimar, learned German, and made friends.

I decided to share my feelings with her about my problem, and how my dad did not want to let me go to study. She immediately went to my dad, and I was horrified that I would cause a scandal on a festive evening. She resolutely told him: "she will go to study in Baku and I will go with her."

Mom's eyes filled with tears; I was trembling because we both understood that my dad could get mad. But I already said that traditions are honored here, and therefore, it is impossible to argue with the elders. Therefore, my dad stepped over himself, and showing respect to grandmother, agreed. We were all in shock.

It's been 6 years since that moment. I entered university, graduated with honors, and now I work as a freelance translator. And all this thanks to my grandmother, who stood up for me. Now I make good money, and even send part of the income to my family. I see how dad and mom changed their minds and are even proud of me now, and no longer look at me as someone's future wife, but respect me and my actions.

I know that I am not the only girl with a similar story in our country. There are a lot of girls who dream of something more than just getting married, but parents do not allow it. I urge that all the girls listen to their heart and move in unison with it, and never give up. Because this is your life, and when your parents are no longer around, you must learn to stand on your own feet and always move towards your dreams, even if these are small steps.

My Life As A Woman: Bahamas Edition #1

The Bahamas is a real heaven on Earth, where you can relax and enjoy year-round tropical weather. And thanks to nature, it is the most visited tourist place in the world, especially for newly married people who come to the Bahamas and have their sweetest honeymoon here. Oh, I am Carmel from the Bahamas and I am a tourism manager. My job is to organize romantic traveling for couples from different places in the world and I adore my job. It's the best thing to make other people happy and make their voyage interesting. My job is to find good offers for hotels, places to see, cafes and restaurants, other tourist attractions, and add a little romance to it and it is done.

I was born in Nassau, Bahamas in a well-earning family, where I was a loved child who was always in the center of attention. I got a great education, studied psychology at Bahamas College, and marketing in the university. I am happy with the education I have; marketing was always one of the most required professions which every company needs, and psychology you need to master everywhere. For example, when you deal with people and service, you should act like a real marketing specialist-psychologist. I try to combine all this at one table, and still, I have received exceptional words of gratitude.

I always wanted to be a singer as I have a good voice, but life is full of surprises, so I became a tourism agent. Not complaining, as I really reached some success and proud of my career which I built for a long time. I'm already 15 years into it and I'm dealing with the tourism industry on a daily, and I can say it is one of the most interesting jobs. Now I have another dream-goal now, I want to open my own travel company, but it is hard enough for a single woman, so hoping for the best.

The only struggle I had when I was a young girl was to be more than a wife and a household. I wanted to be an independent and courageous woman, as in my opinion, being independent as a woman is a great success. And good for me, I reached it. The only thing I understood is that I am my one and only inspiration, I found out that nothing can motivate and push me up like me. And only now I realized that I am, and I will always be my own inspiration. I would like to say to all women in the world that they are enough the way they are, they should do everything to be self-confident and courageous. Remember the strength comes from inside not from outside. I would advise them to increase their self-awareness to realize how valuable they are when they are being just themselves. Never be a victim of a life situation, be a winner everywhere. People are being mistaken when they say that women are the weakest, women are the strongest!

My Life As A Woman: Bahamas Edition #2

Hello, my name is Chenique Wallace formerly Chenique Whylly. I am a twenty-four (24) year old Bahamian, I was born and raised on the island of New Providence in The Commonwealth of The Bahamas. I am the fourth of five siblings, two girls and three boys. I am a daughter of two wonderful parents and a beloved wife of one Mr. Wallace.

I grew up in Windsor Lane off East Street in a three bedroom apartment that we all shared, growing up was rather tough being a victim of mental abuse by my third grade teacher, who always told me that I would never amount to anything in life, which crushed me. After that, I became more focused and determined to prove her wrong. I started to work on my grades, I took extra curriculum activities and became a prefect with an outstanding G.P.A. of 3.24. Also, as I graduated with honors, I received many awards including designing the Top Logo for my graduating "Class of 2007". Growing up I always wanted to become a Business Administrator because it was my goal! My passion! I knew now what I needed to do. As the years passed, I became involved in the field of business in junior high and I was accepted in a Business Magnet Program later in senior high. It was at that time I met the love of my life, Mr. Wallace.

I have always been inspired by my late grandmothers the way they handled life. I looked forward to the weekends because I can count on my grandmother having prepared meals and baked bread for us. My grandmothers were always financially stable in the way they handled money. On Mondays through Fridays, my father's mother would open her 'Tuck Shop" selling baggies and snacks throughout the community. My mother's mom would always send her grandchildren to the food store. She would show us how to keep an account of what we were spending and how to count the funds that we received. They were such a big inspiration in my life.

In 2013-2014, I enrolled in Success Training College to study Business Administration, I was offered a partial scholarship to complete my studies at Bahamas Institute of Business and Technology from 2014-2016, which I received my Associates of Art Degree in Business Administration. Despite the obstacles I continued to face during my studies, I still managed to obtain a 4.0 G.P.A. with Mr. Wallace at my side. To further my education, I decided to take a QuickBooks course at the University of The Bahamas in 2017.

Due to my recent accomplishments, it led me to be promoted as a full-time receptionist at my job, not only that, but months later I was proposed to by Mr. Wallace, I was so surprised and excited at the same time! The restaurant was so magnificent, the food was great, and everyone was involved. I was so shocked, when the waiter opened the dish to reveal a ring in a dessert tray.

In 2018, Mr. Wallace and I got married in December and we finally tied the knot. Dealing with our wedding has inspired me to become a Wedding Consultant and Planner. It was then that I enrolled while Wedding Planning and Coordination at New Skills Academy in 2019. Following my certification, I then launched CC's Reliable Service and became a wedding, event planner and coordinator. I am currently enrolled with Shaw Academy to focus on my Leadership and Management Studies.

I am proud to be a Bahamian but what I love more is our culture from Junkanoo wearing custom costumes, beating goat skin drums, playing trumpets, trombones, shaking cowbells and dancing until the morning comes to eating Bahamian dishes such as; conch fritters, conch salad, peas'n'rice, crab'n'rice and guava duff. Also, the scenery of our beautiful beaches with pink sand.

As a woman, I struggled with having to be subjected to harassment in the business world and everywhere I go. My success as a woman is my achievement that led me to becoming my own boss in Business Administration.

My advice to women everywhere is to follow your heart, be true to yourself, and always lead by example. Women should never sell themselves short and present themselves accordingly. Never give up on your goals, work hard to achieve your dreams, never let anyone tell you that you CAN'T and in life you will succeed. "If I can help somebody as I travel along, then my living shall not be in vain".

"It's amazing when women can come together with a collective intention, it's a powerful thing."

~ Phylicia Rashad ~

My Life As A Woman: Bahrain Edition #1

These paragraphs are rather emotionally challenging for me to address because I've struggled with talking about certain features of my life. I've also faced unfortunate sexism in my childhood, so my identity as a woman is one, I find myself strongly attached to. My name is Fazila Nasoordeen, I grew up in a small residential area called Muharraq, where my family shifted between houses confined to that region. I remember my youthful years of riding a bike in front of my house, and a fond memory of me strolling alone to a cold store with monopoly money stashed in my pocket. Regardless I was yelled at by adults because I dared to step outside without supervision. A pattern of restriction and rebellion that continued throughout my and countless other female companions' lives.

My brothers were my inspiration, or at least my oldest brother. I thought he was cool like any younger sibling. Like every other child, my career priorities shifted, I was never forced by my parents to pursue a medical degree or become an engineer like the fate of students I grew up with, my parents just hoped a prestigious organization would pay me well. I look back at a nostalgic day in first grade where kids could dress according to their desired profession, and I was the only girl in the entire batch of students who wore a military uniform. I wasn't tomboyish or any of that sort, but I always stood out in that sort of way.

Thankfully, military aspirations didn't get the best of me, I have been working on my business career goals since high school. I've put a large chunk of my time learning about leadership, business, and arts, sowing seeds for my future. Bahrain's culture is guided by the Arab heritage, diversified by fishing and pearl farming practices. Mosques stand mounted at every corner of a street, one mosque calls for prayer, and every subsequent mosque follows, it's mesmerizing echoes take over the atmosphere and reverberates down every home.

The island is home to a large expatriate population, and as cultures change, Bahrain's rich middle eastern culture merged with the refined south Asian practices from Pakistan and India. Another aspect that's special about this culture is its tolerance towards other faiths. I have experienced nothing but hospitality despite coming from a mixed background. I currently work as a freelance artist and writer for blogs.

Being a woman in Bahrain can be both restrictive and have its fair share of boons. It was the first gulf state to implement education for women and it's one of the safest countries to live in, especially for a woman. But there are slight restrictions on how to dress. Since I've lived here my whole life while traveling to other destinations often, I can contrast how parenting here is much more restrictive towards girls than boys. Daughters are treated as a God-given miracle, a key to the gates of heaven, but a more "difficult" and "spineless" child to manage. As a result, the patriarchs in the family hold the duty to "set women right" in the family. I've had to grow up in that sort of environment, and one could hypothesize how it would affect a girl's self-esteem.

Yet I've managed to graduate from high school with a strong sense of self-worth and remained a dreaming, goal-oriented spirit. I immediately planned on what activities I must take part in to boost my leadership skills, honing my crafts as an artist and in acting, and finding accessible ways to earn money, all with balancing my education in a restrictive environment.

My advice to women from a woman living in Bahrain is to take risks, this doesn't just apply to financial risks, but the risks of facing a Goliath in the shoes of David or making that phone call you've been postponing for fears of rejection. You need to constantly re-evaluate yourself, introspect and be unafraid to make drastic changes in your life. Be aware of trends and ask yourself if you're doing something purely based on style vs. something you can really gain from career-wise. Try out new things that not many people are interested in and gain the wisdom of experts. Because no matter what background you come from, "knowledge will set you free". I've heard that statement repeatedly, and now as an adult, I truly understand how much people underestimate it.

My Life As A Woman: Bahrain Edition #2

Where did you grow up?

I am Esraa Hamid, a Bahraini, and I was born in Bahrain in 1983 on 10 May. Bahrain means life to me and if I could achieve something one day, then it is my gift to the homeland.

How did you grow up?

I grew up in a family of three brothers and one sister. I'm in the middle among them. I thought that this family was simple or normal until I became a mother and became certain that God had blessed me with a mother whose life was dedicated to us, teaching us principles, values , and respect for others. And a father… a great father, he taught me all pure qualities... not in words but in deeds.

My mother taught me that values are my treasure, my father taught me that humanity is above everything.

Did I learn that easily? No, I didn't, but life helped me to establish that value and didn't give me a chance to choose. I was the youngest girl in the house, so obviously, I was the little pamper who didn't know, couldn't, wasn't able to. And I believed it for a while.

As for my adolescence, I lived that rebellion to the fullest extent, and I don't regret the misery and the adventures of adolescence, for it taught me what nobody else did. As for after adolescence, I do not remember that because I became a mother when I was twenty.

Now, I am 37, a mother of three sons, the eldest among them is in high school. And the wife of a chivalrous man who endured together the obstacles of life, and today she became what I aspire to, and he became a person he aspired to be.

Did you have parents or maybe a grandmother who inspired you?

My father is my number one source of inspiration. He taught me the true origins of life with his actions. Today, he is my best friend, my advisor, and my strength. As for my husband, he is the motive of love in my life, the reason for my success, and my persistence, and he is the one who has the credit for my knowledge and work.

What did you study / What did you want to be growing up / Why?

My childhood dream was to become a gymnastics teacher, being very social, I like team games and I was sportive as a child. I participated in all sports competitions in the school and I was so special.

My story with studying was difficult. When I graduated, I did not get the major that I was dreaming of. I studied a major and deluded myself that I could not stand it, that's why I failed and didn't excel in it as usual.

But the dream of studying came to me for years and years until it became real in 2016, and here I am today, in the final semester of studying a major that I got to know and loved and excelled in Media and Public Relations. Here I found myself and here I will prove myself, God willing.

Today, I am grateful to my Lord for that academic failure that taught me, disciplined me, and taught me that studying is a girl's weapon and support. Also, I am a certified professional trainer and a certified coach, specializing in Life Coaching and Leadership and self-development.

What do you love about your culture?

I adore my society despite its so many contradictions and other things, but I belong to a historical civilization whose people have been known for goodness, sophistication, generosity, and beauty of spirit. I am very proud of being brought up in a society like the Bahraini society that unites all my highest values, simplicity, culture, and Islam.

What are you currently doing for work?

Today I am fully devoted to training and coaching. Life Coaching is my passion that I got to know after years of soul-searching and life experiences that were in the form of lessons that refined my personality. Empowering people and improving their quality of life is my passion, and I practice my profession with love. Believing that man always needs a shadow, but in light, He can create a plan for a meaningful life. This is my profession now that I am proud of.

Tell me about your struggles as a woman.

My failure in the course taught me the meaning of science later. I faced so many obstacles as a mother, wife, student, and employee for a while. At the beginning of my training career, I encountered many people who believed that I would not be able to excel in the field of training, and I disappointed their expectations by my hard work. I suffered from a financial crisis that almost brought me to scratch, and I am still facing it with full force. I submitted my resignation while I was in love with my work and I apologize for not stating the reason, but God knows it and that is enough for me.

Tell me about your successes as a woman.

I was able to break the housewife's chains. I turned into a housewife, student, and employee. I've trained more than 1,000 young men and women to lead and have made an impact in their lives years later. I trained in the best Bahraini institutes and represented Bahrain abroad in several courses, forums, and forums.

I managed to transfer marital relations from divorce to stability and I was able to help draw up life plans for many people, some of whom later starred. I have nearly 100 certificates, shields, and medals. Despite this, my biggest achievement is that I am a mother of three children whom I was able to raise then in principles.

Provide some advice to women from a woman living in Bahrain.

- Don't discriminate
- Don't compare yourself to any man or woman on this earth
- God created every woman in a unique way that is full of beauty that no other female had.
- Believe this, and be certain that once you answer these three questions, you will be able to find yourself that is incomparable to others.
- Who am I? What do I want? How will I achieve that?
- Women should support other women and be helpful to each other
- Strive with all your strength, so the pain of jihad is much more merciful than the pain of not trying.
- Build yourself and make yourself the project of your life
- Remember that God didn't create us with no vain, each of us has a message to deliver.
- Search for your message in this universe that benefits all of us, and always remember that, You are more beautiful than you think... Whatever you are.

My Life As A Woman: Bangladesh Edition #1

Once upon a time, there was a little girl, named "Sernaz", in a small family living in a tiny small town, with hundreds of dreams blossoming in her mind. Yes, that's me. I was born in Bangladesh as the 3rd child of my parents amongst six. Life was full of rejoice when I was little kid growing among the kinfolks. South-Asian culture is always ritualized, plenteous of traditional celebrations. It's extensively reflected in my culture. The architecture, literature, diversified colorful clothing, traditional music, dance, arts, everything tells you the story of its heritage. One aspect of my culture is a combination of attitudes as cordiality, heartiness, companionship, in a word-hospitality. This extraordinary nobility of my people is beyond comparison. I've traveled to some other countries, never came up with that level of hospitableness. Poverty, illiteracy, population problems, none of the negatives of my country can bid this undeniable positive.

I turned to be a dreamer as I grew. My parents, family, nature, culture, all were my pedagogues for cracking the book on the way of climbing dream-trees. This journey was not velvety, my parents stood by me each time I backslide from my dream. I waded through all the obstacles one-by-one. After high-school, I started studying Computer Science & Engineering. Later, started thinking about studying higher. The education system in Finland is the best, I learnt. I made up my mind to apply in Finland for higher studies, though I knew it would arise so many hardship-blocks. Especially because I'm a woman. I applied to three universities. Fortunately, I got admission in all the three with 100% scholarship-grant, I had to choose one. I preferred MDP in Software Development at Tampere University. It was a rough-house to finally reach Finland, however I made it. Nevertheless, parents were my comrades always. It's the time, my biggest dream came true.

I started my life in Finland on September 2018. As an international student, I've always been honored in this multicultural society. I kept my pace going higher to accomplish the best outcome, started working part time in a local service company. For day and night shifts, since Finland is a secured country for women, no fear, no harm, at midnight for girls to walk on the street alone. Finland has the same right, same priority, same respect for men and women. However, I've completed all courses successfully within 2019, started writing my thesis. A month ago, I've got an offer from a Company as an IT-Intern. I'll join it from June.

In Finland, there are tons of opportunities for you in diversified field of work. Teaching, Nursing, Accounting, Sales and Marketing, Tech and Services, whatever you prefer, several ways to explore as a woman. Some jobs require Finnish-Language skill, not all. Nonetheless, the local government provides language courses and integration programs, free of cost. So, it's no big deal, just learn it, and get a job. Some other organizations arrange diplomas and trainings for those who need more expertise to compete in Finnish market. For expecting or working mothers, Finland is the best place to live. Maternity leave is 2 years, or more. The government will also give allowance to bring up your child happily. Day-care centers are in every corner of a city, surely your child will get the same care there as you do.

Little by little, I've been carrying out to climb all branches of my dream tree. Now, my goal is to become an IT Expert and enjoy life here as a successful woman. My prescription to all the women, dream big and be the change. You'll win in life.

My Life As A Woman: Bangladesh Edition #2

I would like to introduce myself. I am Sudipta Dey. I completed my bachelor's degree and master's degree from Shahjalal University of Science & Technology of Bangladesh. My major was Anthropology. I am a freelancer as well as a news presenter, a reciting artist and program presenter.

Where I grew up:

I was born and brought up in Sylhet, located in northern-eastern region of Bangladesh. As both of my parents used to live in this divisional area due to their job postings; I, along with my two junior brothers, grew up in this city. Sylhet is one of the eight divisions of Bangladesh. This particular city is famous for religious '360 Auliyas or Saints' as well as also named as the city of "two leaves and a bud" for its massive number of tea gardens producing quality tea for domestic and international market. It is also a very renowned tourist place for its wonderful scenic beauty worldwide.

How I grew up:

I grew up in a different way unlike others, because both of my parents were working people. My mother was also a banker like my father. So, they both had to work hard to grow me along with my two siblings. As there was nobody else in our family to help, especially my mother had to work hard to maintain time properly for taking care about our studies, social communication, etc. along with their working schedule. She fixed the timetable for doing separate works in such a structured way that there wouldn't be any remaining tasks. Besides these regular activities, she also provided us the opportunity to take participation in several cultural activities, which was commendable.

Who inspired me?

My parents always inspired me; provided me quality adequate time. If I can't do any work, they made me understand how to proceed it patiently. They always took care of me, my wishes, and tried to make me happy and eventually they were successful. I was fortunate enough to have such parents from whom I learnt the ideology, ethics, honesty, hardworking attitude.

My Background:

I completed my graduation (bachelor's degree) and post-graduation (Master's Degree) from one of the public universities of the country in the subject of 'Anthropology'. I have educated myself to the highest level because I firmly believe proper education can help to develop your own understanding. Of course, my family members helped me a lot to achieve this. As I studied in this reputed public university, which provides me an opportunity to introduce myself to several sectors apart from study resulting a firm strong knowledge, which helped me in my next steps of life. I always wanted to be a human being with open-minded facilities, not only limited to a certain boundary of conventional work time.

My love for my culture:

In our indigenous culture, the social bonding that joins us each strongly is very important. Here we connect in such a special bonding, where everyone shares his/her joys and sorrows equally. The way we enjoy the celebration of an individual's program together, similarly when someone falls in danger or in an uncomfortable situation, all try to solve the situation. Apart from it, we do have our indigenous cultural activities, being inherited from our ancestors; teach us to nourish our culture from our childhood. Overall, this social strong bonding is one of the key features of our culture.

My current work:

At present I am concentrating hard in my freelancing career. Apart from this, I am also taking part in news presentation, program presentation and dancing. These activities provide me with soothing feelings, which in fact boost up my mental strength.

My struggles as a woman:

In Bangladesh, there was a poet named 'Kazi Nazrul Islam', who is considered as our national poet, wrote a poem named 'Woman' stating that "In this world whatever work has been done, half of them been done by women and the rest half have been conducted by men." But unfortunately, this has not been justified from our country's perspective. Rather, you'll find just opposite scenario. In this country, a woman's work has not been acknowledged properly as like as man. In my case, I wished to do lots of things, but due to some limitations like social obstacles and family responsibilities, I couldn't fulfill them yet. I don't know, if I am able to fulfill them ever!

My successes as a woman:

I don't know whether it's success or not. I am trying hard to continue my work. The work, whatever it's small or big, I always tried to finish it with honesty, concentration and hardworking attitude. That's why I always receive positive feedback in my work.

Advice to women from a woman in Bangladesh:

I strongly believe, I am lucky enough to get such supporting family members. But in my country, there are lots of women, who are deprived of such supporting family members. So, I would suggest gaining self-confidence first, and then must be self-dependent, which is mandatory in this society to fulfill your dream. So, nobody will help you; you must set your goal and set the arrangements by yourself only to fulfill your wish. If someone is honest, has firm belief in herself, has strong willing power with hard working attitude, nobody in this world can stop you from fulfilling your dream.

My Life As A Woman: Barbados Edition

I was born and raised in Barbados, which is a small island in the Caribbean. It's sunny, hot and very tropical—I spend lots of time at the beach and I love the water! I grew up as working class, in the southern part of the island in an area called Grazettes with two brothers and a sister, of which I am the youngest. My mother was a primary school teacher, who raised my siblings with help from my grandmother who also lived with us.

Since my mother was a teacher, we grew up strict—which is generally the culture in Barbados. There is a big emphasis on education, as Barbados boasts quite a high literacy rate and this was doubly important in my household, considering my mother was a teacher. My siblings and I were jointly raised by my mother and grandmother, and those two women both serve as a big inspiration in my life. I have quite a large family with lots of aunts and uncles and cousins and I love having such a big family.

When I was 18, I received a scholarship to study at a university in the US, which is where I received my bachelor's in psychology. While I enjoyed my time in the US, I ultimately returned home because I wanted to make a difference at home. Upon returning to Barbados, I started working at the Child Care Board, which is the state-run organization dealing with children's rights, etc. I always wanted to work with children in some capacity, probably inspired by my mother who also worked with children, and I've enjoyed my work as a social worker so far.

Besides the wonderful weather and delicious food, I love how close-knit and family-oriented the culture in Barbados is. It's a very small country so everyone usually knows everyone, even though it means very little privacy, it also means everyone looks out for each other. Everyone is very jovial and lighthearted—Bhajans love to laugh and make lots of jokes!

It is also a very maternal society which means women are held in high regard. It is not uncommon to see women in high roles in the corporate world, as well as doctors, lawyers, and accountants. Women especially are encouraged to get their education as it is seen as a means of elevating themselves. I would say my education and working in a career that I enjoy is one of my biggest accomplishments thus far! In terms of struggles, I think dating for me is quite difficult because the dating pool is quite small due to the size of our population and lots of men are intimidated by me.

If I could offer some advice to other women, as a Barbadian woman, I'd say focus on working hard and that education can open many doors. My own mother, who grew up quite poor, was able to become a teacher by applying herself and focusing on her studies and she passed it off to myself and my siblings.

My Life As A Woman: Belarus Edition #1

When I was a child, one of my favorite hobbies was reading. First, I was interested in adventure stories such as "Treasure Island" and "The Adventures of Tom Sawyer". As a teenager my tastes had changed. I was delighted to dive into Jane Bennet's story from "Pride and Prejudice". I was inspired by her independence, confidence, and thoughts. The next woman to have influenced me was Scarlett O'Hara from "Gone with the Wind". She is not completely a positive character but her persistence, intelligence, and, sometimes impudence, must be admired. All these characters especially changed my mind.

I was born in a little town where I had been spending my childhood and youth. I have an elder sister who supported me. After her graduation, she moved to another country where she lives now. She has always inspired me with her purposefulness and confidence. She wasn't afraid to move to another country with a different culture and mentality. Now she is a mum of two wonderful children.

During my last year in school, I didn't have any idea what to study in university or what to do next. At the end of the year I chose an economics major as I have always loved Math. My university was in Minsk, the capital of my country, and I had to move there. It was my first step to adult life. The first two years were not so easy as I blew tests, had success and different situations which students meet in their life.

As a student I had always tried to help my parents. Furthermore, I took a job at McDonald's where I gained great experience. It taught me to handle stressful situations, to be a part of a team and to communicate. I earned my first money and could not be more independent. My first job wasn't perfect, but it gave me a push to self-improvement and hard-working.

In my free time between university and work, I appreciated the moments with my friends. We often explored our city and visited new places which we found interesting and had an ambiance. In Minsk, one of the most popular and modern places is Oktober street. There are stylish cafes and restaurants, for instance, "DEPO" where you can try delicious food, particularly pancakes. People make this place special. The vibe is so inspiring and free, especially people who are friendly and kind. Soulfulness is a specialty of our people and what became a part of our culture.

I graduated from university over one year ago. Now I'm a part of one of the best IT companies in my country where I communicate with clients and elaborate on our business. It was not an easy path to the true me and I continue to go on to find myself. I proceed to self-improvement and fulfillment. In my job, it is significant to learn new things and to keep pace with the times. Within the job, I can use all my skills and realize myself. I'm so glad to represent such a wonderful company where every person carries value.

I know it's difficult to find yourself and do what you want to do in your life especially in my country. Don't be afraid to try something new that you didn't do before. You can learn a new language or watch useful videos on how to improve your skills. Books remain a source of information where you can even find yourself. Don't worry about failure. Every problem and failure teach us something and makes us better. Love yourself and give your love to others around you.

My Life As A Woman: Belarus Edition #2

I was born in Hrodna, a town in western Belarus, close to the Lithuanian and Polish borders. It can be hard to believe for some, but Hrodna is one of the main towns in the country, and during my childhood (which was in the XXI century), there were no shopping centers or amusement parks. My family lived in a "social dormitory" – a place for families that don't have their own home. There was shower only on the first floor and one kitchen on each floor.

Everything was stuck in the USSR. People crossed the border to buy clothes or TVs or even food. It was all cheaper and better in Poland. It was called "shop tours" to Bialystok and my first one what at the age of 11-12. Spending 15 hours on the border control is not some funny game for children, believe me.

During my childhood, I wasn't keen on peaceful professions. I wanted to become a policewoman, soldier, or cosmonaut. When I was interested in journalism, I thought only about war journalism, when my parents tried to convince me to become a doctor, like my whole family, but I thought only about war hospitals. Mainly, I wanted to fight for all the good against all the bad, but no one had told me that aggression is not the only way.

We have preparation for army in Belarusian schools, but only boys can attend it. As a girl, you can learn to cook and knit, or listen to information about contraception. To make this even worse – before the lesson about menstruation, my teacher checked and closed all the doors so that no boys could come in.

Frankly speaking, I'm still fascinated by the concept of war and how something so ghoulish can happen repeatedly. That's why I started security studies and moved to Poland. Moving to Poland wasn't so hard, as my family is half-Polish, as well a majority of families in our region. I wanted (and still want) to become an academic, which is more studying throughout your whole life.

Speaking about my culture, I love everything about it except for one thing – the fact that it is dying. From 1937 and till nowadays, we are under huge Russian impact everywhere, they even changed our school history books to fit their story and political agenda. I try to do anything, like speaking Belarusian or helping Belarusian book publishers, but it never seems to be enough. It's still hard to believe that anyone has power to change something, because in Belarus you learn that you don't and that you can't.

That's why firstly I didn't react to catcalling or even worse situations. As most students did, I worked as a waitress. Once I had a strike – 3 days in a row as I was working till midnight and every time, some guy aged 30+ came to me drunk and started trying to convince me either to go for a beer with him or once even to have sex with him. I've done nothing, but now I clearly understand that they had no right to urge on anything after my "no".

The same "no" we can openly say to anyone, who uses reproductive violence. The President of Belarus ("the last European dictator") wants women to have at least 3 children, pro-life activists in Poland want women to give birth even after rape, and still proceed even if it can be harmful for the woman's health. However, we are people and we can choose what we want in this life.

I cannot work in Belarus in my field, because it's for politically suitable men only. I cannot abort a child or openly love another woman in Poland, but I can have a voice. It is sometimes frightful to speak, it is sometimes dangerous to share your thoughts and you don't have to do it but remember that we are the change. There is so much that we can do, online support matters, activism matters, showing your thoughts on a topic matters, anything that raises awareness matters. No matter what your views are, don't let anyone make you believe that you are not enough. Because you matter. Each and every one of you. Time flies and every new day is not the same as the previous one and that's what inspires me.

My Life As A Woman: Belarus Edition #3

I was born and raised in Belarus, the country that has opportunities but not as developed as the USA, France, or Austria. Living here definitely isn't bad, but my modern views and my gender make my life a little bit more complicated.

I'm living in Minsk which is the capital of Belarus and I think that I am lucky, because this city has many opportunities, while other cities in my country don't have them. There are many stores, restaurants, and cinemas in Minsk, although there are cities that don't have any theaters or concert halls. We have a lot of universities and different courses. Minsk is developing fast, that's why a lot of people from other areas are trying to move here. But I didn't deal with it. I have a small but wonderful family that consists of my mom and grandparents. My parents divorced when I was 15 and it made my life easier, so when someone says: «I'm sorry», I think: «I am actually glad that I don't see my father anymore because his hysterical character created many troubles for me». I don't think I'm unlucky, because some of my friends have an awful family experience because of alcohol-addicted members.

I was the best student in my school always getting the best marks. I started to dance when I was 13. I was playing tennis. My mom and granny did a great job developing my skills and I am forever grateful. But childhood doesn't last forever, so 6 years ago, I needed to choose a university. That was the time when I needed to figure out who I wanted to become.

I always wanted to be a director in the film industry, but the diploma of our university doesn't mean anything in other countries, and Belarus doesn't produce many films. So, I chose the international marketing sphere. Studying wasn't fun, sometimes I felt like I was wasting my time reading books that were written many years ago although our specialization requires learning new approaches.

I remember one day… it was a lecture by our teacher who was well-educated and intelligent. She never shared anything personal with us. But she said: «I have a daughter. Yesterday she wanted to play in the yard, and I needed to sit there for several hours because I couldn't leave her there alone. She was playing with other children and I was sitting near their moms. We started to talk and damn… They didn't know anything about politics, about other countries, about psychology. They could only talk about some discounts on clothes or food and their children. So, girls educate yourself! » There was nothing unusual in her story, but it made me realize what I really want in my life.

I got a diploma and started to work. I changed several jobs until I found the one which I liked. I'm working as a marketer in a logistics sphere. I've improved my English level by watching American movies. I'm learning Spanish. I've been dancing for 10 years and I'm trying to improve my skills as it's more than a hobby, I want to succeed. I'm taking many online courses trying to improve my knowledge of marketing and analytics. I need to get 3 years of working experience to be able to get an MBA degree and that's what I'm planning to do. I didn't betray my dream and I want to work in the film industry after getting an MBA degree. My dream company is «Netflix», I love its culture and I find it beautiful that it's possible to create and promote films that can educate or help many people. Once my friend betrayed me and I was broken, and one movie is what really helped me because I watched it and felt that I wasn't alone in my vulnerability.

As a female, sometimes I need to deal with people who say: «Why don't you have a boyfriend? » Or something like: «Your purpose is family, not career». Many people in my country have traditional views. But I don't care, because my role models are my mom and some strong female social influencers. And to everyone who feels what I'm talking about now… Don't be afraid to be you! Educate yourself! Think about what you really want to do! Get an education in universities or offline! Meet new people, move or stay at home… but don't be afraid to get rid of toxic friends who don't believe in you.

My Life As A Woman: Belgium Edition

"You live because it's your turn." I figured on myself into the matured lady setting in Ghent. I sprouted intellectually apart from my brothers. They were younger twins. My foremost concern was to oversee them as an elder sister. I accepted them politely that I would be the one to take care and look after them. Like a mentor, I concentrated on pragmatism and discipline. This outlook was in actual the necessitation for them to move forward in their own lifetimes. I reinforced them at every pace of perceiving the globe. Like a messiah, I communicated to them how to inspect the formalities of present creatures and their attitudes. Also, I directed them on how they should mend their behavioral attitude in the logic of humankind. In the same way, I consumed my own journey keening on the account of my hard experiences.

My father joined me during all these moments. Occasionally, my granddaddy used to come and spent time with me. He taught me that bearing and competing hardships is a refinement to achieve prosperity sooner than later. He was a common villager. His stories were, in fact, the root of all my encouragement. Once, he narrated; a group of military force of Western Europe was training in the forest to develop supreme armed forces of their land. Three of them fell into the morass. All other men refused to relieve them. They argued that they did not have any source to escape. If they tried, they would face certain death. So, there was not any expectation of breath for them. However, the three firmed to disregard what the others were uttering, and they continued to attempt and jump out of the morass. Besides their struggles, the group of men at the right side of the morass were still uttering that now the three men should leave, though it was not possible. Finally, one of the drowning men noticed what the others were verbalizing, and he stopped, dipping down, and went to his grave. The other men proceeded to jump out as tough as they could. Again, the crowd of individuals shouted at them to quit the suffering and just allows themselves to die. They fought even harder through the hint of hardest stones fixed at the banks of the morass and they eventually came out. When they got out, the other men asked, "Did you not perceive us?" Both men, the remaining, clarified to them that they were deaf. They believed they were encouraging themselves via their inner voice. The lesson of the story is that despite what the public opinion is, listening to your inner voice is more important, as it was during that night, in which one man attempted to listen to others and died, but the other two kept strong, steady, and paced themselves, so that they could continue to live.

You should also ponder about what you speak before it speaks out of your mouth. The story also suggests that you should not focus on the others' blatancy. You just must hold on to your objective and do what you must do. It does not matter who are you, rather it matters that you are a woman and you need to be more successful like the men of our nation.

I completed my education from the public University of Pascual Bravo, Belgium. I took in English Literature in bachelor's and moved on with journalism. Today, I am running my own website, though it is not having much more high publicity but, in the future, I want to grow the web traffic more. I publish my English articles on my website. Without greediness of income, I give it my best. I also lead a circle of women in a non-government welfare society. I love cultural music in every social language of Belgium and own a musical brand with my brother. I think music is a light of soul. My positive vibes are with the brand that soon it will appear like a well-known brand. I am active and loyal with my work because work is such a thing that you need to be passionate with anything you do which helps you create your identity forever. I am fruitful as a woman as I looked after my little brothers from the early life. Today, I have earned much respect from my younger brothers and they trust me for everything. They consider me as their best friend. So, I found my best relations because good relations are a source to take a more slothful breath. In a goodbye manner, I will advise you; do not depend on others. Create your own path. Your created path will correctly guide you to the fresh and fragrance plants. And with that, relish your plants.

My Life As A Woman: Belize Edition

My name is Divine and I live in Belize City, Belize. Belize City is the largest city in Belize and was once the capital of Belize before it was moved to Belmopan. Being the largest city and the most populated city in Belize makes it the hub of business, tourism and entertainment. It comes with its benefits, and unfortunately, with disadvantages as well. One of the major disadvantages of living in Belize City is the crime and violence prevalent mostly in the south side. Belize, as a country itself records high crime rates annually. Due to the country's small population and high murder rates, Belize unfortunately ranks in the top 10 countries in the world for homicides.

This violence also leads to gender-based violence which is targeted at women. Sexual harassment, sexual assaults, and even rape are rampant in Belize City with women and young girls mostly being the victims of these heinous crimes. Perhaps, more damning than the crime itself is the lax and indifferent attitude of Belizeans towards these crimes. Victim shaming and blaming are prevalent attitudes, and this leads to scenarios where victims, instead of getting justice, are instead, re-victimized.

Having lived in the city for years has meant being subjected to catcalls (with explicit innuendos), being touched and grabbed by men to get my attention, sexual harassment in the workplace, among many other issues. It has also meant being very careful in turning down the advances of male admirers because I feared for my safety. It has also meant having to walk in groups at night on my way back from work or school. Living in Belize can be very unsafe.

Another challenging aspect of being a woman is the negative attitude and the push back that comes from others when they come across an ambitious woman. I can't speak for everyone, but I can say that personally when I have shared my goals and plans of getting multiple graduate degrees and being involved in policy making, I have rarely gotten positive feedback. Being a good Belizean woman is often equated to being in a relationship with a man, remaining faithful and loyal to the man regardless of what he does, having many children with him, and raising these children and taking care of them. While there is absolutely nothing wrong with women who make the choice to follow this lifestyle, the imposition of this lifestyle on women who want something different is oppressive. I have noticed the dissatisfaction and disapproval, especially from my fellow womenfolk, when I share my ambitions with them and let them know that I will not be getting married or popping out babies anytime soon. A lot of women are unconsciously forced into being content with a high school degree, even if they might want more for themselves.

Additionally, I am a very opinionated woman and I enjoy political banter. I have often found myself side-lined and overlooked and interrupted whenever I want to share my take on a political situation. The common notion is that women cannot understand politics; and this notion can be seen clearly in the under-representation of Belizean women in politics. Living in Belize has made me tough and soft; breakable and resilient. It has made me appreciate the complexities associated with womanhood and has also made me aware of how wildly capable women are. The Belizean society could make use of the input of women and would be better off empowering women. Belizean women can do great things if given the opportunity to.

My Life As A Woman: Benin Edition

I'm a native of Bassila, a town located in the department of Donga, in the west-central of Benin. It is a crossroads city, nicknamed the lively city to be a point of attraction for the other districts of the municipality, and even for the neighboring Togo. I was born and raised between its lakes, its marshy trails, and its listed forests. It is a place where vegetation is natural. It is characterized by a mild climate alternating between monsoon and harmattan. However, this climate can be rough.

I had a beautiful childhood divided between tradition, modernity, and religion. As a mischievous little girl, I grew up in the warmth of a Muslim family that taught me the essential values of life. I was taught to be honest, hard-working, empathetic, and to have compassion for others. As for my education and my studies, I was an average student. I worked hard to succeed. That's how I became a woman too demanding with myself, always trying to do better.

My mother, my model

You will say that all our parents are considered role models, but I kept my mother's image as a strong woman. The one who struggles off the beaten track to achieve their goals is worth it. And it was this woman that I became.

Childhood Studies and Dreams

Curious in nature and in view of the way, I worked in literary subjects. My entourage saw me become a senior professional in audiovisual or print media and a great journalist, which ended up being my dream too. As a teenager, I was already imagining myself behind the cameras presenting the TV news. Throughout my schooling, I faced this dream with the best possible reality I could. After my bachelor's degree in literary series, I continued my studies in the field of communication. So, my parents enrolled me in a university of audiovisual and communication in my country and I graduated as a journalist.

What I love about my culture

I love my native language, Andi. It is a bit complex, but it usually arouses the curiosity of people outside the language. And the main characteristic of my culture is that people are very social. For example, I can go to the neighboring hut and ask for food without there being any refusal.

What I'm doing now for work

Today, although I am a little less in the spotlight, I live my passion as an actress of the cultural world more specifically in the field of events and audiovisual services. And, a writing enthusiast.

My struggles as a woman

For me, every day of life is a new challenge in this world that is not often tender with women. I struggle to impose my opinions and my choices. To demonstrate my ability, to have the freedom to do what I want and to fight the prejudices that describe women as weak and submissive, whose place is only at home.

My successes as a woman

A smart businesswoman, I'm a fighter and I am responsible. I managed to open my own event box when I was 28. I am inspired by my power, a source of inspiration for the women around me.

Advice from a woman in Benin for her colleagues around the world.

Be yourself and believe in your abilities. Don't be affected by the vagaries of life, fight to achieve your goals. Only in this way do we impose respect.

My Life As A Woman: Bhutan Edition

I am Phu Zam, a 25 year old woman, from Punakha district in the western part of Bhutan. I was raised up without much problem or struggle under the affection and care of my parents. Both my parents are farmers and they worked hard to see me grow up healthy. My parents inspired me to work hard and to be strong in life, no matter how tough it was.

Generally, in Bhutan, ladies care for the family, getting ready the food and weaving materials for family use to make available to be purchased. However, my parents had enrolled me in school and started my primary education at the age of 6 and I studied up to high school. I am very much interested in teaching and my aim in life is to be independent and become a teacher, but I could not reach my dream as I was not qualified for college. Still then, as of now, I do teach my sister's children during this COVID-19 pandemic due to the close of schools.

Every nation has their own social and customs, similarly my nation of Bhutan has distinctive social and conventions. Out of all, I love our national dress gho for men and kira for ladies. Bhutan's customary dress is one of the most unmistakable and obvious parts of the nation. It is necessary for all Bhutanese to wear national dress in schools, government workplaces, and in formal events. Men wear a gho, like the Tibetan chuba.

The Bhutanese hoist the gho to knee length and hold it in place with a woven cloth belt called a kera. The kera is wound tightly around the waist, and the large pouch formed above it is traditionally used to carry a bowl and money. Women wear a long floor-length dress called a kira. This is a rectangular piece of brightly colored cloth that wraps around the body over a Tibetan-style silk blouse called a wonju. The kira is fastened at the shoulders with elaborate silver hooks called koma and at the waist with a belt that may be of either silver or cloth. Over the top is worn a short jacket-like garment called a toego.

Being a lady is at some point favoring and at some point, hard as we must face challenge when nobody underpins us. However, as the country steps up with development, Bhutanese women are moving beyond household chores and becoming main income earners in the family. Nonetheless, the female unemployment compared with male unemployment is high and the individuals who are utilized have poor professional success possibilities and the nature of employments held by ladies will in general be second rate compared to that of men, as ladies work in low-paying divisions.

I am still young and I have nothing to reference about my prosperity, but I will accomplish what I had dreamed to be one day, as I am determined and hard-working woman. Along these lines, the main counsel I can give, or offer is to be unassuming and steadfast lady and consistently be thoughtful and empathetic to every sentient being and above all be an independent woman.

My Life As A Woman: Bolivia Edition #1

My name is Sonia, I was born in Tarijia, Bolivia, 53 years ago. I come from a home of four siblings and separated parents. It was not easy being the oldest in a home where our father abandoned us, and my mother worked while I took care of my brothers. A welcoming town, palm trees, parks and cafes adorned the streets and a warm climate, fortunately. Four women, four sisters, in a very small house where Mom had to leave us all day, in order to go out to find daily sustenance and return very tired for us to take care of her so she could rest. It was not a very familiar panorama, but like this, the monotonous days passed.

Fortunately, we all went to school; my mother had all the faith that someday, one of us, or even all of us, would get ahead to try for a better life. Roxana, Lidia and Rosmery, the best sisters: naughty, happy, supportive and loving. In the middle of a rather difficult economic situation, we were a large family of women with a great mother. To describe mom is to speak of a very brave woman, working in the vineyards like any man, fighting shoulder to shoulder, to defend her work amid a very macho era. But life changes and for the good of us, we went to live in the country's capital, where Mom had the great fortune of having better jobs that allowed her to give us a better life.

Meanwhile, we older ones each made our lives. For my part, working with my mother in a store, I met a great man, an Italian who had traveled to "La Paz" for business and who worked with the gemstone business. My mother began working with him and gradually learned about the business, where he supported her, seeing her as capable and so full of business vision.

Little by little, we fell in love and went to live in Italy, in a city called Napoli. He was older than me and already had a son almost my age. Quite a particular situation, but it was not any problem. Although it seemed like a fairy tale for me, it was not. A wonderful mature, wealthy man, and I, in Italy, living comfortably, but my personal reality was another. I greatly missed my family, my city, the food, the customs, and costumes. In conclusion, I was not happy.

I was very young and could not measure what was happening in my life and the fact that I thought I would not have children was also something that filled me with sadness. A man with his life made did not think about babies. At almost 50 years old, you don't think about it anymore. I tried to make my life in Italy, but I couldn't adapt. So, I decided I would go back home. I came back with a great dream: to work with my mother and my sisters. They were fine, but life in Bolivia is not easy and I did not want them to continue having difficult times, in jobs that were sometimes not very well paid.

Once I returned home, I looked for them and I told them my great desire: to be the owners of a school, to teach all of them and Mom was the director and manager of the coffee shop, because she was very good for business, money and finances. A simple job for her, with her great organizational skills. Of course, supported by us.

At the beginning, it was not easy and my sisters did not believe in this project and they said to me "No joches los petos", which means, "Do not look for trouble", but my spirits did not drop. I knew that having a business like that, would give us financial strength and a better quality of life. I had studied art and language in Italy and to be a teacher, it would be very useful. Roxana was fortunate to have studied English, Lidia was an expert in crafts and sports and Rosmery could help with systems and coordinate the discipline, because she was very organized. The rest would be covered by hired teachers.

So there we were, again together, fighting together, at Mom's side and taking care of her. The family is the greatest treasure and when I left the country, I felt that I lost that treasure that was not bought, nor compared, with family love.

My Life As A Woman: Bolivia Edition #2

I grew up in a small city of around 1.4 million people in the little-known South American country of Bolivia. Unlike most of the people in the country, I was lucky enough to have been born into an upper middle-class family that provided me with an education and the comfort of financial security. As a result, I experienced a less harmful version of the misogyny so heavily ingrained in this society. Unfortunately, others aren't as lucky as I have been and are victims to sexual abuse or violence by their husbands, fathers, or employers throughout their lives. At times, it can be hard to even watch the local news since not one day goes by where you don't hear of husbands killing their wives or fathers impregnating their daughters. And this is only the small percent of abuse that gets reported.

On the other side of the spectrum, sexism is not as outwardly displayed. From a young age, girls are indirectly, and sometimes even directly, taught to value their appearances as if their future depends on it because, in a way, it does. Most of my classmates' mothers were young housewives who had married wealthy men. Perhaps this is part of the reason why women aren't as valued as men but how can women be expected to become powerful and successful in such a limiting society? In my case, I was lucky enough to have been raised by a divorced grandmother and a divorced mother, both of whom were the greatest role models anyone could ask for.

In her youth, my grandmother had followed the typical path set out for women. She was a pageant queen who married a landowner twelve years older than she was. There is no doubt that they married out of love but, as most marriages go, it didn't last. After their divorce, she flew herself and her two daughters to Florida to start a new life. She took English lessons at the local university and began an import-and-export company that didn't pay much but was enough to get by. Once the divorce was finalized and my mom and aunt were in college, she came back to Bolivia to find that she had received a few acres of land and cattle as part of the divorce settlement. With no source of income and no experience in the cattle business, my grandmother knew she had a lot of work ahead of her. And so, my mother gave up her dreams of being a stockbroker and flew back to help with the new family business. Together, they developed the land entirely by themselves in a way that only men had previously done. With such independent and hardworking women as role models, I knew from a young age that I could build any life I wanted for myself, so I chose a life in architecture.

Growing up in what used to be a Spanish colony, I couldn't help but admire the beautiful architecture created by a combination of the Spanish and the indigenous cultures. Walking along the streets of the city center, I marveled at the great arches and brick walls. I created stories for every one of the large houses facing the main plaza. I imagined the great Spanish generals hosting celebrations in their homes and all the ladies dancing in their beautiful ball gowns, their elaborately done curls swaying with the rhythm of the music. Eventually, I decided that through architecture, I could build the setting for stories of much greater beauty and depth.

Despite its faults, I found it impossible not to love my culture. Some of my fondest memories are a direct result of this beautiful culture. I remember how every year on Bolivian anniversaries, the school would organize celebrations in which students read poetry, danced to the traditional songs, and read about the history behind the event. I loved being a part of something bigger and feeling connected to everyone in my community. In some ways, the idealist within me wishes modern society could be more like in those days, where everyone played an equally important role in the eyes of everyone else.

I suppose most of the challenges I faced growing up in a superficial society have been a result of the competition and stress that this superficiality created. I distinctly remember that ever since I was ten years old, my actions and opinions were dictated by what was considered "socially acceptable." From the way I talked to the way I walked, every decision I made was considered in the context of society. I was so preoccupied by being accepted and sought after that I didn't develop my personality until I recognized what I had done. This epiphany came around high school and I decided that I would no longer live to please anyone other than myself. Looking back, I see this as one of my great successes. I learned not only how to be my own person but also what it meant to be a woman today; an independent free-thinker who needs nobody but herself.

If I had any advice to women or young girls, it would be to live for yourself. You are under no obligation to meet society's expectations if that is not what you wish to do. Don't be afraid of being judged or criticized for what you believe in, especially if it comes from the heart. Work hard to open doors that would otherwise have been closed. Invest time into developing your mind, because today, it's your most useful asset.

My Life As A Woman: Bosnia Edition #1

The story of Bosnian women begins with determination. I have known that ever since I've overheard the bits and pieces of my grandmother's story, at my early age, abroad, not fully able to grasp the meaning behind it, yet somehow feeling the weight of it, of what I'd later learn to be a story of so many women in Bosnia – a story that continues and, though ever changing, has the same roots, those always leading back to the same thing: determination.

I did not know my grandmother because she died in a war in Bosnia when I was very little. She had four children, all whom she has raised while being enrolled at a university. She was studying to be a teacher, and she was one, to my mother and her siblings, guiding them through one course that was more unpredictable and under the pre-war time necessary than any other life. Upon coming back to Bosnia at the age of seven, I discovered the fundamental drive that my mother always spoke with and about, something cultural, beautiful and nurturing, and all – I realized then – ingrained in Bosnian ways of living, thinking, feeling and giving, in stories of other Bosnian women, narrated in my grandmother's voice. Though I hadn't met my grandmother, I got to know her well in the everlasting heritage of her life, and lives of so many other grandmothers, in their stories of love, success, but also pain, grief, and struggles.

I was taught, and so was my mother, to seek for ideas, in everything, even in places where they do not seem to grow, and then to explore their seeds, nurture them, hold onto them tightly to be able to grow alongside them. In Bosnia, which means understanding the past and all the pain women have been through during war in Bosnia, and letting it give us a will to rebuild ourselves and define womanhood with the strength we owe to our grandmothers, ourselves, our daughters.

To be a woman in Bosnia – today – means to use that strength as determination to be independent, and to deprive we of somewhat still present expectations for women to fill in the role of a traditional housewife and have their aspirations rooted in the old Bosnian customs of people who didn't know any better. Instead, the roles of today's Bosnian women are versatile, striving for inclusion. In economy, in business, in sciences, in politics, in activism, in making their strength visible and heard, acknowledged even by those who haven't found their own.

To be a woman in Bosnia – to me – means to embrace the culture in ways that would serve as a motivation for both personal and professional growth, but never to take traditional practices as a priority over my subjective aspiration. Growing up, I have found my greatest passion to be in storytelling and in – what is, according to my mother's words and views, I grew up developing and nurturing the ideas, holding onto them, embracing the creativity; and finding inspiration in history and culture and appropriating their practices into my own modern story, in being able to tell my story – or, as a writer, any other story – my own way. While that can be fulfilling in the long run, and while so many aspects of the process make me grateful, there are occasional struggles that I must face, just for being a woman. After all, Bosnia has kept its tradition for a long time, and some of it is reflected even onto workplace perspectives and habits based on gender stereotypes.

A woman is, even in a competitive and professional environment, simply viewed differently. She is doubted more, she is always monitored more, and different expectations are set upon her, even if she hasn't chosen to be a part of them. A woman that is successful has her credibility constantly questioned. Job interviews are different for women – we are never caught off guard when asked if we're dating and about our plans to start a family, no matter how professionally put, or sometimes entirely direct and without a single layer of masked professionalism. I have personally faced the reality full of obstacles based on a preferred gender role in the system of academia and professional environment in Bosnia, just out of a possibility that one day I might choose to be a stay-at-home mom, and people's assumption that such possibility is an instant drawback in maintaining my career. Some norms, views and stereotypes, though ingrained in Bosnian culture in ways that made its history, need to go away. They need to be spoken about in order to be acknowledged by majorities and recognized as something that needs to be changed.

That brings me back to the drive, and determination I see in Bosnian women daily, in the ways and will in which they tackle their struggles and create the future for themselves, through hard work, activism, healthy mindsets that empower other women, and encourage them to rise. We have embraced the history and, though often having to face the consequences of misappropriated Bosnian customs, we take our grandmothers' stories as an inspiration and motivation to build a better life for ourselves and our daughters. We nurture the seeds of ideas, and watch them come to life, having the knowledge and power of growing alongside them. And all the women in Bosnia I encourage to embrace their strengths and not settle for anything lesser than what makes them happy. Our grandmothers' stories are guidance for us, today, and a reminder to never lose the determination of Bosnian women. And all the pain and struggles are there to teach us a lesson, but never to make our home.

My Life As A Woman: Bosnia Edition #2

Growing up and living in the post-war Bosnia and Herzegovina, a small country in Southeast Europe known for its unique mix of East and West old and new, modern and traditional, and for the way different cultures, lifestyles, and traditions blend into something you cannot see anywhere else in the world, has always been interesting. People usually have prejudices when small countries like mine are mentioned, but they come from not knowing enough about us and seeing only the outer shell, such as major historical events that seem overwhelming and like there is nothing else to be said. However, they are missing out on many beautiful things, simple everyday things, which are the ones that make life great.

I was born in 1995, the year that the Yugoslavian war ended, and Bosnia started healing. Growing up in Sarajevo, the capital of Bosnia, with my mum and twin sister, I lived a happy life, a life that could, I feel, compare in everything with living in bigger and more well-known countries. I have never had an experience, growing up, where I felt like living in Bosnia was a bad thing. Even as a girl, and later a woman, I have been lucky that I have not had much experience with misogyny and sexism. Of course, I am aware that this does not mean that misogyny and similar things are not present in Bosnia, but I have always tried my best to fight them in any way I could, either by educating people, supporting someone who has had a bad experience, or even simply by telling people who said sexist jokes that they were not funny. Revolutions can start small.

My sister and I grew up with a mother who left our father when we were still babies. Even though she loved him, she was aware that the relationship was not good for her, and she gathered the strength to leave. My grandmother did a similar thing, back in 1960, when divorce was much less common or socially accepted. The two of them are the strongest women I know, and I admire them immensely for taking their life into their own hands and fighting for their place in the world no matter the circumstances. That is how our mum raised us, to always respect ourselves and know our worth, and not to shrink ourselves for anyone. Ever since we were little, we knew that we had her full support for any kind of path that we chose in life.

While growing up, I have had many ideas of what I could do for a living. A forensic scientist was a long-time wish, thanks to binge-watching of crime procedural shows. Later I decided to major in English. However, soon I realized that while I loved learning about language itself, I did not feel like completing my degree, as I wanted to focus on some different things in my life. Instead, I started freelancing, and I have discovered I enjoy it quite a lot. Being my own boss and deciding exactly what I do or do not want to do is very liberating. Freelancing is quite an unknown territory in Bosnia, but modern technologies have made it possible for anyone.

One might expect that living in Bosnia, considered probably by many to be quite old-fashioned, I would be expected to behave and live a certain way. Maybe I was by some people, but I never cared about such opinions. When I think about my life, I am happy and grateful to say that I have never had an issue doing anything I wanted because of my gender. I guess as time passes, people do feel more awkward about being sexist, as they are aware it is becoming less and less socially acceptable, just as it should be. Of course, I have sadly seen other women struggle with sexism in different ways, but they always fought back. I have always been surrounded by strong women, and I am proud of all of them.

If there is one thing, I would want to say to all the women in the world, from this lovely little corner of the world, it would be to love and respect themselves.

No matter whether you live in a small village or a bustling city, whether you are a CEO or a housewife, live your life the way you want. Do not be afraid of change, as change brings growth. Do not be afraid of getting rid of toxic people in your life, as that will only open the door for the right ones to come in. Know your worth and make the world know it too. Do not settle for anything else than you deserve. And you deserve the world. If your vision of your world is traveling across the globe and having adventures, go for it. If it is living a peaceful life with your pets, go for it. If it is having a husband and children, guess what? Also go for it. If it is being the CEO of a multinational company? Yup, you guessed it – go for it. Live your life for yourself, as no one else will. And once more – love and respect yourself.

My Life As A Woman: Bosnia Edition #3

By Tanja Kosanović

I am a 27 year old female marketer, raised by loving parents: an open-minded stay-at-home mother, and a traditional father. This is a typical Bosnian family set up where a woman is taking care of the home and a man is making the income. I was their first child, a daughter, so they were a bit overprotective and I got too sensitive to the outer world. I became an introverted young woman who struggled to fight for herself.

When I was a little girl, I wanted to be a doctor when I grew up. I have no clue what brought me to that idea, but that was all I ever wanted. Or that's what I wanted until the point where I had to make that decision. I went to medical high school and had a lot of practice in the local hospital; it made me change my mind about my future. Seeing all those doctors not actually doing what I always envisioned they would, which is helping people and saving lives, but instead getting into politics, made me realize that's an environment where I cannot nor ever fit in. You're probably thinking: "you should just be yourself and try to change things". Let me tell you one thing: this is Bosnia, you cannot change some things on your own, especially as a woman. I could either fit in or get going.

So, I had to figure a different future for myself. I had no other desires or wishes, but to be completely independent. The one thing that I never wanted was to be a typical Bosnian housewife, raising kids, and asking her husband for a new T-shirt or whatever. After a lot of thinking, I somehow landed on the idea of enrolling in the Faculty of Economics. I thought it would give me plenty of options and I'd figure something out along the way.

Guess what? I haven't figured it out. I ended up being a marketing assistant in a small company, doing everything one marketing assistant could do, for a minimum wage. I thought it should get better, but I was never brave enough to ask for more. After a while, things started to change.

After nearly three years of working for a typical Bosnian boss, I met the right people and was employed in an amazing International company which, up to this day, values and appreciates my work the way one company should. I ended up loving my job and my company, and there are only a few minor things that I'd change. But let's say that it worked out for me without too many struggles. Also, being a part of a serious company changed ME — I became a little fighter.

I am lucky enough to say that I haven't had any serious struggles as a woman, so far. My inner struggles are more related to life in Bosnia in general and the way most women in my family used to live as stay-at-home moms with no "real power" in their hands. Knowing the difficulties, they had always kept me going towards my goals. I'm doing it all to show them that it's possible not to depend on a man. I'm doing it to make them proud.

Also, I'm doing it for YOU out there! Don't let anyone tell you that you're there only to give your husband babies, because you're NOT. There's so much more out there! There are so many fields in which you can succeed. You can do everything you want, you're stronger than you think. Trust me, you are!

My Life As A Woman: Bosnia Edition #4

I'm a 19-year-old girl from Bosnia and Herzegovina. I was born in Mostar and spent almost half of my life there. My parents were in a bit of a pickle, but they managed to get out of it and eventually opened a shop together. That's where I come in. I was born and everything was going great. When I was 1-year-old, my father cheated on my mom and she found out. She immediately left him and my brother, mom, and I started living on our own. I can't say we lived under the best circumstances, but mom managed to put a roof over our head, and eventually things got better. She did everything she could for us to be the people we are right now, and it inspires me to be the best version of myself.

We eventually moved to Sarajevo, the capital city of Bosnia. Mom got a job here and we rented an apartment. By the time that happened, I was 13 years old. My aspirations at the time were to be a police-girl. I figured that being a policeman wasn't the job for me, because I'm not what'd you call the handiest person in the world. I had bad grades in elementary school, the whole moving thing didn't do me a favor, so for high school, I ended up going to an electrical engineering school. My grades drastically changed, I studied because I wanted to be able to go to any college I was interested in. I met my boyfriend in that school, we're two years together now and live together. I've never been happier. I guess it was destined to be. I finished high school this year and managed to enroll in the best college for graphic design, which I'm really into now. I found myself interested in graphics design somewhere in high school.

The culture in my country is very specific. Some things can't be explained, you must feel them. Bosnia is a multicultural country. There are a lot of different nationalities and no one has a problem with that. As far as I know, we have a bunch of traditional foods like ćevapi, baklava, different types of pie, etc. that are amazing, as well as traditions. I love the spontaneity of people here. It's like everything here happens accidentally.

I work part-time as a graphics designer at a firm, but I'm not very good. It'll need some time. I worked as a swimming coach for a few years back, but I gave up because it's too time-consuming. I'm working on an Instagram page for selling used clothes as well. It's going well. Nothing too large, but it's going well. My boyfriend's idea is to open a clothing shop for me because he sees my interest in it.

Throughout my childhood, men were constantly shutting down women because we're not built the same. My dad didn't end up being a saint. As a kid, I was constantly wishing that women would be treated equally. I'm not saying that they should do what they can't. Both genders have their purpose. Women shouldn't be discriminated against.

I've been working a lot. I'm a 3-year cantonal swimming champ. I've been through a lot and still managed to stay on the right road. I made a comeback in school regarding my grades, and it was quite easy. Everything I planned for eventually happened. Things are going great, can't wait to finish college and work on my graphic design skills.

Every woman in the world has at one point in their life been in a rough spot. It's the meaning of life. Without hard times, good times wouldn't feel so good. That's the balance. The point is to stay motivated through the hard times. Never let someone tell you your dreams are unachievable. Everything is possible, if you put work into it. You go girl!

My Life As A Woman: Bosnia Edition #5

When I tell people that I live in Bosnia and Herzegovina they usually ask me if I speak Russian and they ask about the difference between Bosnia and Herzegovina. Russian is not our native language and regarding the difference, you are welcome to visit and experience the culture of the north and the south region. I want to use this opportunity to tell you more about my life as a woman living in Bosnia and Herzegovina in her mid-twenties. Although my whole family is from Bosnia and Herzegovina, I was born in Germany and lived most of my childhood in the city of Munich. This beautiful green city made me fall in love with the outdoors, especially the endless English Garden.

When I moved back to Bosnia and Herzegovina, I didn't experience a huge difference as a child. My childhood continued playfully. The thing that I love most about my country is the feeling of community. Because it is a smaller country, with smaller cities, knowing all your neighbours is a common thing and you don't feel weird when a stranger greets you on the street.

Growing up, I didn't experience any kind of different treatment because I was a woman. As I was approaching my mid-twenties, I realized that there was a stigma surrounding women in Bosnia and Herzegovina – no matter how successful you are, if you're not married, you didn't make it in life. As a woman, people don't really ask me about my education, job or goals. What they usually want to know is if I'm married and when I say that I'm not, they aren't afraid to discreetly tell me that my clock is ticking. The struggle here is not the lack of interest and appreciation for your achievement. It can feel very lonely when you can't talk about your real interests and when you keep all your creativity to yourself.

It used to bother me, knowing that all your efforts and successes aren't appreciated, for the simple reason that it doesn't matter, because the ultimate goal for a woman is to become a wife. The real hypocrisy here is that I'm not talking about a stay-at-home wife, but a woman who is still expected to go to work, make dinner after coming home, take care of the children, and also take care of the husband.

My mother had a positive influence on me for which I will always be grateful. She wasn't the type of mother who would give advice, tell me how to or how not to do things. The biggest gift she gave me is freedom, the freedom of thinking for myself, freedom of trying and failing without judgement, freedom of finding what makes me happy and the freedom of never settling for something that is not the best for me. And with her humor and a healthy dose of sarcasm, no problem seemed too big. This way of thinking taught me not to seek validation from others for doing something that matters to me.

This led me to where I am today. In the city of Sarajevo, I found a place for myself, still trying and failing to make my dream of becoming a successful writer and blogger come true. Even though not many people want to know what I as a woman have to say, I will do my best to live my inner world on the outside. There is no need to work for recognition, because life is not a competition.

I know that women in Bosnia and Herzegovina, and all around the world, have bigger struggles than me but always remember to appreciate your worth and creativity. Never forget what you used to dream about. Express your thoughts even if no one seems to care but share your life with someone who does care.

My Life As A Woman: Botswana Edition #1

My name is Elizabeth "Nkuku" Molabi, as you might or might not guess, "Nkuku" is a Setswana name. It's actually a very rare name, Nkuku is a Setswana word for grandmother, I know by now you're thinking, "How does a parent name a child Granny?" Funny story, so I'm named after two people who passed away before I was born. The first one was my aunt, my mother's sister and my great grandmother, my father's grandmother. Both their names were "Elizabeth", but I was named by my grandmother, my mother's mother. When my father heard that I will be named by his grandmother's name, with very teary eyes, he said "Ke Nkuku" meaning, "She's Granny." The nurse on duty when I was being delivered, either taking her job very seriously, and writing everything down, or being extremely goofy, she wrote "Nkuku" on my birth certificate, as my dad said it, hence my middle name today, Nkuku. From this story alone, you've probably figured out that names are important here, in Botswana, and as a matter of fact, in Africa as a whole.

I was born and raised in the capital city of Botswana, Gaborone, by a single mother (70% of families in Botswana are single-parent led, 90% of which are female). I remember part of my childhood, when my mother rented out a servant's quarters in the city, where we lived with my grandmother. My mum did what single mothers across the world do for their children, she worked hard. She went to night school and worked during the day. She became my first source of inspiration, from the early days of my life. My grandmother was an entrepreneur, she was a tailor, and worked from home while she took care of us while my mother was out, working or at school. I like to say, I was raised in a family where women made it happen… with, or without a man. Every one of the women in my family is a dreamer, and an achiever, influenced by my late grandmother, she wore her heart on her sleeves, and did her business with love. She passed away in 2006, I was young, but I remember the lessons she taught me, even when I was too young to comprehend. She taught me to do it with love, or not at all. My grandmother was loved by everyone, she taught me that "Thong, botho", which means "your dignity is your humanity".

Four years after I started my Primary school, my mother had completed her second house, the first one was reposed and destroyed by the government because it was apparently built on land that belonged to the government. We moved to our new house, in Tlokweng, a town just 11km from Gaborone. In junior high, in 2009, I finally discovered what I truly wanted to be when I grew up, I had previously wanted to do all the conventional professions I could think of. From a doctor, because I watched a lot of medical shows, to a cop, when I started watching rookie blue, to a lawyer, when almost all the shows on TV were crime shows, and finally an accountant because my mother was one. Then finally, one day, I'm sitting in class and I had an AHA! moment, I wanted to start a school magazine. This is where I would grow up to the woman I am today.

I'm a qualified Broadcaster in Radio and TV, having completed my Associate degree at Limkokwing University of Creative Technology. Those were some of the best years of my life. After graduating, I did internship with one of the national radio stations in Botswana, Gabzfm. I knew I was home for a very long time on the first day. I volunteered at this radio station for 2 years before I could get hired, from 2016, I finally got hired officially as an Executive Producer, and stand-in Presenter. I stopped working for Gabzfm, in late 2019.

Now, I run my own production company, which produces shows for both Radio and TV, offers creative and effective writing services and a hub for social media management for different sized brands. My intention getting into the media industry was to change the narrative around Botswana and Africa. I vowed to produce content that matters and empowers Botswana and her people and Africa and her people. I love Batswana, for deciding to be different, and respectful. Although culture is diverse and constantly changes with the times, we have decided to make it our mission to incorporate our culture into our everyday lives, especially respect. If you walk anywhere in the streets of Botswana, city or small town, you will be greeted with a smile.

Even though we have ample love for our culture in Botswana, there are cultural practices that should change and be abolished such as the cultural saying, "Monna ke selepe", which means, a man is an axe, and he can be shared. Although, we don't use this saying anymore, practices show that we still believe it. We are a patriarchal society, with a rape culture. According to the national statistics on GBV crimes, there were 1,208 recorded cases of defilement in early 2019 compared to 769 in 2018; indicating a 57 percent increase, or 439 more cases. I must admit though, there are organizations, corporations and individuals who are constantly fighting the battle against Gender-based violence. I, for instance, took part in the 'I am tomorrow" conference to help empower and girls and women. I am also a mentor at TAWLA, The African Women Leadership Academy, which teaches women how to be leaders.

In conclusion, I want you to know, my fellow Goddesses, that you are your words, when you say you're a Queen, you're a Queen. The Universe will back you up, and everyone and everything in it will recognize. You must keep reinventing yourself, learn, unlearn, and relearn. There are infinite opportunities out there for you, claim them. And finally Love yourself.

My name is Liz, The Queen to Queens.

Thank you.

My Life As A Woman: Botswana Edition #2

I grew up in various parts of southern and northern Botswana. We went from living in Mochudi, Molepolole and then Maun. Maun, dubbed the gateway to the Okavango Delta, was where most of my favourite childhood memories were made. Where Maun is vibrant and quirky, I always found Mochudi and Molepolole lacklustre and depressing. Maun, dubbed Botswana's gateway to the Okavango Delta, is Botswana's most popular tourist hotspot, giving it an exciting vibe unlike any other around Botswana.

Growing up in Maun, we immersed ourselves in outdoor adventures including climbing trees, taking long leisurely walks with friends, outdoor games, fearlessly swimming and canoeing in the crocodile- and hippo-infested Thamalakane River! Our house overlooks the river, which in full flood comes right up to our fence. To this day, the fresh, earthy scent of the river remains deeply ingrained in the memories that I hold dear. Just hearing the grunts of a hippo sends me down a much-cherished memory lane. Stumbling across a cobra or monitor lizard in the backyard or seeing a massive crocodile leisurely soaking up the morning rays along the riverbanks of the lush river were just a few of the experiences I enjoyed.

At night, the river would come alive with some of the most heavenly nature sounds on earth, including my all-time favourite, the tiny bell frogs. Under the canopy of millions of breath-taking stars, the fireflies would also come out to play. For me as a child, this was mesmerizingly magical.

My dad, an avid reader, started taking me to the library from a very young age. By the time I reached high school, my favourite subjects were English Language and English Literature, which I naturally excelled at. I went on to do a Setswana/English double major in Linguistics and a French minor. That led to working for the state radio station as a journalist - a job that entailed writing, proofreading, editing, and translating news bulletins.

As a proud Motswana, I love that we readily embrace the spirit of ubuntu, a running theme across African cultures. Ubuntu is the idea that "I am because you are"; that we are all connected and that you can only grow and progress through the growth and progression of others. I love that as I was growing up, it was woven all the way through our daily lives and upbringing.

My success as a woman is the resilience that I possess to rise and do anything I set my heart on, despite the challenges I face. I co-own a Graphic Design company with my husband and work remotely as a translator/editor/proofreader via freelance sites.

To other women of the world I say, as clichéd as it may sound; on our own we are strong but together we can be phenomenal. To women in Botswana, I would like to say; rather than tearing each other down, let's strive to band together and build each other up.

97

My Life As A Woman: Botswana Edition #3

In Botswana's southern district, about thirty miles southwest of the capital Gaborone lies the village of Ranaka. I was born in this village, the 7th child and the only girl in a family of ten siblings. I spent most of my childhood in the village. I had no role model growing up. I had no one to look up to. As a girl child, I was supposed to fit into my parents' template of how a girl child ought to be. Get a decent education. Learn house chores. Get married to a decent man and have children.

In my father's compound, there was one house made of mud. Both my parents were illiterate. Daddy earned a living by carving wood to make traditional items such as chairs and spoons while mom joined a drought relief program to supplement my father's meager earnings to help put food on the table.

I started primary school in Ranaka. I didn't have a school uniform when I started. No shoes. Many times, during winter, I'd shake in class because of the cold. There was nothing to keep me warm. Even my brothers had no school shoes. By the time I was doing standard 4, all my elder brothers had shunned school for better opportunities in the city. Being the only one to wake up in the morning to go to school was a challenge. I wanted to be like my siblings. I also wanted to quit school. I thought it was for the privileged few, whose parents could afford school uniforms. I started to abscond from school.

Every morning, I'd hide somewhere all day and wait until I saw the other pupils leave the school compound, and then I'd join them and pretend as if I was coming from school. My class teacher alerted the family of my absenteeism. Furious, daddy sent me to live with his sister who was staying in Mochudi.

It was during this tenure with my aunt that my life changed. My classmates were advanced in all subjects. They won awards. I envied them. In one of the awards ceremonies, I noticed a Coca Cola bottle in the hand of a certain guest. He stood up to speak. "Education is like this bottle. You all start at the bottom," he said, pointing to the bottom of the Coca Cola bottle he had in his hand. "As you continue with your journey, many will fail. By the time you reach the top, only a few will make it. You'll be anything you want to be in life."

I wanted to reach the top. Maybe I'll be a nurse. Or a doctor, or a teacher. Maybe I'll get a better job and build a modern house. That inspired me to strive to better myself. I excelled in my schoolwork. I won awards. I left the country for Kuala Lumpur in 2002 on government sponsorship to study broadcasting and media studies. I loved journalism. I was inspired by top CNN journalists such as Anderson Cooper and Arwa Damon. Although I wanted to be a journalist, I didn't like the journalism course I was pursuing. I didn't finish the course. I quit after two years and enrolled in a multimedia course. I excelled in this course and graduated with a BSc in Multimedia technology in 2007.

I returned home to proud parents ready to implement the skills I learned in Malaysia. Although I struggled to get a job upon graduation, I didn't give up. A year after graduation, I landed a job as a tutor at a private university. There I taught my students how to design websites and how to edit graphics and videos.

Did I achieve success in life as a woman? It depends on how each woman defines success. Today I'm a full-time freelance writer. I also own a catering company though I still can't cook. I built a house for my parents. I refused to get married because I dream of Tinsel Town.

My Life As A Woman: Brazil Edition #1

Hi, my name is Bianca and I was born and grew up in Rio de Janeiro, the second biggest Brazilian city. As I am an only child, my mom taught me how to be independent, so I started to work at a very young age. I never left my studies behind, but when I was 15 years old, I felt like I needed to earn my own money, so I asked my uncle if I could work at his computer store.

After a year and a half, I quit to take my university exams. In Brazil, you have two types of universities, a private one and a public paid by the government. This latter being the best one. However, to enter a public university, you need to study a lot. I graduated in business administration at Universidad Federal do Rio de Janeiro.

My mom was always an inspiration for me, starting her business by herself, and a large part of my education came from that money. She had a sandwich shop at a private university. Since I graduated, I worked with finance in Treasury and Budget Control on multinational companies. However, Brazil is a sexist country, and women used to face prejudice to get a new job. Besides that, we usually earn less than men.

Questions usually are: "When do you expect to be pregnant?", "Do you have kids?", or "Are you married?" are very common at job interviews. Sometimes it seems that the country is changing for better because lots of companies are starting to get more women in strategic positions, such as CEO and Director, but we are still far from the ideal.

Meanwhile, we are friendly and receptive people, always trying to help each other, Brazilian people are emotional and festive, and this is what I love most about being a Brazilian.

Nowadays, I am unemployed due to restructuring at my last position. Since last year, I am currently looking for a new position in the financial area. But a lot of good things happened in my life last year, so I can't complain about it. I've just bought my own apartment with my husband and we got married and had a nice wedding reception. Also, as a pet lover I have rescued a new dog that lives with us and is treated like a son.

For my career I expect to achieve two goals, first I need to get a new job, then hope to become a manager in a few years, besides numbers I love to work with people and see them growing up with my help. The second goal is to start to teach business and finance; this is an old dream of mine. For that, I would need to start at a master's degree program, which I can't afford to do at this moment.

As a businesswoman, I have achieved a lot of things in my life, I graduated in one of the best universities of Brazil, I work with numbers which I love most, and I have had a large career in good companies where I learned a lot. However, Brazil is becoming a bad place to work, we are having some economic and political issues, especially at my city. Due to all of that, the opportunities are shorter in regards to our life quality.

While I don't have a new formal job, I am working as a freelancer and trying to launch my business as VA – virtual assistant. I have been working with this to earn some money and I am enjoying and learning a lot. Launching a business is part of my dreams as well as have an NGO to rescue animals from the streets, but I don't know if I will achieve it.

Since I was a child, I've always struggled to keep my studies and work to help my parents, my life was not so easy although not too hard, as a lot of other girls in Brazil with no opportunities of study or work. In the inside of the country, we have people living in the margin of poverty and a lot of women and children sell their bodies to get some money.

If I have any advice for Brazilian women it would be to keep studying, learning, working, and never give up because of a prejudice or a lack of opportunity. You will find that when you never give up, the world will open its doors for you. Never try to go the "easy" way, these paths will lead you to a terrible life and it's just not worth it.

We are born facing a lot of challenges just by being women, life is not so easy for us, so do everything by yourself and become an independent woman as soon as possible, never let men tell you what to do with your life, never rely on men, roll up your sleeves and fight! You got this!

My Life As A Woman: Brazil Edition #2

What a great opportunity to talk a little bit about myself representing a community of Brazilian women who are avid for impacting the world. Let me introduce myself... my name is Camila Rossi and I grew up in a city called Salvador, capital of Bahia.

Salvador is very famous to hold one of the biggest carnival parties in the world. We have a saying in Brazil that people from Bahia tend to be lazy... maybe it's because of the Carnival or the amazing beaches. Either way, this saying is far from being true.

Since I was a little girl, my parents always focused on giving me the best education possible. They always thought ahead of their time, and at the age of 16, I went to study for a whole year in the United States to become fluent in English. I always dreamed about becoming a scientist... change the world... and becoming bilingual could really open a wide range of opportunities. And it did!

Coming back to Brazil, I started college at seventeen, studying to become an Industrial Engineer. Through my academic life, I worked hard to become relevant in my profession. I was an intern in two multinational companies in Brazil and even got a scholarship to study in Spain for one year – and that really was a game changer. I could interact with young international professionals, understand how our world is connected, and we must respect our differences to achieve higher goals.

After this experience I was so proud to be a Brazilian and represent my country abroad. I could show that I had the skills and knowledge to interact with great students from big international universities and never forget my warm Brazilian roots.

My academic background gave me a lot of advantage to enter the professional world very early. I got my first full-time job as an Industrial Engineering Analyst six months before getting the diploma at the age of twenty-two! After four years, I still work at the same German company and I couldn't be happier. It was not easy, I must say...

Being a woman in a company that has 98% of male employees has its challenges. I worked close to the production site and it was easy for men to think I was another girl from the Human Resources department. Nothing wrong with HR, but they never thought I was the engineer in charge. After so many years, I could prove my value and having a master's degree really changed my life.

It was not really about the title, but more about the impact I did after my research (Yes! I became a scientist in a sort of way). In the beginning, the people from headquarters didn't really believe in my work and how it could influence our workers efficiency... but after everything was done, it only projected me to a higher professional level but elevated the potential to test more technologies in Brazil. I opened the doors with English and a lot of education (thanks mom and dad!).

Thus, it is easy to say that yes... as a woman, we must work harder and prove ourselves in ways that men never think of. But stay strong to yourself, get educated because knowledge is the only thing people cannot steal from you and... I almost forgot... never listen to old sayings! (especially the ones that call you lazy!)

My Life As A Woman: Brunei Darussalam Edition

I was born and grew up in Kuala Belait, Brunei Darussalam, which is located in South-East Asia. My childhood was a relatively simple one. I attended traditional dance lessons during my primary school years. I was also an active trilingual child speaker for school competitions, in storytelling, and poem reading. Art lesson was also my favorite subject.

My great grandmother was an inspiration to us all. My late grandmother would tell us stories about her mother and how she came to Brunei Darussalam with her on a boat from China during the 1930s.

I have always wanted to be involved in the art industry while I was growing up, but, when I was younger, I wanted to be a news anchor woman. When I was much older, I wanted to be involved in arts so I studied interior design and worked as a graphic designer, and eventually, I became a portrait artist.

I love all cultures because each of them is unique. Diverse as we are, our different cultures bring colors and celebrate life and universe as diverse and unique on its own! As a portrait artist, I am involved in direct art lessons in my atelier.

I don't find any struggle as a woman. I believe my environment has provided us well-balanced opportunities, but I find struggle as a person and not gender-related, in which art is sometimes overlooked and under-appreciated. However, it is just life and it just gives us power to want to work and prove better.

As a woman, never be afraid to share your thoughts and express your opinions even if they contradict the majority. Be strong and resilient and never let anyone to dim the light in your heart. Believe and shine as you are. Work hard, stand proud, and be humble. Love your life and wear a smile even when it is raining.

My Life As A Woman: Bulgaria Edition

The worst part of growing up is a life change that tends to be not as exciting as a childhood. My life as a woman, the story short — I got a job, rent an apartment, and now I go to work, spend weekends at home, run the same streets, travel sometimes... the time starts to pass faster and faster, and the more adventure-less my life becomes, the faster time is passing.

Childhood

That is why the biggest part of my memory is from the place I grew up — the small village in Ukraine. Remember the summer that lasts forever? And this first good book, and the first birthday with a real cake? The first bike, the first picnic? I remember wearing my brother's clothes — the comfiest clothes I've ever worn. I remember eating a sandwich with butter and sugar as a dessert — still, none of the desserts I can afford to buy today is better than that. I remember my young parents that worked hard saving every penny for my education and future life. I always wondered how they were never giving up on me, even though I was bad at school and was fighting with every girl and boy I saw. I was just a terrible child! When every teacher was predicting the darkest future for me, my mom and dad were believing in me. Beliefs of my parents made me who I am today. They are the kindest people I've ever known.

Growing up

The only problem with the village — it is a boring place for a teenager. If you're a girl, you either get a boyfriend or read books to have fun. No Internet, no cable TV. I wasn't the one with a boyfriend, so I had fun reading books. I could start reading before breakfast and end at midnight hiding under the blanket with a lamp, so my mom didn't notice I was still not sleeping. I am very thankful to my parents that they let me read days long because usually, girls in the village have responsibilities — clean the kitchen, help cooking, wash the dishes... I was living a "boy's life", I can tell because only guys were able to do whatever they wanted. Girls had more rules and often they were contradictory, like 'Don't be ugly, but don't be too beautiful" or "Don't wear a skirt that is too long, but not too short". This is the thing I don't like about our culture — Eastern European girls are growing up with an often defined future, to be the one that goes to university, gets married, takes care of the kids, and does all domestic duties... and goes to work. Now we can officially call it "double shift work", but everything stays unchanged. I can honestly say that I had the privilege of not having such an influence from my parents. All they cared about was for me to be happy and get an education. For all the good things I have in me I need to thank my parents.

Being an adult

When I was twelve, I decided to become a writer. I said to myself, "One day I will write an amazing book that will make this world a better place". Following this dream, I decided to study Journalism in Bulgaria. I just turned seventeen! This is the part I love about my culture — Eastern European parents are brave enough to send their only daughter to study in another country. I do not think this is common for all parents, but most of them value education and save money for years to provide this to their children.

At the end of the second semester, I found a job, and after that, I found another job, and another job, and here I am working in the Google Street View project helping photographers and Google teams to improve the user Street View. Finally, I feel that I do something meaningful and helpful for people and this makes me happy sometimes. Also, I found my new passion — translation and content writing. I consider it a part-time job that helps me improve myself and continue moving forward.

Conclusion

If I was asked to give only one piece of advice in a lifetime, I would say — admit and accept your privilege, enjoy it, be thankful for every chance and opportunity that was given to you. Wherever I am located, I appreciate that I grew up in a great family, got a great education, work in a good company and run in a nice park.

My Life As A Woman: Burkina Faso Edition

My name is Lydia. I was born in Burkina Faso, one of the ten least developed countries in the world. My father was a taxi driver and my mother's only occupation was "taking care of the family". It was getting harder and harder to find a job in Burkina Faso and my father was doing his best to look after us at least as much as he could.

My studies

I went to business school and I couldn't finish it because of lack of financial means. I wanted to study so much, and I was passionate about it, but life decided otherwise.

My difficulties as a woman

As a woman living in Burkina Faso, difficulties are part of our daily lives. Despite the efforts of the state, the number of gender discrimination, early marriages, and restrictions on economic rights will never stop increasing. Girls are forced by their parents to marry already at the age of 17, even without the girl's consent. And the girl finally finds herself financially dependent all her life on a man who never stops marrying other women. Men can marry up to 12 women without any problems. I was forced to marry a stranger when I was 18 years old. Since I didn't have a job and couldn't go home, all I had to do was hold on and spend my whole life with him.

What I like about my culture

Burkinabè are warm-hearted, however, demonstrations of affection in public should be avoided, as should the display of naked flesh - especially in the Muslim North. This is not a matter of prudery, but rather of respect for the privacy of both sexes. Long Bermuda shorts can be suitable for both men and women. Burkinabè traditionally offer gifts to each other when they visit: fabrics, shells (cowries) or fruit, but any everyday object is welcome. When you meet someone, it is customary to ask how he or she is doing, and to ask about the family, even if it is a stranger.

The one that inspired me

As finding work for women became more and more difficult. A woman, the only one who could do the work that only a man could do. She became a taxi driver. Everybody talked about her and she did well in that job and made a good living. That's when I saw an opportunity in her.

My successes as a woman

In a country where only men can have a job. I started working as a taxi driver. This is something that women have been doing in Burkina Faso for the last few years. I earn a pretty good living and I take good care of my children. This is what I can call success in a country like this. As a woman, I have had many difficulties to which I had only one option.

"Become strong and endure"

Don't go on living a flawless life. As a woman, you have the potential to build a dream life. Don't give up. The sera break rocks not by her strength but by her perseverance.

My Life As A Woman: Burundi Edition

My name is Izina, I was born in Burundi, the second poorest country in the world. My father was a lumberjack and he earned a few dollars to support a family of 5 people. We were extremely poor and there was nothing we could do about it. Being in a family like that, education was just a luxury we couldn't afford. I was able to study hard in a business school with what little my father earned. I went to sewing school... that I didn't like just because my parents wanted me to be socially nice. It was the only girls-only school in Burundi.

I grew up in a country where civil war was imminent. A civil war broke out when I was 15 years old. We had to flee our country to take refuge in Tanzania. Burundi was becoming more and more a Source of all evil things.

My Culture

Speaking of my culture, it's nothing to be proud of. In my culture, women represented absolutely nothing. Men didn't value them at all. A man could marry five women, which is normal. In a country like Burundi, we couldn't even afford to dream. It wasn't easy.

My difficulties as a woman

A civil war broke out in the country and we had to flee to Tanzania, we left abruptly with nothing. I suffered so much to find a place to sleep, something to eat, even to cover my basic hygiene needs as a woman, etc. It was hard to find a place to sleep and wash at times. It was the apocalypse for me and my family.

My successes as a woman

I finally found a job in Tanzania and there I also met the man of my life. I had two boys and two girls with him. And our lives are almost bright. I found a smart and kind husband who accepted me despite my sorrows and my history. I've had 4 children with him and I'm happier.

My work

I work as a secretary in a small bank in Tanzania. I am respected and taken with a little more value than in my native country. I finally had the chance to be accepted as a woman, which could not have been any dream in Burundi.

Things are getting better

The State has made efforts and succeeded in establishing peace in the country and is working to destroy social discrimination, civil wars, etc. The State has made efforts and succeeded in establishing peace in the country and is working to destroy social discrimination, civil wars and so on. From 2018 onwards, Burundi is a little quiet and everything is getting better and better. No more wars as before, but there is no guarantee that this will last. We must always keep hope, things will surely get better.

As a woman living in Burundi, continue to fight, if only for your children. It is your duty to give them a future and hope.

My Life As A Woman: Cape Verde Edition

I was born and raised in the Bao Vista island of Cape Verde in the year 1985. I was the third born in a family of five siblings with two girls and three boys. My father worked as a security guard with meagre pay while mom was a housewife. As such, the family income was never enough and so we lived from hand-to-mouth, sometimes going to bed on empty stomachs, but I'm glad our father did his best to bring food on the table most of the time.

As fate would have it, dad passed on when I was only eight years old, leaving us under the care of our mom. At the time, three of us were already enrolled in primary education. Life became even harder with the passing away of our dad since our mom had to seek menial employment in the neighbourhood. Jobs were hard to come by, but she could occasionally got a few jobs here and there. Our house, at one point, became so inhabitable due to a leaking roof that we could hardly sleep while at the same time we were expected in school the following day.

I detested the kind of life we led because I didn't always get the provisions for my basic needs like my peers. My desire was to one day be in control over the situation. This drive helped me to clear primary education amid the difficulties. At the time, my elder brothers had cleared primary education and went out of our home to vent for themselves.

On clearing primary education, it was clear my mom couldn't support my secondary education due to the heavy load she already carried. My fortune was when one day in my search for a house help job, I came across a lady who was a secondary school teacher. After sharing my ordeal with her, she really sympathized with my situation and offered to help me out while I lived with her.

To cut a long story short, this lady sponsored my entire secondary and tertiary education where I studied pastry and graduated with a diploma in pastry. Over the years I had developed a desire to work in the hospitality industry in Cape Verde. I worked in various hotels in Praia and gained wide experience in the pastry field.

I opened a pastry shop in Praia where I am the Director and the establishment has employed ten workers. I have also sponsored two needy girls through their secondary education. This is my way of giving back to the society just as I was helped. I am indeed grateful to the lady teacher who came through for me in the day of need.

My advice to the woman of Cape Verde is to value education and be determined to succeed in life against all odds, and when you succeed help fellow women succeed too.

My Life As A Woman: Cambodia Edition #1

Being Cambodian is very funny and interesting, as in my opinion, it's one of the most adventurous and full of new openings type of country. People here are really kind, generous and gentle, especially women who are modest, well-mannered and household. I am Mony from Oudong which is a town in Cambodia. I was born and grew up in an average family, with my parents and two sisters. My childhood was the best, it passed by playing with my friends in the yard, not in the phones as a big part of nowadays children do. But times are changing and our lives do too.

I remember when I was a child, my dream was to become a business lady and still, I do not stop thinking about it. With time, my dream became a goal and I only thank my family who inspired and helped me with a step-by-step approach to it. I was always watching TV and inspiring by women in classic suits and imagining myself in their place. Today I'm studying marketing in Cambodian Mekong University and together with it trying to build my career. I am grateful, especially my father, who played a big role in this. Now I am a human resources assistant in a company named 'Decathlon', I love my job, but this is not what I am dreaming about.

As I have already mentioned, Cambodian women are modest and household, and in our country, there are less women who have their own businesses. There are many things I like about Cambodian culture, like you must be a virgin until you get married or our weddings are interesting. For women, it is very important here to merry, have children, do home stuff and if a woman will become financially independent, people can get it wrong and one day, you'll hear different rumors about yourself. This is my biggest struggle as I have experienced this kind of social problem before and now it's a big fight in my head. Sometimes I am thinking about giving up and live a standard life, but my inner voice was always telling me 'DO NOT GIVE UP'. When I grew up and became more mature, I understood that no matter what I will reach my goals, maybe it will be later, but I will do anything to become rich, and to assure a good life for my children. I don't do anything bad or illegal, I go to my dream with every logical and possible way.

I understand that society is the biggest barrier between you and your goal, so let them speak, let them be jealous, but never let them disturb you. Do everything you want; this is your life and you decide what to reach to. Even if you don't do anything wrong and you get a strong support from your family and friends, there always will be people who will rumor about you and your success. Be mentally ready for that and patient.

My Life As A Woman: Cambodia Edition #2

Numerous individuals are living in this world and everybody has various characters. There are no two individuals who have precisely the same characters. Everybody in this world is remarkable in their specific manners. One's character is something that doesn't change, which makes each person one of a kind and extraordinary.

Before going into nuances, let me uncover something to me. I am a Filipina woman, 46 years of age, I grew up in Manila, the main city of Philippines. I studied Bachelor of Fine Arts, major in advertising.

We are two siblings of our parents and I am the youngest. My mum is a full-time housewife and my dad is a salesman. I have learned from my parents the value of time, honesty, hard work and commitment to the purpose.

I am also a single mom of three lovely grown-up kids. Supporting three of them was not easy for me. Up until my friend mentioned Cambodia. So, I decided to visit the country. When I first came to Cambodia without anybody else passing on one baggage, it was a challenging experience for me. Around that point, I knew nothing about this area. That day, I thought to stay as I now had a fresh start of life, and from that day onwards, my life would take an extraordinary turn, knowing I ought to set myself up for positive or negative or anything that comes my way.

Undoubtedly, moving to a substitute country isn't as it was, a straightforward choice, either to explore or to start a livelihood, and was by all accounts, overpowering. Regardless, it ensured opportunity and a self-supporting way of my life. Coming out of this security and put communication on the greater canvas, is something that women are making an advance toward, as it was very empowering for me. Remaining calm in a country I knew nothing about and had to learn from scratch was scary, but I did it. No matter what I went through, and I was pushed and sneered at, I was always carrying on with my life.

However, making it work in another country, without my family, not even having my kids there, can be really testing. Starting a calling in another city, setting up a hangout with the central area and letting the hair down, there's beyond any doubt, an adrenaline rush to it, and it's a feeling of opportunity. Times are advancing. On the off chance that it was simply stressing, I did alter my needs. The prerequisite for money-related opportunities is one of the foremost grounded fundamental pushes for women and I did find opportunity in the country.

For me, life was not about almost living off my people. I realize they are there, yet I couldn't depend upon anyone. The goal I'm currently striving for is to make this world a better place to live in by starting the changes with myself, even if only for the sake of my kids. Sure, I've had bad experiences in my life too. I believe that it is manifesting day by day and I feel even more **responsibility** for what I do and where I go.

I think, when we grow older, we seem to lose or forget about those crucial qualities and for us to be descent human beings, we should consider re-educating ourselves on morals and values.

My Life As A Woman: Cameroon Edition

Hi, my name is Eleanor Visas, but everybody calls me "Small", a pet name which was given to me by my mum not because I was small, but because I was the youngest of two people that shared the same name with me. "Gegah" my native name, was the name I shared with my two cousins which means "A way to talk" and, we were named after our grand-mum which is actually a very common phenomenon in Cameroon.

I grew up, I would say in different parts of Cameroon, my dad being an electrical engineer employed by the government contributed to my continuous moving from one part of the country to another. I was born in the northwest region of Cameroon (Bambui), but spent the most part of my childhood in the Central Region (Yaounde) the Capital of Cameroon.

I had a pretty normal upbringing with both of my parents raising me and my three siblings. We attended the Catholic nursery and primary school which was just 100m opposite the house we grew up in.

A typical day for me would be to wake up early morning at 7 a.m., take a shower, have breakfast and then walk off to school. After school, it was an obligation for me to observe siesta after my lunch and then do our homework before going outside to play. My day would end by 9 p.m. when my Dad would come home from work.

By the time I was 10 years old, we moved to the Littoral Region (Douala) which is the Economic capital of Cameroon, where we lived for 2 years and we had to move back to the northwest region. With all these constant relocations due the nature of my Dad's job, I got to encounter different people and lifestyles, which helped to shape my life in a way I think is impacting me in a positive way.

Cameroon has two official languages, French and English, and more than 250 mother tongues. French is spoken in many regions with the exception being the northwest and southwest regions which are the English-speaking parts of Cameroon. Because I grew up in both parts (English and French parts) of Cameroon, I developed a mastery in both languages.

I did my secondary education in a boarding school in my mother's village. Seven years in a Catholic boarding school; if I were to start talking about it, we would need a book. But let's just say it was an experience of a lifetime. The moment you step foot into a boarding school, you just automatically become an adult as you start to fern for yourself, sticking to the same routine every other day, being disciplined in the most un-traditional ways (humane of course) and disciplining yourself among many other things. Boarding school was a place to be when you are not there (funny but true), keep in mind that I don't regret any of my experiences there and will still do it if I were given the chance because some of my best memories and adventures were made there.

Growing up, I had a lot of strong women around me that inspired me so much, with my mum being the biggest inspiration. I always dreamt of being a Banker or a corporate woman, because I wanted to be like my mom. She was a corporate woman and it inspired me so much that, I went ahead to study Economics and Accounting in the university. Even though I was going on that part, but my priorities have shifted. Right now, I am more interested in social protection especially in the areas of health and gender equality. So, I am not working now but currently doing a Masters in "Analysis and Design of Social Protection". I took this course because of the experience I had at my Undergraduate level, where I was almost raped. There I realized how powerless I was and how much violence is going on within our society and communities, with very little being said or done about them.

Even though I love our culture, I don't agree with some aspects about it. The thing I have always struggled with, especially being someone who is strong minded, is how our culture always finds a way intentionally or unintentionally marginalize the woman.

The most challenging thing I faced with that was how the culture would say a woman should aspire to marriage no matter how educated they are; the woman should not eat certain parts of a chicken because "they are not meant for women", women should not dress a certain way; we are not allowed to sit or talk when men are talking; we should not always say what's on our minds because that might scare the man away from us, and these are just a few among many other things.

I am just 27 years old and still have a lot to learn in life but one of my biggest successes up to date is that everything I have always set my mind to, I did, I tried, and I did not let anything hold me back from trying and speaking my mind and making my voice heard in the smallest ways. The best advice I can give to women in Cameroon is to make sure they do what they want to do in life, try not just to sit at home and complain even though there is much to complain about. We should be strong and be inspiring to the younger girls that are coming behind us and for those of us that might have kids or already do have, give those kids an education at all costs, especially the girl child.

My Life As A Woman: Canada Edition #1

"Speak English and only English!" The factory supervisor shouted these words constantly. Workers from all over the world who were newly landed immigrants in Canada worked in factories just like this one. Times were difficult and discrimination was rampant and unbridled in the workforce. That was my mother's experience when she arrived in Canada from Italy in 1955. Things have certainly changed. I am a first generation Canadian, born in Toronto and thanks to the trailblazing of so many brave immigrants, my life has been privileged in comparison.

I was born on the fourth of July in the late sixties, to Italian parents and have five siblings. I always cut my first teeth on crusty Calabrasi bread and had smeared tomato sauce on my face. My first junk food consisted of ricotta cheese spread on Italian bread sprinkled with sugar. And yes, the rumors are true, getting disciplined with a wooden spoon or a designer sandal from Milan was really a thing. Saturdays were always set aside for house cleaning and it's a wonder to me that I still have a sense of smell since bleach was all we used to clean anything. We lived on a residential street in Toronto and spent almost all day playing with the children who lived on our street.

We lived in Canada, however, we still maintained many of our Italian customs, we were very blessed to be able to do so. That is why I love Canada so much; it truly is a mosaic of many cultures, a crescendo of voices and customs from the far reaches of the earth. People here find a way to blend in while still maintaining distinct cultural identity. In the city of Toronto, we have concentrated areas of one culture or another. There is "Little Italy'" in one area, "Little Greece" in another, "Chinatown" in yet another, where you can go to shop in quaint little stores and eat at amazing restaurants all representative of each culture. We celebrate our unique blend of people.

As a child, it was my dream to be a doctor. I wanted to help people. I yearned to someday have my own practice and live my ideal life, but as we all know, sometimes our best laid plans can be trumped by circumstance. My parents separated when I was just thirteen and our lives were plunged instantly into chaos and the inevitable adversity that followed. I had to get my first job at fourteen to help my family survive during that difficult time. I witnessed my mother struggle to keep our heads above water and no matter what impending doom hung over us, she overcame every issue like a champion. My mom is my hero. Little did I know then that I would need to cling to the hope her perseverance and strength had taught me.

I married shortly after high school to a traditional Italian man (marrying young was very much a cultural thing back then). My husband had a family business and I worked in that business alongside him. I told myself that I would delay my continued education for a short time and "one day" I would go to university to begin my journey to become a doctor. The problem with "one day" is that one day, you wake up and realize that that day never came.

I began having children and loved being a mom, my dreams and ambitions all faded, became distant thoughts, but never off the table. As I settled into my role as a mother, I decided to start working towards my continuing education. My time was so limited as a mother to five young children, so my best option was to do home study courses (not online at that time). At first my focus was in psychology then later changed to anatomy, physiology and pathology. Just as I was getting into a groove of balancing motherhood and study, I became a single mother. I found myself going through the same struggles that I saw my mother endure and I was consumed by fear. I was terrified that I would drown in the sea of responsibility and impossible adversity. During the storm, something beautiful happened, I discovered my strength as a woman. Somehow, from beneath the crushing weight of the impossible, emerged a warrior. I cried a river of tears, prayed like I had never prayed before and one day, I simply put the tissues away and decided to fight.

I found a job at a large wellness center in my area and soon became the clinic director. After a few years and further training, I facilitated the inclusion of therapeutic medical laser, began treating patients and witnessed their improved health and wellbeing. I have been with the same clinic now for 20 years. Furthermore, I consult for other practitioners and clinics to help them implement new modalities, patient education programs and develop improved practice protocols.

My children are grown now and have become beautiful, compassionate human beings. Do I have any regrets? No, not one! Some would say that I did not hit the mark or achieve my original vision for my life, but I say, I used my circumstances as a springboard instead of a weight. You may grieve for your unrealized dreams, but I tell you, if you open your heart to new interpretations of your original vision, you may find an even more glorious reality. Beauty from the ashes.

Franca Turturici

My Life As A Woman: Canada Edition #2

Hi guys! You would think that writing about yourself would be easy, but it's a little tricky when bits and pieces of you are from different parts of the world, you don't really know where to start! So, let's begin from the beginning.

My name is Maida Affan and I was born in Karachi, an extremely fast-paced, energetic, metropolitan hub of Pakistan. Since my dad was working in the Middle East (Oman) at that time, much of my early childhood was spent there. I have vague memories of pre-school, sandy blue beaches and valleys in between gorgeous, towering mountains there.

Funny how people from this part of the world are mostly depicted as fear-mongering terrorists, oppressors and camel-riding nomads who don't know any better in mainstream media. In hindsight, I only remember being exposed to the most giving, respectful, and cultured people. They invited us into their homes, broke bread with us and called us family. If anything, living in the desert had only grounded and humbled them, not hardened them.

When I was around 7, we moved to Canada. The small, but beautiful city of Halifax in the province of Nova Scotia became my home for the next several years. I had a very nurturing and wholesome childhood. Being the eldest of only two siblings, I didn't really have to prod for attention at home.

My mother has always been a very invested parent, always at the top of her game working relentlessly to provide a healthy environment at home, raising us to be strong, secure and confident in our own skin. As a child of immigrant parents, you don't realize the struggles your parents face in order to provide for you and shelter you from the prejudice against minority groups. I can't say that I've experienced any of that first-hand, but even if there was some passive aggressiveness, I probably took it in stride and didn't let it get to me, and I owe this sense of self-assurance to my mother.

My formative years flew by with the coming and going of colorful, crisp autumns and harsh winters. I transitioned into a typical nerdy teenager. My social circle comprised of an extremely diverse set of people with different backgrounds, cultures and skin tones. It was a beautiful bond. In between weird celebrity crushes, hanging out with friends, parties and the works I grew up! Don't we all?

It was time to make tough decisions. Important decisions. I had always wanted to become a doctor. Well, my passion and love for writing compelled me to aspire for journalism too. However, life intervened and due to certain circumstances, I had to move back to Pakistan.

Now, remember that this was the first time I really lived in Pakistan. I knew of it, had visited maybe only once in the past decade or so, so the culture-shock was real! As a young adult woman with an unconventional childhood, raised in a more progressive part of the world by broad-minded parents, the adjustment in a conservative setting was very visceral.

Having said that, it would be fair to say that I had a biased view of life in Pakistan myself. You must live there and spend time with the amazing people and be exposed to their warmth and energy to gain perspective of that backdrop. Today, I can say that Pakistan is one of the most hospitable, charitable and resilient nations of the world! I've met some of the strongest and smartest women in Pakistan fiercely pursuing their goals as teachers, scientists, journalists, pilots and activists- playing their part in changing the narrative.

On my mom's side of the family, I was the first female to get a professional education and the first to become a doctor. There were feelings of pride and joy, but also gossip of 'settling down', marriage and kids. I wasn't ready to commit to someone yet, and my parents supported my decision. After getting my degree and 2 years of professional training I got hooked!

Then you know what they say. Life seemed to have boosted exponentially after that and my fate brought me back to the Middle East as a wife to the towering mountains of Saudi Arabia this time. Today, I'm a mother of 3 amazing boys and trying to be half the woman my mom was! I know how important it is to be there for your kids during the formative years, so I currently work from home and am privileged to have this opportunity.

I consider myself extremely lucky to work as a telehealth Physician providing remote patient care through virtual communication and pursue my passion of writing. I've been a freelance content writer for over 4 years and run a microblog by the name of Dr. Mama on Facebook and Insta. I share my insights, opinions and health facts that not only stem from my background knowledge in Medicine but also from the beautiful amalgamation of the different cultures I grew up in.

From Riches to Rags to Inner Peace

"It's never too late to be what you might have been." – George Eliot

Hi! My name is Casey. I am a proud Canadian citizen. I grew up in Oakville, Ontario Canada. An affluent town situated by the shores of Lake Ontario. I lived in a middle-class spacious home on a quiet street in the suburbs. My education consisted of public schools from kindergarten to high school graduate. I had an excellent education. Incredible teachers. A plethora of resources.

Winters were spent playing in the snow, building snow forts, ice skating on rivers, sledding down gigantic hills, and hot chocolate with tiny marshmallows! And I can't forget to mention our indoor fireplace! In the summertime we swam a lot as we had our own pool. My friends and I went roller-skating, kite flying, played indoor and outdoor games, we went cloud busting, star gazing, and attended theme and water parks.

My high school years were some of my favourite times. I played soccer and taught swimming lessons in the summers and enjoyed hanging out with my friends during the school year. One year in gym class we had a karate instructor join us for a short duration to teach us self-defense moves! I'm deeply saddened I cannot remember his name or what he even looks like - but I do remember his essence. He came across to me with such a deep inner spiritual wisdom. I remember wanting what he had but at that time I had no idea how to achieve even acquiring it. I would carry his essence with me my entire life in search of what he held within him that captivated me. It was a pivotal moment in my life. I am inspired deeply by people who live unconventional lives and thrive! Those who choose to live off grid, on a sailboat, in a van, a yurt, a trailer....my list could go on but those are the people that truly rock my world. They are free in my eyes.

After high school I studied office administration at a prestigious college in Oakville. I never had any clear direction about what I wanted to be growing up. I'm not sure why. Everyone else had suggestions for me and I did try those - but I still felt incomplete and lost. I found myself missing my old high school days and friends. It was years beyond that now and yet for me it seemed like just yesterday because I thought about everything so much.

My life had reached a point where it was just too stressful and overwhelming. I fell into a deep depression over regrets I had. I began to shut down. The depression resulted in loss of work and friends - which only made things worse. I was now living in poverty by Canadian standards. I was struggling with my past life and unable to accept my present circumstances. For someone such as myself who was addicted to materialism and living in a consumerism society thing were very difficult for me. Or so I thought....

My greatest success through those dark years for me - was finding minimalism. Minimalism is a beautiful lifestyle! It's about living with less stuff and just having what is needed. For me it's about rarely shopping any longer. And it goes much deeper.... I choose to look at it as being able to enjoy the present moment. For the most part, and it's a pretty big part, minimalism freed me from my depression and negative thinking. I am under a doctor's care and taking antidepressants which do help. Minimalism has just become a way of life for me.

I practice it every day. It has completely changed how I live, think, and even breathe. I no longer desire what can be bought in a store but only what I can nurture within - which is my spirit, my thoughts, and my body. I spend a lot of time in the quiet of natural sounds. My favourites are birds singing in the early mornings and crickets chirping at dusk. A basic campfire and tent suffice my inner yearnings. I enjoy being in nature surrounded by tree's, a creek, wildlife, a walking path. Minimalism has brought me much inner peace. It is my compass towards simplicity. I am grateful every day.

If I could encourage any woman, it would be to say to you that the quote at the very beginning of this article is true. The best suggestion I have and what has worked for me recently is just to take little small steps towards what you would like to achieve in life for yourself. A very close friend I had once asked me, "what matters to you?" It was another pivotal moment for me. That question stunned me. I'd never been asked it before. The question intrigued me. I would think about it and process it for years - because I just didn't know. Until now!

Remember my high school gym sensei who I wrote about earlier? Because our paths crossed in such a short moment in time - he led me on a self-discovery journey. What I discovered is that I have chosen to slow down and stay in the moment. It takes a lot of discipline for me to stay in the moment. I have much more inner work ahead of me. But it is inner work that I enjoy immensely. Today I have begun to enjoy a completely new direction in life filled with a gentle pace and a set of personal values I adore. I have embarked on a new journey as a digital nomad. It feels right! And I love that feeling!

"I had learnt to use my fears as steppingstones rather than stumbling blocks, and best of all I had learnt to laugh." – Robyn Davidson

My Life As A Woman: Newfoundland Edition #1

Hey everyone, I am Dorothy. I am from Newfoundland, Canada. Newfoundland is the most spectacular place ever. I lived with both parents and two brothers in a little house on the coast. Growing up I lived for exploring, my siblings and I would go hiking, whale watching, and going to the beach. We had an avoidant relationship with our parents, they were always busy with work or at home, tired and sleeping. They were there, but not there in the same sense. So we were left to fend for ourselves and do what we wanted. We still had great respect for them because they tried their best to provide for us, in a sense. I was the middle child but both my brothers treated me as if I was the youngest. When our parents were at work and we came from school, they would make lunch for us and we would go fishing. Growing up my eldest brother was my hero, I wanted to be just like him. He was very outgoing, free-spirited, and determined.

I attended Cowan Heights Elementary, where I was successful and moved to O'Donel High School. I didn't do the best at school, I just could never get the concept. I did better at the creative tasks, I could do many things with my hands, they were my gift from God. I started drawing at a young age, it started as doodles on my brothers, as I grew my skills improved. Like every young child, I want to be in the typical profession; doctor or lawyer., but that was not going to work for me. So before finishing high school, I decided to follow my creative path. I have been selling my paintings since then.

Newfoundland is very diverse, with a range of beautiful summer days, to winter nights. There is always something fun to do here from hiking, fishing, going to the beach, snowshoeing, and whale watching. Newfoundland is the safest place ever, there is very little crime. Our people are super friendly, helpful, and outgoing. The only downside of Newfoundland is that the weather is terrible.

Growing up, I didn't trust people a lot, the only people I trusted were my brothers. That affected how I interacted with others in my surroundings and the life choices I made. I had a lot of opportunities but I didn't make use of all of them because of my trust issues. If I was more trusting, I would be further in life than I am now. Over time though, I became more trusting and started to take more risks. I think my brother would be proud of me. My biggest accomplishment is following my path and not the one people think I should. To all the women of Newfoundland school isn't for everyone. Not saying you should stop school but if you're putting in all the work and it is not working, find what works for you. It may be that you should be a blogger or a writer. So from me to you, create your path.

My Life As A Woman: Victoria Island Edition

My name is Isabella Jades from Victoria, which is the capital city of British Colombia. In this city, I learned what it needed to take to prosper as a woman in Canada. As a young child, my parents went through a divorce, and I had to stay with my mother, who struggled for work. Despite her struggles, my mother was a significant influence in my young life. I grew up in a city that is considered to be one of the best for a woman to live in, but as a young adult, I was still concerned about my safety. This is because regardless of the great conditions in the city and the support structures for women, there were a couple of sexual assault cases. Even though these cases were isolated, women had to be cautious constantly.

I loved that Victoria had a diverse culture, and one of these was ice hockey. This sport was a great pass time activity, and despite being labeled as a man's sport, I still got to participate. This was my early realization that the only restrictions that women face are those they generate. The struggles that my mother faced did inspire me to want to become a journalist, and I went to journalism school. Today, I work at a famous media house and run a blog to give women a voice and ensure social inclusion for women like my mother.

Through the journey to my current position, I have faced many struggles and successes. Victoria is advertised as one of the best cities for women, and while this is true, wealth disparities and other challenges still exist. As I was starting my career following my graduation, I got a gig in a small media house. In this role, I was assigned the task of covering fashion news or articles and other types of work that could be considered "for women." This was frustrating in my life as requests to write serious articles about the welfare of people were consistently declined. At one time, I did present an article detailing the opportunities of women in the construction industry. The manager declined the article on the basis that I was inexperienced, but what he meant is that I would not understand the industry based on my gender. This subtle gender discrimination limited my opportunities, and I had to resign and look for independent ways of conveying my voice. Through my earlier struggles, I found success by using the internet to target women going through the same struggles that I was. This effort attracted a large media house to acquire my talent, and this has allowed me to reach more women and inspire them.

My advice to women in Victoria Island is that the city does provide the perfect conditions for women to succeed. However, changing the culture of society is usually a daunting task. Hence, the struggles that you face should not be an inhibitor but a motivation to pursue opportunities. Women that have been successful across the world do not really on society setting the perfect stage, but it is through the grind that they have achieved their goals. Victoria may perform great in terms of gender equality, but more needs to be done, and this is a cue for women to get involved in support of other women.

My Life As A Woman: Central African Republic Edition

Where did I grow up?

I am one of the people of "the Forest" (laughter) as we say in our country. I was born somewhere in the northern edge of the great Congo Basin forest. My people, called Aka, are hunter-gatherers who have had commercial relations with Ngbandi farmers since the dawn of time.

How did I grow up?

One of the social characteristics of the Akas is the strong bond between fathers and children. Aka fathers spend more time and want more on their children than any other society. Therefore, we grow up with an impressive physical and mental strength and a strong character regardless of our gender.

My Model

My father logically. I loved his way of handling the bow and the boar spear. I called him "master" and he was a formidable and incomparable guide to me. He taught me a lot about nature, including climate change, trees, medicinal plants and their uses. It is thanks to him that I know the forest and the benefits of certain plants.

Education and childhood dream

I had an education that can be described as "normal", I was never the last in the class or the first, I was the assiduous but very attentive student. It was necessary because the school was, in a way, our way out to go on a big adventure to the city after graduation. And I can count myself among those brave women who have achieved this achievement. I studied for several years and brilliantly graduated from business school with my bachelor's degree. And yet, when I was a child, all I wanted was to be part of the amazons of my people. Except time passes and priorities change.

What I love about my culture

I cannot express myself in terms of one culture because the Central African Republic is full of very rich cultural practices. To speak of the Central African Republic is to say of a diversity of cultures relating to various national communities that form it. Each community has its own customs and customs, its artistic manifestations, its religions that characterize it and that distinguish it from another. For my part, I like folk dances in my home as well as culinary specialties. I also love Sängö, which is my vehicular language.

My occupations

Currently, I'm continuing my little way to integrate the conglomerate of the capital's richest merchants.

My struggles as a woman

You know how to make a successful life as a woman in the middle of the age, you don't necessarily make happy around you. I am a little more every day the target of evil eyes and nocturnal persecution, but that's not why I give up.

My successes as a woman

I can spend a whole day talking about it, because everything I do is successful through the grace of God. I hear testimony from older women in the marketplace who are asking each time how I have achieved this level of trade despite my age. It must be said that having the character forged since childhood has made me a born leader.

Advice for Central African women: The only advice I can give them is to try to be better at what they will do.

Eve Ndindia

My Life As A Woman: Chad Edition

"Here she is beautiful as a pearl" my mum said to my dad handing my little sister to him, hoping to wipe the confusion and sadness on his face, but his reaction was not pleasant, his words cut deep into her heart he said: "well congratulations to you at least a third set of hands to help you out around the house." He didn't even take her in his arms and he left the room. The midwife took Leila out of my mum's hands and gave her a pat on the shoulder for comfort, "SARAFINA, SARAFINA hand me the bowl" my mum was calling my name. I was 13 at the time but I was standing there in the middle of the room with the bowl of hot water and a cloth in my hands, speechless, wondering if my dad had the same reaction when I was born, wishing that he was rather happy and thrilled when it was me, but at the same time I was so pained for my mum, because somewhere in her heart she was not fully happy, she blamed herself for not having a boy this time around. Before he left the room, I saw the disappointment in his eyes, I handed her what she needed and left the room.

The midwife put my clean still crying sister back in my mum's hands and I could hear her saying that if she had followed advice since the beginning of the pregnancy, she would have had a son, all the advice she gave her like sleeping more on her right side, drinking some specific herbal mixture, visiting the "old man" as they called him so he would pray on her belly and other weird witchcraft that I just could not grasp. I was baffled they were not excited she just had a healthy beautiful little girl, with no pregnancy complications, as many women in our city due to severe hemorrhage and they were rarely saved. The hospital was miles away by the time they got there, the women would have already lost her life, even my older sister screamed on the phone AGAIN. She was 16 at the time, married, and had a baby boy of two months so she could possibly not understand my mother's pain.

In our small town in Chad called DOURBALI, words fly by fast. Once my mum gave birth, an hour later, the whole area was aware that she had a daughter again, Leila being the third daughter, and my dad was wishing by this point to have a little boy so the family legacy would live on. People came by to greet and congratulate him and quite frankly, we could've done without, it looked like they came to a funeral telling him that it was God's will and Allah will not forget granting his wish, that he shouldn't lose faith, all that fired a flame in my heart so I asked my dad, why was he so upset. He explained candidly that having many daughters has no use, they will help out in the house, yes, but only boys can make a good living out of their education. Boys are more willing to take on hard jobs that need strength, that boy he dreamed of would help him with his plans and he would have grand kids to carry his name, he said he forgave my mum by now and he is not mad at her anymore. Sadly, he had no clue that the kids gender is mostly the male's doing but he was my dad I could not get into details with him. He said it was not too late he will just keep on trying. He wished not to have many kids because of his salary, as he was working in a small rice shop, but he wouldn't stop trying until he had a boy.

All this talk gave me the rush to prove him and everybody wrong, that as a girl, I can be the kid he wishes me to be. I was very lazy at first and did not want to go to school every day, but I was suddenly adamant to graduate from school and make them proud, if not surprised. As my sister was growing up, I did my very best to teach her everything I knew so she could be as brilliant at school as I started to be, even my teachers were surprised by the sudden change in my grades. I started to help my dad in his work carrying heavy material with him to the shop, it was quite handy, but I wanted to prove a point, people started talking saying I have boy blood in me and I would laugh and move on. I graduated with honors and got a scholarship for a Tunis university to finish my management and business classes. My family couldn't be prouder now that I'm 24 and I work night shifts to provide for them and visit whenever I can. My dad is the man to say one good girl is all I needed. After the sixth daughter, he just accepted that he will be surrounded by strong females and he couldn't be happier.

My Life As A Woman: Chile Edition #1

It is very true that we cannot choose anything when we come into the world, many times I asked myself; What would my life have been like if I had been born in a first world country? Right now, that doesn't worry me anymore. The reality is that I was born in Venezuela, a wonderful country; I don't think I can find friends in the world like the ones Venezuela gave me. The fortune of being born among its beaches, with that fresh breeze from my city, transmits everyone with a warm and friendly spirit, they love to share life with joy, and there is no way that sadness is the protagonist; This characterizes almost all Venezuelans.

I am the youngest of brothers, my dad is a man with a very noble heart; he always has a right word at the right time. My mother is a talented housewife, generous hands for sewing and cooking, and she loves to teach; Once she told me that if she had studied, she would have been a teacher. I carry so much of her with me, her talents, her tastes, her kindness and even her fears; I've already recognized myself a few times reacting and acting like her.

We are a large family, and I love that! Humor is a constant, as is faith in God. My father's family had an upholstery company, and I remember seeing my Aunt Ruth and Uncle Angel working in the office; I loved being there. During my childhood, I liked to play "the little office", writing on papers as if I were sending letters, use fake phones and calculators. Now that I think about it, that influenced me a lot! Well, I thought that when I was older, I wanted to work in an office. So, when the time came to choose a career, I chose something comprehensive from "Business Administration", I wanted to be part of the business world.

I started at the University at the same time that I started working in the administrative building of a Free Zone, it was an incredible learning experience, in fact, the professional level that I currently have is due in large part to the experiences obtained in that company. One of my biggest professional challenges was facing Human Resources management at just 25 years old.

Unfortunately, while my professional and personal life was in a facet of balance, my country was going through one of its biggest economic and social crises. Migration became daily news, and it was heartbreaking to think of leaving my country, because by then I had achieved many goals. But living in Venezuela had become an exhausting process! And feeling that I had much more ahead, I decided to emigrate to Chile.

"If you are what you do, who are you if you don't?"; This phrase came to me a few months after being in my new country and I immediately identified myself; It was a fascinating reflection of what I had been feeling since I arrived. When we emigrate, we cannot bring in our suitcase, our job, and our entire professional career, we lose previous references from us (personal and professional); but finally, we must completely reinvent ourselves.

This reinvention has been my struggle, and the strongest internal and external process that I have faced. And this type of perspective, you only develop it when you grow up, when you get away from your loved ones, from your customs of those irreplaceable energies, when part of learning you realize who you are and why you fight.

I know that these reinvention processes in your life can come in a different way, what you must remember is that life brings many difficult moments and we must have the tools to overcome them. Losing the fear of continuing to learn. You must form a team, because nobody can do it alone. Change, transform, have the life you want so much, to become the person you want to be. At this moment I remember a wonderful phrase from Eleanor Roosevelt, which is: "The woman is like a tea bag. You never know what it's made of until they put it in hot water. "

Without a doubt, these processes teach you more about yourself than anything else and the decision is to reinvent yourself or nothing. Believing in us gives value to everything and in the end is what we reflect! Let's be the person we want to be, no matter where we are.

Lisbeth Martínez, Chile *14 de Mayo de 2020*

My Life As A Woman: Chile Edition #2

I grew up in the city of Santiago in Chile. I grew up in a hostile home, as my parents were always arguing. While the arguments subsided, the violence started, and I would helplessly watch my mother receive a beating. In such cases, I would flee from home on foot and stay with my aunt, who was residing just a few miles away. Unlike my mother, my aunt was a single mother, and she always taught me to make a stand in my life, or I would be exposed to the problems facing my mother.

Talking with my aunt was inspirational as I could dream again of what I wanted to do in the future. I always wanted to open my salon. When I went back home, these dreams would disappear as I had to face an abusive father that was not interested in my education. I felt lost knowing that my dreams would not be realized, and I would have to settle for just being alive. The society was geared towards patriarchy as women faced economic barriers. However, it was not all gloom as the festivals each year allowed me to forget the problems and feel that I did belong somewhere.

While my aunt was a great role model, I fell into the same trap as my mum as I started jumping into relationships too early and got married at 18 years old. As fate would have it, I utilized my husband as a scapegoat, but this did not last long as he too was abusive. After years of violence, I stopped giving excuses and joined a community organization to empower women. This was the first time I felt happy in a long time knowing that other women were suffering the same troubles I had, but they had also successfully managed to achieve a great life. This was a challenge as I was a young single mother.

This was the beginning of my success story, and through the community group, I was able to challenge my preexisting notions that a woman would not succeed in Chile. I got a job as a receptionist and was able to put myself through school. After completing my studies, I got a great job as a financial consultant, and through this, I was able to raise capital for my dream business. In a moment where I had lost hope, I was inspired by women through a community group, and I found my footing.

As I tell my life story to many women going through difficulties, it is apparent that these women face societal barriers and those of their making. I also had brainwashed myself into thinking that my situation was not that bad, which exposed me to more violence. My advice to women in Chile is that they should have the courage to escape any form of abuse. This is the first step towards empowerment, and life can be quite great. Many community centers support the empowerment of women, and joining these centers can be helpful. Generating a positive mindset can also be the difference between changing your life or suffering the same problems daily.

My Life As A Woman: Easter Island Edition

I grew up on Rapa Nui, known as "Easter Island," to people across the globe. The island is located in Chilean territory, and I grew up in Hanga Roa village, a small community of at least 5,000 people. Growing up on the island was exciting as the sceneries are quite extraordinary. As a young child, I would dress up in feathery dresses and join dance groups to showcase our culture to visiting tourists. Despite being 50 years old, I have never once failed to appreciate my culture, especially tattoos. This is because it is one part of the culture where women and men could be considered the primary audience.

As a young child, I had wanted to pursue a career in aviation, which was primarily influenced by the interactions I had with several tourists. I had imagined how I would leave the island and attain success in America. This was the first time that I learned of the patriarchal nature of society. My dad discouraged my dream by stating that I would be best served to be a nurse in the local hospital as it was a career that suited me. My father meant no offense and was reciting what the culture had taught him in his life. I had to drop out of school due to a lack of funds, and this allowed my brother to advance his education. My experiences exemplified the struggles that women face as they are consistently regarded as an afterthought.

I am currently working as a tour guide on Easter Island, and getting to this point in my life has been an achievement. While a tour guide position may not seem like significant progress, it is a job that I had to get by putting myself through school. I faced plenty of struggles, especially on what I could or could not do as a woman. I have not experienced much outside of Easter Island, but engaging with tourists from different parts of the globe has been crucial in understanding the many struggles women face worldwide. Not once have I met a tourist that has hinted at any gender equality in their country.

I have always tried to create relationships with most of these tourists, which has led to me being connected to inspirational women who are fighting for equal rights. Such women inspired me to encourage women from my community to form a group that would create a voice. The group has been critical in raising alarms on sexism and the lack of equal opportunities in education on the island and the mainland. I may have failed to achieve my dream, but I consider myself successful by ensuring that future generations do not face the same obstacles that I did.

My message to women is that they are not the only ones experiencing challenges in society. Thus, they should not give up on what they want because society is set up to favor men. By following your dreams, you ensure that other young girls have a role model to look up to in their battles.

123

My Life As A Woman: China Edition #1

The life of my grandmother, who is an old housewife, was not easy. My grandmother, born in the 1960s, experienced the hardest time of China during the Great Chinese Famine. Unfortunately, with the lack of foodstuffs, when she was still a little girl, her father and her little brother starved to death, leaving her mother and three sisters. So, when she was about 7-8 years old, she was forced to work to earn "work points" to exchange the foodstuff for living. Compared to today's children, it's the age that enjoys the parent's love most.

As she grew up, she met my grandfather and married him. It seemed that she finally had found another person to bear the heavy burden of life to be with. Nevertheless, my grandfather always worked outside so that my grandmother always managed on her own. Even if my father, uncle, and two aunts were born, my grandfather just found several days off to come back. To perform well at work, my grandfather spent more time focused on it. One could imagine that my grandmother raised all the children by herself. At that time, my grandfather achieved success owing to grandmother's assistance behind the scenes. When she told me about the story of those years, it was as if I was listening to the story of a firm and strong heroine.

I don't want to be a fatalist, but it seems that everyone can't escape from their fates. My grandmother also believed this. Life is not so merciful to her later years. It is universally acknowledged that each family has its own problems. As a peasant family, with the shortage of fortune, education, the relationships of family members were not so good sometimes. From my perspective, the most terrible thing is not the fortune, but the family harmony. Whereas, different people have different emotions. There are twelve members in one house, so quarries are inevitable. Hence, this time, my grandmother would be stuck in the dilemma, for she was always after trying to help and keep the family united. Although sometimes her sons did something that hurt her, she still loves them forever, even the unforgivable things. Every time I feel overwhelmingly depressed. I can't imagine how she can tolerate this. I am not a mother, but I see the mother's love from her, how a woman tries her best to manage her family, as a mother and a wife, also, how a person struggles with life and never bends her head.

When I was young, I didn't realize that life was a big challenge. We were born, but it's not the point, the most crucial thing is how to live. We require facing everything that we don't want to meet, but in order to live, we can just enjoy it. Sometimes, when faced with a problem, I realized my grandmother had no choice, but after several days, she still performed to live with passion. She lives like a heroine, fighting with the life and always lights the lamp of life with passion for all her life.

My Life As A Woman: China Edition #2

I am a woman born and grew up in China. I was born in late 1990s in Shanghai. Like many children who were born in this age, I am an only child because of the one child policy. In order to prevent people in the city to have a second child, the government started to propagandize gender equality. My parents always told me that girls should be independent and are able to be good at math just like boys. At that time, parents in big cities were laying more and more emphasis on education, they considered children and their education as the best way of investment. So, my childhood is relatively lonely. No siblings, lots of homework, little play time and extra-curricular classes on weekends.

I started to learn how to play Erhu, a traditional Chinese instrument, at a very young age. I started to learn it not because I like it, but because it was my grandmother's dream. But she didn't have the chance because of the economic situation when she was young, and my mom also failed to realize her dream. So, this dream passed on to me. It is a ridiculous reason when I think about it now, but at that time, I accepted this explanation and spent seven years of painful lessons learning it. Almost every day for an hour-long in practice.

Like many parents in China, or maybe in east Asia, my parents also tried to choose the best way through life for me. My first rebellion in adolescence was about Taekwondo. When I was 13, I fell in love with this "masculine" sport and decided I would open my own Dojo in the future. I spent plenty of time in Dojo, practicing, making friends there: that small Dojo became my second home and my emotional support. I started to spend more and more time there and less and less time on studies, and my grades plummeted. Facing high school entrance examination, I didn't care that much. At that time, I was not mature enough to make the "right" choice, but I started to try to free myself from the control of my family and society. My parents thought that I should stop practicing, not only because of the big exam, but also because it was not a hobby "suitable" for girls. Despite this, I kept fighting with them, until one day my coach told me that I could do better and I should study while practicing.

My coach served in the army before and taught me a lot about being brave, patience and strength, which I should have learned from my father, but I didn't. He was right. Why are these two things contradictory? Am I avoiding my responsibility as a student? Why did I resist? Is it for Taekwondo's dream or is it just the rebellion of an ignorant teenager? I refused to give up training and studied hard. Finally, I got into a good high school.

This is the first experience that I said no to my parents and received their approval by myself. This experience gave me and my parents the confidence to let me make my own decisions in the future. There years of high school life passed by soon, I entered college and studied engineering. I was struggling because I liked philosophy and literature, but it is hard to get a job if I studied these majors.

Another experience which had great influence on me was my trip to Uzbekistan. I went there at the age of 19 with a local friend. I almost knew nothing about this country except that it was a Muslim country. And at that time, my impression of Muslim was not so good because of terrorism and strict rules about women. So, as a girl from a "civilized and equal" country, I kept asking questions about women's rights there, hoping that I could change something in their country and maybe do something in "saving" these girls from all these strict rules. I was young and arrogant, thinking that it was a "fault" if a girl cooks for the family or cleans the house: girls should all study in Universities and be economically independent!

Until one day, I asked my friend's sister, who was the same age as me, "do you like doing housework?" She answered me, "yes, I enjoy making things clean and tidy makes me happy." Then I asked myself a question, is she born like this or did her culture and society's influence make her love cleaning the house? On the other hand: do I really enjoy studying science and engineering, or engaging in sports? Or I just kept trying to prove to others that women can do just as great a job as a man? Who is free? Becoming a housewife seems to be an embarrassing thing in the eyes of our generation, but is this really the case? If a woman loves the family, chooses to serve the family, educates her children and their families have such economic ability, why does it become a politically incorrect thing? What makes me think that all woman should hate doing cleaning stuff?

After that, I realized that there is no right choice for women. Women don't need to be man or like men because we're not men. We should be ourselves. We can enjoy practicing Taekwondo or doing laundry. We should also be proud if we love doing girls' stuffs such as cleaning or cooking: that is equality. We can all be ourselves without being judging. Not by man, not by society or culture, not by ourselves. Of course, we should work hard, contribute to the society just like man. We have the right to say "no", when parents said that "girls don't need to work so hard, just find someone to marry." And if our dreams are a happy family instead of successful career, we should also be able to admit it frankly.

To this day, some friends around me still struggle with their future life: but in my opinion, it is also something man should face in their life, confusion about the future life, including marriage. They all have some achievements in their careers and independence. At my age, I still don't need to consider too much about that, but finally I need to face it. What makes me happy is that no matter whether they are married or single, they have made their own choices.

My Life As A Woman: China Edition #3

Born and raised in a small village in southern China, I had lived with my grandparents until I was eight. Children of similar age played together before we could vaguely perceive the difference between boys and girls. The absence of parental love reinforced a strong tie with my grandma. She was a traditional Chinese countrywoman who was illiterate for there was no chance for her to accept education at her age. However, her instruction made an indelible impression on me especially on the important years of my life. When I was four, my sister was born. Grandma cuddled the little baby and told me she is my sister. I had no idea about the notion but was curious about the new life. I kissed her and murmured that I am your sister stuff. Each time she spooned the little baby, she would remind of old times and retell those stories to me. Senior sisters had responsibility to take care of their younger siblings, which is a basic tenet of clannism. The sense of family responsibility penetrated my mind even though I always got into fights with my younger sister in my younger years. I was also illuminated by the truth of family responsibility.

The lifestyle of a traditional Chinese village offers a snapshot of some outdated minds, which meanly put pressure on women. Nowadays especially in big cities, it is a shadow of its former self. I transferred to a prestigious school in town when I was in grade three. When I went back to the village years later, I found some of playmates in childhood became housewives the moment I was going to apply for college. Most of them dropped out of school early and had worked for several years before their parents hastily made blind dates for them. The upside to this choice was the freedom to steer their own lifeboat. In a sense, staying at school kept me away from a premature period. Luckily, being a child had the privilege to enjoy my good time instead of being bothered by life troubles. The only big deal was to get a good grades which was also the best comfort for my parents. Those girls' rumors would sometimes be raised again by seniors, which offered a lesson for us to study hard. Advanced degree is regarded as an honor for whole family and an easy way to find a good match. In some seniors' mind, it's better to marry well than to learn well.

Those minds surround me along the growth. It is ridiculous to find the truth that education gives female freedom to be themselves while social stereotypes never stop degrading them. I am lucky enough to receive a better education for my parents realize it necessary.

Now, as a sophomore from the northern most province, I do enjoy my campus life which presents a whole different world. My parents give me freedom to choose my major. The dream of being an interpreter enlightens me to pick another language. Growing awareness of the preference of literature gives me the pleasures of reading. It also empowers me to be sober to clear out stereotype that society imposed on. When I look back to the old times, I realize that we don't need to live a life that others want us to have. Each step that we choose paves the way for a bright future.

My Life As A Woman: China Edition #4

My name is Rosie, an ordinary girl from China. I'm a college student in a Chinese university and I think my family is a traditional Chinese family. I've finished my primary school through four different schools, because sometimes my parents were having to go and look for work elsewhere. But I can adapt effortlessly to my new surroundings, making new friends soon. And I often performed well in school, being awarded a prize for excellence in my studies.

The members of my family are my parents, younger sister, younger brother and me; my brother is the youngest. I'm the oldest child. As the oldest, I think I was often under the pressure. Considering that I should be the one to set a good example for my younger sister and brother, and I must do everything as well as I can. I guess it has something to do with my cultural background. In traditional Chinese concepts, the older one has a responsibility to lead the young and take good care of them. For example, in China, when a group of people go out for dinner, the oldest one is most likely to pay for it, but some occasions, like the birthday parties for the old, are not included. In a word, as the oldest child in my family, I must try my best in my life, and I will keep trying to become a better person.

In order to become a better woman, I often want to do something to improve myself. I believe in no pain no gain. When I was very young, about 4 years old before I went to school, my mother started to inspire me to learn something like simple calculations, a few Chinese characters and Songs of the alphabet, etc. which helped me a lot in my future life and I owe my mother my best thanks. I often learned what I was interested in by myself and I would benefit from it. For example, I'm learning how to use Adobe Photoshop to create some beautiful pictures or polish photos. I also like reading. I often read some books before going to bed. The book I read this week was named The Willpower Instinct by Kelly McGonigal, Ph.D. And maybe soon, I'm going to learn Korean. I think what I'm doing or going to do are all out of choice rather than compulsion. I enjoy learning new things, which improves me very much and could provide me with more opportunities. In addition, it's worth mentioning that some people in China hold that there's no need for women to go to school, because women will get married and should be a housewife, and they also consider that in becoming a housewife, they don't need high education but some life skills and common sense. I see such remarks as a put-down of women. I feel I was very lucky that my parents see their daughters as equal to their son. It's the fact that some parents from a small, one-horse town would give up educating their daughter at schools but support their son to go to school because of the poverty. Though it isn't a universal phenomenon, it can't be overlooked.

As women, we ought to be independent, because only you will not betray yourself. When it comes to my future, I want to go freelance. I don't like to be controlled, and I want to control myself. My perfect life is that I can plan my own schedule rather than being led by the nose. I would like to freelance as a translator and writer, and I think I would enjoy in it and at the same time, I could earn my living. Wow, what a perfect life! Even now I can't do that, but I'm keeping towards my goals.

Now I'm in my second year of university, and it's a pity that I can't go to school this term because of the novel coronavirus (COVID-19) pneumonia. I sincerely hope that this disaster will end soon. My plan for these 2 months are to complete my course well and keep fit. I also want to learn Korea if I have enough time left and energy. I'm Rosie, a hard-working and energetic girl, and always keep running towards my goals.

My Life As A Woman: China Edition #5

I was born in a small village in China, my family condition was not very good, but I had a happy family. My parents who love me and my sister were always considerate. Midsummer eighteen years ago, a little girl was born. This was a very happy moment, but for the already poor family, it was somewhat of a burden, and yes, I am the girl, but my childhood memories are full of love. They took after me carefully, and I'm also a career-best, leading the way then I got into the city with priority high school, and did very well, eventually starting my life.

When I was in high school, my sister failed the college entrance examination, seeing her sad tears, my heart was saddened by the event. So at that time I swore to study hard and enter the best university. The first test in my high school, I did horribly and was not even close to being in the top of my class. At that moment, I really didn't know how to describe my mood, unwilling, sad, fear...all kinds of emotions flooded me, but on the other side, I was pretending to not care about my grades in front of my classmates. My face was laughing but my heart was crying and I didn't let anybody know my mood, including parents sister and friends.

I felt like a trapped animal, living in prison, muddled in the school every day, grades getting worse and worse. I complained about everything while dawdling. That period of time, I read a lot of inspirational articles to cheer me up. My senior year suddenly started up and the people around me settled down to start taking their studies seriously so I also began to study day and night, did the exercises crazily, extra credit, whatever was going to get me ahead. Some night I slept less and even slept when I was standing up. Inspired by my classmate, I refreshed myself, all the way by leaps and bounds, scored high points very quickly, and my heart had comfort finally, with a little bit of light appears in front of my eyes.

In a way, I was going through a jedi rebirth and felt wiser. I still was afraid of the university entrance exam, seeing how my sister was, but I was wrong and got lost in a mess, thinking about it during my waking hours and even dreaming about it, before I even saw the test, or knew the result. One day, I finally took a much-needed break and had a long lunch to recall the past three years. Suddenly, everything seemed to be understandable and make sense to me, but still in my heart, I tried to suppress the pain. That night, I was awake all night and had thought about the tough requirements of my parents with their hard-earned money to go to university. I was sad when I envisioned their pale hair, always feeling a twinge of regret and irritating sensation in the nose. But regret is useful for the reality one is living, and that completely woke me up. I understood from the beginning of the prison that I was lost...later in the days, I began to cherish my time more, grasp every minute, every second, live in the present, now I'm heading towards my way of life bravely.

Maybe you have heard of nirvana reborn, you will have boiling passion because of other people's stories, but please don't live in someone else's story, only experiencing this despair will make one cherish the hope. If you are going through the pain, please don't give up hope every time the growth is accompanied by pain, I began to appreciate my experiments firmly in the footsteps of my life, and I won't stop, you can't stop.

Life is beautiful and we are just one of millions of ordinary people and wish that through my own experiment, I can give you some encouragement, believe in yourself, God helps those who help themselves. Each of us has a different definition of success, but the road to success is bound to be difficult, you must believe that you will never fight alone, the people who love you will always behind you.

My Life As A Woman: China Edition #6

I grew up in the Chengdu of Sichuan which is a capital city on the southwestern side of China. I am the only child in my family. My father is an engineer, and my mother is a sociologist, they both love me very much. My mother is a woman with strong career-ambition. She is bright and energetic. The relationship between us is more like friends instead of mom and child. Her stories and thoughts motivated me a lot and had a great influence on me as well.

In the 1980s, my mom was in her early twenties. She loves reading and traveling. At her 25, with the strong desire to go out and travel around the world, she started to learn English from ABC by herself. At that time, many of her peers formed a family and delivered a baby. I was born when she was 31, but this still didn't stop her from traveling. She always educated me to have a worldwide view. When I was 7-years-old, we moved to the Philippines for about one year. This experience made a great change in my life. It was my first time experiencing another culture and living aboard.

My mother always told me, as a girl, I should be independent, and take the chance to go outside to see the world, experience different cultures. I kept this in mind and started to study and live abroad independently after my twenties. So far, I have traveled around 20 countries. These experiences also have a great influence on me, while reshaping my worldview.

After I got my master's degree in Europe, I went back to China and found a job as a UX designer at an IT company, where I observed that women endure more pressure than men in the workplace. In China, many women older than 25 easily get anxious. On the one hand, the pressure is from gender discrimination in the workplace. The employer prefers to find men or single younger women compared to married women for job vacancies. If a woman just got married, she probably would be discriminated against in the workplace. For this reason, a married woman will probably become pregnant someday. On the other hand, women are supposed to spend more time on family compared to men. There is a proverb in China that says, "men managing external affairs women internal". Therefore, in some elder's eyes, the social success of a woman is supposed to marry a good man and have a baby. A married woman with no job is fine, but a single woman with a great career sometimes is not respected by others. That's the reason why many women in China are striving to pursue more rights for men and women on an equal footing.

Last year, I quit my job and became a freelance designer and started my own business. I started to build my professional expertise and work remotely. I want to find a way that is more sustainable, while I can make money by myself, and balance my family life and work.

If you are a woman who lives in China, I hope that you will have less burden, be independent, and develop a skill to achieve secure economic independence. Don't rely on families or men. Be trusting in yourself and believe in yourself. Follow your own heart, don't just choose someone to get married because of social pressure. Finally, I hope women in China can protect and inspire themselves and other women!

My Life As A Woman: China Edition #7

Growing up in a middle-class family in the countryside of Canada, surrounded by cornfields for as far as the eye can see, is not as rare as it may sound in Canada. Since Canada only has about five major cities, plenty of Canadian born and raised youngins have had a similar upbringing. Looking back now, I can't remember a time when I didn't dream about living in the 'big city'. Growing up in rural Canada, the big city for me was Toronto. A glorious three million people and a thriving daytime and nighttime scene, my dream for most of my young adult life was to live in what I thought to be the most vibrant city of all time.

As the years went on, I felt so lucky having friends in 'the city' where I could easily hop on a train and go enjoy the bustling city life for a weekend. But surely, the more I visited Toronto, the less it appealed to me to live out the rest of my life just a short three-hour trip away from everything I had known growing up. That's why it shouldn't have come as a shock that I was soon bored of Toronto. I wanted something newer, something I had never known. I had no idea where I would land, but you better believe it wouldn't be Canada if I had anything to say about it.

Cut to months later, stepping off the plane in Shenzhen, China, which was unlike any other experience I had had to date. My hair agreed: it frizzed out in 2.5 seconds due to the 100% humidity of Southern China. My first week in China was challenging. More than a few people who arrived at the same time as I did packed up and went back home, lasting less than a week and proving China a difficult code to crack. I didn't blame them. China isn't for everyone, but my perpetual lack of homesickness and longing for a new culture kept me thriving and never doubting I would grow to love my new home.

My new profession in China was an English teacher and having never been to Asia nor having taught a class in my life, I knew I had some hurdles to overcome. I will never forget the overwhelming nervousness I felt that first day in the classroom. I had no idea what I was doing and looking back on my lesson plan, I must chuckle to myself. Being a female teacher in China also came with its struggles. I didn't initially know it, but the students tend to respect the male teachers over their female counterparts. Whether male or female, as a foreign teacher you can expect 75% less respect from your students than any Chinese teacher would receive. Teaching wasn't without its hardships in the beginning, but I soon discovered a passion for my new role.

There is one question, asked by many women, myself included, before I moved to China: is it safe? If you have never visited China, I would be willing to bet a hefty wager that the first thing to come to mind is cheap clothes and sweatshops – I know that was the first thing to mind for me. How can a place like that ever feel safe for women? Trust me when I say, China is one of the safest countries I have ever been to. Having travelled to 30 plus countries, China is one of the few I felt completely comfortable walking home alone at 4 A.M. This is one of the benefits of China, as there are video cameras everywhere. It's a trade-off sometimes between your freedom and safety, but how many other countries can women feel undoubtably safe walking home alone all hours of the night?

As any foreigner in China will tell you, the second you step foot off the plane you are an instant celebrity. Being a Caucasian female, this is especially the case. If you have blonde hair, watch out or your face will quickly be plastered all over Chinese social media. Thankfully, my dark hair helped me be slightly more incognito (at least from behind), but once your non-Asian facial features are noticed, you can guarantee a good handful of Chinese people will try their darned hardest to use their broken English to ask for a photo. Or maybe three. Or five.

The instant fame for simply not being Asian soon wore off, and now I often try to hide my face if possible, in the hopes of avoiding photos, or even worse, stares. Being a foreigner in China will never be an easy feat and being a woman even less so. Chinese women are expected by their families to live a very different and more traditional life than western women. While most of us in the West have the freedom and blessing to travel the world and not have to worry about procreating before we hit 30, or even ever if we so choose, the Chinese women are expected to honour and make their families proud. Most are told to find a good job, have a child, and then often let their parents raise that child while they continue working for the next twenty years. However, the times are slowly changing in China, and I enjoy seeing some of the Western views I know so well being adopted in my new country. There will always be some things that will be traditionally China and will never change, but as the phrase goes: If you can't beat 'em, join 'em.

Nicole Vilaca

My Life As A Woman: China Edition #8

I am an ordinary girl from China. I am an undergraduate reading student now. I want to share with you my story of growing up in China as a woman. When I was a teenager, my lack of confidence was visible to all. I was born and brought up in Xi'an which is a famous city for her ancient culture. Under the influence of a rich cultural background, I like Chinese traditional culture, especially poetry, because it full of lingering charm and artistic conception. My favorite line is that Wildfire can't burn them up again; They rise when vernal breezes blow.

My parents are barely literate with no idea of the how the world works, but they put my education first. Particularly, my mother considered it very necessary for me to get an education. I had some best friends and very general grades in school. I was shy, obedient, a mediocre student through my high school days. However, there was one thing that I couldn't get through—national college entrance examination, the fairest examination in China, probably determining most people's lives. I agreed to go to college. In addition, my mother inspired me to try again. So, I decided to study for a whole year and take part in the test. Eventually, I was admitted to a good normal university, although my math score was bad. My major is English education. I want to be an English teacher when I graduate, because I want to teach more people about the fascination of English.

After I began university, I found that I had more time to know and improve myself. And, I was no longer confused. I gradually fell in love with reading and excising, which enlightened my mind, pointed out the direction and gave me endless strength. Of all the books I've read, books about women incredibly motivated me. I love the freedom and innocence of Samoa in the Stories of the Sahara; I love the woman's fortitude and kindness in A Thousand Splendid Suns; I love Scarlett's nature and courage in Gone With The Wind. Moreover, I had willpower to exercise every day, which relieved my stress and put me in a good mood. With the spirit of positive and diligence, I obtained a scholarship at the end of my first term.

I am taking online classes at home now. I persist in taking exercise indoors and reading. Despite not knowing what challenges are waiting for me in the future, I have a lot of confidence in my ability to solve them. Looking back along the way, I really appreciate my mother and the education I received. I thank my mother for her hard work towards me. When I failed, it was she who gave me strength to get away from the situation. Although my education background is not outstanding, it transformed me. I am not the girl I was, but I am a courageous and thoughtful woman now.

As a woman, I hope you realize that we are not worse than men or that men are better than us. We are all equally blessed with opportunities and faced with challenges. You should set aside biases from others or yourself as you possibly can and make full use of your time to do useful and productive things, such as reading and doing sports. At last, learn to watch yourself, accept yourself, and enhance yourself.

My Life As A Woman: China Edition #9

Growing up in a countryside in Fujian Province, China, I spent my childhood like many children in China. When I recall the past, I always think of my brilliant mother. For instance, I once failed in a math exam, she didn't get angry at all. Instead, she enlightened me patiently and told me the correct way to solve the problems. It's such a trivial matter that influences my perception. Every time when I encountered something annoying, I would think of her gentleness. As I grew up, I could face situations calmly.

Recently, a lot of bad things happened in my country. Facing the COVID-19, no matter how hard it is, my country never gave up anyone. China invests a lot of human and material resources every day to control the infection of the novel coronavirus. That's why I love my country. It retains one of the essences of Confucius culture: The Benevolent Person Loves Others. In this battle, we see countless medical staff are fighting in the front line. From my point of view, they are the real back waves of China.

But there are some problems in Chinese society. In April, a man called Yuming Bao is accused of violating his adopted daughter for three long years, but to my anger is that the Yantai police safeguard the man. If this matter cannot be handled properly, I feel very scared. Can we even believe the law? Are there any rules in this world? When I think deeply, I will recall the struggles as a woman in China. Society seems to have a big prejudice against women, just like the previous Didi incident. It's obviously a male driver's mistake but to blame the female passenger. After the storm, Didi Dache issued a new regulation to ban female users from riding after 8 pm. I always think that this is the most malicious to women.

Despite the disgusting things that happened and laws and regulations that seem to be put against women rather than men, I still feel the success of women. One hundred years ago, Coco Chanel designed pants worn by women and told all girls: "You can't afford Chanel, or you don't have many clothes to choose from, but never forget one of the most important clothes, this one called yourself." Women can bloom themselves in many ways in China today. Compared with women in countries like India and Afghanistan, we can work in many different industries like business, art, film, writing, etc. instead of being restricted forever. Besides, Chinese women's status has improved. Although the concept of male superiority and female inferiority still exists, it is slowly fading. When women encounter unfair incidents, they can speak out to the society boldly.

Virginia Woolf believes that if a woman intends to write a novel, then she must have money and have a room of her own. As far as I'm concerned, for every woman, whether she wants to write or not, she must have the ability of self-reliance and independent consciousness. That's the only suggestion I give.

My Life As A Woman: China Edition #10

Where did I grow up?

I grew up in a small county in central China. This is not a rural area, it's also not really a city in the true sense because it does not have a developed industry and advanced infrastructure. The area is not large, there are nearly 800,000 people. This population is not dense by the standards of developed regions in eastern and central of China.

I went to primary school for six years here, and after six years of junior high school and high school, I spent much of my time in Changsha, the capital city of Hunan province. There, I have always been boarding, but I still often go home. In elementary school, we had about 65 to 70 students in each class, 50 to 60 students in junior high school, and 45 to 50 students in high school.

In my hometown, the main economic industry is the service industry, but it is not developed. Mainly to privately operated supermarkets, restaurants, small clinics and clothing stores. In addition, some state-owned enterprises and government administrative units have provided some jobs.

How did I grow up?

When I was very young, there were few residential buildings in our hometown. Everyone lives in an old house with two or three floors. (Of course, not everyone owns a house, most people rent them.) These houses have their own specifications and colors, and they are not flat.

Until recent years, local real estate has developed, and many 20 to 30-story residential districts have been built to form neat communities. When we lived in a bungalow, our life was like this every night, many small stools are moved in front of the house. Everyone sits and chats together, looking up at the stars and telling stories or discussing business. If it was winter, we would put a firewood in the middle to warm up. In daily life, we would cook and exchange meals with our neighbors. Old people would go for walks and square dances together, and younger elders would go shopping together. Our children usually got together to do their homework or play hide-and-seek, sometimes we would get together and watch TV (at that time, not everyone had a TV at home because the economic conditions did not support it.)

About twelve years ago, I entered elementary school. China's elementary and junior high schools are free and compulsory. At that time, I think there is no way to compare with the current level of education. First, because information was blocked at that time, the Internet was underdeveloped, and thinking was relatively limited. The second is affected by the economic foundation, the level of education itself is not so high.

In retrospect, my elementary school teacher is far behind the present. My primary school class teacher has some influence. If you want to get her attention, you may need your parents to give the teacher some material benefits. In addition, her professional level is also very limited.

Now, because of the improvement of the education level, the education industry is more perfect, and at the same time, the competition is more intense. Therefore, not only has the overall professional level of teachers been greatly improved, but their moral level has also become higher. In addition, the teacher's behavior is somewhat constrained by the corresponding professional rules, such as requiring parents to give gifts, and corporal punishment of students, who must be punished accordingly.

Most of us have been very concerned about our grades since elementary school. Because China has a large population, the competitive pressure on learning will be relatively greater. In the elementary school, we study hard, in order to be able to enter a good junior high school. In junior high school, we also study harder because we want to enter a good high school. In high school, for three years, we work hard for our goal of studying for so many years, namely, to be admitted to a good university. In the second year of high school, the school divides the curriculum into liberal arts and science, with some schools starting with the division in the first year. Both liberal arts and science students must learn Chinese, mathematics, and English. Then, science students need to learn biology, physics, and chemistry. Liberal arts students must study politics, history, and geography.

In the first and the second year of high school, most of us are boarding, our school is a dormitory, and one room is usually for eight people. We do our own laundry and go to the cafeteria to eat three meals a day. And during school, boarders cannot go out casually, unless there is a leave request. But in the third year of high school, because washing clothes will delay time, and at the same time, many parents think that children need to supplement more nutrition, they rent a house next to the school and let the children move out of dormitories. In the third year of high school, I usually got up at 6:20 a.m., and went to bed at about 12 in the morning. In addition to in-class learning, interest classes are also an important part of our growth.

Most conditional, parents send their children to learn dance, painting, piano and Taekwondo when the children are very young. But after entering junior high school, because of academic pressure, many people will not continue, but spend more time in English, mathematics, writing classes, and many will also supplement physics, chemistry, etc.

In growing up, we spent most of our time in school. Regarding the growth of girls, I would like to talk about adolescence. We must wear school uniforms at school, not the clothes we like. At the same time, it is not possible to dye hair, or to keep very long hair. Some schools may allow it, but the requirements in different regions are different. The original intention of these rules, I think, is to prevent students from generating competing psychology. In other words: if everyone looks mostly the same, they will not be jealous or envious of each other.

In adolescence, many girls are very sensitive. Maybe she will be shy because of the acne on her face, maybe she will be inferior because of her fat body. In short, girls have many scruples, to a certain extent, these scruples suppress the nature. In addition, in fact, whether it is a boy or a girl, in adolescence, dating is not supported by the school and parents, because this will affect the child's learning, and at the same time, it may also cause the child to have a bad mood and not focus on the right thing they should do, so "dating life" in high school is almost nonexistent. However, most girls will like one or a few boys during adolescence and they will secretly pay attention and inquire about them. They might be considered one of the bad girls. In fact, I am one of those girls. I can't help myself.

Any family members who inspired me?

For a long time in China's history, there was the idea of favoring men over women. In fact, in some rural areas, there are still some old people who prefer the birth of a boy to a girl. Because in ancient times, boys were able to do more work, support their elders, and even obtain official positions, while women would be geared towards the married life.

In order to be able to give birth to a boy, many people who are discriminatory against gender will allow women to have children until a boy is born. Sometimes, if things go against their wishes, they will even put the desire of "want of a boy" in the name of the girl in the family to realize the meaning, so many girls might have usual boys' names.

I am lucky that my family is not like that. Even the elderly at my home like me very much, and my sister. While it is just me and my sister, my family accepted it and does not long for a boy. My grandparents care a lot about me and my sister. No matter whether it is clothes, food or education, they will do anything for us. And mentally, they also have a lot of support. Mom and Dad will not stop us from learning more because we are girls and limit our choices in future employment. On the contrary, they invested a lot in our education. And they encourage us to be independent and strong as a girl, both financially and spiritually. I am very grateful for their education.

My personal pursuits and ideals

Regarding the pursuit of growth, as a young woman, I think that in the future growth process, I should follow the following principles. Be independent, whether economic or spiritual, must not become a vassal of others.

Enterprising and constantly learning new knowledge

Love our life, be considerate and filial to my family, and make my life full and interesting. Regarding ideals, I chose a language major at the university. I know that learning a foreign language and mastering it is not a simple matter. But I still chose it, and I already have a mature goal, that is, I want to work hard to become a simultaneous interpreter. I chose it as my goal for many reasons. Firstly, the income of simultaneous interpretation is very considerable. In fact, I'm not a person who values money very much, but I still hope to have a high-paying job that will allow me and my family to live a stable life. So, we can often travel and engage in entertainment activities that I like to do. Second, I think that simultaneous interpretation is a difficult and challenging thing. And I like to be aggressive and challenging. Third, because of simultaneous interpretation, I will have the opportunity to participate in many large and meaningful occasions, to see a lot of wonderful things and excellent people, learn a plenty of things, which is also an attractive reason.

About my favorite culture

When it comes to culture, my favorite is literature. Whether it is domestic or foreign, traditional or modern. If it is an excellent literary work, I like it very much. Among the vast ocean of literature, my favorite field should be fiction. I really like reading novels, including historical novels, romance novels, and science fiction novels. Whenever I have time, I will go to the library to look for novels.

Current work

Currently, I am still in the learning stage. My college is a foreign language college. In the process of learning foreign languages, I need to memorize words, learn grammar, correct my accent, and at the same time, train my listening skills. In addition, we must learn writing and translation.

Struggles as a Woman

Today, in fact, at the legal level, the status of men and women is equal, but not in the view of some people. For example, in the most subtle daily conversations, some people may have sex discrimination, such as fertility choices, for example. And when recruiting, many times, men are more favored than women. You can see on many social platforms in China that men and women are arguing about sexism. As an ordinary woman, what struggle can I make for women? I think that is a bit trivial, but I still must do it. Because if every woman can try, sooner or later, there will be no more discrimination in people's ideas.

First, we must strive to improve our professional capabilities. Only in this way can more people see that women also have considerable value in the job market. Second, don't take marriage as a matter of enhancing your status. If a woman expects to marry a rich man because of her poor family and economic conditions, to a large extent, she will become an accessory to marriage and lose her original spiritual independence. I think that our own growth progress is far more reliable than the appreciation gained through marriage. Third, we must dare to say "no" to discrimination, we can start with small things around us, and eliminate the discrimination concept of those around us.

My success as a woman

I have no great success; they only exist in a very small part of life. For example, when I was studying, I could do better in many subjects than the boys in the class. Even running, I can surpass some boys, and have the power in a power duel. In addition, I had explained to the teachers that the boys in the class bullied the girls and asked him to make a ruling. Therefore, those girls are protected from being bullied. And in the future, I will continue to stick to my ideals and be an excellent woman.

Recommendations for women

In fact, I can talk about the successful women in my heart and make these suggestions through them. I want to talk about Wu Zetian in ancient times, Lin Huiyin in modern times, and Dong Mingzhu after reform and opening. Wu Zetian was a famous emperor in Chinese history. Unlike the situation in European history, in ancient China, women could not even go out often, and could only teach children and do housework at home. They are not supported in reading and are not allowed to talk about politics.

Therefore, Wu Zetian is a special existence, she is not like the other emperor's concubines, but she dares to do something politically and she has made a female political voice in history.

In modern times, Lin Huiyin, an excellent architectural designer and a writer, has a very good background and knowledge. In the era of poverty and turmoil, she could have chosen to continue to live a stable life, but she was determined to contribute to China's construction cause, and she was wandering around most of the time. She never shirks the hard things, and even if she was very sick, she insists on working while educating her children. Not only is Lin Hui so devoted to her work, she is also strong and independent. She does not easily obtain other things by virtue of her beautiful appearance but focuses on inner cultivation. And, she also has high attainments in literature.

Dong Mingzhu is a successful female entrepreneur in China. On February 12, 2020, Forbes China released a list of the most outstanding businesswomen. The 65-year-old Gree chairman Dong Mingzhu once again boarded the rankings, and she is likely to become the first female professional manager to be listed on the Forbes global billionaire. Dong Mingzhu chose to endorse for the company's products and shouted the slogan "Let the world fall in love with Made in China".

Today's success does not mean that Dong Mingzhu has always been successful. On this road, she experienced many hardships. When her child was just two years old, her husband died. Later, she needed to bear the burden of her family, so she kept learning, going on business trips, and working, instead of being reunited with her child often. She started at the grassroots level of the company, and after decades of hard work.

They are all representatives of countless women in China. Although they are in different eras, they can affect that era, even now and in the future. I think we can learn about their independence, their dedication, their strength, their dreams, and their courage to fight. These qualities, whether in peace or when we encounter difficulties, are very valuable spiritual assets.

My Life As A Woman: China Edition #11

"A citizen of the world, in you two worlds are combined together with kindness and determination." The sentence comes from a letter my dear aunt once wrote to me. An aunt who was like a second mother to me and who unfortunately died of cancer during the same time as my first trip to China. I've lived in China ever since. But I'm not Chinese. I'm Italian and Tunisian. In other words, I'm a living cultural cappuccino.

Like all good stories, the beginning of my life started in a very small town in the nearby Venice. Never have I ever seen more than a hundred people walking in the streets of my hometown. I grew up in a version of Italy much different from now. In the 'ol times, mixed couples were far from mainstream. I had to go through decades of self-talk and self-reflection to understand who I am. I had to define who I was most. I would say I am half Italian and half Tunisian, which is a common saying among mixed-race children. We define our cultural identity as two halves, as two sides of an Oreo. And we are the white cream inside it.

I bet you, too, went through some hard times as a teenager. You want to feel understood and appreciated. Your body is changing, and so is your vision of the world. As a mixed-race child, every doubt was enhanced to its peak. I am not like other Italians, as much as I am not entirely Tunisian either. I have dark curly hair and brownish skin. Despite being ethnically Italian, my mother is the stereotypical representation of the typical North European lady with pearl-white skin, blonde hair, blue eyes. My father, on the other hand, couldn't be different. I inherited his curly hair and brown eyes. His skin is darker than most Maghrebians. Some of our relatives live in the South of Tunisia, a place surrounded by sand and dunes. That might be the reason behind our darker skin complexion.

I come from a very small town. I've always felt different. I am different. It took me a long while to realize and accept this. But I'm glad I finally did. I know, reading about other people's first-world problems and boring childhoods is not exactly the recipe for an exciting piece of literature. Keep reading, as we still haven't reached the most interesting (and complex) part of this story.

"China enters the chat"

I've always loved languages. I still do to this day. I could get lost in analyzing the complexities of each word. How do we say what we do the way we do? Don't get me started with this. To communicate with my Tunisian family, I had to learn French from a relatively early age. In case you are asking... no, unfortunately, I can't speak Arabic. French is the closest I can get to avoid getting lost when traveling to Tunisia.

Anyway, in 2012, I decided to make one of the bravest decisions of my life. I went to China alone, without much money, a computer, or a decent phone. I couldn't speak Chinese, besides the very basics "hello" and "how are you?", "I'm Elisa," and such. To tell the truth, that same year, I started studying Chinese at university. But I soon got so lost and upset that I was incredibly close to giving up. I didn't learn much of Chinese that year. It sounded and looked way too complicated for me back then.

Anyway, again, when I left that summer, my aunt was in the hospital in critical condition. I knew too well that I would have the chance to see her only at that time before my departure. Indeed, when I came back from China, she was already gone.

It was also my first international flight. I was barely past 18 years old. I didn't know what to expect from China. The information about this immense country was too scarce even to get a very general idea about what was in store for me. I could only base my judgment on stereotypes and trust that everything would be fine in the end.

I remember I felt exhausted at my arrival; the jetlag was proving much harder to cope with than I expected. As I walked towards the driver, the summer school called for me. He drove for 3 hours back which then felt like an eternity. And then, I arrived at the school campus.

As you can imagine, communicating with one of the teachers wasn't exactly that easy. I hadn't practiced English for a long time. I finally had access to my dormitory room. It wasn't a presidential suite, but it was far better than nothing. However, it was covered in dust, and a whole family of big hairy spiders was living in the toilet. And I have arachnophobia.

That night I didn't sleep well. I cried like a baby. Everything felt so different and, in some ways, even scary. What if I went outside and forgot my way back? How was I supposed to communicate with the locals? How could I ever call my parents for help with barely a Nokia-3310 type of phone? Would I have died of hunger if I didn't step outside that room?

You might feel I was overreacting and that you would act differently had you have the chance of being in my position. But think back to when you were 18, even just for a second. Imagine your 18-years-old self going through all of this. It wouldn't have been easy, right?

I'm not trying to portray myself as a hero or a role model. I'm not trying to sell you a training class where I coach you how to be your best self if you wake up at am, make your bed, and learn Chinese. I would react differently right now, but I just want to narrate my story to you.

In the end, the day after, I woke up with a strong resolution: I had to make the most of that trip, no matter what. My parents didn't pay for my flight just to be in a dormitory room crying off myself. As an immigrant to Italy, my father had to go through years upon years of what I was experiencing at that moment. I feel both grateful and ashamed for even reacting that way.

So, I left my room looking for food. I got lost, indeed. But I was also able to find my way back home. Then I did the same that evening, the day after, and for three months after that. I was lucky enough to make amazing friends, especially a young lady from Sichuan province who treated me like a little sister. I owe her a lot; she showed me how welcoming Chinese people could be. Talking to her also drastically improved my Chinese. I gained a long-term friend, too.

What about after that? I came to China the year after, during the summer break. And two years after that, too. I've been working in China since 2015. At first, I came to complete a 3-month internship. Then I decided I wanted to take a year gap. That year gap ended up lasting five years and more. I don't regret making that decision, even though it's sometimes very hard. The hardest challenge I had to overcome was to build my career. As a foreigner. As a female foreigner. Most foreigners who end up in China work here as teachers. Kindergarten teachers, high school teachers, English teachers, Italian teachers. You name it. I didn't see myself going toward the same path. I didn't want to become a teacher. Nothing against teachers - if you love teaching, I fully support you and admire you - but it's just not my cup of tea. Most teachers in China can earn a competitive salary and receive benefits like travel allowances, long summer holidays, a flexible schedule. Just to name a few.

Despite all of that, I still would have rather worked in any other profession. I started as an Italian translator and market developer in a Chinese cross-border e-commerce company in Guangzhou (South-East China). In three years, I climbed the ladder by working first as a CRM specialist in the Customer Service team. Back then, I was the only foreigner in the whole 200-people department. I soon became a Customer Experience Management Team Lead, and I managed a team of 3 international colleagues to improve our overall service experience.

In 2018, I decided to resign. Despite my years of experience and polyglot background, I still found it hard to prove myself. I would go for interviews where the job position kind of matched my current situation. The skills and experience I was asked for, however, were not always a perfect match. I had to learn everything by myself since the beginning. On my first day in that e-commerce company, I was immediately asked to create content and ads for two of our Italian Facebook pages. How and where was I supposed to start? I figured out a way, slowly and by going through tons of mistakes.

I then moved to a Chinese marketing agency. I started as a Senior English Copywriter in charge of managing 10 SEO clients. I know it doesn't exactly make sense, but that was the best I could find. At first, I felt writing articles was far below my ambitions. I spent the whole first month teaching my colleagues about their English mistakes. Did I work so hard to become an English teacher in disguise?

One year went by, and I became a Content Operations Lead. After two months, I became a Content Marketing Manager. And I still am. To this day, I'm working in the same agency when I'm writing this article. Everyone already left to celebrate the weekend. I decided I would take some time off my schedule to tell you about my story.

It might not be a story of heroes, or an inspirational novel you can't take your eyes off. But it's real and authentic. It's who I am and what I have been, no strings attached.

A lustrum of challenges and discoveries

The way Chinese society sees women is not always flattering. You are surrounded by images of ladies with a high-pitched voice, a cute appearance, a soft and well-spoken tone. Things are starting to change, but China is now a completely different country from the first time I came here almost eight years ago.

When growing up, I didn't dream of becoming someone. I wanted to make my parents proud of me and to change the uncanny perception we have of what is different. Who is different, to be precise? I am now a mix of cultural elements from at least three nations and three continents; I guess I came close to achieving my goal.

Now that five years have passed since I moved here, I'm proud to look back and see everything I have achieved. I'm glad I realize how those days and the challenges each of them brought compiled together to create so much. You often don't notice an ant unless you're looking at an ants' nest. Now that I see all those little moments combined into memories, I can give each ant the meaning it deserves.

I have learned a lot from myself. However, I wouldn't have been much without my parents' support. My mother taught me always to keep an open mind. Keep in mind that she decided to spend her life with someone from another continent. It was not mainstream - or accepted - back in the 80s in Italy. It is hardly accepted even today. My father taught me to wake up every morning and work the hardest I can. He works an average of 15-18 hours a day. I didn't miswrite these numbers; he really does work that hard.

The world is not always an easy and nice place for a woman. You know that too, for sure. But if there's something I would like you to keep from my story. Don't let others define the way you should look, act, or speak. Don't let others impede your progress towards the career and life you want. At the same time, however, don't expect a different treatment as a woman. Put all your hard-working self in every little thing you do, work your bum off, and only then demand what you deserve.

I'm grateful for being who I am, and I haven't felt more powerful than now. I hope you feel the same way, or that you'll feel even stronger soon. Without realizing it, I've become one of the millions of immigrants wandering between worlds that are at once so captivating and exigent to live in. And I'll soon work my way to becoming better than my best self.

My Life As A Woman: China Edition #12

I was born in a small city in Guangdong province which lies in the south of China. I was not a lucky girl and my childhood was not so happy. When I was just a little kid, my parents were divorced, and I was left to my mother. There goes a famous saying that misfortunes never come alone.

A few months later, my mother suffered from serious illness which needed immediate operation. As a result, she couldn't take good care of me, which directly led me to live in an environment without restriction and either much care from my mother.

Though a large proportion of my childhood, my mother was not by my side, her inspiration and encouragement were always in my mind. She encouraged me to do things confidently and try not to give too much consideration to others' unreasonable criticism. She exerted herself to stand up with terrible pain to set me a good example—to be brave and firm when facing crisis. It was my mother who bought me into future.

My childhood was full of setbacks, but to be frank, I did have many wonderful moments with my friends. At that time, homework was not so heavy as it is today, I would finish my homework as quickly as possible in order to squeeze out more time to play with my neighbors. And sometimes I would get asked by people around about what I wanted to do and who I wanted to be in the future. My answer was to be an English teacher because I was so interested in English and I believed I could get along well with kids.

Time files fast, nowadays I am a mature adult. But deep inside my heart, I always look forward to Spring Festival. In China, Spring Festival is the time for family reunion. Every year, we Chinese will get together with families and friends to set off fireworks, hold fantastic parties and share big meals. Everyone will be consumed with happiness and be full of great expectations of future life. Those awesome things are the true reasons why I like Spring Festival and my culture.

It seems like everything is getting better and better. My mother is in good health, my dream to be an English teacher has come true, the pain that I have suffered has turned into experience and chances for me to become a stronger person. As an English teacher, I must handle many things, such as communicating with students, teaching them basic English knowledge and skills, etc. Although it really runs me out of my energy, I do love my job. However, sometimes it is hard for me to balance life and work. For life, as a typical unmarried woman in China, under the pressure of my mother and other relatives, I am often forced to date with strange men to get married as soon as possible. For work, the pressure of work almost tears me apart, students are too naughty while parents are too tricky. But when my students progress, my boss praises me for what I have made, and my salary gets raised, I feel like my hard work and efforts were paid off.

To sum up, as a Chinese woman, my life is full of ups and downs. If you want to live in China, I'd like to give you some suggestions based on my own experience. Firstly, try not to care too much about what others think of you, just to be yourself. Your own feeling is the most important thing. Secondly, try your best to take good care of yourself. Although social environment in China is relatively secure and peaceful, you still need to watch out and protect yourself. Don't come back home too late and don't walk on the paths alone under the dark. It's not always safe at night. I would appreciate it if my advice works, hope you have a good time in China!

My Life As A Woman: China Edition #13

Hi, I am a Chinese woman. I come from Shenyang, a beautiful city in Northeast China. Maybe because of the growing environment, I have the forthrightness of Northeast Chinese people. I have a very strict mother, and a very amiable father, as if most Chinese families are like this. Because of my mother's strict requirements on my study, I am also very self-disciplined at ordinary times, and because of such strict discipline, I sometimes have no confidence. My mother was afraid that I would be too excited and become arrogant after being praised, so she seldom praised me. Therefore, now I very much lack self-confidence, sometimes I don't believe that I can do something well. I do know my mother loves me no less than any other mother in the world, so I also understand her education to me. After realizing this, I will often encourage myself from the bottom of my heart. I hope I can be confident as soon as possible.

Now I am a sophomore majoring in English. Although my English level is not very high, I am trying my best to learn and improve constantly. Because of this international major, I often try to learn more about other countries' cultures. The more I know about these cultures, the more I love my country. We all know that China used to be very backward in the past few hundred years, but now we have made great progress. The Chinese people have indomitable courage and indomitable will, which is why I am proud of being Chinese. China is the most populous country in the world, and the imbalance of gender ratio is also a problem that China is worried about now, because in the concept of my grandparents' generation, boys can inherit the family business, and girls will marry after all, which means that after marriage, girls will no longer help their own parents. I believe this is a common phenomenon in many traditional Asian countries. I know that this concept is very old-fashioned. Over the years, everyone has been updating their own ideas. I am always willing to believe that our ideas will become better and better. There will be less and less gender discrimination in the family and work. Let's break the prejudice and take a more inclusive view of the world. I also believe that soon, more traditional countries will realize the importance of gender equality and hope that everyone in the world can be treated equally.

If someone wants to come to China to live or work, as a woman, I want to tell you: China's public security is really good, you can go out in the middle of the night without fear of being robbed; the Chinese people are very friendly, you can make friends with everyone; Chinese food is really delicious, you can eat three meals a day for one year without any repetition. If you want to experience life in China, please come to me. I'd like to introduce my country to you.

My Life As A Woman: China Edition #14

Where did you grow up?

I was born in a city called Guangzhou on the coast of southern China. I have lived here for twenty years and never left. Guangzhou is a city with four indistinct seasons. The climate is warm and humid with plenty of rain, which is typical of coastal cities. Guangzhou has many unexpected nicknames. One is "the City of Flowers", because the climate here is very suitable for the cultivation of flowers, every season this city is full of flowers. Moreover, the larger flower sales and wholesale markets in southern China are concentrated here or in surrounding cities. People or businessmen will come here to buy flowers, especially during the Chinese New Year. The other Is "Yangcheng", which is Chinese for "Antelope City". You may infer that "it is because Guangzhou's antelopes are famous", but this is not the case. "Yangcheng" comes from a legend: It is said that five years ago, there were five fairy people who came here with wheat ears. In order to help the poor people here choose to turn into five antelopes and stay here forever. Guangzhou is the capital city of Guangdong Province. Many years ago, it was a trading port between China and foreign countries, creating a trading center in Guangzhou. Although the name may sound relatively unfamiliar, here was the venue of the 2010 Asian Games.

Guangzhou is my birthplace and my favorite city.

How did you grow up?

I was born in a family that was not wealthy. I live in the old city of Guangzhou with my parents, but I feel very contented. My family is not considered a well-educated family. My parents did not attend college. In their childhood, it was already a very happy thing to be able to go to school. It is even lucky to be able to go to high school. They are very kind and work very hard to support me and let me receive the best education.

Since I was a child, I learned a lot from my parents that I could not learn from books. They taught me to be strong so that I wouldn't be overwhelmed by the setbacks in the future; they taught me not to be proud, because if I am proud, I will easily make low-level mistakes, and I can't do what I want; they taught me not to be inferior, not to compare myself with others, because my parents always love me, I will always be their beloved one, and I should also love myself; they taught me to work hard, be independent and don't rely on others, they said "Because you are always the most reliable in this world". They taught me a lot and what I learned from them cannot be learned from school. This is how I grew up while studying hard and accepting the influence of my parents.

Did you have parents or maybe a grandmother who inspired you?

My parents inspired me, a lot, especially my mother.

What did you study / what did you want to be growing up / why?

Now I am studying mathematics, which is a hit major recently. I used to dream of being a scientist, or a doctor, or a businesswoman. A lot. Just because these jobs are of value in our society. But after I went to college, I found that there is no such fixed path that everybody should follow if she wants to be successful. If it's something you really want to do, just go for it and put forth your effort.

What do you love about your culture?

My culture has both good side and a bad side. I appreciate the good side, and for the bad side, there is still space to improve.

What you are currently doing for work?

I am still a student. I am studying at a university famous for studying foreign language. My major is related to mathematics. Moreover, I often do part-time jobs online, such as translation, writing, or data analysis related to my major.

Tell me about your struggles as a woman

Even though now the city I live in is modern, opened and comprehensive, struggles as a woman are still experienced frequently out of school. For example, employers will prefer male to female. Also, the concept of "be a lady" is still deeply rooted in a great portion of the female's mind, such as always be fit (and I think that's why in China body-shame is more familiar than western countries), be obedient. The gender discrimination and bias are not that serious as ten years ago, thanks to the development of social media and "metoo" in China, women became much braver to stand up and tell the society their stories. But the misunderstanding still exists, with males and even females. In a word, even though a woman has dreams to achieve, restrictions in our society still makes them hard to realize.

Tell me about your successes as a woman

It is hard for me to define "successful". Everyone will have his own definition, right? For me, being happy means successful. That is, if I can do what I want to do, instead of being restricted by any of the social norms. If I want to enjoy food, I don't need to think about others' opinions. If I want to wear beautiful clothes, I don't need to think about that other people may criticize me. If I want to become a doctor or a boss, nobody can stop me if I want to, instead of telling me "be lady".

Provide some advice to women from a woman living in China

In our society, social norms and misunderstanding towards women is frequently seen. That's not your fault, so don't be sad and lose heart. What you now can do, and always can do is, love yourself and try your best. Don't put much attention on others, they're just strangers, forget them and their critics. BE BRAVE. BE CONFIDENT. LOVE YOURSELF.

My Life As A Woman: China Edition #15

I grew up in a family in a big city in northern China. As the only child at home, I can enjoy almost everything I like. My parents will give me the best, but I always feel a little guilty because they ignore themselves for me. Life. My mother seldom buys clothes. There are only a few clothes in a whole season. She is actually very beautiful, but she gave up herself for the family. I feel that all I have is given to me by my parents. My personal material is rich does not mean that my family is rich but may be under a lot of pressure behind it. Perhaps ten million Chinese homes court like this, Chinese people are always very tough and patience.

In China's mainstream values, the mother has always been an unselfish, with a hard-working image. The mainstream media promotes such a mother image to limit people's understanding of the mother to this. Such propaganda is for the patriarchal society. Men are more at ease to enjoy the services of women; all the women's contribution is only a void of Happy Mother's Day in exchange for Mother's Day. Men do not help their wives with household chores, but rather it has always been home to be shared by two people, so there are numerous Chinese stereotyped thinking, this is just the story of the city, a child, a husband's life, perhaps behind the mother, is her sacrificed chance of being promoted in the workplace and she sacrifices her love of herself for her family. In the countryside, there are still girls who are forced to give up their studies because of their preference for men. China's economy is constantly improving, but these deep-rooted ideas are not so easy to change.

Growing up, I experienced a gray time when my body was very fat. I had to pretend to be a boy to cover my inferiority. Pretending to be a boy would not go to compare with other girls. Girls think of me as a boy, I feel a kind of safety, because men will receive a lot less physical examination in society. The stage of puberty is often the most beautiful stage, but I feel that I am excluded from the ranks of young girls because of my body shape. I cannot devote my energy to appearance. Women's beauty is diverse. China's Internet is very malicious for intellectual women. Many people think that intellectual women are useless for reading, and no one will want it. But in fact, the meaning of female life is not to be selected, but to realize yourself and your value.

I observed that as if overnight, consumerism invaded China. Chinese women suddenly entered a new stage from the past, facing the sky, without transition, and entered the world of consumption confusedly. Due to the extreme lack of material life before the reform and opening, the Chinese people at that time only wore one color and one style of clothing. The previous lack of aesthetics and aesthetic suppression created the current trend of crazy shopping. Many women do not know what they like but feel that they should have more. Merchants connect consumer goods and identity. You have these things and you are a delicate and beautiful girl. However, the status of Chinese women has not been improved because of the rich material life of a small number of people, allowing women to have more material, or advocating men to give women expensive gifts. These so-called pampers are to suppress women's spiritual pursuits. The real advancement of women's status is that women can freely choose what is beautiful, they cannot accept men's gaze, and can have the right to speak on more important occasions in addition to these insignificant aspects.

Chinese men always say that women's status is high enough. In ancient China, polygamy was still their favorite. They always liked which one was worse, rather than seeing how women were treated in more developed regions. Under the baptism of a culture, many new families are dominated by women, and their husbands must pay their salaries. Many men regard this phenomenon as a sign of the advancement of women, but they are not. This is just another kind of gender inequality. Women play the role of men in the traditional sense, and squeeze the freedom of men in the family, which cannot be used as a sign of the advancement of women. The advancement of women's status is that women can have equal voice with men in social work and on the political stage and can receive equal pay for equal work with men. Instead of superficial women managing household finances, women receive gifts from men, etc.

I am currently paying attention and hope that I can help Chinese women who are confused. I hope that Chinese women can get rid of the shackles of beauty. Beauty is a good thing, but don't be kidnapped by it. As a Chinese woman, it's not easy. In the context of China's low education level, women's choices are still limited, social inclusion is still insufficient, and the affirmative action environment is not very good, but I am still willing to work hard. After I talked to my parents about these things, I think they were inspired. This is a very small family progress, but everything needs to be done step by step, so it doesn't matter.

My Life As A Woman: China Edition #16

I was born in Beijing, in a 3-story building not far away from the embassy area. It was a fall day. Beijing's fall is the most beautiful season of the year. It is neither hot nor cold in September, the air is pleasant, and the overall scenery is very picturesque. However, the weather changes when winter comes. As a result of the cool wind in infancy, I was in bad health for some time. In addition, I was very naughty. That is why my mother always told me to stay at home.

Therefore, books and toys became my great friends. My elders are intellectuals. They often bought me many books. My mother encouraged me to find the answers to all my questions, so I started to look up dictionaries and literacy books by myself when I was four years old. The first word I learnt is Beijing, because there is a company outside the window, with the word Beijing in red particularly conspicuous, and I kept it in mind as it appeared so frequently.

At that time, we still needed a stove to boil water. Every day, I would ride a small tricycle around the stove in the house. When I was tired, I would read a book. Therefore, I remember few playmates in my childhood.

I had a good time at school, working as a student leader. I was president of the student union in high school and college, but I skipped grades in the middle, so I felt lonely for a while.

Even now I still miss the time I spent with my school friends before I was ten years old, when I could see flowers blooming everywhere and people's sincere smiles. There were very few cars on the road. I never worried about safety when going to school with my friends.

My grandpa was a translator. I was his favorite among his grandchildren. He had great expectations of me. He always bought me a lot of books, with each of them carefully inscribed and written with a message. Unfortunately, my grandparents died when I was young. I spent more time with my grandparents like most Beijing children. Here is the model given by my family: enrich your own inner world and dare to face challenges.

My major at the university was international trade and Chinese language and literature. I got a master's degree in Business Management and Developmental Psychology. I wanted to be myself, the only one in the world. I was determined to know right from wrong, value friendship, think independently, and master my own future direction.

I love my motherland and my nation. In addition to patriotism, I also love the national spirit of diligence, brave, love of peace, perseverance and self-improvement. These spiritual details have also contributed to the splendid Chinese culture. Myths and legends, literature, art and food culture are my favorites.

I am currently a translator, and I am also engaged in general planning. There are still many injustices towards women across the world today. These injustices exist in education, school choice, job selection and treatment, spouse selection, marriage and childbirth, etc. Fortunately, I did not encounter too many issues, since I lived in a relatively fair and just environment.

In large cities in China, women have had significantly higher status over men, thanks to the protection for women's right to receive education. When they are educated, they could give back to the society, which makes people aware of the power of women. Women's wisdom plays an important role in the development of the whole society. We also have a strong voice in our families and in the society. However, women's success is not just about getting out of the household. And from the point of view of physiology and psychology, it is impossible for women to leave their families completely. Most women choose to give birth regardless of their natural or social pressures, but the best time to give birth is precisely at the golden age for young people to get promotion in career. It is surely difficult to have your cake and eat it too. Most men cannot understand that the psychological and physiological changes brought about by fertility to women are irreversible, so the issue turns to the problem of gender contradiction.

Success is far from being absolute. It's relative. At least I haven't yet achieved the success I want. As a woman who grew up in Beijing, I can give women the following advice: never give up on personal development! If one wants not to be eliminated, whether it is by the time, the work, or being disgusted by the spouse, it is necessary to improve oneself. Either you keep forging ahead or you keep falling behind. If you don't put your feet on the ground, life will teach you a lesson soon or later. Those wasted time when you indulge in nothing will affect you at a certain point in a few years later, you could possibly be a middle-aged woman who has no advantage, a wandering life with no sense of happiness, or a sensitive woman being swayed by considerations of gain and loss.

Therefore, please keep working hard!

My Life As A Woman: Macau Edition

My name is Kiko Hu. I left my parents for family reasons from my earliest years. I lived independently since I was 13 years old and I was a homeless street child at that time. Later I lived with friends. Finally, I rented a house and lived alone.

In terms of learning, I dropped out of school for three years after graduating from elementary school because I didn't want to learn. But then I realized the importance of study and began to study hard. Fortunately, Saint Rose Middle School and Saint Paul Middle School gave me the opportunity to continue my education and it took me three years to complete the junior high school study with my grades always being the first one among the entire students. When I was in high school, I came to know that I should start preparing for my future life, so I chose to study in the Macau University of Science and Technology majored in Chinese Medicine and started my own business.

My grandfather was a very wise man who had experienced wars and reforms in China. Although he was not rich or famous, he lived a happy life. When he was alive, he often told me to study and work hard. "You don't need to make so much money, but you can do much contribution to the society", He said. Every word he said deserves savoring to me now.

I am currently studying for a bachelor's degree in Chinese medicine, and I want to be an excellent Chinese medicine doctor in the future. At the beginning of the medical study, I simply wanted to protect my family. Later, I noticed the health care conditions of Macau needed to be improved. Since then, I was determined to engage in the medical industry and do something to contribute to my community in Macau.

I am very interested in traditional Chinese medicine culture, and I really admire the ancients who came up with the yin-yang theory. Moreover, I love Macau, a city witnessing the fusion of Chinese and Western cultures. Inclusiveness can be seen from churches/temples to daily meals.

I am working in a hospital as intern and in the meantime, I'm running two restaurants as a side business. I feel that women now have more opportunities than ever before, and I believe women's social status will become higher and higher in the future. My father is a typical patriarchal male and he was unhappy after I was born knowing that I was a girl. However, his dissatisfaction with me has gradually changed with my long-term hard work. I understand that the world may be unfair, but I can't give up without really trying to change.

I do not think I am a successful woman and I am just like the normal person. For me, success requires both hard work and perseverance. The temporary success to me right now is to struggle to pursue what I believe to be.

From my perspective, women in Macau benefit from the promotion of gender equality and we should make good use of these conditions to make more progress. With the development of Macau's gambling industry, women in Macau can easily get work in casinos, but it is detrimental for them to slowly develop laziness and not study themselves or consummate unceasingly.

On the other hand, in terms of getting married and having kids, I would like to suggest you should not have children or marriage when you are young if you are not ready, as this will not only be harmful to yourself, but also affect the next generation. Today, women are no longer as before and we have the right to choose how to live, but we also need to be responsible for ourselves as well as those around us, so we should think twice before making decisions.

My Life As A Woman: Colombia Edition #1

My name is Joimar Fernandez, a Venezuelan migrant who has lived for more than 2 years in Colombia and has experienced a roller coaster of circumstances. These situations have helped me to mature, to project myself as an entrepreneurial woman and to be able to achieve everything I set out to do. I lived most of my life in a fishing village of 500 people, with freedom as the first benefit. A child surrounded by nature and silence, learns to look inward and that is what happened to me: I was always aware of my being, dreams and individuality.

My first inspiration was my mother, with a successful educational career and always proactive with her daily activities. The second person who has been my role model, my maternal uncle, who always had a prosperous life without limitations, as a result of his effort and fidelity to his work.

Since I was 9 years old, I knew that I wanted to study psychology, but when the time came, my financial situation did not allow it. I was furious with my situation and promised not to give up on a dream again due to lack of resources. I studied Public Accounting at the 7th best university in my country, with high hopes of getting ahead and achieving my goals.

Unfortunately, the economic crisis in Venezuela forced me to escape in search of a better future, just months after graduating; and Joimar Fernandez, who vowed never to give up on anything again, had to leave everything for the love of her family.

The first months in the Colombian capital were difficult. I was a street vendor and "bus musician" for a long time; until, thanks to the brothers of a local church, I got a great opportunity in an office where I would earn much more than I expected. Unfortunately, a year after I started, my colleagues and I lost our jobs and I had to think of a new strategy to avoid going back to the streets. Although they were unsuccessful months, I had decided to start an advertising creative writing project and after 7 months of living on savings, great projects began to arrive, and I was able to dedicate myself completely to this.

This journey has not been easy, but it was a great learning time. Many think that women are dependent, emotional, or that instability can break them; but it's not like that. I identify myself with the reeds, that as much as they bend, they never break and endure even the strongest storms. I think my greatest successes in Colombia have been being able to position myself in the labor market, I could keep my little family in Venezuela and, having been able to independently undertake and monetize one of my great skills: writing.

Currently, I am fully dedicated to my digital projects, in which I provide services to companies and professionals with the positioning of their digital channels, the creation of attractive content for traditional media and web pages.

Although I love my country and miss everything that links me to it, in this time that I have lived in Colombia, I have learned to love the culture and its people. I have found beautiful persons who are willing to help someone who is not a compatriot and I owe my successes to everyone who has given me opportunities and has got me their friendship. As a woman and a migrant, I have had to struggle on many occasions with verbal harassment, xenophobia and abuse; that has hardened me a lot and I went from trembling in a dangerous situation to facing anyone who wants to break my dignity. Thus, with each passing year, I feel more able to bear the difficult circumstances that sometimes hit us, while still enjoying life.

I always advise women not to settle for their current situation. Everything is temporary and if they cling to a circumstance that makes them feel uncomfortable or incomplete, it will take longer. Don't be afraid to ask for help, don't walk alone and don't give up your personality. Instead, polish your being with an unbreakable character that serves as a wall for everything and don't yield your decisions to the emotions, since these are more harmful than exterior things. Acting under moral principles and logical actions is best. The road is hard for everyone, and no matter what dreams we have, obstacles will always appear. Keeping your vision fixed on the goal while enjoying the path to it, is one of the best ways to live.

My Life As A Woman: Colombia Edition #2

I am Paola, a 44-year-old Colombian entrepreneur who loves to dance. I was born in the city of Cali, in the south of the country, a region where dancing salsa is almost like walking or talking. As a good daughter, only very spoiled and with the adoration of my dad. I was a good student, judicious, responsible, and with a very marked religious vocation, due to education in a nun's college.

Exaggeratedly cared for by parents who were very responsible for their role, so much so that they watched me grow up, together, without having any minimum of love for each other. Great sacrifice in honor of blessing to be parents. I was an obedient girl without many friends and excellent in my school education.

I finished high school and decided to study Social Communication - Journalism, although I really wanted to be a Psychologist. Today, I am very happy with my choice. On the other hand, I felt from my school years that my dream was to be a dancer, and to always be on stage, accompanying singers, performing in large groups and on stages full of lights and colors. But I must confess something, I was of a thick build, the typical chubby of any group of people, who may have danced in school groups, with cheerleaders and in performances, but always behind everyone, where they wouldn't notice me, and this allowed me to be a little happy in silence.

In those years, my life had no incredible things to tell, as I was studying and going to the gym for hours in the afternoon. In Cali, women are distinguished by having very harmonious bodies and it is part of the culture, taking care of yourself, exercising a lot and of course, dancing and dancing. And being "the chubby", I did not feel well at all, so I spent much of the day trying to stay in shape.

I finished my professional career and I know who my husband would later be for 10 years. With him I moved to Bogotá, the capital of Colombia, to look for a better quality of life and got a job for both of us. But things did not go well at all and it was 10 years of failures at work and failures in the relationship. Fortunately, the best of those 10 years were my two daughters, whom I love deeply and today, I live back in Cali. Yes, I returned to my hometown and that was 10 years ago too. I came back with my daughters of years and two months, without a job, or anywhere to live, without money, but with an enormous desire to get ahead. Being very overweight after my second pregnancy, my damaged self-esteem, it was difficult to adapt to the city, where the culture of beautiful women bored and disappointed me, since, in the workplace, this point is also reflected.

Fortunately, I decide to work from home, in Digital Marketing, a topic that was very current at that time and did not require a great body, but yes, a great brain and a lot of creativity. A few months after turning 40, I began to rethink my life. The maturity of that age makes you think about what you really want. I started thinking a lot about my old age and how I wanted it to be. So, I decided for self-love and health, to lose weight. It was something I had longed for since I was young, but I wasn't serious. It was not an easy task because I gained 15 kilos. but this time I wanted it to be something definitive. I wanted to become an example to other women and my own heroine. I wanted to be the pretty lady where I was eating healthy by decision and conviction. I didn't know where to start, but I knew I was going to make it.

I knew dancing would be my therapy until I reached my old age and throughout. I didn't know how I would do it, but these two goals made me wake up full of energy, every day. One day I came to a park where people were playing sports, and I saw a group of people dancing! And I thought: here is what I need! I joined that group, which was Zumba®. I was very happy that day and decided to return at the same time each day to dance with them. Dancing outdoors with many Latin rhythms made me filled with energy and happiness. My mood began to change and of course, my body too. This marked my life so much that I could not believe that I was beginning to materialize something in such a conscious and mature way.

To summarize my story, I lost 15 kilos in 6 months dancing Zumba® every day. In this process, my self-esteem grew stronger and I wanted to take care of my diet, and take care of my body. This dream changed my life so much, that nowadays I am a Zumba® Instructor. I teach and dance on the platforms of many stages to dance. As you can see, age, rather than being an impediment, was a motivator for me. I managed to be a woman with the body I had always longed for and with the healthy life I loved so much. I managed to be part of a dance group, get on many stages, participate in events and the best thing: help other people to improve too.

Today I combine my work as a digital marketing journalist and writer with my Zumba® classes and I confess something to them: I am the pretty woman with the big brain. 4 years have passed since then and today I share my story, so that women everywhere can be convinced that dreams do come true, when you work from the heart for them.

My Life As A Woman: Colombia Edition #3

Every time I think I can't do something, I breathe and think about everything I've accomplished thinking I couldn't do it. My name is Erika García, I am a Colombian woman who was born in Cúcuta, the colorful and warm capital of Norte de Santander. I had a childhood that I can still remember at 33 years old with some precision and affection, those memories always fill my head with smells remembering my mother's food, with noises and laughs when I think of games with my cousins or family parties characteristics of Colombian people. I think that is part of everything that life and my parents gave me during my early years. I am the daughter of a marriage between a Colombian and a Venezuelan, so my education was a meeting of two very similar cultures, but with certain differences and although they seem obvious, you must immerse yourself in the history of each country to understand them. I have an older brother, and in contrast to what many imagine, that machismo in Latin culture comes from family, in my home it never had acceptance, because my mother always educated the two of us equally. I could say that I am a lucky person, as I did not lack a bed to sleep, food or education that in a Latin American country, is quite common.

I was always very applied to my studies, but not very decided about what I wanted to do in life, which led me to study a career that I love and hate at the same time. I'm a social communicator, but I consider myself an autodidact woman free soul who is dedicated to what happy does, yes, I know that this thought is not very lucrative, especially if you want to survive day-to-day with some money and food. Maybe I was indirectly influenced by my cousin Elba, who lived a few years with us. She represented the free, smiling, somewhat rebellious woman that I wanted to be at that time. Now that I am an adult, I can see a lot of her personality in me.

Currently I live in Bogotá, the great multicultural capital of Colombia, life here is much more hectic, and it is a city with a lot of life during all hours of the day. A few years ago, I became passionate about gastronomy and became an international cuisine chef, I also married a wonderful man and we have a beautiful daughter, and although I never imagined it, I am a 100% housewife with a few hours to dedicate myself to freelancer work doing gastronomic photography and content creation.

My work in Colombia is not a work with many economic benefits, but it allows me to raise my daughter, and that is a lot because I am concerned about the considerable violence that is seen every day against children. I know that many women feel guilty for leaving their children in daycare while they work, because the opposite happens to me, I feel guilty for believing that I don't do enough, but I understood that feeling bad and being stuck with that thought would not be the right thing is not typical of the Colombian woman who always seeks to continue to support her family. Therefore, I think that one piece of advice that I will give to my daughter when she will be older and that I would also like to reach out to more women is that it is okay to cry, it is okay to stop when you do not know the right direction, the only thing that is not It is good to lose identity and trust, we are our worst enemies because we fill our heads with doubts, but we are also our own saviors, because only we know what we are capable of achieving what we want.

My Life As A Woman: Comoros Edition #1

Hello everyone, my name's Hayirati Mmadi Ali and I am delighted to be here today to talk to you about my life as a woman. I am a 24-year-old woman who was born in the Comoros and was raised in France from my 4 years and I'm still living there. Following my health problems, my mother wanted to find competent doctors in France because it was still impossible to find people able to help me in the Comoros because of the precariousness present in the country.

All my life, I've been inspired by my mother. She left her family and the life she had built to help me; she fought alone to achieve her goals and save our lives. In general, it is easy to say that our mother is our greatest inspiration, but all my life I have seen her more as my savior than my mother. Love is such a complex word, right? If we should impose a definition of this word, we would all agree that everyone has their own definition.

We can relate this word to a name, a person, a place... but I relate it to my mom. She taught me about "pure love" and how much it was important to keep the people we love the most near us. After high school, I studied business. I had to mix work and studies, little by little, I realized that I haven't found my place in what I was doing. It was then that I discovered my passion for makeup and my new goal was to become a makeup artist which is still currently my biggest goal. I love how my culture mix is Islam and their own tradition: religion is important in our country, around 97% of the population is Muslim and our traditions really lean on the Coran which I really appreciate.

As a woman, I have suffered a lot of criticism in all the things I did. In school, I often tried new things, I tried new methods of makeup, which often gave the boys the opportunity to judge me. In the professional world, it was sometimes difficult to find work because of my skin color, my age, or my physical features. I started working at the age of 17, which often caused me trouble with clients. Some of them held approaches or sent me insults. I quickly learned to become independent and strong by myself. But today, thanks to all these experiences through which I grew up and gained knowledge, I know who I am and who I want to be. I want to depend on myself and achieve my goals alone. I think that's my greatest success.

The road is still long before I learn to love myself in its entirety, but I cling to everything I have built so far to get there. I may no longer live in the Comoros, but I still continue to visit the country when life gives me the opportunity to do so. If life forces you to leave where you come from, keep in touch with your origins. It's important to know where you come from to know where you're going. The person you are is the reflection of your origins, you should be proud of your experiences and grow with all your knowledges to be a woman who'll support all women equally.

My Life As A Woman: Comoros Edition #2

The rich and rare species wildlife, ceremonial dishes, festivals marriage ceremonies with female and male dances in the celebrations, the violin concerts and recitation off important literacy texts, the religious and musical events. Those all always made me love and miss my culture. I was born and grew up in Anjouran, Comoros. My father is a fisherman and my mother sells the fish in the market and sometimes she fishes at low tides using a piece of fabric as net or a plant that releases a substance that paralyzes small fish. I have one brother. I help my parents by collecting wood and fetching water. And my brother helps me cut the trees. I also help my mother in drying the fish and selling them by moving from place to place. I attended a religious school where I memorized the Koran. When I was a child, I wanted to study marketing because I wanted to build a solid foundation skill, to understand the consumer relation, communication and to benefit society in general to improve people's life. I also wanted to change the traditional belief of the society, for example, they do not separate sickness from other misfortunes, the grand marriage and in dining wife eats in the kitchen with the children but the husband eats at the dining table where he might invite a parent or a friend.

There were always enough fish to feed all our families, now the work in the sea has become harder and harder and about ten thousand residents depend on fishing for their livelihoods. There are fewer fish now and we must go further and further out into the open sea. My parents spent a lot of money to purchase a canoe, engine, oars and nets so that my brother could fish. My brother was the best teacher for me ever since I was a little girl. My brother stood by my side and helps support our lives. He was with me through thick and thin. He helped me to grow stronger and wiser. He was the one who showed me how to catch a fish, how to cut wood, how to deal with snakes, and the one who helped me memorize Koran.

I did all the heavy domestic work. But still, the income did not meet our basic needs. We all worked very hard though. I was always afraid to go cut wood alone because sometimes I would get bitten by snakes. Most of the time I got tired of moving from place to place all day long without having a meal. There were also bad men who stole my fish and earnings on my way back home. After my job was done for the day, I would go home and prepare dinner. I had to wake up again in the morning to fetch water and prepare breakfast. I barely got any time to sleep at all. But I never showed any sign of weakness or tiredness. All I thought and worried about was how to survive and how to meet and satisfy the basic needs of the family. But I could not always fulfill this depending on the sea and I wanted to make a change. The life on the sea and the challenges that I had faced inspired me to know that I deserved a better life.

One day I told my parents that I wanted to go and live with my uncle in Moroni so that I could learn and make a living. As expected, my father refused. I begged him for months. But he would not change his mind. I cried and asked my brother to persuade my father. My father still said no. He left me with no choice but to run away. It was the hardest and most difficult time for me to leave my family. But it was for the best. So I went to Moroni and settled with my uncle and his wife. I told my uncle everything. He helped me gain access to education. And I was one of the top students there. Right now, I am studying marketing and working at a fish drying facility as a part-timer. I am helping my family financially.

We women must believe in ourselves. We should participate and play a crucial role in improving the income of our family and our country; we should never depend on other peoples' minds. Only dead fish go with the flow. Have confidence and do not give up. Dream big and you will get what you want. What is meant for you will never pass by you. Just look forward, think positive, and face the challenges and you will find yourself on top of the world.

My Life As A Woman: Costa Rica Edition

I grew up in a "small town in a small country", I was born in Naranjo, Alajuela, it is a town of 1,814 people, founded in 1886, its located in the center of Costa Rica, near to everything but far from everything at the same time.

My country has a lot of history values, economy, and sources. Costa Rica is internationally known for its coffee, Naranjo is a village full of coffee, and a certain percentage of the best coffee in the country is from our farmers.

Sadly, I grew up discovering that Costa Rica is not a country to develop me to what I wanted to be, less Naranjo, we have not so much opportunities like other cultures. We have to work a lot and go to other countries to have more opportunities, but my parents and sister have always believed and supported my ideas. Their experience made me believe day by day that I can get everything I want, they had me when they were so poor, the three of us had nothing in that time. My dad was finishing college, and starting at his first job, my mom had a lot of complications while she was pregnant, had to quit her job, but they got through all of that, teaching me the values I needed to know in order to become the enterprising, brave woman I became.

Today I am a student of Biology with an emphasis in Biotechnology at The National University of Costa Rica. I am in the third year, hoping to graduate within the next two years. Also, I am an integrant at the theater group, started this year at college, and in scenic arts at 11 years old, we practice twice a week.

I have this little company in my town that sells products made by the farmers and workers of Naranjo, I founded this market at the end of last year, and its development is growing slowly but successfully. Costa Rica is a country where people are so extroverted, nice, humble, modest, helpful and as we say, "Pura Vida", "Ticos" are so kind, we are happy like all the time, we say hi to everyone and are always dreaming. We believe in "La virgencita de los Ángeles", she is our queen, we have a day to celebrate her, she grants the miracles we ask of her, and we believe we can do everything if she is with us.

The best of Costa Rica, beside the people, is the food, we have delicious recipes like gallo pinto, arroz con pollo, tamales, plátano, ceviche, when I am out of the country, I really missed our food. We defend our culture so much, our rights, our history, our environment, our nature, and our lovely ones.

However, we, women, have a lot of struggles, we suffer a lot of insecurity, a lot of disrespectful comments on the streets. According to my experiences, I can't wear shorts or a skirt and walk peacefully outside, I receive yelling, name-calling, catcalling, vulgar comments. My friends have no peace, every one of us has teasers or pepper spray because we don't feel safe walking alone, during the day, nor at night.

Still exist a lot of maleness in our culture, men get a major salary than women, more opportunities in jobs than women, more peace, and security than us. Even with all of this challenge, I have to get over them and convert into the successful woman I am today. I am 20 years old, with my own company, studying a great science and engineer career, and also doing what I love, staying with my family and friends.

Of course, I want to be more, to reach more, to get more, someday I wish to travel the world, to work as a scientist, to have my own fabric, and bring my products and solutions to other countries, to help the people and become a great woman.

Costa Rica is a great place to live, with beautiful beaches, nature, opportunities, great food, dances, clothes, culture and people.

But, if you live here, you have to raise your voice, fight for your fights, don't let any man disrespect you, or anyone to tell that you can't. You can reach your dreams, achieve your goals, and have the life you always wanted.

If you want to live in Costa Rica, I recommend you eat all you want, to discover all the nature and beaches we have, to believe in God, in faith, in yourself, this is a country to be happy, to reach your goals with energy, effort, to fall in love and the best part of it, to be you.

My Life As A Woman: Croatia Edition #1

My hometown is Split, the second-largest city of Croatia. When I say the second largest, you might imagine a big city with at least a million inhabitants, but this isn't that case - in Split, you 'll find around 170k people. I love my life here – this is the city where I was born, where I grew up, where I studied, and where I now work. I grew up with my mother, sister, and grandmother. Since I can remember it was just us girls. And we were like a true girl tribe.

When I look back on my childhood, I see flashlights of me playing with my sister in the backyard till our mother yelled "Girls, it's time to go home", watching Mexican telenovelas every day at 12.30 PM, and day trips to the prettiest beaches near Split, where we would sit on the sand and eat meat slices and tomatoes, that, I am not kidding, had the taste of the summer. It was truly a carefree period, even though the odds were against us.

Looking back now on my childhood, I realize that my mother was (and still is) a wizard - as a child I had no clue that we didn't have a lot of money. I mean, I had clothes, books, warm meals, and similar things but anything "extra" was off the table. A simple example, almost all my classmates would buy sandwiches during the break, but I always had one from home, prepared by my mum. I just thought my mum was the best, she prepares my favorite sandwich every day. But, as you get older, you become a teenager, you realize your mum doesn't have that 10 kn (around 1.5 €) to give to you on daily basis, so you can't go on that school trip to Italy in Garda land and that you can't have those jeans like Marta from your class.

So, when I was old enough to work, I did. I did all kinds of jobs, from cleaning the yachts, selling postcards to working in a retail store. I was always a good student, in school and after in college. Especially in college, because I knew I had to pass all exams on time so I could have free summer for work. I'm not one of the lucky ones – that one from day one knew what they wanted to become. I studied Italian language and Art history – because I love languages and architecture so, in my mind, this sounded like a reasonable choice. So, I finished college, finished an internship in an elementary school – only to realize this wasn't something that I wanted to do for the rest of my life.

I decided to change everything. I googled "most wanted jobs", "popular jobs" etc. and came across "digital marketing". That is when I got interested – I started reading everything about marketing, I paid for various online courses and sent a dozen emails searching for an opportunity to gain experience in this field. Finally, I was called for an interview, in an agency in Zagreb. That was my ticket in. I was lucky to have a place to stay in Zagreb because this wasn't a paid internship, so I needed every penny. But it was worth it. I met interesting people, real experts in this field, and learned a bunch of new things. Now, I had something to offer to agencies in Split.

I went back to Split and sent a lot of open letters to different agencies and companies. Right around the time when I started to doubt my choice, my effort, and my knowledge, I found a job – my dream job. I am proud to say - today I am a social media and content manager in an agency in Split. I am so lucky to have listened to my heart and that I dared to change my career – I can't even imagine how miserable I would be and how much I would regret if I didn't try. My message to you all that have second thoughts about your career – DO IT! CHANGE IT! You only live once – you don't have the time to wonder what if.

My Life As A Woman: Croatia Edition #2

Lana Bitenc, Croatia, Professional writer, author and ghostwriter, an actress and director, skipper and world traveler, and chocolate eater

People say it is completely normal that I have become a writer. As my father is a writer too. But, nearly no one knows that the greatest inspiration of my path for writing was my grandmother. Ok, both. The one from my mother's side was a tiny woman that was always laughing and was suspicious all the time. On the other hand, there was my father's mother – she was not an ordinary granny, but there was something in her behavior that was inspiring to me. Having just four grades of primary school, Biba, even her real name was Rose, and I named her Biba as she always had some different opinions about everything. She was, of course, always the smartest. She knew everything. One time, I checked her crosswords and everything was fulfilled. I was searching for the answers in the end but there was not anything. So, I began to check Biba's answers. Who asks himself: "To be or not to be?" she had answered: "Not possible." And in fact, I was living all the time near her thinking that she was normal and that almost all grannies are like that. She came from Switzerland, working in the Lindt & Sprungli factory, and was always wearing leggings. And on Friday evening she was going somewhere, even when she was 70 years old, with me to the gym. She was sitting in the corner observing young fit men. After a while, she stood up, whistled, and invited all the gym to drink a beer.

Somehow, at first, I subconsciously realized that all my characters in my books and comedies for children and the audience were having Biba's piece of character. Of course, I wrote a comedy about her, but it was rejected for financing by The Croatian Ministry of Culture as they wrote to me, she is not a real character. That hit me to my heart. And it was the beginning with my struggle with windmills. I was alone all the way. At first my parents wanted me to be a professor in a school. And I was, from the beginning, in a completely other movie. I wanted to have my theater.

I grew up in a small town, with just 7,000 inhabitants. The name was Ivanić-City, 40 km from the capital Zagreb. And where the hell is Croatia? Europe, for sure. On the Mediterranean Sea, near Italy. Sometimes I am not so pleased when people do not know where Croatia is, and sometimes they mix it with Ukraine. But I suppose it is the same if I mix Tennessee with Connecticut.

Today I have my own professional theater company for children in Croatia. It is called Theater Don Hihot. We perform our shows in kindergarten, schools, cultural centers, other theaters in Croatia, but also in Valencia, Hamburg. In 2020, we celebrated 10 years. Beginnings were difficult as we did not even have a car, and still do not have one. I was handling all on my own with a positive attitude and with lots of failing, I always had a solution and I was moving forward. I was constantly thinking about solutions, especially while I was swimming or taking a shower. And of course, the best ideas were in the moments while I was eating chocolate. After the gym. Without the beer.

My Life As A Woman: Croatia Edition #3

Growing up as a Croatian girl to becoming a Croatian woman is something I have always been thankful for, despite the challenges experienced as a child. I was born in Stradun, the main street in Dubrovnik, Croatia, the same place where I grew up. Growing up to become the woman I am today wasn't fun or easy at all, 'so many tears and fears beneath my smiles'. When I was a child, I was not so lucky to experience that fatherly love like every other kid in the neighborhood. I was told the man who happened to be my father left us when I was just a year old, to marry a rich woman. I grew up knowing my mom and her parents; grandparents to be precise. These people had a huge impact on my life, and I can boldly say they furnished and molded me into the woman I am today. As a young beautiful innocent girl, I used to support my mum who was a photographer and at the same time attended afternoon classes as my mom wasn't rich enough to afford school fees. Yet she was a strong and persistent woman who never gave up on herself, and left alone her child. She wouldn't tell any of her secrets or pains to anyone, even her parents. We lived like this for years fighting for survival.

When I was a child, I'd dream of spending every weekend at a very beautiful location far from home with families, visiting new places, and exploring the world, without affecting my job. I'd always dream of enjoying the beauty of life, living a carefree life, but so sad I never enjoyed any as a child. I had to face reality at an early stage of life. My granddad would always say to me, each time I told my dreams to him, "you have to fight for whatever you want. Always remain positive, strong, and optimistic, irrespective of your gender. Make that dream of yours a reality. Focus, avoid distractions, and have that tenacity of purpose, face your fears, and always remember that nothing good comes easy". These are the words that kept me going as a child. I've cherished these gifts for years. Of course, not only had he shared these sayings but inspirations. Then I started seeking stories of those people going from rags to riches, most inspirational while building my own foundation for success.

Grateful to my mom, she raised a queen, I've always been intrigued by the subject of intelligence. As a child, my mother would refer to me as "smart ass," she did all she could to support me, and encouraged me to be more focused. For as long as I could remember I have always dreamt of working on my own terms, and at my own convenient time, so I chose to become a freelance writer as freelancing is the only work I can do and still have more time to explore the world without having to affect my job, as it permits me to work from anywhere in the world even if I live inside a cave, as long as I have the right equipment with me. After high school, I got an offer from my uncle to go to the UK, where I got to learn everything I'd come to know today. My uncle worked as a freelancer rendering a web development service, he does most of his work at home. Knowing this, I felt relieved and half-way accomplished. I told him about my dreams, and he promised to help me out. After so many days watching my uncle complete his freelancing task, I developed an interest in writing, and he helped me bought writing courses online to furnish my writing skills, before fully going into freelancing.

I was so happy to take these courses as I knew within me that I was close to bringing my dreams to reality. After a year, I established myself as a freelance ghostwriter, completed over 200 tasks both online and offline all on my terms, and at my own convenient time. I made enough money to finance myself and my career just at the age of 22. I had visited three different African countries to see and understand life from their own perspective. This made me believe what my granddad said to me, a day he noticed I was broken "You only accomplish what you believe. Not what you want, not even what you work for but only what you believe. Just keep believing, sooner or later, everything is will be fine".

When I was 23, I moved back to Stradun, the same city where my mum lives. There I got married to my husband. You are probably wondering why I had to move back to Croatia. Well, I moved back to Croatia, because I am so much in love with our beautiful culture, and our men, if you are lucky to have met a good one, you wouldn't want to leave. I can't withstand staying years outside my country without having to taste my favorite food 'Lobster Pasta'. Our culture practices 'The Dubrovnik Gargoyle' which I so much enjoyed. Strolling around the peaceful old town with my lovely husband is just something I wouldn't trade for anything. Staying far away from home will be quite hard for me as I'm so much in love with my beautiful people and my lovely culture.

Now I am 31, happily married and blessed with two kids. Well that has not been easy as a woman if I'm being honest. Combining my career with having to take care of my husband and my children have been my challenge as a woman, but because I was taught and raised to be a strong woman, I found it easy to cope with. So, my success so far as a Croatian woman is that I'd been able to carve for myself a niche, which helped me actualized my dreams and overcome my challenges.

My advice to all Croatian women stuck in one pains or challenges goes thus; the first step to dealing with challenges is to learn how to manage your emotions for you to be able to think clearly about the situation. Bear in mind, no matter how bad a situation may appear, there is always a way to limit its impact, and use it to your own advantage. Never, ever be consumed by any situation that can be solved.

My Life As A Woman: Croatia Edition #4

Zrinka Bertović Skračić

Until my 13th birthday, I lived in Yugoslavia. After that, my country (Croatia) declared independency, and although all our lives changed dramatically, once the war started (that's a whole other story), all my family members were alive, and only that mattered. Looking back, my early childhood was wonderful. Kids were free as birds, always outside, always playing. My family was pretty well off, so we even traveled around Europe, which wasn't common those days in my country, but my parents raised me and my brother to be humble and always appreciate everything we have and pave the way through our lives ourselves.

Growing up, I was really close to my mom, grandma, and aunt. But it wasn't till years later that I recognized their strength and struggles. Much later I realized how lucky I was to have them in my life, and how ahead of their time each one of them was. It's a shame that it's also another story (waiting to happen).

My mom always told me to follow my passion and that I can achieve whatever I want. The thing is, she was told, at the age of 28, that she had one more month of walking before she'd end up in the wheelchair. Instead, she returned to the university and started studying something new, plus raised two small kids with my dad. Although the rest of her life was filled with physical pain (because of her medical condition), she became a social worker and helped others.

I always knew that I wanted to write because writing came as easy as breathing. The words just kept coming. I dreamt I'd be like Marija Jurić Zagorka, a famous Croatian writer and a first European professional female journalist. So, studying journalism seemed like a natural path. Although that freelancing path hasn't been easy at all (especially when I became a single mom at the age of 21, while still attending university and working), I can't imagine it ever going any other way. I still write (plus edit, proofread, and translate) for work every day, but I wish I had more time for myself, my own writing, my other passions, and my loved ones. Maybe one day, you know, isn't it what we all say to ourselves...

Ground control to myself! Let's return to Zagreb, as did I after I graduated from high school in Canada. Although I loved living there, I missed the Croatian way of life: mostly going out, rich culture life my hometown had to offer and partying, of course. Today, I love how we're all still connected, how my kids can go out and about without me worrying, how we go for long coffees, and the older we get, the more connected we become with our families and a close circle of friends who we can trust with our lives.

I love how grandparents still spend a lot of time with their grandkids, and that it's normal to go outside. I love how the younger generations (like my older son, who's now 20), don't obsess over the war, they're mostly open-minded (like my grandma was), and think for themselves. I enjoy watching more young men equally share the family/household/financial responsibilities with women because most women of my generation talked much about it, but in the end, we took everything upon ourselves. You know, children learn from watching their parents, and having such a strong mother as a role model made me think that I must be a superwoman myself. And I'm not, OK? No matter how long I can go on without sleep. And no matter how many months I can work without a single day off.

You see, it was hard being a young single mom and a female journalist always surrounded by men in power. Not letting their comments touch you. Just work, work, work, and prove your worth. And although I accomplished everything myself, that little voice that tells you that you must keep proving yourself is still alive and kicking in my head. In the same way that it's persistent in the heads of most of my girlfriends. Our biggest asset, though, is that we have each other. And we always find time for each other, even if it's for a short coffee (that turns into 4-hour-long drinks). That's how we are. And I wish that women all around the globe could have the same.

163

My Life As A Woman: Cuba Edition #1

I am María Ángeles, more Cuban than "the mojito" (laughs) and I want you know the true power that love for children has. I was born in a very humble home, between fishermen and fighters to survive. I don't want to talk to you about politics or Fidel, only about my Cuban culture. Of the rest, much has already been shown and not exactly such certain things.

My childhood passed between laughter, the coast, the beach, fish and bare feet. Of course, I could not miss at every stage of my life, dance, art, bohemian life. I lived with my grandparents because my parents are gone. A tough stage but really, my grandmother taught me to stand up for myself from a very young age. A dominant and radical grandmother, but thanks to that, I was able to achieve who and what I am today.

It took a lot of work to educate me, I was always jumping around and playing barefoot around with other kids, some my same age and others older than me. The street was my home. There was always something fun to do together and school and books were not my priority. I always felt very free, despite living in a country like Cuba. My grandmother said, I was rebellious and that it was not right and would bring me problems. People in Cuba who are citizens resign to their fate and I, maybe was not going to serve for this lifestyle.

The years passed and without realizing it, I became part of the humble and modest population with a home business and a husband working in a factory.. the typical Cuban life. But inside me there was something that did not let me be happy or that was missing in me, I did not know what it was, but it was clear, that it was not the life I wanted to lead. I got pregnant and the illusion of leading a life within me, made me also awake to the illusion to leave Cuba.

I knew from conversations of neighbors, several cases of rafters who, in a great adventure to the open sea, managed to escape, and arrive to the United States, the country of opportunities. What would this mulatto do with a baby in the United States and without knowing English? Well, fight and get ahead. I spent hours dreaming about everything I could do when I arrived in this great country. This sounded crazy, but I did not want to see my son or daughter grow up in the middle of nowhere, without much to offer and much to do as it happened to me and I wanted to change, for love, that story, I felt responsible to try and change my son's story and make it happen.

My baby was born, a boy, with dark skin and great weight. Seeing him filled me with even more anxiety to leave the country. Time went by and I started looking for people who had the same dream, men and women fearful but full of illusions, like me. The day came. I knew it was going to be a dangerous journey and no one could assure us that we would arrive and in fact, we would survive, but in my heart, the strength was so great that there was no place in my mind to think about the bad.

Without going into details, because they are too many, I achieved what I dreamed of. I arrived with "Franco", my son, in this great country, which today is our home. We go through many adventures, some very difficult, but the force of love can be with everything. Time has made us wise and today, after 20 years, we are very grateful to this country, for the opportunities it has given us and for teaching us to live in freedom.

My Life As A Woman: Cuba Edition #2

Where you grow up?

Hi, my name is Marion Duranona. I'm from the country side of Cuba, a small city named Las Tunas and was living there till 15 years old.

How you grow up?

I was a very happy little girl, living with my lovely family, my mom, dad and brother. They were always really caring about me and supported my dreams and aspirations.

Did you have parents or maybe a grandmother who inspired you?

I think my all family inspired me, mostly my parents, they thought that I should always fight for my dreams and become the person I was meant to be. Thanks to them I know that you will be whoever you decide, you and only you are able to build your own future.

What did you study? / What did you want to be growing up? / Why?

I always wanted to be an artist, that's why I began when I was 8 years old with a small character in a movie. When I was 10, I got into a Vocational Art School to study dancing and prepare my body and discipline my mind to become a professional actress. When I got to the edge of 15, I traveled to the capital city of La Habana, and got into the National Art School, in acting specialty. Now I'm happily graduated and living in La Havana.

What you love about your culture?

That's a difficult question because there is a lot of things about my country I can't stand, but there is something about the people, it's amazing to see how strong they are, how they expose their feelings, they are natural people, and I appreciate that.

What are you currently doing for work?

Well, I'm a professional actress and model, I just ended shooting a Soap Opera for national TV and YouTube. My last movie is about to premiere in Berlin named Ernesto's Island starring Max Riemelt. I'm playing as one of the main characters. And as a model, I just represented my country in an International Beauty Contest named Miss Europe Continental in the World celebrated in Italy a few months ago.

Tell me about your struggles as a woman

I think one of the biggest issues of being a woman is currently dealing with the expectations of people around you. As a woman, you can't let them decide who you have to be or how you should live your life. They can expect you to be a mother, a housewife, etc., but you are the only person to decide what you want to do. You are not a mother or a housewife, you are a free, independent person.

Tell me about your successes as a woman

I think my freedom is my biggest success as a woman, because it can be kind of hard in this society, especially in a country like mine, to set yourself free, to liberate yourself, or your mind of what the society tells you to be. In the moment, I am sure of who I am as a free person, and I have become the happiest person in the world.

Provide some advice to women from a woman living in Cuba

Work hard, believe in yourself, don't let yourself down. You are the strongest being in the universe.

My Life As A Woman: Cyprus Edition #1

I am Gery Nikolova. I am a Bulgarian girl living in Cyprus. Do you dream to live in a sunny small island with friendly people and beautiful beaches? If the answer is YES, I am your guide. I was born in the early 80s in Sofia, Bulgaria. My city has 2 million people and they are all in a rush. Life never stops. The way to meet the perfect man is almost a mission impossible. After several unforgettable men in my life, I decided to go on a journey to Cyprus.

I had an idea from friends that the island is sunny mostly all year round. I was dreaming about funny moments and maybe a new job opportunity. When I was studying mythology, there were amazing love stories. I was sure that on the island, there was one Adonis for me.

Before continuing about big love, I have to tell you that my family taught me to be very closed with men. I have to be polite and I should always forgive my man. I knew that a man is nervous and that is because they bring the money into the house.

What is my background? What did I learn at school?

I was studying at the English language school with two extra classes of French and Russian. I had my college degree in Tourism. I have been working eight years in a casino as a supervisor. From 2009 until my beautiful flight, I was the Assistant Front Office Manager at a five-star hotel in Sofia. I spoke at least three languages at the time. I have to tell you most of the staff where I manage are men, ever since I landed in Cyprus in 2012. In Bulgaria, we had a lot of women in higher job positions than in Cyprus.

Do you think the women in Cyprus are better paid than a man even now?

NO! I came at the beginning of the season of 2012. I was six months working in Agia Napa. It is a beautiful place to enjoy if you are in your twenties. Party town with half tourists from England and another half from Russia and has been my best place to work. I had started as a waitress in a restaurant on a beach.

Why did I start to work as a waitress with that CV?

First, no one wants to know my experience if that experience was not in Cyprus. I had an idea to spend an exotic holiday. And maybe I would make some extra money. I have to tell you that working in Agia Napa was my real dream. I have been working early in the mornings and later in the afternoons, I was free. I was spending time reading on the beach till late and drinking nice cocktails. If you like to meet sexy men on the beach, this is the place. I had fun and it was superb. I like my boss as he was very honest. I give him a lot of ideas on how to get more Russian clients. We get a lot and he gives me bonus after bonus for my work.

Did I meet a Cypriot?

Not at all, I was thinking they are honest and happy people, as my boss. I fell in love with this positive and easy-going life. In the middle of October, I understood we were closing the restaurant very soon. Did I tell you? I was in love with that easy life, how can I go back to the rush and stress again.

I found a job online in Paphos for Front Office Manager in a big hotel. They sent me an appointment for an interview in November. My last days in Agia Napa were so great, partying with friends and my boss, sunny days on beach, and lots of wine and cocktails. Nowadays I have my wine company which sells private wine-tastings. I am a professional Sommelier with world wine and spirit diploma.

Let's talk about my love experience.

I went to Paphos and the offer for the interview was fake. Turns out, Cypriots are not all honest. In a week's time, I was on a beach far away from Paphos in one small village of Polis Chrisouhous. It was so small and so green. The extraordinary place with amazing Bath of Aphrodite. I met an old woman on the road. She offered me a job in a coffee shop and she had a small house to rent for me. I was so excited. The small village was a touristic place with a lot of people even in the winter. My boss and his wife were very helpful and they are my best friends till now. They told me - "never fall in love with the Cypriot".

You have to know all the men were coming and offering me money, dinners, and presents. I was like a trophy. I was not very impressed because most of them were very dirty and hairy. I thought it was insane. A friend told me, all men try to make love with you first and that makes them very strong and handsome among the men in society. She told me to be careful because that is the game. They are not feeling the love as they try to get as much as possible from all the women on their lists. You have to know that most of the cafes are only for men. Cypriot women are not going out alone with friends. They stay home to cook and look after their children.

I have many stories about this beautiful country. Cyprus has old fashion traditions and tourists from all over the world. And how I make a company as a woman in Cyprus? And how much did I pay for my dream to come true? All it took was a move and a dream from Bulgaria to Cyprus.

My Life As A Woman: Cyprus Edition #2

As I grew up in Nicosia, Cyprus. The only home I knew was the SOS village home, which catered to orphans. The matron during my time at the orphanage was great, and I learned most things about life by listening to her. The matron was strict but loving and treated each one of us as her child. The orphanage was one huge family, which shielded us from most of what was going around the world. One particular culture that I enjoyed in Cyprus was Christmas. This was an opportunity to see new faces as strangers would bring us new clothes and other gifts. During this early age, I always wanted to be a doctor, and I studied hard to achieve this goal.

Before I completed my medical education, I got pregnant, and my boyfriend agreed to marry me. Despite the inconveniences caused by the pregnancy, this was a happy time in my life. However, the happy times did not last for long as my husband became abusive. At first, I assumed he was just stressed out because of the newborn baby. However, the psychological abuse would turn into physical violence, and at one time, I got admitted to the hospital. I loved my husband, and I would convince myself that he was going through a phase. While the abuses continued, I went to report the case to the police, but I was sent home, and they told me that my husband loved me and that it was a wrong course of action. Even some of the authorities I was reporting the case to were women, but they just sympathized with me. I attempted to bring the matter to the attention of the police, but my efforts were fruitless.

It reached a point I could not take the psychological and physical abuse anymore, and I decided to flee with my child. We escaped to a shelter in Cyprus, which accommodated women that had experienced domestic violence. While I felt regret for leaving my husband, I did not know then that this was a blessing in disguise. During the first few days in the shelter, I met an official who was impressed with my credentials, and she offered me a job in running the asylum. Having gone through domestic violence, I was motivated to ensure that no woman would have to undergo what I experienced. My successes in helping women in the shelter inspired me to take on more roles with non-governmental organizations. I may not have achieved my dream of being a doctor. Still, I got a chance to protect women by increasing attention in the domestic violence cases happening in Cyprus.

My advice for women in Cyprus is that there is no reason why anyone should abuse them even if it is their spouse. Healthy relationships are loving and do not involve abuse. Thus, one should not be ashamed to ask for help when they are victims of domestic violence. Together as women in Cyprus, we can change the structures in place to protect women. Making a change is as simple as donating to organizations focused on women or even volunteering at shelters for women and children.

My Life As A Woman: Czech Republic Edition

They say diamonds are made under pressure, and that's what I feel like about many Czech women. The Czech Republic has only become independent from the Soviet Union some 30 years ago, a system within which both men and women were taught to settle for the basics and be part of a uniformed workforce with little ambition or desire. The pressure to conform drove all the decisions of Czech women (and men) at that time.

While this taught many women to sit still and look pretty, some have had enough and would not conform to the regime even if it were to cost them their lives. Every Czech schoolkid knows the name Milada Horakova: a lawyer, politician, feminist and a beacon in the fight against the communist regime, who was executed in 1950 for standing up for what she believed in. It is women like her that inspire me, and many Czech women who are now free to believe what they want, do what they want, and stand up for it.

Being born in the free Czech Republic

I was born eight years after the Velvet Revolution. This was a time in the Czech Republic when everyone was still getting used to the newly gained freedom, the ability to travel wherever they wanted and the endless career opportunities. Because of this, not many people wanted to settle down and have kids, and so it was always easier for me to get into better schools – there wasn't as much competition in my year!

As an infant, I was a study partner to my mum, uncle and both grandparents – they were all preparing for important exams as they took turns taking care of me! Not only were my mother and uncle finishing their studies because they were both around 20 at the time, but my grandma and grandpa had decided to get a high school diploma at the age of 40! Why? Because they could, there was no pressure to become part of the manual labor workforce as soon as possible, and education was becoming more and more important. As a kid, I wanted to be a lawyer, a writer, a journalist, a psychologist… it is these ambitions that drove me to go study in the UK for my university degree in Marketing with Psychology and then choose a master's degree in Media and Communication.

Czech women are beautiful

No matter where you go, people tend to repeat that Czech women are some of the most beautiful women in the whole world. This has had a real impact on me as a teenager because I simply did not think I was beautiful. While I do agree that I know so many stunning and gorgeous-looking Czech women, sometimes it feels like we are being reduced to just the looks. I have never heard anyone say that Czech women are successful, smart or inspirational. Do I have to be beautiful to be a Czech woman?

Taking the jokes

Another thing you should know about Czech culture is that Czech humor knows no boundaries. Whether they are jokes about ethnicity, religion, gender roles, or even the holocaust – Czech people will make them, and everyone is expected to laugh and take a joke. While this has led to a more light-hearted outlook on life for many people, these 'innocent' jokes can be incredibly hard to take if you are struggling with self-confidence.

But for me, this is another example of many Czech women being diamonds made under pressure. More and more women are speaking up against some jokes just not being okay and personally, this kind of humor has helped me learn that sometimes, you have to be the bigger person and let a meaningless comment slide. This was especially beneficial to me as a woman of the 21st century on social media full of anonymous trolls. Do I think it is okay to joke about a woman's appearance, weight, or level of intelligence (jokes about blonde women being stupid are particularly popular in the Czech Republic)? Of course not! But looking back, growing up with them has helped me become a tougher, more resilient woman in adulthood.

Value your freedom

As a woman who grew up in a country that has only recently liberated itself from the grip of the Soviet Union, the message I want to leave other women with is - value your freedom. Every day, listening to stories from my family and others, the history of my country makes me so grateful for being able to study abroad, choose the career I want, and speak my mind. These are some things that we often take for granted, but a mere 30 years ago, they were unimaginable in the country I come from.

My Life As A Woman: Democratic Republic Of Congo Edition

My name is Sephora, I grew up in the Congo in a pretty cool family, my father was a carpenter and my mother did not work. We weren't rich but we were still happy. I grew up in a country strewn with troubles, wars, conflicts and violence around minerals (gold, coluant, copper), a tactic which emerged from the rape of women and sometimes even children. We have never been so insecure without escape. So you had to be strong and stick to it. My father had a car accident and he couldn't continue working as a carpenter, it was a pain. And maybe it was time for my mother to take over, she taught me the best lessons in life.

My mother managed to feed a family of 8 people and this for years until today, I was convinced that women too could do better.

My sewing studies

With the little money she made, I was able to study thanks to her in a sewing school. My only goal was to start a sewing business later, I was so motivated than ever. Despite everything that we were facing in the country, we still had something to be happy about and that is something that I like in my culture.

What I like in my culture

With us, "History is written orally". Reading the book of memories of a griot therefore consists of sitting near him and listening to him. To make the rooster, it is enough to ask him questions, pretending to want to draw morality thanks to his experience. This is the game our griots love. To successfully get them on board is to steal their time. This is how I managed to steal from Granny almost overnight. The central knot of my questioning consisting in knowing how her contemporaries married, she preferred to reveal to me also why they were getting married.

My difficulties as a woman

As a woman, I had a lot of difficulties which I would never have thought of being a kid, the disrepute for women is huge in Africa especially in my country, women are not taken seriously, their work being said "babysitting, taking care of the kitchen, raising the children" to go ahead further was a danger for the family. I remember once, one of the scenes that completely hurt me and that at the time, my mother had a new boy, there was joy in the family, everyone was in a good mood and happy, until then, everything was fine. Years passed, my mother got pregnant again, imagine that. She gave birth to a daughter, but what hurt me the most was the fact that my father was not happy in the same way as when it was a boy, he didn't care "almost", quite indifferent. That day, I wondered why women were discredited.

Taken with low regard

The women in Congo were only scarecrow, they even went so far as to prohibit university studies for women on the pretext that they would be married and that their sole objective would be to "raise children" for long periods. Studies will not help them and even see that they could be prevented from taking good care of the family. A good girl must obligatorily marry when she reaches the 17 years threshold.

More or less good improvement

Despite all this, things have improved in recent years, we have never had as much freedom of expression as at the time, a more or less sufficient consideration, since these days, makes them reveal that things will never stop improving.

My successes as a woman

I started a small sewing business where I work with men now, everything is going great, they respect me, and give me more and more say and need my opinion to make important decisions. The success I now have is the certainty that women can, these days, pursue their goals which could not have been at the time and once only a dream in a country like the Congo.

Trust yourself, with strength and perseverance, you will always get there, do not be intimidated by anyone, the future belongs to everyone, whether you are a girl or a boy, men or women, pursue your dreams and you will reach them for sure.

My Life As A Woman: Denmark Edition #1

By Camilla Malm

My mother has always told me that I was very fortunate to grow up in Denmark. As a kid I just thought that it was because we didn't have any war, starvation, or dangerous animals. The older I'm getting, the more I'm starting to realize that it is way more than that.

Growing up as a woman in Denmark has given me freedom and equality. Denmark is ranking 13th on world basis when it comes to gender equality, according to World Economic Forum. We are free to wear, do, or speak what we would like. These are factors that you don't value or think much about as a child, but as you grow up to become a woman, you start to appreciate it more and more.

I grew up in Denmark, just outside of our capital of Copenhagen. I grew up in a safe neighborhood in the suburbs, where everyone knows everyone, kids play on the street and ride their bicycles between their house and their friends' houses without having to be followed by an adult. My childhood was very safe and probably what most people will describe as perfect.

In my family we were always told to appreciate everything we had. We were not allowed to leave the dinner table without finishing everything on our plate because "kids are starving in Africa". We had to pray an evening prayer every night before bed and thank God for all that we had. We were indeed very lucky to have all that we had.

All of my family lives in Denmark and I've grown up very close to all of them (we are 64 just on my mother's side). I've always been used to seeing all of my grandparents at least a couple of times a week and I often spent time with them after school. My grandmother was never shy to tell stories about her upbringing and how they were children sharing one bedroom and two beds. She grew up not too far from where I grew up (less than minutes to be exact) and she sometimes showed us photos of how our familiar neighborhood streets looked like when she was a child. It was always fun to see the difference and it was hard to imagine our pretty suburban neighborhood with gravel roads and farmers. My grandmother has always been a big inspiration to me, as she is always just positive and has a lot of spirit. She believes in hard work and that you get what you deserve, so she has always been kindly pushing my sister and I to grow up as independent and strong women.

Growing up I always wanted to be a veterinarian or a coroner. I never took school very seriously, so when I was about to go to college I found out that I did not have the required GPA to become either of that. I had no clue what else I wanted to do, so I went travelling around the world for 2 years after high school, before I settled on getting a bachelor's in marketing. This bachelors was not even my idea, but my fathers. I'm very grateful for his advice today, as it has truly shaped my life in a direction that I love. I have now been working with marketing on a freelance basis for 3 years and it has allowed me to travel the world even more. I am still based in Copenhagen, but now I travel most of the year while working on the road. I feel truly blessed to have these opportunities and I am happy with where my life has brought me.

Travelling has also taught me to appreciate Denmark and my culture even more. It has shown me how lucky I am to be Danish. We have a strong sense of community and we truly take care of everyone. In Denmark, we pay some of the highest taxes in the world, but we get so many benefits from that, such as getting paid monthly to study (yes, you read it right), one of the world's longest maternity leaves and free healthcare. We are a Christian country, even though we are mostly Atheists nowadays, but we still celebrate a lot of Christian holidays. One of the biggest things in the Danish culture is "hygge". Hygge is a Danish word, which can't be translated, but it means to be because, comfortable and to enjoy the time with the people that you love.

Growing up in Denmark as a woman has thankfully not given me any real struggles in life. Denmark is very safe, there is space for everyone, and we all have the exact same rights – as it should be. It has never been a thing that women were not equal, here it is expected. My only struggles as a woman has been when I have been abroad, where women are sometimes not seen as equals or where women have to be cautious when walking the streets. In other countries I have sometimes even gotten the question if I shouldn't just get married and take care of the children – and find my place in the kitchen as a woman should. NO, I should not. A gender is and will never be your guideline to define success. There are millions of successful women out there and success will always look different to different people. I like to not define my success in money, but in happiness. If I am happy then I am successful in life. It is up to us to define and find our way to success. To me, happiness should be the goal in life, and I base my decisions on what makes me happy and I change what doesn't. You can do it too. It will always look different, easier or harder based on your situation, but it will never be impossible to change your life. Remember, that whatever you are not changing, you are choosing.

My Life As A Woman: Denmark Edition #2

I am a Danish woman. I grew up in a smaller town with 60,000 citizens in Jutland the main land of Denmark. I grew up with my mom, dad, and sister in a very safe environment. We always enjoyed travelling but we didn't have much money when I was a kid. So most summers were spent in Denmark in a camper or we drove to Italy and lived in a camper there.

When I was 15 I had a year at boarding school, which was really good for me. I made good friends and I grew up in a different way and felt more secure and my self-confidence grew a lot. When my little sister turned 15, she moved to America and lived in Michigan. She studied in high school over there for a year. It was a super tough year for me in many ways. I missed her deeply. After I graduated, I moved to New Zealand to live there for 7 months. I worked as an Au Pair and travelled the whole country.

I came back to Denmark, and my home wasn't home anymore and everything felt boring and small. I moved to Copenhagen, the capital of Denmark. Growing up my aunt has always been an inspiration for me. She travelled the whole world with her backpack and she lived and studied in Copenhagen for some years, before she returned to our hometown.

So to Copenhagen I went and started nursing school. My mother has always worked at the Hospital, so that was my dream too. After half a year I needed to end the studies. I liked the idea of being a nurse and I wanted to help and work with people. But the subjects were not for me.

Instead I started on a Marketing degree. I was good at it and I enjoyed going to school and learning. During my education it was possible to study a semester abroad, and I knew what I wanted that. I thought about Europe, but my boyfriend always had a dream about living in Dubai. So we found a solution to move there, while I was studying one semester at a University in Dubai. It was so different and I felt very left out and different in many ways. Those six-months felt very long. But I didn't quit. I finished and after that there was an opportunity for us to stay in Dubai if I could find an internship. It was a long struggle but I managed and it was a better time in Dubai. I took my exam in Denmark and I then had a bachelor's degree.

We then needed to find out if we wanted to stay in Dubai or move back to Denmark. The first year was very tough, but after one year, we had a really good life in Dubai. We knew the city, we had good friends, and were used to the different culture. So we decided to stay and we are still here. I got a Marketing job a few months after graduating.

I miss Denmark and I miss the Danish culture a lot. The culture I miss most from Denmark is the food, the celebrations, and the traditions. And of course, the times spent with my family. I can now cook almost all Danish meals and we stick to our traditions and Danish food. What I love about the Danish culture is all the old traditions we have all around the year. The time we spend together and eat and drink.

If you are also thinking about moving to the UAE or other counties I would say DO IT. I would never have thought how life-changing a move to another country could be. It has made me 10 times stronger. It has made our relationship 10 times stronger. I sometimes still feel insecure as a woman. But sometimes you need to get out of your comfort zone. Even in the tough times. If you last through something really hard, and make it out on the other side, you will feel a liberating feeling and you feel stronger.

I have had some episodes here in Dubai where I didn't feel comfortable being a woman. Men are sometimes staring. Men don't want to answer you if you are talking to them. Sometimes you can feel that there is no respect for a young woman like me. But honestly I am used to it now. There is a different culture here in the UAE. Most men do have respect for women, they speak to you nicely, hold the door for you, let you go in first and so on. I feel very respected here now in the UAE – most days. It is hard to be a woman! You work all day long and you still need to get home and do the grocery shopping and clean the house. But you can make it! You are a woman. We can handle anything.

My Life As A Woman: Faroe Islands Edition

Hi. My name is Martia Dahl. I grew up in the 1950s on the island of Leirvik, on a sheep farm near a small town called Toftanes. It's a very small place and it seemed that everyone was either related to each other or at least knew every family very well.

How did you grow up?

My father was a sheep farmer as are most people around here, and my mother was a housewife but also worked the farm. We lived off what we had on the farm and sold the rest to make a little money. It was hard, but I enjoyed growing up there.

Did you have a parent or grandparent that inspired you?

I always loved hearing my grandmother's stories about when she was a young girl – it felt as if she was living in a different time – a more innocent time.

What did you study and what did you want to be when growing up?

Traditionally, when a girl around here married, it would be to either a sheep farmer or a fisherman, and that would define her job and home life. My mum stayed on the farm and she would use wool from the sheep to make sweaters, blankets and things like that. As a child I learnt to knit (we all learn that here) and were learning the skills to be a good housewife, but academically I was very clever at school, and I wanted to see some of the world so when I finished school, I went over to Denmark and studied at the university in Odense. When I graduated I spent some time travelling around Europe then came back to Denmark and started working as a teacher. I decided to become a teacher as I love learning and helping other people learn, and always found it satisfying to help children grow up into happy and confident adults.

What do you love about your culture?

Life here is at a very slow place. Everybody knows each other and has mutual respect. It is a very rural lifestyle so there are not many factories and things like that, and there is not so much pollution as I have seen in other parts of the world – we have fresh air and we all live a simple life, but a sometimes difficult one as we are very isolated and the weather is always cold and wet (that's why we wear the sweaters).

What are you currently doing for work?

Well, I started off as a teacher in Denmark, but came back to the Faroe Islands after five years. I worked as a teacher here in a folk school in Torshavn until recently when I retired. I'm enjoying my free time now as I am able to relax and I do a lot of walking around my island to keep myself fit and healthy.

Tell me about your successes as a woman?

As a child I always wanted to explore the world, maybe that's because I grew up on a small island and so my biggest success as a young woman was finally leaving the island and studying in Denmark. I learnt a lot about life whilst there, and when I came back here I was an independent woman, and there weren't too many of us here at that time on the island. Working as a teacher helped to empower myself as I knew that I was gaining the respect of those around me and that I was playing a crucial part in the development of my students.

Provide some advice to a woman living in the Faroe Islands?

It is good to keep the traditional values of the community but is also good to go and see some of the world before settling down. The islands are a small place and we live in a big world in which there is so much to learn. Go out and learn and when you return you will be a much wiser person.

My Life As A Woman: Greenland Edition #1

I grew up living in the capital city of Nuuk in the beautiful country of Greenland. Nuuk is a very small city which made life simple and sweet. My childhood home was a beautiful, colourful wooden house located on the south coast surrounded by a breath taking body of water. I would spend my time as a child playing puzzles indoors with my older sister since it is always cold in Greenland. I remember only in the month of July, would my parents allow us to play outside because the weather warmed up a little. I was highly creative growing up and loved to draw and play dress up.

I was also a huge food lover but the range of food in Greenland was not vast and consisted mostly of meat and seafood as it is a surplus in my country. My dad worked in the natural resource industry so I would rarely see him and so my Mother took care of my sister and I most often. She was my role model and an excellent seamstress. I admired her hard work and precision. I would watch her sew for hours on end to meet tight deadlines for her clients. She would make me beautiful warm sweaters and scarves to wear to school that would also protect me against the cold harsh winds of Greenland while I walked to school. It was actually my mother that inspired me to pursue a career in fashion design and what led me to create a successful fashion label for women that can be found in numerous department stores all over the world.

It was a tough battle to get to where I am today as a humble woman from Greenland because people in power in the fashion industry are usually males and they do not like to hear ideas from others, especially women. I was resilient and did not let negativity or discrimination bring me down. My mother taught me to carry myself professionally as a woman and it helped me network with people easily. Having the right contacts is vital and helped my business grow so much. In my experience, it was heartwarming to notice that many women genuinely like to see other women succeed and often go out of their way to help one another out in this industry.

It is an honour to represent my beautiful country, Greenland, with such a huge platform that I have created with my fashion brand and I am so proud to bring more spotlight to my wonderful country. Although I travel a lot for work, I will never forget Greenland's rich culture, friendly people, delicious food and its simplicity.

To all my fellow Greenland women, I advise you to dream big and pursue your passion relentlessly until you attain your desired goal. It is not easy to have such humble roots and start from nothing like I did but if I, a small-town woman from Greenland can achieve success with hard work, then so can you.

My Life As A Woman: Greenland Edition #2

Are you new to the globe of Females Encouraging Other Women in Greenland? This article will be a basic intro to what's been taking place around. I matured in Nuuk, an extremely attractive place however very challenging to make ends meet. I was inspired by my mom's struggle to endure the challenge in order to live a good life.

I enjoy the Inuit culture and the abundant history behind it. I function as a tour guide with Qaqortoq Museum as well as I want to take a trip abroad later on the following year to study worldwide relationships. My desire is to make Greenland a better place for all to live in. It is different to be a lady in this part of the world as a result of the many obstacles right here.

You aren't most likely to want to enter without a little prep work, do you? This is something you have to consider in the past doing anything else. Beginning with something you aren't planned for can cost you a whole lot a lot more in the future than you originally invested.

Aikakositika is one more location where Ladies Motivating Other Women in the Greenland job. It's a village that remains on the south coast of the Northwest Peninsula of Greenland. It's obtained a population of around 900 individuals and likewise is mainly populated by people from China, the Philippines, India, Pakistan, as well as numerous other countries. They're also the forefathers of the contemporary Inuit populace.

They have solid connections to the country's financial scenario with their sell minerals, geothermal power, and also metal ore. So they're a big deal in addition to an effect on the financial situation. Nevertheless, they aren't particularly normal in Aikakositika because it's such a much go for most individuals.

Aikakositika is a remote and additionally separated area, so it has fewer individuals. Unlike the landmass, where it's bordered by plenty of kilometers of land and also sea, it's more on a lee shore than being on any sort of landmass. The resources of Greenland are just about 30 kilometers away, which makes circumnavigating Aikakositika challenging. As a matter of fact, the marketplaces are much needed to the Ladies Motivating Other Women In Greenland neighborhood. For a few of them, it's a bit of a challenge to travelling right throughout the nation and much of them depend upon the sources of the resource-rich coasts for their sources.

Waqonqabik has various markets where they sell their items, particularly angling items. It's also the area where they obtain their home heating gas. We pointed out earlier the solid links between the main center as well as additionally the north, yet Manila is essential. It's where lots of people from Aikakositika go to get their residence heating gas and also along with finding their techniques around the town. It's also a large market for their items as well as also services. Trading is likewise exceptionally critical to the group right here. This is because they have a system that functions as an exchange with large amounts of deals happening at all times.

From Manila, a lot of them can fly over to Nuuk along with getting on the boat that takes them back to their homes. By doing this, they do not need to walk around Greenland. In fact, a lot of them head home right from Manila, aiding to make up for the lack of profession happening between the landmass and also the neighboring communities.

Those that can't remain in Aikakositika can typically still come as well. Yet there's less need for certain professions so when an individual heads out to see people, they do so by walking. Concerning the neighborhood worries; it's virtually open for any company, as well as every person to do whatever they want. It's as uncomplicated as that.

Lastly, we women need a voice and to make our voices heard. We have to be strong and use all our resources to safe other women and children to develop our nation. Orientation and awareness programmes through social media, marketplace or sport centers are a very important tool to educate other women and our younger generations. Thank you for reading.

My Life As A Woman: Djibouti Edition

Warning: This story contains graphic content. Proceed to read with caution.

I was born and grew up in a village called Galafi, Dikhil, Djibouti. I have two brothers and two sisters. My father is a farmer and my mother does the rest of the work inside the house and at the field. Me and my sisters always had to wake up very early in the morning to milk the cows, fetch water, help my mother in the kitchen, and my brothers would help my father in the farm, and also to look after the sheep. Since there were no schools nearby, we girls were not allowed to go to school, but I really wanted to go. As our farm was very small and dry most of the time, it was hard to make a living with it so for source of income they forced my eldest sister to get married at the age of fifteen to an old and rich man.

Once upon a time I went to fetch water. The pond was way too far from my house. Back from the pond, there was a scorching sun. I carried two gallons of water on my back. I could not resist the heat from the sun. I was so very tired that I had to take a rest. So I put down the gallons and sat under a tree and I suddenly heard a voice, to be more accurate, it was a speech. I wanted to know where the voice is coming from so I went to that direction. I counted and there were twenty women sitting and a woman speaking. She was telling them her story. She said that she was born in this village. "you all know that our country is very poor. There is shortage of teachers. Most of our people die from malnutrition and there is not any health care. There are things that has to be gotten rid of like harmful traditional beliefs, inequality of gender, and also female genital mutilation. So you have to learn to improve all of this", she continued, "twelve years ago, I was like you…. I was in this village and as you know, there is no school nearby so I had to walk on foot for long hours to get the access to education. At the age of fifteen, I underwent female genital mutilation (FGM) and I suffered from a lot of worse things. I constantly had pain, repeated infection, bleeding, and a problem in peeing and holding pee in and most of the time I was very depressed. I had no siblings to share my feelings with and a friend to talk to. But my books became my friends. my books gave me strength, and hope to stand up with my foot. Now here I am teaching you the basic courses. Education is the key to success," she said. Ever since that day, I was very inspired by her speech that I wanted to become a teacher like her to motivate others, to change the villagers, and to destroy poverty through education. Her speech hit me very hard. That was the day that I made a promise to myself to never give up on my education.

When my elder sister underwent FGM when she was fifteen, our living room was filled with guests and neighbors. They all were singing and dancing. Me and my sister were told by my mother and grandmother that FGM is a requirement for every girl. There were also five other girls who were going to be circumcised after my sister. First my sister was blindfolded and then her hands were tied behind her back. Her legs were spread open and they pinned down her labia and clitoris and cut it. She was screaming very loudly but no one cared. I saw unhygienic medical procedures and they even used the same blade on all of the girls. I felt really sad to see my sister in pain but suddenly I heard my grandmother saying why wait till next year let our little girl be circumcised now. I was very shocked I had no choice but to run away. I went to Djibouti city and settled with my aunt and I got the chance to go to school.

I am currently a teacher and an anti-FGM campaigner. Now I am helping my family financially and I am creating awareness to the villagers about the negative effects of FGM and the harmful traditional beliefs that has to be rid of. I also opened a school nearby my village. We women should fight against the practice of FGM; even if the world seems scarier, and unfair we have to face the challenges. We are born to add something to the world so don't give up, have faith in yourselves and together we will play a crucial role in improving everything. In that way we will be able to overcome our problems and our fears.

My Life As A Woman: Dominica Edition

Après Bondie C'est La Ter, after God the earth. This motto represents the authentic beauty of Dominica. Our roots are grounded on being a God-fearing nation with its people overwhelmingly filled with the Dominican dignity. We take pride in our land that is ripened with culture and tradition. Our luscious mountains and alluring valleys infused with fauna and flora are guaranteed to take anyone's breath away, literally. I am Dominica proud! And when I say Dominica, I do not mean the Dominican Republic, I mean the Commonwealth of Dominica. My island between two French islands, Martinique and Guadeloupe, and it is bountiful in luscious beaches and friendly people that will instantly make you feel like you're home away from home.

I am so blessed to be raised in one of Dominica's best villages called Wotton Waven. We usually call it the healing community, and that's because we are surrounded by sulfur. You see, Wotton Waven is a Caldera, which means there is lava all underneath us. You think that we villagers would be scared, huh? Actually, we are a fierce people that turned this predicament into a blessing. By that, I mean the villagers used both the hot water and the sulfur to make sulfur springs; tourists say that we have the most potent sulfur springs with healing components in the entire world, considering that Dominica has not only one but nine active volcanoes. These sulfur springs have a lot of healing properties for the body, both physically, mentally, and spiritually.

Though this all sounds like a dream, a fairy tale, an escape from reality, and for any normal child, it would be, it was not my story. It was never a comfortable journey growing up, I was nowhere near normal. By the age of nine, my health slowly started deteriorating, and I was diagnosed with Hereditary Lymphedema. This disorder affects the Lymphatic System and is characterized by swelling of limbs and a lot of pain! Now you would think that it is just an easy complication. There is no big fuss about it. But just take one minute and imagine you being a nine-year-old in a community filled with kids your age.

All you would want to do is run around in the bush or go to the river with your friends; instead, you're stuck at home in either intense pain or being injected for continuous blood samples from Doctor's visits. Those visits were always the hard part. Tests after tests, injection after injection, and every test saying that you are okay, seeing the pain and disappointment in your mother's eyes every time a Doctor told her that there is nothing wrong with her child. Still, her mother's instinct was just not able to believe it. I love my mother! And always felt guilty for the pain I saw in her eyes. Now at that time, I saw myself as a normal child. Still, everyone else saw me as something completely different until their projections started rubbing off me, and inevitably, I began to see myself wholly different, but through a negative aspect. The abnormal child, the sick monster who has swollen feet and cannot be cured. Now, imagine how the constant bullying from the people I thought were my friends, the feeling of not being able to fit in anywhere, and the rejection all this spiraled my mental health to the ground. As a nine-year-old, the strangely unfamiliar feeling of rejection planted seeds of hurt and over the years, blossomed into a lot of anger towards life and its meaning. I felt unworthy of love and desire, and that in itself harvested my social anxiety and low self-esteem. I never felt like I belonged anywhere, and because of that, suicidal thoughts were rampant in my mind as a way of escaping all the hurt I buried while growing up.

The famous Maya Angelou said, "but still like dust, I arise." As my fresh tears flowed genuinely throughout the years, my strength and self-confidence ascended into something beautiful. I am proud of the strong woman that I am and the woman that I am becoming, I am grateful for my struggles; it made me who I am. The journey of self-love is a hard one, it is accepting and eventually loving the faults and the imperfections that make you unique, making you, you. What is broken can be mended. What is hurt can be healed. And no matter how dark it gets, the sun is going to rise again.

My Life As A Woman: Dominican Republic Edition #1

Hello, I am a Dominican woman and I have a dream. I grew up in Santo Domingo, the capital of Dominican Republic in a family that worked hard for every penny. I had a great childhood, very active. We didn't had good luck with nannies, so instead my mother signed us in ballet, languages, karate, volleyball, football, art classes and more. I remember that she used to say a lot " Yo no naci pa' semilla" which basically means that I have to learn as much as I can about everything because she won't always be around.

During my life, I had two examples about empowerment and resilient: Grandma and mom. My grandmother raised five children on her own once my grandfather left her for another woman. While she used to work day and night, my mom helped her with her brother and sisters, selling lollipops at day and studying at night. Since life is funny sometimes, my father left home 8 years ago and the story started all over again. Mom took the whole package of three children, one dog, three birds, two cars and a house on her own. She didn't have it easy, but she fought back. Nowadays, I still wonder how she could do it all.

Inspired by these women, I always loved to study and learn new things. I have a bachelor's in Hotel Management and a master's degree in Events and Wedding Organization. I love my career and have been working in the industry for the past 7 years along with some micro-businesses such as a home based bakery, online travel agency and online store. My dad used to say that knowledge is power, so I kept that idea. However, when I was teenager I wanted to be a creative writer, even got a scholarship in high school to study in Washington but I rejected it because I thought I wasn't good enough. The "what if" always remain in my mind.

I didn't choose to born in Dominican Republic, I just got lucky. I lived in that beautiful island 23 of my 25 years where everything is joy even in the hard times, food is super seasoned and amazingly delicious and people are very determined. There's a phrase that says: "Dominicans do not run the world because they don't want to."

Women of every nationality have been struggling for their rights since forever and I feel proud every time a woman accomplished something, especially if it's a Dominican woman. I started to work at the age of 18 to pay my university and then I discovered the world as it is. In my first jobs, I had a lot of issues for being a woman and leader of a group of men. Respect was hard to earn and harassing was an everyday deal. Step by step, I noticed that I had to work twice harder to stand out and being a Latina in the USA didn't make the path easier.

I have lived in Mexico and Miami and that was enough to fall in love with my culture even more, and to be sure that I have to represent my country whenever I go, the best I can. I moved out to Miami to join my husband. I left part of my life and my family for love and to start a new adventure. I do not regret for a second. This year has been rough but allowed me to redesign myself and I have confirmed that "what doesn't kill you makes you stronger" (being there, done that). Currently, since life put me in an uncomfortable situation, I am doing something I didn't believe I was able to: being a freelancer and guess what? I am writing!

Today, I dedicate my life to combine the best of both worlds: writing and travel. I have my own blog where I share my experiences and encourage every woman to get to know the world and follow their passions. It is easy to notice a Dominican woman anywhere: loud, confident, goal driven and a fighter. So my advice would be simple: Be as loud as possible so you get noticed, be confident so nobody can take down your dreams, be goal driven because the path is uneven and you will have to be focused. And fight, with all you have, fight for your future, for your family, for your country, and especially for YOU.

I told you I have a dream and if I can dream it, I can live it.

My Life As A Woman: Dominican Republic Edition #2

I grew up in Santiago de los Caballeros city, the main city of the Santiago province, north region of the island. The city is dubbed "heart city" because we're almost at the heart of the island. This is the second most important city in the entire island. Despite being in an island famous for its tourism and beaches, I barely go to the beach, maybe a couple times a year. In this country, we have a culture hospitality in being warm and helpful. When it comes to our relatives and friends, we are noisy and try to be so helpful to the point that codependency is an unspoken part of our culture.

Growing up was as easy as it can be in a tropical island. I grew up middle class, but went to public school in elementary, later transferred to private school for high school and finally landed in one of the top universities here. Growing up, I had no idea what I wanted to be, I simply had too many things that I was passionate about, such as arts, infinite curiosity for science and writing, to name a few. When time came to choose a career, I was pressure to pick from a limited array of choices that the universities in my city offered. "You need to study something that can get you a job" my mom urged, so I went for medical school for 8 years. I thought it was the best choice given that it had science all over it, most people said that doctors were a dignified lot and respected in society and they were always hailed as "smart people".

Along with these things, when I was in high school, my father fell ill with an unknown disease, which left him in a wheelchair for 8 years, battling a cascade of related diseases which later culminated until his death in 2013. My father's disease influenced me enormously to study medicine, I was curious and loved the sciences, it was a perfect match.

As a woman, I've experienced some barriers presented by society outside of my house, because I didn't make such distinctions of assigning roles to women and men: i.e. my mother was the breadwinner and we were all expected to do house chores, go to college and get a job, regardless of our gender. I currently work as a general practitioner and the most annoying things that I can recall is people doubting of my driving skills or professional skills just because I'm a woman. I've had patients in consultation in rural areas asking for the "real doctor" because "women are nurses".

The second hurdle that comes to mind is regarding the topic of driving. I had put off learning how to drive for a long time because of the belief that women are bad drivers and if there's a man that can drive, he's the de facto driver. Slowly but surely I started driving years ago, rolling my eyes when people made innocent comments and suggestion of letting a man drive when possible, that you can't drive in the highway cause it's not safe for a woman and that requires a "man's expertise". Slowly but surely, I began setting myself driving challenges of going to different places in the country and debunked these myths to the most important person: myself. Now I feel perfectly capable of driving anywhere in the country with ease.

Times are changing of course, the newer generation is more accepting of women behind the wheel and at the workplace, these objections mostly come from men and women of the boomer generation. I consider that being a woman has its perks. In my personal experience, by being a woman I can notice things that men don't, and offer another perspective and different solutions to problems in the personal realm and in the workplace. Women are considered culturally to have the "gentler touch" and that may be considered as weak, but I personally believe that not everything can be solved with brute force, there can be peace and gentleness and still achieve the same results.

And finally, my advice for fellow Dominican women is to throw out the window any misconceptions you have collected through the years about what a woman can and cannot do. Study, get a job or build a business, drive a car if you like, go on a road trips like me if you wish. It's time to discard that collective voice we've picked up from our culture that we need a man to provide, we need a man to drive us around, we need a man to pay for our salon… it's all imaginary, these barriers are a prison of our own making.

My Life As A Woman: Ecuador Edition

As you read on I want to make clear that my life is not a clear example of what is normal for women in Ecuador, I've been very lucky with the family I was born in and the support system that they provide. Both my parents come from rural cities but in the earlier years of their lives their families moved to the biggest city of the country in hopes for a better future for their children. They met in college where my dad was a professor and my mom were a secretary on the faculty he was teaching in. They married and went on having two daughters, me being the younger one. Our childhood years were pretty busy, because after school our parents enrolled us in various activities, from swimming, tennis, ballet and piano. Every year during summer we would go to an apartment we had near the coast and we would be put in summer camps where we would swim, have cooking and acting classes and do sports like football, tennis, parasailing and kayaking.

This all stopped when we started high school as me and my sister started speaking up for ourselves and decided we weren't into doing any physical activities anymore, my parents didn't make a fuss and agreed to our decisions. When I was about to graduate high school I had no clue what I wanted to study, my dad saw my despair and one day talked to me about how he saw that I liked art and should explore that calling, not sure what other option I had, I enrolled in the same public university he taught. Over the couple of semesters I was there, my dad realized I was not happy so he insisted I take a semester abroad in Argentina and finally decided graphic design was not my thing. Having the opportunity of meeting people from all over the world and getting their perspectives on different topics, I realized tourism might be for me, so when I returned I changed majors and universities.

Before the COVID-19 lockdown, I was working in a bed and breakfast helping the owner with their social media growth, sadly she had to let me go because I was not essential and she didn't have the income to keep me, she had to let me go. This free time at home made me think a lot about my life and my country and even though Ecuador has been really struggling, I can see that we have come together as one. One of the things I like most about us Ecuadorians is how close we are to our community and families, for example, it is very common for children to not leave home for college and live with their parents for that period of time, as well weekends are spent visiting grandparents' homes which are a must in most households.

My parents are very family-oriented and that is why I admire them so much. Also I have come to admit that my dad is a huge inspiration for me because of all he has been able to accomplish. He grew up in a low-income family with four other siblings, him being the second oldest. Their education was in the public system and even though all his brothers and sisters stopped studying after university, my dad persevered until he was able to study his Ph.D. abroad in one of the top 30 universities in the world. Now he is living in China and is in charge of a leader organization specialized in climate research. He was able to break through from his low class status, putting his name as well as his country on the map, while also getting her daughters through private schooling.

I have been very lucky being surrounded by a good environment but I don't take it for granted. Machismo is a social structure that sadly is very engraved in our culture, so it is common for women to be catcalled on the streets and even more to be forced into a house wife status and treated as someone whose only role is to serve men.

My advice to women would be to not be satisfied with the bare minimum of life, whether that is as big as an university major you don't like or an abusive partner to something minimal as the length of your hair. If something bothers you, it's important to try and change it, even though it might be challenging, as in the end the result of actually changing is so gratifying.

My Life As A Woman: Isabela Island Edition

My name is Floreana White. I grew up in a remote village in Puerto Villamil in Isabela Island. I was brought up by a single mother who broke loose from a dysfunctional marriage and decided to follow her path. Back then, it was tough for a woman to do so, as they relied on men for provision. My father was not any different from the majority of men as a drunk. Other women, who did not see a way out of their predicament, chose to stay in violence-prone marriages, but my mother followed a different path. After the separation, I, later on, came to have a whole different picture of my mother. We were a family of three, but my mother worked tirelessly to ensure we had a better life than we had before. She is my living proof and inspiration of how much a woman can achieve if she chooses not to be derailed by the negativities around her.

Back in my younger days, getting education as a girl was a challenge. Nevertheless, with her small fish selling business, my mother took me to a standard school. That is where my love for education began. Growing up, I vowed to use my knowledge and be a vessel of change for other women, something that my mother instilled in me. To further my agenda, I asserted to join the education sector and become an educationist to inspire young girls in embracing education so that it will open them up to the world of opportunities.

Puerto Villamil had started blooming with tourist visitations. Every year the number continued rising, a factor that was associated with the natives' warm, receptive culture. Growing up here played a vital role in creating the person in me. As I helped my mother in her fish hotel, I got an opportunity to interact with many tourists visiting the port - giving directions, narrations of my native land, and more so selling my mother's delicious fish. My peoples' culture was in my genes, an aspect that drove me to establish the Puerto Villamil School of Hospitality later in life. This institution devotes itself to empowering the girl child and the local women groups in Isabela.

Growing up in Puerto Villamil came with a set of struggles. From being raised in a dysfunctional family with an absentee father to fighting the patriarchal system in Isabela that did not leave room for women to be in realms of success in the business and education sector. I have been able to reach out to girls in schools and offer mentorship and scholarships through the Puerto Villamil School of Hospitality's Sister's Kitty. This initiative has inspired our young girls to remain in school and pursue their dreams. We have also walked with the local women in Isabela, who own small hospitality enterprises like my mother's to equip them with skills to run and sustain their businesses through free workshops and short courses on hospitality.

We, women, are the beacon of hope to the society. We are the small split of cedar wood that possesses the power to light the dark charcoal and the wet firewood. Our job is to be the spark that shall bring to light the darkest and coldest dreams of our community to bring forth light and warmth that will scare the worst fears of the society.

My Life As A Woman: Egypt Edition #1

When people hear of Egypt, they usually conjure up images of impeccable sand dunes, and the moon shining on the great pyramids of Giza. And being a woman in an Arab country will probably make you think I grew up in a patriarchal household. The truth is my life as an Egyptian girl was the total opposite. I hadn't seen the pyramids of Giza outside of television until I turned 18, and I was raised by two amazing women, my mother and my grandmother, who were both very strong in their own different ways.

The Pearl of the Mediterranean

In the coastal city of Alexandria, where I spent my childhood, there was still magic in the streets. Alexandria is a Mediterranean city with quiet streets and fragrant wet asphalt in winter, and a busy summer crowd by vibrant blue waters in summer. There, reading a news article for the first time at the age of seven, I dreamt of becoming a journalist, "for a news agency," I said, after discovering what a news agency was for the first time. Nobody laughed. While the culture here favors medical professions, I was a bookworm from an early age. Pursuing a somewhat unusual career in writing seemed reasonable for me. My mother frowned and later discussed how dentistry might be a better option. My grandmother smiled and said I always told a good story. Eventually, they both nodded in approval as I graduated with a bachelor's in journalism and took my first career steps.

Struggles and Successes

The thing I struggled most with was perceived as being too independent for a girl of my age. Living alone during university was almost unheard of at the time. My managing the situation with relative ease was even more surprising to new friends and acquaintances. Of course, this has become more common now, and that's one of the things I love the most about Egyptian culture: we are always moving forward and embracing change and progress. This has been especially true in the last decade, with the newer generations facilitating change in several areas in Egypt. I think one of my biggest successes is being a part of this wave of societal change Egyptian millennials significantly contributed to. It is an accomplishment I will forever be proud of.

Shape the World

If I could give all the women out there one piece of advice, it would be this: Be fearless. The world tries to instill fear in all of us along the way: fear of change, fear of failure, and even fear of success. And it is only when we challenge these fears that we are able to connect with our true selves and shape the world around us, instead of letting it shape us.

My writing journey has taken me across the country where I ended up settling in the busy Egyptian capital of Cairo. I'm still a writer, still independent, and still pretty excited to see what the world has to offer.

My Life As A Woman: Egypt Edition #2

Hello all, I am Shrouk Magdy, and in Arabic, Shrouk means sunshine, if we consider that each of us carries a share of her name, then my name always gives me hope, optimism, and brightness. I grew up in Cairo - Egypt specifically in a neighborhood called Nasr City, a neighborhood of a commercial nature characterized by crowding and perpetual movement throughout the day, and it is one of the most vital areas in Cairo.

My childhood was somewhat traditional, as I did not practice a certain sport or a certain hobby until the age of 12 years. I liked playing with other children very traditional games such as hide and seek. At the age of 12, my passion for reading started, and that was because of my grandfather. He was, and still is, my idol. He was a teacher of the Arabic language, a lover of books and reading. He fully believed that reading is the weapon of nations to progress, as it contains all the findings of previous nations that have achieved tremendous progress with few possibilities.

I started reading short stories for children, then realistic short stories, then novels by Egyptian writers such as Naguib Mahfouz, Taha Hussein, and Al-Aqqad, then I realized my love for historical stories that tell the cultures and tales of previous nations. Also, one of my preferences for reading books is related to analytical psychology, as it is an extremely interesting field, as the study of the human psyche carries with its complications as large as the complications of that soul.

With age precisely at the age of 15, I was able to write the first short story from my writings. Of course, it was not perfect, but my grandfather encouraged me at that time to continue writing, but with his death, I was unable to continue writing short stories, but later I took the writing of online work as freelancer to write articles, especially scientific ones.

In high school, my interest in the medical field appeared, especially regarding drugs as medicine. Of course, I took this passion from my father as he is a pharmacist, in addition to my interest in biology and chemistry, and from here I made my decision to study pharmacology, and here I am a student at the Faculty of Pharmacy Cairo University, separating me from my graduation only one semester away, so then I can work in this great field alongside my father.

Because I am an Egyptian loves history and her tales, I always find that the history of Egypt is rich in interesting stories about the different cultures that existed on the land of Egypt during the different eras from the first Pharaonic, Roman, Coptic, and Islamic times to the modern era that was established by Muhammad Ali during the period of the Ottoman caliphate. I can say that what attracts me most in the current culture is that it is a mixture of all of these cultures, in addition to the Egyptians' adherence to a great extent to the values, customs, and traditions.

I can say that women in Egypt are still suffering a lot. In most poor areas, women are still deprived of education to provide them as servants working in the homes of the wealthy, and there are many women who are subjected to family abuse by the husband, and other manifestations of persecution in Egyptian society. But to be honest, there are other women in Egypt who were able to make great progress and were able to reach prominent positions in the country and be the owner of a decision.

This causes a lot confusion about whether Egypt is able to protect women, who may be exposed to injustice, violence, and harassment. In my opinion, Egypt until this time is still divided on the issue of women and still needs more time to put in place laws that guarantee a woman's redress from the injustice imposed on her.

To all the Egyptian women, I hope we all have a decent life, and all my best wishes for you. I hope in the future I can help the largest number of women during my work as a pharmacist. Be strong, do not give up on your dream, do a lot, and win the restrictions of society. Let us pray a lot for a better future for all the Egyptian women.

My Life As A Woman: Egypt Edition #3

My name is Aya and I am a medical student in her last year, working as a freelancer (writer and translator). I grew up in my lovely homeland, Egypt. Drawing is my hobby especially Mandala art. It teaches me patience, relaxing when I'm anxious, bringing peace and tranquility, helping with concentration and pushing aside thoughts to let my creativity flow. I've learned to be responsible since my childhood. My mom travelled abroad to work and I was in the 3rd grade living with my father and since then, I knew to be responsible and I learned a lot of things.

I have studied medicine for 6 years. I enjoy studying it so much that in future, I hope I can complete my study in the US and become ECFMG-certified. That will cost me so much and I want to be independent so I decided to begin a work to help me a bit to achieve my goals and invest my experience in Arabic and English language as a writer and translator.

I think the idea that women shouldn't care about personal success or the work that gets them there is disingenuous; it is impossible for women not to have jobs anymore, so it doesn't make sense to expect them to structure their lives around getting married. The real failure is our cultural incapacity to make room for women to live and thrive outside of traditional conceptions of femininity and relationships. After all, we can eat without marriage, but not without work.

I have researched a lot about freelancing work and finally I decided to become a freelancer on Fiverr. Working as a freelancer allows me to enjoy my freedom, respect my own pace and follow my passion. I believe it helps me get the best out of me because I can adjust my working hours with my study and change locations often. It keeps me awake, curious, and inspired. Freelancing has really helped me find myself again, I feel more responsible for my life and alive. I'm not built for office life. I get extremely antsy when trying to sit still for eight hours a day, and that feeling of being trapped at a desk always made me less productive. But freelancing has freed me to follow my wandering spirit. I now have the pleasure of working with clients across the globe how, where and when I want, establishing good communication with others, knowing more people, and of course, new culture.

I love travelling so much as every country and place is a new experience for me. "We travel, some of us forever, to seek other places, other lives, other souls." – Anais Nin said. I used to be afraid to reach beyond my comfort zone. I think work and travel throwing off the so-called safety net of your comfortable surroundings to discover new parts of the world (and yourself).

Finally, I hope I can reach all my dreams one day, keep my passion up and I hope that every woman will be able to take her own path and realize her dream.

My Life As A Woman: Egypt Edition #4

I am Sarah El-Gindy, born in Cairo, Egypt. I have Turkish and Lebanese origins as well as Bulgarian, but I am Egyptian, my grandfather (father of my mom) who has Turkish origin, Saad Othman, the owner of the largest tourism company in Egypt in the fifties which is Memphis tours, who raised me after the death of my father, and my father was a football player (Gamal El-Gindy) who died when I was 3 years old.

My grandfather and grandmother are my role models. I learned from them the love of life, optimism, strength, love of travel, and knowledge of the customs and traditions of different countries.

I graduated from the Faculty of English Language Department at Cairo University in 2008 and I did not work completely in my studies because my goal was to learn cooking, but I didn't study cooking because it was my favorite hobby during the university and I was looking a lot for different distinct recipes and not traditional because I love food from all countries and Because of my permanent travel to many countries around the world, it made me love to explore their eating habits and distinguish each country in its different recipes and spices.

My mother always cooked very distinctive recipes and had a fine taste in her recipes and learned from her a lot about how to present dishes sweetly. I always tasted any dish and asked for recipe details from chefs in hotels or restaurants or even from my friends and family.

The country that I learned the most cooking art from is India, which is one of my heart's favorite countries, because they have many different spices and their famous dishes with distinctive flavors. I used to travel a lot to India, and to go with the biggest chefs of India in the largest hotels of India. I learned pastries and their special dishes, and also the recipes of other countries.

I got married in 2008 to a civil pilot, who is the father of my children, Lilia and Zain El Din, and we separated in 2019 due to many problems and the suffering of 11 years. And my separation from him made me more powerful and I got to know more about my abilities and my self-confidence. I am a strong woman and I can fulfill myself without a man. Since our separation, from here came the time for my self-realization and to prove myself and achieve my goals and my main goal was to love people in the different cultures of the countries in a simple way. Among my goals is to convey a message to every woman: to love yourself and that you are strong and you draw your strengths from within. Never expect to derive your strength from a man, but you have to prove yourself by yourself and know that you are strong, and difficult circumstances may come and make you feel weak, but never give up, take all the circumstances and make some ambitions, goals and dreams, and never despair.

I learned that self-love is what brings strength to any woman, if you love yourself and my idea of your aspirations, you will be able to achieve them with the will of God. Now I'm a food blogger and lifestyle influencer!

Before my divorce, my page was a private account, because my ex didn't want me to work at all. But after we broke up, I made my account public and all my passion and love for cooking appeared on my page from 10 December 2018.

It was a great challenge to prove myself, and by the grace of God alone, I achieved a large part of my ambitions, which was to publish my recipes to them, and in a year and a half my page grew from 300 followers to 47,000 followers and followers of my page are organic followers.

At the top of the problems during my separation from the father of my children, I decided that the time had come to fulfill my ambitions and myself, and I used to work every recipe with love and passion that made people see my success and gave me great support with their love for me and their application to my recipe, and from here I grew my page and appeared in the largest cooking programs in Egypt. And I have my own online program.

This was a simple part of achieving my goals and it came at the top of my weakness, and now I am at the top of my strength and I will always continue to achieve everything I aspire after, by getting close to people, and my constant search to develop myself for the better.

Finally, I offer you simple advice to every woman who reads my story. You are strong, you can achieve whatever you desire with your love for yourself and your confidence in your abilities that neither age nor anything in the universe makes you ever give up.

Start from today and tell yourself that you are strong, beautiful, and distinguished and that you always deserve the best and do not make anyone in the world underestimate your abilities, be strong with your intelligence, beauty, and abilities.

And I would like to mention and clarify that the Egyptian woman is strong and she can always overcome all difficulties and never give up.

My Life As A Woman: El Salvador Edition

When they ask me where I come from and my answer is El Salvador, it is very common that you should give more explanations than that, and that is my country. I must accept that it is not very well known. I love being a Salvadoran, I was born two years before the signing of the Peace Accords, growing up in the post-war period, it has shown me that we Salvadorans are fighters, we recover very quickly, and we face adversities without hesitation.

I was fortunate to be born into a home with a committed father and a very smart mother for business. Even though both of them did not finish primary education, they have been able to teach me the importance of education, for this reason at a very early age I began to love reading, which helped me to see with curiosity everything around me.

I am sure that throughout our existence we have all been asked some question (or several) that have marked a milestone in our lives. That happened to me, at eleven years old when my mother asked me, "What do you want to be when you grow up?" and my answer was: "I want to be the boss!", I knew that I wanted to be an example and pride for the people around me. Every decision in my life I made according to what I wanted to be, I studied at the only public university in my country, I graduated with honors, but I also enjoyed (and enjoy) life, ah but yes, what I have always avoided to do is to say I cannot. I am convinced that my brain takes the word NO very seriously, therefore I am careful to use it.

It is not unknown that there are too many gaps between men and women, political, educational, salary gaps, I knew this, although I came from a home where I was taught to strive regardless of my gender, society proved to be a little different, now well, you have two options, you sit back and complain without taking action, or you do something to decrease that gap. One of the best strategies we have to direct ourselves to success is to invest in ourselves, and that is what I have done every time I can. In getting my MBA, it opened my eyes to all the opportunities that exist worldwide and since then I seek to acquire more tools that allow me to be a Salvadoran woman who represents and makes her country unforgettable.

Remember, no matter where you come from, we all have what it takes to succeed, sometimes the key is so simple that it is there and we do not see it, so it is an honor to be able to share with you, these four tips, which have allowed me to succeed and be totally happy:

- Read and never stop learning.

- Forget the phrase I CAN'T.

- Create unique experiences that give you joy.

- Don't forget to enjoy today as you prepare for tomorrow.

The only person who will help you to be better every day, you will find her every morning in the mirror.

My Life As A Woman: Eritrea Edition

Warning: This story contains graphic content. Proceed to read with caution.

I was born and grew up in a small town called Dekiamhara which is located in Asmara, Eritrea. I had two brother who died in the border conflict before I was even born. My father was a doctor and also a freedom fighter and my mother was a teacher. I was ten years old but I still vividly remember when I heard a very loud knock at our door very late at night. Me, my mother, and my father woke up from where we were. My father went near the door and gazed through the tiny holes trying to figure out who it was. Two armed men stood there. My father opened the door, and the armed men asked for him. We asked them what was going on and where they were taking him. But they didn't reply, they just took my father away. They didn't even give him a chance to speak. That was one of the worst days of my life, that night we didn't sleep at all. I was crying all night.

My mother knelt down and started praying. The next morning, my uncle came and told us that my father and other freedom fighters had been taken to prison. From that day, we didn't hear a word from my father. We had no choice but to assume that my father was dead. I wanted to be a lawyer when I grew up to solve problems like these. I wanted to make a difference in the lives of people through law. I wanted to uphold justice for the protection of lives' and to improve all the defects in my country's system of administration.

One day my aunt came to spend the night with us. I made coffee and my mother served lunch. Then I went back to my room. "After finishing your homework come and spare some quality time with us," my aunt said. I came back from my study and My aunt spoke, "years have passed now and you are all grown up, you are high school student and you know the government policy...you are going to attend the military service." But my mother said, "you don't have to do that because I don't want you to go through that worst thing. Me and your aunt know there is one great guy we know, and you just have to marry him." I was angry at them. I shouted that marriage was not the answer and that I should face my fate. I know my aunt has inspired me since I was a teenager. She is one of the strongest women I have ever seen. Ever since my father died, she was the first to stand by our side and support our lives. She was with us through thick and thin, but I could not accept her saying something like this.

My aunt spoke, "I know how your mother feels and she started telling me story of her life. She told me how she grew up and that she was a mother of four sons. But she lost the elder in the border conflict and two of them in the Mediterranean trying to flee out of the country for better job opportunity and freedom. And her youngest son was a journalist so most of the time he was imprisoned until at last he was killed. She was left alone at her young age, but she said, 'I am still alive. Every day I gather all the strength I have to wake up to another dark day. What I wanted is to see is a change in the administration, to have the Democracy that we never had.'" After finishing telling her story, aunty asked me to look her in the eye...she told me that she is always on my side and that she respects my decision, but stated, "getting married, having children is one aspects of a happy life but for many of us living in this country you know it is stress. You are always scared of your children being taken to the military, prison, and not being able to have a comfortable life. Your mother loves you and she doesn't want you to go through the things most girls have been through. That is why she is like this," she urged on, "never give up, follow your dream and make a change." All the stories I heard gave me a strength.

By the law, every student in Eritrea must spend their final year of high school at Warasai Yikealo Secondary School and Vocational Training Center no matter where we attended classes before. This system was ultimately designed to ensure that all students have equal access to the university and to create harmonized generations. The school is founded inside a military camp called Sawa, however, we have no guarantee that we will ever be allowed to return to civilian life. The day I attended this camp, my life changed. My life was not mine anymore. I lost my youth here. The service is non-stop. It is just like slavery. The military camp is divided into physical fitness training. Military discipline that includes weapons handling and marching and also academic teaching. As girls, we girls were forced to participate in all the same activities as boys. Most of the time, we women were subjected to sexual assault and harassment by the higher ranks in military. We all had to sleep in one room. I was afraid of getting raped and getting pregnant like the others. The punishments were harsh even for a little mistake like over sleeping.

Me and my friends always thought of running away but your family will be arrested until they find you and anyone caught trying to escape the service will be arrested and detained for long period of time in underground prisons where you will never see a light, in shipping containers at blazing temperatures. They even put your legs up and hit you on the soles of your feet. We were subjected to the torture, abuse, and sexual enslavement. But I said to myself, compared to the life in the camp, nothing bad will happen to me, I will just make sure not to die because I have to change this kind of policy. I have to make sure the sovereignty of the law. Thinking of that dream gave me strength to run away. I barely survived the army's bullets when I fled the country with my friends. I had to hide under trees and also under the dead bodies until it was over. I was so dehydrated and I thought I would die there but I prayed to God to give me the strength to keep going.

Finally, when I got to Ethiopia I felt a little at ease and was not all alone. And stayed in the May Aini refugee camp for a year. They gave us the opportunity to work in the field, poultry farm jobs, etc. Now I am working at the poultry farm and making a living with it. My dream of becoming a lawyer is a must and still on the way. I am also taking online law courses. I am waiting for a day to come to reunite with my mom and aunt.

We women should fight for our freedom and rights; we should try to participate equally with boys in all aspects of life because one day everything will be possible. All we have to do is face the challenges on the way because challenges will make you the strongest. We should fear the fear inside of us. We should take down the government and its policies. Other than this, what I love about my culture is the people are very welcoming, patriots, deeply religious, friendly, generous and very respectful.

My Life As A Woman: Estonia Edition

Hi, I am Annie Pea, and I am from Estonia.

Where did you grow up?

Growing up in a family with three daughters wasn't easy. It was a constant power struggle but we grew together to be a very strong family. I was born in Hanila, a small village near the coastline of Estonia. As a child, I knew that family is the most important part of your life and money will never make you truly happy. But supporting your family is essential. And I wanted to offer the best life to my kids in the future. Barely getting by, we never felt the lack of love and care.

How did you grow up and who inspired you?

I was taught to work hard, love hard, and play hard. It had to be equal. I grew up as a farmer's daughter, always there to help out and learned respect from my young age. Thanks to all the things my parents could teach me, they became my biggest inspiration. I wanted to live up to them. And while picking the best schools for me, I had to understand that to grow as a person, you had to let go of your own comfort and dive deeper into the unknown. So I moved away from home when I was still 15 and it was one of the best decisions I ever made.

What did you study? What did you want to be growing up? Why?

Even if I tried very hard, I can't remember who I wanted to become when I grew up. There were a lot of things but when I was a teenager, I wanted to enroll in the best law school in the country. Probably due to the reason, that I can have arguments and still stay calm and strong, and focused on the process. When I finished high school and started to pick the college, I decided against moving too far away from home. Also, it wasn't the easiest period financially for my parents.

I had always loved making food and everything that's connected to culinary. It seemed like a logical way to go and applied to culinary arts in the major service school in the capital. I happened to land the top place on their listing thanks to my good grades in high school. Two and a half years later, I graduated with a degree in culinary arts (national level).

What do you love about your culture?

My love for my country is endless. I am proud to be an Estonian when you know what we have gone through and how we built up our country after the Soviet occupation. Estonians are hard workers, kind, proud and quiet people. Our culture is something we all cherish deeply. I am proud to say that we are the most digital people on the planet and this is something I am truly proud of. We set an example and others follow.

What you are currently doing for work?

My work currently revolves around staying digital and present. Even though I work as a department leader, service manager, and welding instructor in a wire production company, I am more on the production of creative literature, podcast production, and digital handling.

In December 2019, a very dear friend and collaboration partner started a podcast production company Podcastize. I was offered a place as a creative writer but few months later promoted to the COO position. Partnering up with the most amazing team and people gave me so much inspiration and strength to kick up my career and do something that has a great meaning. It has become my passion and so have the people. It's all love surrounding this. I am extremely lucky to have these people in my life.

Tell me about your struggles as a woman

I have never had trouble proving myself in the business, educational level, or private. It takes dedication and time to plan ahead. And taking risks is kind of my specialty. I am a courageous person, who isn't afraid to say what I think or do what scares me. It's just not in my nature.

As a woman, my biggest struggle has been staying grounded with lots of things. I tend to dream a lot and work too much. In a partnership, I never want to drop the financial responsibility on the other half. So I also work a lot to support my family. As a woman and as a wife, I don't fit in the normal paragraph. So my struggle is toning it down to a normal woman.

Tell me about your success as a woman

I don't brag a lot but when I start to count up the things I have achieved, I am pleasantly surprised. I have managed to score a high paying job position in a company where the majority of top-level leaders are men. I have published novels by writing about my girly dreams, have contracts with two major bookstores in the country, written lyrics about love for an amazing artist. I have met the most awesome people and had incredible adventures.

To a woman, success can come easily or hard. I have been lucky in so many ways and been successful in businesses where men usually rule the leadership. I am blessed.

Provide some advice to women from a woman living in Estonia.

Don't listen to the ones who say: "You can't!" You can and you will. There's only your own fear that will stop you from jumping into that sea of new things.

I always say: "A good heart and sober thinking are the best things you can give yourself."

Think ahead but take risks. They will pay off or won't. At least you tried and you will try again. It's called practice. And practice makes perfect.

Learn how to be comfortable with digital life. Don't stay inside the box and reach outward. Europe, the States, the belly of the Earth - you can work globally like everyone else.

My Life As A Woman: Eswatini (Swaziland) Edition

Swazi women rarely lift each other up because we spend our entire lives learning to share without understanding and we also succeed in different ways. We collectively share home duties with our sisters and mothers. We also collectively share in public successes. Have you seen the Reed Dance? We dance in unison, share in rebuilding the Queen Mother's fence, and collecting the reed. With all this collective sharing and collective contribution, Swazi women rarely go on a personal discovery. Yet to inspire change and empower women, more Swazi women need to learn about personal worth, individual talent, and what it means in her collective space.

I didn't grow up in rural Swaziland until returning home from Norman, Oklahoma in 2018. I never shared these collective experiences. However, I was always a foreigner in my own country. I grew up in the Sugar Belt in a small unicorn-town called Simunye. Simunye had its own rules; Friday night barbeques mixed with cultural and western festivals such as Marula festival and Guy Fox. Consequently, I spent my entire adolescence not fitting into Swazi standards. I was an outspoken 2-years old screaming in her uncle's ear to an 18-year old overweight national swimmer who raced with men in the 200m IM because no girl wanted to do the race. My father joked that I angered the top managers because a trainee's child can't be the top three swimmers in school.

It wasn't always easy. My mother taught us to be strong, but she never taught us personal boundaries because it never existed. She never taught us self-worth and confidence. She is reserved, and so are other Swazi mothers. As an outspoken woman, it became difficult in the workplace. I moved away from Simunye and joined the hot city jungle of Manzini. Previously, I tried hiding my achievements because I was berated for studying in the USA. Yet hiding my achievements was futile. It's never worth hiding your achievements because it didn't change cultural dynamics. Older female partners mixed cultural beliefs with work cultures. A young 28-year never dare speak up in meetings, yet I did.

It's become important to help more women know her self-worth and life's purpose. Whenever a person fuses perceived stress with actual stress it creates projected emotions. This became my experience at work female coworkers wanting us to collectively succeed when I was a manager and they were my subordinates.

Both of us could learn something from that moment. I learned self-worth, personal boundaries, and confidence. My coworker could have learned about personal discovery, and emotional blocks in her lives. Personal discovery would have helped her discover her DNA-purpose. Then self-boundaries would have helped us work in unison while maintaining personal goals.

When I became a Finance & Insurance Manager at 28, I learned there are several managers both men and women who do not have self-worth, who are suffering from trauma and other mental health issues. If you're going to empower Swazi women, begin with teaching them the importance of identifying daily triggers. Unspoken emotions that had erupted into dismissive and competitive behaviour. Give her tools to define her own success and independence.

Allow her to feel safe to achieve those goals, so she won't tear down other women who look successful. I know my life's purpose, which makes the hardships easier to tackle. However, when you're beating through the unknown and experience the storms of life it's tougher to gain passion. Women who know their life's purpose outside of the collective are better able to match the community's needs because they are self-aware.

It's easier for me to bounce back because my purpose enables clearer self-improvement. It also encourages information sharing. Swazi women need clarity in life, so she identifies her emotional blocks and learns to overcome them independently. Growth comes from healing, wisdom comes from making planned mistakes and maturity comes from patience in the journey.

A journey begins with a goal. Empower Swazi women with life goals, so she doesn't have to fear when her coworkers exceed board members' expectations. Empowered women share information on how they failed and succeeded. I am happy to tell women my struggles from anxiety, crying myself to sleep for 10 months if it helps her also accept failure as a part of growth. Give the Swazi woman a collective love to see another sister and mother independently succeed.

My Life As A Woman: Ethiopia Edition

I was born and grew up in a village called Maitafat which is located in Shire, Tigray, Ethiopia. I have two little brothers. My father was a farmer and my mother did the rest of the work inside the house and at the field. I always had to wake up very early in the morning to milk the cows, help my mother in the kitchen and then look after my brothers. After that I got ready to go to school. Actually, there was no school near by the village, so I had to walk on foot for two hours. The way to my school was full of bushes and stiff rocks. So most of the time, I got hurt. There are still bruises on my legs from that time. I endured and I said to myself, my education is all I have to change myself and my family.

I never showed any sign of weakness or tiredness. I was always an active participant in class. With my participation and results, I proved to my teachers that I am equal with all the boys in my class. Due to the fact that there was no school nearby plus harmful traditional beliefs and fear of getting raped, girls were not allowed to get the chance to go to school. So I said to myself that I wanted to be a teacher when I grew up and solve the problem. I wanted to make a difference in the lives of the villagers and students. I wanted to impart life lessons that will never be forgotten and put people in a position to influence their decisions, behaviors, strengths and weaknesses. I also dreamt to open an education center near by my village.

Suddenly, after my father died of heart attack, things began to drastically take a turn for the worse. You know when the bread winner of the family is gone, everything changes. Now my mother had to take care of the farm. So all my relatives and neighbors said I should drop out of school and do the house work and look after my brothers. They said it was enough that I knew writing and reading. At that time, my dreams of becoming a teacher, opening a school, and changing the traditional beliefs turned into ashes. All of a sudden, my mind went blank; I could not think of anything else. I thought dropping out of school was the only choice I had. The hardest and difficult moment was thinking of quitting school but I did what I was told because I did not want my mother to bear all the burdens. I helped her 24/7 with whatever she needed.

My mom inspired me ever since I was a little girl. She is one of the hardest working women I have ever seen. Without ever questioning me, she has stood by my side and supported my ideas. She knows how her children are feeling by just looking us in the eye. One day, when I was helping my mother in the field she said, "let me tell u a story of my life that I never shared with anyone else." She told me how she grew up and that she did not get the chance to go to school because she was a girl. Since she was the first child, she had to look after the cows and her six siblings. She did all the hard work and then at her very young age, she was forced to get married to my father who was thirty years older than her. After finishing telling her story, my mom asked me to look her in the eye... "my daughter, doing the house works and the farm is all that I can do; I got used to it very long time ago so I never got tired. I love you and I don't want you to go through the things I have been through." She continued with joy in her tears, "I see a bright future in your eyes. Do not make it go away... you should continue school. Follow your heart, follow your dreams, and make a change." Her words were sincere and it gave me a strength to study up to my potential, so I continued from where I left off.

Finally, my dream of becoming a teacher came true. Now I am helping my family financially and I am creating awareness to the villagers about the use of knowledge, value of women in society, and the harmful traditional beliefs that has to be rid of and so on. And I am also supporting women who still don't get access to school.

We women should fight for our freedom; we should try to participate equally with boys in all aspects of life because if we want something from deep inside our heart, everything will be possible. Don't be afraid of challenges on the way. Face the obstacles because challenges will make you the strongest.

In addition to the plays, dressing style, coffee ceremony, and foods, what I love about my culture is that the people are very welcoming, deeply religious, and friendly. Generous and very respectful.

My Life As A Woman: Fiji Edition #1

I was brought up in an Orphanage from the ages of four to nineteen years old. It was a strict religious Methodist institute, where we had our devotions every single day at 6 am and 6 pm. I only knew of church, school and the Orphanage. I grew up without knowing both my biological parents but not until I left the Orphanage.

As a young adult today, I never did once see them as parents but strangers. My guardian who was also the Matron at the time, was my role model. She was my hero while I was growing up and she still remains one even when I'm old enough to believe in superheroes. She gave me the love I wanted and needed, she held my hands and hugged me when I was a child. While growing up, I was always told that education was the key to better life once achieved. I am only educated with my secondary education (high school) and completed the five years required. Just like any other child growing up, I wanted to become many things and to help people. For example, a doctor, an astronaut, a scientist, a lawyer, and others which I don't remember.

Despite my education level, I have worked several places and have gained many experiences with life skills. Because of my upbringing, I see myself as a multicultural person. I can easily adapt to outlook, attitudes, values, morals, goals, and customs shared by a society. I understand several languages and speak them too. As a result, I feel that I belong to a large family of any culture in the Pacific and I love this.

Due to this global pandemic, I lost my job. But before this, I worked for a Local Tour Company. A few struggles as a woman, is that people see you as weak and helpless. And that you are to be dependent on man, and that your voice is never heard. On the contrary, being successful as a woman is rare in the South Pacific (Fiji). I am an independent woman and I pursue my goals. I was once told and I would advise another woman the same; never let the odds keep you from doing what you know in your heart what you were meant to do. You are a strong woman.

My Life As A Woman: Fiji Edition #2

Fiji is an archipelago of over 300 islands in the South Pacific. My country is most famous for its crystal blue waters, white sandy beaches, and extremely friendly people. Although our population isn't big, our hearts surely are. I grew up in the capital city of Suva, one of the most developed and populated area in the whole of Fiji. Before moving to Suva, my family and I had been moving from place to place, mainly in coastal and nearby rural areas. Growing up, we didn't have much but in saying that, we had more than what other ordinary Fijians did.

Before we moved permanently to Suva, my parents had bought their first home in the coastal area of Sigatoka, which just happened to be right next to a traditional Fijian village. One of my favorite memories from that time is being invited by the village kids to their 'bures' in which they lived in, for a nice hot traditional meal that was made in an underground earth oven.

This was the first time I had experienced the real traditional Fijian way of life. The kids and their fathers would go fishing and visit their farms for fresh produce that would be used for their daily meals because they couldn't afford much from the stores. Traditionally, the food is placed on a mat, on the floor, and everyone sits around the mat for their meals. This was quite new to me as I didn't quite understand why they didn't use tables. I would be treated as one of them as if I was part of the family. After lunch, the kids and I went for a swim in a nearby river and enjoyed the rest of the day. While this doesn't sound like much, this is genuinely how villagers live their lives.

I am of mixed race and growing up, I only got to meet my paternal grandad who had migrated to Fiji from China by boat during WW II. This man was my inspiration. He would tell us his incredible story of survival after being taken hostage by the Japanese during the war and the hardships of making life or death decisions to ensure his family would live. He was also a magnificent artist and would paint every memory he had during his lifetime. This man taught me strength, patience, wisdom, and what it means to be true to myself, and I wish he was still here with me today.

Growing up, just like other kids, I wanted to be many things. I wanted to be a nurse, a singer, an actor, a pastry chef, a shopkeeper, a dancer and the list goes on. When I reached high school, I still wasn't sure what career path I wanted to follow, but because I felt I was running out of time, I made the quick decision to study Tourism at University, as it's the biggest industry here in Fiji.

A year ago, after many ups and downs, I had graduated with a bachelor's degree in Tourism & Hospitality Management. Upon graduation, I worked as a reservations agent for a hotel in Suva and I'm currently working at a non-governmental organisation as an administrative assistant to the CEO.

My favorite thing about Fiji and our culture is the love and kindness we have for each other, which is quite difficult to see in other countries. If we see someone struggling to make ends meet, we provide something to them with the little we're able to offer and don't expect anything to return. We may not have a lot, but we do have big hearts to help everyone and anyone in our communities. Fiji is slowly but surely moving towards a society where we empower and support women for who we are and what we want to achieve. However, our society can be very judgmental of women for any wrong choices we have made.

One of my biggest struggles as a woman, was the judgment I experienced when I became a teenage parent. I was only 18 when I had conceived with my high school sweetheart and it brought a lot of shame to my family, especially my mother. My secret was out before I could even reveal it. I was thought of as a "good girl" before my pregnancy and I later became "the slut", while my boyfriend at the time was praised. My mother was so ashamed that she wouldn't want my bump to show. She would tell me to walk, sit and stand a certain way so that it wouldn't be so obvious and to wear lose fitting clothing. If we were at a restaurant and someone we knew had walked in, we were all forced to leave the restaurant so that I wouldn't be seen "that way". Fiji is a faith based country and a situation such as a teenage pregnancy would be classified a sin and because of that, traditional Fijian families in most cases, would force the expecting couple into marriage befo

re the baby arrives.

Additionally, I struggle with the primitive idea that woman must take care of the household while men are able to get away with anything. I am currently being faced with the issue of being expected to take care of the house, the baby and go to work simply because these were traditionally the roles of women in society.

I would say my biggest successes as a woman would be graduating with my bachelor's degree while taking care of my newborn and gaining my black belt in Karate a few years ago.

My advice to women living in Fiji would be to follow your heart and do more than what society expects us to do because we are capable of being and doing bigger things in life. Get out of our comfort zones and work towards what we wish to achieve.

My Life As A Woman: Finland Edition #1

25 years ago, I was born in the happiest country in the world – Finland. Even if we officially got the title of "the happiest people in the world" recently, it describes my childhood perfectly. Happy. I'm the oldest child of three. In kindergarten, I was timid and shy but loved telling stories and later on, I started living in books and dreaming of faraway lands. The teenager me always followed the rules, never daring to chase her dreams. It felt safer back then. But slowly the way my parents and people around me lived began to mirror in my personality and made me the young woman I have grown to be.

My mum owns a handicraft shop. When I and my sister were kids, she worked from home at her own business. My dad, on the other hand, has owned two businesses in fields I can't even name. Something to do with construction and windmills. But it's not just my parents – my grandpa has his own vet clinic, my uncle owns a business with my dad, and there's a handful of actors, dancers, painters, and artists in my family.

Parents always want what is best for their kids and so my mum and dad have always tried to tell me and my siblings to just get normal office jobs. They don't hide how hard it is to own your own business. In fact, they would prefer us to just live like most people working from nine to five. Instead, the three of us have learned from a young age what it's like to work for yourself in a job you love. "You can do anything you want." That's what our parents have taught us with their own example.

To put it simply – I was never made aware of the fact that I could have a hard time achieving something for being a woman. There are only a few memories from my childhood I can recall regarding gender. My mum trying to make me wear dresses to family gatherings. Girls being jealous of the sports classes boys had in a primary school. Some toys, jobs, or sports classified as boys' and some as girls' even if you could still take part in them without any real trouble.

My life as a woman has been easy when compared to many other countries all around the world. And it's not a surprise. Finland was the first country in Europe to give the right to vote for women in 1906 and just earlier this year, Sanna Marin – 35 years old, strong independent woman – was selected as our prime minister. In fact, 12 out of 19 ministers in our current government are women. Because I live in Finland, I don't have to often think of myself as a woman. When I stay in my home country, the struggles I have are mostly the same as men's. Any job opportunity is possible to accomplish. My voice is heard. Whatever I act girly or boyish as a woman, both are acceptable.

I want to end my story with advice for all the amazing, powerful, and independent women out there. (And don't try to fight me on this – I have yet to meet a woman who isn't all of the above deep down!) In my own life, I follow the quote below by a well-known Finnish author who happens to be an inspiring female.

"It is simply this: do not tire, never lose interest, never grow indifferent—lose your invaluable curiosity and you let yourself die. It's as simple as that." – Tove Jansson

In Finland, we are taught to be curious and always use our brains. That is my advice for women all around the world. Listen to others but never fully believe anyone without first making your own assumptions on the matter. Read a lot. Explore subjects that interest you even when others declare them as unnecessary. But first and foremost, love yourself and be yourself. It may sound corny but we only have this one life to live.

My Life As A Woman: Finland Edition #2

Me

I was born and raised in Finland, in a medium-sized city called Espoo. It's part of the Helsinki Metropolitan Area, which includes Espoo, Helsinki as well as Vantaa. As an area, the Helsinki metropolitan area differs considerably from the rest of Finland: a large part of the entire Finnish population lives here. Despite the slightly larger population, living here is peaceful and safe. As a residential area, Espoo is still very diverse: large shopping malls, events, and a lot of people, but also forests, nature trails, and national parks. So I grew up in the city, but still really close to nature.

Career

My parents are both highly educated, so I always think of them as role models. Because of this, I wanted to invest in education myself. In Finland, education is free, so after primary school, I decided to study two degrees at the same time. I studied in high school as well as a vocational school and graduated with a double degree in economics. One reason why I value education so much myself is because there are always strong social disadvantages luring for women when, for example, applying for a job. It's against the law and norms to decide the applicant on gender, but inevitably, it happens still today. Therefore, as a young woman starting a career, there lurks a feeling that you have to keep more doors open to yourself than even necessary. Fortunately, it is becoming more and more common that you will not have to state your gender nor your name when applying for jobs. This would not only improve women's chances in their careers, but also limit any discrimination regarding ethnicity, appearance, and maybe even age. An anonymous job application would as a method leave room to evaluate aspects that a person can have an effect on themselves; degrees, skills, and achievements. Currently I am working in financial management at one of Finland's best-known companies. Most of my colleagues are women, although in general the economic sector could be imagined to be male-dominated.

Culture

Finnish culture consists of North European, Swedish, and Russian cultures. Some causes behind Finland's diversified culture can be found looking back at Finland's history before becoming independent just over a hundred years ago. Of the last thousand years, one hundred were spent under the Russian empire and a greater 500 under Swedish rule. This arguably - after many ups and downs - forged a social capitalist welfare state, where education is essentially available for everyone, and the disadvantaged are taken care of by the state by redistribution of income and tax income. One of the many good things this allows is that financially unstable people, for example, young students or even low-income single parents can study when they have or want to.

Finnish culture is something that you have to experience on the spot to fully understand it as it will also often differ in detail from region to region. In the world, Finns are known for their quiet and even introverted nature and manners, but this is rooted in the fact that Finns value their own space and modesty. Other values that are important to Finns are honesty, independence, individuality, and equality.

Strong roots

The Soviet Union invaded Finland during the second world war. While war is frankly never straightforward a driver of development, this one did drive women's role in today's Finnish society. When most able-bodied men had to put their jobs and duties on hold to respond to their call-up - including over 20,000 voluntary women who maintained and serviced the frontlines - women had to tend the nation, even under enemy bombshells.

Nationally over half of the whole industrial workforce consisted of women during the war, while at the same time, many had to take care of their families and raise their children. These willful and strong women laid stable foundations for us modern women to stand on today, to further improve equality and progressivity.

Today

As of 2019, the current Finnish prime minister - the second-youngest prime minister in the world - Sanna Marin runs a female-dominated government, being 2/3 female ministers. She has jokingly stated to Time that now the council of state can do decisions while in the sauna. While being a funny remark, it is also a reminder of an important milestone in history, as this has not been possible before, not for female ministers.

In conclusion

My advice to other women would be to study and learn something new every day. Whatever your goals are set your own standards high. It can be something big, small, complex, or easy. And most of all, dare to be right.

My Life As A Woman: France Edition

Hi, I'm Meghane Poulet but everyone calls me Meg. I'm 25 years old and I was born in a town called "La Teste de Buch", just outside of Bordeaux, in the south west of France. I was born in France but actually grew up in the States, in a big city called Dallas, in the state of Texas. Growing up in the States was the best because there's an infinite amount of adventures you can go on with just a car and a love for road trips. I guess that's what gave me the ever-lasting love for travelling and the itch to become a nomad. My full time job is to be a world class touring circus performer but recently I've just been a world class "staying" performer, living in France.

We've been in full lockdown for almost a full eight weeks as I write this, and funny enough, I had the realization the other morning that this is the most I've been in France (at a time) in the last 10 years (not working). It's interesting that I find myself writing this because if you would have heard me speak only 3 months ago, you would have heard me SWEAR that I would never want to be living in France at the moment, and not at least for the next 20 years. I hated France. Now don't be frightened by this sentence as you'll come to see that that's no longer the case, but I need to start from the beginning for this whole thing to make sense.

I hated France. The people were rude and always complaining, women more than men, in my experience, which really upset me even more. The economy was unstable and the country began to feel unsafe in the last couple of years. A bit over 8 weeks ago, I had just finished a French tour with the company I was working with and decided I would stick around to spend some quality time with family before moving on to the next gig. And then it happened. Within days, COVID-19 is officially announced a pandemic, I lose every gig I had planned for the next six months, and France goes into full lockdown, which means I'm stuck. In France, with no work. Until further notice. I was an emotional mess. I was stuck in a country where I felt unsafe, unhappy and estranged. It took me a couple of weeks before I was able to admit to myself that this wasn't going to "be a matter of a couple of weeks". So I made the life changing decision to start learning how to live with it. And guess what? I started to love it. All of it. The city felt safe and calm and the people I would come across in the street would all say hello to me and share a smile: ESPECIALLY WOMEN.

I decided to find out more about performers rights in the country because you may or may not know this but being a female circus performer is quite challenging. We are quickly underestimated, not taken as seriously as men and put into separate categories: pole dancer (who are incredibly strong by the way), "can you do the splits but in your underwear?", "oh but you're clearly not strong enough to be considered for this gig". Turns out living in France as a Woman AND a Performer is incredible; it was the loveliest surprise I could have come across. The equality between male and female performers in France is incredible because there is a special status made just for them that is called "intermittence du spectacle" which basically translates to "entertainment industry".

It works like this: you have to prove you have a minimum of 507 hours of work in the next year, in your artistic activity. When that is done, your revenues are calculated and instead of being paid per gig, you're paid equally every month which is AMAZING for performers. Having financial stability when being an artist is the number one thing you kind of agree to let go of when you pursue your passion so this status is just incredible. Every person is paid fairly for their amount of work and nobody is paid less than 507 hours. No more "how is half of the pay since you probably can't do what that guy does?". What a time to be alive as a Woman living in France.

My Life As A Woman: French Guiana Edition #1

Where did you grow up?

I am a Guyanese woman, I grew up in the town of Grand-Santi in the village of Mofina. It's a city that is west of Guyana.

How did you grow up?

In poverty but I lacked nothing, because I made a living from fishing and our agricultural harvest from Monday to Saturday farming and during my free time, I sewed (Pangui). The Pangui is a traditional towel on which we express our emotions, our thoughts, and our feelings.

Did you have parents or maybe a grandmother who inspired you?

I did not grow up with my parents, my father I never knew him, he left after my birth. It was my grandmother who raised me who took care of me and took me as much as a woman. My grandmother is a hardworking woman, an inspiring woman.

What did you study? / What did you want to be growing up? / Why?

I studied sewing with my grandmother, our culture and traditions, among the Boeshinengue.

What do you like about your culture?

What I like most in my culture is the atmosphere and our traditional in, which is the Awassa. During my school curriculum, I did administration, economic, and social license.

What do you currently do for work?

I am an accountant in a small business of 6 employees. I take stock, I save the results in Excel, I give my opinion on stocks.

Tell me about your difficulties as a woman

At the time as a Guyanese woman, the difficulty is not being able to discover the pleasures of life.

Tell me about your success as a woman

For me my success is to have become an independent woman who doesn't need a man to get by.

Advice to the women of a woman living in French Guiana

Yes, I have a piece of advice for all Guyana women, it is never to give up on our dreams because you only need little to succeed without the help of men. A woman deserves respect and we are pure, family life is one of the best weapons to succeed.

My Life As A Woman: French Guiana Edition #2

I was born in the capital, Cayenne. Nonetheless I used to live by the countryside until the early age of 2 years old, my parents split up and my mother realised that I would have better chances and a better lifestyle in the city. Therefore, I grew up in a monoparental home. Like most families here in French Guiana, I was raised by an immigrant single mother and became a big sister at the age of five years old. It was a humble home and there were so many things we couldn't afford but my mother always managed to reach our needs, up until now, she is always looking forward to giving us the best education possible and teaching us the best behaviors.

There are two main women that inspired and still inspire me today. My mother and my grandmother (my father's mother) they both had a rough and sometimes painful past, lost dear relatives, went through thick and thin without the help of a man in their lives but kept going on until they managed to make themselves respected by their community. These are the role models I intended to follow when I grew up and already follow, day by day.

I had an excellent education, whether it was at school or at home, my mother always helped me with homework, even though she wasn't a native, she would help me in her birth language. I also succeeded thanks to the help of great teachers and all the dedication I had and motivation. I actually have an accountant two-year technical degree and I am working even harder to obtain a second two-year technical advanced course in human resources. Most of my friends gave up on school and a priceless gift that is knowledge, I didn't follow their expectations and kept on my efforts. Why didn't I stop my studies? Well because I want people to see that I can do better and succeed out of my comfort zone.

There are so many things that I love about my culture. Our traditional meals, our folkloric music, the traditional attire, the historical places and the tales behind. I do appreciate that no matter how hard my culture's past used to be due to slavery, it has moved on to bloom into a beautiful society with beautiful citizens.

I currently work at the local McDonalds, it helps me to save money for my future projects, for my driving license, and it also helps me to reach for my family's needs and be part of the working force. I feel useful and actually am useful, I will not stay there for long but I made good friendships and even met strong leading female role models.

As a woman, a daughter, a sister, and probably a future mother and in almost every society, it is hard to make yourself heard, known, respected or even considered as a competent and efficient human being, we are in a constant pursuit of validation, in a constant need to prove everyone else that we are equal to men. It is a long road and we are not even there yet but we are getting there, step by step. Education is my biggest success, it allows me to do anything I am willing to do, it allows me to be competitive in a man's world, it allows me to be a future leader and inspire future generations of struggling women and why not men as well.

If I could give some advice for the generations to come or the current generation, it would be to stay at school as long as possible, gather all the knowledge you can and keep your main goal in mind. Do not let anything or anyone drag you down, real friends will understand, fake ones will distract you from your main objectives. Stay close to your family, or at least to that one relative that will give enough motivation and courage to keep on. Do not follow others, it is okay to not have the latest phone or the latest designer clothes as long as you stay focused on what you really want, the rest is just superficial, do not tell them about your projects, they might get jealous and do anything to see you fall or ruin your ambitions. And most importantly, do not forget that you exist and deserve to take care of yourself and love yourself, at the end of the day, it is just you and yourself, you make your choices, you take your responsibilities, you live your life the way you want to live it.

My Life As A Woman: French Polynesia Edition

Hi, my name is Karerenui Tiare. I grew up on a small island called "Rurutu" in French Polynesia. "Rurutu" is an island located in the archipelago of Austral, it's really far away from Tahiti. Rurutuis is known for its steep cliffs and caves. There are only 2,466 habitants on my island. Most of them are elders and we have a lot of respect for our elders. We had a goat farm and we made milk with my grandmother to provide for the village. We used to have pigs too, one was named "Mata" which means "eyes" because he had brown circles around the eyes.

In "Rurutu" we did not have electricity so we lived with gas lamps, but it was no problem because we were so used to living like that and my childhood was fun, we used to go fishing every morning with my dad. My dad was my real inspiration. A true warrior, fisherman, and he used to work on the coconut tree farm. He provided for our family everyday with food and love. We used to plant taros everywhere in our "fa'apu taro" which means taro field. Taro is our base ingredient in our alimentation in "Rurutu" as it gives us our strength and proteins.

Growing up, I realized that I wanted to do more than just fishing and living on my little paradise of "Rurutu". I would always watch the boat come from Tahiti who came to bring people to Tahiti and I always wondered how it was there. So I moved to Tahiti, the main island of French Polynesia. It was hard to leave my family and island behind but I had to do it in order to explore more.

Polynesians are really friendly, you would walk in front of a house in the morning and everyone would be screaming "Hey! Come eat breakfast" it's a common thing here. The culture and the people are so rich. We love dancing; our dance is called "Ori Tahiti" and is very popular around the world noticeably in Japan! They love dancing Ori Tahiti!

I am currently a secretary at an insurance company, not the most exciting job there is but I can provide for my family on my own. Women are really respected in French Polynesia, I think more than in other countries. A woman can do whatever she likes to do and won't be judged. I'm proud to be a Polynesian woman. My biggest success as a woman is my kids. I love my kids and I am blessed to have them.

Don't ever let anybody tell you that you can't do it. You can do whatever you want to do in life. Women around the world, be strong and be yourself. Love yourself, love your culture. In Rurutu, the women do the copra (coconut culture) that shows how strong our women are. Rurutu girls are known for being really strong and dominant. We are a strong community and we love our culture more than anything in the world.

My Life As A Woman: Martinique Edition

My name is Marie-Louise Dominque. I grew up in a beautiful place called Saint Joseph, it was a small community where everyone lived like one family. Growing up was not a breeze, at the age of 14, I got pregnant and was placed in a government home. As some people think it might have been the worst decision ever, but it turned out to be the best. In that place was my new mother and father (adopted parents), they treated me like their very own as well as my daughter. It wasn't my daughter and I alone; we had company so we all lived like one big happy family.

My inspiration came from a man named Lucide. In Martinique, while attending school you needed to do some form of internship so that you would've been able to put yourself on the market or show recruiters and managers what you're made of. I met him at the age of 15 and it was really hard to deal with. I saw that man as my father and he saw the best in me as his daughter. Upon completing school, he took me to work with him and introduced me to his family. I learned how to cook through him and now we are alike today. I stand here with a big smile on my face, for I am grateful!

I went to Culinary School to become a Chef or an assistant chef. I have always dreamed to have my own restaurant where I can collaborate my own dish. I love cooking! Every time someone devours my dishes, I feel good, especially when they return to tell me about the "moment of truth" they experienced with my dish. The culture in Martinique is a unique one, I really love the togetherness; brothers and sisters will fight but will always look out for each other. No child is ever too old to take directives from his/her parents. Women are being well protected or represented, for example, if you have an abusive boyfriend. It's all about helping each and giving everyone an opportunity to do something. Women and their kids are their priority! I really love it. They assist the women greatly with finances to send the kids to school and to pay rent which work wonders. The people of the land are very friendly for you wouldn't have to be established friends to carry a conversation. At that very moment you become family to them.

Currently I'm a stay at home mom, I get paid from the Revenu Sans Activités (RSA) by CAFF meaning money without work. I bake bread and make bakes for a friend to sell at her restaurant and also sell Ancient African Remedies. I do small jobs but ideally don't have a permanent job.

The men up here are strange, I struggled with them, this why on a day like today, I have earned respect. It's a struggle sometimes to find a job without being harassed or having to sleep with a man for one. You, as a lady need to learn your laws and use it wisely. Don't sell your body for a dime. 95% of women struggle with these men so much, so that they implemented some laws and opened some businesses where the ladies could go in to report and take the men to court. It is difficult to raise kids without a father, which is the reason for the struggle I went through with my kids in the beginning. You, as the mother, I have to play both rolls, however, I did that for some years and it was rough.

My greatest success is my daughter; I slept on the streets with her for four days. I suffered a lot with her due to teenage pregnancy. My family members betrayed me so much so they thought I would never make it. They made me believe I couldn't have made it as well, and this is why I stand here and say my daughter is my success. I've kept her under my wings, love her, shield her, and right now she's excelling in school. I'm sorry to say but I'm hard on her and I am working hard to get her to where she wants to be. My heart races for her, what I went through, I don't want her to go through it, this is why I do my best to take keep her sane.

My advice to the women living in Martinique, is educate yourself on the different laws that is in place. Don't allow men to deprive you of anything. Conquer it all, keep your head up! Always stay positive let nothing over power you.

My Life As A Woman: Mayotte Island Edition

Where did you grow up?

I was born in the Mayotte Hospital Center, in Mamoudzou. Since my parents are divorced, I used to travel back and forth between Mamoudzou (my mom's city, also my dad's workplace) and Kani-Kéli (my dad's village).

How did you grow up?

I've had a happy childhood. Growing up on this Muslim island as a woman was very restrictive. In Mayotte, women have way less freedom than men. But at the same time, Mayotte, being a French department has become an open-minded and relativistic island. However, everything depends on the education that is instilled in the children.

Did you have parents or maybe a grandmother that inspired you?

My parents are the most inspiring people I know. Starting as an electrician/cleaner, my father has become one of the most reliable people in his company. And by working as ATSEM (territorial agent specialized in nursery schools), for about fifteen years, my mother managed to pass her CAP (certificate of Professional Competence), which allowed her to become a kindergarten teacher. My parents gave me love, education, and respect values.

What did you study/what did you want to be growing up/why?

I did a Literary Bachelor's Degree in Mayotte. Then I studied fine-arts at a university in France. I've always wanted, and I still want to become a professional lyricist/songwriter; because the art that runs through my veins is the art of handling words.

What do you love about your culture?

I love everything about my culture. I love the fact that we're an archipelago of several islands. I love the riches we have; the lagoon, our varieties of edible and non-edible plants, the animals that live by our sides, our dialects, our "joie de vivre", our customs, our traditional songs and dances, etc.

What are you currently doing for work?

I am currently unemployed. I offer my writing services on Fiverr because it allows me to get a foothold in this dream job that I want to have, for the long term.

Tell me about your struggles as a woman?

To be honest, I think if I wasn't a woman, several things wouldn't have happened to me. Especially, the fact that, a man sexually abused me when I was five. I managed to stand back up from that drama. But this kind of monstrosity is unfortunately very common in Mayotte, as everywhere in the world. Despite all that, if I wasn't a woman, I wouldn't have been as strong, as open-minded, as confident, loving, respectful, and down to earth as I am today.

Tell me about your successes as a woman?

When I think of success, I think of a perfect job that allows you to have a great life and great life experiences. So, since I do not have a job, I am unable to say that I am successful right now.

As a woman, I am successful because, in spite of my background, I managed to make my own choices and have my own voice, and I've used that power so I don't get pushed around by some people.

As a woman from Mayotte, could you provide some advice to women?

My advice/message to women around the world is: Know your value. And don't let anyone mistake that knowledge for selfish or self-centered behavior. You're worth living. You're worth speaking. You're worth breathing.

My Life As A Woman: New Caledonia Edition

I was born in Lifou, New Caledonia, and it is a place that I would spend half of my life. I grew up in a loving family of musicians, and we would perform as a band during the weekends at various locations. Our performances were carried out in Drehu, an indigenous language, and thus, the performances were targeted towards preserving our culture and allowing visitors to appreciate the culture. I learned most of the values through my music, which addressed the roles of women and men in society. My mother was also critical in my development as a woman and assured me that the biggest obstacle in life would be my imagination. I treasured the trips that we took with the family when going to perform as this brought the family much closer. However, this would not last as the band started breaking when my siblings and I had to go to college. I had always dreamt of performing music and owning my studio. Thus, I pursued a Music and Arts course and started my journey to become a star.

The beginning of my career was tough, especially finding gigs that pay well. But this I knew was a consequence of being in the music industry in the country. One gender-specific issue was how I was advertised for the few gigs I got. The posts focused on me being a woman rather than pointing out my skills or what I was to offer. On one occasion, an unnamed event organizer asked me to dress in fashionable short dresses that would lure more fans. This statement was hurtful, and being treated as an object of the male gaze undermined my music. I was so desperate for money at the time, and I did the most shameful thing I have ever done and dropped my preferred cultural performance dress for the scanty clothes. I did not have anything against such garments, but their implication in my situation left me embarrassed. I had given up my power and abandoned my musical beliefs. This situation introduced me to how women are viewed in some aspects of society and why they have to be strong.

After this shameful day, I swore never to subject to patriarchy demands. However, I would still be on the receiving end of some sexual harassment by clueless individuals who believed they were flirting. I managed to open my studio in my home town, and my sole purpose was to help young women musicians kickstart their careers. This was a huge success for me as I chose to stick with my beliefs even though I did flatter when I was a naïve young musician. The studio is meant to empower women to fight their battles and stick with their values by producing the music that they want.

My advice to women in New Caledonia is that you will always face challenging decisions in the pursuit of your dreams. In such a situation, you should stick with your beliefs. Sexual harassment is not the norm, and women should learn to stand for themselves. You should not allow such behavior to continue, as this means that you will lose your power.

My Life As A Woman: Saint Barthélemy Edition

I am Alaina, I grew up in Gustavia, formerly known as Le Carénage, in St Barthélemy. When I was younger I lived with both of my parents in a little beach house. It was less than 10 steps from the beach. My mother was a housekeeper for a villa in the city while my father was a fisherman. Both of my parents played an active role in my life. We would have family nights every Sunday, on those nights we would have dinner together, watch television, and just enjoy talking to each other.

My father wasn't always home for dinner because he goes fishing in the night, so it's really special when he comes home. My mother inspired me the most, she had a hard childhood growing up, but she still tried her best to have something for herself. Her parents were roamers, they never stayed in one place for more than a few months so she never got a fair chance at an education. When she was old enough, she left and found my father. She then got some vocational training and became a housekeeper. Even though that's not a 'high and mighty' job, I know how hard she had to work to be where she is now.

When I was younger, I always aspired to be a lawyer, because of my love for justice. I attended the École primaire Gustavia, then my parents sent me to St. Maarten to live with my aunt so I could attend secondary school. I attended the St. Maarten Academy, where I achieved 8 CXC subjects and 8 units of CAPE during my tenure there. I received a scholarship to attend the University of California. I studied law while working part-time to support myself. After graduating, I worked at a law firm based in the United States of America. I am a criminal lawyer, I have worked on many cases; for the rich, the poor, the innocent, etc.

St. Barts will always have a special place in my heart. I love our Swedish influenced architecture; I remember visiting places like the Wall House Museum and Vieux Clocher when my father was home. I was always in awe. Our beaches are to die for; Saline Beach and Flamands Beach. The powder-like white sand, the wind caressing my skin, and the smell of the ocean. Also, our cuisine is the perfect mix of Asian, Caribbean, and European.

While growing up, I longed for the feeling of belonging. I have never felt that I belonged. My environment was constantly changing, from moving from Gustavia to St. Maarten, then to the States. I didn't get a chance to make friends or enjoy where I was living, as soon as I started to enjoy something I felt like it was taken from me. Even with the constant changing of my environment, I learned how to adapt to any situation that I was faced with, how to make priorities, and read people's behavior. Another plus of constantly traveling was being able to see different places and experience different types of cultures.

My advice to all the women of St. Barts is, 'It doesn't matter where you're coming from, what matters is where you're going.' Meaning even if your life is a little difficult now, you can overcome that. Don't underestimate your strength and worth, you just need to be determined and keep your mind set on the goal.

My Life As A Woman: Saint Pierre and Miquelon Edition

Hey everyone, my name is Josephine Andre. I have lived in St. Pierre all my life, I have never been outside of St. Pierre. I was the daughter of a fisherman and baker. My parents only had me and my sister. We live in a small house close to the sea. Growing up, I was very close to my parents. I would always go fishing with my father every Saturday morning and bake with my mother in the evenings. We had a great relationship, the only person I didn't have a good relationship with was my sister. She always wanted more, she didn't like St. Pierre at all. My parents inspired me the most, to me, they had a perfect life; they had a home, two children, and a great relationship. I always wanted that type of stability.

I attended the Henriette Bonin School, then to the Émile Letournel School. I honestly wasn't too interested in school, I procrastinated and spent my time fantasizing about the future. I was more interested in other things; beauty, children, and relaxing. I did average at school, I only did enough to graduate. Growing up I wanted to become a model, but that aspiration died after I understood the modeling industry, which was more a specific type of female; skinny, tall, and beautiful. I didn't fit into that category, I was the opposite, I was weighty and short. With that I started to feel I wasn't good enough, I questioned myself; why I didn't fall into that category and why I wasn't pretty enough. Due to that, I tried to change myself, I started exercising or trying to exercise. I realized I was doing all that for the wrong reasons, so I stopped and started to better myself. In the long run, I gained back my self-confidence. I didn't have to fit into society's views of a beautiful woman. I am now confident about being a little weighty and short.

Eventually, I gave up the dream of ever being a model and ended up following my mother's footsteps and became a baker. I have been working as a baker since high school and I enjoy baking. I love everything about St. Pierre, from the architecture to the pastry shops. Our architecture is very vintage with a colorful touch to it. Just by the color of a building, you could tell what store we were talking about. The pastries are amazing, it's inspired by the French, seeing as we are a department of France. St Pierre makes the best croissants ever, I have had my fair share of croissants. I also really love our unity as a community, everyone is just warm and welcoming.

To all the women of St Pierre and Miquelon, it's okay not to fit into society's views. You just need to be you, having self-confidence is mandatory. It will only make you a better person, more productive, and make better decisions.

My Life As A Woman: Wallis and Futuna Edition

Wallis and Futuna is a fantastic island, and growing up in this area was amazing. The bond that people share as a community is amazing, and I don't think that there is any other area where people are this close. My name is Agnes Saputo, growing up, I always loved the ceremonies where each family was able to contribute to the feast. I loved this culture because I got to meet multiple children my age and always made friends from other villages. The feast, too, was excellent as I got to taste plenty of food. My mother was always caring, and she was my role model. As my father and brother went to work on the lands, she would tell me tales that her grandmother told her as we were left back home working on handicrafts. My father was always respectful of my mother, and it is from this family that I learned how a woman should be treated and the values she would hold. I always wanted to see what was beyond my village, and I dreamt of becoming a nurse in a national hospital outside the island.

I studied hard towards this dream, but as my grades were not enough for medical school, I went into business administration. This course would prove fruitful, and I got a job in a corporate office on the island. At the time, there were very few women in the corporate office, and I was proud of this significant achievement. I did not get to work in the corporate office by chance, as it is the values that my mother taught me that made me think that it was possible to achieve anything I wished.

As much as working in the office was a success, there were struggles that I faced. First, I got promoted early into my career and partnered with an employee named "John." The working relationship was fantastic, and everyone respected my achievements. However, I notice that every single time that John and I were presenting a project to the junior partners, it would be recognized as John's idea. This was demoralizing as my role in the project was seen as inferior. The junior partners were not trying to be mean, but it was the influence of society that allowed them to believe that women were incapable of leadership.

I always got frustrated with the subtle discriminations. When I was promoted to junior partner, I recognized that I could influence the role of women in the organization. Surprisingly, my policies received plenty of attention, and the management was supportive because of the rising push of gender equality across the world. I saw an opportunity to push for more policies, which allowed me to increase the role of women in the business world.

My advice for women in Wallis and Futuna is to always push for your dreams as opportunities can come knocking. As challenges or frustrations increase, you should not quit but try to push harder. Wallis and Futuna island provides an opportunity for women to learn from their culture and educate their children on society's values.

My Life As A Woman: Gabon Edition #1

Lauraine, Journalist, Gabon

Hello! I am a young Gabonese woman. I grew up in Libreville, precisely in the Charbonnages district in the first arrondissement. This is where I spent my college and high school years. I am part of a modest family, so I grew up in modest conditions, sometimes it was difficult, I went to school without eating. But I remained honest, because that's what my late father had instilled in me since my childhood, that is to say, to adapt to the conditions of life.

My father is the one who inspired me from strength, courage and ability to face difficulties; always keep your head up and show dignity. I carefully kept the advice of this man who left me too early, while I was still only in CM1 class. It must be said that this led me to live my high school years without complex.

After obtaining my baccalaureate, my arrival at the University, I studied economics during my first years. Then, for the Master cycle, I specialized in project management and sustainable development, always in the same department, economy. Currently, I'm doing journalism because it's my passion and that's what I wanted to become; but also because in my country, it is not always seen as a profession. So I did radio animation on the screen for a while and enjoyed the contact with the public, giving and sharing my knowledge, which I loved.

Being Gabonese, of the Nzebi ethnic group, I love everything in my culture, but especially dance. Speaking of my struggles as a woman, I can say that I came to achieve things despite the fact that it was not at all easy, because there were certain realities to face. And it is still not easy today, because as a woman, we are often confronted with multiple social and economic situations.

From my successes, I retain the fact of practicing today in the field, which was intended for me, that of communication. Today I am in charge of a Media website. It is persistence.

To the women of Gabon, I would tell them that women are the pillar of society. This implies that we must be an example for others. For those who think they are worth nothing, should not stop underestimating themselves, remember that they have potential and that they must make use of in order to positively impact society.

My Life As A Woman: Gabon Edition #2

Stéphanie, Headmistress, Gabon

I grew up in the Cité de la Caisse, near the Bethanie church, at Gaspard Obiang's place, I grew up like all the first born in a family, so always pampered, pampered, in a word, a baby comfort. I don't really have any inspiration from anyone. Maybe if I had it would have helped me stay the course and stick to my goals. I didn't really have a normal education, I didn't do high studies but I followed a secretarial training and as a school educator. I would have liked to do journalism, because I really like to express myself, to be heard, I have easy speech, to make reports cool, I think.

In my culture I like the creative spirit of Africans, I like African fashion, stylists, African hairstyles, etc. My current job is teaching, except that this year I did not hold a class because I occupy the post of school principal. I fight for the valorization of the woman, because some tend to take the woman for the base of stupidity.

My successes: having a job, being independent, no longer being responsible for parents, having a husband (yes, I am married) and above all, having children (because in Africa, when you don't have one, you become a source of mockery). Finally, living a stable life in Jesus Christ.

The advice for Gabonese women: They must not give up, the fight is tough but the most important is to get there, to be independent, to be the one who can get away with it anyway. One problem doesn't rely on someone because there are so many things we can do to win battles. The thing is to have only one idea, and voila!

My Life As A Woman: Gambia Edition

Hailing from Brikamaba, a small village located in Niamina east district of the Gambia, the inhabitants of this village are mainly fishermen, petty traders, craftsmen, farmers, and they are sometimes mixed with tourists from different parts of the world who have come to explore the village.

Growing up in the Brikamaba village as a teenager with an outstanding vision poised with the ability to liberate myself and my family from poverty, my father kicked the bucket when I was two and I was bred and raised by my poor mother who sold groundnuts as a means of livelihood, she suckled me and brought me up to age. At the age of sixteen, I began to have some marriage proposals from men, it was very hard to reject due to the poor economic condition of my family as at that time, being the only child in my family, I was advised by many to choose the marriage proposals so as to ease off stress from my mother who was currently training me in secondary school.

Having being encouraged and inspired by my general science teacher who saw the potential in me, I was able to hold onto her advice of encouragement. I began to summon courage, grew up in faith, and became more ambitious. I had to set my goal of being a medical doctor for myself since I was the best science student in my class. Therefore, as a child with a single mother, I already knew the challenges ahead of me; first, I turned down all teenage marriage proposals from men, I had to devote extra time to my studies. I avoided extravagant friends with lackadaisical attitudes, and I lived a low key life just like a Spartan. After my senior school certificate exams, it was so unfortunate that I was going to have a re-sit for a subject that was not credited. Consequently, the challenge became more intense and deepened since there was no money and no one to clamor for help, then it began to look like a dead dream. Finally I had to move to the combo Serekunda to stay with my cousin's sister who was a spinster and a receptionist in one of the hotels in Senegambia (the tourist base). I got engaged as a bar attendant and worked for a period of one year before going back to register for a re-sit in my SSCE exams which was successful.

Now the journey began, the goal was that I wanted to be a medical doctor and that was my only dream course and I believed I would surely get there but how it would happen I could not tell. So I came back and stayed at home for another two years while engaging myself in some classroom teaching and petty trading business in a bid to raise funds for my chosen career. Some of my colleagues who could not cope with the condition of things had to embark in a journey to Europe through the back-way though some succeeded whereas some more lost their lives in the sea. I was not greedy and I still hold to my faith that things would turn around sooner. Correspondingly, the Gambia government announced a free scholarship award to her indigent citizens who were qualified and are also willing to study abroad. After my application, it was granted, and I was sent abroad to study medicine and surgery, some years later I was licensed as a medical doctor and I came back to practice in the Gambia.

Nevertheless, the Gambia culture is such that does not permit her women to indulge in premarital sexual relationship until marriage, this has kept over 90% of her single ladies as virgin thus making the Gambia ladies to be decent and responsible. Our culture encourages a mother to tie a bid which is sometimes made with animal skin on the waist of their daughters. The idea is that with the bid on their waist, they can never get an unwanted pregnancy; this also performs other powerful role in both men and women depending on the mood for which they were made.

The Gambia dishes are very special one in the west Africa region, the Benachin and Damoda are very special that I could not avoid them almost on daily basis, our tribe is diversified each with its own languages we all came together to live in peace and harmony. The wolof, mandinka, Fula, and Jolaare are all our tribes, this rich cultural diversity has made us more unique and enviable this is the more reason why I like my culture. Again, traditional marriages in the Gambia are well greased with dances, merriments and eateries with a very little bride price paid to the bride's family the aim is to encourage living in peace and harmony. What about the wild birds, monkeys, chimpanzee, lions, tiger, crocodile, giraffe, hippopotamus to mention but a few, you could engage yourself in wildlife-sporting activities and finally relax at the Senegambia beach to chill.

Subsequently, on the other hand, I can say that if you dream for a future without hard work then you can be named as lazy and pathetic, I have gained success and many times I have failed. The struggle was not easy because most times as a teenager I would have to go hawking for groundnuts and some other times as a student, I would stay back in school and read all night in a lonely classroom and I will never forget in a hurry when someone attempted to rape me during a heavy downpour. At a time when the government was not able to provide all my needs in medical school, I had to engage in some part time job so as to be able to meet up with my end needs, I would sleep late at night and wake up very early to meet up with my classes since in the medical school you could be told to repeat or withdraw from the department if your performance was bad.

Indeed, I can say that my success was as a result of career planning and God's intervention, lack of career plan is like a ship without the radar, it drifts and untimely sinks down. I am very happy that today I am a consultant in over 6 different hospitals, both in the Gambia, and abroad, and I am also a senior lecturer in about four medical colleges. I am currently developing my own clinic where I hope to sponsor the less privileged Gambians who could not afford their health bills.

In addition, I would like to advise my fellow women out there to always be focused in the time of difficulties to plan very well and start small in whatever condition they find themselves. Remember the saying that "Rome was not built in a day". Women should not sell themselves for one cent for a daily meal. They should remember that "a bird at hand is worth two in the bush", check for alternatives because there is always one. Visit the internet and apply for grants of any kinds, visit government agencies that take care of welfare, clamor for help when you need it, and you will always see a way out. Note that: Where there is a will there is a way.

217

My Life As A Woman: Georgia Edition #1

I've always associated soft melodies, delicious food, and melancholic movies with my hometown of Tbilisi, where I grew up and spent my whole life. The stories about the big dreamy cities have never been unfamiliar to me but I've never thought Tbilisi was less than any of them. It was my world, a beautiful world full of life, culture, and history but as I grew up, I noticed that the pink bubble that surrounded me and my hometown had some cracks and holes in it.

I could say that I had an ordinary childhood but that wouldn't be true. My sister and I were very lucky kids and had everything a child needs for happiness: from toys and pretty clothes to friends and parents' unconditional love. I won't exaggerate if I say that my father would go to the supermarket at 2 am if we wanted ice cream. But we were clever kids and knew what we could and couldn't ask for.

Sometimes I think that when I was born, the first word my parents said to me was "success". It's not unusual for a parent to think of their child as a genius but I'm pretty sure my parents started convincing me and themselves of how clever I was and how much I could achieve as soon as I opened my eyes for the first time. When we have a fight, the best argument my sister and I have against my parents is that we had 'golden child syndrome' because of them. That's partly true - the feeling of a huge responsibility has been embedded in me from a very young age and I can say that I had never been a light-hearted child. As soon as I started elementary school the anxiety from stress and pressure made me tremble and pick at my skin. I would spend a whole day studying without lifting my head up, that's what I had been taught to do. My parents always deny their fault and say that the feeling of responsibility is like a talent and that I was born with it.

Despite everything, I adored my parents, and still do. My father, calm and wise accountant and my mother, a lively journalist balanced each other out. But my mother's life had always seemed more exciting and thrilling to me. The life of a journalist, filled with adrenalin, interesting people, and lots of unusual stories attracted me. When she returned home, my mom would sit with a coffee mug in her hand and while sipping it, tell us about her day. She was writing articles, making a movie, and trying to become a writer at the same time. But her favorite stories were her experience in the war of Abkhazia that had happened a few years before I was born. The memories saddened her but she tried to hide it with a smile and start telling all the gripping stories, how the bombs used to explode a few feet away from her, how she walked with a group of soldiers and sang sad Georgian love songs with them before they left to fight for their country. When I was a kid listening to these stories, I thought my mom was a superhero. And I still think that now she has six books published. I'm grateful to my mother. It is because of her that I fell in love with writing.

My mother is not the only inspiring woman in my family. It's true that she used to read us a book every night until we started reading ourselves but our grandmother was the first woman who planted the love of books in us. I loved visiting her because it meant spending the whole day listening to different fascinating tales. I thought my grandmother had unlimited supplies of new stories kept in her mind. I remember sitting on a window sill and asking her every other second: "Then what happened, grandma?" I couldn't wait to hear more. Now we are grown up and have read all the books she had been talking about. Every time we visited her with a thought that there's no way she can have a new story to tell, we were always mistaken. We didn't know our grandmother's secret, only maybe she had a great imagination. Whatever it was, it worked. We never got bored of her stories.

Even though I grew up in a family where people talked about art, literature, or mathematics, I chose a different path and started studying social sciences. When I graduated high school and got in my first choice university with a full scholarship, the fear that I made a mistake and was going to learn something that I was not interested in, was eating me inside out. But as time passed and I got more and more familiar with my profession, I realized that as a social science studies major, it includes everything from art and literature to psychology and mathematics. Now I'm working on my bachelor's degree and at the same time stepping into the third decade of my life as a freelance creative writer. Despite my mother's career, I've never thought to become a writer but one thing is very clear for me, I can't live and not write.

As I get to know the outer world and interact with people of all ages, I notice that the old perceptions about the differences between men and women are still very much alive. Most of the professors are up to sixty years old and some are more than seventy. So they have spent thirty years living in the Soviet Union and some of them still remain there, they live in memories, think as they used to think thirty years ago and are not able to progress, to blend in with the modern world. Sometimes I feel that they don't see us women in the university seriously. Some of them freely declare their understandings and say that we are just there to "find a man and get married". We speak up and try to change their mentalities but as you can't help someone who doesn't want to be helped, you can't change someone who doesn't want to progress. These are everyday struggles and we women try to push and break the boundaries but most of the time our efforts are worthless.

Old mentalities are part of Georgia's culture. Despite this, I still cherish our culture, full of history, and beautiful traditions. Our country is exotic not only because of the nature that has the sea, mountains, woods, and modern cities at the same time, but because of our culture too. Delicious food, soothing songs, traditional clothes, stunning buildings, and monuments are part of our culture as well as welcoming people, big and loving families and always having each other's back. I see, acknowledge, and fight the cracks and holes in Georgia's culture but I love it with all my heart.

I've been walking on this earth for only twenty years but these years were enough to make me see the real world. In these years I've learned to be willful, optimistic, and to demand what I deserve. As my mother says, "even if they step on you the 100th time you have to stand up". Of course, keeping calm and focusing on what's really valuable people in our life is important. However for us, women, fighting, and speaking up are a must. The cracks and holes of the world won't be fixed until we try to.

My Life As A Woman: Georgia Edition #2

My name is Salome Kekelidze, a 26 year old Doctor. I grew up in the city of Tbilisi, living with my parents, two sisters, and my grandma. I had my basic education in Tbilisi, after which I moved to Germany for my high school, and later returned to Tbilisi to attend medical school. I graduated from medical school in 2016, and since then I've been in the hospital doing my Neurology residency which is for a duration of four years.

Ever since I was a little kid, watching my mum go to the hospital and going through the whole routine of emergency calls made me elated. I was delighted seeing my mum save lives and putting smiles on the faces of people. Sometimes during my school breaks, I asked to follow her to the hospital, to get experience on how things were done in the hospital, and it was in one of those days I started considering being a life saver myself. My mom inspired me so much and made me believe that I could do anything I wanted regardless of my gender. My dad was and is still her solid support in all the things she has been able to achieve.

After my high school education, I came back to Georgia to begin my med school career. I studied in Tbilisi State Medical University (TSMU), one of the best schools in the country. My parents were my biggest supporters, as they helped me through the tough times and the long weeks of assignments, having to meet with deadlines, write the tough exams and still work the night shift as a nurse assistant in the hospital. My mum's success was one of my biggest inspirations to keep pushing.

While in med school, I joined the students union at TSMU as this helped build me up socially and gain more exposure. I learnt to do public speaking, work amongst other people, and helped solve problems of a large group of people.

As a Georgian, what I love the most about my country is the hospitality of my people, my friends from Germany can attest to this. I also like the fact that we are a small nation, and really look out for each other. I love the Georgian dishes like the Lobiani, Kachapuri and Kinkali. Kinkali is the best meal to take on a very cold night.

Currently, I am running the last phase of my Neurology residency and would be rounding up by January 2021, to become a consultant. Whilst I am doing that, I also run a mini blog where I share health tips to people and let them be more aware of their health. I also intend to apply for my master's program in Public health as soon as I am done with my residency.

Although a lot of things have seemed to change, and with modernization taking over, some things have still not taken their full course yet. There are several struggles women still go through today, such as some individuals in the society seeing them as nothing but a home maker. The inequality in the job place which makes them pay the men higher for same job in some firms. The harassment a woman can get on the street just because she is a lady, women being underrepresented in politics and so many more. There are organizations trying to curb all these, and make sure there is equality everywhere, but every single individual still has a role to play to make this happen.

I have been able to achieve a lot of things, from my college days till date. I helped set up an NGO to help rape victims find cover when they need a voice to speak for them. I have also mentored some teenagers, teaching them how to think outside the box and be whoever they want to be regardless of their gender or background, and most of them are doing really well in their walks of life. I have also done some volunteering programs to help in the Georgian villages where there are shortages of health care staff. These and many more I have been able to achieve, and still have a lot of things on my list.

I would advise any woman, especially my fellow Georgian women to never undermine themselves; you can do whatever you set your mind to do. No one else can be you. Never be afraid to step out of your comfort zone. I am just twenty-six, and looking at the things I have achieved, I know more people can do better than me. We need to put in the right amount of work and surround ourselves with the right people and believe we can. This is my story, from Dr. Salome K(MD).

My Life As A Woman: Georgia Edition #3

In my culture I love that everyone here loves hospitality, they love preparing food and gathering all together and having fun, while playing music, singing and all. I'm currently an assistant manager at one coffee shop, to earn some cash because I recently moved out of my parent's house and I'm staying on my own plus I needed some change in my life. As to being a successful woman, I'd say that compared to what I've been through in my life, I'd say I've achieved a lot because I've been struggling with depression since I was a teen so doing stuff was always challenging and I'd still manage to do things. As for advice for women in my country, I'd say that they should be strong and never let anyone doubt their abilities, and they should do whatever their heart desires and never let anything stop them from achieving what they really want.

From EKA

My Life As A Woman: Abkhazia Edition #1

I was born in Abkhazia, a very beautiful place particularly in Gali in the country of Georgia. I have a very big and beautiful family. I was inspired by my parents. My family lives in Abkhazia, but I presently stay in Tbilisi city. I got into the university in Tbilisi at the age of 17. Georgia culture is very big, and I can't explain it all in details as there are a lot of things to say about it. But one thing I believe we all should do is to try to preserve our culture and tradition which our ancestors passed unto us, not to let it pass away over time.

I currently work in the bank now and love the job I am doing. Every day I know is really a struggle, it is not possible living without any struggles. One of my struggles would be the fact I am living alone without my family, I miss them so much, but knowing being away from them is to be able to get to work, and earn a living, I know it's for the best. One thing I dwell on whenever faced with challenges is that whatever our goals are, we can achieve them because we are able to, we just need to have faith which is very important in other to conquer.

To all the women from my country, I wish them a healthy life, love and success. Just believe that everything will be good, and it will come through regardless.

My Life As A Woman: Abkhazia Edition #2

I was born in Abkhazia and grew up in Kutaisi. I was raised by my grandparents, and they were my greatest inspiration. I love them and get inspired by them also because they gave me the examples of how a parent should be, of which I followed by examples. I love everything about my culture in Georgia, and I like that it is really old, which makes it amazing as well. My culture is my personality. I am currently working as a manager where I manage a hotel. My greatest success story are my kids, they give me so much joy and I am proud of myself that I did a great job raising them, and they all turned out amazing. My advice to the women in my country, never give up on your own self.

My Life As A Woman: Germany Edition

My name is Sheila, I live in Weimar state of Thuringia. Weimar is a very beautiful city filled with historical values and one of the cities in Thüringen where tourists flock. I lived with my family, we are five in number, I, my sister, a little brother, and my parents. It's beautiful how we all go on vacations in different places but I love it more when we tour in my city. We would visit the Goethe Platz, and sometimes I sneak out with my friends to see the Weimer University Library. My childhood was very memorable. Trick or treating during Halloween time in Germany is least practiced but I loved dressing up. My younger siblings also loved it and went with groups for candy.

I remember teaching my siblings the saying, "Süßes oder Saures" as they collect treats from neighbours. I wished we went to the haunted castle for more fun in our spooky outfits but my parents wouldn't permit that. There is so many other cultures I loved. Like in mid-October, the pumpkin festival, and many more. It's a lot of fun as Germans go the extra mile to put life into these festivals. My mum always pleaded with our dad to allow us have fun with our friends. She has always been there for me in every circumstance she's more of a friend as I always confide in her.

I wanted to study theatre art at the university of Weimar as I aspire to be an actress due to my love for acting, as it seems to be the one thing I could be good at. But unfortunately, that didn't happen as planned, as my father wasn't in support of such. He called it foolish to study as he didn't believe in education for women. He said it was a waste of time instead of looking for domestic chores, like my mom, and settling down.

I have always had problems in making my dad understand the importance of education and how it will help one become a better person for the country. But he turned a blind eye. With his request and my mom being a loyal wife, nothing could be done. I took up a job downtown after my high school in a bar, with the struggles of no one recognizing my potential, all because I was a woman.

My father never saw the need to train a girl through school as he felt it was a total waste of time. I didn't get respect either from my male counterparts at my workplace. Making a mockery of me on how weak I was and my looks. No one looked beyond that. I started to despise myself, feeling like a worthless being. Taking up drinking as the only companion whom understood me well. My journey took a massive turn from wanting to be a better person to a struggling alcoholic. It got worse, I was beginning to lose my mind, which gave my mom a great concern. I found peace hiding my pain behind drinks and I wouldn't want to see anyone taking that from me. My parents did their best, took me to therapy and seemed for more help but it seems to get worse. Finally my mom's instinct kicked in. She realised for me to get off my mind from drinking, I had to become distracted with other stuff. She started picking up acting books for me, hiding them from my dad.

I was finally seeing the world in another dimension through my readings. Finally I was free but I needed to go to university irrespective of my father's disagreement, I wanted to become somebody. I didn't want to be weak like they said. So I spoke with my mom and she decided to speak up. She wouldn't want me to go through what I went through. She wanted me to be a valuable citizen and luckily for me It helped out.

My mom understanding what studying could liberate me from and being fed up with his rules jumped to her feet and argues with my father which led to a conclusion I couldn't believe. She wanted the best life for her kids despite not being learned, she knew the value. And as I am the first child, she wanted me to set examples for my juniors.

Even though I wasn't happy with the agreement, coming with an argument, I was so overwhelmed with joy. As I know my journey of becoming an important person in society had just begun, though I ended up studying linguistics because I wanted to convey my stories and ideas through books. Hoping to own a firm soon but nevertheless I write short stories which allow kids know their potential, especially the females. They should know their worth and never be put down. My Mom has instilled in me the true meaning and value of a woman. I am so thankful to her. Without her support who knows the level of trauma and depression I could have been in.

I'm more of a religious person as it's the foundation my parents laid for us, my mom has taught me the true definition. My dad is nice in his own ways just that his beliefs doesn't sum up. I wish one day he would get to know the true value of education for women, Perhaps when I make him see it. I wouldn't want anyone going through what I went through. It's all in past and I feel free to talk about it. As I feel it will help someone out there. As ladies, let us come together and speak up to avoid another kind of this incident. I know that if my mom had the support, she would have spoken up and also tried to liberate herself from her life back then. She would have been greater than being just an obedient wife who does nothing but clean. We should show the importance of studying for women. Let's stand and speak up. Don't let anyone decide your faith.

My Life As A Woman: Ghana Edition

Hello dear, I'm excited to share my personal experiences growing up as a Ghanaian lady. Come along as I take you step-by-step through what it's like to be a woman born and bred in Ghana. I hope you are inspired by my story and pick up a thing or two to make yours even better! I grew up in Accra which is the capital city of Ghana; and like any other country, life here isn't as complicated as it is in the remote areas. The specific part of Accra I grew up in is called Pig farm. Growing up, all of my childhood days were spent with my nuclear family and a few of my extended family members. I grew up in a Christian family, shared a room with my sibling, and we both were totally comfortable with that.

As a little girl, I had so many dreams that were bigger than my physique. I mostly took delight participating in school debates. One of the people I looked up to was my big sister, because she was one of the few people from my family who attained a high educational level and had good moral standards. My culture teaches me that no man is an island and everybody needs somebody at point, and that's what I love about my Ghanaian culture. What I also love about my culture is its rich history and delicious delicacies it comes with – you can never go wrong with a Ghanaian dish! Ha-ha.

During my high school days, I studied Science as a major and went on to specialize in Psychology at the University level. As a child growing up, I had many aspirations as to who and what I wanted to become, many of which were unconsciously suppressed by my African environment. I wanted to be an African Opera Winfrey, Beyoncé, an actress, a singer, a business woman and a doctor. The most 'acceptable' career to my Ghanaian context was becoming a medical doctor. Looking back, I honestly believe I wanted to be a doctor because it is one of the jobs held in high esteem here in Ghana. It's not surprising I didn't turn out to be one. I am currently a hairstylist, an entrepreneur, a freelancer, and still taking a course at the university.

There have been many challenges I have come face-to-face with as a Ghanaian woman with many aspirations. When people saw that I decided to take some 'digital' related courses men are mostly known to take, I get asked some questions like; "You are a woman, why are you looking for so much money?", "Are you going to marry yourself someday?". All these comments meant I am a woman and must not be so concerned with becoming financially stable. A major challenge I encountered as a Ghanaian woman is the lack of financial resources to fully materialize my aspirations. There have been countless occasions where I could have been financially supported but I lost that opportunity simply because I am a woman and not a man. Another challenge is not getting job opportunities due to the gender stereotype attached to getting a job in my country.

Attaining a high level of education would be number one on my achievements list. In a developing country like Ghana, not every individual has the privilege of going to school, of getting a quality University education like I did. Another accomplishment that makes me indeed very proud of myself, and being a woman, is independently setting up a hair business at age 20. This was not an easy task at all to be executed as I was not born with a silver spoon in my mouth. I also engaged in the buying and selling of a variety of products, depending on its demand.

To any lovely woman reading my story, never give up on your dreams and most importantly, never stop believing in yourself. Always remember you are your number one fan in all your endeavors. It's your very own decision to allow comments from wet blankets be the reason you stop pushing or you push even harder. You might have a dollar and a million dollar dream, but that shouldn't hold you back! Start from somewhere, start now, and let your story be an inspiration to others. Here's a toast to success ladies, I believe you can.

My Life As A Woman: Greece Edition #1

My name is Asimina and I was born in Greece. I live in the island of Evia, the second bigger island of Greece, very near to Athens, so close sometimes that it is not even considered an island. Although its size, my island, even though it has many beautiful landscapes, wonderful beaches and relaxing mountains is not very well known and not a famous tourist attraction as other places in Greece. Not even the islanders considered it a tourist and cultural attraction some years ago, even though the Euboeans are the inspirers of the Latin alphabet, have established colonies all over the Europe and the Euboean currency, due to trade, is found in all the numismatic museums of the world! They didn't even know their recent history, the folk culture of their ancestors, our folk music and traditional dishes. They underestimated both history and culture because they didn't know it!

I was lucky to have a smart grandmother who was a means of cultural training. She was born in a village of the North Evia and she was a practical teacher for me. She inspired me to love the Greek tradition, the Greek civilization and taught me most of what she knew about it. She introduced me to the traditional costumes, she taught me how to make the traditional pies and cook the local dishes, she showed me many of the herbs of the local flora and we made folk remedies together for many health issues. She always reminded me to respect the tradition and inspired me to transmit it to my children and to all the people I would meet in my life. I recall her saying to me with her tender voice, "Wherever you go, remember my little, you are always an ambassador of your homeland."

When being raised in that way as a young woman and you realize your fellow citizens underestimate the place you have been born and love, you want to change things. And you try to do as much as you can to help your island come to the light and find the position that it deserves, to the hearts of the islanders and worldwide, if you can. For me the challenge was to make them partakers of my knowledge, to set them on cultural fire, to teach them the local history and tradition. And so, I did.

After ten years of research, I wrote and published two books on the local traditional costumes and language and made many presentations of them in many towns of the island and to Athens. My books travelled all over the world and many people from abroad asked me information on the subject. I inspired my husband to make replicas of the traditional jewellery and participated in expositions all over Greece. With other people having the same interest as me, we participated in a cultural association and organized many lectures on the Euboean history, folk tales, places of interest and history, competitions of local dishes, folk art expositions, all over the island. I also cooperated with teachers and went to the schools to introduce children and teenagers to different aspects of our civilization. I even participated in the local folk dance association to learn and present worldwide the folk dance and music of our homeland.

After six years of action, I believe there are some important steps being made. Since they learned the aspects of the civilization frequently presented, people started to respect more our culture and tried to protect it. Moreover, other younger people were impelled to participate in the actions and became interested in the protection and promotion of the Euboean civilization.

If you are a restive spirit as I am, you always find ways to continue. Everyone is important to find his or her way through life and make something for their self-realization. Remember to follow your dreams, stay focused on your target and do not let the obstacles deviate you from what you really want, even though it is hard sometimes. Don't be afraid to base yourself on your roots, even if it may seem unfashionable. Your cultural roots are the ones to make you rise and bloom. Respect what you are, and, as my grandma said, always be the "ambassador" of your uniqueness worldwide!

My Life As A Woman: Greece Edition #2

Being a woman born and raised in Greece comes with responsibility. Greece has a rich history, a thing that influences you from an early stage. The fairytales I remember most from my childhood are Aesop's fables and stories taken from the mythology. These stories encouraged my imagination and creativity. Talking animals and gods walking among humans are usually things you read in a fantasy novel. This would affect my future, even though I was unaware of it at the time. Now, I'm sure that when I have kids of my own, I will make sure to raise them the same way. This is the only way that Greece's cultural treasure stays in our hearts.

My hometown is a small town in the rural area of Greece. During my adolescence, I would frequently feel frustrated because I wanted to be in a big city. However, growing up in a rural area came with many advantages, all things I realized long after I had moved to the big city. As a kid, I enjoyed the outdoors. I would meet my friends on our bikes and we would run to the fields. I would take our family dog out for a walk and we would spend hours in the woods. Furthermore, I would help my grandmother in the garden. I strongly believe that my love of nature originated from these happy times.

Moreover, while growing up I had another favorite past-time. As soon as I had learned how to read, I would pick any book that would fall into my hands. It made no difference whether it was a children's or an adult's book. Reading all the ancient Greek myths made me want to become an archaeologist. I persisted in that idea for years until I realized that what I wanted to do was to become an artist. Therefore, when I had to choose a university to attend, I picked one that specialized in digital arts.

However, I quickly realized that I'm a reckless spirit and I wanted to discover all kinds of things. This led me to try out different jobs and always trying to learn something new. One of my endeavors was a creative writing course. This was when I realized my true calling and what would eventually become my job. As a freelance writer, blogger, and aspiring novelist, I can always discover new things to feed my natural curiosity.

Nevertheless, it wasn't always easy. As a woman living alone, away from my family, I had to face many obstacles in my working environments. I had to put up with bosses who mistreated me and didn't care about my opinions. Switching into a freelancing career was a challenge that I'm glad I took. The beginning was bumpy but I was able to breakthrough. I still have to face absurd demands and weird clients but at least I have the choice to keep them out of my life.

My experience in life has shown me that you should always try to learn new things. Understand the environment around you and take any opportunity that pops up. When the situation gets rough, try to hold on. Through hard work and passion, you will surely find your way in life.

My Life As A Woman: Greece Edition #3

A woman's life in any country is full of challenges and here in Greece couldn't be any different. I did not have a normal childhood and playing with toys was certainly not what kept me busy. Born and raised in a small city of Serres in Central Macedonia, in a low income family, where my father was a farmer; we had only few acres of land so to be able to earn our living, everyone in the family worked. As children, me and my sister went to the field since the age of 6 or so. In the beginning, we did very simple chores there and while we were growing up our responsibilities grew as well.

Selling our products was a challenge as well. We had to sell our fruit and vegetables to stores like taverns, restaurants, cafes, and so on. We started at about the age of 10 till the age of 16. I stopped because my body as a woman blossomed and men started to harass me. Then I focused on preparing for the national university entrance exams. My dream was to become a doctor or something related to the health industry because I wanted to help the sick.

Later my father got sick with his heart and he couldn't continue his farming so my mother had to work as an old people's caretaker to earn our living. My father got a pension but it wasn't enough. I am very proud of my parents because they did their best to raise us without taking care of themselves first. Their life was the best life lesson I could have. After all the difficulties, I managed to get into a university in Heraklio Crete. So I spent four and a half years there studying and working at the same time. I studied Technology of Medical Systems Telemedicine. In 2004, while I was doing my practice for my degree in Thessaloniki, I lost my father. It was really a shock and I almost became very depressed but thankfully I met my husband and I overcame it.

I had my daughter in 2006 and after three miscarriages due to autoimmune problems, which really devastated me, I had my son in 2013. Besides my studies I loved teaching so I obtained my certification as an English teacher. I managed to work in a vocational institution for six months teaching hospital informative systems as well but I couldn't continue. The competition for a teaching position was very harsh, my Bachelor wasn't enough. Generally, due to the financial crisis is almost impossible to land a job relating to your studies. That's why a lot of the young generation immigrate to other countries especially in the EU to find a better job.

For the English lessons I mentioned, I didn't have enough students and I wanted to do something to help my family so I started working online. In the beginning I offered translation services, English to Greek, and vice versa. However, translation agencies tend to underpay so gradually I included more. I took courses and earned some certificates and spent a lot of time studying till now and I still do. Prejudice is existent of course. A lot of people still can't understand that I really work. They feel that since I am not leaving the house it isn't a real job.

My life feels like this of a true Greek, full of strength and resilience, overcoming war times, and financial crisis. As we Greek people are living our life in full like there is no tomorrow, celebrating each tiny happy event in our lives like everything is going well, the same I feel I do in my life as well. So my message to all women out there is that since I could follow my heart and do what I wanted to do, then you can do it as well. Never give up your dreams and goals. When you give up, everything stops. Don't let other people judge or rob you of your confidence. And don't let your perfectionism and procrastination get in the way as well. I have been there, so I know from my personal experience this is the biggest mistake we can do to ourselves. Build good relationships with positive people. Having someone that believes in your dream and supports you really makes a difference. And keep up being you. Don't change yourself to accommodate other people that don't know you and they don't want to know you and respect you.

My Life As A Woman: Grenada Edition

I am a 20-year-old female who lives in Grenada. Grenada is a country located in the southern part of the Caribbean Sea. I grew up with my parents and two siblings in a small fishing village. My parents always encouraged us to do well at school. My father worked abroad to be able to cover our educational expenses. Since he would be away for months at a time, my mother was responsible for taking care of us three kids. She woke up at six every morning to get us ready for school. She made breakfast, lunch, and break (recess snack). She ensured that we had natural snacks like fresh oranges, homemade cakes, and fruit juice. Everything was made from scratch. In Grenada, it is very easy to get fruits like mangos and bananas because the island is abundant in tropical fruit trees. Also, it is a custom to cultivate home gardens at the beginning of the rainy season.

Planting at my great-grandmother's house was so much fun. Each of us kids would have a duty — one person to dig the hole, one to put in the seeds, and one to cover the hole. It was a lot of work but a bonding experience. My great-grandmother had 13 children and raised them all by herself. She also raised her grandchildren whose mothers had traveled abroad in search of job opportunities. She would ask me what I wanted to be when I grew up. I would always respond with "a veterinarian!" because I loved animals so much.

Everyone knows each other here due to the small size of the island. A stranger may walk up to me and ask how my parents are or how our studies are going, and I would reply because it's logical to assume they know me or my family. I am not afraid for my safety because I have confidence in the morals of my people. Currently, I am striving toward obtaining a bachelor's degree in the field of biology. Usually, after each semester, I work at local stores or as an online tutor.

One of my biggest struggles is pessimism. Although Grenada is home to St. George's University; there are limited educational opportunities. For example, I like astrophysics but it isn't taught here. This can make me feel like I need to defer from my initial plan. However, I am grateful for what I have accomplished so far. I graduated primary and secondary school as class valedictorian and I'm striving to be the second person in my family to obtain a college degree. Although I'm unsure of my career path, I'm certain I will touch the lives of many people.

To my Grenadian women, focus on your goals. Don't put popularity, negative opinions, or meaningless relationships priority over your dreams. Don't let anyone tell you what you can do. Forget the past and do not worry about the future. The world may seem large and scary but your faith will deliver you from fear. Trust in God.

My Life As A Woman: Guadeloupe Edition #1

My name is Maya Condé, and I was born and raised in Guadeloupe. The beautiful Caribbean and French region islands. I am an only child. Many people would think that it's lonely and boring, growing up alone, but I had a lot of family, so I never felt alone. Our native language is French, but you will also hear people speaking Créole around the island. I had to learn how to speak English because my family and I moved up to the states when I was fifteen. I still have my little hiccups when speaking English, but I have been practicing. I can never forget where I am from. I am proud of myself for having made it through life no matter what is thrown my way.

Growing up in Guadeloupe, I was exposed to many different cultures. My family lived in a small town called Champfleury, which is located close to the coast of Guadeloupe. My mother was a French instructor, and my father was an engineer. The education system back then was very good. I was blessed enough, that my mother was in the education system and provided me with the best education possible. My mother made a difference in all the children that she taught because she knew how hard growing up poor was and trying to learn since many parents did not have that high level of education. My father was a farming engineer, and he was the head of his team. I am grateful for their hard work to support me growing up. They were very famous in town for their work for our country.

Growing up was a bit difficult, but I learned so much about myself. I had a family that supported me with anything that I wanted to achieve in life, but as any family, we had our struggles. I knew we always struggled with money ever since I was small, so I still kept everything to a minimum because, since young, I understood the value of money and how hard life was. Growing up with my parents and their determination in life to provide for me and thinking about my worth first opened my eyes. My parents taught me to be independent and not depend on anyone else. I can do anything that I want once I set my mind to it.

Every day we have to face challenges and obstacles, but we must overcome them. We have to learn from each other's mistakes and try again. When you are a woman, you will never get tired of trying and learning new things; it is our nature to be curious and investigate. It is a great feeling to know that you are capable of doing something big and challenging. As women, we can do anything and everything we want to do as long as we put our minds to it. We are so much stronger than we think we are.

My Life As A Woman: Guadeloupe Edition #2

Guadeloupe is an island situated on French territory, which attracts people with its white-sand beaches, beautiful parks, and the most impressive dive spots. This French island is a real secret and many people come to see and discover the beauty of Guadeloupe. This is a place where people can relax, forget their problems, enjoy the beautiful nature, sea, breathe the pure air, and feel the warm sun. I love this place and I am happy that I am blessed to live here in Guadeloupe most of my life. Maybe I seem too patriotic but this is what my body and soul want. It is very important to find a place where your soul will feel free and comfortable.

I am Kiki and I am from France, I was born in Sadirac, it is a city in France, and my hometown. Now I live and work in Saint-Francois, Guadeloupe, and try to survive in this cruel world. My family has nothing extraordinary to tell, I grew up in a normal family with both parents. My family hadn't much money to help me so I could enter a university, and after high school, I stopped my education, unfortunately, till now I do not have a higher education but this is the goal I have in my life. When I was 15 years old, I was in love with a boy from our city, so we dated and a few years later decided to leave the city and start our new life as we had really serious problems with our families. So we went to Saint-Francois where my boyfriend's uncle was living. We found there a job and I started working in 'Le Relais du Moulin' hotel as a chambermaid. I still work there, with many dreams and goals in my mind. My boyfriend and I have strict goals, we collect money to enter a university, and continue our education, as we both have really big plans for life.

Concerning the advice to women and talking from personal experience, I feel like women supporting women is one of the most important things that we lack. I would strongly advise, more like encourage, all the young women to help and care about each other. It doesn't really matter if she's your friend, sister, or a complete stranger. It's quite challenging for women nowadays to keep a positive attitude, as society is pushing some really weird beauty standards, making women more insecure about themselves. Big advice to never let anyone, neither the society nor your circle, to decide what's good for yourself. Whatever you do let it come from your own wish, your own goals, and your own comfort. Another piece of advice for all my strong women out there, always fight for your rights. Never adapt to anything you don't feel right about just because they say you have to. For example... don't stop fighting for gender equality, for a job or a position that most men get, don't think you're not good enough or not smart enough.. wear that confidence and prove the society wrong. Break the stereotypes, and never settle for anything less than your will and your desires! All the ladies who have sons, brothers.. please, teach them to treat the girls the way you wish you were treated.

232

My Life As A Woman: Guatemala Edition #1

My name is Andrea Aguilar, I am 37 years old and I was born and live in Guatemala City, Guatemala. Guatemala, the country of eternal spring, named for its varied and perfect climate, is a beautiful country located in Central America; It has a landscape full of beautiful colors, aromas and fragrances that awaken all the senses and above all, warm people who will always greet you with a warm hug.

What can I tell you about myself, in principle I could define myself as a happy woman? I grew up in a home where I was surrounded by a lot of love and I am the oldest of four sisters; from my parents, whom I love intensely, I have learned a lot about love, hard and intelligent work and of course to achieve my dreams. Fortunately and as a divine conspiracy, my childhood was marked and influenced by music, in my life I had it everywhere, at home, in the car, at school, with my friends, I heard it in English, in Spanish, and I could say that it was always good and varied. Although my parents were not professionals, they spent a lot of time singing and playing instruments, my dad was a singer and my mom played the piano, so they spontaneously instilled me and directed me towards music.

My best memories, happy or sad, I always remember with music and especially with singing. I remember singing in the car with my sisters with all our strength and enthusiasm, the songs that my dad put on the radio while he took us to school, if the garage of my childhood house spoke, it would say that we sang for hours and made harmonies of our favorite songs, we put on great shows for us there. Despite all the musical influence that I had in my childhood and adolescence and that singing and making harmonies for songs was given to me spontaneously and naturally, when I finished studying basic (medium level), I decided to study accounting in high school, it was one of the worst years of my life, this career was very difficult for me and although I went to school and tried to learn everything, in the depths of my soul I yearned to sing.

At some point in that long and boring school year, I decided that accounting was not for me, but for other classmates and number lovers, but as far as I was concerned, it felt like a bird caught in a cage that is in the window overlooking the most beautiful forest and that forest was music. I was filled with courage to talk to my parents and tell them that I could no longer continue studying that degree, and I say -filled with courage- because throughout my life I have had many friends who studied a career only because their parents forced them, but this was not my case. My parents unconditionally supported me (that's why I love them infinitely) and although their only condition was that I win that school year, they asked me what I wanted to do because they would help me achieve what I wanted so much, which was: sing.

The following year I was enrolled in a school to be a music teacher and 4 years later I was proudly graduating as a happy and satisfied music education teacher. I learned a lot during those 4 years and this learning together with all the influence I had in my childhood led me to become what I am now, a vocal producer and professional singer. Despite my musical studies, I did not dedicate myself fully to music from the beginning; I worked in a customs company and recordings in renowned studios, jingles and songs for different projects and companies, this gave me the experience that the school does not give you and helped me reaffirm my talent. Fifteen years ago I decided to set up my own vocal recording studio and start creating my own arrangements as a vocal producer; It has been a difficult journey because when it started there was no woman doing this in Guatemala, I was the only one who produced her own vocals in a home studio and did not need to go to a recording studio to do the work, as was the way accustomed to the moment, Despite being a new way of working, it took a lot of time and effort to build a reputation in which producers and studios trusted that developing professional work and the height of international productions, even many times they would pay very little money for the work or they would tell me how I was starting in the middle and they would not pay me, but this never beat me and I was not going to give up. I did many free jobs so that the producers heard my work. I took all the opportunities that I considered to record and thus, propose my new way of working. This investment of time and effort paid off, because I met many people who were key in my life and learned a lot from them.

Now, fifteen years later, I can say that I have achieved wonderful things as a vocal producer, I have participated in incredible projects, not only national but international, and when I started on my own this was something I just imagined. Sometimes we make mistakes like mine, studying accounting when what I really wanted was to study music. You cannot stay stuck in a mistake, in a decision, in a thought, if you do not feel comfortable you must get out of there, speak, be radical, if you do not like something you must say it, if a path does not seem to you can change the course, because nobody will tell you where to go and nobody will go for you, nobody will do for you what you should do.

When I look back on everything I could have missed because I had studied a career that was not what I really wanted, I admire myself and I think it was a good decision to lose my fear and talk, to be able to tell my parents that this was not what I wanted for myself and even more, that they support me in that change. I appreciate and enjoy every opportunity that is given to me, every song that I record, every note that comes out of my mouth, because they remind me that I do what I love most in life, which is to create and sing what I believe.

My Life As A Woman: Guatemala Edition #2

Guatemala City is beautiful, but it can also be an acquired taste. With its old and new buildings, chaotic traffic, charming people and beautiful weather, Guatemala is a city where you can lose and find yourself, all at the same time. It is also the place I call home. I was born at the beginning of the nineties to a single mom living with her own mother and sisters. We lived in an apartment in the middle of the city. My mom was young and naïve, only 22 years old and still going to university.

As in most Latin American homes, grandma was the one in charge of the family. Nothing happened or stopped happening without her knowing or authorizing. And although we –as Latin Americans– come from very machoistic cultures, it is not unusual for families to function in a matriarchal way. This was the case for my family. I grew up surrounded by strong women, that even though made their own mistakes and carried with the consequences of them, they always found a way to stay strong and independent. I always admired my mother, aunts, and grandmother.

However, the most important woman in my life have always been my grandma. She is the light of the way, the column of our entire family, and the reason I am who I am today. My grandmother not only took care of me as a baby, she showed me, just by her story and by being herself, what I could and could not accept in relationships, in work, and in life. She set the standard for me and I am forever grateful for that. Being the strong, independent woman she was and still is, and having accomplished as much as she did, I can only say truly, she was my most important role model and she was also my biggest fan.

Growing up, I wanted to be everything that is mutually exclusive. I dreamt about being a great singer and performer while also being President. I wanted to be a powerful businesswoman and a hippie; artist and a millionaire. I was always a good student and I got a full scholarship to go study in the US. I wanted to study theatre or music, but they didn't have a theatre degree in my university and my scholarship didn't apply to music. So, I studied International Business and Photography. Two very different degrees, which had nothing to do with each other. My family thought I was crazy for not going for something more complementary. But I always did what I wanted, so that's what I studied.

When I came back to Guatemala, four years after I had left, I went through an extremely difficult culture shock. I was no longer used to many things in my culture that now bothered me. I had also become an adult in a different country and culture, so I had ingrained something in my brain and behavior that didn't necessarily matched what I grew up seeing in my fellow Guatemalans. Don't get me wrong, Guatemalan culture is great, but as any other culture, it has its good and not so good. Guatemalans are warm, cheery people. They love making people feel comfortable and welcome. They will always try to get a smile from you and make you feel at home. Cook nice meals for you or drive you around for you to know the best of their country or town. We're also very generous and kind. We know how hard it is to survive in this country, so we tend to lend a hand to anyone who needs it, even if then we don't get the same in return. Guatemalan culture is a mix of indigenous, Spanish and other European cultures. We are truly a melting pot of old and new world. Guatemalans are usually very conservative in their views – guided by a strong church and small towns – but very liberal in their actions – if you know what I mean. We are very privileged to have such nice weather all year round, and I think that makes us very unaware of how lucky we are with weather. We don't pay much attention to it and focus our energies in worrying about other things like politics, church, and football.

Being a working woman in Guatemala is not easy. I am currently a proposal writer for an international company. I write proposals that our company sends to governments so we can win contracts. I must admit that it is not my dream job, but I enjoy it and I hope to keep it until I find something more aligned with my dreams. Guatemala provides its citizens many struggles as is, let alone if you're a woman. Besides harassment at work, you can also experience discrimination because you're pregnant, because you're married, because you're single, because you have kids, because you don't have kids, basically, because you are not a man. If you're going to work, you most definitely will experience street harassment, at best, and sexual violence and death, at worst. The number of women who disappear and are found dead from misogynistic violence in our country is exorbitantly high. Just being a woman in this country is dangerous, let alone working in a male-dominated industry. On paper, we are equals with men; in practice, we are always the disadvantaged ones.

But being a woman in Guatemala is not all bad. We have very good examples of women who have accomplished great things on their own; we also have stories of ordinary women who triumph against all odds and not only survive in this country but thrive. I have learned over the years, that to be a woman in Guatemala, you must know four things:

1. Stop caring about what people think

2. Be kind, loving and patient with yourself

3. Lift other women up

4. Know that it will be ten times harder for you than for the man beside you, but also know that you will do it ten times better and it'll be worth every second of it.

My Life As A Woman: Guinea Edition

Warning: This story contains graphic content. Proceed to read with caution.

Where did I grow up?

I come from Guinea forest, but I grew up in Upper Guinea. I spent most of my life in Kindia, a small, not too busy city, about a hundred kilometers from Conakry. Early childhood, however, was in Kpetéwolamai, Macenta Prefecture. Macenta means Chief and/or King in the Massa, the people I came from. It is also an endogenous name often attributed to boys during initiation rites.

How did I grow up?

Generally in our culture, women are never far from men. For them, they are a valuable aid for the various rural works. I grew up between food crops, crops, and seasonal picking and also in canoes, between hooks and fishing nets. But also in a community that values family relationships as paramount. As a result, the small family and the large family are closely linked. Nieces are the women of uncles and they never refuse to help nephews. Aunts and paternal uncles are usually substituted for parents, they are the ones who make all the important decisions in the lives of their nephews and nieces. The grandparents then, are our partners in crime (laughter). They are there to advise and protect us even more than our fathers and mothers.

My source of inspiration?

I'll tell the gang that the women of my family are. This is by no means the female ideal, but they are all real role models. Powerful, well-educated, and attached to our mores. From my childhood, they have shaped me in their image and I can assure you that I have many strings in my bow.

My childhood dreams and my school level.

At the moment, I have the BTS level in tourism and I intend to continue my studies. My family will support me and allow me to go this far in order to have a better future. I had been dreaming since my early childhood of being an influential woman and a very long-time student in society because it is very rare to see women leaders in our country. You get married very young because of the tradition.

What do you like about your culture?

I think I've blown it higher, the initiation rites. Particularly the adult-only ritual reserved for women. It takes place in the sacred forest and is an ultimate step to learn traditional dance.

My current profession

I work in part at a travel agency.

My struggles as a woman

The great struggle I'm fighting now is to make money continuously from my forehead. However, in everyday life, we Guinean women and girls struggle body and soul to eradicate violence against us, early marriage, and female genital mutilation.

My successes as a woman

The only achievement I am really proud of today is that I was able to escape female genital mutilation through my grandmother and my mother.

Advice for women

Live your life with dignity! Never let others decide for you, take your destiny in your own hands.

MAKEBE

My Life As A Woman: Guinea-Bissau Edition

Where did I grow up?

I am a Balante, an ethnic group of Guinea Bissau. I was born in a small town called Bissorâ in the Oio region at the heart of the Cacheu River estuary and grew up in the capital. At the same time, the latter is the largest and only city in Guinea-Bissau and therefore the only major economic and administrative center. Long before I was born, my parents traveled a lot in the country in search of well-being and it is in Bandim, a popular area of Bissau that they have packed their suitcases 30 years ago.

How did I grow up?

I grew up in a Muslim-majority community with strong ideologies. This contrasted with the modern education my father advocated. I was raised to the way of always doing better than others, doing things differently, serving as an example. I think it was this duality that made me a pragmatic and realistic woman.

In the footsteps of my parents

My parents are a model for me to succeed, because they were able to brave all the obstacles that stood in their way to achieve their goals. They left from scratch and became sort of leaders in the country.

My education and my childhood dream

I'm a trained accountant, but I've always dreamed of being a stylist and having my personal brand. I am a tinkerer in the soul and I love to fix or repair what has been destroyed or out of use.

What I love about my culture?

I love our ancestral traditions even though I am an evangelist. I am one of those who think that there is nothing better than traditional African values.

My work life

I'm a professional accountant. I work in my father's society. This company markets agri-food products. However, I am also collecting donations and funds for the young mothers of the social assistance association founded by my older sister.

My struggles as a woman

I have always been attracted to social action because of the increased number of disadvantaged families in my country. As a result, early pregnancies as well as unwanted pregnancies. I grew up in a community where 13-year-old girls get pregnant, where most women raise their children on their own, and where girls who have just left childhood are happily engaged in moral drift. It is with this in mind and with the support of my father that I raise donations and funds to help young mothers who are struggling to make ends meet.

My successes as a woman

For me, the most rewarding part is to see these girls and their children thrive. I am working with my sister for their social reintegration.

Advice to women

Through my life experiences, women can do better with will and determination. You should never be discouraged even when you encounter obstacles. Life is worth living.

Tölo Marie

My Life As A Woman: Guinea-Equatorial Edition

Where did I grow up?

I grew up in Ebebiyin in the far north-east and got my bachelor's degree in the port city of Bata and then went to study in Spain before returning to Malabo where I settled definitively. Nevertheless, I feel more like a woman in Bata because this city has been the most important in my life. With its beautiful places, its culture and being the economic capital.

How I grew up?

I came from a Christian family and my family taught me Biblical values and then evolved in an environment where religious rules were the norm.

My mother, my inspiration

Often, my baptism godmother and my grandmother embody role models for me. But my mother is my greatest source of inspiration. She gave me her own conception of femininity. That of a free woman, able to better manage the home and financial independence.

What I studied/My childhood dreams and why?

I graduated from a master's degree in digital communication. Why this choice? Simply because with digital technology, you can easily get a job or you can self-employ as I do. In addition, the digital professions are accessible to all and abound with many opportunities.

At the bottom, I imagined myself as a model and I had the carrot of it. I have always had a liana body that has remained unchanged over the years. A dream that I lost growing up considering the realities of my country.

What I love about my culture

What I love about us Fangs are dowry ceremonies. Among other things, the part where the bride performs traditional dance steps. Also, the exchange of material goods between families. I am also proud of our beauty because we are one of the most beautiful women on the African continent.

My Work

I'm a community manager and I work freelance. I create content such as writing articles and animating Instagram and Facebook accounts. I also do digital advertising and have my team that I often train.

My struggles as a woman

Through my articles, I fight for a truly free and modern Guinea-Equatorial without stigma, without excision, without violence against women and children. I also fight against traditions that violate certain women's rights.

My successes as a woman

As an Equatorial Guinean woman, I find that I've done a good job of my life. I'm not yet 50, but I have what can be called a beautiful journey. I have a degree in a constantly evolving field, experience abroad, and a company of my own. As part of my work, I led a whole team and mostly men. I'm like a boss lady.

Advice for women

It is very important for a woman to respect herself, to be independent financially so as not to be humiliated by certain men. This leads me to say that financial independence does not necessarily mean hiring, let us prioritize entrepreneurship. The state can no longer afford to hire everyone.

Ina Obono Ndong

My Life As A Woman: Guyana Edition

Growing up in Georgetown, Guyana.

I grew up with my aunt in Georgetown Guyana, a place called East LA Penitence. A big house between the ally way to the range houses and a school. I did not see my mother who traded in goods at the time and was off to Suriname and my father was an electrician whom I did not see at all.

I was an only child and the queen among my aunts as none of them had kids. I was spoiled rotten and got away with murder as we would say in Guyana. My aunt worked as a hair dresser and I remember her leaving for work, I was left home alone during the summer holidays. I would play in the fenced yard by myself, tying my Chinese rope (made out of tire tubes) to the post under the house and having a ball with me. Sometimes I would call the neighbor kids over to play getting trouble all the time as they never showered and I should not have had them in the yard. One time I left the yard without anyone knowing with the kids from the alleyway and found myself in trouble as I am terrified of cows, they charged me and I tried to jump over a trench and fell in. Oh the cut ass I got once I returned home was merciful.

I went through school and finished high school and soon after became pregnant at 17 years with my only child. I was determined not to let that stop me with my very big stomach I attended classes to further my studies. I always wanted to own my own business. I did not have many role models in my life, I just knew that I was not going to allow my child to be third generation of becoming pregnant at 16 like me and my mother. I completed classes in Business Administration, Bookkeeping, and Wedding and Event planning. Later I started working at one of the top hotels and got to experience 3 departments within my years there. As a teenage mother in Guyana, you must have support and also have to be ambitious. One child is a mistake if you continue to have more kids, you are going on a downward spiral, as there is no government support for unemployed mothers with kids. My daughter attended private schools and had the best education and still on her journey to becoming an architect.

I opened my own wedding planning business and I am currently working as a Virtual Assistant. As a woman living in Guyana, if you are not earning enough to support your family you can easily fall prey to either having multiple partners just to make ends meet. You must have multiple sources of income. Guyanese women are strong and not afraid of working. Once you go through the market place, what you see are women hustling to ensure their kids have the best and their families are provided for.

We are a people of 6 races and we are intertwined in every way I love celebrating Phagwah festival of colors or Diwali festival of lights. Then there is Amerindian heritage month where you can experience the food, drinks and clothing from another cultural. I must not forget emancipation in August where the colors would dazzle your eyes everyone is dressed up. Indians, Afro, Guyanese, Chinese, and all the other races dressed in their most colorful African outfit and heading to the National park to enjoy authentic African cuisine.

As women, regardless what comes your way, stay strong, stay grounded, and push forward with your goals. Being economically independent as a woman is an important trait to teach your daughters. As women just need to stay true, we may not have it all figured out, however, I would encourage a spiritual connection reading self-help books meditate and affirmations works wonders.

My Life As A Woman: Haiti Edition #1

Hi, I am Marie and I'm Haitian. I don't know if you know my country. It's a beautiful little island in the Caribbean. A beautiful place before the big rural exodus. Indeed, the town was clean, spacious for the number of people who were living there and safe. I know all that because I see pictures and my mum, and my grandma told me about it. Then, my first trauma, it's my birth, I was born premature with a father who didn't care and who almost killed my mom one day while she was pregnant and deeply in love. I always feel that I was abandoned. He cheated on my mum and had two other kids, then two other ones.

In Haiti, a lot of fathers cheat and have other mattresses and don't take care of the children because they don't have money, or they just don't care. So, I grew up with all those questions: why he did not fight to stay in my life? Would I be different? But in the end, I had a good childhood. I had my grandmother who were everything for me. My mother, my best friend, my model. She was also my father figure. Her "Poto mitan" like we say in creole who means the head of the house. And I had my mum who were like a sister for me.

My grandma inspired me a lot as for her character and confidence. I always liked her confidence. At school, I was what people would call an awkward kid, trying my best to fit in. But how? I was so silent, they thought I was mute, so shy I could look people in the eyes. I always thought nobody loved me except my grandmother. She saves life after all (that's another story) and of course, my mom who sacrificed and kept sacrificing a lot for me. Indeed, she sacrificed a dream to become an architect to go work and be able to give me food and a good education as a single mother.

I grew up a little frustrated and confused. I was not allowed to speak my native language which was Creole. Indeed, for a lot of people in Haiti, Creole was not a language, so every time I was speaking Creole, people or my family told me to speak properly meaning speak French! Really?! Like for them, Creole is not proper, so I be used to switch to French when I am in public, I use to be ashamed to speak Creole with my mom in public. Fortunately, people start to realize Creole is a legacy and a language. I had the opportunity to study it in high school and now I'm super proud to speak Creole and share my knowledge of Creole to people around the world. This is why I made a YouTube channel and started being a tutor online.

I did love school, but I was not good at it, always needing a tutor to help me with all the subjects. And I had to redo a class. I had a lot of insecurities, such as not being beautiful because all my childhood, they called me ugly, fat which gave me an eating disorder, not smart, or I was too dreamy. I always wanted to fly, maybe I didn't want to stay in this world. And, because I am super sensitive, the poverty around me, the suffering of other people affected me a lot, I see myself crying a lot and started having suicidal thoughts, and I am still fighting them! I tried twice to kill myself. I failed, I tried pills, but I was just sick once I went to the hospital and I was mad at myself because I didn't succeed. I went back home and fought with my depression. I did not have any treatment or a doctor to help me. It is expensive to see a psychologist. After all, I tried my best to fit in, I wanted to be friends with some girls, and they bullied me, but I still stayed with them so I was like the "le villain petit canard" (the ugly duckling). I was super sensitive, but I forget them over time.

Dreamy as I was, I had so many dreams like having a lot of careers, like it is was possible. I used to want to be an architect after seeing my mum's drawing when she was at a college to study architecture, unfortunately, she didn't finish, but I was thinking I wanted to draw houses, then I wanted to build beautiful spaces for people in Haiti. Especially after the earthquake in 2010. Seeing all those hurt people, blood everywhere, dead bodies, buildings destroyed. I knew I had to do something about it. They had so many deaths because people do not care about how they build houses. It is understandable a lot of them don't have enough money to consulate an architect or even a civil engineer.

When I finished high school, I started studying architecture like I always wanted. I am almost done so I can start to build for the world! Besides that, I teach languages online for fun, but also to save money to buy books and what I need as an architect. I remember when I told people around me I wanted to be an architect, and they ask me why? I guess because I like to eat. I will be poor especially in Haiti, someone even said artiste does not pay. But I'm happy that I'm almost done, and I can show them it's a good career.

I think our society thinks woman are important even though they also suffer. I said they important because in our history, we have many women who were important when our revolution began against slavery. Indeed, for remembrance, we have in our currency 10 gourdes with the picture of the Lieutenant Sanité Bélair, a woman who fought for our independence. Then we had a woman president. I am proud of our history, it's one of the things I like the most about my country. Besides, of course, the food, especially "fritay", so colorful and tasty! Then do not forget our music, our folklore. I used to dance folklore, every time I heard some drum anywhere, I will dance, my heart will start beating hard, and I will smile like never before. This sound means a lot for me, the folklore means a lot for me too. It traces where we came from. It has 101 rhymes, those 101 rhythms, it's each country on Africa where our ancestor came from, we said in Creole "101 nanchon", "nanchon" meaning nation. I also love the traditional dresses we have. I love the Haitian art, I think all Haitians have the soul of artists. I feel this nation is full of talent. If you come to Haiti, you will see beautiful paintings, sculptures, etc. being sold on the street, or the graphitizes. My country is so beautiful with all her beaches and mountains. Did you know "Haïti" means "Terre montagneuse" mountainous land.

Here people of my color, it is called "Grimel" or "white" even I am definitively not white, but Haitians doesn't see it like that. On the street, guys often call me to come talk to them and if I ignore them they call me "white", it's because I'm white but doesn't want to talk to them, which I think it's so absurd because again, I'm black! Another issue is among the pedophiles I know exist in Haiti. I remember being a teenager, going back home, and being called by an older man on the street, like super older man who could be my grandpa! What shocked me was this guy I met at the University and he was older than me and married with kids, so he was 46 years, I was 23, and I always saw him as a big brother or even a father, but I guess he didn't see it like that. One day he offered me a ride, I agree like always, and he stopped the car once and started this weird conversation. He said that his wife and children are overseas, and he is alone, and he offers me to pay everything for me, give me money in exchange for sex! I was shocked! I said no and got out of his car, almost running. I think a lot of younger girls like me who were poor, and innocent are offered those kinds of suggestions. And if they do not have other options well, they do it. I guess it is what in our modern society, we call sugar daddy. It has made me sad to think some girls are selling their innocence in order to be able to eat or go to school. To find a good job in Haiti, you must have people already in the business or try your best to create a job that might be destroyed with all those riots, and of course, prostitution. And they have raping and kidnapping. Because of all of that, I do not feel comfortable to wear shorts or short skirts, or dresses on the street. I get panic attacks when I know I have to go out of my house, especially if they have a lot of people on the street, you never know who can grab your phone or who can point a gun at you to rob you or you can be on the street and you see everyone running… why… because some random riots will start. They are super violent, and the police also may turn to violence, in which people are getting killed as a result. I received many a time tear gas on my way somewhere.

Even though these things happen in my country, I think I am lucky. As a woman, I succeeded in finishing school and going to university. I am proud of myself for not turning to prostitution. Now I'm working online as a tutor. I'm also working through my goal, such as becoming a millionaire before I turn 30 years old, and that way I can help my country. I want to build more useful establishments, such as hospitals, schools, factories, etc. I really love my country and my culture and in this way, I will keep promoting my culture, language, and our values into the world. I try my best to see things on the bright side and keep having hope for the future. We, Haitians, are resilient, friendly, happy, nice, faithful, persevering and are hard workers. Those values are what keep me going and hope for a better life.

To women, I will say to keep working hard and that it will pay off, believe in yourself, if you want to follow a certain path, trust yourself, your intuition, your goth, your heart, and do it. Keep your head up, be faithful, stay focused. Even if you fail, don't be afraid to start again, and again, and again. Educate yourself on all kind of topic. Surround yourself with positive people, people who want the same things as you, and role model people who are already successful.

My Life As A Woman: Haiti Edition #2

I was born in a little village of twenty thousand people called "Marin", located near the main city—Port-Au-Prince. I grew up in abject poverty and lacked everything. My father was a schoolteacher and earned less than $500 a month and my mother was a street vendor with irregular income. My parents were unable to feed me and my two younger sisters. They could neither provide good clothes nor could they pay for quality education for us. Despite our struggles, we were joyful because each family member cared for the other and found comfort in ourselves. This is something I will never trade, even for the world. Such rich heritage came from my cultural background. And if you ever travel to Haiti, you will be surprised to see how the people live. They embrace life with enthusiasm. They are happy despite their struggles and challenges.

Growing up, I was bullied at school and rejected by my classmates. They used to make fun of and disrespect me. Sometimes, they even refused to sit next to me. To them it was funny, but it was a calvary for me. I became angry and harsh. And I thought that this attitude was a solid barrier to protect myself from rejection. During this hard time, I was inspired by my father. He has a strong character with a great work ethic. He has always encouraged me to dream big, have high expectations in life, and believe in myself. Dad was my modal and I wanted to become like him— a schoolteacher. One day, he told me to dream bigger; otherwise, I will not be financially independent. But it was challenging for me at this young age to think of another career because I did not have examples of successful people in my immediate environment.

After completing my primary education at age 10, I passed a contest to enter an American boarding high school in Haiti. This school offered high quality and free education for poor children. In my senior year of high school, I benefited with a full scholarship to study International Relations and Affairs at a prestigious university in Haiti. In 2016, I also received two scholarships to study Psychology in the United States and Business Administration in Italy. After earning my two master's degrees, I held several administrative positions at different non-profit organizations in Haiti. Without God's help, it would have been impossible to achieve all that considering my poor family background.

I am now a Mindset Mastery Coach. I help women to develop their potential and diversify their income. I also train them in business development and management to start small businesses. Most women across the world are left behind, mistreated, and poor. I always wanted to help them and make a difference. Consequently, I quit my job three years ago to focus on that mission only. And to all women around the world who are bullied, rejected, and left behind, I want to tell you that it is not over yet. Your glorious days will come. Like my dad used to tell me, "dream big, have high expectations in life, and believe in yourself".

My Life As A Woman: Honduras #1

Hello, my name is Andrea, I was born on October 4, 1990 in the city of Puerto Cortés, Cortes, Honduras. I was the second daughter of my parents' marriage. My dad always worked in shipping agencies and boat-related issues, and my mom was a housewife who finished high school after my older brother was born, then there was me, his second daughter and my younger sister. My parents got married when my dad was 24 and my mom was 14. I grew up in a Christian home with a couple of intra-familial problems that are common in Honduran families. I grew up around my cousins who I played with all the time. When I was 14, my parents separated and my mother decided to leave my dad and go to live in America, my older brother had left a couple of years ago too. My younger sister of 7 years and I, at 14 years old, stayed with my dad. It was very hard to separate from my mom and we didn't understand anything. My grandmother lived very close to us so she took care of us. My dad had problems with alcohol and it was very difficult to live with him, it was quite a challenge.

My biggest inspiration was my younger sister and my grandmother. I loved my grandmother and I always wanted to be with her, learn from her, do things together like plant trees, drink coffee, cook together and learn her recipes, I love hearing the stories of episodes in her life that transported me to that time. My grandmother always made me feel loved. And for my sister, I developed a maternal feeling of taking care of her and protecting her, I felt I had to do things right to be a good example to her. I thought she could follow in my footsteps and if I was wrong, she would follow, too.

My mom says that when I was little, I told her that when I grew up, I'd be a dentist. I also remember that at some point I wanted to be a veterinarian because I really liked animals. The time elapsed in between to the public university of Honduras, I enrolled in the degree of Chemistry and Pharmacy, which I left after a year because I had to move to another city that was hours from my hometown, to attend the faculty of Chemistry and Pharmacy. That meant leaving my sister alone. So after considering it, I changed to the Dentistry career that I fell in love with and fall in love with every day.

After 6 years I finished my career and I had my first job as a dentist in an ONG that dealt with family planning and sex education for women. In an attempt to expand their services and more comprehensively address the needs of the patients, they included the area of dentistry. Here I had the opportunity to treat many women and know different stories, some were sad, others were good, others were bad, others were successful. I heard all kinds of stories you can imagine, mostly not positive. I realized the vulnerability of women in our country, and it boils down to the fact that justice doesn't exist here.

I believe that Honduran women have many struggles to fight from a very young age in a "machista" country (Machismo is an ideology that encompasses the set of attitudes, behaviors, social practices and beliefs aimed at promoting the superiority of men over women, or self-reliance and pride of men in various areas of life). Sometimes society pushes you to get married and have children which I find very dignified, but you have to do it only when you want it and not because of pressure.

My grandmother and sister taught me to love, to care, and to protect. As much as I realize, to my parents, that they are human beings with their own personal conflicts, that they are not perfect, no one is. I love them. The situation I experienced helped me to be independent, to take care of myself and my sister, to overcome many challenges almost alone. Was that ideal? No, it wasn't. But it's what I touch and you have to take what you have and move on, until you achieve your dreams. Your dreams are precious, your dreams are worth it, and you are absolutely capable of achieving whatever you want.

Despite everything negative in Honduras. There are very noble and talented people here, I like that Hondurans are warm, cheerful, and very hardworking. From my country, I like food, the climate, the beaches, our fairs, our carnivals, our exquisite food, our folk and "Garifuna" music. I like our rhythm "La Punta", the history of Mayan civilization in our lands.

I think if I could talk to some woman who has difficulties in her life, I would tell her that there's no other way forward, nothing in life is permanent, and if you work for something you want, you can be sure you will see results soon. Life challenges each of us, some challenges are more difficult than others. Remember that we always have the choice to take problems, difficult situations, and turn them into wisdom and compassion. One can always learn something positive from painful experiences. Life is about overcoming our challenges, fears and being better every day. Believe in you, trust you, it's all up to you.

My Life As A Woman: Honduras Edition #2

Sit properly! Cross your legs! Don't play with boys!

Growing up in Honduras, these are all things I had heard as a little girl. I was taught by my elders and teachers to follow certain rules and behave a certain way. Questions that always led to childlike confusion because, why celebrate boys for certain actions, and condemn girls for the same thing? It all seemed unjust to me. This confusion certainly escalated during my teenage years. I never fit in because I could never find myself to be bothered with the idea of makeup, clothes or guys, in general. At this stage in my life, I was more concerned with the next big reggaeton hit or watching anime.

I always grew up with the idea that, in life, there are always more important principles than the ones we are taught at that certain moment. Things like justice, equality, and strength are ideals that used to and continue to drive me as a person. Life is certain to test you at several points throughout your life. It is your duty to pass them and get ready for the next one. Sometimes it's hard to overcome these issues but you can always find someone to rely on; be it a friend, partner, teacher or sibling. In my case, the people who I knew I could rely on were my parents. They were my source of strength and endurance for the challenges one must face in life.

The first challenge you are faced with is the dilemma of deciding what you want to become when you grow up. As a kid, I knew I wanted to help people, yet I didn't know how I could achieve this goal. I used to think it would be through dance, but it turns out I lack the necessary coordination, so I decided to drop that and look for a new dream. It was only after I met a psychologist that I knew this was what I wanted to be: a person able to guide people through their painful experiences and let it become something they can learn from.

Education in Honduras is a serious topic. It is the majority of the population that receives a public education which has proved time and time again, to need a serious reform. According to studies, less than one in ten students achieve a milestone goal in reading, math or sciences. This impacts on the lives of students throughout their lives, as many decide to drop out or start working, making the average years of schooling for adults 4.8. Therefore, it is a huge privilege to get a bilingual education and graduate from university in my country, as I was able to accomplish. And to be able, to work with children, is a tremendous opportunity to make an impact, however small, on the youth.

Personally, I think children who are happy, laugh, and play freely are very well on their way to becoming resilient adults. Resilience is a shield formed around a person to help them overcome and transform hardships into opportunities for growth. Working as an educational psychologist allows me to become a part of this process for girls and boys alike.

Another challenge you may be faced with is accepting your personal identity, and part of that is your culture. Growing up as a Honduran there are many things the media tells you. For example, we rank among the highest poverty rates in Latin America and possess one of the highest homicide rates worldwide. As a woman in my country, you are often subjected to misogynist comments and constant fear of walking alone in the streets for reasons such as violence and sexual aggression, something men don't experience much when walking down the streets. Reports have shown that 27% of the female population in Honduras is said to have suffered physical violence at one point or another in their lives. According to Migdonia Ayestas, director of Violence Observatory of the National Autonomous University, every 23 hours a Honduran woman is murdered. When talking about job opportunities, you may find women to be at a disadvantage. Whether it is through an ad you found on the internet or TV, most of the time you will see that the company hiring sets a specific requirement: for the applicant to be male. Reports have shown that a woman is less likely to be hired, and when she is hired, she's expected to work twice as hard to get paid less than the male doing the exact same job as her.

Sparse job opportunities, low salaries, and questionable work conditions are only part of what one can expect as a Honduran. Nevertheless, it is instilled in you to set goals in your life, work hard to accomplish them, and relax when you have the time to do so. You may do that by walking along the beach with orange sunsets painting the sky and the sea. Family gatherings filled with laughter and conversation during Christmas and New Year's wearing new clothes is something we look forward to.

Enjoying delicious cuisine that you can only find here like: baleadas, tapado and chuleta is something that would warm any Honduran's heart.

Another way to warm a Honduran's heart is through holidays. 'Semana Santa' is a week-long holiday that you get to spend reflecting on the Passion of Christ. El Gran Carnaval is another week-long celebration of friendship in honor of Saint Isidro Labrador, who is the holy patron of La Ceiba city. This celebration, you get to spend it enjoying live music, floats, marching bands and delicious gastronomy. When you live through all this, you can only but fall in with this country and culture.

I think growing up as an empowered woman in any part of the world is a responsibility not to be taken lightly. There will be hardships only we women understand, and the expectations may be harsher than you think. But you are more than capable of making this an opportunity of growth. Break the glass ceiling, make that dream come true, challenge yourself, and overcome every hardship thrown your way. It is through hard work and support from my family that I was able to defy the stereotypes a Honduran woman must face from the moment she's born. And this is something I wish for all women: be free, strong, independent. Defy the odds.

"I hate to hear you talk about all women as if they were fine ladies instead of rational creatures. None of us want to be in calm waters all our lives." – Jane Austen (Persuasion)

Lizzeth Romero M.

My Life As A Woman: Hong Kong Edition #1

I grew up in Hong Kong and studied in France since I was 19 years old. I spent years in Paris learning French and my BBA major in Global Business and another 2 years in Bordeaux for the MBA wine. I started my wine business in 2011 the same year I returned back to Hong Kong. I think my parents are quite inspiring on my business path as both of them are entrepreneurs. I was very independent ever since I was young seeing my mum raising kids and still working at school, studying in fashion, designing clothes, chasing her dreams and creating company with partners. Most of my aunties and uncles studied aboard so I don't think I was an exception. I chose to go to France first amazed by its culture and history. I stepped into the wine industry when I was doing an internship in a Wine Tasting company in Paris. I knew that it would be a trend in Asia Market.

By then, I became the first person from Hong Kong finishing a French Tasting Diploma from the well-known Oenology faculty with a Wine MBA in Bordeaux. Establishing my import and consulting company in my twenties, everything was quite smooth and my business grew so fast thanks to my unique profile. It was interesting to work as a wine consultant, a wine writer, and a boss of a small company. However, I didn't want to stop there and I created a media platform to enhance the wine culture and luxury lifestyle ideas through cross marketing. That was the time I got involved in charity and social enterprise. Here, in Hong Kong, we are very open to any ideas of business and welcome the women entrepreneurs to speak out for others. For some reason, Hong Kong women tend to be more interested in social responsibility after being successful in their business. With no doubt that was on motherhood basis.

It wasn't easy to balance family, friends, and work as an entrepreneur. There is no time schedule for running your own business and charity commitments. But you still need to squeeze some time to take care of your family and friends, to make your house, to have me time and to learn new things, etc. The housework doesn't sound fancy for a woman entrepreneur, luckily we have full time domestic helper to manage our house and you can live your life and pursue your dream with the circumstances above. Proper face, proper house, and proper career, which was the ticket to enjoy life in Hong Kong.

If you have new ideas, go for it! If you have something you want to create, go for it. There is not too late or too much in here. We love people who are energetic, brave to tell everybody who you are and what you would like to achieve! Men and women are more equal in our society if you are confident to be a top mom and top boss!

Summary:

Pros

-        Opportunities

-        Open-minded

-        Freedom

Cons

-        Traditional Asian Mindset

-        Stay-at-home Mum

My Life As A Woman: Hong Kong Edition #2

A good sleeping habit is incredibly important for both mental and physical health. It can improve productivity, concentration, emotional intelligence, and social interactions. As a Hong Kong woman, I believe good sleep leads to a good life. It sounds very irrelevant to the topic. Yet, I'm literally writing about my life as a woman in Hong Kong. I spent one-third of my life on sleeping but I didn't realize this basic need has such importance to my life until I felt seriously exhausted.

I'm very "Hong Kong", even though I spent my childhood in Auckland. I studied and work in Hong Kong for more than 20 years. My family is not poor, but definitely not rich. Like typical Hong Kong families, I and my brother are taught to study and work hard in order to survive in a competitive society. Taking rest means I am lazy. Being lazy means I cannot survive in the future. If I cannot survive, I will not get happiness in my life.

When I grew up, I realized that Asian parent's mindset does has its point, because I found Hong Kong is really competitive, not only in schools and working places, but also dating cultures and friendship, and Hong Kong girls are truly hard-working, smart, proactive and pretty. Hong Kong women are often compared with Taiwanese, Chinese, Japanese and Korean women. While people often say Hong Kong women are the worst due to body shapes, attitudes and personalities, I believe toughness, diligence, and kindness are the unique characters of Hong Kong women.

My major was communication study. All girls are especially good at socializing and know well how to present the best of them. I realized being good-looking, clever, friendly and outgoing, as well as having a good career is the basic standard of Hong Kong girls. If I cannot reach the standard, I am doomed to fail because all people keep telling me this is what "women's success".

While I was persuading the dream of being a "successful woman", I couldn't have sweet night dreams every day. My emotion was affected by how people thought of me. Many questions often annoyed me, like I'll wonder "why guys did not reply my text?", "why did my manager not invite me to lunch?" and "did I earn more than my friends?", etc. I always wanted to be a perfect girl in people's eyes and the effort I paid does give me outcomes, like good friendship and career in life. However, these are not things able to touch my heart.

I worked as a journalist for 3 years and I gave up my journalism career due to the closedown of my company. After that, I decided to give myself a long holiday and I got a lot of free time that I have never had before. At first, I did not know how to spend my alone time because I was too used to work and pleasing people so hard. I realized that I was emotional too and relied on my work and friends because I found I have never catered my own feelings. But then, I tried to ask a lot of questions to myself, instead of "why don't people like me?", I asked, "do I have enough sleep?", "Am I healthy?" and "Am I happy?" these kinds of questions are simple but important questions.

Talking to myself helps me to find happiness. If I feel tired, I should sleep. Sleep for 8 hours until I feel happy. Likewise, if I love someone, just love; If I want to do something, just plan and do it. That's how I gain happiness. I do not need to try so hard to be so-called successful and then be happy.

Thinking back, being a "successful woman" was never my dream. My teacher asked me what my dream was when I was five. I said I hoped to go back to Auckland since it was a nice, clean and peaceful place and gave me impressive childhood memories. Last year, I went back to Auckland. Currently, I am a barista and a freelancer. Flexible working hours allow me to manage my own time according to my priority in life. However, before being productive, I believe enough sleep, good mental and physical health is the basis of the pursuit of happiness.

My Life As A Woman: Hungary Edition

I was born and raised in Hungary which is a small country in the middle of Europe. I grew up in a very small town next to Lake Balaton. In this little town, everyone knew everyone. In the summers, there are a lot of people visiting and spending their holidays there, people from our country and from abroad all love Balaton and they often choose our little town as their destination. Thanks to that, everyone paid attention to how the town looked like, so it is always clean, the buildings are taken care of, and you can find flowers everywhere. That always made me feel really proud. I'm not actively living there anymore, but I visit every month and thinking about that place always warms my heart.

Growing up I was blessed to have two role-models: my Mother and my Grandmother. My Grandmother was a teacher in my Elementary school, she taught P.E. for me. Needless to say, that was my favourite subject. My Grandmother taught me a lot of things. Every day after school I visited her and my Grandfather. She always helped me with studying, she taught me how to use utensils correctly (that was a big deal then for me) and she taught me what real love looks like. She always paid attention to my feelings and needs as a kid and she still does. She and my Grandfather met at the University of Pécs (where I'm currently studying right now) and they have been together since. She showed me how to love, respect and care for our loved ones.

My mother is a superhero. She got pregnant with me when she was only 19 years old. I wasn't planned, which I always knew because she often told me the story of how I came to this world. She would always say with so much love in her eyes that one day I just came knocking on the door and I was suddenly just there. It's not a very interesting origin story, but I can still remember the kindness and love she always showed me when she told me these words. She graduated from high school after I was born, but she didn't stop there. One and a half years later my sister was born, and with her, our little family was complete. My Mother started University when we were little. Our Grandmother looked after us every afternoon, so she could go to school and study. While she studied, she was also working at our pub. My Mother since then went through a divorce, she struggled financially, but she always found a way to take care of us. She taught me how to manage under big stress, how to love unconditionally, and how to be a superhero.

Growing up I wanted to be a teacher. Later, that changed and I wanted to become a policewoman, an interior designer, an actress, an artist, a translator and basically everything else you can think of. By the time I had to apply for college, I knew I wanted to be a teacher for real. My Grandma, my Grandpa, and my Mother are all teachers, so I knew I had it in me. I'm currently in a teaching training program at the University of Pécs, where – as I mentioned – my Grandparents met. Pécs is also the place they lived as kids and young adults, so I feel like it was my faith to end up here.

Going back to the small town I lived in, a huge part of our culture is wine. We make wine and we drink wine, especially next to Balaton. We as a family are growing grapes, selling grapes, and we also making wine. When there is a festival, the beaches are packed with little booths where you can try each winery's wines. There are a lot of famous wineries in this area, unfortunately, my family doesn't produce bottled wine, we make it in huge barrels, but it is a dream of mine to make our wine bottled and famous in our country.

Growing up I faced some struggles which I felt were struggles respectively of women. I never understood the fuss around having to dress up "girly", being "pretty" and "skinny". These were sadly said to me by women. Because of these, I became very aware of how I looked and how society wanted me to look like, which resulted in eating disorders and an unhealthy body image. This affects my life to this day, but thanks to these experiences, I'm a preacher of self-love and I plan to teach that not only to my future kids but to my students as well.

In my life so far, I have experienced some successes as a woman. I was very successful at school and I achieved very good grades on my high school diploma. I entered into university, where my studies are free because of my good grades. I got my driving license while I was still in high school. I became more independent, I learned how to take care of myself, and the place I live in. I started to work as a freelance translator and writer, and currently, I'm teaching myself digital drawing, which is also a passion of mine. I'm constantly learning and evolving, I'm proud of who I am, and I believe that is a success on its own.

My advice as a woman from Hungary is that you should not feel like you can't achieve your dreams just because you don't live in a huge city full of opportunities. There are opportunities everywhere. We may not start from the same place, but we can definitely get there together. There are women all around the world, who made it, who made their dreams come true and you are one of them! I am one of them too! Don't listen to people when they say that you have to be "pretty", "skinny" or "girly". You don't have to be any of those things. Focus on what you love and what you need to learn to get there.

My Life As A Woman: Iceland Edition

I was born in Reyjavík, the capital of Iceland, in 1999. I grew up my whole childhood in a small town 10 minutes outside of Reykjavík. I lived with my mom, dad, and younger brother. I was lucky to go to school just next to my street, I walked there every day with my brother. I spent a lot of my time alone as a kid, I used to read a lot. I would spend weeks of my summer break in the library, eating up books about anything and everything. I had a pretty basic upbringing, but it changed a bit when my parents split up. I try to look on to the positive side of things, it does better than looking at the negatives.

I was taught as a kid to not talk to strangers and not to trust people I didn't know. A lot of the families did that in my town. I remember when I was maybe in 4th grade, a teacher sat all the students down and told us about this man who had tried to ask a girl in my grade to get into his car. That was the first time in my life I felt scared like that, like me being a girl could be harmful to me. Although I was lucky to have never experienced anything like that, I still look over my shoulder every now and then when I'm alone outside. I usually don't feel scared, but sometimes when you're walking home alone in the dark Icelandic winter air you start over thinking. I guess it comes with being a girl.

I have a lot of role models, people who shaped me to the person I am today. My grandmother is a huge influence, that's probably where I get my love for art from. She spent so much time sitting with me, just drawing and teaching me about art. Even when she lost a lot of mobility in her arms, she still paints till this day. When I was young I always wanted to be a painter, just like my grandma. Now I have passion for helping people. I studied social studies in college and I plan on going further down that track. I think I get that passion from my mother, she is also a huge inspiration to me. She is always ready to help me, no matter what she is dealing with. I can surely say I am surrounded by strong women.

In my opinion, being a girl here in Iceland is pretty nice. We are definitely well off, compared to other places so I can't really complain. The culture here usually allows both genders to bloom equally. I do know there is a bit of a wage gap but Iceland is working hard on closing that gap. Of course you will meet people that look down on women, though I think they are less. I think times changed after 1970, when Icelandic women started stepping up for their rights and speaking up about the treatment they were receiving. We even had a female president from 1980 till 1996. In fact, she is the first woman to be directly democratically elected as president. It was a huge step for Iceland, and for all the women here. Of course we aren't perfect, there are things that need to be done so women will be on equal grounds. The battle isn't over yet but we are lucky to be this close. I can say with a lot of confidence that most women here are feminists, they just want equality. I can also say that a lot of men here are feminists, I guess that's also a reason why we are doing well.

As a woman, I've done a lot, but I have a lot left to do. I've gone through years of school, and I was working for a lot of it. I'm thankful I had a job, it helps you get ready for the future, whatever it might hold. I feel like my list of things should be longer, but I'm still so young. I want to travel the world, go to university here in Iceland and learn more about my passions. I want to be known for helping people, for caring.

If any woman wants to come here, I really only have one piece of advice. Keep your head up, walk with confidence. You are just as valuable as everyone else, you deserve to speak your mind. If you sent your mind to something, there is no reason you shouldn't be able to get to that goal. Sometimes you have to fight, but you'll only come out stronger in the end.

My Life As A Woman: India Edition #1

When you are born in a small town in India, which falls somewhere between an underdeveloped village and what we perceive as the epitome of advancement as far as the country goes – a metropolitan city – I was acutely aware of the widespread patriarchal society around me. That does not mean my life in Howrah – which most people still believe is a part of the Kolkata City (it's not; both of them are separated by River Ganges) – was extremely discriminating from the start. Childhood was more or less the same for me and my brother, who was three years older than me. We enjoyed similar games, had the same study hours, and also shared equal lengths of scolding from our parents. When my brother became a teenager, he was allowed to purchase a motorbike with the pocket money that he had saved up. Excited at the sight of him leave the house whenever he wanted, including late in the evening or even night with the mere words, "Hey mum, I'll be late, don't wait up" made me start saving up my pocket money too. But after a few years, when I expressed a desire to buy a scooty, my parents exchanged looks and told me, "Your brother can take you wherever you want, you know." It was their way of softening the blow. But it hurt just as much.

When I look back at whom I admired more between by parents, it was always by dad. Apart from the fact that I was a "daddy's girl" I did not really see what the big takeaway was from my mother's occupation, which I still remember cringing when I had to say aloud in front of my teacher at school. "Housewife." This was before "homemaker," the cooler, less sexist alternative of my mother's occupation was in trend. I never understood what the big deal was about taking care of the household. You had to get up before the rest of the house woke up, prepare about six different meals for the members of the home (since each has their own preference), get your children ready for school, wash clothes, supervise cleaning of the house, check on your children to ensure they are studying, make sure everyone is fed, and go to sleep after everyone else has gone to bed. Sounded simple enough at the time. Only when I migrated to Bangalore and learned to live on my own in a big city did I start appreciating everything that my mother did for me and the rest of the family on a daily basis. I still fail to remember that I have to buy detergent and I am not even physically going down to a grocery store.

I was always a bit of a book worm and hence while you would find the rest of the children on the track field, you would find me cooped up in the corner of the library with my nose deep into a dusty old book. But reading and writing was not enough, I wanted to be able to tell a story that matters and make a difference in the world. As a result, I opted to study journalism. Being a female journalist in today's day and age is as exciting as it is scary. And to be fearless is something that colleges and universities will not teach you. So little things start to matter. Little things like calling your parents before going out of the house. This does not mean that I am paranoid. But just that I would not belittle the power that evil holds in this world. In my line of work, negative feedback does not often end with just a hate mail. But I go out of the house everyday just the same and yes, I finally got my scooty.

All I know is Indian society, like most societies, has a lot of potential for changing for the better. I do believe there will come a time when men and women will be able to enjoy the same privileges and women will no longer have to hesitate before leaving their houses at any hour of the day. It might not happen in the present generation but it will happen. All we, especially women, need to do is not to give up hope.

My Life As A Woman: India Edition #2

I have been fortunate to be born in a home where I was loved, well-fed, and well taken care of. My sister and I were protected yet not pampered, we were loved but not coddled. Like all kids we weren't aware of how lucky we were to be born in the house we were, only until much later. We were not stinking rich but comfortably well off. We had a roof over our head, fresh home-cooked food on our table, a good school to go to, and decent toys to play with.

Thankfully, we never witnessed any incident of domestic violence or abuse at home, our father drank occasionally but responsibly, our mother drinking was out of the question since it's a huge taboo for women to drink in India, and we never saw our parents use swear words. They always tried to instill virtues of honesty, sincerity and moralities of kindness, and generosity in us. Our parents tried to provide us with the best of everything and we were happy at home. My struggles as a girl and later a woman started when we stepped out of the house, away from the protection of our home into the clutches of our society and the world.

I cannot pinpoint exactly when the questions of "You are two sisters only?" did, "You don't have a brother?" started being raised by friends and family. Every visit to my paternal grandparent's place was marked by my grandmother always asking my parents to try having a child again for the sole possibility of having a son. All of this happened in front of us.

In India, we worship women and consider them to be "devis" or goddesses but we do not want daughters, only sons. Daughters are considered to be a burden on their parents in our society for several reasons. The tradition of dowry and the practice that requires a married woman to relocate and live with her husband's family being two primary reasons. Once a woman marries, she is expected to devote herself to her in-laws family and give them priority over her birth parents. Hence, girls are considered to be bad investments and the practice of killing them in the womb is still very common in various parts of India. Incidents of education of boys over that of girls for the same reasons were also not uncommon. However, our parents never succumbed to the pressure of having a son and made us feel that we were enough! They focused all their energy into making sure we got the best upbringing instead. That is probably why I always lived with a sense of underlying guilt for not being good enough in school and for not being worth all their efforts.

I was an average kid who wasn't the best in Mathematics and Science, the two subjects my parents expected me to be good at, but I did well in Languages. My father is a civil engineer and a genius one at that, his expectation to have a child who was good at the subjects he loved wasn't entirely unfair. I, on the other hand, dreaded anything that had to do with numbers, facts, and figures. I was always drawn to stories instead. Gradually, I started reading fiction novels and became consumed in them, ignoring my studies in the process because of which my results suffered. Reading and losing myself in the world of fiction and fantasy novels became my drug and my parents initially disapproved of that, worrying I was letting my grades suffer. However, they came around it and accepted my passion for literature and supported me in pursuing a bachelors and later a master's degree in English Literature. We were now tabooed twice over in their friends and family circle, first for being girls and second for opting for humanities and not sciences. My parents continued to have faith in my passion and abilities whatsoever.

The day I cleared the UGC exam which is the eligibility test for becoming a professor in India, the reaction of my parents was all the reward I needed. However, my troubles were nowhere near over. I taught as an assistant professor for English for undergraduate students and was disillusioned with the academia and the shambles in the education system. I felt troubled and trapped in a soulless vocation and dreaded spending the rest of my life caught up in the decaying system and was frustrated for not being able to do anything about it.

Eventually, I quit and started looking for work as a freelance writer. I have made some progress but have a long way to go. It's not a vocation that earns me a lot of money but it's something I am genuinely passionate about and love doing. Although I am still struggling, I have a firm resolve of persevering and evolving as a writer, maybe even write a book someday.

I cannot change the world, no matter how much I wish to, and make it a better place but I can work on myself and I believe that is where change begins.

My Life As A Woman: India Edition #3

As Albert Einstein once said, "The woman who follows the crowd will usually go no further than the crowd. The woman who walks alone is likely to find herself in places no one has ever been before." He was, for sure, true because a woman is not just a mere representation of the female gender, but she entails a whole universe in herself. As Mother Nature made her, she goes through many facets of life being a daughter to a young woman, wife, and nurturing mother.

I belong to a land of rich history and culture popularly known as India. When we talk about Indian women, the topic is quite controversial. It is a stereotypical society where as soon as a girl is born, she is subjected to so many boundaries and expectations of society. In India, it is said that a woman is incomplete until she becomes a mother. Most women get married early in their life and are expected to give birth at a very early stage of their adulthood. She is expected to be a proper daughter obeying her parents to marry whoever they select for her, being a proper wife obeying her husband as God, and his family as well. She is subjected to neglect, her wishes and thoughts, to give preference to others. Some are being brought up in such a way that they do not have any choice at all. If she is not up to the mark of the society, she is not a perfect woman. Unlike me, those who are rebellious, go against societal norms and expectations and prove their mark to themselves only to attain happiness and peace.

I grew up in the slums of Bombay (Mumbai) and my parents passed away leaving me alone with my grandmother when I was 6 years old. My grandmother was a very strong and confident woman who always protected me and guided me to be responsible and independent. She used to tell me, "Never stop dreaming." It is her sacrifices she made that I am where I am today. All my life I grew up facing towards the sky and staring at the passing airplanes wishing to fly to another land someday. I used to hear the screams of women getting beaten up by their husbands every single night over little petty issues. I saw the attributes of respect, honor, love, and happiness torn away from societal traditions. I saw tears and pains very close and made a pact with myself that I will not face this whatsoever. My grandmother worked in a stitching factory to pay for my school. I was a shy slumber girl but a very good student. My aim in life was always clear in my mind that I must achieve success no matter I belong to that gender which has low value in Indian culture. It is a harsh truth, but one must face it.

Growing up, I also worked part-time in a factory and took care of my higher studies. Being a business student at a local university, and then attaining an international scholarship, I went abroad for further studies. I realized that a woman can come out of the slums without any support and achieve her dreams. I never let go of my root values belonging to India. Indian women are strong and powerful because they are more dedicated and committed to their cultural roots. Today, I own a successful clothing line in India. I have a home in the expensive suburbs of Mumbai, my favorite city in the world. At the age of 32, I find myself at peace. I am happily married to a person who treats me like a human of value and respects my dreams and aims as equally as his own. I have a son whose smile is the world to me. My life changed because I let go of the boundaries that were inhumane. I learned one thing in my life that if you want to achieve something, you must break yourself down and then rebuild it from scratch with dedication, motivation, and will. It doesn't matter if you are a man or a woman; the opportunities are open to both and life gives equal chances. It's completely up to you to break the chains of stereotypical ideologies and follow your dreams. My advice to women out there who have buried their wishes and locked them away in their heart forever is never too late to say "No" to demand and expectation of others and be the woman you always wished to be. Remember that your life has not given to you to live as someone else.

My Life As A Woman: India Edition #4

Hello everyone. I know most of you are stuck at home right now and wanted to do something or start something new which you always wanted to but never got enough time to think about it. Maybe after reading my story you will get some inspiration to stop thinking and start doing. I want to share my story as a woman about how I overcame my procrastination, recognised my strengths, and started living a balanced life of work and passion.

I am a middle-class individual who was born and brought up in Maharashtra, one state in India. It is an evergreen state which has a vibrant culture and peaceful nature. From my young age, I always lived with my parents who used to inspire me in everything I liked to do even when my interests were totally different from the others. I was interested in dancing and sketching a lot in my early age. I used to think I would become a dancer. But as I was growing up, I started developing more of an interest in school. Especially science, as it seemed to me fascinating how chemical reactions create energy and beautiful things all around us. Science and math teachers were my source of inspiration for this interest. As they saw my interest and progress in studies, they motivated me to continue my studies in the science field. But still, I wasn't sure what I wanted to do.

At the age of 14, I had experienced one bad turn in my life as my beloved grandmother whom I never thought would leave me so early due to disease made me think and do something that I couldn't do at that time. My grandmother got a dog bite who had rabies and it got worse so fast that every effort after spreading the virus failed. This drove me even more to study biology. From my high school studies, I was determined to study biology but had seen it in only one perspective: that I needed to become a doctor. Since I am a girl who wanted to become a doctor, I was accused by relatives, and my parents were advised by them to not invest their money on a girl who, at the end was not going to benefit their family, whenever I was to marry and go to my husband's house. I don't like this thinking of people which is still remaining in the less developed areas of Maharashtra. Later when I failed to get a high score to get a doctor's seat, I was depressed as I was thinking now I am going to be accused even more that I am a failure. I was totally broken down. But still due to love from my parents, I kept going.

I was admitted to the bioscience university, and later in university life, I realised this is the path that I wanted to follow. Because I always wanted to find something new for people where they don't have access to treatment as soon as possible. And for this, I was unaware that I needed to study bioscience rather than becoming a doctor, unknown of the well-known fact. This taught me that what is meant by figuring out what you actually want in life should be clear to your mind.

Fast forward my life and I am currently working in a research lab happily. To get to this position, I had to face many storms of different colours. One aspect in being a woman is to be considered less intellectual and recessive. This unspoken behavioural existing fact always drove me to get up and give my best to achieve my goals in life and so far, helped me through these years to put myself equally with everyone else around.

It wasn't easy at first to be motivated all the time but when I started doing yoga, giving myself time to think about my health, planning of one week ahead, it started showing results. I also kept my passion for sketching alive which gives me happiness and energy to do work. This helps me a lot in keeping myself refreshed the whole day and be in the moment in meetings and work.

As I said, there are things I don't like about my Indian culture but still, what always keeps me motivated is the environment in which I grew up because people are loving, caring, full of attachments and inspiring you to do something with the examples of great achievers like Savitribai Phule. Today, when my friends and family see me as a grownup individual in my life, they don't compare me with my brother or any male friends who were growing up with me. Rather they notice my success as a researcher. This feeling is very great to cater for the balance and sustainable future of society. What I learned with this small life is that people are good and bad at the same time and there will be people who want to stop you and pull you down. You just need to take a deep breath till the water overflowing above you calms down then everything will be on your way.

My Life As A Woman: Indonesia Edition #1

I am an Indonesian TCK. Being a TCK (Third Culture Kid) might be some people's dreams. After all, who wouldn't want to experience living in other countries? Living abroad does give benefits and personal development. Still, there are also setbacks of it, especially when you go back home, and your original culture is the total opposite of the culture you were exposed to. And I'm one of those people.

My Childhood

My childhood was so-so, it's the typical Indonesian childhood where we go to school from 7 AM to 2 PM, learning more than 7 subjects in a day. I played with my friends on breaks, had crushes on boys, and escaped from the scary headmistress. It was my routine until my father informed me that we're moving from Indonesia to Suriname.

I didn't know how I felt because I was a kid, but it was probably because I didn't feel anything. As a fifth-grader, my head couldn't process the importance of the information. It was when I stepped my foot on Johan Adolf Pengel Airport, I realized that I'll be away from my home for four years. Then, I became anxious.

A Whole New World

Adjusting to the new culture wasn't that hard. Suriname has what traditional Eastern people call as a Western lifestyle. Dating, living together before marriage, being upfront – things that are considered normal in the West. Although I do realize that they are considered taboo in my culture, I slowly began to accept those things as usual.

We were supposed to go back after four years, but my father loved Suriname. So he retired early and decided to stay there. In the end, I returned back to Indonesia after I graduated from high school. I lived in Suriname for 7 years.

A Native That Does Not Belong At Home

There is only one word that described my feeling after my return – miserable. I went to a university in Yogyakarta, and I was surrounded by people I considered as "conservative" at that time. I was too blunt as a girl and was too aggressive as a lover. My words were rough, and I was unfriendly because I didn't smile a lot. And apparently, I was too rebellious by answering my male friends and too opinionated. I barely had friends in my first and second semesters. I felt as if I didn't belong there.

Then, I entered the university press (the club for university students). Since the people there are as "liberal" as me, I vented my feelings to them. From being too foreign, despite being an Indonesian, feeling lonely since I had nobody, I poured all of them to my press friends. They were patient enough to listen to me, but they also taught me to do one thing – adapt. And they were right. I needed to adapt.

Taking The Middle Path

From then on, I changed. I tried to understand my original culture and how it should be applied to my life. I observed other girls to understand what I should and should not do to acquaintances. I tried practising them, and soon, I had more people willing to talk to me. At first, it was two, then it became a few more, and later it became the entire class. I didn't change my personality since I just took the middle path. I'm still opinionated, but I use softer words and tone. I'm still "aggressive," but I use words instead of actions. I'm honest to those who ask for my opinion. Thanks to my developing ability to adapt, now, I'm no longer an outsider. Instead, I can enter social circles quickly, as my adaptability makes people accept me easily.

Adapting In My Career Journey

Surprisingly, adapting helped me in my career. When I was teaching in another city, I was not shocked by the "rough" culture there (Yogyakarta is considered as "soft"). I was not intimidated by my so-called "rough" students. Instead, I try to follow their pace and understand their situation. As a result, the students became my acquaintances. They were not hesitant to ask questions if they didn't understand something. Some of them opened up and told me their stories. I managed to teach in a school many claimed to be" unmanageable" and passed the two years successfully.

The same goes for my new job. Thanks to my flexible personality, I can do things that I've never learned before smoothly (I am currently a writer for a game studio). My opinionated-self also smoothened the communication between my peers and me. The higher-ups are starting to trust me with more roles. By adapting, I'm learning new skills while gaining trust from my teammates. I'm feeling positive about my development for both my skills and my career path.

Adapting Is The Key

My story might be different from yours, but there is one thing we can have in common – the ability to adapt quickly. If you're struggling in your current working environment, observe other people and see what makes them blend with the others so well. Make time for self-reflection and know where you can slip the positive things you see during observation.

When you don't know what to do, ask. Don't wait for others and take the initiative. Asking questions is a great way to start a communication that can spark a discussion. So not only will you have answers, but you can also deepen your bond with your team. This applies to the higher-ups as well. Don't hold back just because you're an employee and a woman. When you've mastered the ability to adapt, you'll broaden your horizon and see new opportunities you've never realized before.

My Life As A Woman: Indonesia Edition #2

My name is Sukamawati, born in Jakarta. Jakarta is a city where little people depend on expectations, as well as a city that is least friendly to them. My eyes always glaze over whenever I see an old man in a worn-out sack carrying a sack, sitting on the side of the road, waiting for something that somehow comes. As well-dressed people passed by, without the slightest turn in the old man's direction. Whenever I see people like that old man, I feel annoyed because I want to help but feel helpless, I feel useless. My only little dream is to make those who are helpless on the roadside smile again. I want to see the city better, friendlier to the little people like me and old people sitting on the roadside waiting for hope.

I admire my great father, someone who is very reliable. He taught me about the mindset I should use. He said that we cannot fulfill all the expectations given by people and be ourselves. Since I was a kid, I lived in Jakarta, but unfortunately, I didn't really know the culture of my area. Some that I know are dance, clothing and food. The food that I like the most is the Egg Crust and Rice Prawn. Egg crust is a Betawi specialty that is very well known especially during the Jakarta Fair event. Egg crust is almost similar to Martabak, the difference lies in the contents and how to load it. The contents of the eggshells are sticky rice and sweet potatoes. How to cook an egg crust, namely by heating it on a charcoal furnace.

Almost all people in Jakarta and even throughout Indonesia are familiar with uduk rice. Nuduk uduk is a very familiar breakfast in Jakarta. Similar to liwet rice, uduk rice made from white rice is cooked with herbs. Rice seasoning includes salt, coconut milk, lemongrass leaves, bay leaves and orange leaves. The taste of uduk rice is very good and tasty. Uduk rice is usually eaten with sliced omelet, jengkol stew, fried chicken, empal, balado potatoes, and peanut sauce.

Now that I am working in a foreign company, I realize that the demands to appear attractive in all aspects are very high. All types of body care products and cosmetics are easily available. I have thought that I must be beautiful to be accepted by people. I am aware of all the physical shortcomings that I have that makes me stressed and depressed because I have spent a lot of money to cover up those shortcomings but still nothing worked. Behind my dark side is a man who always pushes me, and that person is my father. I realize that everyone's expectations are not always the same. If only I wanted to fulfill all these expectations, it would not make me happy, but it only made me suffer more. I am now even a fool with it, even though I am still looking after myself, but chasing expensive products. I believe there is still hope and that's what keeps me going.

For women out there, I am sure you are great people! Beauty is important to women, but I just want to tell you that beauty has no standards. Beauty is diverse, some say that "A" is beautiful, but some say that "B" is more beautiful. All of these are opinions given by others. You do not need to meet the expectations of others, be yourself, you are all beautiful!

My Life As A Woman: Borneo Island Edition #1

My name is Kornelia Anggun, I am a descendant of the indigenous Dayak tribe of West Kalimantan of Borneo. I live with a very large family in a simple village. My family became very big because everything in the village is about family. The location of my village is in a remote area called Flower Mountain in the middle of the forest. Although located in the middle of the forest, there is village electricity available there.

I grew up in an area that still has traditional culture. In our village, everyone knows each other, and has a high sense of family. Different from the atmosphere of the capital city that may be where neighbors do not know each other, we help each other. But after high school, I moved to the city to study. Life in the city is very different, more challenging because in the city, all are required to be active in everything and required to be able to do everything.

The most interesting culture is the traditional dance of the Dayak tribe. There are several dances, each of these dances tell of struggles in the past. The dance I like the most is the Gantar Dance, which is performed by people who pound rice seeds in a container. This dance is now used to welcome guests and events.

The mother is the first inspiration in life, because she is always patient when dealing with anything. Parents are also the main factor that teaches all basic life, starting from courtesy, speaking Dayak language, and the meaning of life. Dayak language is a traditional regional language that could be extinct because no one preserves or learns it. Parents also give meaning to life "Goodness must be at the core of the mind".

To reach my goals, I must be able to divide my time between studying, traveling with friends, and looking for experiences. In my opinion, to succeed, you don't have to be smart, you don't have to study to death, everything has to be balanced. Everything we do in this world, is more concerned with soft skills or communication skills.

My experience from school to college, in my opinion, is rather difficult, because I used to be spoiled. I could not be independent and when I was in high school, I had to go to the dormitory. I was taught how to respect other people, be sensitive to each other (care for one another) and during high school, I had to be able to adapt to new friends from the city while I came from a small village that was a little behind in terms of intelligence. What I want is to grow up and have patience and love for others, because I feel that if we are patient and always believe in God, we can certainly face all the problems, but praying and patience also does not produce results, so we also have to put forth the effort too.

For women in Borneo, you should be able to take care of yourself, especially those who are far from parents, so that the spirit to live life, instill in each of you "must make happy your parents, not to make them disappointed", choose friends who can take you to the positive, do not let the wrong associations let you drift into the wrong directions. For those who are in college, take advantage of the early semester to organize and seek friendly relations, so you can get to know one another. For those who are working, do what is your duty at your job, don't make your boss disappointed with your bad work. For those who are in serious trouble, please don't give up easily, there are many others that are harder than you think. Everything that you do now, one day will become the past, if your past is bad, then the future must be good. All things become remembered, the activity will one day pass and we cannot do it again. The point that my parents were teaching me is to always "do everything as possible you can do, so that you don't regret it someday."

My Life As A Woman: Borneo Island Edition #2

I am Keysha Ramdanhi. I grew up in East Borneo, the city of Samarinda, Indonesia. I was born on September 24, 1994 Samarinda, East Borneo. I am the first child of my parents along with my 2 brothers. I am adherent of Islam. I grew up in the city with my parents and 2 younger siblings.

I was growing up with a family that had limitations economic constraints, my father had died when I was 2 years old. My father died because of an accident, to support his family, my mother worked as a dancer, especially the Dayak tribal dances. At the age of 2 years, I began to go with my mother to dance because no one could take care of my. When my grandmother died, I was the only child of my parents. At the age of 4, I began to learn dance. I learnt dance from my mother. I was very enthusiastic about following my mother when I had a dance work schedule, and at 6 years old I started dancing and I was very talented in dancing gracefully at the age of 6. I aspire to be a professional dancer and wants to establish a cultural arts studio.

I was very inspired by my mother and was very impressed with my mother even though a single parent, but I was very enthusiastic to make my education fulfilled as I was eager to help my mother to help in the economical improvement to our family, and at the age of 12 I had started making money from dancing, selling fried foods I had ever done to meet the economic needs of my family, I had been taught by the situation to be independent since I was a child.

When I was little, I wanted to make my mother happy, when I become adult, a mother who is always there for us, a mother who takes care of me without complaining even though my economic life is lacking, like other common children I want to give my mother a decent home, a vehicle that makes my mother not tired, overheated or rain when I goes to teach dance, and most specifically I hope that when I grow up. I also want to take my mother away to umrah.

I liked all the cultures of my tribe according to him culture is very unique. I really admire the Dayak women who are independent, and especially the Dayak culture that likes is dancing, because from childhood I already had the artistic soul of a mother and flowed on her. And since childhood I had known dance.

I want to establish a dance studio, and he really hopes to make the Dayak dance go international. Apart from being a professional dancer I also have a dance studio and already have many students. And for that I hope to make the Dayak dance known by foreign people. I have gone through many obstacles and difficulties to achieve his goals. I hope the results can be satisfying and as he wishes.

From my childhood, I am already independent and making money, when I was in elementary school (SD) I had become a dancer, while selling fried foods at school. When junior high school continued (SMP) I became an assistant teacher of dancers because of my talent. During high school (SMA), my talent was increasingly prominent. I had won trophies from the district level to the provincial level as a dancer, and when I wanted to continue my education at the university I got a scholarship from the government because of my talent. At that time as I wanted to make an art studio despite difficulties but realize at a relatively young age making an art studio.

I was successful at this time because of a prayer from a mother, enthusiasm from the mother, and encouragement from the mother. Without a mother, I cannot be the successful woman as I am today, I am very grateful that having a mother who is amazing can make me know the struggle and effort that is being done. As a successful woman I have established a well-known international art studio. I also have a business making custom clothing for dancing and it is also quite successful today. I am very grateful that my efforts were not in vain.

In the view of the Dayak tribe in Central Borneo, the women were in the same level as men. Although limited education facilities at this time and most parents are still reluctant to release their daughters to study outside their village to settle there must be an independent soul and a strong mentality and must know the rules that apply to the Dayak tribe. The Enchantment of the Beauty of the Dayak Girls of Borneo To be honest, it is not a myth, before setting foot on the Borneo Earth, not a few people imagined the violence and cruelty of the Dayak tribe. But make no mistake what you will find is not like that, instead the Dayaks who live on the island of Borneo (Kalimantan) are actually friendly and even tend to be very shy. So from all women in Indonesia, we, Dayak girls are welcoming you.

My Life As A Woman: East Nusa Tenggara Edition #1

Warning: This story contains graphic content. Proceed to read with caution.

My name is Maya and I live in Sumba, East Nusa Tenggara. My father and mother worked as teachers at the elementary school in my city. They have a lot of students, who usually come to the house if they have started entering the examination period. My parents always accept them and teach them wholeheartedly. Because seeing their passion made me aspire to be a teacher, the teacher became a hero to rural children like us. People there are hard, hard people, it does not mean that they often fight, however, the life and topography of the region that makes many people from Nusa Tenggara Timur become like that. Various cultures were present in our small village, one of the most famous events being Pasola and special food.

Pasola is a game of agility throwing a wooden javelin from the back of a horse that is being driven fast between two opposing groups. The purpose of the Pasola tradition is to give thanks for the harvest, as well as a form of devotion and acclamation of obedience to the ancestors. The event is usually held at the beginning of the year, February or March. This event is also referred to as "blood sacrifice" because according to the beliefs of the community, blood is a fortune. When eating chicken or eating pork, blood will definitely spill, so it is with humans, that we also need bloodshed. This event can be dangerous and sometimes may take casualties, so the community cannot carelessly hold this event, and must go through the head of ADAT or the RATO of the religious leaders.

Made from corn, Sumba's special culinary named Kaparak is made from corn flour mixed with shredded coconut and white sugar to taste. The mixture is then roasted until it looks yellowish. Kaparak is usually used as a snack and can also be used as food at breakfast, lunch, and dinner because it has a high carbohydrate, protein, and vegetable fat content.

My difficulty in moving to another city or island arose while I was studying at university. Our black race is still often discriminated against "why are you white?" that question sometimes arises between me and my friends. Nearly all over the world, black people have always been the subject of racism. People who do this kind of action do not know what mental impact is happening, they are only concerned with their pleasure. I had dreamed of becoming a teacher ever since I was a child, because I felt that Indonesia's education was lagging behind developed countries. My first lessons would be to start by teaching children not to be racist in order to make sure that Indonesia progresses. I also hope that the future of children from NTT are not like me, and do not have to experience racism in other cities or islands.

For women out there who still feel inferior to the people around, I hope that you don't think too much about it. Being different does not mean you are strange. Being different is a blessing given by God to us, so we become special people. Feeling inferior only makes the talent within you covered and slowly disappears from you. Confidence is the key to success, keep chasing your goals until you achieve them.

My Life As A Woman: East Nusa Tenggara Edition #2

Let me introduce myself, my name is Indriana and I'm the second daughter of two siblings from Sumba. My father is of Australian descent and mother is Sumba. My father has always been known as a foreigner who likes to help the surrounding community even though family life is also difficult. My father planted vegetables and my mother was a craftsman of Sumba's woven fabrics. My brother and I often helped my father pick water spinach, I also enjoyed learning to weave traditional fabrics, yes, our life is simple. Our simple family brings happiness, and Mother is a figure who inspires my life because of her patient nature in dealing with problems.

From various cultures and ancestral heritage, the woven fabrics of Sumba produce beautiful woven fabrics. Making this Sumba cloth takes a long time. A piece or piece of Sumba cloth can take more than six months or half a year to make. Some even have made it for three years. Another stage in the manufacture of this Sumba cloth is what tests your patience, such as keeping it in a closed basket to ripen its color. In this process the weavers let nature interfere in order to make the fabric more beautiful, the dye still uses natural dyes. These Sumba weaving threads are tied using gewang leaves, which are a kind of palm leaf, so that the color on the motif is different from the base color. For coloring, weavers mostly use noni roots to get red, blue from indigo, brown from mud, and yellow from wood. Each weaver has a special secret recipe for this coloring, because it is a feature and uniqueness of the resulting fabric.

The tradition of kissing the nose for the Sumbanese is a symbol of kinship and very close friendship. In addition, if there are parties who are fighting and want to make peace, then they will kiss the nose which is a symbol of peace.

The tradition of kissing the nose is carried out by attaching two noses, which indicates that two individuals seem very close and there is no distance. Although the tradition of kissing the nose has become a custom and habit for the Sumbanese people, this tradition cannot be done at any place and time. This tradition can be carried out only in certain occasions, such as during the process of implementing the wedding tradition, wedding parties, birthdays, major religious holidays, traditional parties, mourning and peace events. In addition, it is also the time for receiving guests who are considered honorable or noble who come from the Sumba region itself.

When I was old enough then I wanted to pursue my dream, when I was little I always learned to make woven fabrics until finally I liked Sumba cloth and dreamed of having a woven fabric business that could be exported overseas. For now my business is small, but I will not give up. I am happy to be able to introduce the culture that our region has, especially my mother's work. At first I tried to sell to other island areas. Even though my business still hasn't had many orders, I'm sure my business will be successful in the future. For the women out there who have the willpower to do something, I'm sure you can do it.

My Life As A Woman: Flores Island Edition

Just call me Ina Kewa. I was born and raised in Tanah Lamaholot, East Flores. I was born in a simple family with two brothers and my parents. The nature of Flores is dry but displays an exotic impression. The cluster of islands that stretches between the blue sea adds to the beautiful panorama of my island. Flores Island, Nusa my flower. Even though it is dry, but God does not let us languish, some plants thrive in the dry land. Corn, moringa, coconut and sorghum grew proudly on our land. They seem to be competing to present and provide the best for the owners of this land. When the maize season arrived, we as a family picked corn from the fields. Sufficient is enough to make supplies for food and to be used as "Corn Titi". Since childhood, we have been trained by mother how to process corn into a special food called Jagung Titi, of course you know why it is named that way. Corn is half old and old, roasted earlier on the stove using clay pottery.

We also have a typical woven fabric from Flores called the Adonara woven cloth. The Adonara woven cloth has three motifs, namely, the first is the Kewatek, monotonous, straight striped motif, and the third is the Senai (shawl) in color and straight stripes. Based on its usage, namely, for Kewatek cloth it is used by women while Nowing is used for men while Senai (shawl) is used by men and women. This woven fabric is made using 90% natural ingredients, namely, cotton which is spun and woven using human hands and with traditional tools. As much as 10% of the silk thread is used to beautify the fabric. The dye uses two types, namely from the plants around their place of residence. For Kewatek Kiwane (original) the manufacturing process can take as long as a month and it depends on the flowering season of the dye (keroke) and of course the cotton-bearing season. For ordinary Kewatek, the manufacturing takes about one week. Corn Titi and Kwatek, are cultural heritage that we must preserve. These two local wisdoms are produced in extremely complicated ways. It takes patience, tenacity, thoroughness, and of course, a happy heart when we produce it.

Family life is difficult due to limited funds, I only went to high school. I did not get a beautiful adolescence. I had to swallow the bitter pill that I had to endure because I didn't want to listen to my parents' advice. I was pregnant and the man who beat me did not want to accept any responsibility. I was in utter pain, especially knowing that the man I thought loved me, turned cold. I had to surrender and accept all the circumstances at that time. I fell and I fell. All my friends laughed at me. But I didn't care. For me it was a dark time. The days passed, I and my son, who I raised without the figure of his father, were so happy he saw the world. Without knowing what kind of pain I was in. Even though his presence was the subject of ridicule from people around my village, I was sincere. I accepted my baby. I did what I had to do to protect my child and did everything to make sure he was happy. Because I am Ina Kewa, the tough woman of Lamaholot. He is now entered school age and he is 8 years old and very social around his peers.

For women out there, unravel the threads, weave them into a sarong, gap all of your wishes in every period of your life.

My Life As A Woman: Java Island Edition

My name is Sitha and I was born and live in Bantul, Central Java. After about 7 years old, I moved to Yogyakarta. There is a slight difference between Bantul and Yogyakarta, which is in a different environment. The environment in Bandul reflects more the rural areas, but the population around Bantul and Yogyakarta is almost completely the same because it is still quite close to around 15 KM. There are indigenous people who are friendly and gentle in speaking and being very polite.

"Budhe" (in Javanese which means sister of my father) was the first person to inspire me, she taught me many things, especially in how my attitude in public should be. She also taught a valuable thing that is "hard worker", because hard workers tend to realize that their dreams are something that is very possible. They also have the principle that education is the main thing and very important. I just want to be a better person who doesn't harm myself or others. Hurting others is a fatal thing to do for me, because it will only backfire when I can't fix that mistake.

Javanese culture is very much ranging from songs, dances, customs, language, magic power, etc. One of them is good manners, especially towards parents, respecting the policies of the Sultan's lineages (ancient kings). From the Javanese way of speaking especially Jogja, it is more subtle. Cultural traditions such as "Sekaten" to commemorate the Javanese New Year, there are many processions organized by the Yogyakarta Palace. Traditional culture at the time of one's death, namely "Tlusuban" (nuclear family enters the coffin that has been raised to form 8 as many as 3 times). Customary marriage has several processions ranging from pairs of "Tarub", "Bleketep", "Tuwuhan", "Siraman", "selling Dawet", "Midodareni", until at the reception there are still many that must be passed.

I like the dance originated from Yogyakarta the most. This dance has characteristics that do not exist in other cities. Kuda Lumping or "Jathilan" is a traditional Javanese dance that tells a group of soldiers riding a horse. Often in lumping horse dance performances, they also display attractions that display magical supernatural powers, such as the attraction of chewing glass, slitting their arms with machetes, burning themselves, walking on broken glass, and others. Perhaps, this attraction reflects the supernatural power that in ancient times developed in the environment of the Kingdom of Java and was a non-military aspect used to fight the Dutch forces in ancient times.

My main job is a student, but I have a part-time job as a music tutor. My goal is to be able to work in a well-known media company. I reach these goals by "persevering" (consistent) in learning and praying, not easily giving up when criticized. Even if getting criticized hurts, it is a way for us to develop. We can develop from the criticism of others by digesting it well and most importantly to respect others even if the person is disappointed, appreciate every effort and learn from mistakes. "LEGOWO" in Javanese, which means accepting sincerely whatever happens. Being a tough woman is difficult, but by "accepting" and trying to prove to others, especially those who have been humble, are the key to becoming a better person.

Sitha

My Life As A Woman: Lesser Sunda Islands Edition

My name's Juliya and I was born in Negare, of Lesser Sunda Islands. Born into an ordinary family consisting of my father, mother, and younger sister. Bali is a beautiful city that is decorated with a variety of amazing natural beauty and still holds close to ancestral culture. My father works as a delivery agent between cities. For some people to travel long distances is not a pleasant choice, to wade a long journey with the hot sun, flying dust, and cold winds hitting the body.

My father is someone who really inspired me, with the family at home, he became eager to deliver goods. He was rarely home with us because of the long journeys. However, my father always said that "Far or near the family, my heart will always be with you." From this, I learned that family is the closest to be cared for and is always connected to each other. Life must have a goal, and to reach the goal requires hard work, enthusiasm, and most important is support from the family.

Bali, Lombok, Sumbawa, Flores, Sumba, Timor, and Alor are stretches of islands in the Lesser Sunda Island cluster. The Lesser Sunda Island group are islands east of Java where at the beginning of independence the islands were incorporated in the Lesser Sunda Province and are now divided into three provinces namely Bali, West Nusa Tenggara and East Nusa Tenggara. Bali is not a foreign island for Indonesians or even the world, especially Bali as a tourism magnet in Indonesia being the largest foreign exchange earner island of the tourism industry. With a variety of unique cultures that are there.

The Ngaben ceremony is part of the teachings of Hinduism. This tradition aims to purify the spirits of the dead. The form is the burning of a corpse which is placed in a container. After becoming ashes, the family dissolves into the sea or river as a sign of releasing the soul to unite with the Creator.

The chanting is held every Pon Sunday at WukuMedangsia according to the Balinese calendar. The purpose of this tradition is for humans to always maintain a harmonious relationship with God, each other, and also nature. Performers of the rituals are Hindus in Pura Pangrebongan. Tourists are allowed to watch the event as long as they want to use traditional Balinese clothes. Women must be in a sacred state, and not menstruating. The program began with traditional music, flower offerings, and penjor-penjor. Next, the ritual performers pray at the temple. Then, the ADAT police secure the road so that the Mangku and Bhatara would get out of the temple. Then, they surrounded Wantilan (a chicken fighting place) and this ritual was carried out three times. Usually, at that time, some Mangku and Bhatara experienced possession. They scream, sometimes cry, and dance to the music. The most terrible thing when one of these people released a sword into his body. Even so, not one part was injured or bleeding.

Kecak dance is a kind of traditional dance drama art that is typical of Bali. The dance depicts the Wayang story, especially the Ramayana story which is performed with the art of movement and dance. This Kecak dance is one of the most well-known traditional arts in Bali. Aside from being a cultural heritage, the Kecak Dance is also one of the attractions of tourists who come there.

I still haven't felt a struggle and how it feels to be successful, because of my father's struggle for us. But I feel that I can't always depend on Dad. Until one day, I ventured to become a tour guide in Bali. As a Balinese, I have an advantage in speaking because there are many foreign tourists visiting Bali and I also know the tourist attractions in Bali. The beginning of my struggle began, I was still very rigid with my first tourist, but I remained confident in my abilities. Success will wait ahead for those who want to try to fight!

I have a message "Start a little thing". All the small things you do will have an impact on your nature and habits. Don't feel that you are the best, so that you can develop, you must always feel inadequate, let others name or judge for yourself!

My Life As A Woman: Lombok Island Edition

My name is Yulia Agisni, now in my 7th semester in college. I was born in Lombok. My birthplace is more specific in Lenek, East Lombok. I have 5 siblings and I am the 2nd child. I have only one brother and the others are tough women, I pray that God will bring both my parents to heaven for raising us. They are my inspiration, because they raised us children, especially the girls, to be well-educated. Many teachings have been passed down from their ancestors to my generation. The Lombok area is still thick with customs, for example, if you are traveling by motorbike or car you will see some offerings on the side of the road. In my area, various regional arts are still held, one of which is the Rebo Ceremony.

Every year, to be precise, on the Wednesday of the last week of Safar month, people in Lombok perform the Rebo Bontong ceremony. They believed that this day was the climax of disaster and disease, so a ceremony was held to deny reinforcements. The community believes that work cannot be done on the day of Rebo Bontong. Rebo Bontong has the meaning of "breaking up". Until now, the ceremony is still being held by the people in Pringgabaya District. Rebo Bontong has been passed down from generation to generation for hundreds of years. People would flock to the riverbanks and throw themselves in to take a bath. They believe, if you take a bath on that day, the disease will disappear for a year and friendships will be more closely intertwined.

The Bau Nyale ceremony is a traditional cultural festival held by the people of Lombok. The name of this tradition comes from the Sasak language, consisting of the word Bau which means catch and Nyale which means sea worm. Sea worms in question are animals that live in holes in rocks in the sea. Bau Nyale is indeed a sea worm hunting event which is held around February and March. The festival is located on Seger Beach, Kuta. That said, this sea worm is believed to be the incarnation of Princess Mandalika. Nyale also appears only once a year around Kuta Beach and Seger Beach. The worms that have been hunted will be sown in the fields or processed into food.

I am a woman who has a lot of dreams, because for me a dream is a goal that keeps us existing. Since I was little till now, I have a hobby of reading and writing novels. One of my dreams was to become a writer who could change the world. I often write stories with different perspectives of other people. The stories I get from the people around me, various ages and various groups. I pretend I am them and write from their perspective. I think this world needs someone who provides a different perspective so that everyone can understand each other. There are many selfish people in this world, only selfish, my goal is to make them understand people from a different perspective.

For women out there I only hope you have high dreams, it will be a goal in your life to be more enthusiastic.

My Life As A Woman: Maluku Island Edition

My name is Meri. I was born from a modest family and live in a modest home. Born and living in the Ambon region, an area that is still thick with ancestral culture. As an adult, I took higher education in Yogyakarta. Living in a small area makes relations between people better than living in cities that sometimes don't know each other.

My parents are the most important people in the world, they teach many things for my future. My parents are my inspiration, even though they live in a small village and live a simple life, they are able to make my life comfortable (economic well-being) with hard work. I know their struggle to make money, I'm really happy to have them. I hope one day I can reciprocate the goodness and their efforts many times more than what I received.

In the eyes of the Ambon people (Maluku), culture is closely related to customs and beliefs. We still believe in the spirits that must be observed and given food, drink, and shelter called "Baileu", so as not to be a nuisance to those who live in this world. Ambon tribal traditional house called Baileo. Baileo is used for meeting places, deliberations, and traditional ceremonies called country art. The house is on stilts and surrounded by porches. The roof is large and tall made from sago palm leaves, while the walls are from sago palm stalks called gaba-gaba by the Ambon people.

People are required to perform the ceremony first before entering "Baileu" through intermediaries between humans and ancestral spirits. In addition it must also be dressed in black custom with a red handkerchief worn on the shoulder. Men are wearing traditional clothes in red and black suits, frilly underwear and belts. While the women wear cele shirts, a kind of short, thick kebaya that is embroidered. In "Baileu" there is a "pamili", which is a stone that is considered sacred (supernatural power), which is about two square meters. The stone is used as an altar in sacrifices and offerings. In religious beliefs, they still believe in things that will bring disaster to those who do not carry them out. For example, running a village cleansing ceremony, which includes Baileu buildings, houses and yards. If it is not done well then people can fall ill and die. Entire villages can become infected or have failed crops, etc.

Eating in Ambon is not complete without eating "Papeda". Food derived from raw sago is very popular in Ambon. Papeda is usually eaten with yellow fish soup. It feels if the word "Ambon Paleng Sadap Ada Lawang" is what it means, which is very tasty and unmatched. Ambon people usually eat papeda first before eating rice.

I'm actually just a student at one of Yogyakarta's universities, but I have a hobby of cooking. I apply my cooking hobby in everyday life as a side job. Usually I make a pre-order system or when the Ketandan event in Yogyakarta is held once a year. I hope that with my efforts, I can facilitate the parents' economy.

For women out there, don't give up easily just because we have limitations, especially in the economic field. Are you aware that the limitations make our efforts bigger? I hope you always thank God for being born into this world.

My Life As A Woman: Riau Islands (Kepulauan) Edition

My name is Geni, I live in the forest with my sister and where my parents were born. Father is a Batam native while my mother is a Sumatran. My father was a fisherman when he was young, but because of the age he always followed, and eventually he switched professions to become a trader with my mother. I was born in an environment with intense competition where everyone competed to get something, even though I was always seeing my father and mother struggling to meet the needs of me and my sister.

Many people think that it is nice to live in Batam, tax-free electronic goods, and a vacation to Singapore by boat alone. They do not know how difficult it is to be a trader, because all goods compete with one another for customers and high living costs compared to other cities. All food, especially rice, is imported from outside the island, such as from Java and Sumatra. The city of Batam is relatively small and there is no land for agriculture, so it is definitely a high price because there are costs of cross-island transportation. When I was little, I didn't know how difficult it was to make money, but after I was old enough, I started thinking about something before buying it. My parents became my inspiration, they are people with broad views and work hard to make us happy. My father taught me that in concluding something, it must be from various sides.

Culture which is usually an annual event is the Dance of Offering, this dance consists of several people with one person holding the betel and then given to guests. Like it or not, guests must also eat the betel leaves that have been given by the dancers. Because the characteristic of this dance is identical to the filing of betel leaf to people or guests who are respected. But for now this dance is only used for festivals.

Singapore colors are very apparent in holidays in Batam, in which people are mainly just eating and traveling. Batam has a special tea, they call the tea as "Teh O Bing". Teh, which means tea, O is intended to refer to drinks without milk but uses sugar, and Bing means ice in Mandarin. So, Tea O Bing is sweet iced tea. Whereas Tea O is sweet tea without ice. The mention of Tea O Bing gradually became commonplace in the Batam community due to the smooth flow of Singapore-Batam and vice versa. Eventually, the recitation of the Bing turned into a screwdriver tea as is known by the people of Batam now.

As a woman, initially my parents were not allies if I had to get a high education because in the end, women were only taking care of the kitchen and home problems. With determination, I convinced my parents to let me study seriously until I was accepted at a state university in Yogyakarta. After living in Yogyakarta, I had a side job at the cafe. Until now, I had almost graduated from the university, but the COVID-19 pandemic has currently delayed my progress.

In an advanced era today, there are still many people who underestimate a woman, they think that women are only dealing with the kitchen and home problems, but I want to prove that women can do more than that. I made a new perspective for my parents, I hope women out there can do it too.

"Proving is better than just talking." – Geni

My Life As A Woman: South Sulawesi Edition

My name is Desi, I'm the second child of two siblings. I was born into a warm family because we are open and are very close to each other. Born into this family is a gift from God. Families support each other when experiencing problems, help each other, understand each other. Parents are the main pillars in our family, they are role models when we grow up someday. But, mom is the one who inspired me because she is a strong figure, when I have a problem I always tell her about the problem, and she calmly gives me the best solution in her mind. Based on the nature that I saw from my mother, I learned the importance of calmness. Being calm makes us think more clearly.

In each region, all of them have a culture unique to that region. One of the cultures of South Sulawesi is a special ritual to celebrate or commemorate something. In South Sulawesi, there are three major tribes, namely the Makassar tribe, the Bugis tribe, and the Toraja tribe. Each tribe has some traditional rituals such as Annyampa Sanro and A'bayu Minnya which are owned by the Makassar tribe. As for the Bugis themselves, they have a traditional ceremony called Makkatenni Sanro, Mappanre To Mengindeng, and Maccera Wettang. Mapasilaga tedong and Sisemba is a ritual that belongs to the Toraja tribe.

In ancient times, each Tribe always waged war in order to gain vast territorial power. Therefore, each tribe generally has traditional weapons which are currently included in the regional culture. For the Bugis and Makassar tribes themselves have traditional weapons in the form of a dagger, each of which has the name Gencong, Tappi, Sambang dan Kaleo. Besides that, the Bugis and Makassar also have traditional weapons in the form of a Badik, a sharp iron blade that has a pointed tip.

One more type of South Sulawesi culture that you should not miss, namely its special food. Well some special foods that you can enjoy when visiting Makassar include Coto Makassar, Konro Soup, Banana Epe, and Palubuntung ice. In addition, you can also enjoy grilled fish, Barongko, Coto Kuda, Nyuknyang, Burasa, Kapurung, Dange, and Patollo Pammarasan.

I sell cosmetics in one of the online stores, initially it was my side job. Eventually, it became more crowded, the demand grew, making it my main job. In working in an online store where there is very tight competition, I learned from my mother the most important thing is to think calmly about every problem you face.

For women out there, if you continue to feel like a failure, you are still a tough woman! Because one day you will be a mother to your children, you are a mother who is able to raise their spirits when they are down. Cheer up for tomorrow! Many successful people start with a failure that is fixed. So, when you fail, don't give up because success will wait for you in the future.

My Life As A Woman: Sumatra Island Edition

I am Hani Siburian from Medan. North Sumatra, Indonesia. I was born into a Batak ethnic family, with the Siburian clan. Actually, there are so many clans from the Batak in Indonesia, I will only introduce the Siburian clans. Each clan has a Tugu. Tugu is a monument of several Batak clans. Some of these clans are considered as their own families, not allowed to marry fellow clans. The rough and brave character of the Batak people is a part of the cultural acculturation of the multi-ethnic population in Medan, so that it becomes the general character of the people in this city. The community where I live is still very respectful of customs and still runs the ancestral slogan.

Batak tribe is one of the largest ethnic groups in Indonesia, of course Batak culture is very apparent. However, I like the songs the most, because Batak songs can describe a person's emotions or feelings. One that I like the most is Tangiang Ni Dainang describes feelings of sadness and Rade Do Au describes feelings of pleasure. The custom for marriage is the most striking in the Batak, the custom is called "Sinamot". Sinamot is the price or money given by men to women when they are going to carry out marriage. In Batak custom, sinamot must be given to the bride as a sign of buying or taking a daughter to be a companion to the groom's life. There are levels of sinamot, if the daughter to be married has graduated from school or a degree then the price is different. For example, if the bride is a bachelor then the price starts from around 25 million and above, and if only graduated from general school the price is usually 10 million and below. The higher the education of women, the higher the price, so the price of the bride depends on her education. Sinamot prices may go down, but it depends on the woman. Sinamot has been a tradition from the Batak since the days of our ancestors.

My sister is a hero for me, in a difficult and bad family economic situation, she can improve the family atmosphere. She taught many things, ranging from morals and behavior in society and the importance of understanding people around. My sister is my life model.

I am a college student, but I aspire to become an influencer. I took the communication department in college. I extended the communication network to other people. I cannot say I am a success, because I myself, feel far from the world success. I believe someday I will be better than now. But one thing that I consider successful, is adapting to a new environment that is quite foreign. Little things that make you able to develop. Learn how to talk to new people, how to adjust to attitudes.

For women out there, I just hope you can be independent. Sometimes women want to show their weak side, but that shouldn't be. You may want to be under the protection of others and always be in a comfort zone, but don't be afraid, there are times when we need help from others. Don't be shy to ask for help from others if needed. One thing I want to say is "Try to be an independent woman who does everything in her own way of thinking".

My Life As A Woman: Sumbawa Island Edition

I was born in the Jereweh District, West Sumbawa Regency. I myself was born on August 17, 1997, which is exactly 52 years after the Independence of the Republic of Indonesia and was named Agustina, because I was born in August. I have three brothers where I have an older sister and a younger brother. Since I was little, I really liked sports especially football, even though my hobby is actually quite strange for women. My passion for sports is none other than because my father is a sports teacher, this reminds me of the adage that "fruit does not fall far from the tree". My life's inspiration came from my father to be the greatest man in my life, he was there to encourage me when I was falling.

Many folk games in my area are still held frequently, the one I like the most is Barapan Kebo. Barapan Kebo is a folk game related to animal husbandry. Barapan Kebo is one of the events that is very popular with the local community. Barapan kebo is not a race to the finish line, but an arena for sandro to compete with spells. Sandro is the name for someone who has supernatural abilities who will later plug the sakak. Sakak is a stick finish. At the kebo barapan, a pair of buffalo that has been prepared will be controlled by a jockey and run fast towards the sakak. During the event the sandro tries to instill a distracting spell on the buffalo and jockey so that they are unable to reach the sakak. The successful Sandro will sing his victory in a typical Sumbawa boasting poem.

When I was a kid, my leg broke while playing ball. The incident started when my friend invited me to join the club tournament to defend his village club. I didn't do the surgery to put the iron in my leg due to the high cost. So I used traditional healing, where a massage therapist who is used to handling these kinds of things was asked to heal me. At night I could not fall asleep because my leg pain could not be ignored, for almost two months, I was active in the same place, namely the bed in front of the TV, where I ate, drank, and bathed. My parents were always there for me, especially Dad, when I was alone in depression, I was afraid I could not walk like before. After 2 months on the bed continuously, I tried walking close to the house in the morning, I managed to walk five steps, even though I was still limping, and this limp was what I had been doing for a long time, but I didn't give up at all, I always walked morning and evening until finally I could walk normally again. My parents and masseuses didn't let me play football anymore, for the next 5 years until my legs really recovered. I often walked until finally I could run again, when two years later, I surpassed myself. I fought my fear and I tried to kick the ball slowly and carefully, although sometimes there was pain in my leg, and I tried many times, until I could really like walking again. I hope that someday I can be like my father, a parent who was always there for his child, in their greatest time of need.

The greatest success in my life, where I was able to rise from my adversity, namely a broken leg, so I could play football again. The point is don't give up quickly, don't stay tired, fight your pain and fight your fear, get past yourself, because we have a very big power within us, namely trying, so don't be afraid to try, and don't forget to always pray. Many people think that success is like when someone gets a Bachelor, Doctor, Professor, gets a prestigious award, is respected by many people and some even think that success is when someone becomes rich and has lots of money. But success, in my opinion, is when you live your life the way you want it, do what you enjoy most, surrounded by people you love and respect. To the ladies out there, I only wish you success, fight all the feelings that hold you back!

My Life As A Woman: West Nusa Tenggara Edition

My name is Dinda. I live in Bima, West Nusa Tenggara. Out of three siblings, I am the youngest with two older brothers. Our area is quite far from the city, and my parents are farmers working day and night for our small family. I also often helped them since childhood, even though when I was little I only helped deliver food to the rice fields and eat with them and that made me happy. The more mature I became, the more I understood the warmth of the family. Father became my inspiration because of the passion he showed me, he was also a good and great family leader, one day I wanted to find a husband like my father. My small village has a variety of cultures, one of which is Ntumbu and a unique dish from my village.

Ntumbu is the attraction to head against two players and is one of the shows in the Bima area. In this show, both players are given immunity first by the show leader called Guru by praying called Nochtah. To enable the performance to take place, there needs to be trust, confidence is concentrated in the heart for both players. The players will divide themselves into two groups, the defending group is called "Te'e" and the attacker is called "Ncora". Ntumbu attraction is accompanied by traditional Bima music, the player holds and waves a handkerchief and greets the audience, then warms up before the headfights.

"Tembe Nggoli" woven fabric is a unique and quality Bima sarong woven fabric. Made from cotton or cotton yarn. This sarong woven fabric has a variety of bright colors and is patterned on typical hand woven gloves. Another feature possessed by Tembe Nggoli is that it is made from smooth, not easily torn, and can warm the body. Tembe Nggoli is unique, when used during the cold weather, it will be warm, as well as when used when the weather is hot, it will feel cold. Based on the function, weaving Tembe Nggoli is divided into several types. Tembe Songke or Sarong as superior weaving, Sambolo (Destar) or headband that can be worn by men who are entering their teens. Weri or belts made from Malanta Solo, Mbojo shirts and scarves are used by Bima men as decoration when attending a party or as a sash for women. At this time, Tembe Nggoli is increasingly rare, because Tembe Nggoli weavers are decreasing. Given the weaving process of Tembe Nggoli, which is quite difficult and still uses traditional weaving equipment, there are rarely children today who want to learn to weave.

After being mature enough to act and make choices, I chose to work in urban areas with my second sister to improve the economic situation of my family. Considering my father and mother who are getting older, my first brother works in the field and takes care of the parents in the village. Where I work in the city is quite large and because of my good performance, I was transferred to another branch in Java with the position of branch head.

For women out there fighting for something, start from the small things that you have. I hope the short story of my life can inspire all of you so that women out there can be independent of their parents and help their economy.

My Life As A Woman: Western New Guinea

Warning: This story contains graphic content. Proceed to read with caution.

My name is Sukmawati, I was born in West Papua, but my father and mother are from overseas in Jayapura, West Papua. My parents lived in the city of Sorong, West Papua until a few years ago ranging from birth to the time when I was 22 years old. The island is located at the end of the archipelago, we then imagine the beauty of the island, a marine park, wilderness and high mountains that make Papua still feels like a preserved paradise island. I understand the portrait of the lives of Papuan people, starting from their lives, their education, and the rules of life they live, but between us can understand each other and help one another.

My father and mother worked as vegetable and fruit farmers in mountainous areas, because working around the mountains, my father was recruited to do side work by migrants as people who guarded the forest. What a beautiful gift God gave me, I was given a great father who is inspiring me. Maintaining and guarding it is the most important thing we must do. It's just that in some places on this beautiful island there are still many foreigners who want to steal resources and try to destroy some of the natural products from the land of Papua. What makes our worries worse is the lack of serious handling from the government.

Papua is the easternmost island in Indonesia which is famous for its extraordinary natural beauty. Not only nature, Papua is also rich in unique local traditions and culture. One of the well-known local cultures of Papua is dance culture, there are still many unique traditions and cultures stored in Papua.

The traditional Papuan wedding ceremony is an area with a high diversity of tribes and clans. There are dozens, even hundreds of tribes and clans in Papua. Even so, their marriage ceremony is in principle not much different, only the name and procedure may be different. The maturity of each can be seen from their ability to carry out their duties and responsibilities in the family and community. Thus, they only get the blessing of the family and can proceed to the Papuan traditional ceremony thereafter, marriage.

Traditional ceremonies are usually held full of songs, called JamoTegaya. JamoTegaya can be interpreted as singing with adult men and women. Men who are looking for a partner will bring a procession, song, and offering to the woman they crave. Migani tribesmen also need to be dressed up with make-up and jewellery that appeal to women. Starting from the color line, to bracelet woven parrot or cassowary. A family of women who are touched will come to a man's house to discuss marriage. At that time the man will pay the belis (dowry) and determine the day of arrival. On the appointed day, they come with a group of elders, introductory accompaniment, and accompanists of music or songs.

Cut finger tradition, this tradition is a sign of deep sorrow for the loss of one of their family members who died. In addition, this tradition must also be done to prevent the return of the catastrophe that caused death in the family. This tradition is carried out after the funeral procession by directly cutting off one of the grieving fingers of a family member with a knife, ax or machete. Another way that is also commonly done is to bite the finger segment until it breaks, tie it with a piece of rope so that blood flow stops and the finger segment becomes dead and then cut.

After I was old enough to walk alone, I decided to go outside the island to find work experience. However, as a Papuan, I feel discriminated against by others just because I am different. It was a difficult situation for me, I kept trying to mingle with people from various regions. However, after a while, friends from various regions began to accept me. For people who are struggling out there fighting because you are different, you are amazing! Not many people can get out of the zone, most of them are depressed because they are discriminated against by their own people.

My Life As A Woman: Iraq Edition #1

My name is Salima Ahmed from Basra city of Iraq. I grew up in Basra. My father was one of the closest friends of Saddam Hussein. My mother is a somewhat modern woman. She works at the government's department of state. The upbringing of children in my country, especially in my family is quite different from others. From the very first days of my life, I had the chance of listening to the beautiful sounds of the instrument which is known as "Oud". My father was a very good "Oud" player, and he was also involved in some political activities.

There was a woman in our home who was a very sweet, very kind and indeed, a very powerful person. She was my mother. She always inspired me to be a powerful woman and fight the gender inequality in our community. With having such a beautiful family, I decided to study politics. Many people told me that women cannot be politicians, but I thought that I could study whatever I wanted.

Speaking of success, I have had and will have so many successes and achievements in my life. My biggest success is my fight against gender inequality. In fact, I have an organisation that investigates the cases of violence against women. In trying to succeed, I also failed to do many things. When I went to university, I always had the idea that I would be a politician one day, but I didn't succeed.

As an Iraqi woman, I should say that I haven't had so many struggles in my life. My father was a rich person and I had so many opportunities in my life which most of the women in Iraq don't have. My biggest struggle in my life was fighting against the allegations made by people against my father. Because he was one of Saddam Hussein's best friends, people thought that he was a partner of Saddam Hussein and helped him in his policies, but as far as I know, he was never involved in anything like that!

Our culture is so bond to our history. As everyone knows, Iraq is one of the world's oldest country. The Babylon civilisation caused so many changes in the world. The thing that I like about our tradition is, the women's sense of responsibility. However, gender inequality is something that should be discussed, but women have always helped men in so many aspects.

My first message to all women in the world is, wherever you live, whenever you want to start, whatever you want to do, just start and believe in yourself. Do not say that you cannot do it! Indeed, if there is a problem, there is also a solution. You might say that some problems are very hard to solve. But remember that you are bigger than the problem. If you can't solve a problem, do not be disappointed! There might be something more to it.

My second message to all people, not just women, is that everyone has many needs, but you may have something extra. Give it to the needy and make the world a better place.

My Life As A Woman: Iraq Edition #2

Manar Shubbar from Iraq, Horsewoman and TV presenter

Where were you born and raised?

I was born in southern Iraq, I grew up in central Iraq. My career is in the heart of Iraq and its capital is Baghdad. Three cities contributed to the emergence of an environment that provided all the additions to me to get to where I am now.

How were you growing up?

I was very spoiled ... I love drawing, sports, and studying. I used to draw cartoon characters and some community symbols as well as fashion design. If you have parents, both father and mother, I feel the father is your example more, but I see in both of my parents as leaders of a special kind and one of them completes the other. My father was very strict and practical, and I inherited that from him.

My mother was and still is persevering and determined, and she is a teacher. After my father's death, I succeeded, according to everyone's testimony, despite the difficulties of life, especially with a family made up of daughters during the war period. They were role models for me.

I studied the Arabic language and literature. I will complete my master studies this year, and proceed with my doctorate after that in a very important field related to media, which is the power of discourse and how to influence the public in a way that serves a specific cause. I find that successful speech must be based on influential tools and these tools cannot be obtained in vain without exerting effort, research and study. The magic of words has a strong effect on the public in all areas of life. The word is the key to the closure.

Undoubtedly, I am Sumerian, so the civilization of Sumer, Babylon, and Assyria have a firm influence on my personality and out of faith in our history, we had to stand as an organization concerned with the environment (the Development Center for Energy and Water) to endeavor support for the vote on the inclusion of the marshes (Southern Iraq) to UNESCO. This site embodies the biodiversity of a country, located between the Two Rivers, "and the vote was an international recognition of its exceptional global value, considering it the cradle of civilization. The mixed site includes four natural components and three archaeological cultural components: Ur, Warka and Eridu."

I'm a fashion designer and work in media on the channel MBC Iraq. The biggest difficulties are in the field of fashion. When I decided to open my own fashion house and register an Iraqi trademark as a national industry (M|SH), I faced a great risk of not supporting the national product as well as flooding the markets with imported goods and the lack of factories and factories implementing the designs. Fortunately, I was able to get past these issues. For one thing, we believe in our goals and hold a cause that goes beyond the word "I". We are looking for industries that represent our country and we will continue.

One of the most important successes that I am proud of was proving my presence as a fashion designer in Iraq and registering my trademark in the midst of the huge flood of imported goods, as I told you. Not to mention the embrace of young talents in the field of handicrafts or everything related to fashion. Now we are working on re-launching a project that seeks to prepare women to defend themselves against bullying of all kinds in life.

My advice to women: A person succeeds when he realizes himself and does not try to imitate to become a copy of someone else. Be always believing in what you are capable of doing. Nothing breaks the impossible like the will.

Iraq is a country that actually has supported women since ancient times. For example, the first female judge in the Arab world was Iraqi. The first captain pilot was Iraqi and so on. But the situation is slightly different now, so Iraq needs to rise again to regain its glory with the strength of its support for women.

My Life As A Woman: Iraq Edition #3

I am Aseel Al-Bayati and I was born in 1976 with Iraqi roots in Baghdad where I grew up. My father is from Basra and my mother is from Najaf. My childhood was in Baghdad, where I lived with my parents and family. We have a strong relationship with the children of maternal uncles and relatives, and my only inspiration was my mother, may God have mercy on her, as she was my idol in her kindness, compassion, and responsibility. I was very attached to my mother because my father was an officer in the former Iraqi army. My mother, may God have mercy on her, was the most important thing in my life.

I obtained a bachelor's degree in business sciences, accounting department, from Baghdad University in the year 2000-2001. I lived the most beautiful period in the university with the most wonderful colleagues, where I joined the Faculty of Fine Arts, Department of Design, and became a fashion designer and decorator. It was my hobby and I still love fashion, quite fond of it and the indication is that I still love fashion very much.

I love the authenticity and the heritage in my culture that binds me to my country. I also respect the Iraqi traditions, especially Baghdadiya, and now I work as a presenter on the Iraqi channel, the Iraqi Media Network, and I did not easily reach this position at work except with fatigue, diligence, and perseverance. And all the time I suffered a lot and that is why I learned and became a successful broadcaster in this organization.

My practical struggle began in 2003 after the wars in Iraq and the struggle for the responsibility that necessitated us to confront, especially Iraqi women in light of sectarian wars, but we bear the responsibility a lot, and I faced many difficulties, but I continued my studies and media courses to be the presenter of many successful programs.

I faced some difficulties, including in 2005, when I was working for Al-Sharqiya Channel, I was exposed to an attempted kidnapping by Al-Qaeda. Thank God, it failed and we managed to escape. Then, I left this aspect of the media in 2006, when sectarianism was prevalent. I traveled to live outside Iraq in the Hashemite Kingdom of Jordan, and then I returned to Iraq in 2008, and after that, I started working in 2009 at Al-Iraqiya TV, and then I worked in Al-Sumaria and Al-Rasheed TV. Finally I settled at Al-Iraqiya TV, all these attempts were part of my practical struggle.

This period was part of the successes that I achieved in my life. Media work is not easy, especially for Iraqi women, as she suffered a lot, especially in this Iraqi society. This patriarchal society that does not allow women to achieve great successes, but after this development in the world. The woman started struggling to achieve success in her life and career and excel in her work. A creative woman must make her way through all the obstacles and difficulties because the path to success is not paved with roses, but rather full of many obstacles. And being a patient, diligent, and active Iraqi woman, thank God, all obstacles have been easily overcome. It was very difficult, but with my will and ambition it became easy for me, this is an important part for every woman, you must work for your weal for a better future. It is a must to persevere and work for the success of its work. For example, we must enter educational courses, and we must enter the field of practicing our profession. Our profession is very difficult, but it depends on culture, tact and the very important knowledge of our studies and proficiency in the Arabic language, journalism, and following up on programs and news, All these things distinguish the broadcaster in this aspect, and we do not forget that culture is very important.

My advice as an Iraqi woman to every Iraqi woman is that she must not give in to every obstacle she faces in her life. She must be patient and persistent in order to succeed in her life, home, and occupation. A righteous woman starts from her home and then from her work. Every human being raised in a good way will be successful and good. The most important thing is preserving work and at the same time maintaining practical honesty because any person must be honest in his home and in his work, and as a result of that, you will be a good woman. Any woman must find support from her family. I wish success to all Iraqi women and to all women of the world Because persevering women are doomed to success. Greetings to you all. Aseel Al-Bayati from Iraq, the city of Baghdad.

My Life As A Woman: Iran Edition #1

As a woman, I have always succeeded in achieving my goals. I am Laila Bakhtarian from Iran. I grew up in the city of Tehran, the capital of Iran. My family is a somewhat modern family. My father died when I was 10 years old. He was a trooper during the war between Iran and Iraq. He was murdered on the border between the two countries. We never did find the body of my father, but the death of my father was a very big lesson for me and my family.

My mother is my everything. She believes that every human being must be willing to consider new ideas and allow her/himself to do new things. I have always been interested in singing and drawing. My mother is a very independent-minded person, so she allowed me to exhibit and sell my drawings in one of the biggest ceremonies and exhibitions in London, United Kingdom.

My drawings are like the modern European styles. At first, I didn't know that, but an American told me when I was at school. Basically, I didn't study at university. I used to take drawing lessons from one of my teachers when I was at school. But I have information about any field and can write anything from the top of my head.

Iran has a very rich and glorious culture and tradition. Iran is a very popular and very famous country because of its literature and architecture. But the thing that I am always proud of most is our literature. Just to mention that among the 10 most influential poets of all time, at least of them were from Iran and its territories.

As an Iranian woman, I had lots of struggles in my life. For example, I was in a big ceremony which was in Yorkshire, United Kingdom. Everyone thought that I was from Afghanistan or somewhere else. But once they came to know that I was from Iran, they all left me alone. I was very disappointed and even today I don't know the reason behind it. And once something happened when I was walking in streets of Vienna, Austria while wearing a hijab. Suddenly, I became hungry and wanted to eat something. So, I went to a restaurant and reached the waiter. He looked at me and said, "Bank robber, what are you doing here!", and everyone laughed loud. I did not let this bother me and assured him I was just a hungry lady. I stood my ground and proved that Muslim women are strong and powerful, but I think that the prejudice against Muslims and Muslim women exists and is very rampant.

I have been a successful woman in some points and also unsuccessful woman. I have many achievements in my life. For instance, I got the art and culture award from Iran's government. But I haven't always been able to obtain all the things that I want. When I was a young girl, I wanted to be a singer but... this would remain only a dream.

My message to all women across the world is that women are strong and powerful. Just be in a middle position. because being in very high and low positions is not good. Be yourself and do whatever you want. You will be disappointed at some points but know that it is not the end of your life. When I exhibited my drawings in streets of Tehran, no one wanted to buy them for even a single dollar, but I continued my work and became successful. My last message is, "Be yourself and get it done".

My Life As A Woman: Iran Edition #2

Some call it a struggle, some fight for achievement, some battle for success but I call it a journey. A journey that not only took me to different countries and cultures but also took me along the path to discover my true goal in life, both personality and career-wise.

I was born in Mashhad, Iran, where there were no opportunities for girls to develop hobbies and test their talents at a young age. Also the environment was not safe. Being born in Iran brought with it the difficulties a woman would face in her career objectives and personal development. The embargoes on the other hand made bonds with the external world difficult, ironically in an era of globalization. I was lucky though to be born in a family of intellectual parents, well-educated and with a broad vision in life. I am grateful to them for supporting me in all decisions I have taken and my endeavors in life. They always inspired me to have at least a baccalaureate degree. They also saw and supported me as they noticed my talents in in sports and music. They always had a full trust in me and supported my personal decisions.

In primary school I started having a passion for sports. I started practicing Kung Fu at the age of ten. By the time I was sixteen, I was a black belt and was elected to the Iranian National team. I competed in Malaysia and Pakistan for the Iranian National Team. Then I had an unfortunate injury. A broken ankle that kept me away from my sports passion for a while. I sat for the exams of Tehran University for Architecture and graduated as an architect in 2011. During my university life, I pursued my passion for sports and travelled to Dubai to attend courses and obtain certificates for personal trainer for fitness and spinning. I wanted to have a post-graduate degree. I applied to Eastern Mediterranean University in Cyprus for my master's degree in architecture where I graduated in 2016.

During this time I attended and acquired certificates for personal training, spinning, Pilates and yoga. I competed in bikini fitness competition in Cyprus in 2017 holding the 2nd position. I am an Iranian woman brought up in Iran, made her way abroad with a career, cherishing freedom and having a social circle where I am appreciated and appraised in the society I live in. During this journey I had been home sick, felt alone, and sometimes weak but I never gave up. Objectives I wanted to achieve in my country I had to achieve abroad.

Currently I am a personal trainer for fitness and also a spinning instructor. I love it. I see it as a means of helping people achieve their objectives for a healthier and better life style. As an instructor, I help my students understand that I am an architect and we design their body and lifestyle together. It is also a means for them for winding off from daily matters. I also train personally towards my personal goals to compete for the next bikini fitness competition.

I respect all cultures. They are the richness of the world. What I like the most about Iranian culture is the close family bond, and the relationships with members of the broader family like aunts, cousins, etc. Also hospitability is one of the values I admire. The Nowruz celebration is something I never forget, the coming of the spring, rebirth of nature, new life to be celebrated with joy and love of life. Food with its orient origin is delicious. Delicacies of meat and rice with spices to share with Iranian cousins.

As each woman walks decisively in the pursuit of her individual career and personal goal, the synergy they create in the path to overall objective of a better world is immense. Can you imagine if the potential of the women in countries where their freedom and potential is suppressed is let free, just how our world would be?

My Life As A Woman: Ireland Edition #1

"When I die, Dublin will be written in my heart." – James Joyce

One of my favorite quotes by James Joyce, an Irish born writer who spent most of his adult life abroad and still wrote mostly about his country. I wasn't born in Ireland; in fact, I didn't set food on the emerald isle until my late twenties when I got a job offer in Dublin. After two years of grad school in the States, I was craving to explore more countries, live and work abroad. And Dublin was a great place to do that, being the "Silicon Valley" of Europe, it hosts the EMEA headquarters of pretty much all big tech firms from Google to Workday. So, I moved, and stayed.

Being raised in a family of teachers, I grew up among a huge pile of books. Loved reading, it was a magical force that'd take me to places I didn't even know existed. Maybe around age 6 or 7 I started to learn about other cultures, that there are many different languages and I can actually learn some and understand these cultures a bit better. Started with English, without knowing I'd end up in an English-speaking country. In college, I experienced a whole new world. It was the happy place of a nerdy girl like me; access to all kinds of books, knowledge and culture. I dipped my toe a little in French, Italian, Arabic, and in later years a bit of Russian through self-study. But of course, it was mostly in theory, and the things I learned only began to make sense once I started grad school and interacted with people from all around the world. It was a true United Nations environment. Then, Dublin, which was another multicultural experience for me. The first few years I hung out with expats mostly, people from Europe, Middle East, Asia… it was only after I started to get outside my comfort zone and hang out with my Irish colleagues, that I began to be more engaged with the Irish culture. If I were to sum up Irish folks in one word, it'd be "easygoing". "Ah sure, it'd be grand!", "Good craic!" or "Feck it!" are some of my favorite Irish phrases which reflects this "lightness", easygoing nature of Irish people. This humorous and easygoing attitude is what I like about the Irish culture, along with their quite welcoming nature.

The reason I moved to Dublin was a tech job, like thousands of expats in the city. Being a woman in tech is an interesting experience. Depending on the company, it's absolutely one of the best work environments in terms of opportunities to grow. Of course, it's hard work and not always rainbows and unicorns, but then again, it doesn't change the fact that this sector offers a wider range of opportunities than any other in today's world. One just needs to be proactive, as one of my favorite managers used to say, "No one would hand you the project you want to work on a silver plate. You need to go find the opportunity and work on it." It can feel a bit aggressive at times, especially for a woman in the workplace, yet there are ways to make it not so aggressive and also, it's how we grow and get to work on things we want to. When you read a job description and you think, "Oh I don't fit in this." You are not alone – most women do not apply for a role unless they are 100% qualified. Men, on the other hand, would take the chance and apply even if they are just 60% qualified. We learn by doing, so maybe next time you see a role you are interested, have more faith in yourself and just take that leap of faith. Even if you fail, you'd have more than if you didn't apply in the first place. I'll finish with another quote from a famous Irish, Samuel Beckett: "Ever tried. Ever failed. No matter. Try again. Fail again. Fail better."

My Life As A Woman: Ireland Edition #2

As an Indian native Irish woman living in Dublin, I have always been fascinated by the amount of warmth and a sense of togetherness this country has. Growing up in the hustle and bustle of Dublin city centre, visiting the countryside with its beautiful scenery and calm atmosphere has been a family favourite. This is the time I cherish the most as I get to pause and reflect on my life, which I hardly get time to do with the busy schedule of the week. This is the time when I get to feel the grass on my feet and feel the sun on my face (that is if we are lucky that day). In one such weekend getaway recently, my mind wandered off to think about childhood its connection with my gender and the society's role in such aspects of my life.

Since childhood, discipline and a sense of responsibility were instilled in our family especially for girls as we were told in the family that world cannot always be trusted so we needed to know how to take care of ourselves. Hence, studying in a convent school ensured that the lessons in discipline and being a 'good' girl was carried forward. This included on the tone of the voice training to hairstyles that are appropriate in a social settings. They were lessons on behaving in this society in a sophisticated manner. Thus, sophistication became a strength in the subsequent journeys in life as I learnt how valuable it is in the workplace and daily life. People do judge women from the very first appearance and for our own mental health's sake, it is better to put our best foot forward. Since childhood, I wanted to be a 'truth-seeker', but I did not know the discipline of psychology at that age. I knew my ideal profession would involve talking and listening to people from all walks of life. Maybe these questions brought me to do my bachelors and master's in psychology and ultimately work as a psychologist to better understand society, women, and people in general.

On the note of sophistication and traditionality, my grandmother was the epitome of grace. She knew how to put together a great social gathering, how to tell stories and how to keep the decorum of a social setting. I was highly inspired by the way she carried herself as it spoke volumes about how she was raised. She married when she was very young at 20 so she learnt a lot of lessons on responsibility very early. I know many of my friends' grandmothers who got married very young, which just shows how women worldwide follow certain trends regarding responsibilities. For example, in this generation, it would be almost frowned upon to marry when we are 20, but in the earlier generations, it was considered the norm. No matter how we evolve it seems like women can't escape the norms set by society.

My grandmother had a habit of wearing a beautiful ruby red lipstick when she wanted to boost her confidence, I picked up this habit along the way too. So, whenever I am nervous or not feeling myself, I will throw on the mac ruby woo lipstick on and I feel like I can conquer the world. What is it about lipstick that makes us girls feel invincible or is it just me? I guess there is one tradition that I know will be passed on to generations in our family! When I look around in my culture, I feel makeup is a powerful expression under soft culture. We can communicate a lot with just a little makeup. I love this little culture of us women who understand and use makeup the way we want. In our Irish society, another norm that is a little different is the inclination towards having tanned skin through spray tans and similar products. Again, another way makeup and culture merge because the inclination towards tanning is prevalent in our culture but I heard that in some cultures such as India, the inclination is towards 'lightening' creams and makeup. It is fascinating how cultures and makeup combine so powerfully. But these small quirky expressions are what I love about our culture.

One thing I have understood over the years is that no matter how evolved a society becomes or if it attains the title of a 'developed' country, escaping sexism is not straightforward. In my workplace, in society, I have to prove that I am serious about my career and have to work hard to be taken seriously. Although we have come a long way from the gendered roles and restrictions, our societies still have a long way to go from here. I have learnt in my life as a psychologist that young girls often blame themselves for their low self-esteem or other such issues, but on dwelling deeper, we discover that certain standards and notions of self are not even set by ourselves but by the society, which clashes with their notions of self and creates a feeling of discomfort. Thus, this write up reflected life's small instances where gender norms come up and hopefully, it encourages you to also reflect or pen down such normal instances where gender norms might have merged. The purpose is not to be angered or trigger extreme emotions but to take a step towards being aware of subtleties of the societies as it will help us to process and understand our life events and choices better.

Ladies, my advice is to put on that red lipstick, enjoy nature with your loved ones, and keep marching because women quite literally bring life to this world, we owe it to ourselves to live this life in our terms, never let yourself forget this.

My Life As A Woman: Ireland Edition #3

Hello, my name is Ali, short for Alison, and I grew up in Limerick in Ireland. I come from a family of seven, four sisters, and my parents. I am the youngest and the oldest is 13 years older than I am. I walked to school with them daily and my Grandad walked me home from school. My Grandad had such insight into the future. He would regale me of stories of trams in Dublin and how they will soon be there again and he was sure of it. He told me that everyone will soon have their own personal computer. He had a lot of reader's digest magazines of inspiring stories with how-to guides and do-it-yourself stories as well as 'against all odds' stories, he had such a thirst for knowledge.

Cut to several years later and my Dad would buy me old laptops from the Saturday market so I could pull them apart, my sister had been working at Dell and we had an old remanufactured computer. I knew how it worked straight away, I didn't know how I knew, I just knew. I was in school as the mentor for the computer room and we even got training on a Saturday from a teacher in the school, Mr. McKenna. Apart from using the computers in the computer room, we also learned how to type with Mavis Beacon and the object of the game was to get the car on the screen to drive by typing accurately and quickly. I knew I wanted to do something 'with computers' but didn't know what. I did a project on my cousin who was a Senior Test Automation engineer and I was intrigued. I thought he tested computer games for a living and I thought - yes - that is what I want to be, that sounds incredible, what a job to have in your life.

I applied and was successful in attaining a place at National University of Ireland Galway and so I started studies in Information Technology. It was a challenging course with the basis in the first year being mathematics, physics, and programming. I come from an all-girls schooling environment and the "boys will be boys" culture allowing boys to be boisterous was not something I expected or liked. I mean I was used to being surrounded by strong-minded, motivated girls and women who knew what they wanted to do and study and be. This was like walking into a jungle and for all accounts it hasn't changed that much in the workplace. I currently work as a software developer in a technology company and the stories I have would sound unbelievable to most.

I think this is where, as women we create, we can come up with ideas, and we may even be socialised into engagement and creation from a young age. I look at how if something is wrong with a young girl how we rally around and ask what's wrong if she's crying and we support her. We, as girls, are conditioned to speak more, do more, play more, interact more from a young age.

Some of the successes of women can be down to taking initiative and seeing communication as a way to cooperate, making things more team-focused and getting the best out of people. It also means that as a creator, pushing from idea to creation is part of the success and I see this time and time again. I see this in my colleagues and also friends who are working in technology. The women are the ones to jump in and play with the team to coordinate and organise naturally as that's what most have grown up with. The ability to communicate in this fashion is an acquired skill, however, we have the edge if we've grown up with this from a young age.

Yes, we, as women in a male-dominated environment are different, it is almost like having a different culture, remember that by this, I mean some workplaces encourage competitive communication and this clashes with cooperative communication. Be who you are, grow, understand, learn, thrive in an environment that works with you and get what you want out of life. You can do it, after all, you are a creator, you are a woman and whatever you do make sure you laugh at least once a day, it's one of the survivor's guides to looking at the absurdity of some of the environments.

My Life As A Woman: Aran Islands Edition #1

Interview with Peigi O Beirne (Inishmaan, Ireland)

Good morning, my name is Peigi and I come from the tiny island of Inishmaan in the Aran Islands. It is just off the west coast of Ireland. It's a small place and I don't think there are even 200 residents, so we all know each other. I was born there in 1954, and lived in a small farmhouse with my parents.

Both my parents worked on the farm – they farmed sheep. I grew up alone as I didn't have any brothers or sisters, but I had a happy childhood. My parents were always very kind to me and looked after my needs very well. My mother had an amazing sense of humour, I can't remember her ever being serious or angry, so as a child I always wanted to be like her – and I think I am, so I have taken that from her at least. I went to the local national school, but it was a very basic education and I don't think I ever learned that much. Growing up I wanted to be a farmer, like my parents, so after school I would work on the farm and I enjoyed that very much.

I love living here on Inishmaan – the island is so small that everyone knows each other, so we have real trust in each other. There is no crime so it is a very safe place to live and I wouldn't like to live anywhere else. Our home language is Gaelic, but we all understand English too. I think and dream in Gaelic and it is a large part of my culture of which I am very proud. Nowadays we get lots of tourists – they come here to see how we live, but sometimes I think we are more interested in them and seeing how they live, as they always seem so different from us.

My struggles as a woman are that it is difficult growing up here on Inishmaan - the only work is farming or fishing so if I wanted to do anything else I would need to go to the mainland for that, but I'm happy here and as I've already said, I wouldn't want to live anywhere else.

My successes as a woman is that I now run my own farm, or rather my parent's farm, which I inherited. It's difficult work, but it's my life and I've known nothing else, but I'm happy to work for myself and keep our family's land alive. Had I been on the mainland doing something else, I don't think I'd be happy at all. The island is such a large part of me and I can never leave it behind, so that is how I measure my success and happiness.

If I were to give any advice to a woman growing up on Inishmaan it would be to tell her to follow her heart – we must all find our own journey in life, and for some that means leaving the island and their culture behind, but for the lucky ones who choose to stay, they can be happy here in our community and never be lonely.

My Life As A Woman: Aran Islands Edition #2

Interview with Rosie Mullen (Inishmore, Ireland)

Hello, my name is Rosie and I come from Inishmore in the Aran Islands off of Ireland's west coast. I grew up on Cill Ronain, which is the largest town on the island. I was born there in 1964, and lived in a small home with my father Peadar, a fisherman, and my mother, Muire, who was a housewife.

We lived also with my brother and sister, so there were five of us in all. My grandmother was an amazing woman – it was her that taught me to knit, and that's a skill I'm proud to have. She seemed to sit and knit all day long and that's how we got our clothes. I think everyone here knits and Aran sweaters are famous all over of the world, so my grandmother gave me a skill that makes me fit into that tradition, and I'm proud of that.

I went to the local national school, which was just an education where we learned to read and write, basic math, nothing much more. If you want to live on these islands, you can't learn how to do that in any school, so I was never too interested in school. I learned more about life through what was happening in the village and on the rest of the island, and that made me the person that I am now – I still live here on Inishmore, but most of my friends went over to the mainland to work in Galway, but that was never for me.

Growing up, I never really knew what I wanted to do, but I did know that I wanted to stay on the island, and I still live here. This is a special place, and it's different from the rest of Ireland, too. We speak Gaelic at home, and until recently, there were people here who had no English, and our language is a big part of our culture. Whenever I go to the mainland, everything feels so different from here and I guess that is why the place is so special.

Everyone knows about our islands because of the Aran sweaters, but there is more to us than that - we still live very traditional lives. I got married to a man on the island, and I now work on his farm – we look after the sheep, and their wool is valuable to us as we use that for our sweaters, which is a large and important part of the island's income.

Thinking about my struggles as a woman, I think the main one is that my prospects is limited living here – there is not much work you can do if you choose to live here, but that was my wish and I'm happy that I live here. Maybe if I'd went to the mainland, I'd be rich, but I feel rich here as I have a happy life.

As for successes as a woman, the main one is that I am still on the island that means so much to me - I'd be sad if I were anywhere else. And seeing my children grow up has made me feel successful.

If I could give some advice to a woman living here, it would be to go where you are happy – if you're happy on the mainland, then go there and you will find your success, but if you're happy on the island, then please don't go.

My Life As A Woman: Rathlin Island Edition

Interview With Alice Campbell (Rathlin Island, Ireland)

Hello, my name is Alice and I grew up on Rathlin in Northern Ireland. I was born there in 1933, so I'm at 87 years old, but Rathlin is where I'm from and where my heart stays. Rathlin is a small Ireland halfway between Ireland and Scotland, and growing up, I wasn't really sure if I was Scottish or Irish – I just came from Rathlin. I grew up with my parents - I was their only child. My mother was a housewife and my father had a very small sheep farm – just a smallholding, really. It was my grandparents farm, and we lived with them, but my father did all the hard work.

I loved living with my grandparents, they taught me so much about life, and I think that nowadays the young people have lost that – they don't respect their elders so much. That's a pity, but they have busy lives – much busier than when I was young. As I am an old woman now, when I look in the mirror, I see my grandmother's face and that reminds me where I come from and that things just keep happening over and over again.

I didn't have an education. There wasn't really a school on Rathlin when I was young, and nothing they taught at school would ever prepare us for a life on Rathlin anyway. I didn't have any ambitions, but I did want to have my own money and there was no way that that was possible on Rathlin, so I moved to the mainland and started working in a hotel in Portrush. That was when I first managed to gain my independence. It wasn't much money that I was making, but I could still send a little money home, and on a clear day you could see Rathlin in the distance so in some ways it felt like I'd never left.

What I love about my culture is that it is a mixture of Scotland and Ireland. We speak Gaelic at home and the dialect we use is a Scottish one rather than an Irish one, so when I speak Irish on the mainland, everyone thinks the way I speak is interesting.

At the moment I'm retired, but I worked in hotels in Portrush and that area most of my life. While working in one hotel, I met my husband, so that always gives me special memories.

As a woman, my biggest struggle was that there would be no life for me on Rathlin unless I wanted to stay there and become a housewife. I loved my island, but felt that that wasn't me so that is why I left to get a job. And that is how I measure my success – each time I returned to the island with my own money I felt that I was successful – I was never rich but my island friends would look at me like I was a millionaire as I had my own money, so in their eyes and in the eyes of my family, I was successful.

My advice to any woman growing up on an island is that you should always love your home and family, but remember that the island does not define you so you can find your own way in life.

My Life As A Woman: Tory Island Edition

Interview With Sinead O'dochartaigh (Tory Island, Ireland)

Hi there. I'm Sinead, and I grew up on Tory Island. It's a really small island off of the west coast of Donegal. It was a very lonely place to grow up as the place is so remote. In my house, I lived with my parents and my elder sister. My father was a fisherman and my mother was a housewife. I didn't envy my father in his job, as the seas around here are always so wild, but there's not much work on Tory apart from that. My mother just stayed at home all the time, a typical housewife I suppose, but it was her that kept the home together while my father brought the money in. I was born in 1972, so I'm nearly 50, but Tory never changes.

I always loved my grandmother – she was living with us until she died. She saw so many changes - I said that Tory Island never changes, and it doesn't really, but where she saw changes most was in technology and people's outlook on life. When she was a child, life on the island was much the same as it was 500 years ago, but she saw electricity arriving, TV, things like that. And all these changes she just took in her stride. We didn't get a TV until about 1980 and we were one of the first on the island to get one – my grandmother was proud of that for some reason.

Growing up, I got taught in the small local school. That was the only way I really ever found out about things that weren't happening on the island. As a child growing up on a small island you kind of feel that is it, but it's interesting to hear that the world is a much bigger place. My education was good for where I grew up, nothing amazing. Here on the island we all speak Irish, so I didn't start learning English until I went to school. It's strange that, I'm Irish but I didn't speak English until I was 5 or 6. Growing up, I wanted to be a housewife – I know that sounds weird nowadays, but growing up that was all I really knew. I loved my mum and wanted to be just like her.

What I love about my culture is that we speak Irish first and foremost. It's the language I think in – sure, my English is really good now but I still have to stop and think about how to say things in English. My language is special to me. Tory Island has a strange tradition in that it has its own king – he's called Patsy Dan and he's an amazing old fellow. Everyone on the island knows him and he seems to be involved in everything on the island.

At the moment, I no longer live on Tory, first I moved to the mainland and spent a lot of time working in various shops in Letterkenny, the big town. I never really liked that and around 10 years ago I trained to become a social worker and I'm now doing that in Derry.

As a woman, one of my biggest struggles had probably been because I grew up on Tory Island, I wasn't as well educated as some people on the mainland so I found it hard to get work, and also because I mainly spoke Irish. My successes can be gauged by the fact that I got through all that and now have a good professional career as a social worker.

My advice to any woman growing up on the island is that, no matter what you do in your life, never forget where you came from.

My Life As A Woman: Israel Edition #1

While other 18-year-old girls all around the world choose which college to go to, we don't. We keep that important decision for later and we join the army. Yes, just like men. For us, it would be normal, something you look forward to after high school graduation, another phase in life, and our little contribution to our beloved country.

As a kid, or as a young woman in Israel, you believe you can become anything. You are taught to believe you can be anything you dream of. Not many people know that, but women at the Israeli army can be pilots, women can be Special Forces, women can take part in the Intelligence corps. Women can have meaningful service as commanders or officers. We are allowed to do anything men can do, and we do it. We do it well.

Putting your life "on hold" for 2 years and dedicating 100% of your time to defending your country is a privilege, although you go through ups and downs regularly and you ask yourself countless times if it's worth it. When you feel down or homesick, it's the people around you who make the difference. The "new family" you did not choose yourself, but very lucky that fate brought you together, fellow soldiers, which I am proud to call my sisters.

The training, the base camp, and the everyday tasks are the places where you gain your professional skills. The female dormitory is without a doubt the place where you gain your social skills, the place where you create memories. Midnight chats about life, different backgrounds we came from (and of course girl talks and boys!) are priceless. Sharing secrets, sharing delicious homemade food, and sharing everything you got is something you can't take for granted. Inspiring one another and being there for each other is a precious gift. We never felt the need to compete with each other, because we had a massively important goal in front of our eyes. And it made us stronger. It is also probably one of the most meaningful things I learned during my military service.

In the "real world" or everyday life, we tend to forget it. The never-ending competition between women over attention, power, position, or yes, even ego is taking its price. So here is my message to all women out there:

You can do anything. Even if it considers as a "men job" and even if you are not sure of your abilities - you have it in you. No matter which path you decide to take sharing your skills, your strengths, your wisdom, with other women along the way will bring out the best of you. You are unique and you have the power to make other women around you shine, which is a power we all should use more often. You can be a powerful independent woman on your own, but when you have other strong, intelligent, brave women all around you, always there to support you - you are invincible.

My Life As A Woman: Israel Edition #2

I am a young woman. I am 24 years old. I have a master's degree in linguistics and philology. I have lived in Israel for 23 years and my childhood past in a small town. Everyone in my family has a university degree and everyone became a specialist in their field. However, my grandfather on my mother's side had the greatest influence on me. He was an outstanding person. At work, he was a chemist and chief engineer at a large chemical factory in the Soviet Union. At the same time, he was an excellent husband, father and grandfather at home. This educated person helped me understand the idea of the value of education, no matter the gender, age, or race. He always supported my childish hobbies, exploration of the world, and self-development. Thanks to him, I realized how important it is when a close person supports you.

My family is traditional, but education and self-realization are an important part of life for every member of my family. As a result, all the women in my family have higher education and development in their fields. As a child, I did not know about the inequality and the impossibility of self-determination, because our family's friends were prosperous in this sense. When I grew up and started communicating with different people, I saw that their reality was very different from mine. Now I see that there are destructive families in which a person is not free for various reasons. It is important to note that these people have difficulties in self-realization no matter their gender. I know both men and women who cannot be who they want because of the pressure of family, traditions, and society. Thus, we have a society of people who cannot combine their desires and reality in their mind.

Due to the complexity of these circumstances and reasons, I cannot support only the women's movement. In my picture of the world, there is no struggle between women and men. I believe that we are at a stage in the development of the world where people need to struggle for education and freedom of choice, no matter of gender, age, sexual orientation, or race.

With the consolidation of people, especially men and women, we can achieve mutual respect and build a society of equal opportunities. In my opinion, instead of making each other an enemy and fighting, we need to become allies and learn from each other what was previously impossible.

I believe that it is very important not to forget that we strive for equality and freedom of choice, not for conquest. The media every day speaks of a war between countries, between women and men, but I see people who want peace. Many men support me and help me develop. Also, there are many women who have chosen to be a businesswoman or housewife, and I support each of them. Acceptance of each person's peaceful choice is the secret of equality. Meanwhile, the rights of certain categories of women and men can still be unequal and violated. I think that this problem at it relates to the absence of clear and modern laws and universal education. Our generation is ready to solve these tasks.

I have a husband and he supports my forward movement. Today, I work as a translator and copywriter, but the sphere of my interests is much wider than just work. In addition to languages and journalism, I am interested in literature, making music, and currently participating in a cover band. I am also learning with my mother to sew clothes, studying political science through online educational resources, and actively monitoring the political processes in Russia, the countries of the former Soviet Union, Israel and America. Moreover, in a year, I plan to resume classes with the Rabbi in the study of the Torah. My husband and I follow a healthy diet and cook at home. Unfortunately, we do not always find time for regular sports, so we try to do outdoor activities on weekends: walk in parks or in nature, shoot archery, or ride to the sea on bicycles. I have a dream of being a mom of two children and taking care of my home and family. I understand that raising and caring for children will take several years. Therefore, I prepare and study the psychology of family life. Thereby, I hope this time will be a very happy time for my family. Our world is changing so fast, and perhaps in the future, I will get a new profession in the field of sewing and fashion or even make a Ph.D. in Russian literature.

I hope people who read my story develop talents and fulfill their dreams. By our example, we can inspire thousands of other people to become themselves and make our world a better place. Let's stop fighting and unite to achieve the world of the future!

My Life As A Woman: Israel Edition #3

I grew up in the north of Israel, in the Western Galilee, in a small village. For a big part of my life I was homeschooled. Later, I studied in an alternative school that was founded by some local parents, including mine. Only at age 14, I joined the regular education system. In high school, I majored in theater and literature. I've always loved art and wanted to do something related to it. Art always felt like the best way to spend my time and express myself, sometimes by collaborating with others and sharing that feeling with them. As a homeschooled child, my mom played a big role in my life. She was my very first teacher, taught me how to read and write, which opened up for me the world of books, and sparked my love for reading and writing.

As for my grandmothers, I was the first granddaughter for both of them, and I believe this affected our relationship, and probably also my perception of myself (as I'm also the firstborn in my nuclear family). Though these women all had great impressions on me, especially during my first years, I didn't lack male energy around me as well. I am the big sister for three younger brothers (I've only got brothers, no matter how much I wished for a sister). And my father and I also have a meaningful connection, as he, too, was my teacher, but unlike my mother, he taught me martial arts (as I said, I love arts).

Growing up with such prominent male energy around me surely had a big part in shaping my identity as a woman. I've learned I can be as strong and fierce as my brothers and father, but also as gentle and embracing as my mother and grandmothers. I got the perfect mix of lessons from both sides. And let's not forget the culture I'm coming from. In my culture, women's parts are very diverse. From the religious point of view, as the wonder-woman housekeeper, to the modern point of view, as the successful independent career-woman. I like my eclectic culture, and the fact that it allows me to choose what kind of woman I want to be, what many different things am I made of.

Currently, I'm a freelancer, working in translation (between Hebrew and English) and in writing content, and when that's not enough, I make an extra income with multiple, occasional jobs – teaching kids as a private teacher, babysitting, typing, cleaning and more...

Thankfully, apart from the regular stares and some mild arrogance, my struggles as a woman weren't too bad. Growing up, I felt like I had to prove myself around my brothers, as they outnumbered me (I went through a tomboy phase as well), until I've learned I don't need to be like them, which was relieving.

The biggest success I had as a woman is the sisterhood I found and the help I got from other women when I needed it. When you can't have real sisters, you find them in your friends and the women around you. Obviously, being kind and helpful is not limited to women, I had the honor of getting help from some great men, but the advice and guidance – and of course, the steady hand to support me when I stumbled – that I got from women that understood me and my troubles, cannot be replaced, and I'm happy for being a woman in this women's world.

Giving advice seems strange to me, as I'm barely 19 years old. But as an Israeli woman, I can say this: reality can seem very fragile for the most part. But you can be strong and steady and peaceful inside of it.

My Life As A Woman: Israel Edition #4

I wouldn't claim that I'm much of an inspiration to other women, but I can say I've come quite a long way and gathered quite a few life experiences along the way. I grew up in the Beit She'an region of Israel, precisely in Palladus street. I grew up in a family of five; two parents and three children, being the second child, I didn't have a lot of responsibilities placed on me except to go to school and be responsible for my younger sister. Being a parent is to inspire their child/children, my grandmother inspired me most through my offensive act to anybody around us then. She also taught me a lot about how to live a decent life.

I study Healthcare Management in the University center in Florida, Israel. I graduated in 2010 with B.Sc. Since my young age, I like anything related to health, and my sister works in a hospital where I visit her, so I stay there most of the time to see how they treat their patients. One day, the doctor in charge called me and asked me, 'what is your future ambition?' I responded I wanted to be a doctor and he replied to me, "That sounds good." Since then, I was impressed with the healthcare sources, this made me want to study healthcare management in higher institution.

Culture is the total way of life. The culture in Israel is splendid. Being a citizen of Israel, it creates and supports the mission, vision, and values. Our culture also transforms employees into advocates/critics. It also helps keep the best people. I work as a nurse working on cardiology and the coronary care unit in a flagship emergency care hospital, and I also write content about healthcare, health blog, research review, and a lot more. I struggle as a woman to feel worthy of good things, and I have trouble focusing on the positive and seeing my worth. I also see myself as damaged and not worthy of recognition or friendship. I wish I didn't have to deal with a lifetime struggle of anxiety and depression. I struggle to find meaningful support and community as a mom. I'm a perfectionist and an over-thinker, and it's exhausting. My heart says let the day job go, but the head says stay. I'm struggling to find my purpose in a new stage of life. Success as a woman includes progress over perfection, recognition of their accomplishments, motivation of each other, being a mentor to another woman, sharing of ideas freely, and getting out of the norms.

Advice to women from a woman living in Israel, procrastination stems from fear, caring for yourself is the most important thing, reputation is everything, and always keep claiming your spot. To women around the world, keep learning, keep reflecting, and keep improving and stay safe there. Thanks for reading.

My Life As A Woman: Israel Edition #5

Ever since I was a little girl, I loved creating stories. I could make up entire galaxies, filled with wonder and magic. When I grew up, I started writing them down. I thought of myself as a character in a story – the hero, to be exact. It didn't stay like that for long. I grew up in a small community in the north of Israel, and I was homeschooled until the age of twelve. My parents were patient and loving, and although they weren't perfect, they always tried their best. My mom told me that after several attempts, they realized sending my sister and I to kindergarten wasn't right for us, so they decided to raise us at home. I used to take her patience and devotion for granted, but over the years I've come to understand how much she gave us, and how truly inspiring she was.

I joined school in the seventh grade, which was a pretty shocking experience to a girl who had never even been to school before. The first year was difficult – not only was I the new kid, but I was also a really strange one. I was picked on quite often, even bullied by certain kids from my class. I think that's when I had the painful realization that maybe, I wasn't pretty and "cool" enough to be the hero of the story. I was just too tall and chubby, too sweaty and hairy, and overall, just too different.

I tried to remind myself how stupid it was, and that it didn't matter that I didn't look like the girls in the movies, but sometimes, remembering that was just too damn difficult. Sometimes I felt overwhelmed by the sadness and anger, and I would look at myself in the mirror and ask helplessly – why is it so hard for me to love myself?

In high school, I majored in theatre and Jewish bible studies. Jewish bible studies were a bit dry, but still interesting. The thing I really loved was theatre – it was so colorful and expressive, and I found it fascinating. After a while, I discovered that even while performing, which was one of my favorite things in the world, I still felt insecure and too vulnerable.

After graduating from high school, I moved away from home to the big city, where I got to experience a new side of my country. Israel is a country of immigrants, misfits who found a shared home. There are so many different cultures mixed together, with different habits, traditions, and world views. It was as overwhelming as it was beautiful.

After I moved, I started volunteering at an after-school child care facility, where I was exposed to the darker side of life. Seeing the most helpless and innocent human beings get hurt by the people who were supposed to protect them, was painful. There were times when I wondered whether what I did had any meaning. I felt helpless, like I wasn't in control of my own story anymore. But then, at the end of my two year period there, I finally realized how wrong I was, and how strong I was to do this. I finally understood that I didn't have to change myself, because being different wasn't something that was holding me back. Being MY kind of woman, living life my own way – that's always been my strength.

So, if anyone ever tells you that you're not good enough to be the hero of the story, tell them that being the hero of THEIR story must be pretty damn boring.

My Life As A Woman: Israel Edition #6

I wasn't comfortable being a woman up until I moved to Israel last year, so today I want to share the story of the stereotypes I had and how I overcame them. As a kid, I wasn't happy to be a girl. I refused to wear dresses, play dolls, hang out with girls. In my entrance essay for the university I wrote, "I want to be a journalist, not a journalistka" (feminitive of a journalist). Because being a girl seemed to mean being weak, tearful, dependent, even stupid. I wasn't any of those.

I wanted to be equal, and that was the way my parents raised my brother and me: same education, opportunities, freedom of choice. In my family women always worked the same way as men – soviet culture promoted the idea of making no difference between genders. And our family values were universal: learning, exploring, honesty, good intentions. On the one hand it taught me that expectations from me are the same. But on the other hand, I saw that women get less promotions, possibilities, and even respect for the same achievements than men do. On my faculty of journalism boys were always teacher's favourites, and I had to work twice as hard to finish university with my red diploma.

So I learned how to be equal to men, but it meant that I had to hide my gender. I never knew how to be equal and be a woman at the same time. My mom wasn't teaching me to be feminine: she never dressed or wore makeup, and she was ashamed of her body. When I was a teenager and my body started to change, parents were making fun of me because I was "sticking out my butt" - though it was just the way it looked. Wanting to be beautiful, to attract attention weren't the right things to want.

It was the women mentors that taught me that – at my first job in the international IT startup. My colleague was confident, professional, respected. She wore short skirts, knew how to take care of herself, but at the same time she was brave, adventurous, and creative in a way that I only saw in men before. From her, I learned how to be proud of myself and not shy about my achievements. Later I teamed up with a woman manager, with a brilliant education and important role in the company. She was stunningly beautiful and didn't hide it as other women on high positions would do. She taught me how to allow myself to be feminine without feeling threatened, afraid to lose respect, or perceived only for my looks.

It was when I moved to Israel that I finally found the right contact with my femininity. Women here are truly equal: the girls go to the army, they are allowed to love other women and less expected to start a family as soon as they are 18 (the pressure in Russia, you wouldn't believe). But more importantly – they don't have to pretend to be men to be excepted. They look naturally beautiful and express freely their sexuality. Here I felt in the right place and take it as the best compliment when people tell me that I look Israeli and fit in.

So here is my message for all women out there: be equal but be feminine – in a way that you understand and want it.

My Life As A Woman: Israel Edition #7

My name is Michal Lehman and I grew up in Ma'ale Adumim, in a religious home, where we followed the Jewish heritage. However, I never grew to understand it, so when I was old enough to question, I stopped observing. My parents grew up in strict, religious homes, where it was shoved down their throats, so they never learned to love it, and in turn, had no idea how to pass it on.

My parents divorced when I was six. My two sisters and I stayed to live with our mother, while our brother moved in with our father. I don't remember much from that time, or when they were still married. I was young and naive; all I thought about was double presents on birthdays and Hanukah. Despite being a "broken family", we still felt whole, because both parents made efforts to give us all the support that we needed.

In the past few years I've been reflecting on it more, about the deeper ramifications it had on my life and personal views. I've never had a prime example of what happy, married parents look like. When visiting my friends' homes as a child, it was strange to see two parents. To me, having two homes with one parent in each, is the norm.

My mother is a hard working woman, from morning to night and at least two or three jobs, yet she always found time for her children. Instead of sending us to summer camps, she took us to local arts & crafts shops, spent hundreds of shekels on buying supplies, then hours of crafting and creating. It's admirable for a parent to actually spend so much time with their children, and really enjoy their company.

Not only did it develop my creative side, but it also showed me how to be a hard working mother and still be present. She taught me how to be determined, adamant, strong willed and not let anyone push me over. To fight for my dreams and refused to accept no for an answer. To always find another way, to follow through and never give up, my mother showed me how to be kind to others and accept people who are different. She taught me how to be open-minded, tolerant, and patient.

I'm now almost 30, living in Tel Aviv, and working on my first novel as well as my new personal blog. Soon I will receive my degree in creative writing, literature, and psychology. I get a lot of frowns and raised eyebrows at that, but I refuse to let it get to me. I'm learning what I truly love, I've been writing since I could write, and will fight to be successful in it. Life is about so much more than going with the norm and studying for money. I truly believe in the power of art in all its forms, that it's essential for us as humans to stay sane and happy.

I'm asked all the time about marriage and kids, especially since both my sisters are married. Apparently, I'm not getting younger, and the older I get, the harder it is to have kids. I'm told that I need to find myself a husband, as if I can easily just snap my fingers and one will appear. I'm not going to marry just anyone, for the sake of it, especially coming from a divorced home. Also, life has so much more to offer than just starting a family. I have much to do and discover before settling down and dedicating my time and energy to raising kids.

My Life As A Woman: Israel Edition #8

Sarah Lichtenstein

What does the snowy east coast of North America have in common with the Land of Israel? Upon emigrating from North America to Jerusalem in 2017, I discovered the answer: very little. That's the joy of my emigration story: the excitement of a life-altering experience such as coming to a place that offers a different spin.

Growing up in America, my family was a close one. The inside of our home always felt "warm," even though it was cold outside. On nights when the snow was especially fierce—actually piling up against our front door many days—we stayed inside all together. My siblings and I sipped cocoa and read stories. It was a lovely life.

My father grew up in a traditional Jewish Orthodox home. His parents worked hard and kept the mitzvot such as Shabbos and kosher. My mother's parents were taken to the cause of settling in Israel and left America for Jerusalem in the 1960s. They say that growing up in Israel was the best time of their lives. My father and mother met, and together, they built in me a love of Judaism, Jerusalem, and Torah. That's why I am in Israel today.

My personal interests played a role in my emigration, too. I'm a writer, and I was drawn with a fiery passion toward spirituality. There is something in the act of writing that centers me in the midst of that fire, allowing me to express my Neshama (soul). Being in Jerusalem is a natural extension of my yearning to live a life inspired by closeness to the Creator.

One similarity between Israel and North America is that the regions are home to people of many origins. Regarding myself, I live among the Israeli ultra-Orthodox. From my apartment I hear prayer services during the day, see people walking to synagogue or to yeshiva and children outside helping their parents or playing. There is not much materialism in my neighborhood—what you need is around the corner: fresh challah, great coffee, and wine for Shabbos eve.

As a writer/editor, I work freelance from home (called "Osek Patur" in Israel, a designation that is not hard to get when you immigrate). I started off freelancing simply by emailing all the relevant businesses I could find who might need a writer and editor and asked them if there were projects I could do, however small. It took a few years to build up a clientele. This little business has been my greatest success because to do it, I had to boost myself up daily to carry on. It challenged my commitment to myself but by continually pressing on, I am succeeding.

When it comes to life in Israel, so much depends on one's own community. As an ultra-Orthodox woman without a family, it is, for me, a quiet life. Given the focus on spiritual development and closeness to G-d via studying Torah and fulfilling mitzvot (good deeds), there is less of what one might call "entertainment." This can be understood by the following idea.

Years ago when I was still in North America, I trudged over to my local Starbucks for a morning coffee. A woman sat there working. We started chatting and she explained that her life was once very different. She did not have many responsibilities when she was younger; travelled and shopped and had lots of material enjoyment. But now, she said, there are many responsibilities, many projects and people to care for. She explained the difference in the following way.

"When I was younger, and free...there was more fun...but where I am today...there is more joy."

I believe this aptly describes the experience of being in a peaceful place of Torah. There are more obligations, yet more truth. I have traded downtown shops for the hum and song of Gemara.

Thus, my advice to women coming to Jerusalem to settle in an Orthodox community is as follows. Even if you were raised in a Torah home in America, the culture might differ here slightly. Do not be put off by its peace. Think of the differences between the home you loved and your new one, always imagining life here as an adventure. Study, pray, and explore. Be still with your feelings and with G-d. Enjoy the spiritual life in Jerusalem in an internal way, because this is the home of G-d's presence and yours.

My Life As A Woman: Israel Edition #9

I was born in Moscow, Russia in the mid-1980s. It was the time when the Soviet Empire started to crack and fall apart. A mixed sense of fear and excitement was in the air. The Iron Curtain was slightly moved by the first breeze of possible freedom, and some people dared to dream of the outer world.

I belong to the first generation of Russian people who studied foreign languages. It was a pure madness: kindergartens, schools, courses, seminars – our parents used every slight possibility for us to learn any foreign language. As long as I remember myself, my parents told me, "We already stand no chance, but you will definitely go abroad and make it there". Going to the outer world in the soviet conscious was almost the same as going to outer space. Actually, as much as I know history, going to space appeared to be easier.

I was 22 when I met David. The most attractive thing about him was that aura of careless freedom around him. Grabbing a backpack and going somewhere to Europe for the weekend or taking me by surprise to Amsterdam for my birthday was absolutely natural for him and an impossible adventure for me. When our relationships became serious enough to talk about common future, I realized that I was going to move with him to his motherland – Israel. To explain to you how I felt about it back then and what I actually knew about the country, I will have to tell you some of my family history.

My great-grandfather was a very educated, intelligent, and respected man. He was a teacher, writer and an editor of a local newspaper. He was arrested, announced "The Public Enemy", and executed in 1937 during the biggest wave of Stalinist Repressions. One of his neighbors notified local NKVD (KGB) brunch that a very weird language that suspiciously resembled German, was spoken in the family between him, his wife (my great-grandma) and their children. Back then; this kind of testimony was enough to accuse a person of being a German spy. This was the death sentence. The "weird language" was Yiddish.

After his arrest, my great-grandma was so terrified that she fled the town, forged her documents, erasing all possible evidence of being Jewish and baptized her children. Jewish culture and connections became a taboo in the family since then.

I have learned all that after several years that I've been living in Israel already. By the way, I also learned that the neighbor, who stipulated my great-grandfather, got his apartment as a reward for his vigilance. He hung himself in it several years later.

So what did I know about Israel, when I decided to move there with my husband? Whatever they showed us on the TV. News mostly. This means that in my imagination, Israel was an open desert with terrorists patrolling it riding camels and shooting RPGs from time to time with no particular reason. And Israelis were supposed to dress like ultra-orthodox Hasidic community representatives.

Imagine my shock when the plane landed in a beautiful land on seashore, drowning in flowers. I was driving smooth clean roads past Tel Aviv skyscrapers and could not believe my eyes. As long as I was not Jewish neither by documents nor by religion, when I came to Israel, I had to go through quite a long and complicated procedure to get Israeli citizenship. Sometimes it seemed a little bit absurd, when we had to come to our local Misrad Ha Phnim (Internal Affairs Office) with my husband, our newborn daughter, in order to prove that our relationship was real. Sometimes it was funny, when among my husband, my daughter, who was born in Israel and got her citizenship automatically and even our dog, who had Israeli international veterinary documents, I was the only person in the family without the citizenship. But I am grateful for the path I had to follow as it taught me a lot. And the main thing was not to expect anybody to give me any discount. Whatever I wanted, I had to roll up my sleeves and work hard to get it.

I knew from the beginning, that to assimilate in the country and to become successful in any way, I had to learn the language. And let me tell you something – Hebrew has nothing to do with any language that you might have ever learned before. To tell you the truth, it has much more common with Klingon then with any earth language. Israel has a network of Ulpans – special community centers, where immigrants can learn the language – but going back to dusty classrooms was not for me. I already got my BA and MA degrees in engineering back in Russia. I decided to start working and communicate with Israelis as much as possible and learn Hebrew on the way.

But where could I work? I wanted to start a new life in a new country and thought that the best way to do it was to give a chance to my childhood dream. When I was a little girl, I wanted to become a hairdresser. So I went to work in a fancy hair salon in the heart of Tel Aviv. I started as an assistant and a shampoo girl. For about half a year I didn't say a word. I was just listening, analyzing, absorbing. And then one day I realized that I'm strong enough to start cracking the shell. I cannot explain this feeling when you start speaking a language that you have learned all by yourself. No teachers, quizzes, or vocabularies. Pure observation. I guess, this is that long-forgotten feeling when babies learn to talk.

Anyway, either the owners of the Hair salon were impressed by my learning abilities or the fact that I knew how to operate a Nikon camera and boosted their Instagram up to 20K followers, or they just got scared that they have blabbed out too much in front of me, when I already understood Hebrew quite enough, but having started my career as a shampoo girl, a couple years later I became an art director of the place. The interesting thing is that in Israel, the beauty business, especially hair care, is an all-men's world. So I even became kind of famous in the country, being one of not so many women on the top of the industry.

Not so long ago, I opened my own beauty salon and things were going pretty well, but then COVID-19 came. I won't tell you one more story of how the business went down, how it's trying to get back on the track in the atmosphere of a deeply damaged economy and general apathy – you have seen, read, and heard lots of them. I want to tell you that I have realized that a time has come to give a chance to a brand new dream. As corny as it sounds, I also wanted to be a writer.

My Life As A Woman: Italy Edition #1

Hi, my name is Sara, I'm 23 years old, I'm Italian and living in Italy since I was born. And yes, as you can imagine, I eat a lot of pasta, use my hands a lot while I talk, love wine and good food, but there's also a lot more than these funny stereotypes. It's weird how sometimes the ideas we make in our minds influence our judgement of someone or something.

I consider myself lucky to be born in Italy. It's a wonderful country and a good place to live in – don't get me wrong, nothing's ever perfect, but Italy is plenty of art and beauty, modernity and history dance together everywhere, its culture is so rich and yet its inhabitants are so diverse. I live in Northern Italy, in Lombardy, an area that has recently been severely impacted by the coronavirus outbreak, in which many international companies, universities, industries and small businesses are located. I feel lucky to live here, many opportunities are accessible.

I remember that when I was a kid I underwent several "dream job" phases: first I wanted to be a vet, because I like animals a lot, then a medical examiner (I used to watch CSI: Crime Scene Investigation a lot) and then a cartoonist, because I have a creative mind, and these are just a few examples. As a result, after high school, I had no idea what to do with my life. I've always had an aptitude for languages since I was a little girl and I always dreamt of moving abroad, so I chose to get my Bachelor's in Foreign Languages and Cultures. During my bachelor's studies, I decided to fulfill a great dream of mine: living in Australia. This experience was the greatest, most enriching and happiest of my life so far. I could spend hours and fill several dozen pages writing about the places I visited, the wonderful people I met and what I learnt from this, but I will just say that the months I spent in Australia helped me figure out better who I wanted to become.

After my Bachelor's, I decided to enroll in a master's degree in International Marketing Management: I felt like I had a lot of theoretical knowledge thanks to my studies but lacked concrete skills for the workplace. I'm satisfied with my choice, and even though these are hard times due to the COVID-19 crisis, I see for myself a career in marketing. In the future, I'd also like to employ my knowledge both to do something on my own and also be a writer. At the moment, I'm in between marketing jobs and I try to earn extra money by freelancing as a copywriter: my favorite topics to write about are environment, sustainability, climate change and sustainable innovations.

During my master's and my first work experiences in marketing, I sometimes became more aware that in Italy we have several valuable female role models, but that they're somehow underrepresented in business or politics, and that's something we definitely have to work on. Yes, women have the same rights as men, but there are still subtle differences between them: the gender pay gap of 10% in favor of men is just one but significant example. Italy's plenty of inspiring women in all fields, from fashion to entrepreneurship to science, and I wish we could focus more on the positive things rather than on the criticisms.

If I had to give advice to my younger self and to other women, I'd say:

- Opportunities are behind every corner, you just have to learn to recognize them and seize them;

- If something scares you, do it twice: it's better to do something and then regret it than regretting not doing it;

- You cannot control others, focus on yourself and improve yourself;

- Don't doubt, trust yourself, you can do it!

My Life As A Woman: Italy Edition #2

Growing up as a woman can sometimes be difficult, even if you live in one of the most admired countries in the world. Yes, because life in Italy isn't always easy, or romantic, as a lot of people tend to think it is. I am Stefania, and I am a 37 years old Italian woman, with all the ups and downs of living in a small, but complicated country, and here I will tell you my story to inspire you and open a new door on living in my environment. I was born in Italy in 1983, on a beautiful sunny day in March. The city where I started breathing for the first time, and saw me growing up, is Turin, in the northwest of Italy. Turin is a very beautiful city, complicated and with a lot of contradictions, but with a history of kings and noblesse. This has been the first capital of Italy and you can notice that from a lot of little things: for example, Turin has a lot of big palaces, of statues, and one of the most important museums of Europe, the Egyptian museum.

So, I was born here, but I lived in Settimo Torinese until my grown up years. Settimo is a very little city near Turin. My parents decided to move to Settimo when my brother, Cristian, was little, and so I grew up there too, because Cristian is older than me. I started to explore the world of words and books when I was very little: I learned to read and write when I was three and never stopped! When I was six years old, I started to go to school, and decided, since the first day, that I would became a journalist (fast forward to now: I am a journalist, indeed!). I grew up in a very genuine environment: my parents are from the South of Italy, and have a predilection for good food, family and simplicity. So, we always had a lunch and a dinner made by my mother, a lot of time to play in our courtyard and, for me, to dance. I started to attend ballet classes when I was four, and I stopped studying dance when I was 27, but never stopped dancing! Nowadays I teach Yoga dance, a style that I invented and that combines yoga and modern dance.

I finished my school in Settimo, obtaining my diploma as a computer programmer and accountant, and started university, at least, in the big city. I chose Law, and I graduated as a Penal Law specialist in 2007, magna cum laude, of course! After my master's degree I started to work as a journalist in a little newspaper, and after five years they decided to fire me because the recession was destroying Italian communication world. In the meantime, I decided to study to become a yoga instructor and, so, in 2012 I started, after my diploma, to teach yoga too. In these days I divide myself: during the day I am a writer and a freelance journalist, and in the evenings, I teach yoga in my beautiful yoga studio called Shanta Pani Torino (Shanta Pani in Sanskrit means "Slow water").

I love you, Grandpa

My first, and most important, inspirational figure has always been my grandpa, my mother's father. His name was Vincenzo, and, unlucky, he died from lung cancer when I was 11 years old. Although I miss him every day, he inspired me the most because he built what I think is an "empire" from nothing. He was very poor: he lived in Melfi, the city where my mother is from in the South of Italy, in a cellar when he fell in love with my grandmother. He prayed my great-grandfather to have the permission to marry his daughter, and since then he decided to make her his queen. He worked a lot as a countryman, and when my mother was fifteen they had the opportunity to move from Melfi to Turin. He was a very tireless person, and until his death, he loved his nieces and nephews with all his heart, always saying to us that all was possible if we were able to dream it.

Italy, a place called home

I can say that Italy is a beautiful place, of course, but it's also a very contradictory country. We have a lot of issues, the most at a financial and social level; for example, finding a job here is difficult, the most if you are a woman. For that reason, I'd like to move one day with my fiancé, because we have ambitions that here are very difficult to accomplish if you are not rich. But Italy is also a place where you can always find a smile, a place where kids can grow up in a genuine way, where nature is all around you. So, I can certainly suggest you make a visit here, maybe beginning from Turin, a city that a lot of people don't know very well, but that is full of surprises.

The struggle of growing up, and the gifts of my life

When I was 17 years old I started to suffer from anorexia. Now I have totally recovered from it, but this mental disease really changed my life during the period of six years in which I had to fight it. I learned a lot from anorexia: to always have the will to live, to appreciate life, to work on myself, to be compassionate. But my life as a young woman has also been beautiful. I had the opportunity to study, to accomplish a lot of things, to become what I wanted, to meet a lot of people thanks to my jobs. I also had the opportunity to study at Oxford University last year, getting my diploma as a fiction writer. And, as my grandpa taught me, I had the chance to create my life as I wished.

My advice to you

As an Italian woman I can give you simple, but effective, advice: don't ever give up on your dreams. Here the society is not "women-friendly" and we learn, since we are little, that we must work harder than men to succeed in life. My story can say to you that success is possible: study, believe in yourself, and always aspire to become the woman you want to be.

You can do it!

My Life As A Woman: Italy Edition #3

It wasn't always easy to dream of being an artist in the little town I grew up in. While the beautiful landscape surrounding my home hugely helped my artistic flair to blossom, the not-so-open-minded approach to life that little town presented often left me discouraged and sad. On the other hand, however, I was blessed with a helpful and close community my family and I could always turn to in times of need. Growing up on the gorgeous shore of a colorful lake in Northern Italy, in a point where different regions and countries all meet at their respective borders, I spent a peaceful and playful childhood. I grew up in a nice house with my numerous family, spending most of my time with my grandparents.

Having manifested my artistic side early on, I immersed myself in books, the arts, and music while I was still very young. This often led me to spend time in solitude, although people would almost always consider me an extrovert, due to my talkativeness. After middle school, I decided to enroll at a grammar school, where I cultivated my knowledge and love for literature (and started fantasizing about what being a writer would mean). I learned to appreciate the richness of my country's history and culture, especially from an artistic point of view, while also developing a strong curiosity towards the outside world.

I discovered a visceral love for American music, Indian philosophy, foreign literatures. I went on studying English by myself, doing way more than what was requested in class, and I started writing my own words in what, to me, was still an alien language. The thrill of shifting from my everyday language to another one to do some writing is still exciting and interesting, as it helps my writing grow and it keeps my focus sharp.

After University, I finally lived my dream of staying abroad, as I moved to the United Kingdom for a few years. I have always felt at home in a foreign place, so that experience was incredibly valuable. I later moved back, realizing I was missing the warmth of my family and relationships. This also meant I needed to come to terms with what life as a grown-up adult - no longer a student - looked like in my Country of origin.

Being a young woman in Italy is not always easy. There are a lot of expectations to meet from all sides. Whoever grew up in a more traditional family might feel the pressure to get married and build a family. On the other hand, who was raised in another context might feel the pressure to build a profitable career, in a Country where, frankly, the job market and the economy are often very fragile. Our only antidote to this contradiction is being very honest with ourselves, being true to our goals, and our desires. Do we really want to build a family? Do we really want to build a strong career? Are we ready to pay the price for each of these choices?

I think my generation has finally shown that women have the right to choose for themselves, whatever the course of life they decide to embark on. This will surely make things easier for us and the next generations - if we are ready to keep fighting to preserve that freedom.

My Life As A Woman: Holy See Vatican Edition

I was thinking of leaving my country having great hope in the refugee camp. I was trying to escape from my country's crises as violence, persecution, and poverty continued to escalate. I was born and grew up in Benghazi, Libya. I have lived a very comfortable and wonderful life until the civil war a raised. I was expelled from my home during the Libyan civil war and fled to Europe across the Mediterranean. It has been a long and dangerous journey that has brought me from Libya to Greece Lesbos. I saw the Mediterranean sea take many migrant lives. A boat carrying about five hundred migrant sank in the ocean just in front of my eyes. Thinking of that day still causes me a heartache. I could not help but cry.

We arrived in the Greece island of Lesbos. We walked into an olive grove and started lighting fires to call for help. We were shivering in the cold, some of them sat closely and huddled together rubbing their hands to warm up. Some of us sat near the fire and warmed up ourselves as we were waiting for a bus to take us to Moria camp. Most of us were craving food to eat, some of them were expecting to get coats. The children also hoped and expected to start school soon...I also asked myself, will I be able to work soon?

My hopes were gone as soon as I arrived, I was shocked to see the camp overcrowded. There was no shelter and I slept on the ground all night. There was no access to electricity, and when it rained, I feared that I would die of the cold and the wind and I had to walk fifteen minutes to the closest bathroom. We lived in extremely bad conditions with no electricity, not enough water to drink, not enough food to eat, and no medical care. The lines to get food were full of people. There was no space to move and it was hard to breathe. There was a lot of shoving and pushing.

We were not allowed to buy property outside the camp or work in professions. There was no hope. We just spent our time there. There is no life here. It is humiliating, there is no humanity in the camp, it is unbelievably bad. It was the worst experience my life ever had. There was no hope, especially for the elderly, pregnant women, who are forced to live there. For me, Moria is not a camp, rather a place of violence, deprivation, suffering and despair. Animals live better than us. Libya was even better for me. The pain and desolation that I have witnessed have really hurt me in many ways.

One day things started to change when pope Francis, the bishop of Rome, chief pastor of the worldwide Catholic Church, and head of state of the Vatican city state came to visit the camp. I really want to thank Pope Francis, as I was born again. He gave me hope, dreams, and a new life. I could see he felt the humanity, when he came to help all the way. He showed other countries how to help people, how to be kind and acknowledge humanity. I was lucky to go to Rome with five other families from the refugee. we were hosted by the Vatican and Sant'Egidio charity. The Vatican cover the expenses that we new arrivals would have otherwise incurred, while the community of Sant'Egidio helped secure our housing, enroll us in Italian lessons, and place the minors in school and find employment for the adults.

The Pope dedicated mass to us, saying "no one is a foreigner." He warned, "fearing migration leads to racism." He helped us to overcome our trauma, make sense of our loss and rebuild our lives. Now we have access to health care, minimum wage education, and shelter. He gave us freedom to choose where to live. He also helped in reuniting families, provided us quick, safe, and an accessible path to citizenship.

I still sometimes cannot believe I am safe now and have the freedom to work. Though I am Muslim, they help us all the same without any discrimination. I am very thankful for Pope Francis of the Vatican, Sant'Egidio mediation and apples to global leadership to help each other to be friends and to stop the wars and fighting. It is a miracle.

Thinking back on those I left behind, I wish all of them had been as lucky as me. I will not give up on this awe-inspiring opportunity. I want to follow the footsteps of those who made it possible. Just looking at the good jobs, the work, inspiration, determination and action of the Pope, I learnt a lot and still learning more from him.

Pope Francis once said it and I will say it again, "We are not alone, God sustains us. We people must give in turn the gift that we have received: we are called to share the comfort of the spirit, the closeness of God."

My Life As A Woman: San Marino Edition

My name is Sofia, I was born and raised in San Marino, which is not only a city but also a state located in Italy, like Vatican City. I grew up here in San Marino with my parents, I don't have brothers and sisters, but I am still surrounded by the affection of my cousins. San Marino has about 33,000 inhabitants, if we talk about relatives among friends it always comes out that there are distant family ties. After years of friendship, I discovered for example that my grandmother is related to my best friend's grandmother. Living in San Marino is like living in a large family, almost all families know each other, and it is very often that a relative or friend becomes Captain Regent, or one of the two heads of state; a truly particular reality.

My father is a policeman, while my mother is a housewife so especially as a child I spent a lot of time with her. My mother is the woman who taught me everything I am and everything I want to be, taught me not to give up, to start again and to pursue my dreams. Thanks to my mother, I learned to reason with my head, not to be afraid to say my opinion, to pursue my goals, and to have the courage to be myself.

I studied letters in Milan, I graduated with 110 cum laude and today I am a teacher, the job I have always dreamed of and for which I have struggled so much. I love children and I am happy to teach them my knowledge. Often children without speaking teach us the reasons to live. I hope to be able to teach children also what my mother has transmitted to me, to help future generations face the world with strength and determination.

I consider myself lucky to have been born and raised in San Marino, I love the importance given to our city, to the history of our city. At school, teachers immediately teach us the history of San Marino, an independent city just like its citizens. Fortunately, I have never had to face difficult challenges, but if I think of a fight as a woman, satisfaction immediately comes to mind on the day of my graduation. Some girls who had always "underestimated" me, attended my university and were present on the day of my graduation perhaps with the intention of deriding me. I graduated with 110 cum laude, top marks. My successes also include the fact that I graduated with full marks and that I found a stable and satisfying job. I hope that a child will be added soon, that would be the most beautiful success ever!

I recommend not only to the women of San Marino, but to any woman, to always believe in themselves and in their own abilities. I advise you never to fall, even in the face of challenges that may seem impossible. So women, be strong, stubborn, fragile, dreamers, silent warriors. So incredibly powerful that you believe that the fate of the world is in your hands, because it really is!

My Life As A Woman: Ivory Coast (Cote d'Ivoire) Edition #1

Where did you grow up?

I grew up in the town of Yamoussoukro, the official capital of Côte d'Ivoire. Specifically, in the Lakes region of Tie Ndiékro. Yamoussoukro is a city in Côte d'Ivoire and West Africa. It has picturesque buildings such as the Prefecture, the President Félix Houphouët-Boigny, and the Basilica.

How did you grow up?

I grew up with my family in a relatively stable environment, between minor headaches and great complicity. The society in which I live advocates listening, caring, and knowing how to live in a community. But the inhabitants have no shortage of anecdotes.

Do you have a parent who inspired you?

Alas! I didn't have time to know my grandmother well enough to inspire me. But my older sister does. She is the one who inspires me every day by her courage and tenacity in the face of the different adventures of life.

What did you study? Why?

When I was younger, I wanted to be an ophthalmologist because I had vision problems and my parents would take me to an ophthalmologist for care. But I ended up studying law instead. The reason for this choice is that fee studies are relatively cheaper than ophthalmology studies. However, these law studies offer more professional opportunities.

What do you like about your culture?

I like certain morals like the importance of the family, the respect of the elders, and the modesty that is common to all African traditions. There are also traditional festivals such as the Abissa in the N'zima in Bassam, the yam festival in the Agni, especially those in Aboisso and the celebration of the generations in the Ebrié in Abidjan.

What are you currently doing as a job?

I work as a legal assistant in a law firm.

Did you encounter any struggles as a woman?

My struggles as a woman in Ivorian society exist at several levels. First, professionally, I had to make a lot of effort to prove my intellectual abilities. Secondly, on the social level, there is the ongoing effort that I make to make myself respected by men. For here in Côte d'Ivoire, depravation has reached an extreme level. And men take all women as sexual objects. No consideration of women. Finally, at the family level, there is the challenge of being able to combine professional obligations with those of a housewife.

Talk about your successes as a woman

I am regularly called by a local NGO for consultations on the rights of children and women through my legal actions towards women. I even go on tours with members of this NGO to meet women and talk to them about their rights and the family code in my country.

Do you have any advice to women?

I have always been nourished by a belief that drives and supports me: everything is possible, and I can realize my dreams whatever happens. Therefore, the advice I can give to other women in Côte d'Ivoire is first and foremost to allow themselves to dream about their future. Second, they must work hard to make their dream come true. Nothing is impossible when you have self-confidence.

Emeny

My Life As A Woman: Ivory Coast (Cote d'Ivoire) Edition #2

My name is Antoinette and I am an Ivorian woman, 41 years old, married and mother of 3 boys. Coming from a modest family, with a father and a mother exercising both in the public functions, I had a rather peaceful childhood inside the country precisely in cities located in the center of the country: Toumodi and Yamoussoukro (political capital of Côte d'Ivoire).

I lived with a tutor when I was very small because my parents wanted me to be very independent and to learn to live away from them. Later after my primary school diploma, I joined a Catholic school in Yamoussoukro where I lived in boarding school with several other girls my age. This experience of my life made me quickly open my eyes to the importance of cultural diversity and acceptance of others. So very young, I learned these values that have served me in my socio-professional life.

My maternal grandfather who was extremely kind has always been a source of inspiration for me, and was very attached to the family. He taught me the generosity and the culture of solidarity that people of my ethnic group have: the Baoulés. We are renowned in the country for our kindness and our openness.

After a good school career, I studied accounting on the advice of my mother, but I wanted to do communication or law. At the time, there was not yet a higher school in Côte d'Ivoire providing good communication courses. In addition to solidarity, sharing and generosity, I like the traditional outfits of my ethnic group. Beautiful gold ornaments or even large loincloths called "KITA" are part of our cultural heritage and that is what I prefer. This makes us beautiful during ceremonies. We are also renowned for being the biggest consumers and connoisseurs of good wines in the country.

Today I work as an accountant in a local company, and I am passionate about numbers. I think that having a respected place in society today and a fulfilled family remains my greatest success even if my goals have not yet been achieved.

In my opinion, the biggest difficulty as a woman in Ivory Coast is to go to the end of studies and find a good job to make the family proud. Indeed, traditionally, the woman must silence her personal ambitions to give a good education to her children and be always available for her husband. Basically, she finds herself in a scheme where you must be an executive in a big company with well-behaved children and a husband to support while helping financially his family.

If I must give advice to Ivorian and African women today, it is to tell them that times are changing and with them the challenges that lie ahead. It is no use comparing ourselves to the women of yesteryear because we do not live the same realities. Also remember that only work pays, and that we must review our current thinking to hope to gain our place in society. More and more feminist movements are making this awareness of Ivorian women. The world, innovation, development must be built with us women.

My Life As A Woman: Jamaica Edition #1

Hey, I am Mona. I reside in Kingston, Jamaica. I have lived here all my life. Growing up I lived all out on the island, we never stayed anywhere too long. Initially, I lived with my aunt, my mother wasn't able to take care of me at that point. The treatment at my aunt's place wasn't the best, I was always treated like a "black sheep". After turning 9 years old my mother came for me, I've lived with her ever since. We didn't have much but she tried her best to take care of us. It was me, my sister and my mom; my father wasn't in the picture until I was 13 years old. Growing up I never really had a role model, I just knew that I didn't want to be like anyone I was raised around. Until I met my father's mother, she was something else. She was strong, outgoing, caring, and smart. She was my only inspiration because everybody else was so complacent in their poverty, they made it look like it was the only end goal. Generation after generation and no change. That was not what I was looking for.

Seeing as I didn't have my parents at a young age I didn't attend an official school until I was 7 years old. I attended Franklin Town Primary School. Then attended the Convent of Mercy Academy. During my school years, I wasn't an outgoing or active child, I always kept to myself. I never had any friends and did very little playing. I always wanted to become an oncologist after my grandmother (father's mother) died of cancer. So I ensured I did well in school and had my mindset on going to medical school. All those dreams shattered when I realized, my parents didn't have enough money to pay the tuition, even though I got a scholarship. That was my biggest disappointment in life so far. I quickly realized I had to edit my plan, to let it better fit my budget. I decided to study chemistry at a local university, I am currently in my last year of university. After graduating I plan to work and save money for medical school. I am currently working part-time at a clothing store and offering freelancing services.

I love my Jamaican culture, I just don't like how the world sees us. We are more than Usain Bolt and constant crime. We have the best coffee in the world, amazing spicy and some of the best beaches. Other than our natural resources, the people are amazing. We are extremely nice and welcoming, with a fiery sense of humor. I remember going to the markets on Saturday mornings; we would spend hours just looking at all the items. It was like a trip every week. We are also very religious people, I think we have the most churches per square miles, there's a church on every corner. Children were raised in the church, and we take our faith seriously. The next thing I love about Jamaica is our love for tea. Jamaicans will tell you tea can cure anything.

To others, I am confident, fierce, and perfect, but on the inside, I am far from that. I had self-esteem problems growing up because I had no parent to show me love or tell me I was okay and that I didn't have to fit in. the lack of having my parents around really affected my perceptions of life, I became withdrawn and lacked emotions. Over time I worked on my self-confidence, it took a while to work on it but now it's a little better. I still lack emotions but now I am trying to be more empathetic. My biggest success was being accepted into medical school and getting a scholarship. I came from not attending an official school to getting into medical school; I can now empower little girls in my community. I ensure I volunteer in the community, so they know it's possible and that they are not stuck at that level forever.

To all the women of Jamaica, not because your family is currently poor means you are restricted to that level. You can be the change in your family, I believe. So believe in yourself, as much as we believe in tea, and you know how much we believe in tea.

My Life As A Woman: Jamaica Edition #2

Paula, (that's me) was born and raised in a remote district in the hilly regions of St. James, Jamaica. I am the third oldest child in the family, following the birth of two older sisters. Our community was a low socio-economic community, where everyone was family, whether you were blood-related or not.

We were poor, but my father who was a farmer ensured that food was always on the table for his children. Mama was a housewife. She stayed home and took care of the family's needs while Dad went to the farm every day. Even as children, my younger brothers and sisters had to help our Dad out on the farm.

Life wasn't easy. My dad planted sugar-cane, bananas, ground provisions and vegetables. Cane reaping was an annual event, but banana was a weekly event. We had to help dad out when it was reaping time. While the house was located on the land where my dad planted sugar cane, the banana plantation was located roughly 3 kilometres from home, far in the bushes, away from civilization.

Every Sunday my dad would head off to his banana plantation before day break. My siblings including myself had to walk that distance and carry the bananas on our heads to the main road. We had to make several trips to get those bananas out to the main road. However, my two brothers who were a year and two years my junior started doubling up for me because I usually would start having headaches after my third trip.

I remember waking up as early as am every morning to go to a standpipe in the community to get water. We had to get up very early to carry and fill at least two barrels every morning before we left for school. Getting up early was a must if we wanted to miss the long line of waiting community members at the standpipe. We would sure get into trouble with our parents if those barrels were not filled each morning.

Although the primary school was roughly five to six kilometres from home, I loved attending school. Mama ensured that her children were in school. I attended school at times without lunch money, but my teachers always ensured I had lunch. Moreover, I was a good student and my teachers loved me. I spent more time doing my school work than actually playing with friends during recess and lunchtime at school.

Regardless of the time, we left home, we had to be at school on time. Everyone feared to get a flogging from the headmaster for being late. So if we're running late we would make up for it by running most of the way to ensure we are on time. So much running made me tired, I remember one morning I got to school late, I was about ten years old at the time. All latecomers were lined up outside the principal's office door. He was using a leather belt and each child had to stretch out a hand to receive the "licks" (that's what we called them in Jamaica). When it was my turn, he simply looked at me and said, "Go to your class because I don't see anything on you to get a flogging." I didn't wait for him to repeat, I hurriedly left the line and went to class.

Because I was small-bodied, I was bullied at primary school at age ten years. Children often teased me and picked a quarrel with me. I never fought back, so I was constantly bullied because they thought I was soft. My two younger brothers made sure to defend by taking care of the bullies. After a couple fights between them and the bullies, the bullying stopped.

At age 11 years, I passed the Common Entrance Exam for high school. I won a full scholarship and my parents were proud of me. A full scholarship meant that my books and tuition and other school-related expenses were paid. I still had to trek the five to six kilos from home to get the big bus to attend high school in Montego Bay. Mama was there for me. She would wake me in the mornings, fix breakfast, so I could eat something before I leave for school.

That woman was my inspiration. Every morning religiously she would accompany me on my way to school. We would usually leave home before it was daylight and she would stay with me and would only turn back when daylight breaks by then it was light, and I could see my way clearly. For all my years at high school, my mom made sure she walked with me every morning.

I watched my mom struggle and fight the odds to care for her children even after my dad died. I promised myself that I would hold my head up high and never disappoint her. I stayed in high school and completed my course even when other girls within my age group in the community were getting pregnant and dropping out of school.

I wanted to be a public health nurse but after failing one key science subject in my GCE O levels exam, I never met the entry-level requirement for nursing. After high school, I got a job as a pre-trained teacher and discovered that I actually liked teaching. I taught for four years and saved enough money to pay my way through teachers college, earning a certificate after completing my studies.

Due to financial constraints, I wasn't able to pursue my first degree until after I had my three children. That too was another sacrifice. The university was in the central region of the island. That means that I couldn't reside at home. So began another two years of travelling. I spent every weekend at home during those two years. Every Friday, I headed for home and every Sunday evening or Monday morning, I was on the road seeking transportation to get back to the university, which at times was unreliable. In spite of the challenges faced during my studies, it paid off because I graduated with honors.

Looking back, I'm not sorry I didn't become a nurse. Why? I found fulfilment in teaching and challenging my students to rise above their difficulties to be who they want to be. It doesn't matter your upbringing, you can be successful in life if you believe in yourself and your dreams. Being poor is no reason to throw your hands up into the air in despair.

The black in the Jamaican flag symbolizes the struggles every Jamaican woman faces, and behind those struggles, the will to overcome. If we can dream about our success, we can achieve them by sheer will and hard work.

My Life As A Woman: Jamaica Edition #3

My name is Kaylene M. I grew up in the beautiful parish of Portland, Jamaica, with my mother, grandmother, and younger sister. Portland is said to be one of the most beautiful parishes on the island with its calm serine natural feel, warm weather and beautiful rivers, beaches and streams.

Growing up in a small community in a rural area, you are not aware of the level of poverty you face until you go out of your town and begin traveling the world at large. While my father was absent for most of my childhood, we were not poverty-stricken. My mother worked tirelessly, rearing animals, washing clothes for various persons to provide for my sister and me. My mother is my true inspiration as I have always been amazed by the things she has accomplished with limited education and being a single mother. My grandmother was of great assistance to her, as even though she was visually impaired, she was instrumental in attending to my sister and me while my mother worked. While not having an extensive education experience, our mother ensured this was not the same for her daughters. I graduated from one of the most prestigious universities in Jamaica, with a Bachelor of Science degree in Management and Economics. My sister also obtained a degree in Tourism and Hospitality Management.

Jamaica is indeed a beautiful country; while being blessed with the opportunity to visit many different countries, my conclusion is always the same. Jamaica's foods, my simple and humble beginnings, the island vibes, and way of life is not one I would trade for any other lifestyle. Presently I work online as a Digital Entrepreneur, which has blessed me with the opportunity to work anywhere there is an internet connection. While not a usual practice in Jamaica, it is now a fast-growing trend in the country.

Like many other countries, women living in Jamaica have faced their own unique set of challenges. While there are those challenges, we seek to fight daily like gender equality and being respected as being able to accomplish anything our male counterparts can. Some Jamaican women also face poverty due to limited opportunities in the country, forcing them to be with less than desirable partners. While 70% of university attendees in the country are women, you will find some women graduating without being able to get the job they qualify for. Another challenge is the number of women being forced to be single mothers as some fathers choose not to play an active role in their children's lives. Some single mothers do not have formal education and struggle with what is called "hand-to-mouth" lifestyle. This lifestyle forces them into being sexually exploited and forces them to attain partners for money and provisions.

While there are grim moments of being a woman living in Jamaica, there are women who lead by the examples we all want our daughters to follow. There is Shelly-Ann Fraser-Pryce, yes, the fastest woman in the world is Jamaican. Ms. Toni Singh, who became Miss World in December 2019 who is also Jamaican. And of course, there is also former Prime Minister, Portia Simpson Miller, who became the first female Prime Minister of Jamaica in 2006. While women have always been involved in politics in the country, Mrs. Miller's accomplishment swung the doors of the political arena open to the females in the country.

You will also find that in recent times, women in Jamaica have come into their own, where entrepreneurship is concerned. Many women are striking out on their creating opportunities for themselves, where no changes seem to be found. A vast majority of this success should be accredited to new advances in technology. Women are taking advantage of social media and the option to sell online without a physical store to become influencers and YouTubers. You will find that many young women in the country use these methods to generate income for themself.

Despite the negativity, Jamaican women are beautiful, healthy, vibrant, notwithstanding, they are also nurses, doctors, scientists, entrepreneurs, journalists, world travelers, and dream chasers. I, for one, am on a mission to ensure my children will never know what poverty is and will be able to partake in life in a way I was not afforded to as a child. But no matter what, we will never stop evolving and growing. Most importantly, I will always take it as a privilege to have been born a Jamaican woman.

My Life As A Woman: Japan Edition

Women living a single life in her 30's overcome discrimination and rejections. Forced dating and forced marriage are often a hot topic in company gatherings. In Japan, women struggle to choose between careers over getting married. Traditional Japanese forced women to get married in early life. Isn't it satisfying to get married when you have already established yourself?

Before getting married, women should learn to become independent, learn to manage herself before accepting a new role, and strengthen her abilities in managing tasks without parent's supervision. Leaving my parents' home for the first time was a bit lonely, and daily tasks seemed daunting. With a few adjustments and time management, I get to handle work over personal life. My concerns are always my finances, security, and health.

My mother is my biggest influence. Since home helpers are not common in Japan, I helped her with the house chores. I am grateful that she trained me to prepare healthy foods without spending too much. One lesson I learned from mom was to be creative and mindful of my spending. Mom urged us to get a degree and find a better job to finance ourselves without needing others. Her philosophy in life was, "the higher education you have the more you can chin up".

Although mom never shared how Japanese guys treat women, we saw our father's situation. Father was a hard-working man. We sometimes misunderstood him loving his job more than his family. He never did anything at home, even clearing out his table. Mom did all the heavy family obligations.

Seeing mom in that situation made me scared of getting married at an early age. I chose to pursue my dream of working as a bank clerk and delayed my marriage. Unfortunately, my first application after graduating college caused me frustrations. Rejected. Too many companies need women for their administrative work. After a few attempts, I was hired at an e-commerce company and am now working as a project manager. Now I'm in a company of hundreds of employees. Some are very kind and considerate. Some may question your status in life. I get questioned all the time. Sometimes inspiring, but most of the time annoying.

On Valentine's day, colleagues tease me to date other single men in the office. Or on Christmas day, they will settle for a blind date. If you take their words, it will break you. Being a single woman in Japan is a big issue. While co-workers questioned my marital status, close friends are very supportive and appreciative. Most of my friends are like-minded people. Like me, they also enjoy their single life and travel to foreign countries.

Every woman has the freedom to chase their dreams. They can choose which path to walk through which is why I love living in Japan. There is no escape, trolls are everywhere destroying us and our career. It's about how we deal with them. Focus on what makes us comfortable and happy. Being alone doesn't mean we are being neglected or lonely. If you're a single woman living alone, embrace it with all your heart. It is your learning opportunity to better define who you are as a person. Discover what you want and where you want to be in life.

My life as a single woman in Japan teaches me to be independent. I've learned to live a minimal life and spend only what's needed and save for the future. It gives me the chance to squeeze myself even tighter and learn to get out of my comfort zone. My life as a woman is very challenging, fun, and exciting. There are also stressful and depressing days. But in Japan, you can have anything that can wipe your tears and fears.

Don't expect your happiness from others. True happiness is what's inside of you, the real you. Take time to organize your life so when you're ready to settle down it is easy to balance family and work.

My Life As A Woman: Jordan Edition #1

Imagine that our society is free of women, do you think life will stay in its state!? The principle that says: "Women make up half of the society" is a wrong principle, women make up the whole society. I was born and brought up in Saudi Arabia until I reached the age of 15, and that put a great responsibility on my shoulders − as heavy as a mountain − to show the best shape of the Jordanian girls. And that was a major factor that made me fall in love with working and learning. In addition to that, my family's interest was focused on learning and working so I loved hard work and nothing but that.

Then we made a fateful decision which was to move back home. We moved back to our lovely home in Jordan and that was a great decision. In that time, I encountered many difficulties with communicating with other girls because I came from a completely different environment even though we were from the same country. Above all of that, our returning to Jordan was synchronized with the period that my personality was forming and that made me have many problems with socializing.

However, I don't want to forget my great parents and teachers who stood with me to pass this stage. They supported me, never left me and of course helped me to find my own passion. Nevertheless, women are used to facing some challenges. I got into high school, but unfortunately, I didn't get the average that I was dreaming about. As I mentioned, we fall, but we don't give up. We face problems, but problems never win, women are always the winners, so I tried again and got it finally. During this period, I had the opportunity to think again about my passion and my university major.

At the same time, despite my hesitation that accompanied me all the time, my whole mind was focused on how I could make an obvious impact during my life and after I die especially in the medical fields. That was because of my grandmother and how she died with the Sly Syndrome disease, so I directed my compass to accomplish that goal.

After many hesitations, I felt that I would achieve that by enrolling into the major of Chemical Industrial Engineering. I preferred that because I thought that major would let me know more about substances from the chemical side, which would lead to a better and faster reach to help cancer patients. In order to do that, I did many things to develop myself, so that I could reach my passion faster and faster. Nowadays, I started studying for longer periods and became more concentrated on the subject. I also read many articles about my major.

I had some difficulties in keeping a balance between my social life and my university life, but if you live in a society filled with successful Jordanian women who support you, you'll always be motivated, and that made me aspire to follow their path to achieve what I really wanted to achieve. In addition to that, our Jordanian society consists of families, not separated individuals, and that is what distinguishes us. Every single individual here has a great family behind him that supports him powerfully, so no matter what I wanted to be, my family was always willing to help me do it. And that's what I hope to happen with me in achieving my aim, which is focused now on completing my high studies in pharmacy science. I hope to be one of the best pioneer women in the world of drugs and chemicals. I want to give advice humbly to all the girls that are reading my article now, especially the Jordanian ones. Do not ever think in giving up. Your lives are your treasures and your goals, no matter what they are, are the keys for these treasures.

My Life As A Woman: Jordan Edition #2

Where did you grow up?

I was born in Amman, Jordan, and I still live there today.

How did you grow up?

I grew up in a Jordanian family, but it is not your typical Jordanian family since our childhood was eventful due to my family's critical political state. This situation opened my eyes as a kid to a lot of things, I learned how to be an entrepreneur and to have a strong character, but this was a blessing in disguise because I was a girl in a world that revolved around men and men have control over everything in it. I was into arts from a young age: singing, drawing, and poetry, which is something I got from my father.

Did you have a parent or grandparent who inspired you?

As I said I grew up in a political family and that left a mark in me. On a smaller scale our house was full of art and that was my dad's touch. My mother had a different impact on me, she was a kind, simple person with nothing to ask for and in a world that revolves around men, it led to a lot of unfairness to her, and that made me realize that I hated to be weak, I had a strong urge to get all of my rights, and I wanted to live happily the way I wanted.

What did you study?

I majored in psychology, and I fell in love with it. Since I was a kid, I wanted to be a fashion designer, and now I am living the dream.

What do you love about your culture?

In general, Jordan and Palestine have warmth, something about the importance of the family and the traditions. I travelled a lot but the warmth in my country and the nobility you cannot find anywhere else.

What are you currently doing for work?

I work in beauty and fashion designing, I started my career a few years ago, and in a short time I became a well-known name in both fields. I never miss any chance that comes my way, I worked as a radio representor and had my own morning show, I also worked as an antiquate trainer for kids.

Tell me about your struggles as a woman

I always had an ambition towards success, but I got married young and made a family and got busy with it, until I decided to file for a divorce when I reached a dead end in this life, which made things harder. I used to have my urge for success shot down constantly, I was scared to dream, and I thought it was fine to give everything up while maintaining a family and a home, but when I got my divorce I believed that I had no other option but success. I considered it as a new chance in this life given to me by God and I wanted to make the most of it.

I worked hard in training women in cosmetics, I worked in bridal makeup, I designed my own fashion line for modest clothes, and I used social media platforms to advertise my work. All of this did not go well with the community I came from where women did not appear on screens, but that did not put me down and I kept working on my dreams through all the hardships. Every year I reached a new dream and I never looked back. I travelled a lot and saw a lot of countries and learned about their cultures and that itself was impossible at some point, but I believe we live only once so we should live it the way we like.

Tell me about your success story

With determination I reached my small goals, but my main goal in life and the thing I consider a success is to raise two happy children even with a divorce. Today, I am Zeinab Tamimi, a fashion designer, I own my personal brand, a makeup artist, and an influencer on social media. I can still see my dreams at the end of the path, and I am on my way towards them.

My Life As A Woman: Kazakhstan Edition

Since Kazakhstan is trying to reach the same level of life as highly developed countries, I have always been optimistic for living here. However, as a woman of the traditional and conservative nation, I face some obstacles and challenges, which I will describe below.

First, let me explain that it is very important in which part of Kazakhstan you are trying to realize your ambitions. If you want to reach anything, you better to get an education or work in the current capital (Nur-Sultan) or former capital (Almaty). These two cities have the best universities and wider opportunities than other regions of the country. Unfortunately, I was born neither in Nur-Sultan nor in Almaty. My hometown Shymkent is located in the South part of Kazakhstan. This city has preserved traditions probably more than anywhere on Kazakh land. People are still more conservative there, maybe because of Shymkent's bordering with Uzbekistan, where customs are highly esteemed.

To marry a daughter is the first issue southern parents have to solve. Preferably, a future groom should have wealthy or at least not poor parents. If a bride's family is not so rich, they try to find someone more or less equal to them. Luckily, my parents were wise and educated people who think that a girl should have the proper education and career opportunities. The reason for such an approach is the education they received in Russia from ten years of living there before moving to Kazakhstan. After graduating school in Shymkent, they helped me to move to Astana (former name of Nur-Sultan). It was a very difficult decision since we had not enough money to pay for my university. It was a hard time. I do not like to think about it because I still feel pain inside. However, my parents did not want my destiny to relate to marriage at eighteen years without any chance to become who I have always wanted to be. They said that they would do anything to make me happy.

My big dream was to become a lawyer who can protect everyone who needs it. I studied hard at university in order not to fail. In fact, Nur-Sultan showed me that some traditions can be abandoned. People I studied with inspired me because the majority of the best students were…girls! I think that girls study and work harder than boys do, because they feel inequality everywhere, and try to prove that they are worth something more than sitting at home with children.

It should be mentioned that there are many female entrepreneurs in Kazakhstan who run their own business and can be independent of their husband. Also, every year a big number of students apply for bachelor's or master's degree to the best universities around the world. Girls and women are among these students. I am writing about it because even if Kazakhstan is a conservative country, it gives young talents to achieve their goals, regardless of gender.

One of my professors at university was one of these young talents. She was born in a small village in Kazakhstan without any chances for the bright future. She had a strong will to break all stereotypes and get a proper education. The Harvard Law School Admission Office considered her application and decided to give her the opportunity to study in the best law school all over the world. It happened in 2005. Kazakhstan was less developed than now. This professor really inspired me with her story.

My main advice to women is that they should not think of their gender when they have goals to achieve. We, women, are the first people who limit our abilities. If their country is more traditional, they can use it as a free space to become first in any sphere (law, medicine, or engineering). They can inspire such young women like me.

My Life As A Woman: Kenya Edition

When I was a child, I watched the beaming headlights from my mom's SUV deluge my dark bedroom. I exhaled in both excitement and disappointment; happy to know that she was home but upset that it was going to happen again. My mother often left before I woke up in the morning and returned in the evening after I was asleep.

It wasn't until I grew up that I realized what a rare quality it is for a woman from the village to start her own company and successfully lead hundreds of people. I watched my mother's character evolve; from harsh and loud, to stern and composed. The latter was a survival skill she had to augment in order to maintain peace at home and effectiveness at work.

Before I could start thinking about my career, I had to think about what it meant to be a woman first. I explored different clothing styles and even practiced my walk, trying to strike a balance between feeling wanted and feeling safe enough to be wanted. Some days I felt flattered if a guy noticed me, and other days I wished I had a gun to shoot them in the knee for impeding my freedom to be a woman.

I remember when I first developed the awareness that I was being judged for how close or far I was from society's standards of a beautiful woman. In Western culture, slim bodies are often elevated in the unforgiving eyes of the media. But in Kenyan culture, you weren't worth a glance if you didn't have round hips.

While the rest of the women in my family had beautiful curves, I was a hair away from being confused with a 14-year-old boy. I sometimes got remarks from guys two or three years older than me asking, "Your sister is hot, what happened to you?" One day during lunch break, a boy asked me if my butt got punctured. I remember struggling to find the correct response, unsure myself of why I didn't turn out like other girls. Women of colour often pride themselves in being curvy and thick, which left me feeling like a disappointment, not just as a woman... but as a black woman. For goodness sakes, it's what we are known for.

Beauty is no longer my only concern now. While it's nice to feel desirable, I have to think about what value I want to have contributed before I depart from this earth. I am young in my career and find myself frustrated when it comes to being taken seriously in certain professional settings.

It's in the little things like being interrupted, talked over, judged about my appearance or belittled when I try to be assertive. It's in the calculated frustrating comments that are diluted by the dispiriting "you're being too sensitive." In fact, I remember an older guy in high school rubbing my thigh in the school bus and I laughed it off because I didn't want to look like I was overreacting. Or the barrage of insults that follow your disinclination to a romantic request. It's scary. If you're too stern, you beckon aggression. If you are too gentle, you find yourself enduring uncomfortable situations. So how can you be strong and kind at the same time?

What I have learned thus far is that each woman has a different leadership style. Some have the physical power to intimidate and others use their empathy and assertion to deliver results. While painful experiences will force you to toughen up in order to survive, you should not have to mute the beautiful aspects of your personality, you just need to harness them to get the result you want.

For instance, I have never been a fan of raising my voice. I also happen to be a petite woman, right at 4"11, so if I'm not careful about the impression I make, I can be easily drowned by those around me. Fortunately, I'm naturally a very curious and empathetic person. This has helped me to develop respect from others and have something interesting to contribute. I tend to be strategic and not necessarily the person leading down the crowd.

If you find that you are a naturally free-spirited person but have had to hide behind baggy clothes because of harassment, my encouragement to you is to embrace your femininity but be smart about it. It is a good rule of thumb to carry pepper spray and go to uncomfortable places with a group of people. Other things you can do are practice being assertive yet respectful, and if it is affordable, take fighting classes. I have a good friend that's fearless in nearly every situation. Once a man that was messed up by drugs started yelling and following us on an empty street. She was so confident and kind, which caused him to bother us more. I asked her how she could be so calm in such a situation and she told me she's really good with knives and had one in her pocket. Little things like these can take you out of a victim mentality. Don't seek out trouble but be prepared if it comes.

You have this one life to live and every part of your personality is like paint; if you don't express them you limit yourself from creating a masterpiece.

Be strong. Be kind. Be bold.

Sincerely,

Just another woman.

My Life As A Woman: Kiribati Edition

Hello, ladies, my name is Halani from Tarawa, Kiribati. I grew up in a religious family that was bounded by traditional beliefs. My society does not encourage personal wealth and other achievements. Connections to traditional and family land are highly valued. Since Kiribati women are entitled to taking care of the homes, each day before going to school, I would help my mother with the house chores like cleaning and cooking breakfast. After school, I had no time to waste; instead, I would still join her in doing the remaining tasks before going to sleep.

I loved Kiribati because of the different economic activities like fishing, mining, seal salt extraction, and cloth-making that generated income. I would spend my school holiday helping my mother with the cleaning and packing of tunas already fished from the ocean. I would sometimes join her in making traditional beverages for domestic use. I would also participate in traditional dances that portrayed our customs and sports activities like volleyball. Being a Roman Catholic, every Sunday, I would join my parents to the church where I spent the whole day.

Since attending primary school was a must, and only the chosen few had a chance to join secondary school, I had to work hard until I had the opportunity to join a government secondary school. I worked hard and scored good grades that would enable me to achieve my dream. I dreamt of becoming a doctor who will help my community to live a healthy life. Because I wanted to be the best doctor, the only way to achieve it was to study overseas. By looking at my background, we did not have enough money to further my studies. Therefore, my community and other church members held a fundraiser that enabled me to study medicine in the United States.

The hard work and determination my mother had was my inspiration. Each day I saw her doing all kinds of jobs, I reminded myself that tomorrow's journey starts today, and I want to be a successful woman, I better start preparing today. I finished my studies and worked as an internee in the State before being employed in my region. Presently, I am a professional doctor helping my community with the fight against different kinds of diseases. I also offer my support concerning protective gear for my fellow women who wake up early in the morning regardless of the cold to sustain their families.

I advise women in Kiribati that being a Kiribati woman is the best thing ever. Our region has the resources that can make succeed. Tomorrow's success requires today's preparation; therefore, the struggles and hard work they have today will eventually bear fruits tomorrow. Success requires hard work and determination to accomplishing their dreams. Relying on the community will not make you a successful woman, but following your dream and working on it will make you successful. A successful woman that makes her society proud of, because if you succeed, the community thrives.

My Life As A Woman: Kosovo Edition

"Each time a woman stands up for herself, without knowing it possibly, without claiming it, she stands up for all women." -   Maya Angelou

I grew up in Prishtina, the capital of Kosovo. I did have a pretty normal childhood and I was raised by my parents. I studied Marketing on a Master level. Anyway, that's not what I wanted to study! I love art and everything that has to do with it but because of some personal circumstances, I ended up in the marketing area.

Located in Southeastern Europe, Kosovo, it's landscape consists of broad plains, hills, and mountains. Kosovo is known for its incredible hiking opportunities and quaint mountain towns. About 93% of Kosovo's population is ethnic Albanian. The other 7% includes Bosniaks, Serbs, Turks, Ashkali, Egyptians, Gorani, and Roma. That's the thing I like about my culture because we respect each other's culture, religion, and ethnicity! Another thing that's interesting is that, many Kosovars value "besa", which roughly translates as "trust" and manifests as a general sense of responsibility and hospitality. We are very welcoming, polite, and friendly people. The other thing that I love is the value of family! It is an extremely important part of us. Families here have an average of two children, those in rural areas may have more. But, while today's families experience greater equality between men and women, the patriarchal structures still exist in some rural areas.

As a female adult and degreed in marketing filed, right now I am unemployed, so I don't have a regular job. However, I did find myself in a different area and that's art. It is one of my passions since I was a kid, always surrounded by pencils, papers, and colors. And growing up that passion became bigger and bigger and I started using my talent into different categories of arts and felt free to give my personal thoughts or messages through drawings and paintings. Currently, I work as a freelancer, mainly as a design artist and photographer. My art work is concentrated in illustrations, sketches, hand drawings, logo designs, calligraphy, and urban pictures.

In terms of my position as a woman, I struggle a lot. The biggest challenge I face is the patriarchy. Regardless of experience, education or abilities, the patriarchal nature of Kosovo society, fosters the perception that women are less qualified and less competent than men. What patriarchy has done is convince people that a strong and intelligent woman represents a problem; a disruption to the social order rather than an integral part of it. The other thing I struggle with is sexism and economic inequality. The extremely potent combination of these two - this may seem like too broad an answer, but it pretty much covers it on both a domestic and global front. All of the individual challenges I may be tempted to rank are symptomatic of these massive systemic power imbalances, working in tandem. The other issue that concerns me is the lack of financial independence because in my state, as a woman, it is difficult to find a stable and long-term job. This is because gender inequality still exists! Inequality is always present in the job market, starting from the job position, payment, decision-making, duties and responsibilities thus creating strong barriers to career development, financial stability, as well as standard of living and lifestyle.

Some of the successes I have achieved so far as a woman are that I have a habit of self-improvement and I do it every day. The daily habits help me succeed, like exercising, getting up early, reading and being serious about my to-do list, which helps me to be healthy, informed and highly productive. Also, I don't apologize for what I want anymore. It means living life on my own terms and going after my dreams regardless of what anybody else thinks. And this is the most freeing and powerful feeling in the world!

Despite decades of notable progress, at home and abroad, a reality in which opportunities are not defined by gender has yet to be universally achieved. Even more disconcerting, in too many places around the globe, women exercising or even seeking their basic rights is interpreted as a direct and destabilizing challenge to existing power structures. Some regimes are now trying to roll back the hard-won rights of women and girls. This means that we have to work still and harder so that our voice can be heard. Some advice I can give to other women out there, no matter the culture or the language are these; have your own life, independence and identity, look at the all-good qualities and love yourself the way you are, don't apologize for who you are, be brave, define successes in your own terms and speak your mind! Let the emotions out, because you deserve respect and to have your voice heard.

I hope that one day governments, the private sector, and civil society reinvigorate and reinvest in the policies as well as in the legal and social frameworks that will achieve worldwide gender equality.

My Life As A Woman: Kyrgyzstan Edition #1

Throughout history, the central role of women has ensured the stability and long-term development of nations. From global volunteering to being educators and caretakers, they are pivotal for the whole world right alongside men. With that being said, the following is an interesting insight to what Nurzada Beshbakova, a teacher of Anatomy in International Medical University and a Kyrgyz native, has to say about her life as a woman of Kyrgyzstan.

"I was born and raised in Bishkek. There are three sisters in the family. When I was 4 years old, my parents got divorced and I grew up without a father. Despite all this, my mother fed us and raised us. Each of us have been educated well. My mother was a Mathematics teacher but later, she had to quit her job at the school. Keeping in mind a teacher's salary, she knew that it wouldn't be enough to provide for us all. No one helped her, not even my own father. But did she give up? No. She overcame all the odds by building her business from scratch, bought an apartment, and took care of our needs and wants. After all, being a mother of three and more importantly, being a woman, the difficulties are tremendous. However, it has just struck me now in my adulthood, the struggles of my mother, since I grew up like any other child and was oblivious of all of this.

Nurzada goes on to emphasize the key lesson she learnt from her mother's life.

"Mom always told us to study and receive education. Indeed, in our country, many go to university but don't graduate. Some get married and their husbands do not let them complete education. Thus, their studies are left unfinished. Many girls, especially from villages and rural areas, are told that education is not necessary and that they'll simply get married and stay home." Nurzada condemns this and says, "This isn't the way at all. Even if a woman does not work, she will have to raise children. That's why education is important for them." She goes on to state another major reason why education is so important for women. She says, "Education for women is like a perpetual safe haven. If, for example, a man divorces his wife and the wife has to carry the child alone with her, she won't find a good job anywhere since she's not educated. Cases like these lead to abortions, which, for the record, I absolutely despise."

Nurzada's Inspiration

"It dates back to 9th grade when my grandmother fell severely ill and I had to take care of her all the time. That's when I realized how nice it would be to have a doctor in the house. This was because it was getting harder day by day to find nurses and doctors and to get them to come by. It was only then that I decided to become a doctor as many people in my family were engineers, lawyers, and in the police. So, after graduating from high school, I enrolled in Kyrgyz State Medical Academy (KSMA) and studied with all my heart because the most important thing for me was studying. That spirit led me to graduate with honors. In the 6th year of my studies, my academy sent me to the Olympics in Obstetrics and Gynecology in Novosibirsk, Russia.

To be honest, from that moment on, I fell in love with this field of medicine. Due to the fact that I won prizes in various competitions, my university trained me for absolutely free in Obstetrics and Gynecology. My happiness knew no bounds since this training was the most expensive, to obtain specialty in Gynecology, and I received this for free. Then, I went on a competitive basis to the "School of Young Leaders of Kyrgyzstan." I learned a lot there and it currently helps with my work. Our aim is to travel to rural schools every year as a volunteer and deliver a lecture on women's health and also on the dangers of smoking. Also, I often go with my students to orphanages for the disabled. I come face to face with children who are disabled and abandoned by their parents. It literally breaks my heart to witness this. How could someone ever break all ties, these little gems? But then again, this world is far away from fair."

The Kyrgyz Culture

Nurzada says that there is value of respect for elders in her culture. "You come to Kyrgyzstan, you'll observe how in public transports, if the elderly climb aboard, almost every youngster on the bus will stand up themselves in respect. This is observed vastly here," she says. "The value of kinship and family relationships as well. Our people are also very hospitable. This is something I admire very much about Kyrgyzstan."

Nurzada currently works at a maternity hospital. She also works as an obstetrician-gynecologist and in her free time, she teaches Anatomy. "I really love my specialty, despite that it's very difficult. Other than this, I also study English in parallel." she says.

The Billion Dollar Advice to the Women of Kyrgyzstan

"Trust only yourself, never rely on others. Always strive for your education even if you've married and that marriage is a success. Education for a woman is confidence in the future. Engage to improve yourself in everything and the world will be better for you."

As time passed in her professional career, Nurzada came forth to say that several women wanting abortions because their boyfriend and even husband left them. While in other cases, she has met women from some areas of Kyrgyzstan where they are abused and that too, occurs on a daily basis. When asked about the possibility of divorce, their answer was always the same. "If that happens, who will provide for my children?" Therefore, they withstand all this damage and remain in a state of unprecedented turmoil. And as the children grow up, they do so by hating their father all the way up to adulthood and we can all imagine how that will turn out for the family.

The word 'motivational' would belittle the story of Nurzada Beshbakova since her resilient effort and drive made Kyrgyzstan one woman free of dependency and vulnerability.

My Life As A Woman: Kyrgyzstan Edition #2

A different approach towards life has been taken from Medina Berdibekova, a school teacher living in Naryn, one of the many states of Kyrgyzstan.

"Life has been pretty basic for me ever since I was born. Had a normal childhood with normal parents. Both of them were teachers. Therefore naturally, my inclination was towards this profession. My childhood was ordinary with minimalistic challenges but nothing too strenuous. I studied in a foreign language faculty and quite customarily, became a teacher."

She currently teaches in Naryn Kyrgyz-Turkish High School and is nothing but satisfied from life. "I love my job!", she exclaims.

"My culture involves immense respect for its elders.", she says emphasizing on this prevalent quality of the Kyrgyz youth.

Medina has her say on life in the following way, "I fight for justice and I always try to be independent. I think for me, this is success. Today, I have everything I wanted from life."

Her Advice for the Women of Kyrgyzstan?

Be strong and be independent. Whatever life throws at you, remain steadfast and deal with it. It's the only way you're going to survive if you don't want to depend on anyone and I think that's the best way to live life. Independently.

My Life As A Woman: Kyrgyzstan Edition #3

Now, look at things from an entirely different angle, a Pakistani woman living in Kyrgyzstan has also given her two cents on life abroad.

The Pakistani Perspective

"My name is Alisha Asim and I hail from Khanpur, Pakistan. It's been five years since I left my homeland for Kyrgyzstan. This was only because of my husband who got a decent job here and told me it was time we stepped to the outside world."

Alisha says that before we go on any further, she wishes to inform the audience about this little culture back home that daughters of the family are wed off early. Sometimes, even before they complete their education. Afterwards, their husband would decide if their wife can continue to study or not.

"Nevertheless, I, luckily, am from a fairly rich family in Khanpur where the women are given their fair share of choices involving marriage. They can decline or accept as they wish. I had no interest in all this in the beginning. I studied, graduated, and even started a job as a graphics designer online. It was only then that I met someone and got married. No regrets though. Life's as it should be. Anyway, as I mentioned before, my husband started out small managing local businesses but after a considerable amount of time, he strived for a job somewhere abroad and he fortunately found Kyrgyzstan. After everything was double checked, we bid farewell to the life of Pakistan and entered a new phase of life."

The Difference

"Truth be told, my first day in Kyrgyzstan, I was awe-struck. Everywhere my eyes rolled, I saw a woman at work. From local shops to luxurious supermarkets, everything was being run by women! Such a spectacle took me by surprise because in Pakistan, you'll only see women working professionally. Most people are terrified to send their daughters out to work if the job isn't going to be respectable, in an office and well-paid. However, in Kyrgyzstan, it seems no one has the time for such insecure thinking. I see women out here all the time, working 24/7. It doesn't matter to them, nor does it matter to their parents."

Alisha lives with her husband now who makes enough for the two of them. She doesn't have any particular struggles as a woman living in Kyrgyzstan although she would like to shed light on the fact that she is heavily inspired from the women of Kyrgyzstan.

"In the beginning, I had to face the language barrier in Kyrgyzstan. No one spoke English here, instead, many natives felt that we, being the foreigners, we should learn their language, not that they should learn English. This concept resides in the minds of many to date. When I started making some friends after a while, everyone told me that English is compulsory in every high school here. Whoever graduates knows the basics in English. Thus, it was pretty evident that many were not educated here."

Alisha further talks about her observance here. She says, "At first I thought, in such a female dominated society, this country would be far better in terms of domestic violence and abuse towards women but how wrong I was. It turned out that women here were also a subject of mistreatment. Particularly, those who weren't educated at all."

"Everywhere you go, it's basically the same, really. The takeaway here is if you're a woman, you have to be independent if you want a hundred percent secure and a happy life." Alisha concludes.

My Life As A Woman: Kuwait Edition #1

I am a doctor born and raised in Pakistan and currently living in Kuwait. The house that I grew up in is located in Punjab, Pakistan. It's a big double story building with a huge garden, a big living room, 6 bedrooms, and an enormous kitchen. I can remember having evening tea in our garden where we have so many birds in different cages on one side. The sunsets and birds chirping while having a little walk after tea was so soothing. We still have the same house in Pakistan where my parents, grandmother, and my siblings live and whenever I visit my home, I relive those childhood memories.

My father is not very educated as he started working for a living at a young age to support his widow mother. But he always wished that his children get well-educated. We are four siblings with one brother and three sisters and what we are today is because of his struggles. My mother is a housewife and I've always seen her working for us and making the house a peaceful place to live in.

My parents and my grandmother are the ones who always inspired me. They have made me understand what life is about and how to find the little ray of happiness in difficult situations of life. They have made me sincere, disciplined, and dedicated. I consider my father the biggest role model in my life. He always says that don't sit idle, keep your mind busy in useful thinking, and plan to make your future well for you and your family. He taught me the values of working hard but at the same time seeing the bigger picture. Most importantly, my parents never compared us to other children and never ridiculed us in a way that affected our self-worth.

I always wanted to be an engineer while I was in school because I loved math. When I was being admitted to high school, everyone asked me to go for pre-medical as in our Pakistani society, medicine and teaching are thought to be the noble professions for a woman. As I wasn't bad in biology also, I chose pre-medical and studied hard to get into medical school, and here I am today, a doctor by the grace of God.

I love Pakistani culture where our society is not led by individualism but rather by collectivism, where family and other relationships stand strong. Pakistanis are very hospitable. In our religion, a guest is considered a blessing from God. Pakistanis welcome the tourists and visitors with open arms and show love and respect to everyone.

Pakistani weddings introduce you to many local traditions and are laden with a multitude of colors with heavily embroidered flowy dresses of women, tantalizing food, traditionally decorated stages and halls, and a lot of dance and music that lasts from three to six days. And then there are dinner parties thrown by the groom and bride's side of the family after the wedding festivities end. Pakistani culture is very diverse, and I love it.

Currently, I'm not working any job as I've got a toddler to look after. I'll pursue my career as a doctor for sure when my child will be school-going. Until then I'm a housewife which is a 24/7 job. It's a lifetime job actually without any pay, increments, or incentives.

My struggles as a woman right now include:

1.   Learning to be authentic and just be me without thinking of other's expectations.

2.   Staying calm with my kid and finding patience at the end of the day.

3.   Learning how to deal with the constant comparison with other mothers and working women. It feels like there's a lot of pressure to be doing something beyond just caring for your kids these days.

My successes as a woman, rather I would say as a homemaker include:

1.   Keeping the schedule of each day with the kid

4.   Keeping everything at home in order like laundry and cooking.

5.   Keeping myself sane with all the tantrums thrown by my kid and having some me-time

6.   Deciding what is important at one time, focus on it, and rid the guilt

As a woman, I would advise other women living in Kuwait to never miss any opportunity to go and get a life that you always wanted and dreamed of. Struggle hard for yourself and your family. You are no less than men and you have every right to live your life according to your own choice. Life in Kuwait has its ups and downs, just like any other country in the world but remember that many good experiences are waiting for you in this little country. You just need to reach out and find them.

My Life As A Woman: Kuwait Edition #2

My name is Ghadeer Al-Qattan. I am a 50 year old Arab Muslim from Kuwait and unlike the conception that the media will promote or most will mistakenly think that women are oppressed by Islam, their rights are undermined and need spaces in order to empty their problems and concerns. Quite the opposite, I am a well-educated computer engineer, and I have not had any feelings of injustice as a woman in my whole life. That is because I have understood very well the description of Muslim women' rights advocated by the Qur'an and the Sunnah of the Prophet, so I knew that my high position and all my rights are well preserved and I am very satisfied with that.

I was born and raised in Kuwait. My father, may God have mercy on him, was the most influential person in my life and raised me on the necessity of the pursuit of knowledge. For me, he was a father, a best friend, my main source of security and safety. His death 25 years ago left a scar in my soul that I still suffer from psychologically to this day.. After his death, my mother took full charge of all the family responsibilities and has been the most efficient homemaker! When I think about my mother main traits, I think about her strong personality, a mastermind woman who takes the right decisions and recites Quran nonstop. I grew up in a very stable home. The priorities of my parents were to raise me and my seven siblings securing all our needs based on a set of values. Family and family ties are very important to us which I highly admire in our society; the interdependence of individuals within each family, and within larger circles outside the family.

I excelled in grade school then I studied computer engineering at Kuwait University. I was not sure then if this was my desired field of studying or I just chose it because it was a growing prestigious field and highly on demand back in the eighties! I graduated and was appointed in the government sector where I worked hardly and sincerely. In every action, idea, or step I take, I put in mind a verse from Surat Al-Nahl:

"Indeed, Allah is with those who fear Him and those who are doers of good (128)"

I later concluded that computer engineering was not what brings me the satisfaction and value that I longed for my job was not of direct and clear benefit to others, such as a teacher or doctor's job. What I really want is to provide a valuable service to others and from here I retired from my government job and started the journey of studying and memorizing the Holy Qur'an and voluntarily teaching others the correct intonation and recitation and this is what literally satisfied my need for a sense of actual value.

As for my hobbies and interests, I love sports, scuba-diving, hiking and photography. After retirement, I discovered the beautiful world of agriculture and gardening and this completely changed my idea that the weather in Kuwait is not suitable for gardening, because the gardening season usually lasts nine months of the year, then I spend the rest of the year in my indoor nursery in preparation for the next season. And like my Quran studies, in the field of agriculture I find myself happier and more content when I share my knowledge with others. I do that through Instagram or online courses on training platforms and this is one of the positive aspects of COVID-19 on all of us. Distance learning has become easier and more diverse than the past!

I find my successes in my marriage, my home and my children, in giving to others, in doing what I love with privacy and freedom disciplining myself according to the Sharia regulations that protect me.

I grew older, I found myself distancing away from women who obsessively focus on material things, external beauty, and outward appearance, neglecting the value of time, because time is wasted with nothing to satisfy them. In my life: Time is one of the most important things.

Allah says in Sourat AlSharh : "So when you have finished [your duties], then stand up [for worship]. (7)"

That is, once one act of obedience ends, it is joined with another act of obedience. Women and men should fulfill three main purposes in their life:

1: The spiritual purpose, religion, which has to have a clear reference, i.e. Quran and Sunnah.

2: The physical purpose, by incorporating sports into one's daily routine so that he/she will age strong and healthy, both physically and mentally.

3: The mental purpose, by always learning useful science because learning has no age!

Gardening nourished these three purposes In my life. Quran and Sunna repeatedly mention plants, trees and fruits. This encouraged me to think about the wisdom behind Allah's creations. So during my gardening activity I invoke the relevant citations, accompanied by constant movement and physical activity. Also, my knowledge is continuously enriched because I love reading about organic farming and the soil food web.

A person who fulfills these purposes, will not search for anything else that is worthless and the material world will not be his/her obsession. This is by far the most guaranteed recipe to remain young at heart, happy and content because in order to move to a more beautiful and immortal world, the hereafter, we must work right in our life to win at the end.

I think that the challenge that I face and is suffered from by those who live in a blessed and luxurious life and prosperous welfare is anxiety and constant thinking I try to remain productive and psychologically stable and resist any urge to be idle.. by fulfilling the three purposes I mentioned above.

Ghadeer Al-Qattan

My Life As A Woman: Laos Edition

My name is Khambay Soulivong, I was born in Lak Sao, Khamkeuth District, Bolikhamxay Province. The 'Lak Sao' means kilometer 20 from old French Solider Camp during the war in the past. It is spectacular scenery of karst mountain landscapes and considered to be one of the most impressive passages to Vietnam from the center of Laos. There are 8 members in my family, I have two older brothers and two sisters and one brother. Even though, I have a big family, I was treated very well and started school at an early age.

There are many people living in Lak Sao, some of them are Vietnamese since it is bordered with Vietnam. When I was in primary school, my mother was a rice vendor in the market and occasionally went to Vientiane Capital for her small business, but my father was a farmer, he raised poultry, pig, and fish. I loved the way of my mother's doings and she inspired me to study and communicate with people. After school, I went to help my mother sell rice in the market and later I could speak a little Vietnamese language. I had been taught to be a good rice vendor as my mother was, I had practiced calculating mathematics for exchanging money as well as collecting and saving, which everyone nearby loved me as a kid. I said to myself that one day I would be a good businesswoman like my mother.

I had a big shot in my mind when I graduated high school; some of my best friends were not interested in continuing higher education, since they had to move to the big city and there was only one University in Vientiane Capital that we thought of. I started to talk with them on many reasons, but it steals my mind when one of my friends said, "women do not need to get higher education, women have to take care of family and woman living away from family is risky". It was not just my friend who said that but also my parents. They asked me to think about myself and what I wanted to be in the future, they insisted getting higher education was the same, just how well people could manage their life for a better well-being and for a happy life. I checked with my older brother who was in University ahead of me and found that the number of women in higher education was less than men, women had a very small number in the field of science, technology, and engineering. Then, I started to think about myself and my family. I knew that the man is the head of family and will take care of the whole family. This was the reason that I thought that they had to get higher education in order to bring more success to the family and I decided not to continue my education in the University, instead working with my family business.

I have been working with my mother and father on a small business in my local area for many years and I traveled with my mother to Vientiane Capital quite often for another small shop. I learned how to manage business and connected with many royal buyers in many provinces. Now, I am married with a man from Vientiane and we have a small business for living, too. We planned to have three children and earn more money for travel. Since, my English is not very good I decided to join an English class near my village. I study English every day in the evening and practice with my new customers.

I still remember many lessons from my mother not only for the business but also a way of living to achieve a happy life. I practice every day to stay in the present, not in the past and the future, learn something that I need to know, be confident and stick to my goal. Of course, sometimes my big goal can make me feel tired, but it is valuable enough to continue working for the goal.

My Life As A Woman: Latvia Edition

I grew up in Latvia in a tiny country and all in all, quiet provincial where people appreciate a lot being close to nature. Until about the age of 4, I was living with my grandparents on the farm. My mom at that time worked in the ambulance and could be called up at any time in the middle of the night and my father worked night shifts in the factory. In the years that followed, I was coming to the farm every weekend and spending there my summer and winter holidays.

On the one hand, it was time I will never forget. A lot of warm memories. Me and my grandad getting up with the sunrise and going to get the grass for the rabbits. Going mushroom and berry picking and exploring new paths in the forest. Watering the garden at 10 pm and it is light outside. I had responsibilities and was taught to work hard. Every day. In my family as a woman you grow up taking care of everything and everyone around you and rarely consider your own needs. At that time, I spent a lot of time alone. Quite frankly, I never felt bored. I loved it. Up until today I appreciate my alone time and always find some sacred peace in it.

On the other hand, when I got to about a teenage age, I was sick and tired of the same life and being around the family who would decide what I would do and occupy every free minute that I have. I started to wonder about breaking out of these routines and living a life where I would be in charge. That was my dream.

I turned 19, finished school and went to the UK to study at university. I had no idea what awaits me and how a bigger change it would be for me to make sense of this huge foreign world on my own. After I finished university I traveled to Denmark and worked as a Key Account Manager in sales. That pushed me way beyond my limits. Not only did I struggle to sell but also being unable and insecure to have small talk to someone in their 50s and me in my early 20s. To me it was more of a pride question, to be able to sustain myself and never going back to the farm and someone else's orders.

Now I am almost 30 and I feel that only now I entered smooth waters and I am truly on the path that was meant to happen. I met someone I love, and I am a mother of two boys. Being a mother is a blessing. And yes, you are endlessly busy from dawn to dusk. When I play with my boys, I return to be that small girl in the woods, observing the nature around me and playing with whatever I can find in nature.

I work as a researcher for a Canadian company and have a pleasure to do it from home, in my peace. In all these years, living in different countries and seeing different people, I realized that there is nothing wrong with appreciating simple things. As a Latvian girl who ended up living in Denmark, I learned about feminism and fighting for equal rights. While I appreciate equal opportunities, I do believe that the beauty of a woman is to share love through everything we do and remind everyone through what we do about harmony, beauty, and peace.

My Life As A Woman: Lebanon Edition #1

My name is Naema Ahmad from Beirut city of Lebanon. Basically, I grew up in Beirut, but once my family migrated to Germany, I lived there for some time. My father is a lawyer in the Islamic court of Lebanon. My mother is a housewife. My family is very open and at the same time a very traditional family.

The way I grew up was very joyous and also very interesting. My father and my mother are very kind. When my brother and I were young, we used to listen to a short story from my father, and then we used to sleep. Because my father was a lawyer and was very busy working on some cases, sometimes, he came home late at night. But if he came late, my brother and I used to wait until he came home to tell us a story and then we went to bed. Still, we are a very sweet and nice family.

Actually, I didn't study a specific field. I studied a traditional Indian music which is known as "Dhrupad". Once I was in France and my friend invited me to go to the concert of one of the most renowned Dhrupad singers, "Ustad Sayeeduddin Dagar". When I listened to his voice and the way he elaborated, I said, "One day, I will learn this art form and will try to make it a part of my life!" Soon, I went to India and started learning it. Apart from music, I have a bakery shop in Beirut.

Basically, Lebanese men and women enjoy equal civil rights. I think that Lebanon is one of the most diverse countries in Asia. The way different ethnic groups live together is unique in its own. Once a Persian poet who was from Pakistan said that god gives victory to that nation which can maintain its own needs and make its own future. Lebanon is a country which has made its own future and has given equal rights to both genders. I think that there are still lots of things to change, but our people have made such a country that can be changed very easily.

We have a multicultural society. Different religions have different laws and every person can practice his or her own religion. For instance, if two Muslims want to marry, they can go and marry in an Islamic court and if a Christian couple wants to marry, they can go to a Christian court. The same rules apply to other things like inheritance or divorce.

I had many struggles and meanwhile, big successes in my life. When I decided to learn music, my father said that Dhrupad is bad music, so it was not permissible in Islam. But I tried my best to explain it to him. My father and indeed, my whole family were against my idea. But after two months, I finally got the permission of my father to learn it.

I wanted to start a small blog and make it as a way to express my ideas. Because I am a person who wants to have her voice not only in one place or the other, but to have my voice all over the world. I want to convince all women across the world to have patience toward their goals. As far as I can see, there is always something that one should achieve. But the most important thing is patience. Try to be patient when it comes to your goals, but do not procrastinate to get it done.

My Life As A Woman: Lebanon Edition #2

Sabine Nehme

Where did you grow up?

I was born and raised in Lebanon Zook Mikael. I lived my whole life there until I was 20.

How did you grow up?

I grew up in a family of boys in a small city in Lebanon. My mom was overprotective and always kept me around her as she never trusted anyone with all the war history and trauma she faced. I had a different childhood than any girl in my age and was a focused on the artistic side of me. I found my passion for writing and music and focused by teaching myself how to write and create content. Of course, not to forget that I played boys games, since I had three brothers to play with, but at a certain age, I found the girl in me caring and loving life and hungry to explore and this was the day I packed a bag and moved to UAE.

Did you have parents or maybe a grandmother who inspired you?

My family were all an old generation that could not understand me well. But at a certain age I always found myself curious about Lady Diana and opera. It became a dream for me to always be motivating to women, especially as they inspired me to change. I always wanted to love unconditionally knowing I was stabbed many times and heartbroken but the faith in my heart kept me believing. My grandmother was a great cook and that's the only thing I could say I proudly took from my family.

What did you study? / What did you want to be growing up? / Why?

I studied graphic design and web design with a third major in Interior Design, but I found my passion for content when I moved to Dubai. I always wanted to be a singer but sadly in the Arab world, I always had the fear to do so. So I decided to focus on the media content part and I could have my own stage where I became a public speaker and motivational coach by supporting women and parents around the world. I always felt I wanted to be on a stage communicating and motivating people to believe and dare to change and move on.

What do you love about your culture?

I struggled at the beginning to adapt into my culture. I was always needing to know more and curious but at a young age a girl was forbidden to ask. After travelling and exploring the world, I noticed that I was so close to my own culture that I thought, I need to connect back with our traditions and life changed in an educational way in Beirut knowing the current situation keeps on dragging its people but with the faith the power I felt, I knew I was a strong woman and this is where a lady stands in a city where they appreciate strength and power. I could see the culture changing into working women who were decision-makers and life-changers and that's where I found myself coming back from Dubai after 14 years to adapt back to my own culture.

What are you currently doing for work?

I work currently as a TV presenter, Agency owner, and an ambassador of love for awareness whereby I share my voice and support unconditionally.

Tell me about your struggles as a woman

A woman's life is never for her own, she always has to sacrifice something for someone. When we meet someone, we sacrifice changing for them and then we sacrifice a dream or a job to make sure we are positioning ourselves in the perfect image of a woman. I struggled always giving up my dreams for someone and always lived for others until I reached a point where I forgot myself. I always felt the competition to prove myself to reach something.

Tell me about your successes as a woman

For a Lebanese girl living alone with her daughter being a single mom and risking everything and moving on is my success story. I made major decisions and turns in my life and all to show my girl that a woman can be whatever she wants to be. We deserve to be happy and we are. We deserve to achieve dreams and I did. I am living my own dream and not to miss in parallel being a perfect mom to my daughter. I could move to a country and raise my own kid alone working and starting my dream and achieving. Today I am living the dream and sharing my love and being multitasking for me and all the special people around me. Today my success and believing I could and I did and still moving toward making changes for a better world … full of unconditional love.

My Life As A Woman: Lesotho Edition

I was born and grew up in small village which is found in Maseru, Lesotho. I have five brothers. My father works with the livestock and sometimes he goes to South Africa's mine to work and send my mother money. My mother does the work in the agriculture and inside the house. My brothers are responsible for the livestock. I always had to wake up very early in the morning to milk the cows, do the kitchen work, and look after my little brother. I would go to the field and help my mother by hoeing, planting, weeding, and harvesting the crops. I would walk a great distance to obtain firewood and carry the load home on my back. I also carry water that I fetched by walking miles from the well for cooking, drinking, washing and for laundry. I sometimes even carry my brother on my back and pail of water on my head. After that, I wash the clothes and scrub it and hang it on the bushes to dry. I know it is a lot of work for the day, but I have to endure to survive. After all that, I got ready to go to school. I always wanted to make my mother happy and help her financially. I always try to make her happy by my school results.

As higher education is very difficult to pay for in Lesotho, my mother had not enough money to send me to high school, so I dropped out of school. My mother always told me not to give up on my education. My mother did not want me to follow the path that most women went. She said, "This is for the time being. Don't feel sorry for quitting school. I will work hard and save money so that you can continue." she continues "My daughter, I am your mirror. You have to smile for me to smile, you have to follow your dream, your heart and make my sorrow wash away." I still always remember all the words she spoke because it always motivates me.

Once upon a time, my father and mother were talking loudly late at night. They were quarrelling whether I should get married or not. My father was the initiator of the idea. And for not agreeing with his ideas, he started throwing things and had a fit at her. I wanted to run away but my father would think that my mother helped me run. I knew he would make her suffer day and night until I returned, so I decided to stay. Months later my father forced me to get married and I settled in the capital city of Maseru. Now that I am a wife to my husband, I became his slave. He forced me to have sex with him wherever and whenever he wanted. I was his property, a slave to him. He always came home late and would take out his outside frustrations on me.

I knew my potential, but I was limited by my surroundings. I did not want to rely on my husband for money and food. I did not want a man's support to help me live. I also did not want to push away my dreams and focus on being my husband's slave. I was not willing to give up on my dream for anything. I hated the traditional beliefs of my country and mostly I hated the legal laws that affect women's existence.

In Lesotho, if we women wanted to take out a loan, we need our husband's permission. We also must get approval to open a bank account, or to go and see a doctor to take contraceptives. We women cannot inherit property and are barred from running a company. We have no legal power to refuse sexual relations or demand use of a condom. As a result of our inability to refuse forced sex, most of the time, women carry HIV AIDS virus.

Once we get married, men own us women. Unemployment tops higher percentage, especially for women, because we struggle to get loans and open businesses. We also are not allowed to inherit or own property. I wanted to make a change, a change in the law.

I did not want to be defined as housewife, so I decided to be independent. I divorced my husband and started working as a waitress in a restaurant. I made a living with my tips. After my shift was done in the restaurant, I would go and work at the textile factory. In addition to working my two jobs, I volunteer any extra time to improve the lives of Lesotho people. I am working with the local leadership to compact the challenges that young women face like early marriage and gender-based violence. What I always wish for is for the boys to find a way to become different from their fathers. I need them to understand the hardship that women face. We women are very vulnerable and we should be given basic human rights. The bad traditions must go. We don't have to give men a chance to lay their hands on us and we women should take control of our life. We have to fight for our freedom. We have to have a dream and we have to make a move.

The traditional music, dance, literatures, storyteller's, dancers, and musicians all join with the audience chanting, clapping, singing to retell ancient folktales, tradition of singing and dancing males with high kicking group dances and singing with handmade instruments which include whistle, drums, rattles, stringed instruments are the things that I love about my culture.

My Life As A Woman: Liberia Edition

I was born into a family of five children in Zwedru, a small town located in the southeast of the capital city, Monrovia, in Liberia. It's unfortunate that we had to spend our childhood away from both parents due to separation. It didn't make things any easier for us. Like many other village children, I was tasked with many morning duties before I finally set off. These ranged from fetching water, washing dishes, sweeping, among others.

Remembering my experience when growing up in the village brings me both good and bad memories. I keep thinking about how learning at night would have been more accessible if there was electricity in the town. I was supposed to do my homework in the class after school or the next morning because the lantern in the house was not meant for reading. Some children were fortunate to get lights from their friends whose parents could buy an extra candle for their children to learn at night.

Having no role model, growing up in the village, presented me with three options: learn a trade, go to school or go into farming. The fear of ending up in the streets and the zeal of making a meaningful life, which we believe can be achieved through education, made almost all other children, and I chose school over the other options. Although going to school in the village was not easy, because it came with its challenges.

The ever-existing challenge with schools in the village is a lack of structure, learning, and reading materials. The story is not different from my school. The absence of a computer laboratory and library made teaching and learning of some subjects hard. For some of us who could not afford to purchase textbooks, we were at the mercy of classmates who were not ready to lend us theirs.

One common thing about the teachers in Liberia is that they encouraged us to work hard to achieve what we couldn't. It is believed that if your performance was below that of your school teachers, you had failed. This motivated us in our studies. Today, I have a degree while most of my teachers' then boasted of their diplomas. I hold a degree in Medicine from Adventist University of West Africa.

Working in rural areas, the profession has taken me to lots of places where I have left marks in the hearts of many. I still get messages from those I met and speak highly of what I have done for them. I worked in Elwa Hospital, where I specialized in Mother's and Children's Healthcare. I moved to Mascho Hospital as an MCH district coordinator. I was able to start my medical center at Bong County. I can't say I have succeeded yet because my fulfillment is to see the lives of many people being saved.

I believe that every woman has potential in them, and all they need is to push a little. If I did it under limited infrastructures, as well as learning and teaching materials, nothing should stop you.

My Life As A Woman: Libya Edition

My name is Farah from Tripoli, the capital of Libya. I was born in a middle class family. I grew up in Tripoli, but we lived in other cities as well. My father works at a bank in Tripoli. My mother was a secretary of ministry of human rights when she was a young woman. But because she lost one of her hands during the Libyan civil war, she decided to put an end to her political life. My family is a middle class family and my mother was a politician.

When my two brothers and I were young, my father used to tell us the stories of civil war and how people were fighting against inequality. My father and my mother always convinced us to study and fight against gender inequalities. The other thing which was common on those days was, children used to go to the Elders and take lessons from them.

I am currently studying Engineering at the University of Libya. I like to do hard things in my life and try different things. I think that this specialty makes me different from others. I always had the idea to have my own business. However, I tried so much, but I didn't succeed. I hope that I can make that happen one day. Because having financial freedom is a very good thing, in my opinion.

Arabic culture and the Arabic world have influenced so many things in our country, including our culture. Our culture is very different from other African countries. The way we live, the way we study, and the way we think is unique in its own way. The thing I like about our culture is the role of women in society. We have a higher women labour rate among the other African countries. About 30% of the women work outside their homes. The other thing is the number of educated people. About 80% of them are educated.

My biggest struggle in my life was my religion. I was Jewish in the past, but when I was in high school, I had many Muslim friends. They used to talk about their religion, and I was convinced by them to accept Islam, and I did. Soon after my family came to know that I accepted Islam, my father told me to change my opinion and stop doing my prayer. But the interesting part is that when they saw the way I worshiped God and the things that changed in my life, they slowly converted to Islam. Although our family was said by my uncles and relatives not to allow that to happen, today we are all Muslims.

My message to all women in the globe is that we females are unique creatures, do not let yourself be abused by men in any way. Be strong and do not let others decide your future. Be the player of your own game. If you have no one to support you, do not worry! Because it might be in your benefit. Lastly, I want to point out that every human being has weaknesses and also strengths. But do not let your weakness overcome your strength!

My Life As A Woman: Liechtenstein Edition

Liechtenstein is a small European country, located between Switzerland and Austria. Liechtenstein's flora is really stunning, this country is famous for its adorable castles, royal rich heritage, historic sites and pure nature. This country is an aesthetic one, full of really beautiful and dramatic scenes. People fall in love with Liechtenstein, as here they can find peace and enjoy nature and tourists are always leaving this country with sadness in their hearts. What I love about Liechtenstein is that it is very safe, like there is no crime at all. You will never hear about any murder or a robbery.

I am a Russian woman who lives in Vaduz, in the capital of Liechtenstein. It is a small peaceful city. Originally I am from Russia, Saint Petersburg where I was born and passed all my childhood. I grew up in a traditional Russian family with my two sisters, went to a local school and when I became an adult I started to seriously approach my future. I noticed that I was fond of design and I adored the profession of a designer and I was always imagining myself working in a famous company. Actually, from the time I turned 18, I started a long and challenging journey to my dream. With the strong support of my lovely parents, I went to Edinburgh to continue my education. I entered The University of Edinburgh, Faculty of Architecture, and immediately found a job in a local flower shop, where I was a florist helper. After that, I found a job in a business school for women, where I was a web developer. So you can see a quick improvement in my career because I am not that woman who will wait for luck or something else. After this, I got a raise in my career and became a marketing specialist. But this was not what I would like to be, I went to Liechtenstein and entered the University of Liechtenstein and studied another branch of architecture. This was my final station at this moment, actually I found my man and now we live and study in Liechtenstein with big goals for the future.

My life is kind of a mess, I was living and working in different cities, I passed a really hard route and I do not avoid future difficulties or changes. Life can change in 1 minute so never give up and strictly go to the life you were dreaming about. This is advice for all the women living on this planet, be strong, purposeful, and courageous. This life is for strong people, it loves invincible people and always gives chances to them. If you show that you are scared of something nothing will be easy for you, but when you show that you are ready to bear every difficult situation and pass it so welcome to the club. I was a girl when I went to Edinburgh and started life from scratch and nothing could stop me, and I want women to be that much stronger.

My Life As A Woman: Lithuania Edition

I was born in a small town. My country had declared its independence and was recovering from a long soviet union occupation. A few years after my birth, my town's name was changed, but in my certificate, the name of my birthplace remained the same. It turns out that I came from nowhere, a woman from a place that does not exist on the official maps anymore.

I grew up in a typical working-class apartment. My mother likes to say that I was a very quiet child. But, I was quiet only while being under my parents' watch. I was an explorer, a risk-taker. I was wandering around the abandoned buildings, which we had plenty in my town. My older cousins and their friends were my companions in summer adventures. They taught me how to ride a bicycle, how to hold my breath under the water for minutes, and I even learned to fight and to curse, something, my Catholic mother would never approve. Yet, I was pretty good at pretending to be shy and fragile. I did not grow like most of the children, surrounded by joy, love, and care of the grandparents. My mother's parents died early, and I did not have time to know them better. My father is an orphan. All that I know is that his mother had a beautiful name, which means a "flower".

He almost named me the same way but decided to give me another, more powerful one. "Life is full of struggles, you'll learn it soon. You need to have a strong name, so people see that you are not weak.", that's what he used to say to me when I was little. I knew then, my life as a woman might not be as easy as I thought. I did not see my father often, as he worked a lot. I rarely spoke to my mother about something not related to my scores or what I had for lunch today.

I promised myself that I will never be, as cold as my parents were to me, to my children if I ever have them., I became my own inspiration. I learned to solve my problems and how to be a young independent woman.

When I turned 16, we moved to a cottage in a small village. I had to get to school by bus, which was full of angry, dirty local children. Those kids used to beat me. I was not like them - smarter, clean, and always polite, like Andy Dufresne from The Shawshank Redemption.

When I was 18, my only aim was to pass exams to get a university scholarship and leave the place where my parents brought me without my consent. I was not sure who I was going to be then. I wanted to create something big, make people notice me, talk about me. I was very good at the visual arts, and even won a couple of awards. My writing was pretty successful too, and my essays brought me some valuable prizes. Yet, writing and art did not seem profitable to me by that time. So I went to Medical school. I was good at science and languages and loved to fix things. A science degree in Health and Molecular Genetics seemed like a perfect match for my abilities. After graduation, I changed a couple of jobs when I found the one that satisfied me.

I work for a multinational company as a data analyst. One of the best things about working for a huge company in Lithuania is that people embrace other traditions without hate or disrespect. We managed to learn how to respect other nations and that is what I like about our culture the most. But, I had some struggles in my life, related to my parents' attitudes. The main challenge for me as a woman was to prove to my family that I could be accomplished without being married. Also, that dating without marriage is not something terrible. In addition, I managed to show them that I can enjoy things which they think are only for men: army, combat training, carpentry, and fixing computer hardware.

As a woman from Lithuania, I wish that women around the world would learn to find strength and joy inside themselves. I never had somebody to look at, whose example I could follow. So I made myself my motivator. Learn to be your inspiration, and you will see that life is not as hard as somebody once told you.

My Life As A Woman: Luxembourg Edition #1

Sometimes dramatic changes happen in life and you have to be strong and able to start everything from scratch and do not hesitate to prepare for something that may not work for you. This is exactly what happened to me about 10 years ago when I was a young girl looking for a job to move my life to another level, become independent, and live my best life. Everything was just perfect, I found my job, doing my favorite thing, improving myself to conquer new heights. But love doesn't ask before coming, I met a guy and had fallen in love with him. He was living in Luxembourg and a moment came in my life that I had to choose, either marry him and break up with my dreams, or stay in my motherland and follow my goals. I chose the first one as my love for him was really strong. For an Armenian woman, it is very important to marry, have children, and become an exemplary wife wherever you live.

Yes, I'm an Armenian living in Luxembourg with my lovely husband and son. I was born in Yerevan, Armenia in an average family of teachers. I really love my parents, they invested in me every coin they earn, to provide a good education, a good profession, and assure me a good future. I studied insurance in State University and immediately found a suitable job with a good salary for that time. A year passed and I met my future husband, at that moment everything was like in a fairy tale, and thoughts about leaving my country were not a place in my mind.

It's really difficult to leave everything and go somewhere, where you know neither language to communicate nor any people. Actually, my parents inspired me and helped to live through it, they were always with me although there was the distance. First of all, I decided to learn French or German to be able to communicate with people, and I started my courses towards a good life.

Even though my husband supported me financially, I wanted to find a job and work in Luxembourg, which was one of my best choices. My husband could find a job for me according to my profession, at that moment 'PwC Luxembourg' was looking for an auditor and I started working in that company. With the time I got used to my new lifestyle, I could make friends, could communicate in different public places, could become an Audit Manager in the same company. Everything seems too difficult and unbearable, we think that it will not be better, we think that we will not achieve more, but often life gives us the best, but the path to the best is the most difficult.

My status for life is not to be afraid of cardinal changes, everything that is done is done for the better. This life is full of surprises, you can fall asleep with plans for your future but wake up with totally different results. Women! Find a man who will support you in every difficult moment of your life, I am grateful to my parents, and my man whose support I will feel till the end.

My Life As A Woman: Luxembourg Edition #2

My name is Juliet Jades, Luxembourg is the only home I have ever known. Born and raised in the capital city, I have never thought of ever moving away from this lovely city. I have not been to many other countries, but growing up in Luxembourg felt like I had been to multiple countries. This is because the city is populated by individuals from other neighbouring countries, with each individual bringing their perception of culture into the country. One of the best cultural traditions I enjoyed as a child and continue to enjoy today is the hopping at St. Willibrord.

Despite this being a religious event, it is characterized by so much fun, and over the years, more people are participating while many others spectate. Besides the cultural events, I learned about my Portuguese mother's traditions, and these interactions made my mother a role model because of how much she treasured the preservation of culture. I always wanted to be an engineer when I grew up, and my parents supported this dream. My dad was the inspiration behind this dream as I followed him to work several times as a child and loved how they could make buildings appear out of raw materials.

I took my education very seriously and would end up in engineering school, where I graduated with first-class honours. I got a job as an intern in one firm and would proceed to secure a full-time job in the company. The working environment was excellent as I was achieving my lifelong dream. The one thing that bothered me was the few numbers of women in the construction industry. As I got promoted in three years, I instantly became the only woman in meetings, the only woman speaking in an expert's panel. It felt quite lonely to stand out so significantly. This was a male-dominated world, even especially in the leadership bracket. I did learn to embrace standing out, and pushing on changes to the board was stressful enough. This is because limited ideas influenced decision-making, which was a struggle I experienced in the industry. The low number of women in this industry made it difficult to amplify the woman's voice.

I suggested a program that would go to schools, inspiring young girls to consider the construction industry, and this was approved, becoming my most significant achievement in the industry. I would also take any new female employees and interns under my wing and try to inspire them. This was significant because 15 years later, the firm is composed of at least 39% of women employees with a considerable number of them making it to leadership positions. Even today, the school program I started is active, and the enabling of women roles has been turned into a department as the firm has realized that there are benefits in pursuing diversity.

My advice for women in Luxembourg is that the journey to the top of any industry is lonely, as men dominate most industries. However, it would help if you were not afraid to stand out as this generates opportunities to inspire other women to achieve. Pursuing tough goals can also enable you to influence promoting the participation of other women.

My Life As A Woman: Madagascar Edition #1

I was born and raised in Madagascar for most of my life. For many of you, when you hear "Madagascar", perhaps the cartoon or a fantasy land may come to mind. For me, Madagascar is the place I call home. Growing up as a little girl and now an independent woman living here is, as you would expect, different from your upbringing. I am, what you call a Millennial, born in 1994, and had a childhood marked by beautiful skinny barbies with shiny blond or brunette hair which after a few play dates (with my mom's makeup tools) would turn into horrifying figures. I lived with my mum, dad, two younger sisters and spent a lot of time with my circle of friends. Long before the time of iPad, iPhone, and limitless Wi-Fi, in fact as long as I remember, my playdates involved climbing trees, playing basketball or running errands.

Perhaps like most families around the world, my mom was the strongest and the most present figure in my life. Not to say that my dad wasn't there. He was, but because of his career choices, he was traveling around the island for more than six months in a year. Thus, for half a year, my mum had to 'play' both parenting roles. She brought us up with a steel rod, not hesitating to raise her hand whenever my sisters and I were out of the line (Don't worry, that's just how African mums discipline their kids!), screaming at the top of her lungs for bringing home bad report cards and as I am sure many can concur, being forced to stay up past midnight until you master your math times table. Although I hated those moments back then, as I look back, it was in these instances that my mum had taught me the value of hard-work, self-discipline and righteousness. But, my mum was also a 'softy'. She would melt down whenever we hurt ourselves or whenever we had heart-breaks, e.g. when our dog died. I remember how she would murmur comforting words, when we didn't feel well, and hug us tightly when we were sad.

Like many little girls around the world and as cliché as it gets, I looked up to my mum without realising it. She was, de facto, the only inspiring woman in my life and thankfully she was and still is, a pretty good one. She worked with resilience to build herself a name and a career, to provide for us and to help out her parents. When I was, she made the decision to move to another city for a fresh start, privileging challenge over comfort and freedom over emotional bondage and a toxic environment. With us in the back-seat, and a not-so-happy-to-leave dad, my mum organised everything to move from the capital, Antananarivo, to the province of Majunga. In the span of seven years, she moved from house-maker, to Area Manager and to finally land herself a job as a Director in one of the biggest companies in Madagascar. She carried her work duty with honesty, walking the hardest path of righteousness in a world where corruption, theft and money laundering are common practice. While maintaining her dignity, my mum has passed unto us the value of integrity, truthfulness and moral uprightness. I carry in my professional life her hard-work but most importantly her belief to do good.

Now you may be wondering what did I inspire to be when I was little and what am I doing instead? Here is another cliché for you: I wanted to be a stewardess. For me, stewardess was synonymous for luxury, fun, glamour and beauty. As a little girl, it seemed as though they had their life sorted out together and I think Hollywood has played a role in shaping my mindset. In movies, the stewardess was always the one with a beautiful and slim figure, pretty face and well-mannered. Little did I know that it wasn't a job as rosy as I thought. So, at this point, you may have guessed it right, I didn't end up pursuing it. Instead I went on to study International Relations, simply because I was passionate about history, international economy and world affairs and eventually I wanted to become a diplomat or even better, I wanted to work for those international organizations, such as the World Bank, WHO or GIZ, who've been present in Madagascar for a long time

Why diplomacy though? Madagascar and I have a love and hate relationship. There are many things that I hate about this country and many more that I love. I adore the fact that family is still an essential part of our culture. No year passes without at least two family reunions with my mum or dad's great-grandmother's children, her children, the children of her children and so on and so forth. The festive seasons are another excuse for a family get-together with no less than 30 members packed into the house. Respecting the elders is another Malagasy culture that I appreciate about my country. 'Ny tso-drano zava-mahery' which is translated as 'blessings are powerful' is a core belief that makes or breaks Malagasy lives. We believe in the power of blessing from our elders, meaning grand-parents and parents. My mum used to tell me stories of family members getting married without the consent of their parents. Passionate love ended with a sour taste, was what was left of the marriage.

On the other hand, I hate the traffic in the capital, the shabby and dirty streets and feeling scared, 75% of the time, of being robbed. So, when I was 18, I decided that my life mission was to enrich the life of Malagasy people so they could feel safe in their own hometown, walk on clean streets and drive miles without spending hours stuck in the traffic. Anything that would enrich the lives of my compatriots, I was down for it.

Nine years down the road and here I am. On a completely diverging path again but somehow on the same mission to enrich the lives of my fellow Malagasy. When I was at University in Europe and Asia, I did what most students do, eat, study, drink with little sleep. I also jumped on every opportunity to travel to neighbouring countries and grew really fond of it. I love the excitement and anticipation that came when I packed my luggage. I loved it when I spent hours googling the best food to eat in Vietnam, the best place to go in Cambodia, what to do in London for Christmas, seven unique experiences only found in Amsterdam, etc. I loved it when I finally landed, checked in my hotel room, dropped my bags and ran outside with my eyes wide open (even if I didn't sleep enough on the plane), and my mouth, ears and hands just waiting to feel the adventure and mesmerising experiences. Traveling made me feel good and alive so I decided to be in the travel industry. As of this writing, I run my own travel agency, helping to enrich the lives of Malagasy people with authentic travel experiences and memories.

Nevertheless, living in a traditional society as a woman is a bit of a challenge, since everyone has high expectations of you. I grew up with the idea that being an employee is a norm so naturally when I decided to start my entrepreneurial journey, the idea did not sit well with my parents. I have learnt to trust my intuition and forgo external advice on many occasions. People always have their say and set of beliefs they try to ingrain into you, but you also have your own, and an idea of a life you wish to live. That's when you have relentlessly work on getting your own personal approval.

In my society, women are expected to attend to daily chores-such as preparing meals, doing the laundry, cleaning the house, cleaning the dirty dishes and many more. I am lucky to be married with a man who equally contributes on doing the house chores, who with love, would offer to take over from my house duties and anything else 'women are supposed to do'. I used to receive funny comments from my parents that I would brush off but deep inside they were uncomfortable. 'You are working on your computer and he is cleaning the house, that's odd', 'You are chitchatting with your friends and he is cooking, go help him', they said. I have learned to attend the house because I love to take care of the things that I have. They say women are supposed to serve food to their husband, to be of service to their husband. I say I am serving my husband because I love him, and I love myself even more to be faithful with the things that I have.

The best advice I can give you as a woman living in Madagascar, or anywhere for that matter, is 'Be it in your career, fitness journey, self-development, sport or relationship, always strive to do it from a place of love and appreciation'. Because I love volleyball, my team and I won the Tri-Campus Championship. Because I love challenging myself, I can now do 15 push-ups. Because I love traveling and empowering people through, I wake up every morning with ideas to fill people's lives with joy and discoveries. And to date I have travelled in over 10 countries. Because I loved the idea of studying International Relations, I secured a place in a top University although my English was pretty basic, and also obtained a scholarship

I do because I love it.

I progress because I love it.

I succeed because I love it.

My Life As A Woman: Madagascar Edition #2

My name is Nosy, I'm from Madagascar. Madagascar is the largest island situated in the Indian Ocean. According to the World Bank, my country has among the highest poverty rates in the world. Anyway, I'm proud to be a Malagasy woman, living in a beautiful country, a unique population and an exceptional culture and traditions. I'm now 32, I was born in Antananarivo, the capital of Madagascar. I'm the first child of the family and also the only girl. I have two younger brothers. I'm now married, but no child yet. My father comes from "Ampanihy", a place situated in 1200 km from the capital (in the south of Madagascar) and my mother is from the capital. I'm, then, a kind of mixed race as Madagascar has around eighteen ethnics, and each ethnic has different cultures and traditions. My father is a soldier and my mother is a seamstress.

I can say that I've lived in a peaceful family. My parents gave us everything we need, as long as they could afford it. For a country like Madagascar, "everything" means, "food", "clothing", "private school" and vacation from time to time. Apart from that, it is a luxury that I can't claim. I've never, for example, been abroad, I've never taken a plane. I could only afford a smartphone at the age of 30. As long as I can remember, my father told me to work well at school. He pointed out that only education could help me to live in this very poor country. To guide me on the right path, my parents sent me to "Ampanihy", my father's city of origin. The travel was terrible, I was alone, and I had to travel for two days from Antananarivo to Tulear. And another three days of travel, from "Tulear" to "Ampanihy", through a secondary road. When I arrived in the city, I witnessed the poverty of the population. No water, no food, no electricity, living in a very small house, no education for children, eating only cassava and corn every day. There, until now, most of the people are still living by hunting and agriculture. It was only at the end of that trip that I realize the value of my father's words. I, then, began to study seriously. As a teenage girl, I had to do a lot of sacrifice. I didn't go to parties as teenagers do, I hadn't any boyfriend as the other girls had, I haven't tried alcohol or cigarette. In a word, I didn't live as other teenagers do. Anyway, I got a best friend, and my mother was always with me to support me in my studies.

I'm now a civil servant in Malagasy administration. I studied law. It was not easy to achieve that goal but with effort and faith, I could do it. Thanks to my parents. Sure, I'm not very rich, but at least, I can support myself financially. I can also have the opportunity to dream, to get richer. I'm not depending on my husband (very important). The world is open to me as I can manage to adapt to any situation. The proof, beside my work as a civil servant, I'm now a writer, working as a freelancer.

Now, I want to create an association that can help people living in the south of Madagascar. And, on the personal side, I'd like to visit the world and to give to my future children, the best inheritance I've ever received, it means study. Personally, I think that we, girls and women, compared to men, are still facing many problems. We are still living in a society limited by a "glass ceiling". Through my experience, I know that we can overcome this. We just need to take on our responsibilities. As a woman, try to give all your best to achieve your goals. Try to study, study and study again. It is not a waste of time at all. It will pay one day. There is no age of when you should start to study. Having a husband is not a rush. If you are independent, it will be men that will come to you. You'll be spoilt for choice. I think that having a baby from 28 years old is not late at all. And remember girls, it is never late to start studying and to begin to have a goal, wherever you are in the world. Take care of you girls. And Good Luck.

My Life As A Woman: Madeira Edition

Bruna Di Staso, aged 47 and a mother of 3, speaks as a woman who grew up on the southwest coast of Madeira called Calheta. "I grew up in the south of Madeira in a very nice place, sunny and full of happiness. As life progressed, I left to venture towards north and enrolled in a university."

Talking about her education, she says, "I studied Law and graduated. Shortly after that, I began working as a lawyer in many different law firms. Now that I had gained vast amount of experiences, I thought of opening my own firm and after a while, I did that. I launched a law firm with some of my friends, all women, and worked with them for a couple of years. I loved this tale of my life, but it was a lot of work for such little money."

The year of 2009 was a big turnaround for Bruna. She says, "In 2009, my mother offered me a big opportunity. She wanted to start a brand-new family business. Therefore, we took an initiative to form a company of ice cream production and retail with up to shops all over the island."

She says that the business ran very well for a couple of years and it exceeded our expectations. But then, with the economy crash, her family had to close down all their shops and concentrate on opening up a big one combined with a restaurant as well in the center of the city. Very sadly, that was short-lived as she says, "When issues started to arise with the space owner, we definitely had to close it all. Nevertheless, my brother kept the company while I got into other things."

Talking about work next, she says, "My husband and I invested in a small boutique hotel afterwards and I've been searching for something more profitable for the family. Therefore, I became a real estate agent for Sotheby's International Realty. Right now, I'm in search of a new challenge to work from home while studying keenly the opportunities the market has to offer."

Bruna says that she's always had a middle-class family with normal people. "My mother though, has always been ambitious and my grandmother as well. I guess I'm just the same woman as well, following their footsteps. I'm not really a competitive woman, I just want the best for my family and myself. I've been together with my husband for 24 years. Our marriage has been a success since we're really good friends as well.", she says.

Talking generally, Bruna says, "Madeira is a beautiful place to live and be in. It doesn't give many job opportunities and I'm sure my kids will fly away soon. That's why I want to get a job that'll set me up for good. But to work in Madeira, it's really essential to make your own business and there's a lot to do about that."

Life puts up a lot of hardships for us. For Bruna, it was the fact that she had to leave the job that she had studied long and hard for. She also had to leave her company because according to her, "People are unfair." She says, "My only struggle is to find my place in this world which is not easy at all. Now, I'm going to invest on me and that's the struggle. Find the perfect way to be a great woman. Despite everything though, I'm a happy woman, mom, and wife."

To the woman of Madeira, Bruna says, "Madeira is a great place to live. I take pride in knowing that we, as women, are natural born fighters. I could only advise them to keep lifting their heads up as they march along life. There's a lot to learn out there so do adopt a curious mind. Knowledge always seems to pay off, I know this for sure. Someday, I hope, we'll all get there, where we wish to be."

This concludes My Life As A Woman: Madeira Edition.

My Life As A Woman: Malawi Edition

The story of my life begins in early March 1995, in the small village of Kafukule in Mzimba, northern Malawi. I was born in the middle of the night, in a hut miles away from the nearest clinic. The only other person presents at my birth – my mother's aunt, wrapped me up in her coat and journeyed with my mother and me to Lilongwe - the capital city a couple of months later. And while my mother went to nursing school, I was raised by my adoring paternal grandparents and my dad's siblings who pinched me more than was necessary.

Growing up, my grandmother was the breadwinner and a very capable matriarch of our family. Looking back, I realize I never asked her what exactly her job with the ministry of finance was, but I do know that she built the sprawling bungalow I grew up in, my great grandmother's house right next door and also managed to send all of her kids to pricey universities abroad. I would, in a heartbeat, say that she is my biggest inspiration, and so is my great grandmother who was the second female presenter/producer/correspondent for our state broadcaster and the first to be trained by the BBC in the early sixties – four years after our country had attained independence from Britain.

Another strange thing I recently realized is that I don't remember desiring a specific vocation when I was a kid which I think is rather odd. I remember telling my uncle that I wanted to be an astronaut and my stepmother that I would become a painter. Somehow when I was through with high school, I went on to study travel and tourism, but I ended up dropping out because I had lost interest and more importantly because the college had a strict attendance rule and I desired a bit more freedom. I eventually settled for a business management program, but ironically, I have only worked exclusively in the travel and hospitality industry since I graduated.

For my first job at 19, I moved to Senga-bay, a town on the beach of Lake Malawi where I worked as a hotel receptionist. I learned very quickly how to live on my own, ration groceries and pay bills, how to stretch my meager salary to last the month, and also that while paying rent sucked but it didn't suck as much as being heckled by my boss and hotel guests. If you have worked in the hospitality industry before, you know you must be pleasant at all times, even when getting harassed. And because I am an introvert, it was especially hard for me. Everyone I tried to talk to about it told me I should be flattered by the attention, it meant that I was attractive. I started to resent going to work and it took a toll on my mental health. Every day became heavier than the last and I fell into depression.

After a year, I quit and moved back to the city. I got a job as a travel consultant and I traveled around the country for work. I started to write creatively and share my stories and I also started a travel and lifestyle blog. I did not know when I began that these were the things that would bring me fulfillment that they would come to define who I am. But even more importantly, bring me communion with my fellow creatives and sisterhoods with phenomenal women I would not have met otherwise.

In all my life and everything that I have been through, I have come to understand that most of the time we have no choice but to be resilient and that is absolutely admirable. But we should also be honest with ourselves and we should be decisive. We should not stay in unpleasant and crippling situations (jobs, relationships - romantic or otherwise) for a second longer than necessary. Life is really short, and we must strive to live a life we really love, a life of our choosing. Amidst the setbacks, self-doubt, and anxiety - you have to discover the things that you love, the things that bring you joy, and pursue them relentlessly.

By Xara Hlupekile

My Life As A Woman: Malaysia Edition #1

The first step to be good at something is to fail countlessly. English is my second language. So, it's only natural that I struggled and had a difficult time adapting to it. But, that didn't stop me. I was 9 when I first started writing - after being forced to write a daily journal by my English teacher. I continued practicing until one day, my father sat me across from him as I was bracing myself to receive the yelling of the century.

Growing up, my authoritarian father and I have never seen anything eye to eye. My father could talk (read: nag) for hours. Meanwhile, the cat always caught my tongue during the heat of an argument which is why I found writing to be therapeutic. Unfortunately, 11 year old me did not think things through especially since my father discovered my journal. As fear filled me from the inside and made its way to my trembling hands, he said, "Your words flood my heart." I knew then that words could have a powerful impact on someone. Albeit, my journey as a writer was not as smooth as I hoped it would be.

I am a daughter to a civil engineer feared by many, and a respected chief clerk. Born on red soil at the heart of Malaysia; a country rich in culture and beliefs - like many, I was brought up with an expectation to become a prestigious doctor. As I pushed my passion aside, I focused on what I thought would bring me afar in life - scoring A's on exams. I soon realized the inequality of education systems that are fixated on only one (emphasizing the singularity) type of intelligence - the ability to memorize. Sadly, a 15-year-old does not have the power to cause a ripple on the pre-existing system. So, instead of fighting the system, I followed the stream of the river. What's sadder is forcing to love something you don't and becoming someone you're not.

Have you ever heard of a theory called "The Butterfly Effect"? A tiny trivial thing in the now could cause a small or great impact in the future. Powerful. I believe the struggle I faced during high school led me to the decision to fight for my passion's rights. I believe it made me value both writing and learning as much as I do now. I believe it made me who I am today. So, that's my story – the beginning of my story.

"A journey of thousand miles begins with a single step"

I pursued my tertiary studies on Mass Communication majoring in Journalism. Throughout this particular chapter in my life, I have met a handful of inspiring people that have widened my perspective on the world. Even so, it didn't feel right. It felt as if I took a wrong turn. So, I made my way out of the maze and entered into the world of Psychology where I completely have fallen in love. I found the perfect balance - understanding human behaviors while still being attentive to my passion in writing. I strived during the first year but, slowly, I crashed and burned.

"So, this is it", I thought. "This is the bump on the road. It's okay. It's only a flat tire." However, the truth is, mental health is not as easy as changing a spare tire. To this day, I have never worked harder in my life than I did on myself and yet, my accomplishments were next to nothing in comparison to others. That was the golden moment I learned the negative effects of social comparison. Women should not be intimidated by the beauty or accomplishments of other women. I had to transform my old ways of thinking and change the feeling of intimidation to inspired. It was the darkest and hardest years of my life and thankfully, I managed to graduate.

"A ship in the harbor is safe, but that is not what a ship is for". I carried my hopes and dreams along with my degree and set forth into the real world - only to found out that it only gets more difficult. As if being a female writer isn't hard enough, having to deal with people's low expectations on you for being "just a woman" is painful than it sounds. Not to mention the sexist stereotypes such as "the hotter you look, the dumber you are" and not be taken seriously if I wasn't "dressed up" or didn't put on any makeup. Again and again, I tried changing their views and gave my speech on how beauty is only skin deep but it's pointless.

Apparently, these behaviors and mentality are considered to be a norm especially for a woman working in a male-dominated industry (although it is the 21st century). I used the rage to fuel my motivation to aim higher and achieve the impossible. I wasn't going to let a group of pretentious entitled men have a say on what I can or cannot accomplish.

As of now, I am merely reaching the top of the hill – I'm not even sure if I'm even halfway through it. But, who does? Success is subjective and there is no one way to achieve it. Each individual has their own road to take. Every single road is bumpy and twisted in their own unique way which is why we should never really compare our hardships or accomplishments to others, especially with the intention to put ourselves down. Every story is different, and this happens to be mine. So, what's your story?

My Life As A Woman: Malaysia Edition #2

Malaysia, being one of the developing countries in Asia once consisted of rural areas, villages and small towns populated by moderate people. Even now there still exists these areas, but the past struggles will never be the same. In the olden days, Malaysian women are expected to be housewives, farmers and small-town folks. I was born on 23rd February 1972 in a small village located near the province of Yan, Kedah, a state known for its great paddy field. I was raised in a poor family, living from hand-to-mouth, unlike other people who seem to have it easy. But I'm still grateful for having food on my plate and a roof over my head.

I grew up with 6 siblings and I have been taught on how to farm and when I was 6 years old, my job was to distribute seedlings to other farmers on the field. Unlike other 6-year-olds, my hands were rough, but I continued to work to help my family get through our daily struggles. From when I was young, I always wanted to be a teacher, especially in teaching the Quran to kids. Back in my day, I often compete between schools and states on who could read the Quran beautifully. That was when I thought of becoming a Quranic Teacher to pass on the little knowledge I have to my community.

The ones who inspired me the most are my mother and my late teacher, Ismail bin Long. Both of them are the reason for my ambitions towards becoming a teacher. To pursue my dreams, I worked hard. I focused on my studies and was determined to change the fate of my family for the better. As the world's going through modern changes and there are rising costs in my own country, I had to be able to support my own family. However, as fate decided, I had to choose between furthering my studies or give the chance for my younger brother to pursue in law. We were in a poor family and even though education costs are not that high, my family can only bear the university's costs for one child at the time. Thinking that my help at home was more needed, I sacrificed my dream for my brother to achieve his. Things got worse, my father suddenly became ill and I had to give up working afar and helped my mother earn a living for us to continue to live.

As the years went by, I got better at what I do and got a job as a factory supervisor to help ease the burden of my family. Our luck began to turn for the better and finally, we had enough for all of us. What I love the most about my culture is its simplistic and moderate living. Most of us have been taught to be grateful for the food on our plates and the roof over our heads. By being grateful, we struggled not to obtain luxurious things but to provide comfort and ease to our children and grandchildren in the future.

As a woman and as a mother specifically, I often think about the kind of world we're leaving behind for our legacies. Currently, I'm working as a manager in my husband's law firm and in my part-time, I teach Quranic lessons to children. My only struggle as a woman is constantly the lack of respect towards a woman just because of my family background. However, I succeeded in helping my own family and supporting them until now. Even if I didn't have the chance to continue my studies, I worked hard to secure my own family's future while sacrificing my own.

To women all around, be us. Stop pretending to be something or someone that we're not and don't give up in pursuing your dreams. Even though some people may look down on us, just remember that our fate rests in our hands. Our failures are our fault. Follow your dreams and beware of men who are only here to hurt and use you. Lastly, be sincere with what we do. When you do good things, don't expect to be returned the favour but instead do it for the good of mankind without expecting something in return.

My Life As A Woman: Malaysia Edition #3

It was the first day of school. The teacher handed out pink cards with our names on it and instructed us to write our ambition on it. At 7 years old, I had never given much thought about what I wanted to be when I grew up, not until my class teacher insisted that we fill up our report card with a definitive job-of-our-dreams. I peeked over at my classmate and copied her answer: "Doctor".

Over 19 years later, I find myself laughing at this memory. What I do today is nothing close to what 7-year-old me thought I'd be doing. I don't even have a college degree! Growing up in the small town of Bukit Mertajam in Penang, your life could be mapped out against your parents or those around you: you finish high school, graduate from university, (ideally) get a good job as a doctor, teacher, engineer or lawyer, get married, settle down and have 2.5 children. My life today is nothing close to that.

I currently work for an e-commerce startup that operates across the Asia Pacific region doing operations and find myself striving for non-conventional "wins" which do not include the checkboxes mentioned above. If you're curious, operations are essentially an umbrella term to cover all the administrative/back-end work that helps a startup maximize productivity, scale fast, and achieve product-market fit. I never thought I would be working for a company that has so much emphasis on culture and attitude --- so much so that 50% of our performance review is based on culture fit!

How I turned out today is a result of how my parents brought me up. At first glance, my parents are almost opposites: where my mom is the kind of person who works behind the scenes, while my dad, with a memorable laugh and noticeable presence, is the life of the party. However, they were both very much aligned on my upbringing. Aside from "typical" Asian values (which I absolutely value) like working hard and striving to do our best in whatever we do, they also gave me a firm foundation in the Catholic faith alongside the freedom to be me. They never stopped me from being curious and exploring unconventional paths like freelance writing for the nation's leading English daily or taking part in a ridiculous amount of after-school activities.

As an adult, it did take me awhile to be confident enough to accept that I can be successful on my own terms, even though I don't check all of the supposed boxes of what makes an adult successful. My parents not only gave me the space to make my own decisions (such as quitting my full-time job to take a few months off to "work freelance", or dropping out of college after realizing it's not for me); they also stood up for me when I needed it most and trusted that I would make the best decision for myself.

This gave me the confidence to chart my own path, which most times, goes against what my culture would deem as "successful". I consider this one of my successes, especially as a woman, in a culture that is hyper-focused on women living up to what an ideal "wife" should be. While I value these ideals, I do think it is these very expectations that form a large part of the struggles of a Malaysian woman. Dress too provocatively, and you're termed as attention-seeking and "asking for it" if anything were to happen to you. Dress modestly, and you'd be called a prude.

Looking back, I recognize that I am blessed to be brought up by parents who never imposed these expectations on me. But, I still don't know what I want to "be" when I grow up (sorry, 7-year-old Ann-Marie!). I do know, though, that whatever path I end up choosing, I will prioritize my happiness and personal growth, and that's more than enough for me. If there's one piece of advice I could share with any woman living in Malaysia, it would be this: It is impossible to live up to these ideals or to please everyone around you, so the best thing you can do for yourself is to create your own ideals and what you want to be, and strive to be the best possible version of yourself. Not for anyone else, but for yourself. Be the kind of person that 7-year-old you would be proud to be, and don't allow society's expectations of the way you dress or your job title to define who you are as a person.

My Life As A Woman: Malaysia Edition #4

I must begin to say that I believe WOMAN is the backbone of the society. WOMAN is the complete package, who has not only to take care of home affairs but also raise kids into responsible citizens and good human beings. Besides all this, she is contributing to the society by working equally like men.

In year 1987, my family had then shifted recently from Libya to Pakistan where my father had been working as a civil engineer. A different environment but I got settled being with family, relatives and friends. Respect for the teachers, never ending chats and playing innocently with my friends were some of the highlights of my school life. After school, then college and finally a day came when I had got my honours degree in management sciences.

I must admit that the guidance and support given by my parents paved my ways to achieve my desired goals. The trust and faith of my parents in me never let me go off track and I remained focused to achieve my aims one by one. After graduation from College, I had a desire to get a degree in Business administration. However, things got re timed by my parents', mine 's and my now husband's mutual consent. That was to get married first and then continue with further studies.

So, I married a guy, who was an Airforce Pilot. After 2 years of our marriage, we had our first baby boy. I decided to pause my desires for a while. The quantum of responsibility was even more on me being the wife of a military guy. I had to manage driving, cooking, and looking after our baby. It took me three years to get admission in the Virtual University in order to pursue my studies, but finally, I was able to achieve this dream.

Moving along the timeline, God gifted us with a beautiful daughter to complete our family. Since we had always planned to grow with our kids in a foreign country, we had started to speak with them in English from day one. We had some resistance from the family members by not teaching them the native language first, but we kept on with our plans. In the meantime, kids grew up and I could take a job as a Primary School Teacher for some time.

My husband took early retirement from the Air force and got a job in Malaysia. Malaysia was more than our expectations. The people are very nice and kind., the climate is awesome, and the place is peaceful. The challenge I faced as a mother was that there are no international schools in Langkawi (where we are based). So, I had to study with kids at home and got some online schooling for them. They have made new friends, who they go out with, play with and socialize.

Since my kids are now grown up, I can spend more time with books or internet to feed my desire of gaining knowledge. I am freelancing as well as looking after home schooling (online education) of my children. I also encourage and teach my kids to cook, bake, clean their rooms, drive and buy groceries. Though our society is male dominant, but with the self-confidence boosted in me by my parents and my husband, I achieved all my desires. Now currently my aim is to help my kids grow into the best human beings to spread love, peace and harmony in the society.

About life in Malaysia, I must say that it is simply amazing. Here men and women are treated equally. As I mentioned that we live in Langkawi, which is a beautiful island. The society is free with equal chances for men and women, Women are seen working in every walk of life, from taxi or Grab drivers, salesgirls, working as labour on construction sites, business executives and pilots. At the same time, they are seen working in the fields, as well as selling food. I think they contribute greater than men to the society here while living with respect and dignity. This is something I must appreciate as it is not seen in countries like Pakistan or other Muslim countries may be. I would advise the men in all conservative societies to give respect to the women. Give them confidence and encourage them because women can equally help men to contribute to the nation and the society. To the women, have confidence and give time to yourselves also.

My Life As A Woman: Maldives Edition

Story of Myeha – Maldives

Sunny Side of Life, with crystal bluish ocean surrounding a bunch of tiny greenish islands is my home with warmth, The Maldives. Story of Myeha begins before city of Male the capital grows concrete than trees, in a ground floor which is quite rare these days as the ground floors barely used for living in modern apartments. It was a fantastic gathering, as most of Maldivians have an extended family culture, which a few families live together, which was mine as well, a bunch of uncles and aunts around me and eight cousins to move along, made the nest warmer and happier.

Looking at life as a grown up, in aspect of searching which made me an influencer, there are them whom I adore, my father, mother and my lovable superwoman, my grandmother. My father was a teacher, who has never went to school but self-studied to enlighten himself and started teaching others at the age of 15 in our very own tongue, Dhivehi, and currently possesses degrees and master's in various topics. He is popular with his students who are very grateful for making them more expressive and presentable. My brother and I would later also become masters in these areas with the teachings of my father. Then comes the woman who brought me up, my mother who is a kindergarten teacher, I still wonder how she manages to cope with a bunch of mischievous (in loveable manner) kids, as her daily routine and who broke the Asian rule of "Men work – Women cook". Here comes my attitude influencer, my adorable grandmother (mom's mother), who was a single parent with six kids and with whom I spent most of my days as a child. She was a routine housewife who has to wake up early, cook, laundry and apart, a struggler for an income to feed her children and did numerous jobs to earn the daily bread for the kids who later became responsible educated citizens where three sons work for national defense and another other as an environmentalist whilst daughters work as hotelier and a teacher. That is where I learned that giving up or quitting is never an option and her can do attitude with zero complaints with barely cried eyes made me what I am today, with her adopted attitude, "If I say I'll do it, I'll find a way and do it, wait and trust me kid.".

Having all these back stories, I made it through my Ordinary Levels and Advanced Levels in Science and later was a blank break, latterly followed by my bachelors in Shariah & Law which I gave up in last year and moved to Medicine. There starts my confusion, whether to become a doctor, detective, photographer or the list goes on and finally halted in museum. There I was a kind of bookworm to read a lot on history and various aspects. Maldives culture is neither Sri Lanka nor India, but a hub of cultures which has differed cultures in every island, that at times pretending them as separate countries as the islands had their own independent lifestyles in old days.

Departure from museum and the break afterwards made me do research on coffee and finally flagged me as a Barista who makes people's day with essence of coffee and hosts TV shows in the youth sector of PSM, State broadcaster of Maldives, YesTV. Not only that, but also an oratory coach in Male and other islands schools as well as an Instagram influencer in aspects such as fitness, lifestyles and business which I did for fun later become remarkable with a bit of vlogging.

Achieving all these was never a piece of cake with the judgmental mindset of people around since my childhood; as I differed as a girl with my thoughts, as well the looks. Later on, pressure was on my parents as I was coming home late, had a lot of male friends and yes, some unique interests, such as being fond of riding bikes, which is not girly.

Having a look at my journey, with the struggles I faced, the biggest achievement was recovering from three years of depression and anxiety which sent me away from Maldives for a month, losing over 15 kilos of weight to get back to a new level of mental and physical stability. That was the turning point which made me believe in myself despite gender or judgmental vibes around to become what you are. Sharing all this positivity in Instagram, it's speechless the feeling I get when someone meet me and say, "I was inspired by you".

Myeha, who never thought would become this "Myeha" she is now, is the emblem of success I see in myself who broke the stereotypes in society with freedom and power that drives me now, despite the waves that rise against!

My Life As A Woman: Mali Edition #1

Where did you grow up?

I was born in France, I lived there a large part of my life, but I also lived a few years in Mali during high school.

How did you grow up?

I grew up between two cultures France and Mali. But I feel closer to Mali by the fact that my parents have always taken the time to teach us the traditions and the history of our country elsewhere. I can't go anywhere without an accessory or a cloth that reminds me of Mali.

Did you have parents or maybe a grandmother who inspired you?

My parents are the people that I admire the most in the world because they have sacrificed themselves so much for me and my sisters. I am so grateful to them because they educated us of Malian culture and the best part of my culture is the cuisine, for which I recommend you the best dish in the world (cooked by me of course); Tigadégué, a rice dish served with a peanut paste sauce. We also spent all our holidays at Mali. It was their way to inculcate us with values of tolerance, sharing and love, and values close to the Malian culture. Moreover my parents pushed me to go back to Mali and it was the best decision I made in my life.

What do you love about your culture?

What I particularly like about Malian culture is the importance of maintaining social ties. Being Malian is like being part of a big family. No matter where you are in the world, Malian people will always have food and a door open to welcome you and help you.

What did you study / What did you want to be growing up? / Why?

At the end of high school I didn't really know what to do as a graduate, I was a pretty reserved girl with very few friends. I told myself that I had to choose a profession that could make me grow and open myself to others.

What are you currently doing for work?

I studied communication without really knowing where I was going. Surprisingly I discovered a passion for organizing events and advertising campaigns. Today I am the advertising manager of a major communications agency in Mali. Every day I discover a little more about my country, and create connections by meeting inspiring people.

Tell me about your struggles as a woman

Ss a modern African woman I feel little lost because in Mali, the woman occupies a prime place in her capacity as a wife and mother at home because she was raised to be dependent and subject to her family. She is taught to fade away and play a second role, while man must be independent and dominant. So for me it's a constant challenge to prove that women have as many skills as men and that I don't belong in the kitchen looking after children.

Tell me about your successes as a woman

What I am most proud of today is to be back in Mali and to be part of this new generation of Malians back home with lots of great ideas to change the future of Mali.

Provide some advice to women from a woman living in Mali?

You need you more than you need others; you are the only person who can change your life. You are strong and beautiful women, your future is in your hands.

My Life As A Woman: Mali Edition #2

I grew up in Mali in a town called Mopti. Life was hard, since I was brought up by a single mother. My mother was raped and got pregnant when she was a teenager. The man who impregnated her was an older man who died before I was born. Her parents never supported her; therefore, she had the responsibility of taking care of me. Since my mother had no permanent job, she had to go to other people's farms to cultivate so that we could get food. Even paying for my school fees was hard for her. I had to stop schooling and joined her in farming for other people's farms. Sometime we could go fishing so that we could sustain ourselves. Despite the struggles my mother went through, she was my excellent role model. She taught me to be firm and optimistic. In Mali, women are usually given the role of taking care of their home and family, while other positions are meant for men.

The struggles that my mother went through reminded me of how my future needs to be prepared. I wanted to be a leader in future, a position that was meant for men according to Mali culture. As I went fishing and farming, I had to save some money, hoping that I would go back to school one day and achieve my dream. I even participated in traditional dances that attracted both local and foreign tourists. Each season the tourists visited, they could leave some money for us. The money I saved helped me to go back to school. The hard work and the determination I had helped me secure a scholarship offered by a foreign country. I finished my studies and graduated with high marks. I am now a woman leader representing voiceless women like my mother in society. I support projects that empower girls and young women through education in Mali.

My present life is as a result of the struggles I underwent with my mother. Mali is a country that is rich in agriculture, fishing, and mining. However, poverty, girl abuse, rape, and violence are major problems. These problems prevent most girls from realizing their dreams. Most girls and young women lack education due to early marriages, early pregnancies resulting from rape, and poverty. Seeing girls and young women going to school the same way boys do, pleases me.

My advice to Malian girls and women is that, despite the challenges such as poverty, rape, and early marriages, they should join hands and fight hard. Enough is enough; they should engage in activities like group farming and fishing. These projects will enable them to sustain their needs. It will also help educate their girls, who will be our tomorrow's leaders. Girl child has rights just as a boy child has; therefore, educating them is of great benefit. My mother strained alone because she lacked support; if women can support each other, they can build a better society. They can make a society that is free of violence, early pregnancies, rape, and violence.

My Life As A Woman: Malta Edition

I was born on 5th February 1990 in Malta, to two very loving parents (Marthese & Joseph). They are my backbone and I love them to the moon and back. I am an only child and so the bond between us is very strong. I still live with my parents to this day, even though I am now 30 years old. One may find this very odd even more so since I am a very independent woman. But expenses are very high in Malta and to start renting out apartments is just not worth the money. I grew up with a very loving family, infinite number of cousins, school friends and music. Yes, music and singing have always been a substantial part of my life and they will remain so until my dying day. They are the factor which make my life worth living to the full and to always experience new things which in turn inspire me to create new music.

My Mother is my ultimate idol. She shows me that it is not impossible for women to be independent and to live their life fully and equally like all men. She gave birth to me and stopped working for 3 years. Once I started pre-school she started working again and is still working to this day. I was brought up with very independent virtues and at 9 years old I was arriving at home alone from school, opening the front door and disabling our home alarm system. These virtues have grown and developed with me and I believe that I am stronger because of them.

I always loved going to school. I studied accounting and graduated as an accountant in 2016. I liked being an accountant, but life is fluid and that drive towards numbers faded away by time. So, against all odds and cultural rules, a year ago I decided to start studying again. This time a completely different subject, that is, Digital Marketing. This was not taken too well, especially by my parents. But I was determined to change my career and to find a job that I love doing. This determination led to success and I started working as a Digital Marketing executive during January 2020.

This goes to show that no one should ever settle in a 'comfortable' routine. We need to challenge ourselves and to evolve along the years. This does not mean that I did not encounter struggles in my life. When I started telling people about this change, most of them looked at me in a very weird way, like it was a very unusual thing to do to change a career when you are reaching the 3rd decade of your life.

Malta's culture has developed substantially. Although, one can still find people with the mentality of 50 years ago. One case that I still remember and that frustrated me to no end is when my fiancé and I were going around bathroom suppliers to choose a bathroom set for our new apartment. We were looking at bathroom sinks and the salesman was doing a good job until he turned to me and said, "you naturally love cleaning and so this bathroom would be ideal for that". At that very instant I turned to my fiancé and told him to go out of that outlet and to never return. At the time, my fiancé found this really amusing but he understands me and treats me as his equal. We do everything together and he sometimes takes care of our apartment more than me.

Never let anyone put you down or tell you what to do or not to do as a WOMAN. We are all equal and we all need to take our responsibilities seriously. A quote that I keep as my mantra is:

"SHE is not fragile like a flower. SHE is fragile like a BOMB."

My Life As A Woman: Marshall Islands Edition

My people are friendly, kind, caring, respectful and peaceful. Strangers are received warmly. Consideration for others is a must and important in our culture. Family and community are also important. the traditional stick dance, tattooing, and the beat of drum played while a mat covered the face of the person being tattooed, and the most significant family event celebration which is the event of a child's first birthday, music, The condition of the environment, view of the islands, the trees, the whispering wind, beach the dressing style, and marine life are what makes my country alive. They are also the things that I love about my culture.

I was born and grew up in the beautiful city of Majuro, Marshall. I have two brothers. We were raised by a single mother. My mother worked really hard to raise us, send us to school. She is a weaver. My brothers do the job or work involving climbing coconut trees, papayas, and sometimes fishing. Like most of the women living in Majuro I always deal with things pertaining to the home, I usually make money on the side by my talent with hand crafts and excellent weaving. I know it is a very hard and tiring job, but I need to go on working to make an income, to help my mother. It is strange the way time moves here because the seasons do not change. It feels as though time stands still, yet every time I ask my mother, another month passed by. Life has become harder. I have worked, faded for my family for years but nothing seems to change my life. I was always afraid of not meeting our daily basic needs and mostly I was afraid of the flood; I always pray to God not to wake me and my family up in the underwater.

Most people value their health above everything else in their lives whether they know it or not. So when I grew up I wanted to be a doctor, helping other people in an extra ordinary sufficiently great way. And I will be able to positively affect patients every day. Being a doctor will allow me the potential to impact human life in a way that is truly unique and from what I saw and heard, the job satisfaction you get is unparalleled. It is a field in which one needs to put others first, medicine is truly a service. And as there is scarcity of physicians in Majuro, I wanted to give the service. My biggest fear was, not accomplishing my dream. In order to my dream came true, I have to study.

But I only sometimes go to school, after finishing the house work, and weaving, and only if I have time. I always wanted to go on time and learn properly. But with the situation at home I was always late. I am a quick learner though. I never forgot what my teacher taught me in class. I listen attentively. My lips cannot stop smiling while I am in class, my mind will forget the entire situation that I am in for the moment. I was very active in class, but as a time goes by and with the work at home and weaving were too much to handle, I often become really tired.

Once my teacher asked me why I am always late for class and why I do not come regularly to class. And also why I am not active as always. I told her the truth about the situation I am in and that I need a break until things at home change. But she said, "my dear student, you have to Take care of yourself; speak what is in your mind. Do not just be a people pleaser, have your own life. Go with your gut, find your focus, chase your dreams, be a lifelong learner. Do not just make assumptions that you have helped your family your entire life now is the time they help you." Her speech hit me very hard and inspired me.

Thanks to the best person in the world, my teacher, I survived and followed my dream. Ever since my teacher met my mom and talked her about value of education and punctuality, I now always go on time. She is my biggest cheerleader, inspiration for life, and she gave me the biggest gift that is to believe in myself. Now I am studying medicine in the US. and also providing free tutoring for the poor.

So women, don't just give up. Do what you love. life is really short, focus on making an impact. you are born for a reason. On the way, create the environment that is right for you. In order to get, you have to give, remember luck comes from hard work, and be your best at all times.

My Life As A Woman: Mauritania Edition

Mauritania is one of the biggest Muslim countries, where you can find traditionally dressed Muslim people working all day. You all probably know about Muslim's lifestyles and views on life, we are enough conservative and maybe old-fashioned for you, but this is what Muslim means and how we live. As a traditional Muslim woman, I adore my country and culture, I adore the way women must be. We have to be modest, household, and a humble family woman, who has to be an ideal spouse for her husband, a perfect mother for her child, and an exemplary woman in every way.

I was born and grew up in Nouakchott, in a standard Muslim family, where I had great parents, who were a really good example for me. I saw how it is to be a perfect father and mother, they are still my best lessons which I tried to learn well. Now in my family, I try to act like my mother who was my best teacher and to whom I am grateful for many things. Life for a Muslim woman is hard enough, we live in a conservative society where the role of women is really big. Our rules are limited, our freedom is also limited. We grow up in a family, we marry, have children, and that's all. I studied in a local school and after in a local academy, after what my father helped me to find a job in 'Attijari Bank' after who I married, and my life moved to another level.

When we are children we do not have any imagination about real life, about what we will go through, and what it is to be a Muslim or Christian. I was dreaming about becoming a singer when I was a child, and I remember myself singing everywhere, but it is actually not so accepted, so I had to leave my dream behind. I can advise women to find a worthy man, who can be an inspiration for every woman, a place where you can feel at home, a best friend for you, and a good father for your children. Also, on the other hand, you have to provide all the mentioned points to your husband, try to be a perfect wife, and support your man.

I found every woman has a right to be happy, to make a strong family, have children and mostly all this depends on her. Try to combine work and family and be in time for everything, sometimes it is difficult to be the best, but at least we all have an opportunity to live and be an example for our children. Also, I wish everyone on this planet to be harmonious with mind and soul, find calmness in someone you will love, and live your best life. Life is one and you will try to enjoy it in every possible way. I enjoy it with my family, my children and my husband.

My Life As A Woman: Mauritius Edition #1

I always thought my life was sort of ordinary. Not mediocre, but not extraordinary. However, when I take some time to look back at the past 33 years, it has been quite the journey. While I always considered myself a strong independent woman, I never realized how dependent I actually had become, being in a relationship for 12 years, doing the same job…talk about living deep inside my comfort zone. But then one day, life happened, and I left both my job and my partner of 12 years, and suddenly I truly started to understand what it meant to be an independent woman and mother in Mauritius. So, buckle up and let's ride (even if I still don't have my driving license, but that's another story!)

When I lost my father, a few months before I turned 18, taking care of the household was my only option, with a mother who had never worked in her entire life, and a teenage younger brother who had other priorities. Right after getting my HSC, I should have started going to University, but I decided to start working right away. Someone had to provide for the family after all. However, with a little push from my childhood friend, I still enrolled for a BSc in Communications Studies with Specialization in Journalism.

Remember when I said someone had to put food on the table? Well, I worked a night shift in a call center while being a part time student at the University of Mauritius. In a perfect world, I would have been juggling perfectly between the two, acing my classes and still having a social life. But this was not what happened. I missed classes and was sleep-deprived. But I refused to give up. Long story short, I stopped working night shift, my mother got a job and I made it through my last exam while being 6 months pregnant. And as soon as my daughter turned 6 months old, I got back to work.

To this day, looking at her motivates me every day. No matter how cliché it might sound, my daughter is my greatest source of inspiration, she keeps me going because I know I have to be a role model, I have to provide for her and support her dreams and aspirations. I don't only want her to have the life I never had, I want her to have the life she dreams of, and to achieve it on her own. Having to live on my own, pay rent and manage a whole budget on my own after relying on a partner for 12 years has been a real eye opener. And it has also made me realize that all the reasons that were holding me back were only based on fear.

No matter how happy and in love I was at first, at some point I knew I had to leave because the relationship wasn't meant to have a happily ever after. But, being a woman in Mauritius, I had so many doubts, so many apprehensions about what would happen next, what people would think of me, where to go, or if I could even afford to live on my own and still provide for my daughter. But guess what? To all the women out there who hesitate, who settle or who are unhappy, you can do it! One of the beauties of Mauritian culture is that people will help you! They will look out for you and make sure you don't fall apart. Also, you are much stronger and resilient than you think. Sometimes you just need a little push to get going, and from that point, you become unstoppable.

At some point, my life was a real financial mess. I was working 12 hours or more every day and still living paycheck to paycheck. It had to stop! I come from a family where 4 people had to share a bedroom. And even if we always had food on the table, I know just how many sacrifices my parents had to make. I know that sometimes we missed weddings my mother "didn't feel like attending" only because it would cost too much in terms of new clothes for everyone, transport, gift for the newlyweds, and so on. We never even traveled abroad as a family.

Meanwhile, I would look at my godmother, who has always been my greatest inspiration, and dream of having a life like hers. She started to travel around the world at the age of 17, she moved into a country where she had to learn a new language, and ended up learning five, but also raised two kids on her own, never complaining, never asking anyone for anything. And this is the woman I aspired to be, and hopefully am becoming.

Today, even if some days I still feel a little overwhelmed, I remember how far I've come: I love my job as a Web Editor/Copywriter, I got out of the financial mess I was engulfed in, and most of all, I have goals which I am slowly but surely achieving. And this is the woman I want my daughter to be one day.

My Life As A Woman: Mauritius Edition #2

I go by Misha as my pseudonym name. I am from Vieux Grand-Port, Mauritius. Mauritius is an independent tropical island situated in the Indian Ocean. I basically grew up in a village which is very much community-based. My country in itself is a multi-ethnic society, descended predominantly from Indians as well as from Africans, Chinese and European people. So, I am from a lineage of Indians that came to Mauritius for work back in the 1830s. Here is the story of a Mauritian woman who was raised in a middle-class family.

As a millennial, I have been part of both the 20th and the 21st century which has made me witness the struggles of my parents trying to climb up the social ladder. My biggest inspiration is my parents who have worked so hard to raise their kids. Be it about my father who had to give up his studies to work in a sugar cane field as a labourer to support my grandma or be it my mother who is a housewife never off duty. My biggest goal as a teenager was to become successful enough so that I could give my parents everything they had deprived themselves of just because they had to save money.

I never had a direction of what I exactly wanted to be as a kid, I only knew that I had to succeed anyhow. Other than jumping around and being a tomboy, I really loved to read books and I later developed a fascination in literature. I mainly studied literature in English and literature in French in high school. I then completed a BA English. That open two career doors for me, one was journalism and the other one teaching. And I decided to go with teaching as that made my parents happy and proud. I also see it as a noble job as when I had my training at the university, I had an opportunity to interact with students and I kind of knew that this is what I wanted to do, to provide help and guidance to kids. Currently, I am following a full-time post-graduate training course in teaching, so I have not been posted in a school yet. What I do for work is, I give tuitions to lower secondary students and I am a freelancer. The process that I went through to be what I am today is what I see as my success even if I have not reached my goals yet because every small step is bringing me closer to my goals. Every day is a struggle, overcoming small challenges every day are still small success stories that one should learn to appreciate.

I have been lucky that I grew up in a patriarchal family who believed that a woman should be independent but that does not mean that I am not facing prejudices. I love my culture because of its customs and traditions but very few of the Mauritian communities understand that a girl should be allowed to do whatever she wants without the fear of public scrutiny. It's always about what people will think about your upbringing if she is out walking with a boy or drinking alcohol or wearing short clothes. Even if my parents are supportive they are still very engrossed in the idea that a woman is 'wife material' when she knows how to do household chores, talk respectfully, willingness to marry and get pregnant at a 'reasonable' age and one who listens to male authority. There is a lot of pressure due to expectations of how a girl is supposed to be in society. As Asian parents, my mother and father always projected themselves as strict and I could not really talk to them about my insecurities as I would to a friend. There are hundreds of times when I wished I was comfortable enough to talk about heartbreaks and failures to them. There was a time when I faced depression because I felt I was not good enough, I was not going to succeed anywhere in life, and I started questioning my existence. In those times, I wished I could have communicated easily to them without the fear of facing judgements. I grew past that phase and realized that was the thought my parents were brought up with and it was not their fault. I should see the good side of it, appreciate their sacrifices and be forever thankful.

My advice to all the women out there, just be yourself and stay strong. Keep struggling and keep rooting for your dreams. Do not measure your progress to that of someone else's success. Most importantly never fear public scrutiny because people will always have something to say about you even when you are doing well in life. And keep believing in family bondage, they are the ones who truly care.

My Life As A Woman: Mexico Edition #1

Where am I from?

The first daughter of a married couple between 25 and 26 years old, almost the age I am now but in a totally different situation. I was born and raised in a small town in the state of Coahuila, this is in the North of Mexico. A small place with only about 800 inhabitants, and where all the people know each other. Walking down the street and saying good morning, good afternoon or good night was considered an act of kindness and good manners, I remember my parents saying to me: Say hello! Whenever you meet a person. At first, I found it hard to talk to older people, but little by little it became a good habit, a habit that remains to this day.

If you don't study you will work in the countryside

In this village, agriculture is the main job, most of the men work in some plot, growing melon, and watermelon during the months of May and June, and others grow tomato, onion, cucumber or chili. If you don't study, you'll go to the country and work! This was always a reality, few of the men and women showed interest in continuing with their studies, so finishing high school was already considered a great achievement, if you finished high school it was something very rare, not to mention a college career, but if you did not decide to follow this path, one would surely wait for you, the daily road from your home to the country for work.

I saw how some of my classmates stopped going to school and went to work instead. The salary in a field job is not much so the living conditions do not evolve much being in that environment. As was the custom, and still is in some parts of the country, I was raised mostly by my mother as she has been a woman totally dedicated to the home. While my father was away working my mother and I kept each other company and were our own family for a few years. Growing up in that town meant growing up with a series of traditions, customs, and even a certain stereotype marked by society.

Why did they do this or are they still doing this? "Because she is a woman, that's what women are for, to take care of the house, to have children and to take care of the husband".

Another Brick in the Wall

It seemed that nobody thought outside the box, many times I hear mothers telling their daughters, "find yourself a good husband", or "the day you have children you will know what it means to take care of them", or "learn to cook because when you get married you will have to do it". These comments were most common, what was not common was listening: I bought you a new book, we will save for you to go to college, study, travel, grow!

I must confess that I got to have those comments too, during my adolescence, and when I started my adulthood. I think my mother at first had that kind of thinking too, that is, she wanted me to get married and have children, but as I grew up she noticed a difference in me, and she has always supported me.

The weird girl

When I was in my teens and already in high school, my friends and I made that transition from childhood to adolescence and some things changed. The talks were already about makeup, 15th birthday parties, boyfriends and "bailes".

A "baile" is a party with live music that is usually held during a wedding or a quinceañera. Usually these events are public, and people can go to enjoy the music and dance. For the young people in this village this is a very common way of having fun.

My cousins and other girls would get together to put on makeup, look pretty and find a ride to the baile, usually this meant going with boys who would also attend. During the weekends when there was no "Dance", the usual thing for young people was, or still is, to meet up with friends and go for a walk, maybe drink and be there until the early hours of the morning.

- "Hey, come on, let's go to the baile, we're going to introduce you to a guy."

- "How is it possible that girls younger than you are already at bailes and you don't even go?"

These were some of their comments towards me, of course they said them as a joke, because for them I was the weird girl, who doesn't go to the bailes and prefers to stay at home, a weird and boring girl. With time, the relationship between my cousins and me was changing, we distanced ourselves until it seemed that we belonged to totally different worlds.

There were also comments from neighbors, aunts and other people in the village asking: when is the boyfriend due? Aren't you going to get married? By the time I was 18, I was in college and all my high school classmates were already starting a family. I honestly never worried about that. The last time I received a comment inviting me to find a boyfriend to become my husband was about 2 years ago. One of my aunts who I love very much always insisted on "introducing me to someone", she was very excited to see me with a couple and always took the character of Cupid, shared my cell phone number with the best prospects who she said were good for me: "Hey, this guy is very hardworking and he's single, I'll share your cell phone number so you can send messages and meet each other."

It was always a funny thing, of course I never accepted her proposals, and she stopped making these kinds of comments and realized how happy I have been living a life in my own way. The day I told her about my travels, my friends, my work and my plans for the future, she was as excited as I was, she congratulated me and gave me her support. If there was one thing I had been sure of since I was a child, it was that I did not want to follow the same path that all the girls in my village followed. Why should I?

There's a world inside books and magazines.

For my fortune, I was always a very dreamy person. While I was an only child, my only entertainment was playing by myself and inventing the characters, doing the different voices and creating imaginary scenarios. Many of my characters were cut out of magazines, of which we had quite a few at home. I liked to look at those magazines, I didn't know how to read yet but just looking at the images made me imagine many things, in them there were things that didn't exist in my environment and that helped me realize that there were other lifestyles.

I must say that television is also part of that, I'm not saying that is the best hobby but during my adolescence in my free time I was dedicated to watching movies, or some television programs. I remember Saturdays on Channel 7 (At that time cable television was not very common). I was looking forward to the announcements for weekend movies, if they were of my interest I watched them, and if I spent time being bored or doing something else, but there was not much to do so those were my options.

The typical American movie, where the teenager studied in high school, had friends, fell in love, went to parties, made trips to places whose name was not known and in the end everything was perfect, those were the movies I always saw, I must say that the stories were not my favorite. What I liked about those movies was what I saw in them: huge cities, forests, beaches, high schools, or universities. I saw how people moved to college and lived in groups, different types of food that I did not even know existed, all these things may sound very common to many people, but they were not common to me some years ago, and I'm sure there are many young people who are totally unaware of the world outside the usual environment.

All this that I saw in books, magazines, and movies made me want to live that kind of experience, it awakened in me the curiosity to explore what was out there by wanting to follow another path, and that's what happened.

I want to go to college.

I always liked school, maybe it sounds funny, but it was, I would rather get up early to go to school to see my friends, have fun than stay home bored and do nothing, in fact, weekends were not my favorite at that time.

I was a very dedicated student, I was always in first place and that made my parents proud, and my grandparents, they all saw me as a very smart girl, and I didn't even know what that word meant. I finished my high school and enrolled in a high school where I chose the specialty of Computer Science. High school was the most normal for me, I kept up my good grades and my circle of friends got smaller. I think I became more reserved, from middle school to high school, but that changed in college. College was one of the most beautiful stages of my life, and I would definitely go back there for all the experiences I had. My outlook grew and my ambition to learn more grew as well. It was a little different, but the important thing for me was that I was already living it, and I really enjoyed it. At that time I was one of the few people in my village who attended a university, some men had already done so, my friend Mary and I were the first women to do so.

Leaving home to follow a dream

To go to college I remember I had to get up at 4:30 am and take the bus at 5:30 am. I would leave my house accompanied by my mom who would drop me off at the station and wait with me until I was on the bus.

Then I had to leave my house and move to a new one that my father built, a because little house in the city, so going to college would be even easier. Living alone sounds exciting but it wasn't easy.

Leaving the state to follow a dream

An opportunity presented itself for me and I took it. I've always thought that opportunities don't come twice in a lifetime and you have to take them. At the company where I worked I was offered a new position, a position in a totally different environment, outside my city, and totally outside my comfort zone. That new job represented a very big challenge for me and also the opportunity to grow professionally and economically, so I accepted, with fear but accept, I remember that the next two nights I didn't sleep thinking about the "what am I going to do?.

For this new job I had to move again, this time to a town in the state of Chihuahua, I discussed it with my family and as always my parents supported me from the beginning: "Sometimes you have to make sacrifices to get the things you want." My dad's words of wisdom to me.

By March 2016 I was traveling with a group of 15 men and I was the only woman. To be accepted in an environment totally dominated by men and to become one of them. Being in that new job meant a total change in my life, I can say without a doubt that I left my comfort zone behind and entered a totally unknown area for me, and that was very exciting.

It was easy to make friends, very good friends that we still keep in touch to this day. I also knew the betrayal and the bad times were there too. My companions and I went from laughter to a cold silence when we heard about the death of companions. The risk was always present, and we knew what we were risking day by day. This new job was an area totally dominated by men, there were few women working there and even more, women who play a leadership role and with personnel management, that's what I had to be. The most difficult part was to be accepted by the other workers, honestly, in some areas in Mexico there is still that kind of ego or machismo in some people.

"How can a woman come and tell me what to do?"

"We are in charge here and things are going to be done as usual."

The atmosphere was hard, and I had to be strong, I knew I had to catch up with them and I did. Luckily, not all the workers were like that, other colleagues of mine always offered a hand to help, they were kind enough to teach me about the processes and even made me part of their teams. We created a family of employees, we spent Christmas together, the end of the year parties, birthdays, days and nights, and talks that made the long workdays a little more enjoyable and helped you forget a little about the stress of a hard day's work. In this job we were all away from the family, a place in the mountains where the work never ended.

During the year 2019 many things changed both professionally and personally, I felt that professionally I was growing and I would have a lot of future in the company that everyone told me, but something was happening, personally I was not satisfied, I had little time for myself and I also had other dreams which I wanted to fulfill. So I looked for other options, I proposed a date to quit my job: December 2019! And so I did.

Undoubtedly, being in this job has been one of the most representative experiences in my life, not only for professional growth but for personal growth, helped me create a strong person, which is not easy to knock down, gave me independence and above all helped me to value everything that really matters in my life, and helped me define what I want for my life and what I do not want to be.

By March 2019 I began to have other concerns, I was beginning to think about what I wanted to do for the next few years, where I wanted to be, what dreams I had to fulfill, all of this led me to dream, to dream again but also to work for those dreams.

My new wishes were:

- To go and live in another country, how would this happen? I do not know, but I did not want to stay with the desire to live the experience of living in another country.

- Learn the English language

- Getting a new job

- Study a master's degree at a good university.

- Get my personal life back.

- To have a balance between my profession, my dreams and my personal life.

Leaving my country following a dream.

Before I quit my old job, I was looking for job offers in other cities and even in other countries. I had nothing to lose so I sent my resume to several foreign companies, many of them didn't even want to answer, others said they didn't hire non-citizens and suddenly I received an email from a major telecommunication company saying they were interested in an interview.

They told me no.

The first interview I did in the English language, I understood and could speak some things in English but having an interview was something totally new and I felt very nervous. Obviously, I didn't get the job but that didn't make me feel bad, on the contrary it gave me hope that I could make it another time and continue studying the language and looking for a job.

Something that will always exist is the word "No", many opportunities will be denied but that should not stop you, after many "NO" you will find a "YES".

One day a job offer came to me that completely challenged my comfort zone, Here we go again! This new job was a totally new area for me, and in a new country, it was everything I was looking for and I accepted without hesitation.

I think my family is used to me being away all the time and this time it didn't surprise them to say: I'm going to the United States, again, I had all their support and I can say they feel the same emotion I do. I said goodbye to my family, my little nieces, my friends and my country, to go and fulfill another new dream. My inspiration.

The man with the newspapers and the books

Throughout my life, different people have been my inspiration, during my childhood I remember a lot, especially my maternal grandfather "Toto", which was my name for him. He was a hard-working, disciplined man, in love with books, history and writing, (I think that's where I inherited the taste for it).

Toto had quite a few notebooks that he used to write reviews of the days, the most important thing of each day was written there. If there was a new birth he would write down the date, name and parents of the baby, including details such as weight and height measurements. If he started a new job, he wrote that down too. As well as the purchases he made, if he made any changes to his bike, among many other things.

He was one of the first people to tell me: Lala (that's what he called me), study, read the books and study to become a teacher or a doctor. I was 14 years old when he passed away, I don't remember what we talked about before that happened, now I ask myself: How would a conversation with him be now, would he be proud of me?

My father's words

I practiced Taekwondo in high school and college, while watching the 2008 Olympics, my father and I, he asked:

- "When are you going to go there?"

- I just laughed and said, "yes and no".

To which he replied with a phrase that will stay in my mind forever, and that really helped me to trust, he said:

- "Why not? Hey, you can achieve everything you want as long as you set your mind to it."

At that time, I didn't understand that phrase very much, but now it is a very important memory for me. Study, prepare and never depend on anyone. But my greatest inspiration and main driving force has been my mother. I will always be grateful for the advice she gave me since I was a child: "study, get ready to be someone in life, so you can have a better lifestyle and never depend on anyone". Their support and education have been essential for me to grow up.

Me actually.

I live in the United States and I am dedicated to developing mobile applications, apart from that I have another vocation focused on copywriting, I provide writing services for different clients. I have worked with people from many countries, Australia, Germany, Spain, Canada, Costa Rica, Switzerland, Mexico obviously, and some other countries, writing for me is a hobby and I turned it into a part-time job which I enjoy a lot. Previously, I created other businesses that I plan to retake and my digital marketing agency is also on the list.

I have had the experiences I wanted, met wonderful places and people, I am very happy with what I have achieved, and I can say that I am currently living another of my dreams, of course this does not end here, we must continue to work for new goals.

Advice to other women

- Trust yourself, if you trust yourself I am sure you will achieve everything you set out to do, this advice was given to me and has become my life's motto, and now I share it with you.

- Don't forget your dreams, we are all dreamers but when we grow up many people forget them,

- There are no unattainable dreams, everything can be achieved.

- Things are not easy, the pink world does not exist, you will have to face different obstacles but each one of them will be worth it.

- Do not give up, even the smallest effort is a great advance.

- You are stronger than you think.

- It is also worth falling, crying, have bad moments, those also make people strong.

- Respect yourself, give yourself respect and also respect others.

- Break the stereotypes, you have every right to decide what you want to do with your life, life is only one so live it doing what makes you happy. Create your own path, you do not have to follow the path of others.

I want to be like you.

I have two beautiful little nieces, one is 2 years old and the other is 5 years old, the oldest is obviously the one with whom I have created the most bond. We have a relationship not only from aunt to niece but from friend to friend, I was very surprised one day when she told me:

"I want to be like you, I want to work like you on the computer, I want to drive like you, I want to travel by plane like you."

And that made me think: Am I going to be a good example for her?

Well I don't know. What I do know for sure is that I want her to achieve everything she sets out to do, she and all the people who read this experience, change happens trust me, it's up to you.

My Life As A Woman: Mexico Edition #2

Like the rest of the world, we fight every day. Sometimes we are mothers from an early age. And others, we have to be father and mother at the same time, in a country where the rates of violence and insecurity are high. However, it is a country with people who work hard. We are not afraid to try new experiences. We just want to grow.

I grew up in a "Green place"

I grew up in the tropics of Mexico. It is located in the southeast of this huge country. The current population is around two million habitants. Unlike northern Mexico. Here, economic development is slower. Although the nation's oil is located in the Gulf of Mexico. Everything is exported to the north. However, I can assure you that where we were born, we are fortunate.

You will never see the same landscape when you see the state of Tabasco from an airplane. The surfaces are covered with trees, and we have 80% of the country's fresh water. In conclusion, at the place where I was born, we have natural resources. Wherever you look, there are trees everywhere. The landscape in Tabasco is green.

Tabasco is sunny, right now as I write, we have a temperature of 40 degrees. I grew up studying, because it is an opportunity that not everyone has.

My mother gave birth when she was 21 years old. My father was 26 years old at the time. I am currently 26 years old. When I was little I used to go to a public elementary school near my house. I grew up in a quiet neighborhood, 10 minutes from the capital.

6 years passed. And I did middle school and high school. I grew up wanting to study the most difficult subjects. But, finally, I decided to study communication at the Public University of Tabasco, it is called UJAT.

My father used to tell me, "Study what you want, if that makes you happy, you will find success." The reality is that now women go out to the labor field more than before. And I had the opportunity to prepare myself to be able to work professionally.

Here in Mexico we have access to education, however, there is a high dropout rate due to factors such as poverty. The positive part is that we learn to work from a very young age. That way we can pay for our studies. In many cases. Our parents do their best to get us to school. Either way, that forges a character in each person, facing difficult times with the best face from a very young age.

Inspiration was born with confidence and freedom

My father gave me the freedom to make my own decisions, make mistakes, and learn. As for my education, he never said no. He inspired me to prepare professionally. I think I was always excited to have his approval to let me study. I was always a good student. At the end, when I turned 20, I told him I wanted to go to Europe for an exchange. And he said "yes". The key to my inspiration is him because I fully trust myself. And it gave me real freedom.

My dream was to be on a television set

Studying communication has been one of the best experiences in my life. I know that in Mexico it is a high risk race. Specifically, journalism. However, there is much to tell about Mexico, the passion of its people, the daily events, the way they react and how they face tragedies.

During my university studies, I specialized in journalism. I learned to write and practice in one of the most widely circulated newspapers in Tabasco.

I made a two-month research stay in Guadalajara, Jalisco, Mexico. The researcher worked on Latin American studies and the latest free trade agreements. That gave me a more global vision of Mexico's relationship with the world. In the last semester of my career, I managed to be in a television studio. That was my first professional experience.

Three different views on being a reporter

In Mexico people are hardworking. To get my first job, I decided to give my professional practices, on TV Azteca, it is one of the two most important television stations in Mexico. I did it, I was a reporter and television host for two years. Later, the Government of Tabasco hired me as an official reporter for the state to write and report through official bulletins. Currently, I am getting to know one of the noblest sides of being a reporter. I returned to my university, UJAT, to be a reporter for educational, academic, cultural and scientific events.

In conclusion, my first job was in a commercial medium, then I learned about the world of politics and later, I am in an educational communication medium.

Mexico: a hectic life, with flavor and joy

People here, scream, and we don't realize it. When I was on a bus from Europe, it seemed to me that everything was silent. Here all the time it is about talking. We always have new jokes. And we have a special code to laugh at ourselves. The Mexican can be everything, except a quiet being. As I said, what I love about Mexico are its incredible contrasts from north to south. We have 32 states in total. The magnificent thing is that each one has at least one dance and a traditional meal. Knowing each state of Mexico is a unique experience. Wherever you go, you will never miss a very spicy sauce and a taco stand on the street.

People in Mexico love beer and partying. They love competitions, and soccer. And they like to have lots of friends. I love from Mexico that disturbing daily crowd on the streets, the noise, the burning sun, the music, and of course, any Mexican cannot live without their food. There are more delicious dishes besides tacos.

We have a strong identity for our ancestors. It is a mystical culture that teaches us that we had a great empire and many cultures before the arrival of the Spanish. Mexico is a rich land, our gods described the treasures they had. Today, we maintain a unique identity throughout the world.

The daily struggle of women in Mexico

The biggest fight is deciding when to be a mother ?, here in Mexico the culture marks that you must be a mother before 30. Today we are winning that fight, to say when to be mothers, decide to work and be able to share household chores with men.

Also, the way we women dress is a problem. My constant struggle has been not to go out at night, much less with very low-cut clothes. Men don't measure up to look at you and throw compliments at you. Walking alone, as a woman, is not a good option here. That is a fight that we have not yet won.

Visualize your dreams

My greatest success is being able to choose what I want to be in a country with few opportunities and still achieve every professional goal that I have wanted. My father told me that who is good at something will be everywhere. And I have been able to perform as a professional in the world of communication in a state that has second place in unemployment. That means I have found my personal success in the midst of many difficulties. Whenever you set your mind to it, you can do it.

Living alone in another country with a culture very different from yours is a successful experience that every young person should live. Living away from it all helps you find yourself.

Difficulties cannot limit you

My message to all women in the world is that we can always overcome obstacles. There are places where there is more peace and health, they are lucky places. We must take advantage of the dreamy mind that women have to dream big, beyond having a home (something very good) but also dreaming that they would not make us happy in this world anymore. Fight for it, despite the difficulties, whoever seeks, finds a way to achieve it.

My Life As A Woman: Moldova Edition #1

My story is probably atypical, but it is typical for the country I am from – the Republic of Moldova. The Republic of Moldova is a very tiny country, sandwiched among Romania and Ukraine. It is a picturesque country, without access to mountains or sea, but with beautiful rural landscapes and many forests. Many know it for the high-quality wines we produce and export all-over the world, others know it for the very difficult history we have had, being situated in-between two great geopolitical powers: the European Union and the Russian Federation. Consequences of the being annexed by one country or the other for a long time has determined us to be a country with difficulties in keeping united, who manage to get in conflict with our own kind because of the language spoken or the views we have about the past and the future. Probably, this division of views is common for many other countries, however to me it seems like a distinctive feature for mine. My country is beautiful, however the difficult history and the lack of a people-oriented leadership has determined many people to emigrate, about 1/3 of the population to be precise.

My story starts with this: emigration. I was 3 years old when my mother and my father decided to try their luck and create a new life somewhere abroad, somewhere better, where the authorities think about the people that got them elected. Because at the point Italy was on the list of countries where it was relatively easy to emigrate, they have decided to take that destination. They left me with my grandmother, an extraordinarily kind woman, who grew me up for two years in the countryside. I had as friends a cow, a cat and a dog, I helped feed geese and chickens, I played with the other kids in the village. A village of which, nowadays, remain some tens of houses standing and even fewer people inhabiting them. I was a happy child who didn't feel like anything was missing. What could a four years old girl understand of this anyways? When I was almost five, my parents, who in the meantime had managed to find work and rent a place to live in a remote Italian village, have decided that they cannot bear the distance anymore. They managed to raise enough money to make me documents and pay for the travel and came back to Moldova and took me to Italy.

This is probably the moment in which my destiny parts from the one of many other children of my country, whose parents didn't have the means to bring their children with them. Those children who have been raised by their grandparents, hearing from their mothers and fathers only once in few weeks by phone and, lately, seeing them once a week through Skype conferences.

I have lived in Italy, in a democratic society, being privileged by the fact I had a natural inclination towards learning languages, a quick mind and a very European look. I have spent there 8 years and a half, without even visiting my country, without thinking about it, except for geography classes when I was seeing it in the atlas. I had lost completely the Romanian language, a language that I didn't even know in the end, because how well can a 5 years old child know a language? In 2009 in Moldova there has been a revolution. The people in the country were tired of fraudulent elections, of the same people winning even if everybody was voting for a different path. And they all went out in the streets, in the center of the capital, protesting. Protesting hard. For a European future. Nobody knows the truth about how the violent acts during the protest started, both from the police, and from the protesters. What I know is that we were watching the news on YouTube, as there was no other source to check them, and seeing people shouting and screaming, violent clashes, the Parliament building half destroyed, the Presidential building as well. And then, silence. The revolution was over, the European path was decided, and my mother had decided that she'd had enough of feeling like a foreigner in Italy. My parents had already divorced at that point, so she asked me if I wanted to go back to Moldova, and I said yes.

And here, my path becomes completely different from that of any child from this country, as many have been left by their parents to the care of their grandparents, other have been brought by their parents to foreign countries, for a better life. But an extremely small, microscopic number of children and parents, after having created a life abroad, have decided consciously to come back and settle in.

When we came back, I didn't know my native language. I couldn't read it, nor speak it. I could understand most of the words. I started speaking it after a few days, but nobody could understand a word of what I was saying. My essays in school were all red of correctios, Italian words which had slipped in my Romanian writings. I was feeling like a foreigner in my own country. I still do sometimes.

Somehow I went on through life. The first years in Moldova I cannot recall anything except the uneasiness of living in a country which I did not understand, with conflicts everywhere, with regions where there was no water in the houses and toilets had to be improvised outside. But also with limousines, like the ones I was seeing in Hollywood movies, with Porsches and Ferraris, which I had never seen in Italy, but I could see here. All of them running on streets so full of holes that you needed to be careful not to chop off your tongue accidentally while talking. A country with women so beautiful, wearing skirts, dresses and stilettoes, but where if you walk outdoors for more than 50 meters in high heels, you risk breaking your neck. A country where, in the public transportation, there is still a person employed to come and pick up your ticket, a person payed miserably to do a difficult job, but who (if it is a woman) will surely have astonishingly long nails, in the latest gel manicure trend.

Growing up, of course, I observed some of these absurdities, but didn't really process them. I didn't have a purpose in life. The first ambitions I had, becoming a Chef, and then becoming a doctor (neurosurgeon or heart surgeon to be precise) had joyfully been smashed down by my lack of cooking skills (which even I could observe) and the light-hearted remarks of my parents regarding the impossibility, in their view, of me becoming a doctor. Therefore, I didn't have a purpose in life, a career in mind. But growing up and getting involved in volunteering projects, I started to observe and analyze more and more the inequalities I had been seeing from the beginning. And thinking about what I could do to make them disappear. This is how I ended up volunteering, at the age of 17, for an international charity based in Chisinau. Soon after, I managed to get hired, and have worked my way up to the point where I could grow no more. I have spent five years in this charity, working to improve the access of terminally ill people to professional medical, social and psychological assistance. Paradoxically, I ended up working with doctors, without being one. Raising funds for the development of palliative care services has been my purpose and it could have been still, if it wasn't for the global COVID pandemic which has affected my country as well. I have lost my job, as many others in the country, but I have been lucky enough to find another path to take, and I have been working for a while now in monitoring the activity of the local public authorities and making it their decisions, proposals and so on, more accessible for the people who live in the capital. In the meantime, I have been working also in the cultural field and doing freelance work online.

If there is one thing that I have learned until now, one principle that I follow, is that we are all alone in this world. That yes, parents exist, and friends exist, lovers and maybe later – children. But, in the end, it is all up to yourself. Counting on others to solve your problems of help you in moments of struggle is not only a privilege, but also a limitation, as it impedes you to puts your brains into motion and solve the problems by yourself. However, it comes with a great price – loneliness. And, in the end, it is up to each one apart to make this decision.

My Life As A Woman: Moldova Edition #2

To talk about life from a feminine perspective in the country of Moldova, a certain person has come forth while wishing to keep their identity anonymous.

"Being 30 years of age, I was born and raised in the heat of Chisinau, Moldova. I am the only child in the family so having a brother or a sister remained only a dream. Since the very beginning, I was always interested in doing something out of the norm. I demanded more from life and also from myself. Therefore, I started to go to a dance school when I got 3 years old. I began to love dancing. It could've been my profession today because I danced for more than 10 years and learnt different styles and really dug deep in the methodology of dancing. Couldn't pursue it as a career though. Anyways, I later went to a school of art where I learnt to play piano."

Over time, she started developing an interest for crafts like floristry, embroidery, crochet, toymaking and drawing and she learnt doing all these after school hours and on the weekends.

"After graduating, I studied Economics at the university. My specialty, however, became Tourism. As time passed, I realized I've loved travelling more than ever. I also know that deep inside, I'm great at my job and I feel confident in this.", she says.

Our woman from Moldova speaks several languages. She's fluent in Romanian, Russian, English, Swedish, Ukrainian and at a basic level in Italian.

For the past 6 years, she's been working for Swedish companies. The first 5 years belonged to a Swedish call center in Chisinau and after this job, she moved to Sweden herself for one year. "I worked with some kind of dispatch, planner of trips and also worked as a customer support representative.", she says.

Moving on towards the feel of life itself, she describes her personal experience. She says, "Now that I'm living back in Moldova after all this time working abroad, I understand how much I love my country. Although there was nothing to complain about in Sweden, it just didn't have that ring to it. To me, home is where you're born and where your family is."

During the last 10 years, she has travelled around the world whenever she had the chance because according to her, "Discovering different cultures and different places is pure happiness". Speaking of culture, she says that her country is amazing. "Perhaps, it may be far from perfect but, I love the nature Moldova has to offer. One thing's guaranteed that I've never ate such succulent and mouth-watering fruits and vegetables anywhere else than Moldova. I love how we dance and I adore how we sing our songs. Our unique meals are an absolute treat and our traditions are a breath of fresh air. But what I love most about my country is that special feeling of freedom that you don't feel elsewhere. It may be because of other places' busy schedules, restrictions or plenty of rules and regulations. I can't say for sure how but the feeling here is unparalleled."

Growing up, she always wanted to help people in one way or the other. That's exactly what she does now as she's always worked in the service department of different companies.

The Inspiration

"Definitely, my grandma.", when asked who inspired her. To quote the Moldovan, "She was an exceptional woman. A mother of six, insanely strong and nothing but a sweetheart. She was the living embodiment of hard work and at the same time, she was a perfect housewife and a good mother. That's why I called her exceptional because she was the jack of all trades. The person who went through war and   hunger   but   never   gave   up."

To talk about struggles, she says that life itself is a struggle but she tries to focus on herself. Sometimes, she struggles with her laziness which is perfectly humane. She specifically talks about those moments where she doesn't want to do anything but she has to. She says, "I've struggled to assert myself as an entity at work where a woman is usually at a disadvantage compared to a man. I've always felt the need to be better and do better than the men around me to prove that a woman is sometimes even stronger. I try to do my best because I'm a perfectionist and by nature, that's a struggle all in itself. To speak in general, I try to do as much as I can because I always had the feeling that life is too short."

"My success?", she asks thoughtfully, "I really don't know. Maybe, it's a success not to have enemies. At least, not the type that despise me. Perhaps, it's a success that I'm able to sleep at night with the door open or take a walk at midnight without the sense of insecurity. I'm the one blessed with the ability to behave decently and adapt to rapidly changing conditions in an instant. I'm also proud that I'm able to earn money, manage my budget. That's what makes me independent and free. I guess I can call this success. Moreover, the fact that I can keep myself in good physical shape despite of my busy schedule is something I treasure as well."

She addresses the women of Moldova in the following way, "Dear women, each and every single one of you is unique in your own way of being. Therefore, I urge you to believe in your own strength, to keep getting up no matter how many times life puts you down. More importantly, dream. Dream and always do more than what you think you can to achieve your goals because take it from me, you can never know if you'll wake up tomorrow. Think positive and don't be afraid to fail. There are only two outcomes to every endeavor, you either win or you learn."

This concludes the life experience of the fascinating woman from Moldova.

My Life As A Woman: Transnistria Edition #1

Hi, my name is Natalie H. I am originally from Transnistria, I was born and still live here. I grew up in a small town Bender, which is located on the western bank of the river Dniester and used to be a river port. My first and the brightest childhood memory is our nice tradition to visit Dniester beach with my parents. I was the youngest in the family and I also have an elder brother. All my childhood, my parents were traveling and having a very active way of life. They traveled all over the Baltic states and I joined them first time when I was 6 years old in their trip to Lviv, Ukraine. But then the dissolution of the Soviet Union happened and of course all our family travels were over.

My parents always inspired me: they always preferred a healthy life style, they were into healthy food and yoga even before it became mainstream. I still have some yoga tutorial books of that time. Our house was always full of books, because my father had a huge book collection and it wasn't just fiction literature, but scientific literature too. We had books on Psychology, Philosophy, Religion and World Art Culture. In this way, my parents inspired me to read a lot, to research and discover something new and exciting. My most favourite book of that time was "Myths of Ancient Greece".

Other role models were my grandmother and grandfather from my mother side. Grandmother lost her entire family in World War II and so she became an orphan. They were purely self-made people with my Grandfather. Both were originally from very small villages, but managed to move to the town, where they had been noble workers at the factory and had a very active social position. Grandmother also became an MP. So I had examples of my mother and grandmother, who are the strongest women, who could overcome any difficulties for the sake of their children and stay positive and harmonious at the same time!

Thanks to my childhood family atmosphere I grew up being very interested in literature and languages, especially English language. My passion about English language started from "The Lord of Rings" by J. R. R. Tolkien and some TV shows such as "Twin Peaks" American TV series for example. I was very excited to read my favourite books and watch favourite movies and shows in their original language - English. Later I became a student at university in the philological department, where my main three subjects were Literature, Russian language and English language.

Literature and Russian language were always a great source of beauty, wisdom, depth, which helps me to move forward, analyse this world with curiosity and appreciate it even more! On a daily basis, it inspires me now to read books and tell fairy-tales to my little daughters!

English language was my preference and the most favourable subject. So, after graduation I worked 3 years as a teacher at the university and primary school, but as soon as I got the possibility, I changed my job to Russian/English translator at a garment and textile factory. It was a precious and happy experience for me, and it gave me an opportunity to travel the world a little, because we had some abroad trips to work meetings and exhibitions.

What do I love about our culture? Well, we are people of sunny South country and South people have always sunny souls - they are always open-minded, hospitable, welcoming to everyone and if you come to the house they will always greet you with a table generously full of delicious home cooked meals!

I know that our citizens of Transnistria are extremely strong people, because they overcome difficulties everyday which they face as citizens of a mostly unrecognised country. Frankly speaking, people here are survivors and fighters due to local life circumstances, but at the same time they are always ready to help others and always extremely optimistic people.

What do I do for life now? I am a house wife at the moment and stay home with kids (3 and 7 year old daughters). Of course, I am fully involved in parenting and do my best to pass to my girls all traditions of my family and to make them strong and happy as my mother, grandmother and me.

I am into photography and the main motivation to start it was the birth of my kids. I wanted to catch each and every happy moment of their life and to have precious memories in various photos. And very soon it became my second profession.

Talking about my struggles, I can confess that it's not easy to find time for self-development and constantly grow in profession when you have two small kids. Because kids are always a priority and so you always have less time for yourself, but I always try my best. I don't think I have any other struggles in Transnistria.

Talking about my successes, I can say that I value and highly appreciate our happy family – with an always supportive, loving and understanding husband and our lovely daughters. As for professional achievements I have some achievements in both areas of my interests. As a photographer, I was published multiple times in the Ukrainian fashion magazine and I also have 20 million views at free stock photos platform Pexels and my photos from this site are published and appreciated all over the world every day. As a freelance English/Russian translator, I completed the translation of one science fiction book for a Ukrainian writer.

My advice to women from a woman living in Transnistria is simple - please never give up, achieve what you want in spite of any difficulties. If life gives a woman a problem, she must consider it as a lesson what will only make her stronger, wiser, better and more experienced and she will solve this problem as a real winner! Even if right now you feel like you are giving up, just remember: "The night is darkest before the dawn!" Just be grateful and happy and try to find harmony and inner peace within yourself and your family and be an example for your kids.

I believe that woman power can achieve everything in this world! And I wish you all to be happy and positive and best of luck in following your dreams!

Regards,

Natalie

My Life As A Woman: Transnistria Edition #2

I grew up in a small and picturesque country Transnistria, in town Bender as a very happy and loved by parents and grandparent. We had a big family house with a garden full of different types of tasty berries, fruits, vegetables and also pets kittens, puppies, ducklings and chickens. It was a child paradise in a way! My favourite game was to play in "traveling and adventures" exploring our garden or to read my favourite books, comfortably siting at my favourite big apricot tree. But in 1992 everything had changed - crucial war came into our country... it was a war between Transnistria and Moldova for independence in 1992. I was 10 years old then and saw everything with my own eyes... a military tank was standing directly opposite our house and its barrel was aimed at our window! My life and all my family were in real danger!

Very soon we lost our house, it was totally exploded and ruined, and nothing left.... war finished in a few months and the government gave us a new apartment. But we had nothing left, and my parents were divorced till that moment already, so my Mom started a new life with me and Granny from the very beginning. She was always my hero and role model. In the difficult 90s, she managed to feed me and take care about me with a salary of 13 dollars per month - it was difficult times for all countries of post-Soviet Union. And she managed everything in such a way that I never felt I was missing something. I continued being totally happy, positive and a life-loving child because it is how she behaved too, and I saw this example in my family every day!

Right after the war I entered the best school in Bender, Lyceum. As you remember I loved reading and literature from the very beginning, so I chose the humanitarian department, where main subjects were languages and literature and I enjoyed this a lot! But I was bullied at school right after war - even by mine so called "friends". We lost everything, I was considered "poor" and used to wear clothes from charity what the government provided for us in a parcels from abroad or clothes what granny sewed for me with a greatest talent from old clothes. Also I was super skinny, and they laughed at it too and my most cherished dream was to gain weight. As you can guess in all these circumstances, I didn't favour myself a lot... let's face the truth - opinion of friends or classmates of same age can be more appreciated by kids than opinion of loving and supportive parents. So I gave up and felt myself not attractive, not beautiful and I was very sad that classmates were treating me like this. Looking back I can say that in reality, I was just slim, usual shy, and humble girl, who was surrounded by books much more usual than with friends and school parties and nothing was wrong with this. But it was a long way ahead for me before I learned to love myself!

Mom and Granny always supported me, and they kept being best and my most positive friends with the wisest advice! It was Mom who gave me the idea to concentrate on the English language, because it would be very appreciated in the future. It's Mom who tried her best to buy for me many precious English books and to make me passionate about the English language. As a result, languages and literature had been always exciting and very easy subjects for me at school, in university and throughout all my life. On top of it my both school and university languages and literature teachers were just geniuses in what they did and loved their subjects with all their souls, and they were another inspirations and role models for me! When people have so much passion in what they do - I naturally responded to them with the same kind of passion and highly motivated them to learn their subject really well! Mom dreamed of me being an English/Russian translator and I wanted to be that as well, but I had no idea where I could find such job in my small town and country.

My second inspiration was "Twin Peaks" TV series - this USA TV show was out of this world in the 90s... I was inspired and in love with each and every character and artist from that show and created a lot of diaries and fandom handmade books, carefully gathering articles about this topic. I was dreaming to speak English languages as perfect as THEM - my star American artists!

I entered the University without need to pass any exams, because I was a winner of the Republic Literature Olympics contest. I was tired of being invisible and I started to "build myself". Once again, I have chosen philological department with English language, Russian language, and Literature specialty. My teachers were perfect, subject were various and interesting. I met so many new people, had good and bad experiences with them, but I was much stronger than at school and just learned my lesson from these situations. I began to learn how to love myself, celebrated life with an open soul, coloured my hair in new bright shades every month, and visited all student parties and felt myself like a star there!

After 5 years I graduated from university and worked in a few schools as a teacher of English language. It wasn't what I want frankly speaking: I felt more as a friend than a teacher for children who had just a few years age difference with me. I needed to work at school in my country for 3 years - it was a government rule for those who studied in university for free. So, being a teacher, I kept my dream of becoming an English/Russian translator. And suddenly me the most cherished dream came true!

One translation company from the capital of Moldova Kishinev were trying to open their experiment department in my city - just to check how it would go, and they were looking for translators and interpreters. And you know what? I was scared like crazy, because my English level was just intermediate, but I pushed myself to go for it and not to lose my chance! I applied and was accepted immediately! It was one of the happiest days of my life! Company bosses brought super old equipment. It was 2006 and I used to get internet access only visiting internet clubs and it was unusual to have your personal computer, so even those old computers felt like a luxury. Our office was in the oldest hotel in the town, but the way from my home to that office was a paradise for me, because it was my dream job, where I could fully use my creativity and passion about the English language and constant communication with people! In two years, my boss offered me with the opportunity to open my own department in a neighbour city Tiraspol, and of course, we did this! I had my office now and great team and we brought lots of good results to clients!

Since 2008 I started to participate in creative photo shoots as a model and photographer. Everything was for free - just as a hobby. Modelling businesses don't exist in Transnistria at all, but at the same time you can find lots of brilliant photographers, make-up artists, and beautiful girls as models. In a small town and small country where lots of things are missing, you must entertain yourself with your own creative ideas and projects, that's what we do there!

Also after finding my dream job, I got more possibilities and I immediately started traveling. My first trips were to Ukraine, Russia and Turkey. My best friend and classmate got married in Istanbul and invited me to visit her and stay at her house. In one of these trips, I found the love of my life, my future husband. He was a foreigner, an Indian man from London, UK and that's where all my English speaking experience was useful. One year later we married and I moved to London. For the moment we raise our one-and-a-half year old son, I am a housewife and also shoot product photography and video for my friends and friends of our friends.

Also if you remember I was simply addicted to "Twin Peaks" American series in 1993-95 when I was a child, so in 2017, a third season of these series was out on TV, which was actively discussed in Internet and Instagram. I started my Instagram account about "Twin Peaks" - I had a lot to tell! And after that I was very soon noticed by almost all the artists from this show and was lucky to communicate with 90% of them! With some of them I became good friends on Instagram and we still communicate in direct messages, others I was lucky to meet and hug in Twin Peaks UK Festivals, which took place in London, and with one young actor from season 3 we became the greatest friends and he visited our "Twin Peaks" home parties with fans of the show. Who could tell that a 10-12 year old girl from Transnistria, who just lost her house, that her dreams would come true and stars will become so close in her life?!

What do I love about the culture of my home country? Transnistria is very beautiful! Her nature is a real enjoyment for the eyes, it's very green, clean, and full of colours. The climate is Southern and amazing - we have a proper four seasons and summer is pleasantly hot and welcoming to the local river beaches. Food is tasty, natural and home produced. Citizens are beautiful inside and outside and positive. What is not to love about this country?! In such atmosphere, most of the people are gifted to appreciate and enjoy the simple things around them. Yes, maybe we are one of the poorest countries comparing to Europe, we don't have much, we have only one theatre in our country, just one cinema in my entire town and a very difficult economic situation, but this teaches people to be creative and find new exciting activities and hobbies.

We can appreciate the beauty of flower, a cup of coffee in cafe early morning, a walk with friends and - in my case - when with this talent you move to another, much bigger country, you are over the moon!

But I would have never left Transnistria if it wasn't for the love of my life! I was quite stressed and depressed to start my life in a totally new country at 33 years old. I left my Mom, all my friends, my 10 years of friendship with theatre, my amazing job and my own apartment, what my Granny gifted me long ago. And all for LOVE! It was not easy at the beginning, but by now, I love London with all my heart and it's my second home. And when I am looking in the most beautiful, kind, wise and understanding eyes of my son, whose eyes are the colour of coffee, as his Indian father and hair is blond and curly as his Russian Mom and heart more golden that any of us - I know all my sacrifices were worthy!

We try our best to visit Transnistria every year and in 10 days, we are going to be there, and I can't wait my 14 days quarantine in Moldova with my Mom, husband and baby son! Even Mom, who is always the wisest woman accepts the fact that it's better to be far from her, but happy in family life - with loving husband and kids, then to stay in Transnistria and always alone. Why alone? Because I know 100% there is no man for me in my home country. The difference between our local men and most of the foreign men are huge. Our Transnistrian men are a bit spoiled, because they are very over numbered with amazing girls and women. They have too much choice in finding partners and unfortunately this doesn't make them trustworthy enough. Also they like psychological games - if you like man, you absolutely must not tell or show this to him, otherwise he will lose his interest immediately. If you run away from him and he is interested in you - he will most likely chase you. It's funny enough, but for me it was not funny.

I am a very simple person with an open soul. I was just enable to play. If I like the person - I want to scream about it all over the world! If I don't like - I will not be able to hide this fact, either. I think that most of foreign men psychology is much more straightforward, where YES is YES and NO is NO and that makes things clearer and more honest and life easier and that's perfect for me! I think it was only a struggle for me in Transnistria and it was a really huge struggle. Because I love being a woman, I really enjoy of achieving my career goals, but at the same time I am very family-oriented and loving, a family and child is a main happiness for me. And many women in Transnistria can't find a good man to create a family, just because there is not enough men there and those who left are not suitable to them. I would sincerely advise to all Transnistrian women to make their search of love and happiness wider and not be afraid of looking for abroad too! It's not easy to leave your comfort zone, but it's much better to act and to give yourself a chance to have a really happy and full-of-love life than to be afraid to make a step and keep complaining and be unhappy year after year. You can't find your love, just keep sitting at the home sofa, you better act! As I always tell everyone: "You can find your love anywhere - may be next door, may be in the other part of the world. There was nothing next door for me, so I preferred the second option."

As you understood one of my biggest life successes was my family. I am married to the best man in the world and we have best son in the world. Even our surnames, with my husband before marriage were similar - my maiden Russian surname is totally the same as his Indian one, but with a Russian ending. It was definitely destiny, which I found just because I got out of my comfort zone and enjoy of achieving my life goals and dreams!

My second main success in life is my attitude toward life. I just adore life and this love is mutual! I am happy most of the time and totally thankful for good events in my life and treat bad events as useful life lessons and important experiences. My life is full of amazing surprises and luck. There are lots of psychological books such as "The Secret" which teach you how to be thankful, how to stay positive, how to become happy. For me it came naturally, it's in my blood and it's a family tradition, my Grandmother was full of life and humour and my Mom is the same. I am very blessed to have these qualities and it gives me the possibility to have everything that I want in this life - just be positive and work hard and dedicated. I never worked in my life at boring jobs, because I try my best to choose only those jobs, what will be my real passions. So, as soon as our son Amir is old enough - I will continue my carrier as a photographer, make-up artist and model - all in my most positive 38 years old.

And I would advise all women to love life and themselves, never give up, be positive and thankful and just go for it! - for any life adventure and take a chance on what you suppose can make you happy in the future! Yes, it's like a jumping in unknown cold water, but you can suddenly find out that you are perfect swimmer after all! I wish you all real happiness, love and best of luck in everything!

My Life As A Woman: Monaco Edition

The author has been verified and the story is authentic.

Princess Charlotte Casiraghi of Monaco – My story

Being a celebrity is not easy; everyone knows something about you. People have said a lot about me, my family and my life. However, today I will share my story. I was born in a Royal family in Monaco, and you can imagine the pressure that comes with all that popularity from a young age. Everyone wants to know every bit of my life. Here is my life story;

My childhood

I was born in Princess Grace Hospital Centre on 3rd August 1986, in Monaco Mediterranean Principality. My dad is the famous Italian industrialist and speedboat racer, Stefano Casiraghi. I have two amazing and supportive brothers Pierre and Andrea. After my birth, I was christened in accordance with the Roman Catholic traditions and named after my great-grandmother Princess Charlotte, the mother of the Rainier III.

Unfortunately, my father passed on when I was only four years old after he was involved in a powerboat racing accident on 3rd October 1990. I came to know much about my dad later. I was too young to understand what was going on when he passed on.

Nevertheless, my mother Caroline or the princess of Hanover moved all of us to the Midi village in Saint-Remy-de-province, still in France. A move that she said was to protect us from the Media that was too interested in covering our story after the incidence.

Education

My childhood education started at the age of two to six years in Les Dames de Saint Maur,' which is part of the Catholic schools of 'François d'assisi Nicolas Barré' in Monaco. Then I was taken to the state school education system at École de la République,' Saint-Rémy-de-Provence.

Later after doing well, in my "baccalaureate" exams, I enrolled in the University of Paris IV and graduated with a bachelor's degree in Philosophy in 2007. I then pursued my internship at the Robert Laffont publishing house and "The Independent London".

My career life

My career life could be very interesting. I have moved from my profession to doing publications and even tried my luck in the fashion industry as well. My first job was in a publication firm where I was a writer and editor for "The Independent" Sunday magazine after my graduation and joined "AnOther Magazine" in January 2008. My passion for fashion also pushed me to start my annual ecological and fashion journal known as (Ever Manifesto). In 2009, I published 3,000 copies of the magazine to support sustainability in the fashion industry, a project that I'm proud of to date. I have worked with FXB France, a non-government organization that has been helping the state to alleviate poverty and AIDS.

I'm currently working on an upcoming film that might be released later this year. The movie has a fantastic story, motivated by the "Our Lady of the Nile" book that was published in 2012. I wouldn't say I like talking much about my private life, but I'm married to famous film producer Dimitri Rassam. He's a supportive and loving husband, and he's really helpful in my upcoming film project.

My last say;

I believe anyone can achieve anything in this life. You just need to work towards achieving your dream and don't rely on anyone to lift you.

My Life As A Woman: Mongolia Edition

"You are the one that possesses the keys to your being. You carry the passport to your own happiness."
- Diane von Furstenberg

I grew up in a country with vast land, full of richness underneath the soil but not enough resources to discover it. Corruption and inflation are making it harder to live year by year. I grew up in Mongolia, the birthplace of Genghis Khan. I spent the majority of my life in Ulaanbaatar, our capital city. In the thirteen plus years I grew up in Mongolia, I'm proud as a society we have immense love for our mother figures. That would also imply to women, Women's Day (March 8th) is a big celebration in our country. For many of us, our mothers are our inspiration, which includes me as well.

I am most thankful to my mother and my aunt. My mother taught me how to be more optimistic and have a positive view of life. I have been battling depression for many years now. The biggest lesson I've learned from it is that your life is what you make of it. You have all the power to choose how situations and people affect you. Instead of focusing on your wounds, you can learn and grow from it. You will be happier when you let go and then it will no longer have power over you.

My aunt taught me how to be a fighter, how to fight for your rights, and your place in the world. No matter how hard it gets, everyone falls but only some get up. If you are a woman, you will inevitably have difficulties at least once or twice in your workplace. Women don't receive the same treatment as men, even if they are more qualified for the job. You will have many doors shut on your face but that shouldn't hold you back from succeeding.

When I worked in mostly male-oriented places, I would often receive remarks such as, "Such a young girl like you shouldn't be working here. You should try more 'feminine' jobs," or "This type of work must be too boring for you. Why don't you try fashion or makeup?" from both genders. Whether it's selling generators and cars or working in the fashion industry, as long as I'm good at my job it shouldn't matter if I am a woman or a man. I take pride in my work and my work ethic, so comments like that would rile me up in the past. Instead of getting mad and ruining my day, I took the frustration from feeling undervalued and made it my motivation to do better and be better.

All the doubts and remarks stating I won't be much in life or I can't do anything on my own has led me here. Now I'm 21 years old, I've lived in 3 different countries for a good amount of time, can speak 3-4 languages, and am now on my way to graduate in Taiwan. Coming from a poor background, I had a few opportunities and many difficulties. But, I also have big dreams and goals. To obtain them, I learned how to carry myself and not let people's judgment and opinions affect me.

If I could give you any advice, it would be 'you have to focus on yourself and your goals in life'. Find your passion and everything else will find you in time.

-Enkhjin (Enji) Enkhbayar

My Life As A Woman: Montenegro Edition #1

Montenegro is one of the smallest European countries, with rich history and incredible geographical diversity. It is situated on the Adriatic sea coast, and it's known for its numerous large mountains, from which it derives its name. The legend says it was named by Italian sailors who called it the black mountain, after they've noticed the mountains appear as they crossed the Adriatic sea. I am very proud of my country's landscapes and history, especially all the brave women thanks to whom I grew up living a carefree life.

The women of Montenegro have had a long fight for their rights, the first big milestone being the right to vote, which they got after the WWII, as was the case in most of European countries. Still, their fight didn't end there, it barely begun. Although they acquired some legal rights, culturally and socially speaking, they remained in the disadvantaged position compared to men. Sons were significantly more valued than daughters, and as the secondary education became more widespread, it was only them who got the chance to get educated, of course not counting the women from upper class families, which were a minority.

Being born just a couple of decades ago, I can't say that I experienced any of those hardships, but that is precisely why I'm so thankful to the women that came before me and paved the way for all the upcoming generations of young women. Nowadays, Montenegro is completely modernized, and the only crises that I remember growing up were of political and economic nature, as the country switched from communist to democratic and free market based economy, but that was an issue of all of us living in Montenegro, men and women equally.

My biggest inspiration has always been my grandmothers, who grew up in the time of war and crises, yet still managed to gain their independence and teach their children the values of hard work, equality and peacefulness. If it wasn't for them, I never would have been raised by such open-minded parents, and I am forever grateful for that. My two grandmothers had very distinct experiences, as one was raised in the city, and the other in the rural countryside.

My mother's mother was a child in the family of six children, the youngest one being a brother. Her family decided to send her brother away to get education and he needed someone to look after him and prepare him meals. My grandmother volunteered to look after him. In the bigger city, where he studied mathematics, she soon realized that she could get education as well. As soon as the new school year started, she enrolled in medical school, and not long after, she returned to her city and became one of the first women working in the hospital.

My father's mother was slightly older and had a very different upbringing. Her brothers were among the first people of Montenegro who left for Minnesota to work in the gold mines. She remained with her family in the village. She was a teen with only elementary school education when her village became occupied by the Italian military. For several years that her village had been under occupation, she learned and perfected Italian language and later became very successful in trade.

I fondly remember both of them. I often recall learning first aid from one, and how to count in Italian from another. These moments shaped my childhood, and thought me the power of knowledge, both formal and informal. They fought for their rights in an incredibly cunning yet peaceful way, working with what they had to achieve the most. From then on, it was my dream to become an educated and independent woman who will dedicate her life to helping her community, especially women in need.

I decided to study sociology and then get a degree in public health, and I could definitely say that my grandmothers inspired me to do so. Compared to them, I was incredibly privileged in life, but spending time with the two of them, and then later studying sociology, helped me understand women from various walks of life, that is, as much as I could.

My advice to everyone reading this, no matter how old or financially stable, is to learn as much as possible. Learning shouldn't always be focused on getting a formal degree, not to mention the fact that not everyone is able to get one. Learning should be about expanding your horizons and building up courage to gain independence from family and marital partners. Whether it's a foreign language, a craft, or something in the academic field, never feel discouraged to try it out. Everything is the hardest at the very beginning, but what once was a difficult task, over time becomes a deeply fulfilling and empowering habit.

My Life As A Woman: Montenegro Edition #2

Determined by our DNA, gender seems to be nothing more than a set of coincidences. Or rules. The product of an equation discovered a long time ago. However, I believe it is much more than a number. It is a gift we carry throughout our whole life. One day, in the small store, at the bus station, a clerk asked me for my name. She said the way I looked is how she imagined her daughter would look like as a teenager. She made my day. I mean, it was nice getting a compliment, but that's not a point of the story. Being a woman is like having a special power.

I was born and raised in the capital of Montenegro. With my sister and a brother, I am the eldest in the family. I always reflect on my childhood with a smile. Being loved and well-taken care of made me strong and confident in my qualities. Both of my parents were working, so I needed to learn to be responsible early on in my life and take care of my younger siblings. It didn't only strengthen our bond, but also made us capable of holding our own in life. Over everything else, I remember the time I dedicated to taking care of my mother. Last year, fighting breast cancer, she proved yet again to be a strong role model and figure in my life. She supports, and inspires us, teaching us to deal with setbacks in life and to love everyone around you.

Currently, I am working as an English as a Second Language Online Tutor. This is the full-time job I am enjoying, after finishing high school and taking a gap year. International experiences were a big part of my life in the last few years, and now having them daily, I look upon my own culture with different eyes. As you may or may not know, Montenegro is a small country on the coast of the Adriatic Sea. The Balkans are proud of their trembling history. As a product of such circumstances, Montenegro developed a strong patriarchate. Although it was reasonable - father was a protector of the family, but when it came to security and economy - we had a hard time dealing with remains of a system that was so unsuitable for the twenty-first century.

Before, I was assured the downsides of our systems were huge. Then I realized that gender inequality here is part of the old culture, but it is not as present as in other countries. While working on projects with some of my international colleagues I felt a lot of discomfort. Me being a woman made them underestimate me, and I hated that. Especially since I never experienced it in my small home country. I also found out that in other parts of the world, many women abandon their work and careers for marriage, and they usually don't opt for careers of doctors, mechanical engineers, or similar. Although it is not a rule, it occurs more often than not. Conventions of my culture may have seemed strong. But even though we aren't encouraged enough, nobody is dragging us down to conform to old stereotypes. We can freely pursue any career path we want and choose the life we want. My dream is to become a scientist. That is my own long-term goal, based on the strengths I believe to possess. Yes, there are grandmas that are nagging you about getting married soon. But, forgive them because there will always be someone else saying that you should finish your schooling first.

I believe there were, and that there still are issues. It's the story everywhere. But the truth is that the bad side of the patriarchate is progressively fading away in Montenegro these days. In different regions or particular families, the situation may be difficult. I witnessed it before. If you are in this situation, have in mind that the world isn't as cruel as it seems at the moment. Your power is not limited. We don't always agree with our families, nor are we always supported by them. However, if you treat yourself with respect and dignity, others will treat you too. That's the law of nature that doesn't depend on the gender you inherit. Anyways, there is that little power of beauty, the ability to provide life and guidance, which should make us proud of who we are.

My Life As A Woman: Morocco Edition

I'm finally graduating college! Wait.. Coronavirus?

It seems that just yesterday I was at my internship, with a job promise in a big multinational company and the friendliest office I had ever seen. My career was on the rails to a great start. The picture perfect dream of every college student. That was 2 months ago. Right now, reality is working remotely on my thesis, scrolling through memes for hours and eating my feelings away. It really feels like my life has been put on hold before it even began. We all dream of our college graduation, the forever freedom of studies and the ceremony that marks the beginning of a new life. Somehow I had to make that beginning myself, on my parents' couch.

I was studying and doing my internship in Tangier, on the north coast of Morocco, if you're wondering where that is, picture a map of Africa, it's right at the top peak of the continent. I could see Spain's coast on my way to work every day. Soon after the first Coronavirus case got recorded in my country, obligatory lockdown took place. I came back home as soon as we heard the government was considering a national lockdown. Else I would've been stuck 180 miles away. So now I'm home with a master's degree thesis I need to work on and a not so promising career anymore, well, at least not in the near future. The job market froze, companies are lucky enough if they keep their employees.

We never really realize how fast the years fly by until we are confronted by the reality of it. I have been away from home for over 5 years, coming back on summer vacations and a few times a year. I thought I was still the same person, but how could I be? Another city, other friends, another school, I didn't get ahold of the changes that were occurring in me since I first started "adulting" when I moved to college. Living alone came naturally, I have always been an independent person. But it also came gradually. Being home again, I was surprised to feel like I was putting myself in someone else's shoes. I felt trapped body and mind in my teenage room, even found myself listening to the same old 2012 albums on repeat. It took me a while (and a lot of motivational podcasts) to realize that I wasn't the same 18 year old girl who left 6 years ago, I was the 24 year old woman I have become, through hardships, relationships, studies and real life battles. So why should I cram myself to fit into who I once was?

I acted, picture this: Rom Com movie room makeover, it took me 2 days, I put a board on the wall, with all the plans I was determined on taking. I dedicated a notebook to my to do lists (a very cute notebook.. it had to be cute!) I put on two big goals: start drawing more and make an Instagram page, because everyone who ever saw my sketches told me they loved it, what was I waiting for? And secondly, start a business, my chances of getting hired anywhere were slim, so why not create that chance myself! That's how I got into freelance writing. I was a butterfly blooming. I have always been an avid reader, and always wanted to write but lacked motivation, getting paid to do something you love is the best way to go. In three weeks, the endless flow of everyday pouring into the next wasn't so senseless anymore. I had a purpose to every day, a reason to wake up and put myself to work, short and long term goals to achieve, all while my bank account is getting fat, not me.

Your body might be on lockdown, but your mind isn't. Be creative, find what you love and let it set you free.

~ Sofiya, 24 years old, May 13th, 2020

My Life As A Woman: Mozambique Edition #1

Where did you grow up?

I was born and raised in the capital of Mozambique, Maputo.

How did you grow up?

I had the privilege of going to the school from my first year of life until I was 5 years old, something that at the time was only for families with more luck, my grandmother worked in a company that was entitled to a place in a school, and at 6, I started the first year of basic education, I had a typical childhood of a Mozambican child going to school, playing with friends at the end of the day reviewing the material.

Did you have parents or maybe a grandma who inspired you?

My father is my greatest source of inspiration, without taking away the space of mother, I say this because I always wanted to be intelligent as my father is, and to be his pride.

What did you study / what did you want to be when you grew up / why?

I studied business management, and I always wanted to study economics, I am happy with the course I took because it resembles the course of dreams.

What do you love about your culture?

What I love about my culture is the cultural diversity that exists, in my country 43 languages are spoken, some of them Macua, Tsonga (Shangaan), Sena, Lomwe, Chuwabu and Nianja. In addition to languages, we also have dances and each region has specific dances in the south, we have marrabenta as the main dance, in the center we have the Nhau dance and in the north we have the Mapiko dance.

What are you currently doing for work?

Besides being a model, I am currently working in the commercial area on a project of ecological houses, I also work as a makeup artist and I have a partnership with petevonreflex, but of course modeling is what I do with passion.

Tell me about your struggles as a woman?

My biggest struggle is to be able to conquer a space as a model, which is difficult due to so much competition and undervaluation of fashion.

Tell me about your successes as a woman?

I feel happy as a Mozambican woman, being trained and having the job I like, as a model I made several achievements such as having won the 2015 inter-university contest, having achieved the miss personality in the miss African heritage contest in South Africa and representing Mozambique in the contest miss CPLP in Portugal, I am part of the KLD agency that organizes the annual Fancy fashion week and various other fashion events with brunch and fashion.

Do you have any advice from a woman living in Mozambique?

I advise Mozambican women and everyone else to fight to achieve their goals, whatever they may be, as nothing comes in vain.

My Life As A Woman: Mozambique Edition #2

I am Mari, and I grew up in Mozambique Maputo (which is the capital city of Mozambique). Mozambique is located at the South East region of Africa. I grew up in a humble family, and I was also brought up knowing that money is not everything, you should always be humble.

I always thank God for having both my parents alive and they raised me up in the best way they could. The greatest inspiration I have is my mom, who inspires me all the time on different things.

I studied Sustainable Human Development in the university because I have always wanted to help the poor people and also to make a difference in their lives by teaching them how to fish, and this as well means that I am helping them to look for solutions to their problems, by them having a source of livelihood.

There are so many things I love about my culture, and this includes the fact that we are always willing to help one another without wanting anything in return (that indeed is pure love) and also the ability to express certain emotions such as: "You are a true friend", without having to be embarrassed about it. I also love the hospitality of my people towards foreigners and to one another as well.

I am currently still a student right now, who also has great plans for her future, some of them I have been able to carry out, some are still in the process and many more are yet to come. I hope to help as many people as I can although I have started doing this already.

My struggles about being a woman are in different variants, but some of them includes having trouble listening to myself, and as well as seeing my own worth. I also tend to listen to what people say about me, and that affects me a whole lot when it comes to focusing on something in my life.

My success as a woman that I currently am involves a lot of things, for example: when I first began my job over three years ago, I struggled to meet a deadline for a multi-part project. This situation taught me a major life lesson of which I am grateful for, and still practicing. I have since then developed a new strategy for managing my time, and after implementing this new strategy, I have been on time or ahead of time for every project I have done since then, both individual and team projects. I think this ability to keep a group on a task will make me a strong team leader in an office, or anywhere I would find myself in the future.

My advice to other women living in my country and to the rest of the world is that, Women should always be willing to make a difference in people's lives, internal motivation is key, and strife to be the best you can ever be in all areas of your life.

By: Mari, a Mozambican.

My Life As A Woman: Mozambique Edition #3

INTERVIEW

NAME: Carla Josefina

How did you grow up?

I grew up in a humble family with my parents. Respect, discipline was what prevailed. In my childhood we were definitely more social then kids are today. We were always joyful because we were very social, the games were connective and that made us very close and easy to socialize, unlike today where each kid lives in their own corner, parents barely know what children do or learn.

Just like any other kid we were also into dolls, playing house and many other games. I also practiced sports at the institute, I liked to play basketball and handball as well as running, but handball was the sport I most identified with, having decided to join the club of Ferroviario from the age of 14 until 26.

Did you have parents or grandparents who inspired you?

Fortunately, I had grandparents and parents. My grandparents were very kind, always concerned about their grandchildren, very hardworking, used to working in the fields, at that time I was a child. I had someone very special who is the most inspiring person for me - My mother.

I was unfortunate to lose my father when I was 10 years old, I was a clueless child at the time. My mother was widowed at a very early age (40), she was a domestic worker with four children to raise, it was extremely difficult. Having one less parent had a really strong impact on us not only emotionally but also financially.

My mother never failed us in any way, she was always firm and determined, she looked for ways to make money to support her family, she started selling chickens, she grew her own food to sell she also used knit and crochet baby wear etc.

It was with her that I started learning how to be a woman, what she did I also tried to learn, together we made baby clothes out of wool, we also did tablecloths, napkins and quilts. They were products with a lot of demand that helped a lot for our livelihood. I even forgot that I was a child and I embraced the work and valued it because we were never hungry, we never lacked bread or food on the table.

Today I am what I am because of my mother's education and guidance. She gave us the best education, we all studied, we learned to be humble a have respect for others.

What did you study?

I completed a degree in education and training in 2008.

What do you love about your culture?

As far as traditional music and dance I like Marrabenta and mapiko as far as music food I enjoy eating Matapa, it delicious dish, made from stewed cassava leaves blended with ground peanuts, garlic, and coconut milk.

What kind of work do you currently do?

I am currently a bank employee.

Tell me about your struggles and challenges as a woman.

As a woman, I have managed to develop in our recognition especially in the workplace, I have been blessed with opportunity to make money to support my family. The struggles have become more of lifestyle, manage the house, the people who work in the house, raise a daughter, make sure I make good investments so that my children will not suffer when my time comes.

Tell me about your successes as a woman.

My success started in adolescence, because I always liked to work, to do anything to occupy myself, I always liked to learn without laziness and without choices.

- I'm valued in my family

- I'm the pillar of the family

- I have the same capacity as any man

What advice does a Mozambican women have for other women?

May they remain firm in their purpose as workers, educators and mothers or wives. Many of them are the ones that guarantee the support of their families and much more that they continue to fight for their rights, in favor of the elimination of all forms of discrimination, we must know our rights, be self-determined to build our future regardless of what culture says. We are the same as man. God created two human beings, a man and a woman, and nowhere is it written that one is superior than the other.

My Life As A Woman: Mozambique Edition #4

INTERVIEW

Where did you grow up?

I was born and raised in the city of Maputo, capital of Mozambique.

How did you grow up?

I grew up surrounded by a lot of love, care and protection. My parents were not wealthy, but they always tried hard to give all the best for me and my sisters, especially when it comes to education. They've always put us in good schools, always made sure that my sisters and I played sports, that we were not sedentary people, and above all they always taught me that I should put God first in my life. So my routine was basically this, going to school, playing sports such as basketball, football, volleyball, handball, swimming, and I've always kept my spiritual routine.

Did you have parents or maybe grandparents who inspired you?

I grew up with my parents, they got married even before I was born and are still together until today. They are my biggest inspiration. As a woman, I mirror myself in my mother, who is a wife, housewife, worker and grandmother now. And despite these multiple tasks that she always had, she never did anything for the halves, everything she does she does perfectly. She is an excellent housewife, an excellent wife and an excellent professional too. So I grew up watching my Mother doing all these things. For me, being a woman has always been that, someone who unfolds but is always whole.

What did you study? What did you want to be growing up? Why?

I am finishing my degree in Applied biology. I am currently developing my final project on the "Occurrence of microplastics in drinking water".

Since I was a teenager, I have always been fascinated in courses related to well-being and aesthetics. So I decided to direct my Biology to that area. I took a distance clinical nutrition course at an Institute in Brazil. I managed to finish successfully but then I found out that it was not what I was looking for. I had to study to understand that it wasn't my dream.

The Nutritionist's job depends 75% on the patient or maybe 80%. Then I discovered that what I like to do is something that shows results, which depends more on me than on others. That's when I decided to take a second training in basic facial aesthetics. Love at first sight! It was exactly what I always wanted. I had cousins, uncles, and close people who had hairs stuck in their beards and that sometimes made it look bad. I had friends and some family members of mine who suffered from acne, and when I'd see it I'd wonder how uncomfortable it could be.

I've never had acne but being a vain person who cares a lot about appearance, I imagine what it must feel like to have something on your face that you can't hide. For these reasons I always wanted to bring the solutions to these problems.

As I said earlier, I like to see results, and here I could see results that depend more on me than on others. I also like to make a difference, meaning, what I do is not just a business, I intend to restore people's self-esteem and solve the problems that are within my reach so that my customers are as comfortable as possible. I intend to continue with my studies and do my master's degree in Advanced Aesthetics that will allow me to carry out more complex works, with more modern resources.

What do you love about your culture?

The gastronomy. I'm a food lover, so I couldn't talk about anything else (laughs). In our cuisine, basically two ingredients cannot be missing: coconut and peanuts. It's wonderful!

What are you currently doing for work?

I am setting up my Beauty Space (Spa) - Renovar, which will be able to perform aesthetic treatments and various pathologies that affect the skin, using individualized protocols and combined therapies.

Our Mission is to offer aesthetic treatments with results, raising our client's self-esteem, providing them a better quality of life and well-being, using ecologically correct products.

Tell me about your struggles as a woman?

I am a mother of two, divorced, student and worker. It hasn't been easy to reconcile this, but I always try to give my best, especially as a Mother. I am not just talking about giving my children better conditions, it is important that I am a present person for them. Life is very busy these days, but I always try to have quality time with them.

People talk a lot about women's empowerment and gender equality, but the truth is that women will always be less privileged because they end up having more responsibility at home. It may seem that I am against feminism, but no, it is how I see things. As much as we have professionals who help us at home or even our companions, we will always worry about supervising to see if things are really going perfectly. It is our nature, the so-called maternal instinct, and no one will take that away from us. So I really admire women who manage to be excellent professionals even though they have all these responsibilities.

Provide some advice to women from a woman living in Mozambique.

My advice is that women in my country should be trained so that they can have more opportunities in life. In my country, as in many African countries, women end up subjecting themselves to abuse or mistreatment because they are financially dependent on their husbands. My wish is that all women study and become financially independent so that they can achieve whatever they want and not just accept what life gives them.

My Life As A Woman: Mozambique Edition #5

My name is Fredelisa Dirce Simango, I am from Mozambique, and I am 25 years old. I was born and raised in the country's capital, Maputo, in an area where all the neighbours are close. I am my parents' third daughter, and I was raised in an extended family environment. Both my parents always held a job. My mother, just like the majority of the Mozambican women while working, put great emphasis on our education. She strongly believed that good education would be a crucial factor in the success of her children. My father was even though concerned about our education but mostly played a passive role in decisions.

Currently, I am studying "International Relation and Diplomacy", at Joaquim Chissano University. I hope to work for UNICEF after completing my degree. I strongly believe, it is my duty to pass on the values that my mother so carefully passed on to me to young children in my country and other parts of the world, who were unfortunate to not receive guidance and care that I was given by my mother.

Currently, I am working as a project coordinator at a local marketing firm. I spend my spare time managing a project that I founded. The project's aim is to link the children who are unable to afford education with the families that are willing to support their education and extracurricular activities. I do believe that much of that love for education comes from the legacy of my mother.

Even though I grew up in a family where I had access to education and freedom to make my own decisions. I am still not free from societal pressure. Even though the time has changed, but people expect from women to accept the traditional role of getting married at an early age and raise a family. We need more education and awareness and open discussions on this subject.

As a woman, I also believe that I can be an agent of change in my community, especially concerning the lake of support and constraints that women face. I wish and try to support these women so that they never give up on their education and dreams.

I believe that as women, we must support other women on their path, whether educational or professional, wherever they are, women must be supportive to other women.

My Life As A Woman: Myanmar (Burma) Edition

My name is Nang Aye Nawe. I was born in Lashio, which is the largest town in northern Shan State, Myanmar. I considered myself pretty lucky when I was young since I grew up in the caring and loving environment. My parents loved me unconditionally. The whole family of my father lived under the same roof. My father had 8 siblings meant I had lots of uncles, aunties and cousins. It was the best moment of my life unlike other people who cannot live with their parents or had family problems.

Heroin, opium or similar types of cocaine are largely available in Shan State and that leads to many people especially men who will abuse those drugs. It is common to see many families with problems and fights. My grandmother said the mothers in nearby villages are scared to give birth to sons and they preferred only daughters.

One bad thing about my parents is that they are conservative, and they don't allow me to do what I want. When I was young, I wanted to be a detective after I watched so many wuxia movies and Chinese movies. It was just my childhood fantasy. My actual dream is to become a successful businesswoman. But my parents insisted me to pursue a degree and follow a normal traditional path means working as an employee. Frankly, I do not have any ideal women who inspired me although I do like strong women not only physically but also mentally.

Being conservative, my parents did not allow me to go out at night time until I was 22 years old, which was also because I left for Yangon to work, the largest city in Myanmar and the industry and commercial center of the country. If I stayed with them, I still would not be able to go out no matter how old I am. Every time I came back to Lashio to visit my parents, they still don't allow me to go out alone or at night time. In my opinion, it is not good for parents to be too strict on children especially on girls. If you asked Myanmar girls, I think most will answer the same. It is the parenting style of typical Myanmar parents.

I graduated from Lashio University with a degree in Geography. I wanted to study Economics, but Lashio University did not offer that. I needed to go to either Yangon or Mandalay to pursue that. But that time my parents thought I was too young and asked me to choose the major that the Lashio University offers.

Currently, I am working as a sales promoter at the famous jewellery shop in Yangon and get a good pay because I can speak Chinese and Shan languages other than Burmese, Myanmar's official language. My father is Chinese, and my mother is Shan, that's why I can speak those languages. I am also learning English at the time being as I believe I will have access to a greater number of career opportunities in the future.

Different countries have different culture. I have been to Thailand, Indonesia, Singapore, and Malaysia. But I found that I love my country culture most although most Asian countries have similar cultures (maybe it is normal for most people to love their homeland). The culture of my country is greatly influenced by the neighbouring countries like China, India, and Laos and also influenced heavily by Buddhism. We have one distinct strange manner that is like a hesitation, reluctance or avoidance, to perform an action based on the fear that it will offend someone. We are also considered as the world's most generous country.

Some of the struggles as a woman I noticed include lack of women in leadership roles and positions of power. Besides, there are still some men who ignore or don't care about the gender equality and treat women as dirt.

I suggest women here in Myanmar to try and rely on themselves rather than rely on the spouse, relatives or other people. If you don't have social status or earned income, there is a higher chance of your relatives, neighbours or your future in-laws looking down on you. Be yourself and be strong.

My Life As A Woman: Namibia Edition #1

My name is Helen lithete. I am currently a citizen of Windhoek, Namibia. Everyone agrees that I am a serious person nevertheless, I enjoy socialising with family and friends. An interesting a fact about me is that I am multi-skilled. I do both the work for the men and women, for instance, I sometimes walk with the cattle and cook in our village.

I was born in November 1985 in the Oshana region in the northern area of Namibia. I grew up in a village deep in the "bush". As a curious child, I would often wander deep into the trees by myself and my older relatives had to look for me. In my early childhood I would get myself in trouble and there always were consequences for my immoral actions. I mostly grew up with my grandparents and relatives as my parents worked in the capital.

My mom and dad play a significant role in my life. they taught me valuable lessons through times of joy, sorrow, and neglect. Despite them being there for me and being my parents yet looking up to my granddad at a young age was nothing but a source of inspiration. All grandparents are full of knowledge and wisdom, however, Mr. lthete was a true warrior. On a sorrowful approach, he passed years ago. I continue to honour him and remember the memories I shared with him and hope to meet again in the next life.

Our culture, the Ovambo-speaking group is the majority of the country and make up 40 percent of the total. I'd say our culture is far better than the rest and many do agree with me. What I love about most, and what makes me proud of being an Ovambo, is the wedding ceremonies that we celebrate. A wedding is a significant event that happens in one's life and I think that it is wonderful to gather with our extended families and socialise.

After high school, my parents couldn't afford to send me to university. I struggled to get money for university and decided to raise money to start a small business. My business grew and had enough income to put meals on the table. At first I looked on being a businesswoman, then my grandmother unexpectedly approached me and advised me to work in the health and medical field. I did not figure out what she was trying to say since they couldn't afford for the University. One day, my dad found a program at the town for me join. I gained experience in it and suddenly got an offer to work part time as a student. Today, I work full time as a nurse in the capital, Windhoek.

I have experienced obstacles in my life as a woman. When I had my business, I lacked certain skills that were business related and knowledge. Gender equality was another challenge as hiring became much difficult. We women where seen as housewives and not seen to handle work that men do.

I have achieved a few things that I can say I am proud of. Firstly, I had and continue to have perseverance in everything I do. People saw me as a liable person, they had great respect towards me and to top it all, people agree in describing me as an authentic person. Lastly, after all my sufferings, I have reached the position of being a professional nurse!

Advice that I would give to my female companions in the country and probably the world is to be who you are, never give up when challenges arise and continue working hard. Your quality and actions determine who you are and has a great effect not only on your peers but your future as well.

My Life As A Woman: Namibia Edition #2

I grew up in a small country called Namibia in Southern Africa, in the capital city Windhoek in a quiet suburban area surrounded by the modern setting of the ideal family life. I grew up around many siblings and a large portion of my extended family. Like most children in Namibia who are privileged enough to go to school, I started school at the age of 5 with kindergarten and moved onto primary school at age 6. I then went to a private Catholic primary school that helped shape me and my beliefs to this present day.

My parents are very involved in my life and are always very supportive and made sure we always had everything we needed. Growing up my mom was always my biggest inspiration the way she juggled her career and still kept both her family and her intact. I grew up watching her every morning putting on her gorgeous high heels, doing her makeup and still having time to make each and every one of us breakfast. Her work ethic was one to be admired. Her professionalism was absolutely outstanding.

I am currently in medical school in my fourth year and it honestly hasn't been an easy task. Countless sleepless nights and many hours of hard work and plenty of sacrifices. Growing up I always wanted to be a doctor, I never saw myself doing anything else. That white coat was all I knew growing up, saving lives and gaining the respect of many whilst doing something so noble sounded absolutely amazing to me. I aspired to be the best and most sought after plastic surgeon in Southern Africa then to the world and beyond.

Being a woman is the most glorious gift from heaven above. It comes with many struggles such as living in fear of being raped whilst walking alone at night. Not being seen as a worthy opponent by the opposite sex in any aspect outside the kitchen. No matter how much further into the future we advance into, a lot of people have that same notion that a woman's place is not beyond that of the affairs of the kitchen. Ignorance is quite bliss. In the year 2020 there are still men that will ask me why I'm in med school, shouldn't I be a nurse or something? One of my biggest achievements is successfully making it to medical school and maintaining high levels of achievements whilst inside school.

Growing up as a woman in Namibia has proven not as hard because of all the amazing women who have forged the path for us already. We are both blessed and lucky enough to have had them come before us. I would advise them to work hard and not be distracted, to know what exactly it is you want to achieve and work hard to achieve it. Don't be distracted by anything meaningless. Focus on building yourself, your faith whatever it is you believe in even if you only believe in yourself. Keep your head on straight don't let your crown fall, and know you got this, Girl!

My Life As A Woman: Nauru Edition

Have you ever heard about Micronesia and about an island-country called Nauru? I am not surprised at all because many people are really surprised when I tell them where I am. So this is okay for me that people do not know about Nauru, about this beautiful place which is rich with its white-sanded calm beaches, tons of palms and amazing nature. This is tropical heaven for us, for people who live in Nauru. Although our isolated location, we keep our contact with Europe, which has a big influence on the formation of our culture. What I really adore in my culture is our rhythmic dance and singing, which we perform on special occasions.

I am Meruwa from Malem, Micronesia but whole my life I was living in Yangor, Nauru. I grew up with my father and brother and I was the only woman in my family. So it was pretty hard without a mother, but I guess I did my best. I went to local middle and high schools, finished my education, and to help my family improve financially I found a job in 'Nauru Rehabilitation Corporation'. I am a clerical officer and you will be surprised but I love my job. The staff I am working with is like my second family, I pass a big part of my day with them and every day I wake up I can't wait to go there, to meet my friends, to work and enjoy my life at work. As I already told you I grew up in a family with father and brother, so a lack of a woman in family had a big influence on me, it changed my style, my views at life, and in general on me. I got all the love from my family, and I really appreciate the effort that my dad made on us, he gave all his attention and love, so we became good people. Except being my dad, he is my best friend who is always with me, who always gives me the best advice and support in any situation.

What can I advise? Place your family in the first position, no matter what, they are the people who gave you birth, gave your life and gave you their hearts. I know this kind of warm relationship does not exist in every family, some children do not even talk with their parents, but as a woman who didn't feel the love of her mother, I wish all of you be careful to your moms. Another piece of advice, be ready for every kind of situation that will appear in your life, never be afraid of something, you can handle everything as nowadays women became stronger. Never judge someone, as you can never know what will happen with you in the next minute, and always love yourself, try to enjoy life, help others with every little thing you can do. Be grateful for the life you have and always pray that you woke up and could see your lovely people.

My Life As A Woman: Nepal Edition #1

I was born and raised in Kathmandu. In comparison to people in other parts of the country, I had an easier life. I received a formal education, played with my friends all afternoon after homework, and pursued my hobbies, all at the heart of the capital city of Nepal.

I defined myself as an ambitious girl even when I was a child. Like every other person, I wanted to be something big but didn't exactly know what. I wanted to become a doctor, a lawyer, a pilot, a politician, a social worker, and a librarian. This may sound absurd, but those were the things that fascinated me. I always wanted to become more than just one thing. However, those are the list of things I wanted to become over different stages of my childhood, and after high school, the practicalities of life hit me. I decided to become a Chartered Accountant. I am currently pursuing my career in Auditing.

In my family, there was one person after my mother who motivated me the most. My mother taught me to have patience and I learned about discipline and consistency from my uncle, my father's brother. My mother always motivated me to do the best in whatever I put my mind to and my uncle taught me to be disciplined and consistent at it. Even though I did not grow up in a family where all the members were educated, my family valued education and good cultural values.

I am from a Hindu household. The majority of the people in Nepal practice Hinduism and Buddhism, and most of the culture is based on these two religions. However, there are different people from different cultural backgrounds and religions in Nepal. The diversity in Nepal is astonishing and people live in unity with respect for each other. One thing I love the most about the culture from where I belong to is the spirit of living. People enjoy their lives in each of their vibrant ways. People do not get disheartened by small losses and celebrate every small victory. We have festivals to celebrate the victories, and the losses too.

Having said that, growing up as a woman in Nepal was not as easy as it may sound. Women face many struggles everywhere in the world. It is worse when you are a woman in a developing country.

Most of the struggles a woman faces in Nepal are mostly because of the inequality that prevails in each aspect of life. The education of women is not always the priority. They are treated less than equal to their brothers or other men in the family. They are constantly reminded of their contributions not being enough and their voices not heard.

Luckily, as I said earlier, I did not have to face this inequality in my family but as it still prevails among other households. I faced criticisms from people about simple decisions like what I choose to study, how long I stay out at night, what and when to speak, etc. It has affected my life in all manners. It has influenced my perspective towards my own choices, my confidence, decisions I make, and my overall well-being.

Nevertheless, I consider the awareness to realize, I am above all inequalities of society and insecurities of my own as a success, as a woman. I do not let these things determine who I become and what I want with my life. My successes as a woman include being able to stand among people and be heard because this basic right is a privilege, not every girl in my country has. Besides, these struggles made me who I am today.

One piece of advice I would like to give to a woman living in Nepal and women in general is, seek for more and you will always get more, undoubtedly. Women settle for whatever they are given, and it includes the level of education, their rights, status in the society, their independence, and their voice. Know what you want in your life and work relentlessly towards it against all odds. It is important so that no one can ever tell you again what to do with your life and criticize the choices you make. Be grateful, but always seek for more.

My Life As A Woman: Nepal Edition #2

My life as a Nepali girl is quite a blend of conservative and liberalist approach of living. As globalization paves its way around the world, the typical Nepalese society is reforming with westernization so is my life as Nepali women. I grew up believing my father as the head of our family and obeying every decision my father took for the sake of my life and career. Literally, DAD is the brain of my home and my MOM; the heart of our family. Every day my mom wakes up before everyone else in our family and cleans the entire house. Growing up, I saw my mother managing time to do the house chores, rush to work, and serve us with a plateful of love every day without considering her own health.

I grew up in Kathmandu, the capital city of Nepal. Growing up in the busy streets of Kathmandu actually made my life a lot easier and better than the life of many other Nepali girls. Yes, I'm talking about girls living in rural villages of Nepal. Their lives are gravely affected by gender discrimination and controlled by a patriarchal society. While their brothers are sent to expensive boarding schools, they can hardly manage to attend the classes in government schools. Whether it is about missing the first period of their class while rushing between house chores and cattle rearing, or about missing the career and life goals while unwillingly getting into an arranged marriage at a very young age, they miss countless opportunities in life. I would have faced the same fate if my parents didn't take that one decision that completely saved my life from getting bounded within four walls of our house in the village. I was born in a rural village where life was much conservative and unfair. However, my parents decided to move to Kathmandu when I was 4 so that they could provide me with better living, education, and career opportunities as I grew up.

I grew up to be an amazing woman I'm proud of. I received education in the best schools and colleges and passed with amazing results. After my higher secondary level studies, I enrolled for a bachelor's level of education majoring in Business Studies. I also joined the Chartered Accountancy course at the same time. I'm currently studying both courses intending to become a 'successful woman entrepreneur'. Now, this phrase isn't so familiar in Nepalese society. As I mentioned earlier, women are mainly bound to house chores and marriage at a young age in Nepal. I'm 23 now and I don't intend to get married before I become successful in my career and financially strong. I'm currently working as an audit associate at a renowned audit firm in Nepal. Besides, I do abstract paintings and sell them. I am also a freelance writer. I want to become a source of inspiration and courage for the Nepalese girls out there who don't have the privilege of independent life. I want to become an entrepreneur who can solve the needs of people in Nepal and contribute as much as I can in the national economy.

How I grew up? Well, you got the answer. I grew up being pampered with good education, love, and freedom that my parents provided me with, and wiser vision I built for myself. However, I wasn't provided freedom in making all the choices I had to make while growing up. It is very obvious that our lives are affected by the society we live in. My mother taught me how to dress up, how to speak in front of other people, and how to present myself as I grew up. She told me not to wear short skirts and sexually appealing dresses. I had to reach home before sunset and speak less in front of elders. I was not supposed to give a wide laugh in front of elders because it would make me less disciplined and cultural. I grew up being influenced by one or many of such social norms and values of Nepalese society.

However, I always got the support of my parents who didn't force me to follow unnecessary and hard rules of society that would hinder my personal growth. My mom is my inspiration. She inspires me to become a better person every day.

Talking about Nepalese culture, I like the festivals and Jatras celebrated in Nepal. The major festivals I like are Dashain and Tihar. Most families celebrate Dashain by offering goats, ducks, chickens, and eggs to the goddess Durga. People return to their home and meet up with relatives and friends. Younger family members receive red tika and blessings from their elders.

In the Nepalese society, the woman needs to provide strong reasoning for every choice they can possibly make. They have to accept the decision of father and brothers over their own choices before marriage and once a woman gets married, she will have to accept the decisions and restrictions imposed by her husband. I didn't have to struggle greatly in my life until now, but I know, I must be ready for any challenges the society throws towards me.

As a woman, I have established myself as a professional book writer/editor and abstract artist at a young age of 23. I am professionally emerging as a Chartered Accountant and trying my best to become a successful entrepreneur one day. I'm doing lots of side hustles and working hard to make my dream of 'launching my own business startup' come true.

I've tried everything I can, to possibly have the best version of life for me and my family until today. I still fight to do so by letting my voice be heard, by showing the world and other Nepali girls out there, that no matter how early or late your journey start, and no matter how hard your journey is, you too can do it. You too can make it, you too can survive this, and you too can have the best possible life you can ever dream off.

My Life As A Woman: Netherlands Edition #1

This is about me, a woman named Mirjam (49), living in The Netherlands. But am I living in The Netherlands? Born and raised on the most northern island in The Netherlands, a two-hour sail from the mainland, with the name Terschelling. A quiet island in my youth days. Tourism started to set ground. As children we always played in the dunes and woods with other children from the same street. Everyone was welcome and we saw no harm in the world around us. Everyone's house was always open, and nobody used the front door of the houses. At the age of 13, I had to go to school on the mainland. On Monday morning with the 7 am boat to school and Friday afternoon at 3 pm back home. During the week I stayed with a boarding family. On Wednesdays, my dad called to ask how I was doing and always finished with, till Friday do I need to pick you up from the boat? Well actually it was a 5 minute walk and my dad picked me up with his bike so I could put my heavy laundry/bag on the back of the bike.

Because you go away from home during the weekdays, you start to get more independent at a young age. Around the age of 18, I was thinking what I really wanted to do for a living. My dad was a marine engineer, and this was inspiring me to go to sea. But I did choose to serve in the Royal Dutch Navy on a four year contract. This was in the first Gulf war period of 1990/1991. I was very lucky and had the assignment to go to the Caribbean for 9 months instead of Yugoslavia or the Middle East. With a total crew of 180 pax, including 24 women, you can imagine sometimes there were of course problems on board, but mostly these were little problems mostly relational. The only thing which was not so comfortable was, when we came on board of a ship which used to be a "men's ship" and which was turned to a men/women ship. The men were thinking they would lose their manly freedom in foreign harbours. I had a great time and stayed on for 5 years.

After my navy time I went back to Terschelling, where I got married and after 15 years divorced. After my divorce, I went for 7 years to the Caribbean. What I knew from my years of service and from holidays. Curacao is a beautiful island, and one of the ABC islands, former belonging to The Netherlands. Because it was an island again (a ship is sort of an island as well), I didn't have much trouble adjusting to island life, because once an islander, always an islander. Now I am back on Terschelling since January. And back in Europe since November 2019. From November till the end of January, I travelled around in a small class BR-V with my dog and cat. I had to know if the Nomadic lifestyle was for me.

So what is it to be a woman in The Netherlands? Well for me it is great, and I didn't have any problems at all. I am working in a Bakery and only part-time. In Curacao, I worked as a sales manager and operational planner, which was a very busy job, so I am happy to have more free time nowadays. The hardest thing was to keep my head up financially, on Curacao and especially after my divorce. But to go back to the basics and stay on a budget has given me a boost to now work part-time and have the same income as I had in Curacao with 20 hours less working. To manage everything by yourself is the best success you can ever imagine. The best life is the life you get when you can be yourself at any time.

My Life As A Woman: Netherlands Edition #2

February 14, 1979. I was born at 2:11 PM in a hospital somewhere in the east of the Netherlands. "Oh how nice, a Valentine's baby!" were the first words from the nurse when I looked into the world with my dark hair and blue eyes. At that time, Valentine's Day was still a very "American thing". Of course, I didn't hear these words literally, but that's what my mom told me when I was older. I grew up lovingly in a small village. You walked to school with friends, waved the neighbours goodbye and played outside in the forest nearby. I'm the youngest of the 2 children in our family. My father worked in construction and my mother took care of me and my older brother. We get anything we needed. There was always enough love to give and a tasty meal was available at any time.

"Maybe they looked so big because I was so small"

We lived just outside the village in a luxurious farmhouse that my father renovated all by himself. The house was big enough for our family, but also for my grandparents who lived with us. I only had to open a door to get overwhelmed by the warmth of my granny and her big boobies. But maybe they looked so big because I was so small, I don't know. My Grandpa was an icon. This sweet man was a little rowdy but always sweet and kind. Sometimes I saw him smoking a cigarette in the barn. He quit smoking years ago, so he had to do it in secret, without my Grandma seeing it. I remember how I loved the smell as a kid and still, a cigarette reminds me of my loving Grandpa.

"Nothing could stand in the way of a happy life"

As a little girl, I was hopelessly addicted to horses. I almost killed the pony of the neighbours, because that poor thing was so old, and I was so fanatic. Later, I got my own pony, followed by several horses. Going to school was necessary, but I hated it. My learning capacity was more than sufficient, but I was not paying enough attention to it. If I'm sorry about that? Definitely not. As an "Aquarius", my creativity always brought me where I wanted to be. At that point, I wanted to be a professional rider in equestrian sports. When I was 17 I left home and ended up with a loving family in the middle of the Netherlands. Here I am formed and together with the loving education of my parents, nothing could stand in the way of a happy life.

"I really wanted him as a buddy or a soulmate"

I was a bit cheeky in that time. I wanted to explore the world in my own way and sometimes, that attitude brought me in some very unpleasant situations. But, this attitude also taught me some lessons about life. The recklessness brought me beautiful things, but I also started to lose myself. That also applies to my older brother. I really wanted him as a buddy or a soulmate, but unfortunately, that never happened. He suddenly broke up for unknown reasons. Not only with me but also with my loving parents. This has cost a lot of grief and left scars. And no matter how angry I was at that time, I would now receive him with open arms. That's the power of ageing and I can take my parents as an example of that.

"We were given 5 minutes to say goodbye, perhaps forever"

When I was 22, I met the love of my life. Although he was 21 years older than me, we married 16 years later. Both the relationship and my life weren't always that easy. We have had many setbacks in the field of illness. When we had only been married for 12 months, he came to Intensive Care with an aneurysm. We were given 5 minutes to say goodbye, perhaps forever. The operation was risky but necessary. Besides, there was a real chance that he would not wake up again. And there you are. Full of fear and forgiven with panic. This has been one of the most difficult situations in my life. While that moment lasted seconds, the memory will stay forever.

"If I could do it all over again, I would have filled it in exactly the same"

What doesn't kill you makes you stronger, and that's true. Especially if you have lovely people around you who know what you need. That doesn't mean that you can't make your own decisions. In the Netherlands, we have that freedom. That's what I like so much about our culture. Be there when you need it, and fade into the background if you can. Because in the end, you should be able to do by yourself. At this moment, I work as an author for various clients. I love what I do, and I do what I love. Although I never gave my brains the education they deserved, I do have enough knowledge and experience at this point in my life. Theoretically, my life approaching half the expiration date. And that's fine. If I could do it all over again, I would have filled it in exactly the same. You should not regret the things you did, but the things you didn't do.

My advice to all the lovely women in the world

What I want to say is that every day offers you new opportunities. No matter how dark your horizon is, it will always be light again. Do not doubt your own ability because, in the end, you fight like a lioness. Side by side, or alone if you have to. Act in the moment, because at that point, you know you are making the right decisions.

My Life As A Woman: Bonaire Island Edition

Hello everyone, I am from Kralendijk, Bonaire. I love the city I was raised in, it's also the capital of Bonaire, it's very colorful with European inspired architecture. Growing up I had severe asthma, any and everything would aggravate my asthma. Wearing highly dyed clothes or not wearing a jacket while it's windy would make me very sick. I would have to go to the hospital at least once a month. Over the years it got a little better, my parents and I learned to better manage it. I am grateful for my parents, they were always there for me. My mother was a hairdresser and my father was a builder. They made me a priority, they showed me a lot of love and tried to make my life feel as normal as possible.

Seeing as I had to visit the hospital so often, I had a good relationship with the doctors. Just seeing their compassion and how empathetic they are, really inspired me. I wanted to be just like that, I wanted to be able to help someone, I wanted to be a change factor of society.

I initially attended the Kolegio San Bernardo, which is an elementary/primary school. After I attended the Scholengemeenschap Secondary school, where I did my MAVO and HAVO exams which is comparable to the CXC exams. I also did the MCAT exam in which I was successful. With my MCAT score, I received a scholarship to attend the International University School Of Medicine. I became a doctor because of the doctors that took care of me while I was younger. Before I wanted to become an athlete, but with my illness, I wasn't able to take part in such events. Even though I did become my first career choice, nothing makes me happier than being a doctor.

I love the diversity of my culture the most. We are a fusion of Indian, African, Asian, and European cultures. As a result, our music and dance aren't what you would see anywhere else; the music is a blend of African beats and European inspired instruments. Bonaire is brightly colored and that has a positive effect on our people; we are always warm and welcoming.

Growing up as a sickly child, I wasn't able to experience a normal childhood. I couldn't go out to play and I couldn't wear some of the clothes I like; because of the pigments. It killed my aspirations of becoming an athlete. I was also treated like I was a fragile piece of glass. They would help even when it wasn't needed nor would they allow me to do certain activities at school.

Even with my health problems, I became successful. I learned how to manage my asthma and live a healthy life. My biggest success was becoming a doctor. I am now able to help other children facing similar situations. To all the women in Bonaire, let nothing stop you from achieving your goals. Yes, there will be setbacks, but it's just for you to persevere. You might also need to change your action plan but just remember you can do this and do what makes you happy.

My Life As A Woman: Curaçao Island Edition

Her real name is Alicia, but she is called Lizzy, she was born in Willemstad and her parents are foreigners who settled on the island. Lizzy recounts her experience living in a place where many people go from all over the world to take their vacations and she recounts the good, the bad and the ugly of living in a place like this.

However, the opportunities have been great; and she is grateful that she did not grow up in her parents' country (Colombia) since the politics and opportunities of this country are lacking compared to the "Curaçao" Island.

Alicia grew up on a farm, surrounded by many animals, there she awoke a passion for being a vet. Today she has an office and she is doing very well, however, she does not miss the opportunity to go to the beach once in a while since she loves it. Lizzy's parents married very young, when they were 22 years old; Then they migrated to Curaçao where they had their first daughter, since then they have not returned to Colombia.

Alicia's most gratifying experience is having had such hard-working parents; that helped her follow her dreams and become the great person she is now. She assures that migration is one of the most difficult things a person can do; moving away from her culture, family and friends and then starting from scratch in another country is something that has motivated her and has kept her motivated and self-confident.

Alicia is 25 years old, and she still does not know many of her relatives, since she has only been to Colombia a few times, she has not been able to see them all, but she does have references about them, and assures that they are honest people with great values.

One of the things that Alicia enjoys most in her city is going out to dance salsa casino with her friends and eat delicious typical dishes; as is the Keshi Yená: a giant gouda cheese filled with fish and vegetables. But without a doubt nothing compares to being able to live in such a paradisiacal place to see incredible sunsets and bathe in crystal clear waters, for Alicia this is priceless and unmatched.

Alicia considers herself a fan of Oprah Winfrey, for her she is the most inspiring woman in the world and shares many of her ideologies, but the one she loves the most is the following phrase:

"The best discovery of all time is that a person can transform his future just by changing his attitude"

Alicia says that she has changed many things about her in recent years, and this has helped her become the right person that her mother has always taught her to be. For her, it is very important to have the approval of her parents in most things, since they have been the fundamental pillar to become the woman she is today, something that is also clear and that is that every day is an experience. New and soon she hopes to be able to marry her boyfriend and have a nice family, that is, her wedding will be in Colombia, in honor of her parents.

My Life As A Woman: Netherlands Antilles Edition

Hey everyone, I am Ama Chahun. I live in Curacao, which is located in the Netherlands Antilles. Growing up, I lived with my parents and 2 sisters. I had a closely knitted family, we did everything together. My father was a nurse aid, and my mother was an accountant. We had a serious Sunday family ritual, starting our Sunday morning with a heavy breakfast of maize porridge. Then we would play games for a few hours. After our games then we would then start cooking, Sunday dinner. After having dinner, we would watch movies until we were ready for bed. We did this every Sunday, this made me have a great appreciation of family time and time in general. Growing up, I aspired to be just like my mom, she had a strong persona. She was always trying to empower and help people in the way she knew how to.

My sisters and I all attended Curacao American Preparatory school, from pre-K to high school. I did my exams and went to university. I always had a love for learning; I loved mathematics and English. I did well in school and was very active in extracurricular activities; dancing, clubs, and society. I always wanted to become a painter. To make my dream a reality, it took a lot of practice and dedication. I painted a lot throughout my younger years. After getting older, I decided to lessen the amount of time I spent painting and do something more meaningful to me; I started to tutor children in my community. That way I would impact young lives.

I love my Netherlands culture because of its rich diversity. It was a mixture of Dutch, English, and Asian. Netherland Antilles was like all the other Caribbean islands, we have amazing white sand beaches and amazing history. There was always an activity to do in the Netherlands Antilles, from diving to exploring. The food is delectable; I always loved the Rauwe haring, Patat oorlog, and the Poffertjes. Most of our food is very greasy, but the amazing taste masks it.

Growing up, I didn't have much self-confidence; having two beautiful sisters made my life a little difficult. My family never made any comments on appearance, but the world did. I was constantly reminded that they were prettier than me. I never resented my sisters because they never judged me or said anything like that. I never felt comfortable with my appearance. That lack of confidence affected my overall view of life and the risks I took. Some opportunities were available that I did not act upon, and I should have.

Over time my self-confidence improved, I became comfortable with myself. I am now able to empower young children about the importance of self-confidence. I don't think enough attention is paid to the importance of self-confidence. To all the women of Curacao, Netherland Antilles, you are beautiful. Don't let anyone tell you otherwise, build your self-confidence and you can do anything. believe in yourself, don't wait on others' approval of you.

My Life As A Woman: Saba Island Edition

Hey there, I'm Tina from St. John, Saba. My parents are actually my aunt and uncle, they adopted me from my aunt's niece. My biological mother was young and couldn't care for me, so my aunt took me. My father was a dive instructor, and my mom was a cook at a local seafood restaurant. Even though they weren't my biological parents, they treated me as such. They gave me everything I could ever desire as a child; love, attention, and care. My parents inspire me the most, they have a really big heart. They were just very compassionate, always ready to volunteer and help a friend in need. They volunteered to feed the street people once every month. I wanted to be just like that when I grew up.

I first attended the Sacred Heart School. Then I went to the Saba Comprehensive School, where I did my CXC subject. I didn't know what I wanted to be, so I just did some random subjects; from art to sciences. I did nine CXC subjects and graduated high school. After finishing, I realized my love for the arts. I decide to follow that pathway and become an artist. I went to vocational school and started to sell my craft to the tourists. After a while, I got an opportunity to be featured in a magazine. After the magazine gig, my art career kick-started; I got offers coming from all over.

Like most Caribbean countries, our culture is a mixture of African and European influences. Saba is famous for two major things; Saba spice and Saba lace. The lace-making process is not only to get a yard of delicately crafted material; it's empowering for the women in Saba. It's a source of income and it's a means of socialization for the women on the island. Saba spice isn't a spice used in cooking its liquor. Saba Spice is a mixture of rum, fennel seeds, cloves, etc.

Even though I have no resentment for my biological mother now, when I was younger I truly resented her. I always questioned why she didn't keep me or why she didn't come when she got a chance to visit me. I always felt a longing for attention from my biological mother due to that I acted out. I would steal from my parents and I would just create all types of mischief. I did all that hoping she would at least come and talk to me, but she never came. I could never understand her actions. I think my parents realized that was the reason and properly explained the situation to me.

After that my mindset did a total 360, I started taking school more seriously and stopped stealing from my parents. Even with a unique start in life, I maintained focus and pushed through the situation. I moved from creating mischief for attention to understanding my worth. To all the women of Saba, you just need to understand your worth. When you understand your worth you won't stoop to a certain level and belittle yourself. You will feel strong and empowered just being yourself.

My Life As A Woman: Sint Eustatius Island Edition

Hey, I'm Charlie from Oranjestad, Sint Eustatius. My father was a preacher, and my mother was a housewife. She also sold pastries right outside our house. My parents were very old-school; I was not allowed to do what other children my age could do. I had to dress modestly, not sing certain types of songs nor talk about certain topics. We went to church every Sunday. When I came of age I was expected to teach Sunday school to the younger children. My parents were very nice people, they were just too restrictive with their rules.

Initially growing up, I wanted to be just like my mother. She was always so poised and well-kept. She didn't have to work, all she had to do was cater to my father's needs and maintain the house. To the younger me, that looked so appealing. As I grew up I realized, I wanted to do more than cater to a man's needs for the rest of my life. I remember watching tv and saw Oprah for the first time. She just had a strong persona and was so empowering. Oprah then became my inspiration, I wanted to be as empowering as she was, I wanted to be strong.

I attended the Bethel Methodist School, where I did my literacy and numeracy exams and moved to the Gwendoline van Putten School. I took my HAVO exams which are comparable to the CSEC, in which I got a successful grade. I initially wanted to become a housewife, but after learning about Oprah all that changed. I decided I wanted to be a social worker. There wasn't much opportunity in Sint Eustatius, so after graduation, I left and went to America. I became a social worker and stayed in New York.

When I moved to the United States, I realized the gem I was living in before. I wasn't able to enjoy the simple things I was so accustomed to. Like going to the beach every other day, seeing warm welcoming faces while walking on the streets, or eating strongly spiced food. The saying was so right, "you don't know what you have until it's gone".

Although I have great love and respect for my religion, it has made me feel very conflicted throughout my life, especially when I had to leave for college. As a woman, I felt pressured to fit into my religious standards. I felt like I was forced to be religious and be married. I didn't feel like I had a choice, especially with my parents being so religious. They didn't care about me getting an education or having a career, they only cared about me getting married to a nice religious man.

Now I found myself, I don't feel restricted to anything or anyone. My parents' opinion on my lifestyle doesn't matter, the goals they had for me were way below what I had for myself. I can now openly be me, without caring about the constant criticisms. To all the women in Sint Eustatius, don't let other people's beliefs or mindset determine what you do. Make your own goals, don't let anyone make them for you.

My Life As A Woman: New Zealand Edition #1

'Where are you from?' sounds like a simple question with a simple reply but ever since I was a child, I've found myself struggling how to answer this question. I was born in Chicago as my mum is American but moved to New Zealand when I was 10, as my dad is a Kiwi. So yes, I am one of those lucky people that holds two passports. It is definitely a huge privilege, but it does sometimes leave you questioning where home and which nationality is you identify with more.

Having families from two different countries and holding dual citizenship has definitely made me who I am today. Being adaptable is in my nature. From the age of 10 I've had to learn how to adapt, as I was moved to three different schools in two countries within the space of the six months. Although at the time, I was distraught and thought it was the end of the world, I am now very grateful for that experience. I believe it has made me a much more adaptable and flexible person and triggered this urge in me to challenge myself to go outside my comfort zone.

As much as I love America and identify with aspects of American culture, I do find myself identifying more as a Kiwi as I believe it has formed me into the woman I am today. New Zealand has been a pioneer when it comes to gender equality. It was a world leader in women's suffrage, the first country in Asia-Pacific to legalise same-sex marriage and was the first country in the world to grant woman the right to vote. Although still not perfect of course, I feel pretty lucky to be able to call it home. There tends to be an openness and mindset with Kiwis that women can do anything. My dad also further engrained this in me, teaching me how to do things that stereotypically would be a 'man's' hobby or skill. From a young age, I have viewed many Kiwi women to be independent, strong and resilient and believe I've gained my independence and adventurous spirit from these surroundings.

For a small country with only the population of 4.7 million, New Zealand is extremely multi-cultural. Even when I think back to high school, out of my group of eleven friends, only four were actually born in New Zealand. New Zealand really is a melting pot of all cultures, and being so far away from everything, it only sparks the urge in most Kiwis to travel that much more. Travel and adventure are part of who many Kiwis are.

As a result of my surroundings and parents' influence, I had always dreamed of seeing the world and moving overseas one day. So at the age of 18, I began doing exactly that. From working at a summer camp in USA and Au Pairing in Quebec, Canada at 18, to backpacking Europe and doing a Uni exchange in Edinburgh at 20, I fell hard for the travel bug.

Once I moved back to New Zealand after my exchange, I finished Uni, got my first proper full-time job, had a serious boyfriend, moved in together, you get the gist. It seemed like I was doing everything right and everything I 'should' be doing. However, I still had the travel bug and this dream to live abroad and go backpacking for an extended period. My boyfriend at the time was happy to do the same, so for the next few years I began saving and continuously dreaming about this backpacking trip of a lifetime and where we could move to. But you know, life works in funny ways and of course, doesn't always go to plan.

Long story short, one night only 7 weeks before our flights, my ex got into a drunken rage and ended up getting violent with me. It felt as though my dreams had all come crashing down within the space of 10 minutes. I was devastated to say the least, not only dealing with the trauma of the situation and the heartbreak, but also the fact that this trip I had fantasised about for years may have also come to an end. I considered cancelling and grieving the loss of not only my relationship, but also my travel dreams.

Luckily, I had a wave of realisation. Why should I cancel my dreams because of a guy? Why should I not still go? And I did exactly that. I had plenty of anxious feelings and definitely wasn't mentally prepared to travel solo. So many 'what ifs' ran through my head, but I got on that plane and it ended up being the best thing that's ever happened to me. For a trip that was only meant to be a month or two, I loved it so much that I continued solo backpacking through Asia and Europe for 5 months. After this, I still wasn't ready to go home yet, so spur of the moment I decided to take up a working holiday visa in Ireland, which is where I am still currently residing today.

Don't get me wrong, it wasn't all as easy as it sounds. I definitely did have my moments while travelling and still to this day, but I'm so proud of what I achieved and did for myself. No one to stop me or hold me back, I did it all completely for me and learned so much about myself. The trip was everything I needed and truly helped me heal from the breakup.

In many ways, I do attribute this personal achievement to my upbringing, my parents and coming from little ole New Zealand. I always had a sense of adventure, determination and going outside my comfort zone, but I really believe that the Kiwi mindset and strength of women around me is what further influenced me to achieve my dreams, despite the hurdles that came my way. Like many other Kiwis, I will always call New Zealand home and will end up back there one day, but for now I'm content seeing the world and calling Dublin home. Now, whenever someone asks me where I'm from, I say New Zealand with such a sense of pride.

My Life As A Woman: New Zealand Edition #2

I grew up in a small city in New Zealand. My ancestors came from India, and over generations they migrated to Fiji. My mother was born there, while my father was the first generation in his family to be born in New Zealand. We all followed the Islamic faith.

We didn't celebrate Hindu holidays, I didn't know what Diwali was until I was in my late teens. But my family wore Indian clothes like salwar kameeses and saris, and made Indian foods, when celebrating weddings and Eid. So my childhood was a mix of Islamic teachings and Indian culture, in a western country.

My mother was introduced to my dad through their parents when she was eighteen, in Fiji. Three days later they were married, and they went back to New Zealand to start a life and family.

My life could have been the same. There were times when other families asked ours about wanting to arrange a marriage. I don't know if it was living in New Zealand for twenty years that made my parents not follow this tradition, or something else. I'm just glad it didn't turn out that way. I feel like there would be no time or space to be an independent person.

My mum's arranged marriage makes me think about how it would feel. To be a teenager, be introduced to someone so you could marry them three days later, then immediately moving to a new country to start a new life. And also makes me think of the different expectations of becoming an adult depending on the society you live in. In New Zealand, being eighteen years old means moving out and living away from your parents, making your own life decisions, understanding and entering legal contracts, etc.

I grew up during the 90's technology boom. We would watch movies on VHS. I first used the internet when I was twelve and didn't own a mobile phone until I bought one for myself at sixteen. I was able to start working and driving when I was seventeen. I had planned to enroll for university, but issues with my family affected me, and I ended up being behind in both my education and career. I feel that I was brought up with traditions in mind, but when it became time to be an adult, my life wasn't going to follow a traditional path. I felt unprepared and lost. It wasn't until I moved out of my family home that I started to figure out how I wanted to live my life.

I feel that the different cultures and perspectives I grew up with clash with each other, and I have trouble with this up to today. There are still a lot of things I need to learn. There's been a lot to come to terms with during my teenage years and early adulthood. I think both being independent and being able to access knowledge and people's stories across the internet, is what's helping me learn the most.

Over time I'm identifying more with New Zealand, my home country. I'm discovering things about myself, like even though I like Indian foods and sweets, Mexican, Italian, and American cuisines are my favourites! Mainly I want to work so I can take care of myself. I had the goal to have a career working in an office, which I was able to do a few years ago, and I've really loved it.

A year ago I had some health issues, and I had to stop working. Because I'm a citizen of New Zealand, I received help to get by. My medical costs were affordable, and I received financial aid to keep a roof over my head. I'm really grateful for this. Even though there's some stigma about receiving financial aid from the government, it didn't factor in when deciding to take care of myself. To be safe and make progress, sometimes we need a bit of help. Right now, I want to educate myself further, meet people and have a fulfilling career.

My advice to others: where you live will have some influence on your lifestyle; know the value of family and tradition, but find your independence; doing something different from your family can be scary, but sometimes it's the best way; whatever hardships you face, don't let it stop you from doing what you need to do for yourself.

My Life As A Woman: New Zealand Edition #3

New Zealanders are lucky... and they know it. Including their women, especially me. As a little girl, the world was my oyster. I could be anything, do anything. At least that's what it felt like. Growing up with a history teacher as a mum, I was predestined to a career involving all things ancient. Unbeknownst to her, it wasn't the historical bug that was shared, although it wasn't for her lack of trying. Instead, it was mum's persistence to pick up rubbish during walks that lit the spark that kick-started my professional journey. Little eyes are always watching, and you never know what will catch their attention.

The impressive New Zealand landscapes (we have plenty of those), tiny bugs and gorgeous native trees pulled my heart strings. David Attenborough was my hero and my ultimate dream was to make it as a writer/biologist for National Geographic. I went on to become a high school Biology and Literature Teacher (I know, quite the combination. But it sums me up to a T). However, I never made it even close to National Geographic.

Instead, I bumped into this fascinating, handsome bloke, fell head over heels in love, and became a mum. If you ask me, it was the best thing I ever did (both the husband and the kids). But my career was put on the back-burner. Outside of motherhood, however, writing and nature remained my happy place. When the time was right, and the kids found their own feet, my professional journey returned to my first two passions. At times both combined, at times one more dominant than the other. My big career as a respected writer/biologist however never happened.

To be fair, that probably says more about me as a person than about professional opportunity for women in New Zealand. Aotearoa (the Maori name for New Zealand) was the first country in the world to allow voting rights for women - the suffrage movement in the late 1800s was extremely strong. Jean Batten, the first woman to fly across the South-Atlantic in 1936, had a Kiwi passport. And these days, we have a very popular female Prime Minister. She's not the first woman on our shores to take that seat.

New Zealand has a can-do attitude, and that is extended to its women and the professional opportunities they are presented within life. There is nothing you can't do if only you put your mind to it. But that doesn't mean it's all roses. The topic of gender equality and gender pay issues is highly debated. And domestic violence is probably more present than anybody likes to admit. Add to this that life in New Zealand is expensive, which is especially hard on solo parents - often women.

The funny thing is that most Kiwis seem to be happy to take the high cost of living in their stride. That's because men and women alike really appreciate the work-life balance we have in New Zealand. Working hard and getting ahead is important to Kiwis, but not at all cost. We highly value time spent with family, friends and in the outdoors and it's not something we will compromise on.

Which makes me think... we may not be the richest nation in the world, but we can't be too far off from being the happiest and the luckiest.

My Life As A Woman: New Zealand Edition #4

All my life has been based in the city. I grew up in Auckland, New Zealand, which is a culturally diverse city. Through my interactions with other children in the city, I learned different ways of life. Despite living in the city, the family was an essential aspect of everyday life. Also, after every month, an extended family gathering would be held at a single rented space. My mother taught me values that would guide me throughout my childhood and are applicable even in my adult life. The best part of having a mother from the Tuhoe tribe and a father who is an Aboriginal is that I got exposed to two unique cultures. Additionally, regardless of the distance, the family was the number one priority for both Aboriginal and Tuhoe cultures. My brothers and I attended the same school and were given the same opportunities to succeed. As a young child, I wanted to be an artist, and this is a dream that my parents supported as they only wanted me to be happy. As life would have it, I had a change of heart and started pursuing law, which was the beginning of realizing that the women had different expectations than women. All my life, I had always been taught to pursue my goals, but in the real world, this proved to be difficult.

After completing the Bachelor of Laws course, I first got an internship in a small firm in Auckland but later secured a job. In this role, I watched for seven years as my workmates got promoted, and I got stuck in the same role. Unsurprisingly, all of the individuals that were promoted were all male. I watched as many women got frustrated and left the firm. I hung on until I could not take it anymore, and I demanded a promotion. I made a great case for myself and pointed to my excellent track records. However, instead of a promotion, I got sacked under dubious conditions. Instead of fighting for my job, I was relieved. Day in and day out, I was the subject of flirtish conversations even when presenting critical cases in the office. I was not the only one singled out, but this was a treatment that all women had to face.

After losing my job, I got to understand the struggles that women go through across the world, even in ones that are termed as developed. This was the lowest point of my life, and I felt like the world was against my gender. I almost gave up before coming up across a social media link where women were speaking about their struggles. I was grateful that I could interact with these women, and I would find another job in an organization intending to educate the next generation on social issues affecting society. Through this organization, I have been able to find a voice that has a chance of changing the experiences of women across the globe. I still partake in online conversations about gender inequality, and this helps women like me to find a voice.

My advice to women in New Zealand is that society provides challenges, and the one way to solve these issues is through collaboration. The internet and social media make it easy for women to find a voice. At times it may feel that the society is firmly set up against you, and sadly it is. But rather than feel sorry for yourself, you can find ways to contribute towards the cause of achieving gender equality. Whether it is donations or educating younger generations, there are plenty of ways to get involved in the fight for equal rights. Whether you are an Aboriginal woman or come from any other culture, you can make a difference.

My Life As A Woman: Cook Islands Edition

Hey everyone, I am Maya from the Arorangi district of Rarotonga Island in Cook Islands. I grew up with my entire family being around me; aunts, uncles, and cousins living right next to us. We were very close and had a great relationship. My parents owned a little craft shop in the town and sold items like floral arrangements, Tahitian costume, wood crafts, and bamboo weave craft. They had five of us but I was the only girl. Having that many brothers toughened me up, I would always go exploring with them. We used to go fishing and searching for bugs; it would bring us so much joy when we found a new one. My childhood was rather nice. My aunt Maria made the biggest impact on my life; she was a tour guide. I just loved how she was free-spirited and did what she loves. Maria lived nearby us, she didn't get married or have children like what was expected. She would always say, 'let no one put limits on you, you can do any and everything'.

I initially attended the Arorangi Primary School, I did well on my literacy and numeracy assessments. I later moved to Tereora College for my secondary education. I did average; I lack interest in school so I didn't do as much as was required. I graduated from secondary school and going to university was nowhere in my view. When I was younger I always wanted to become a teacher, but after going through school my mind took a total 360. I wanted to do other things, so I worked at one of the resorts. I saved all my money and when it was enough, I left for Europe and started my travel blog. It took a while to start making money for the blogging business, but I was steadfast in my dream. I let nothing deter me from achieving my goals. I found alternatives to help me save the little I had, my brothers sent me money at times, and I also picked up some odd jobs while I was at it.

I don't know where to start when talking about my culture, I love everything about it. I love our natural resources the most; being able to go snorkeling in a lagoon or just laying back on a white sandy beach. I also love how we openly embrace our culture through cultural shows. Our cultural shows include a lot of dancing, singing flowers, and laughter. We are just naturally happy.

Being a female travel blogger, I had many fair shares of challenges. The first problem was being judged by locals; they would show pity to me as if I was forced to do this, or as if I was vulnerable. I realized the next problem when I traveled to Egypt, women weren't seen as equals. I would have to follow rules a male wouldn't have to. Lastly, there's always a fear of being sexually assaulted, I couldn't trust anyone. It was just me, myself, and I.

Even with the challenges I faced as a lone female traveler, I never made anyone or anything deter me from doing what I love. I pushed through even when I felt like I wanted to give up. To all the women of Cook Islands, let your challenges motivate you not to deter you. Everyone faces challenges, but it's up to you to determine how you proceed. You either make those challenges break you or you make them build you, I chose the latter.

My Life As A Woman: Niue Edition #1

Niue is a small island in the South Pacific and it has been my home for the last 39 years. It is affectionately known as the Rock of Polynesia, one of the largest uplifted coral atolls in the world. Niue has fourteen villages scattered around the coast of the island and I hail from the villages of Fineone Hakupu Atua on my dad's side and Oneonepata Avatele on my mums side.

Niue's population is approximately 1,700 and the beauty of growing up in such a small place is that everyone knows everyone. It is definitely a truly unique place and probably one of the safest places in the world to grow up in today especially since Niue is still COVID-free.

My parents were educated in New Zealand and returned to work for government both eventually holding senior level positions within the Niue Government for many years. My dad was an architect by profession, and he became the Director of the Public Works Department. Dad was responsible for designing many structures in his time, from people's houses, churches, tourism places some of which are still in existence today. He was voted in by the people of Niue and became a member of Niue's Legislative assembly. He sadly lost his life to cancer in October 1996 during his first term in the assembly. My mother was a teacher at the only Secondary School on the island. Many years later she became the Director of Education for a few terms and sadly resigned in 2003 and migrated to NZ not long after. Both parents were very much involved in community work in helping with village and country developments, sports groups, national groups, NGOs and the never ending family and village obligations. They also raised and adopted children as they were unable to have their own until about 7 years after they were married. I take pride in the work they did for our village and country for many years and today my family and I continue their legacy as I am the only child residing on the island. The rest of my four siblings remained in NZ after going there for tertiary education.

I was very lucky to have been raised in the village of Hakupu surrounded by many of my close and extended family and friends. There was never a dull moment. We attended the Hakupu Ekalesia church every Sunday and were a part of all the village groups from Girls Brigade, netball, cricket, Sunday School to youth and more. Our close knit community always banded together to help one another especially during family events such as the traditional haircutting and ear piecing ceremonies, 21st celebrations, weddings, funerals and more. The community was a great support network for families during family occasions especially funerals, something I saw when my father passed away. The overwhelming support of food, money, and love from the many that attended to pay their respects all helped with the grieving process. The same happened when families would play host to big celebrations. This definitely instilled in us our traditional family and village values that we still hold dear to us and practise today.

Our childhood in my eyes was a indeed privileged one, not in terms of money but because of the fact we lived a care fee life, we received free education and free health care. Our family like many others lived off the land and the sea to supplement the income they received from working for government or private sector jobs. We not only got to enjoy the local food but also grew up on western food too, something that has now contributed significantly to the rise in non-communicable diseases on the island. On the flip side we enjoyed the best of both worlds. There was no need to lock doors to our house or cars, so security was not much of an issue. We were free to roam the village and play with our cousins without our parents having to worry where we were. With many of our extended families living overseas they would send us goodies off the boat or plane especially during festive season. These are some of the things my own family still continue to enjoy today.

Growing up surrounded by many strong beautiful women, my grandmothers, my aunties, and my many cousins, they have been my inspiration. Both my grandmothers inspired me through their traditional way of life and their strong Christian beliefs. They both raised big families and spent all their lives raising and caring for them including us grandkids that followed. They were great cooks but were also very talented weavers, each with their own specialties who both lived long and fruitful lives. My Avatele Nena Meleligitia wove the most beautiful hats and my Hakupu Nena Higano wove the most beautiful fans decorated with human hair. As kids we would play while they would go about doing their weaving. Prayer was a significant part of our lives with them, morning night and before every meal. It is only now that I realize how important this was and my only wish was that I had sat with them to learn their craft. Now that I am older I have taken up weaving and I am determined to be just as good as they were. Unfortunately my mother was too busy working and therefore did not inherit their fine art of weaving so I hope that I can continue on for them.

Despite this, my mum was definitely my role model and she had her own talents. She was a very strong women's leader both in our village and our country. When my dad passed away, she brought us up on her own and has supported us through the many milestones in our lives, from our tertiary education years right up to us starting our own families until now. We have indeed been very lucky to have her.

Niue Primary School and Niue High School in my early years was a fun time for me which resulted in lifelong friendships. I don't remember what I wanted to be but one thing for sure was that I always wanted to travel overseas and return to Niue to live. I attended 7th form in Whaganui Girls College in 1998 and that was a major culture shock for me. Surrounded by girls 24/7 was foreign but thankfully I made many friends and graduated allowing me entrance into University. At the end of 2002, I graduated from the Victoria university in Wellington New Zealand with a Bachelor of Science majoring in biology. My intention was to continue on my training to become a pharmacist, but this interest fizzled and I ended up working for the Department of Agriculture, Forestry and Fisheries when I returned to Niue in 2003.

I appreciate and love everything about the local Niuean culture from its history, it's traditions, singing, dancing, sports, local food delicacies from the land and sea. With the continuous influences from the outside cultures, Niueans face the threat of losing its language and its culture. I am a strong advocate for the Niuean culture and widely promote it through every opportunity I get. I do my best to encourage my own children to take pride in their culture especially through traditional song and dance. In 2010, the youth group of our Village Hakupu Young People's Fellowship travelled to the Shanghai China Expo to showcase our Niuean culture, a life time experience for us all.

Like my parents, I returned from studies overseas and worked for the Niue Government in the Department of Agriculture, Forestry and Fisheries. I have been there since 2003. I now hold a Senior position in the Department and my official role is the Deputy Director. I help my Director to manage the 34 staff in our department and coordinate the activities with its five divisions.

In this role I have managed many projects in different fields mostly that of natural resource management, food security, agriculture, forestry and fisheries. This has allowed me to work alongside various stakeholders, international organizations such as FAO and UNDP, government departments, NGOs, schools and communities. I especially enjoy working with our local farmers and fishers whose livelihoods depend greatly on our natural resources.

When I am not working in government, I am heavily involved in youth and village and national development activities. I have helped lead our local youth group Hakupu People's Fellowship and also worked for the local government in the Hakupu Village Council for one three year term but continue them. One of my joys is being a Sunday School teacher in our church for kids under 6 years old, teaching them new songs and bible stores. I enjoy listening to them and how enthusiastic they are to learn.

The biggest struggle I have faced since I started my own family was being a working mother to six children, 5 boys and 1 girl between the ages of 15 and 3. We do not have the luxury nowadays of having our grandmothers stay at home to help us look after our children as most of them continue to work past the age of 60. The difficulty of finding a full-time baby sitter for our children often resulted in me and my husband taking alternate days off. We were blessed to have pastors wives look after our children as they offered. I advocated for a childcare facility for children under four years old when my eldest child was born over 15 years ago. It was only last year that they finally opened a proper childcare facility for children under four years old, a service which my last child can now enjoy. A great burden lifted for myself and my family. I do acknowledge all the support provided to us over the years by our nenas, our cousins, our aunties and our families in helping care for our children when we couldn't find people to babysit for us.

This has been one of the reasons that I have turned down many opportunities to further my working career, especially those that requires me to travel and take on more demanding roles, one including an offer to be our Premier of Niue's personal secretary. I understand the struggles of being a working mother and do my best to provide support and encouragement to working mothers. The four day working week, the child allowances and infant allowance are some of the benefits we have been blessed with under the leadership of our Premier Sir Toke Talagi. I am well and truly grateful for all these benefits because it has been a tremendous help to raising our family.

My success as a woman has been first and foremost giving birth and raising six beautiful children with my husband being there by my side throughout it all. Raising them in my village of Hakupu Atua and my husband's village of Makefu and providing them with the lifestyle that I was privileged to have, so that they can enjoy the best of life is another one of my successes. Growing up in a world with technology especially the internet, social media, mobile phones, tablets and more is the life my kids will experience. The saying where it takes a village to raise a child rings true for my family because the support from everyone, family and community has been overwhelming.

Holding a senior position in government and supporting the developments in the area of food security and sustainable natural resource management has also been fulfilling. The guidance and mentoring I received from those senior to me have helped me get to where I am today. Supporting our village developments is another, a recent achievement for me in this area will be helping to coordinate the development of the Tuhia Marine and Nature Learning Center. A center that will help encourage the sharing of traditional and contemporary knowledge in the marine and conservation area between the young and older generations. This was a project that saw all members of the community, young and old, men and women come together to help with its construction. A valuable Taoga that will be used by many generations to come.

I believe that although it is challenging to be a working mother, anything is possible with the right support system in place. Taking time out from our busy lives to reflect and celebrate our successes is something I feel we all need to do as women, especially investing some time on our physical and mental wellbeing. Often we do not allow ourselves this privilege as we are too caught in our daily lives of raising our families, working and doing other things. Most times women can be their own worst critics. In order to lift women up rather then bring them down, I feel we can support young women by Sharing our experiences and mentoring them so they are able to cope with the challenges they too may face as young women. My only hope is that my children and their children will continue to enjoy and experience the blessings I have had in my lifetime.

My Life As A Woman: Niue Edition #2

My earliest memories would be around the age of three. My father was pretty much non-existent, but when he did turn up I remember well his drunken rages. I remember vividly him throwing my mother around like a rag doll…dragging her by the hair and punching her in the face time and time again. I have several motion pictures that remain embedded and forever running through my mind, until this day, of him doing this. Despite this, my mother stayed with him and gave him four more children after me.

My name is Carmen. I was born in a small town on the foot of the Snowy Mountains in Australia. I was the fifth born child of my mother and my father's second born with my mother. I am of mixed race, my father being an Italian immigrant to Australia and my mother was Austrian born. My mother's first three children were all adopted out before I met them. I have since met two of them during my adult life.

I was a carefree and happy child, for the most part. I took many risks, climbed the highest trees, jumped from ridiculous heights, hurled myself into creeks filled with fat hungry leeches, tore down the steepest hills on a scooter skidding and almost removing my kneecap several times and I would swing upside down from whatever elevation that was high enough for me to hang from. We were a poor family and I was probably the most raggedly dressed child at school, but I was a good student. I took my lessons pretty seriously and I loved school.

However, as time went by my mother must have grown weary with having an absentee husband, of having no money or perhaps she had enough of being at the receiving end of my father's fist when he did come home. Either way, after having six children with him she decided enough was enough, so we packed up and moved on to start a new life in a new town.

I left friends and all that was familiar to me behind. I would turn nine soon and would spend my birthday in unfamiliar surroundings. Looking back it seemed like a lifetime I spent in this new town, but in fact it was only a few short months. During those months my mother started drinking…a lot. We were often left home alone, in a house with no panes of glass in the windows, no furniture, no food, nothing. Sometimes we were dumped at strangers' houses with other kids with absentee parents, other times we were left on the street outside of pubs until they closed late at night. The only constant we children had was each other. My older sister, less than two years older than me, myself, my younger brother, the small twins, and the baby.

During those months of my mother's self-made oblivion I survived being sexually molested, neglected, going hungry, being terrified, running for my life, hiding from police in the bushes so I wouldn't be caught wagging school, shattering my wrist after falling from a great height when home alone and the list goes on. But somehow we survived.

Our mother was reported to the authorities by the neighbours I think, after my younger brother was knocked unconscious falling off a swing when our mother was out again. I tried my best to revive him by slapping his face and pouring water over him. The ambulance came. He lived.

The first visit from the authorities was a warning to my mother to improve our living conditions. The second visit was to take us away. After a court appearance where my father turned up and claimed he did not want responsibility of us, we were removed from our parents care. I became a ward of the state.

Being institutionalized had its moments. Being separated from my brothers and sisters was not nice, but manageable. My world became a selfish, self-centered one where I thought purely about myself. I learnt how to adapt. I became a chameleon and I blended in well with my surroundings. I learnt how to get what I needed by fitting in and at times rebelling against the "rules". I learnt well how to survive.

The girls home I found myself in could only be described as a prison for children, where we slept head to toe in beds sharing head lice and sad stories, where the institution's kitchen walls were alive at night, moving, as a thousand cockroaches made their way into our morning cereal, where if you weren't fast enough and smart enough, you could find yourself in the clutches of a deranged, traumatised schizophrenic sixteen year old whose sole purpose it seemed was to make everyone's life a misery, where the rules were strict, where you had no privacy, where your life was in the hands of strangers.

Almost a year passed until myself and my siblings were extracted from our various institutions and reunited in a family group home. As "ex-cons" we needed to be de-institutionalised and reformed to make us fit for fostering.

At last I found myself with a "real" mum and dad. At last I felt safe. At the tender age of ten I had a mother and father that took care of my needs for me. That taught me what was right and wrong and showed me how things were "meant to be done". This couple, who took us in, saved me as a person and helped me become the woman I am today. Under their firm but fair guidance, I thrived. I no longer needed to look over my shoulder for danger. I no longer had to constantly look out for my younger siblings and do head counts to make sure they were all there and that they were ok. They encouraged me to greatness. They uplifted my downtrodden self-esteem. They elevated me on high and told me anything was possible.

I was in this family group home for three years before I was ready to be fostered out. I was almost thirteen. My foster parents, my new mum and dad, gave me a different perspective on life. They lived on a farm a good distance from the main township. I caught two buses to get to school. I was free to roam the country side, track kangaroos in the bush, run alongside them barefoot and carefree. I loved life, I loved school. I wrote poetry, I wrote songs, I taught myself the rudimentary skills of playing the guitar. I became a pretty good athlete and gymnast around this time as well, encouraged by my foster father. There were a few elements of discontent in this home, however, but nothing compared to what I had already endured.

I thought long and hard what I wanted to do with my life when I finished school. Due to my love for sports, I thought I should be a sports teacher, however, others encouraged me to do nursing. Once that self-centred layer I created around myself peeled away, I developed a great compassion for others, where I would fight for the underdog, where I would stand up for those being mistreated. I guess this was why some encouraged me to do nursing. So nursing I did, for a time.

Once I completed my senior studies at school I went a little crazy for a year, enjoying my new found freedom. No one telling me what to do and when. It was very liberating. I frequently enjoyed nights out, my morals became a tad loose and I generally, as I said, went a little crazy. But after a year of this nonsense I had a good look at myself and said "enough".

I found my life partner and eventually we moved to his place of birth. Niue. That was thirty three years ago now. Niue is now my home. Niue is now my life.

I remember when I first landed in Niue. Emerging from the plane all those years ago I recall being hit by a huge wave of heat, enveloping me in a suffocating embrace. The humidity was overpowering. I looked down from the top of the stairs into a sea of beautiful brown faces...so many brown faces. I recall tugging my sundress more closely around my knees as a gust of wind threatened to lift the hem of my dress up around my hips, Marilyn Munroe style...

It was, for me, like stepping into a movie scene. Once clear of customs and bag collection in the very cramped and small terminal, I waded, dripping with perspiration through a throng of beautiful Niuean's as I desperately scanned the crowd trying to find my partner, who had arrived in Niue several weeks before me. Although I struggled to see him he found me easily enough as I was possibly one of the only palagis on the plane.

The drive home from the airport was surreal. The colours seemed brighter than usual. The air around me held a golden glow. The cars were older and some quite dilapidated. I was driven home in an old van with no door. Then I got my first breath-taking view of the ocean as we descended the higher plateau towards the lower one. Never had I seen a bluer ocean. At last I knew I was truly home. Wow, just wow.

So, here I am. Four children and eleven point five grandchildren later, I am still here, still breathing and still surviving. Not every outsider can live here. It's pointless coming to Niue with a superior attitude thinking you know better than the locals. It's time wasting to think that you can come here and beat your chest saying you know what's best for the people here. The Niueans here know what is best for Niue. I had no problem adjusting to the lifestyle. My chameleon skills learnt throughout my life have served me well. If you have a genuine love, compassion and understanding for the people here, they in turn will love you back, it's that simple really. I often forget the colour of my skin now. I forget I am a palagi.

As a white woman in Niue, I did not personally find it difficult living here. I accepted things as they were and adjusted accordingly. At times, however, in the first ten years living in Niue, it was indeed tough as my partner and I dealt with some very personal domestic family issues. It was truly a struggle as a woman, as a white woman, and as an individual who had no family of her own to turn to. I was, after all, living on a remote island in the South Pacific, where could I possibly go, and having limited income, or none at all, made it even harder. I was too busy trying to get through these times to really notice and appreciate what Niue had to offer and I was ashamed. I worked hard and tried even harder. Although the island, as it were, seemed to accept me and I felt welcome, those closer to home did not. It was a very painful time as my children were small and I tried my best to protect them from the worst of it. To this day I still feel robbed of how it could have been.

It was only when I finally found the courage, finally found my voice that I spoke out. It was only then that things began to change. People can change, if they want to. It's not impossible. Some choose to change, others do not. I was fortunate and the cycle was broken.

As I have no real culture of my own, not having lived long enough with either birth parent to grasp their heritage, I have since fully embraced the Niuean culture as my own. One of the things I dearly love about the people of Niue is how they support each other and embrace each other in times of need. When a loved one is lost, when someone needs help, when a child needs loving, there is always someone there, always, and not just one person, but throngs of them. I love how the people come together to celebrate life, to comfort at times of sadness. You are never truly alone here. If I was born in Niue, I would never have been lost in the welfare system. There would always have been an "Aunty" to take you in. I love the truly giving and caring nature of the people of Niue. I love their passion. I love the people. Their Taoga has become my Taoga.

My partner, now my husband, is very traditional. We don't use chemicals on the soil, we weed our huge bush gardens by hand. We don't use the plough to prepare the land for planting, we use the traditional slash and burn method. Our produce from our plantations are free from pesticides and fertilizers. We also rely on fish caught from my husband's vaka. He is a canoe builder and fisherman. We are a family of vaka paddlers.

I remember the early years as a very young mother I would go to our garden with the family to weed. At eight months pregnant it was hard, crawling around the rocks on my hands and knees, sleeping at times under the leaves of the taro plants when I grew weary. If I had a new born, they would come along to the garden with me and sleep on a pillow in a box, covered with netting to ward of the flies and mosquitoes and feed from my breast if they woke, as I held them with one hand and weeded with the other. Life was a struggle, but I got through.

I have worked several jobs since my arrival into Niue. I've been a barperson, a truck driver, a shop assistant, a journalist for a local paper, a cleaner, ran a small gymnasium, operated a small day care centre and pumped gas for a living. All occupations I took on between giving birth and raising small children. During the time when my children were small I was able to take them along with me to my places of work. As they grew and attended school, I was able to take on office jobs including accounting/administration roles at the New Zealand High Commission followed by a similar but more extensive role for an overseas organisation based in Niue. From there I progressed to managing a company, then a few more accounting/administration roles after that until finally where I am today. I currently work for a Non-Profit Organisation as a project officer for a marine conservation project.

Success is what you make of it and what you perceive success to be. For me, after years of struggle, success meant I could finally stand on my own two feet financially and be a good wife, a good mother and I could provide for my family. Success meant I did not feel the need to have everyone's approval, nor did I need everyone to like me.

The important thing is to learn from history, your own history. If your parents failed at being parents, you make sure you be a damned good parent. If you don't like the way you handled a particular situation, you fix it, you make amends. If something was your fault, you claim responsibility, learn from it and move on. If you don't like something and its hurting you, speak out. Never give up on yourself. Learn to forgive yourself, learn to love yourself.

I don't blame anyone else for my own situations. I chose my own path as an adult and I alone determined how that path was walked. If at any time I didn't like the direction I chose, I would try to change course by repairing and manipulating the path. If I couldn't stop the momentum I was travelling, I would do everything in my power to at least slow things down to give myself time to think of what my next course of action would be.

I am a woman, I am who I am, and I am enough.

Carmen Fuhiniu

12th June 2020

55 years old

Niue Island

My Life As A Woman: Niue Edition #3

My name's Natasha Bell, and this the beginning of my story. When I was born my Mum was told that I was an epileptic baby. It took a while before they could actually diagnose me as being an epileptic, but I was two months old when my mother had to experience something she had never experienced before, as she does. She had only been in New Zealand for two years.

I am born of a Niuean mother and a European father - Kiwi to be exact. Um, but I know, um, I am now currently thirty-five? Thirty-five I think, no thirty.. yeah thirty-five, um. I have led quite the adventurous life, from the age of five I was a ballerina. I got to experience dancing with the Royal Academy of New Zealand, as well as being a netball player, rugby player, tried soccer, but mum wasn't too happy when I didn't get out of the car because there were no boys in the te- no girls in the team. Nevertheless, I have worked many jobs, from a dance teacher, to a fully qualified beauty therapist, to a panel beater, a butcher, a cleaner at Suncorp Stadium, as well as sewing, and welding blinds and awnings.

I have experienced good things in life, such as dancing, with the academy, and I've also experienced bad things in life, such as drugs, alcohol, and love. I have three gorgeous children, who are my world, but unfortunately for me, the grandparent of the in-law is withholding them from me. That is a whole other story of very dramatic proportions and has been as such for the past five years. I lived in Niue for two years, which was my experience of being a panel beater, and a dance teacher of, an American boy - amazing little boy, whose father lives on the island. And I also got to experience my family. Where I came from, where my mum was born, where my mum went to school. My aunty still currently lives there, and I can't wait to go back and visit. But I was lucky enough to experience a couple years of my teenage life living there. Unfortunately, going there was on the purposes of letting my Pop go, and taking him back home to be put to rest, next to Nana.

Being a panel beater there was quite an experience. Our shop was right on the water's edge, so lunch break, I would sit on the roof of an old broken down van that we had, and I'd eat my lunch, watching whales dance in the sea, just for me. It was also the same time that the wharf of Alofi, the main centre in Niue, was wiped out by a hurricane. We had American Seabees come to fix the wharf, and I was one of the islanders that helped show them, well pretty much show them where to drink, as well as where to experience the most beautiful parts. Within the caves, within the waters, within the people of every village, mine being Avetele. I love it. I know, I know this has been a long time coming, um, but this, me writing things down became a little, quite um, hard, tricky, and really emotional. Just seeing what I was writing, so I thought I'd try. I'd try recording it [cough], I thought I'd try recording it and sending you what I have, what I can say for now. And if you want me to carry on in detail, I will, but it is going to take me a little bit of time. Only because it means I have to open up some, some scars that I thought had healed, and I didn't really want to open. But if it's something you'd like me to continue, if it's probably something I should probably do. It has a potential to heal a lot of parts that need to be healed within myself.

Nevertheless, my name is Natasha Bell. I'm a thirty-five year old epileptic mother of three, with an epileptic child who was diagnosed at the age of five, and who is - who suffers it a lot deeper than I do, and the only reason I want to tell my story is for her, in hopes that she knows that it's not a disability, it's a super power. It makes us stronger and it helps that we are Niuean, because that does give us even more strength in a sense, of knowing just how supportive and how far my family will go to ensure we come back to our roots in these times, and my root is Niue, although I was born in New Zealand.

My mum is my life. She raised me by herself. She did it while studying, whilst working, whilst volunteering, being a care worker. Whilst learning to be able to understand how she could better help and support me through a superpower we had no knowledge about. That thanks to my Mum, and a wonderful woman in the studies, Helen Bruce, we got to learn a little bit of something so large, that we're still yet to learn a lot more of. I'm sorry, but now I'm crying, and I've got to go.

My Life As A Woman: Niue Edition #4

My name is Mamata Etaone Salepou Gill. I was born in Niue, in the village called Alofi, on 26th March 1950. I am called Mamata, so much easier than my long name above. I was named Salepou as my surname until I was 17 years old when I learnt that Salepou was my fathers' Christian name. From that age, I adopted Hunuki, for the correct surname.

My parents were Salepou Motuvale Hunuki and Vatasi Mokahemana Hunuki. I grew up with Salepou Motuvale Hunukis' eldest brother Tuhega, his wife Manogiaga together, with my brother Hunukitama, who was a year younger than I. We were raised with five of our cousins from our uncle Tuhegas' side. My parents left for Papua and New Guinea when I was two years old. I did not remember what they looked like when they left to work as church missionaries in Papua and New Guinea.

My grandparents often encouraged me to take up nursing when I grew up. In 1967 I left Niue for New Zealand. I saw an advertisement for a community nursing training, and I applied for it. I got interviewed and accepted for training for eighteen months. I completed community nursing training and I learnt that there's psychiatric nursing training. Again, I got accepted for psychiatric nursing. I did the comprehensive nursing course for 3 years. This nursing training was cut short, because I had five years of nursing courses. At the end of this comprehensive nursing course, I was awarded for excellence in theory and in practice.

I got married after my nursing training and had two beautiful girls, the eldest is Michelle Alevine Gill and Zita Meleone Gill. Mr. Gill had a job as a Director for telecom Niue in 1976. We came and stayed in Niue for 3 years. I had gotten a job as a researcher for wheezing bronchitis.

My advice to women living in Niue, to follow their hearts, go out into the world, if they can and study, gain some working experience, and return to Niue. Most of the Niuean people are kind and everyone are treated like their own family. They gave me food when I needed and drinks when I needed, and they do care for my well-being.

I love being on Niue, although, I can still have goose pimples when some local people ask me, whether I have seen ghosts on the road, especially when there's a funeral. I just tell them that ghosts cannot hurt them.

I hope that you have enjoyed reading my story.

My Life As A Woman: Nicaragua Edition

I am Isabel Cárdenas, I was born and grew up in Nindirí department of Masaya. I lived my childhood within a very believing family of God and under the evangelical religion. At the age of 2, my parents moved to the city of Rivas where I currently reside.

My family is made up of five brothers, my mom, and dad who have served as an inspiration for me in the struggles in which they have been involved in order to bring my brothers and myself forward. For a few years, I suffered from my mother's illness that brought her to the brink of death. Her fight against cancer made her a strong and courageous woman.

My father always brought food to the house with his work. With that effort, I completed my primary and secondary studies at a religiously oriented school. For five years I studied and managed to crown my university career in Criminal Sciences obtaining my Bachelor of Law degree.

I have worked hard to build a reputation that places me among the most prominent attorneys in Rivera society. I had the opportunity to do postgraduate studies in family matters and it is a goal for me to reach other specialties in commercial law and criminal law.

As a lawyer, I have had experiences that have inspired me to help people, always bearing in mind that the just financial reward is the consequence of a job well done. Likewise, I provide legal advice to those who request it without remuneration.

The study of this university career was a difficult decision, looking for a way to help helpless people in the face of some unjust situations, I decided on Law at the Polytechnic University of Nicaragua until culminating in 2015.

MY PASSIONS

Although I live in a country with a macho culture, I feel that I have made some important achievements in my life. I am passionate about being able to conclude my family cases. With this, I contribute to the fair distribution of justice.

From the Nicaraguan culture, I adore the fortress, the hardened character of a people that has struggled for years, and with all of this continues to be a very friendly and supportive people. My town is full of working people and in each town the idiosyncrasy that characterizes them to be unique.

At work, I am covering areas such as property, family, and commercial. Advising and fulfilling the functions of the legal area of non-governmental companies that offer support and advice to sugarcane producers.

I aspire and work to occupy a position that allows me to provide more help from a public institution to people with limited resources who cannot bear the expenses of legal representation.

About 5 years ago, I became a mother, product of a relationship that was not the best, and that kept me submerged in an environment of physical and psychological violence. With the strength that my son has given me, I managed to get out of that relationship to settle as a woman and mother. Always with the vision of seeing my little one grow in health and happiness, I work to always offer him the best.

Along this path, I have come across people who have been very supportive and have given me professional assistance, contributing their knowledge and experiences to provide solutions to situations that I did not see clearly. My professional successes have been in the family and commercial areas, as well as in the civil part corresponding to property.

TIPS FOR NICARAGUAN WOMEN

Job opportunities are not the same for women and men. The macho society does not contribute to the growth of women and physical and psychological violence is an issue that has become the constant struggle of pro-woman organizations.

A woman does not need a man to get ahead. There is always a way to go to offer yourself the opportunity to be what you want to be. It doesn't matter if you had the help of your family or grew up alone.

The woman that I am now has allowed me to realize that only with daily and constant effort can dreams and goals be achieved. Never give up on the pursuit of happiness. The daily struggle of the Nicaraguan woman is admirable and I see it reflected in that woman who slaps tortillas to feed her children, the one who washes and irons others, the one who, despite suffering from thirst, hunger and heat stroke, comes out daily to offer her children a plate of food.

"Do one thing a day that scares you." – Eleanor Roosevelt

My Life As A Woman: Niger Edition

What is the interest with women's rights in Niger? Like in several countries especially the African ones, Niger women are in very specific conditions, very low to limited rights and many restrictions that take their roots from ancient traditions and beliefs. An ongoing fight that we wish one day will do its wonders.

My name is Nadja, I'm 27 years old and I got married when I was 15, my parents thought it was best to marry me to the first man who asked for my hand. What I thought was a good decision, was not the best after all; my marriage at a very young age had more cons than I anticipated. Child marriages are a result of many societal influences and two main issues; poverty and fear of "unwanted pregnancies".

Gifts and money are given to the bride's family during marriages as a sign of appreciation, as a poor country that gesture sadly turns very quick into a trading move and younger girls are usually the target, in addition to that, the fathers are happy because it's one less person to feed and take care of, therefore less expenses for the household, as in for the fear of unwanted pregnancies, it's the lack of education's fault. You can't expect less from a country where the talk about sexuality is taboo, girls never learn about intimate relationships, what is the best way to protect themselves from diseases or even pregnancies. Many other countries with the help of UNICEF tried to establish sexual education programs to prevent these dilemmas, but elders refused in view of that it will mold a perverted society with an increase of sex before marriage, it would tempt the youth's curiosity, but rape and unprotected intercourse are already common, but they wouldn't like to admit that, having to come to terms with that would only mean admitting that the society is already somehow perverted, whilst receiving knowledge on these topics would only have a great impact like controlling rape impulses, decrease of diseases, and less unwanted pregnancies.

I once thought those excuses were valid to marry a girl at such a young age, so when my father saw me being intercepted by this man at a Haoussa meat restaurant, he accepted giving my hand to him after 10 minutes of conversation, he claimed he knew his family and they were a great fit; he was surely motivated, and accepted their status, and just like that I got married at the age of 15. I had to stop going to school because my schedule was not aligning with my day to day chores, but after my first child I wanted more for myself, I wanted to go back to school, learn so I could work and provide for my kids and feel financially independent. I was talking to a friend from Mali who was making a good living out of her selling affairs, she used to travel buy fabrics and jewellery and sell them here in Niger, but I lacked knowledge, my math basics were doomed, and my communication skills as well. I had forgotten how to write proper French, which is the official language, the first hiccup was my husband but after long talks and trying to convince him, he agreed to let me finish my studies. Sadly, he was pressured by his family, as they feared I would let him take care of the kids alone. He started to feel frustrated and begged me to back down, but at that point, I had had enough and I stood my ground, and around that time, I had my second daughter. It was harder to keep up I had no time energy to be going to school, cooking, baring two kids making sure my household is well taken care of but I did not want a bitter taste of failure so I kept pushing myself harder.

Thanks to school and my perseverance, I know how to write, how to keep check of my money, and fructify it. I travel when I can and buy fabrics from other nearby countries in Africa to sell them. If I had let other people dictate my life even as an adult, I wouldn't have had the opportunity to feel as free and as happy, my husband is still not pleased by me flying with my own wings, but my happiness and my kid's comfort is and always will be my infinite fuel to go on further in life and thrive, my dream is to have enough funds to have my own shop and I will make it come true.

What Life Looks Like As A Woman Growing Up In Nigeria

Gone are the negative perceptions and challenges which try to control us, Nigerian women are fiercely fighting for their opportunities and winning. Our strength is being expressed in various iterations from entrepreneurship and our career goals to nurturer, role model, and mentorship roles we play daily. Nigerian women are no longer just struggling to survive, we are taking charge. In this article, I am going to brief you on what life looks like as a woman growing up in Nigeria.

In Nigeria, it takes a village to raise a kid. Your parents are not the only ones who hold the responsibility for your upbringing, there are always aunties, uncles, neighbours, church members, and friends that will put you back on track when you misbehave. You could get spanked at any time by these same "Uncles" and "Aunties". One hand does not nurse a child, so said the proverb of my beloved country.

I have always felt incredibly proud to be a Nigerian woman and privileged to stand on the shoulders of generations of strong Amazon women. My grandmother was a market trader who was the quintessential Proverbs 31 kind of woman. She was an entrepreneur and a matriarch. I have been told when she came home from the market, she always bought a little something special for everyone in the household. I have learned that it is possible to have a family and a thriving career from strong Nigerian women.

Nigerian women are some of the most enterprising women in the world. Nigerian women are also some of the most fashionable and best "packaged" women in the world. From the farmer to the market trader to the head of corporations – Nigerian women know how to dress up and stand up, despite the hardships they often face based on our bad government and economics, education, and so on. Our flamboyant head scarfs, being one of the best mind blowing culture-emulated by many countries throughout Africa, if not the world to the way we swing our hips to good music – Nigerian women express their joy, their femininity, their identity, and their strength with a quintessential Nigerian swagger that is unbeatable. In some cases, I don't like to be associated with that tag of Nigerian woman, but at most, with a title that I am sometimes proud to have to be a Nigerian woman.

As a Nigerian woman, I am proud of our heritage, proud of our culture, proud of our history as trailblazers, our entrepreneurial spirit, our loving nature, the list goes on. But in the same breath, as a Nigerian woman, I feel ashamed that I am still forced to deal with a country where my rights are overlooked for those of my male counterparts despite my struggle towards having a better life still of myself in this process, where the blame culture is strong when it comes to rape and abuse, where I have to work twice as hard and very hard to be recognised for my achievements and where my personal achievements are second-guessed just because of my gender.

As a Nigerian woman, however, I have a sense of purpose and responsibility. I am a citizen of the most populous country in Africa and if I can help to get gender equality right here, I will be helping to create a ripple effect for the rest of the continent and ease the struggle of other women like me. I am passionate about Nigeria and would do all that I can to make it a great nation. I say nation because I'm particular about the people as opposed to geography or topography. Nigeria is not an easy place to live in, however, I can't see myself living in any other country.

Despite tough living conditions, Nigerian women continue to thrive, succeed and flourish in different areas of their lives such as family, career, community, etc. the tough conditions are just what you need to build muscles for greatness. A Nigerian woman is like a rose growing out of concrete. We are strong, resilient, hardworking, kind, resourceful, and fashionable, amongst many other things. Between our parents giving us the same education as the men and telling us we can achieve any goal we set for ourselves, our teachers and professors expecting excellence through our learning years, the media selling beauty and perfection, only to be faced with all sorts of views, more often a very traditional view as to how a woman is supposed to conduct herself, get married, run her home... and it's actually impossible not to be strong.

I find that culture and religion have a lot to play in the place women have in the Nigerian society, but many women are breaking out of the mold and are living life fully and abundantly without worrying about the stereotypes placed on women that are still prevalent in the society. Nigeria is full of energy and passion and as a woman in Nigeria, it's difficult not to tap into it. I respect all women who have pioneered change and have empowered and fought for the rights of women and I pray God uses me to change even one person's life for good. Let us empower the next generation by supporting one another and fulfilling what we have been called to do on this earth to the best of our abilities.

Valerie

My Life As A Woman: Nigeria Edition #2

Becoming successful in a patriarchy society: a personal life experience

It is no exaggeration to say that growing up as a young and ambitious lady in a patriarchal society in Nigeria is but a tug of war between survival for success and a perpetually constraining culture and tradition. I am Azee, the daughter of Mr. and Mrs. Hameed. I was born and bred in the remote town of Patigi, Kwara State, Nigeria, and belong to the minority tribe of Tiv. Having completed my primary and secondary education in the neighboring town of Share, I emigrated to the capital city of Ilorin August 2009 for my tertiary education having gotten admission to study political science at the prestigious University of Ilorin in the preceding month. It was during my stay at the University of Ilorin that I got the spark to life and decided to look beyond the walls my environment and culture built around me.

From childhood, most Nigerian female children are trained to be good wives and mothers to their husbands and children alike. They are meant to perceive the world they live as "the world of men" where little competition is expected of them; while the men are bred to become 'superhumans'. My four years in University was simply a dialectic between the bent-to-subjugate guys in the department and the young lady that is as well committed to being outstanding at practically everything the men get involved into. I began my sojourn to greatness with the position of class representative which I held in my 100 level and 200 level respectively. In 300 level, I took a leap on my campus political life to emerge as the faculty of social sciences' welfare director; a position that earned me the nickname "Nigerian Margaret Thatcher (NMT)". I became very outspoken, started attending conferences, and soon developed an interest in writing essays. I became a regular selection for my department's intervarsity debate team to the University of Ibadan and equally made friends across other universities.

With my convocation in the university and the subsequent deployment to the upper north of Nigeria (Katsina State) for my compulsory one year of national service, I became a bit disengaged from activism and politics and found a new love in writing and advocacy. My articles on WhatsApp, Twitter, and Facebook became the everyday tonic of most friends and associates. As they had a feel of the good articles, constructive criticisms, and analysis of political issues that I constantly roll out to them via my updates, I built on the opportunity their audience afforded to build my writing abilities.

"Why not channel this energy into money-making?", the voice from a friend who is into freelance writing and is already making a good sum from it echoed in my ear exactly one year after my national service, and that was how he started outsourcing his articles for me to write. I was fantastic at it and soon became his most preferred hand. I made a good sum from him and embarked on the second phase of my academic life. I enrolled in the University of Lagos in the year 2017 for a master's degree in political science and graduated with a Ph.D. grade in the wake of the year 2020. Today, I boast a master's degree and I am also into freelance writing. Working for no one gives me the independence I have always sought, and the earning from my newly found career gave me the required financial freedom. I came to realize however that no one is anything except that which it conditions itself to be. The society wanted a kitten from me, but I made a cub out of myself. And an obstacle scaled became a stepping stone for greatness. An open mind and the ability to locate opportunities in adversaries was the secret behind it all. This is my success story!

My Life As A Woman: North Korea Edition #1

Hello, my name is SoYul Lee; I am a North Korean defector. I was born in Tongchon near the coast. As a woman in North Korea, I did not grow up with sufficient amount of food. Our family commonly skipped meals and had to work most of the time. When I was around ten years old, my mother passed away from starvation. Then my father got married with my step-mother. I would go to school and learn basic principles of math, science, music, etc., and when I came back home, there would be nothing to eat. At the time, I really didn't have any dream or goal; it was just living one day after another. My father and my step-mother would constantly fight, due to shortage of food.

And that anger would be aimed towards me and I would get hit from abuse every day, so I decided to run away from the family and live as Kotjebi (Homeless North Korean). I would go to relatives house to house and do any work I could do, such as coal-mining, selling herbs, etc.

After a few years, I heard that my father has also passed away from my relative. Then I ran away from North Korea and went to China. I waited in my grandmother's house near the Chinese and North Korea's border and waited until the water level went down. It was near October just before the river would freeze and I crossed the river to go to China. The water was so cold and my body was shivering.

After crossing the river and walking for a while, I came across a Chinese restaurant. Luckily, the restaurant owner was Korean-Chinese and was kind enough to let me work there. It was going well until one night, the owner came in drunk and tried to rape me. I pushed him away and ran outside. I did not know where to go, so I went to a friend's house who I got to know when I was working in the restaurant. She took me in and let me sleep in her house for the night. The next day, she brought me to a tea house that her aunt owned and asked her aunt if I could work there. Her aunt let me work there and provided me with a room to sleep in. Everything was going well again until the Chinese cop patrolled the area to look for North Korean defectors.

I was fortunate enough to not get caught this time, but I knew it was just a matter of time until I got caught. If I was caught, I would be returned to North Korea and face harsh punishment or even death. This was when I decided to go to South Korea. I talked to lots of brokers and planned to go to South Korea. The broker explained that I would have to go to Thailand first in order to go to South Korea. So, I was put in a van to Thailand, and when I arrived in Thailand; I was immediately put into jail, where I was held for 3 months. I wasn't treated well, partially because I was a woman. After I was flown to South Korea, for 40 days, I was under surveillance of Korea's national intelligence service. They asked me a bunch of questions to figure out if I was a spy. Then, they let me go and helped me to get a stabilized life in South Korea.

As of right now, I am working as a North Korean traditional introducer in South Korea. It was a struggle being a woman and running away from North Korea. I hope all women in North Korea don't give up and lose their hope.

My Life As A Woman: North Korea Edition #2

The author has not been verified, but the story has been proven authentic.

INTERVIEW

Yeonmi Park

Where did you grow up?

I was born in Hyesan, North Korea, where I spent most of my childhood until the age of 13 when my mother and I had to flee the country.

How did you grow up?

I remember our one-story house that was on top of the hill. My childhood was a typical North Korean girl. I remember playing in the Yalu with my sister and her friends. During my childhood, a majority of the commodities were expensive. For example, manufactured toys were costly, meaning they were available to very few people. Therefore, we made animal carvings out of mud and dolls out of cutting paper. My mum would make pinwheels for us, which we fastened on the metal footbridge above the railway and named it the cloud bridge. In school, the curriculum was tailored to make the students worship the regime and follow a doctrine that was against their 'state enemies.'

Did you have parents or maybe a grandmother who inspired you?

My father was a successful entrepreneur, and he inspired many locals. I remember he quit his metal foundry job to pursue business. Around 1990, North Korea started undergoing challenging times, the economy of the country had just collapsed, and there was a great famine. Fending for the family became hard, but my dad got into the smuggling business to make ends meet for us. This was a massive risk for him, considering the government's laws on such kinds of business. My father, unlike most people I knew in the society, was not brainwashed by the ideologies of the regime and fear that was being perpetrated. I heard him complain about the government on multiple occasions, which made my mother very anxious. I picked up the enterprising spirit from my dad, and at 11 years old, I got a loan from my mother, which I used to start a fruit business.

What did you study, and what did you want to be growing up and why?

The experience my parents had impacted on me while trying to engage different business ventures to provide for us made me gravitate towards entrepreneurship. I have a Bachelor of Arts in Economics, and I purpose to work as a human rights activist and also pursue my interest in advancing new business models that will be solutions to the social and cultural issues in the community.

What do you love about your culture?

I recall when I was young, we lived in a community where people would care for each other. For instance, during dinner, you would see smoke coming through the chimneys of different homes. In case the smoke was not coming through a particular home, people would go and knock on the door to check on the family. Despite the rough regime, community members always look out for each other.

What are you currently doing for work?

I am a human-rights advocate whose goal is to speak out on behalf of the millions of oppressed persons in Asian countries. These groups of people include refugees who are exploited in exchange for their survival.

Tell me your struggles as a woman?

In North Korea, I was born in a regime of oppression where the freedom of expression was absent. I had to live through the harrowing experience of human trafficking. I also had a tough time adjusting in a social setting. Similarly, I have had a hard time relating to men, especially after the atrocities I went through in different places.

Tell me your successes as a woman?

Well, my greatest success has been the opportunity and courage to tell my story on international platforms. This has shed light on the various challenges that North Koreans face. I believe my work will act as a motivation for nations to get involved in the human-right abuses that are taking place in my country.

My Life As A Woman: North Macedonia Edition

I'm Irena, 29 years old, born in Skopje capital of R.N. Macedonia. I'm Macedonian but my country is a beautiful mix of cultures and nationalities. On every street, in every coffee shop, in every neighborhood you can meet different nationalities, different religions, people even talk different languages, and yet again in a strange way we all understand and love each other since we are all the same. This is the Balkan (The Land of Honey and Blood) so we have learned a long time ago to laugh through the tears, to appreciate the small daily treasures, to love our neighbors. Our families here in Macedonia are mainly traditional, but with every new generation we are striving for a modern lifestyle. Our society is mainly conservative and patriarchal. Even though the Macedonian woman is emancipated, highly appreciated in both the society and the household, it is also silently expected to be one level degraded by men in every aspect. And yet, there is me.

My whole life I wanted to be a businesswoman. In Macedonia my plans didn't go smoothly, and here it is why...What should I do for a living? Am I worth it? When will I have children? Is my career more important than my family? My whole life I was struggling with questions like this. I didn't believe in myself. I was depressed and hopeless, as many of my peers still are. I graduated from the prestigious University of Economics in Macedonia. I was set to make my dreams come true. As I already had a plan, I opened my first business venture, small business for import of beverages. But soon I realized, It was a man's world that I was living in. How is this possible to be happening today in this society? I was shocked and I was disgusted by the proposals I was getting from men. It was all business and the rules were already set. There was no place for women in it. I was still young and impressionable, and I couldn't believe how this could be happening. I was naive. I felt defeated and soon enough I had to sell my business. Ironically the person I sold it to, was also a man. I felt that this was not a job for a woman, not for me.

I got a new job that was considered more "woman-friendly", as a bank clerk, but it seemed that the majority of the managers there were also men. Where is the woman role model that I desperately needed? And then it hit me. The only reason that I wanted to become a strong woman was because I was surrounded by strong women. My mother was a survivor, businesswoman herself, but also my grandmother who was born in times of war, but also an academic woman that married who she wanted to, when she wanted to in the 1950s and not how she was instructed by society especially at that time, a woman that worked in the first academic institutions in Macedonia when many women were not allowed to work. My mother and my grandmother are my definition of a woman. I often remember my now 89-year-old grandmother's advice to not listen to anyone when they say I can't do it, because I can do whatever I want to, to marry only if I want to not because my society says so.

I lost my dream job, I lost some friends along the way, I lost part of myself in the process, but I gained so much more. Life is a struggle for all of us, especially us as women, but the strength in every woman is in her weaknesses. The night that I decided to sell my business because I wasn't able to grow it as I wanted to, it was my lowest point in life. And at that point my life started. I let go of everything that I cared for at that moment. The hardest but easiest decision of my life. When I lost everything I fought for, it was the moment that I became a woman. I realized how strong I was. Now I set myself up for new challenges and I know I will succeed.

My life as a woman in Macedonia, a woman that is smart, ambitious, strong but set for failure by the male chauvinism of the society, I have some advice for every girl − you will succeed because nothing can stop you from living your truth. If I could survive in my conditions you can too, wherever you are, because no physical or emotional pain can stop us, women, we are magical like that.

433

My Life As A Woman: Norway Edition

Today is May 11th, 2020. My name is Ina Egren, I grew up in a loving family in the Southern part of Norway, with both my parents and my three brothers. We were neither rich nor poor, and I recall my childhood as a happy one. I always had ambitions; my dad always inspired me to think big and expect more from myself. I do not consider my family a big one, although I grew up with both sets of grandparents, aunt and uncle, a few cousins, and one of my great grandmothers.

As a young woman I had so many hopes and dreams for my future; I did well in school, and although I did not have many friends, the ones I had were great ones. I chose to go to a private upper secondary school, and I thought of myself as becoming a Marine Biologist or a Veterinary. However, the requirements to become a vet was out of my reach, and the job market for Marine Biologists was slim, so when we graduated, I chose to go into economics at the university. I quickly realized this was not what I wanted to do, and so I tried several different majors before I made the choice to start working instead. That is when I found my passion. Never had I considered myself as a tech-geek or very skilled in this genre, but when I started working in customer support with telecommunications, I suddenly realized this was my area of expertise. In the current days, I always say that we who work in this business, are not geniuses or all-knowing in any shape or form; we are simply skilled enough to know where to look for solutions and knowing what actions can change which outcomes.

In this business, however, both with women in tech, and in customer service in general, there are many challenges I as a female tech-enthusiast must overcome. I have had to endure rants about customers wanting to wait for male service providers because they do not trust my competence in the field due to my gender; I have also had to explain on multiple occasions why there is no need to ask for the store manager (because "I AM THE MANAGER"!).

I was a store manager for five years, I had three male employees (because it is hard to find women who would like to work in telecom), and we took shifts at the store, so we were rarely at work at the same time.

One time, an older woman came into the store and literally stopped halfway in and just stood there staring at me. I tried to ask her what I could help her out with, and eventually she looked me in the eyes and asked me, "where are the boys?" I kindly told her that I was the one at work today, and again asked her what she wanted help with. Again, she started talking about when the boys were coming, and how she always got help from them. After (still kindly) trying to explain that I was there, I could help her, she said, "But, do you know anything about this stuff?" I was stunned, speechless, so incredibly offended, but I managed to keep a straight face and when I finally got to fix her issue (which was done in about two minutes), she left very happy and I think I might have changed her attitude towards women in tech just a bit.

However, this is not a one-time incident! After almost ten years as a young female in the telecommunications industry, I have experienced that there are many minds and attitudes out there that need changing. And mind you, it is not just the older generation that has reservations, although they do represent a good amount of them. There is a saying in Norway: If you make friends with a Norwegian, you will have a friend for life, but if you get them as your enemy you will never know it. I consider Norwegians in general to be an open and accepting people, but there is a deep and imprinted unwritten law in all of us saying that we are not supposed to speak up, be better than anyone or be anything but pleasant at all times. That is why I always let the comments slide, I smile and pretend everything is alright, and when they are gone, I hope I changed yet another mind today.

My Life As A Woman: Oman Edition #1

My name is Maya Javed. Most of my childhood belongs to Oman but Pakistan too. My maternal grandparents are living here in Oman and they are taking care of me until now. My parents belong to Pakistan, so my motherland is Pakistan.

I got my preliminary education from Oman and then I move to Pakistan for higher studies. I have done Premedical and master's in computer science from Pakistan. Unlike most of the people, my Inspiration was my name, Maya. I was quite young when one day I got the meaning of my name. Maya is an Arabic word meaning "Matter" and Javed means "Forever". And what I thought is matter is everywhere and it remains forever. So I decided to do something extraordinary that will be everywhere and remain forever. After getting enough education, I decided to do something to make money. But I wanted to be independent so doing a job was not in my list of ideas. I decided to start freelancing and I completed a course on freelancing and then I started professional freelancing on many platforms. Other than freelancing, I started dress designing and Abaya designing. I am doing it side by side but have not launched my brand yet. Now I have decided to launch my brand and want to provide such a platform to the ladies of Oman where they can come and get what they need without any embarrassment, so my idea is a Ladies Accessories Store.

Oman's basic political atmosphere has been changed now after the new rural Sultan Qaboos. In the era of Said bin Taimoor, there was no freedom for Omanis ladies specially to get proper education and serve their nation but now the atmosphere is changed. Now Omanis are getting higher education and serving their nation in a very comfortable and flexible environment and nearly every sector.

The basic culture of Oman is Islam that requires a woman to be covered all the time especially when going outside. The Abaya is the identity of Islamic culture and also a symbol of honor for an Islamic woman. It's a symbol of rank as well. Mostly the middle-class Omanis wear Abaya and both the extremes usually do not wear Abaya. One extreme is the rural family and the other is very poor villagers. The basic design of Abaya is now going to be changed with accessories so now some modern ladies also prefer to wear Abaya.

The ladies of Oman love their rich culture, so I want to launch a modern yet cultural platform for culture-loving and modern Omanis too. I want to become an inspiring girl for Omanis to stand on their own feet and serve their nation and family. After launching my brand, I want to extend it nationwide and I also want to make it a source of income for Omanis as well. I am working on my ideas with my family.

I consider myself a successful and independent lady and I want to give a message to Omanis to get the education and become independent and my message for other ladies worldwide is that every woman can do anything if she wants to. But the matter lies in "IF". So get up and explore your world on your own. Do not give the authority of deciding your destiny to anyone. It's time to stand up and carve your path that will lead you to your ultimate destiny. All the best.

My Life As A Woman: Oman Edition #2

Early Life

I was born in the early nineties in a small-town South of Oman, called Nizwa. We had our ancestral home there, several of our generations had lived there but since the renaissance of the 70's, our financial status improved, and we were able to afford better housing. I only remember fragments of that crumbling structure, adorned with traditional hand-woven carpet, wafts of burning frankincense rising from an ornate burner and a round metal container always filled with my grandmother's sweet Halwa. Whenever I went to see my grandmother, she would always place a piece of Halwa directly into my mouth and it was one of the reasons I loved to go there. Even though the house had seen better days, my grandparents continued living there till their final years. Our new house was quite near the city centre (the Souq) and had better living conditions such as air conditioners, running water, and a modern kitchen. Children in Oman are loved by all, there is a spirit of mutual empathy, irrespective of their gender. During my preteens I would spend my evenings roaming about aimlessly around the narrow streets of the Nizwa Souq (or marketplace). I still love that place; Omani culture is so deeply embedded there whether it is the pottery shops or the amazing fabrics or the hand-woven carpets.

Molding my Aspirations into a Career

The education system in Oman is quite rigorous and promotes gender equality. I went to a private school, where the primary medium of instruction was in Arabic, but English was also a focal language. Religious teachings play a huge part in our education and knowledge of the Quran is a must for every child. In my early years, my grandfather used to teach me, but when he passed away, my mother took that responsibility. As I grew older, I was expected to dress more modestly, especially while going out we had to don a long loose-fitting garment (often black) paired with a head covering. The transition wasn't much of a hassle nor a difficulty for me because Omani women more or less dress in the same way. Contrary to popular opinion, the younger generation rarely covers their faces, though the older women would don a face shield called a Batoola.

I always knew as a kid that I would be the proud owner of a beautiful jewellery shop (a side effect of roaming in the bazar). With the passage of time this idea blossomed into an entrepreneurial dream. As soon as I finished high school, I applied to a business program in The University of Nizwa. The institute was only a couple of years old when I started there. The thought behind the architecture was mostly functional, with trees planted here and there for effect. The entrance to the campus was through a concrete arch adorned with the Arabic words 'Jamia Nizwa' (University of Nizwa). The classrooms were a pretty standard single story affair with whitewashed walls, ugly false ceilings and boring furniture. The students, however, were the exact opposite, they were exciting, clumsy, funny and ambitious. The only entertainment value the campus had to offer was the students.

Our class population was quite small, so everybody knew everybody else. We were like a family, everyone had respect for the other. Though the university was co-ed, women usually kept to themselves, which was because of their upbringing rather than societal pressure. Perhaps the most enjoyable time I had spent was on campus, I loved what I learned, my classmates never failed to make me laugh and the faculty was quite supportive of my entrepreneurial ideas. I honestly think that time flew by these four years, and I had learned a lot, especially on managing a business. Graduation ceremonies in university of Nizwa are an elaborate affair. I remember mine clearly, we were all cramped in the huge amphitheatre of the university campus, it was the middle of June and our spirits were high. Our academic robes were silken emerald green floor length gowns with gold trims. I thought it looked really beautiful and dignified.

Life after graduation was dull for some time. Upon my father's request I started applying to various firms around the city and after a struggle of a month or two I was able to secure an entry level marketing position in a mid-level firm. Work life was a little hard, a little bit more so because my heart was in opening up my own business. The good thing about doing a job was that I was able to save quite a lot since I practically lived with my parents. Eventually, I learned to accept the 9 to 5 routine and kept my job for more than three years. After that, I quit to finally pursue my dream of owning a jewellery shop.

My father helped a lot and with him I made visits to several of the local markets in the south of Oman. I was particularly fascinated by the statement necklaces called 'Maknakh', only found in the southern region of the country. These necklaces came down to the chest, with prominent pendants depicting mostly a floral aesthetic and in-laid with hints of gold. I met with several vendors and silversmiths and finally decided to partner with a local craftsman in the interior of the Al Dakhiliyah region. Very recently I rented a tiny shop in a more happening area of town and plan on giving the shop an ethnic interior.

My Message to the Omani Women

I shared my life's successes in this short feature, but it doesn't mean that I didn't have a few hiccups along the way. Life is a challenge with its ups and downs, and I choose to focus on the positive. My advice to Omani women would be to think beyond cultural norms and work towards being more self-sufficient.

My Life As A Woman: Oman Edition #3

Dr. Nawal Al Sharji

Where did you grow up?

I grew up in the capital of a country with a mesmerizing natural beauty with stunning coastline, Oman. My country is one of the safest countries and its people are known to be polite and very friendly.

How did you grow up?

This question brought up a lot of vivid childhood memories!

The memories of the days I spent playing with my siblings and friends joyfully and with a lot of happiness, with lots of outdoors activities. To be honest, these memories made me so glad that I had my childhood before technology took over.

Saying this, I did not spend a lot of time playing as I grew up in a family that had education as one of the priorities. So as a child, I used to read a lot and I was even reading complex mathematic books as a hobby! Yes! I was one of those nerdy kids but those readings helped me so much that I was able to compete in a mathematic competition when I was in high school in the national level and I was in the top three finalists.

What did you study? / What you want to be growing up? / Why?

"What one loves in childhood stays in the heart forever." – Mary Jo Putney

At the age of five, I was 100% sure that I wanted to be a doctor. That was crystal clear. I wanted to be able to help others who are unwell, to cure them from sickness, and of course I wanted to be called "Doctor Nawal".

Hence, I pursued my dream. I got into a medical college. I must say I am very thankful that I have a supportive parents who would always allow me to live up to my dreams and support me all the way.

What do you love about your culture?

Omanis share a common Arab, Muslim, and tribal culture as many middle east countries. However, due to the great trade history in Oman, the Omani culture was influenced by other cultures and became a more open-minded culture where it accepts new ideas while maintaining the core characteristics of our own culture. This also have made the society more open to the idea of having well educated Omani women in high ranks in the country and having women in almost all different jobs.

What are you currently doing for work?

I have complete five years of training in general surgery in Oman and currently further training in Canada in a specialty you rarely find women in, pediatric urology. I have chosen this specialty as I wanted to specialize in a field where I can help my society more.

Tell me about your struggles as a woman.

Being a female surgeon was a big struggle in a world that is male-dominated. It was very difficult at the beginning to work with them. As a woman, you had to work double the work of your male colleagues, just to prove that being a woman is not a reason to be less. Many have accepted us in the field, but yet there are still some who continue to keep obstacles in our way for which we have to continue fighting.

Tell me about your successes as a woman.

My success as woman is that my dreams and achievements were never limited to the fact of being "a woman". At the age of 5 years old, I dreamt of helping people, and here I am living my dream. I love what Michelle Obama said, "Success isn't about how much money you make, it's about the difference you make in people's lives."

I do believe that I am making differences in my patients' lives and this is my biggest success not only as a woman but as a human.

My Life As A Woman: Pakistan Edition #1

Since my childhood, I had seen my mother and other females struggle to make a career, balancing both work and home nicely. Seeing this while growing up, I also wanted to get done with my education and step into the practical world. When I got enrolled in one of the best universities in Pakistan, my feet were not touching the ground, as my dream to become a pharmacist was coming true. On my graduation day, I was more excited about entering the next phase of my life rather than the completion of my Pharm D degree. During my pharmacy education, I made my mind to start my career in hospital pharmacy. So, right after my graduation, I was hired by one of the best public hospitals in town. Entering into the professional world as a hospital pharmacist was like a dream come true. Little did I know that this passion would fade away.

Starting my career from there was an achievement, but little did I know that the practical world was different from what I had experienced in my life up till now. With the job came new responsibilities. I, not being a bossy person, found it a bit difficult to adjust. Bullying at the workplace looked like the norm because you are a fresher and being a woman adds more to it. I noticed that the lower staff thought of themselves as superiors because they have more work experience or they have been working in that organization for a longer time, hence having more seniority. This realization made me angry. Initially, I decided to ignore and give some time. At times, things improve with time, especially when you are new, people take time to trust you. But to my dismay, nothing changed. Then, I decided to talk to my in-charge. My in-charge turned out to be a nice person. He immediately understood my problem and straight away called all the trouble makers and directed them to rectify their behaviors.

The next day, they all apologized, and we worked as a team. From this incident, I learned that it's better to always address your problems rather than keeping it to yourself and hoping that things may improve because struggle is always required to make things change. After this, I switched between a few more organizations. Every place came with more challenges and different kinds of workplace harassment, but with the help and precious advice of my parents, I fought them all bravely. I also made sure that none of my colleague, especially female colleagues faced these problems and would always be there for their rescue if I would see any problem. Because females are the easiest victim for workplace harassment and bullying, they already have a lot of societal pressure they don't raise their voice but trust me you should never remain silent, raising your voice and exposing the person /situation is the best thing.

When I was excelling in my career, many proposals started coming in for me, as there is a culture in the country where I was born and raised that search for proposals starts as soon as the girl steps into the twenties, but luckily my family considers education a must thing so this was not my case. Most marriages in my country are traditional arranged, semi arranged or love marriages. Mine was an arranged marriage. When I came to know the details of my now-spouse, I was confused as he was settled in the Middle East. Saying yes to this marriage meant moving to a new country, embracing a new culture, being away from parents and a lot more insecurities and fear came in my mind. But seeing my parent's happiness in this, I agreed on the proposal and moved to the new country. Moving to a new country brought a halt to my career as starting a new life in a new country is a bit difficult and a slightly time-consuming process. For now, I am settling in a new country, enjoying my husband's company. Working on this new relationship, to make a relationship a long lasting one, you should be your partner's best friend. It takes time to know each other, so for now I am taking one thing at a time.

My Life As A Woman: Pakistan Edition #2

Hi, my name is Saima Sajjad. Well, the story of my lifetime struggle and my firm motivation is not any different than the millions of women of the world, especially those who born in the developing countries like in the sub-continent of Indo-Pak. I grew up in a joint-family-system, in Pakistan with my siblings and other relatives.

After the completion of my university education, in my family, I was the first girl who got permission to work outside the home. According to the local custom, normally, it was not allowed for girls to work outside the home. So I struggled and fought for my rights to be a useful citizen of society. My father allowed me to work outside our home. So, I was the first one who was allowed to go outside and do my work. Then I started a marketing job, and later I developed my marketing company. But later, I had to close my company because of my marriage and went to Switzerland to join my husband.

There, it was entirely a different world for me, a different weather, different language, different life style of people living in a nuclear family system as back home, I used to live and spent all my life living with many people in a joint-family. Here, It was completely a different culture in general. I also had to work here, where back home, I was not working outside home and even at home there used to work few servants for household tasks.

In European culture all women work outside home. My first barrier was a new language and without having a good command on language, it was hard, rather impossible to find a suitable and white collar job. Therefore, I had to accept odd end jobs. My husband got ill and stopped going outside home so to meet the everyday expenditures and run home I had to work two jobs in two different areas of our town, existing in entirely opposite directions. I used to finish my first job at midnight and starting the other early the next morning at 6 a.m. Once I missed my last bus on a cold, windy and snowing winter night. Therefore, I had to wait for the next bus arriving after one hour. Finally I reached home at 3 a.m. and started to prepare for the next job starting at 6 a.m.

During my struggle, I had to work till midnights and travel alone at night, which I was not used to traveling alone. Sometimes I had to take the last train back home, and I had to wait and stay on the train stations alone. Sometimes it was so scary in the winter nights. I had to think about my ill husband, my home, my job, and myself. At times, even I forgot myself; due to language problems, sometimes I forgot to change trains between the stations.

On the other hand, I developed worries about the health and nutrition needs of my sick husband alone at home and his nursing. It was a very stressful period for all family members, especially for me to get suitable earnings to run home and take care of him. This crucial time developed a new sense of motivation and polished my desire to obtain success in life. My aim to get successful in life became firm and strong. Regardless of the whispers of many around me, I focused on my aim and kept it up to work hard with devotion.

Finally, I got a reasonable job in a Beauty Salon as a part-time worker. There I worked hard and showed my skills on being a hard worker, punctual, loyal to the job and my employer. Later, I succeeded in becoming a fulltime worker. There I worked for four years. Now I am an entrepreneur myself. This is basically; my non-stop struggle and I have a very strong and concrete motivation towards my goals. My biggest goal is to achieve success, no matter what I do! No matter whether I work on odd jobs or am I a successful entrepreneur, my flesh and blood motivate me to work for success.

I ran my household, took care of my ill husband, and worked morning till evening in and outside of the home. I wanted to be successful in the eyes of my family, my husband, and the world existing outside home. I am inspired by my father, who made a lot of struggles in his life, indeed he is a brilliant person. I have learned and established my business and developed marketing skills I learned from my father. I followed his strategies towards his business and clients.

I love to love in the family-system, as I am a family oriented lady. In our Eastern culture, as I have mentioned before, we used to live in a joint-family-system where all family members live together.

I am a self-employed person and doing my online working, content writing, browsing and selling. I have struggled to achieve my passion as it wasn't allowed for females to work in my family. After all hurdles, I am successfully earning and working on my own.

I would say that women should pursue their dreams and passions and never give up. My message to my fellow women is to "never give up", "work hard", "and be committed with your goals", "honour yourself and honour your words". Then there will be nothing that can stop you from achieving your goals.

As in Switzerland, women should be financially independent; otherwise, we can't enjoy our lives and living standards.

My Life As A Woman: Pakistan Edition #3

Hey! My name is Aiman. I am a born Pakistani citizen and I feel proud of it. Pakistan is a country that follows Islamic teachings and principles. Life as a woman in Pakistan is lovely, as it's the culture and religious belief of the people to give women more respect as compared to men. This doesn't mean men are neglected in Pakistan.. Hah.. no!

Both men and women are treated equally and both genders are offered equal rights and opportunities. Talking about my life, I was fully satisfied with the environment of my country because here I could easily live my life according to my own choice. There was no fear of hiding my religion or my tribe. I can practice my religion and cultural ethics very comfortably here in Pakistan.

Today, where I am standing, it actually took a lot of struggle to be here. Let's have a look at my life journey so far and I hope you'll find it inspiring!

My early life:

I was born on 12th December 1998 in the city of Punjab, Pakistan. My family is small, there are only four more people other than me. My father was a businessman and my mother was a housewife. I have two brothers and no sister. So it would not be wrong to call it "Blessed Childhood" because I had everything I needed at that time. Everything went quite well till I reached grade 5 in school.

After that, suddenly some financial issues just triggered our lives. My father's business went all in loss and after almost one year, he had no work to do. No business, no job!

It was a very tough time for my family. Then my mother started teaching in a nearby school. And she worked very hard to fulfill the basic needs of the family. At that time, my mother was the only one who was working and had to feed the whole family including my father because after bearing the huge loss of his business, he became depressed and his mental condition became very weak. So it was only my mother who fed the whole family until me and my siblings could reach a good position to be independent.

My struggling phase:

I was good at study from the very beginning and didn't require any kind of help or tuitions. My school life was complex because I felt that I was not compatible to sit there with other children as this privilege belonged to elite families. So I was battling daily a fight in my mind and that had a very bad effect on my health. But I didn't tell such things to my mother because I didn't want her to add more to her plate, or because of me, she would become more stressed on top of already being stressed due to her job.

It was just because of my mother's hard work that she made me study in the best school and college of the city. And I was lucky though that I completed my early studies from the top and well-known institutions, but this was also challenging for me.

As I mentioned before that my whole family was struggling from financial crisis so meanwhile, I became a victim of inferiority complex. But I never lost my hopes and continued studying with the same enthusiasm and completed my college with 88% marks.

The University Life

Here in Pakistan, when you pass college exams, you have to get admitted to University for undergraduate degree programs. My subject was Computer Science, so I got myself admitted into the "Bachelors of Computer Engineering" program. During this phase, I got myself engaged in searching for some instant ways of earning money online. I tried so many shortcuts, but all in vein!

Working as part-time writer

Writing was something I had always been good at. Even in the theory exams I scored more than the practical examination. So, writing was a God gifted skill for me. What I can express by writing it on is much better than through speaking. So, that was the time someone told me that you should try writing articles for my company. So I started to write someone's articles which she used to outsource from me at very cheap prices. But as I didn't have any other choice, I agreed to write for that price. I worked really hard to improve my writing skills and provide the best content to that lady. It became very hectic for me to manage study and the part-time job which was now almost becoming a full-time job for me because of heavy work load.

I was very much committed to my work and I started earning some money monthly. Those were enough for me to manage my daily expenses as a student. But then my boss suddenly became very bossy and used to curse me every time I sent her my work. Even though she always got good remarks on those articles, which I wrote for her but when I asked her to increase my writing rate a little, she became rude and even more bossy. At that time, I felt like this is the end of this writing journey and I am not going to have any work in the future. I left that job, but I was worried too because I didn't have any other option in so long.

The emergence of "Happy Days"

It was about 6 months now, my friend helped me to create my account on some freelancing websites. I managed to add my services but didn't get any orders for about 6-7 months. But as soon as I left that annoying job, I got 2 orders on my account. The first order I got was of 20$ and the other one was off 5$. It was like a life-changing moment for me because I really needed work at that time and the price per article was very good this time.

It was the time when my own freelancing career started, and I began to enjoy my work. I always satisfied my client with my work and started getting 5-star reviews. Ahh... Thank God! My life was really starting to change. In less than 6 months, I started earning enough to pay my university fee which was not at all affordable for my mom. I was actually studying on a merit scholarship, but I had to pay around 25% fee. It really helped my mom to get stable now because my fee was quite a huge burden for her. I bought my new laptop, my new smart phone and many other things which were needed at that time.

Final Words

Today, where I am standing, as a LEVEL 2 seller, it's all because of the hard work and enthusiasm. What I learnt from mine and my mom's life that it doesn't matter whether you are a man or woman, you can achieve everything you wish for with your enthusiasm and devotion towards your goals. Today, my family is living a very good and happy life. Me and my mother are completely independent now and can do whatever we wish for ourselves regardless of being dependent on the men in the house.

This is my life struggling story being a woman. It was like a rollercoaster but at the end of the struggle, my hard work paid off!

I hope you learnt something positive and got some inspiration from my story. Summing up all my discussion, I would say that just stick to your goals, stick to what you want to achieve. Be very sure about yourself that yes you can change your life yourself. Once you start working on sincerely, God will definitely help you achieve your goals!

My Life As A Woman: Pakistan Edition #4

There are so many things that I want to share with you, but when I start writing, I feel that the words are not enough for me or for any other woman to share their experiences about their life journey of being a woman. But I motivate myself that I have to do this not for me but millions of women living a life, not for themselves but their parents, siblings, husbands, and kids.

Today, I am going to talk about my life as a woman and answer critical questions. I hope my life journey will motivate some of you.

Where Did You Grow Up?

I am Hira Rana, 25 years old girl, grew up in Gojra, Pakistan. I was born in a Rajpoot family. If you don't know about it, let me inform you that there is a caste system in Pakistan like Bhati, Jatt, etc., and Rajpoot is one of them. After the death of my father, there were four remaining family members, my mother, sister, brother, and me.

How Did You Grow Up?

I grew up like any other Pakistani girl, our religion is important to us, and there are some restrictions that come with being a girl like a dupatta or hijab is a must while going outside. When I did not know about my religion, I only did these things to please my loved ones, not for me.

Did You Have Parents Or Maybe A Grandmother Who Inspired You?

I cannot say they inspire me because my inspiration is something else. But I truly appreciated my grandmother and my mother for living in hardships with so much courage. My grandfather had died at a young age leaving seven children brought up by his wife, and my mother married a man with two children.

What Did You Study? What Did You Want To Be Growing Up?

It's quite funny, but at a very young age, I wanted to marry a rich man and live a peaceful life like any other fairy tale. But I studied just for my mother and did my BS in chemistry.

What Do You Love About Your Culture?

If our culture is a real picture of what Islam tells us, then I love my culture the most, but some flaws need to be solved.

Tell Me About Your Struggles As A Woman

I knew about my religion, my life, and this world at the age of 23 because before this age, I was not a girl who could inspire others.

Let me tell you just one incident; when I planned to do teaching, I dropped my CVs at every school & colleges of Gojra, and no one called me to interview until one call from a school principal, he interviewed me and hired me.

When I started doing a job, I realized that he had no respect for women. I continued my career with his negative comments because I deeply connected with my students until one day, due to my father's severe illness, I did not attend the school, and he insulted me in front of the crowd.

I resigned from this school, and that time he said to be the most heartbreaking words;

"You cannot achieve anything in life because you are an irresponsible and nonserious person. I will meet you after two years, and you will remain in the same position, and you will have achieved nothing."

The most heartbreaking sentences, multiple rejections, and hard works were for just a few Pakistani Rupees. That's enough that I had to do something for myself, not for money, fame and any materialistic thing, but my woman pride and I did a lot.

Now, I am a tuition teacher, and an article writer, and both jobs pay me enough and give me the respect that I deserve.

Tell Me About Your Successes As A Woman

Again I said earlier who I become a tuition teacher from a private teacher. I did not say that I have gained a lot of money, but the thing I achieved is myself respect that if I want something from my life, I can make it.

I am also a content writer at Fiverr, and I exploded with happiness when people like my content and give their inspiring remarks.

Provide Some Advice To Women From A Woman Living In Pakistan

A few things from my life as a woman for a woman living in Pakistan;

- Before expecting respect from others, respect yourself as a woman.
- Not demand ease from life always prays for the courage that you can stand every hardship with patience.
- Stop demanding equality from the society, especially Pakistani women, you have your own worth so, recognize yourself.

Summary

This is my story from an immature girl who demanded nothing from life but a handsome husband with a luxurious experience to a mature Muslim woman who recognized her worth and stood for herself and her family. You can also do it for yourself, and you are not different from me or any other woman. You can do wonders, believe in yourself!

My Life As A Woman: Pakistan Edition #5

Pakistan is one of the beautiful country with very hostile people and many natural resources but on the map, it is still under the label of underdeveloped 3rd world country. When it comes to gender discrimination especially talking about women, then it is quite systematic like it depends on class, rural and urban division, the impact of feudalism, capitalism, and tribal social formations on women's lives. I am a woman of Pakistani born and raised and I am no different in terms of facing the hardships throughout my journey from being an Air Force brat to an ex-pat living in Saudi Arabia.

I was born in the small city of Mianwali Punjab Pakistan. My father was an air force officer and I must say a huge support system for me to achieve what I am today. I begin my studies from various air force schools. I completed by FSC in pre-medical and then started my real struggle of getting into the line of medical colleges. In Pakistan only there are few professions which are considered reputable, one is medical and the other one is engineering. I must say that's not my case I failed in the medical entrance exam twice despite being a hardworking student but still couldn't make it so that disappointed my parents. Then I decided to peruse a master's degree in one of the largest universities of Pakistan LUMS in biology and failed. After that, I applied for MBBS in NUST college, another reputed university, and guess what I again failed to get admission. I remember the year 2009 was very hard on me. My parents lost hope in me and even I lost hope in myself in considering that I am useful enough to start a career. But miracles happen might be it was just for me, I got admission in PHARM-D and I couldn't tell how happy I was that at least I got accepted in some university. I had a remarkable journey in my university where I groomed myself as a debater and won many awards at the university level, I was a topper in my studies, and it was beautiful 5 years of my degree.

Then the honeymoon period got over and came the time to face the reality of being in the profession. Well as I mention Pakistan has only 2 careers that are good in terms of paying you back and pharmacy professionals are without the pharmacist, the pharmacy doesn't have pharmacists, so where these professional will go? That was a huge equation mark for me. I never lose hope and kept trying for a good job and you know what? Did I fail again, surprised? Yes, I have numerous failures in my life than success stories. So I ended up doing a hard job as an industrial pharmacist in a pharmaceutical firm and I was earning just 17000 rupees per month with a doctoral degree. But my parents supported and encouraged me not to see what you are earning, just see the experience you will gain. With this hectic job of 10 hours, I started my M.Phil. degree as well and completed it.

Now I am a woman who is holding a post-graduate degree in hand and is well-groomed because I learned lessons from my failures and never stopped my struggle of being successful. In Pakistan being married and having a career is also considered a mismatch but I married a man who was not only supported me in my every journey but also help me in polishing my potentials. Unfortunately, I had to leave my job to move with my husband to Saudi Arabia but that wasn't hurdling for me, so I started giving consultation to people online regarding their prescriptions, medicines, and interactions to remain in touch with my profession.

My life becomes quite different when I landed in Saudi Arabia because first the country was different for me and I am an ex-pat, so I have some restrictions as well, like no going outside alone or driving on my own. which makes me dependent on my husband for a lot of things which I can manage myself but still this doesn't hinder me to peruse what I like. I mean it is ok I don't have opportunities much outside but inside home, I can utilize my potential and that's the reason I started writing as a freelancer most of the time. I know I don't have a lavish job now but still, I am good at paying my bills along with the potential to use my time in a constructive way for which I am happy.

Opportunities are not something that always comes in your way especially for women. Women life is not as easy as it seems to be. She has to think in multi-dimensional way to achieve without hurting anyone. Women have to be strong and flexible because in our culture rigid women are not considered brave. This is the reason to create your opportunities, make them yes literally make them, and then ascend the ladder it is not something about becoming rich rather it is survival of the fittest.

My Life As A Woman: Palau Edition

An amazing island-country in Micronesia called Palau is my hometown. Best known for its unspoiled beauty and interesting nature, people often visit to celebrate their marriage, pass an amazing honeymoon, or to enjoy breathtaking places. You will only see a clear sea, feel an amazing culture, and enjoy a friendly atmosphere. The most beautiful thing is waiting for you in the evenings, you can admire the iconic paradise on the beach of the sea, and this view you will definitely remember for a long time. This place is really peaceful, calm, and friendly, you will be in love with the people's behavior towards you and their smiles everywhere.

My name is Nathalie, I am 23, I was born in Koror, Palau but unfortunately, I moved to Makawao, Hawaii to work and live. I grew up in a complete and perfect family, where I felt nothing except deep love from my family members and this is what made me so kind and happy person. I studied in the local school, after I went to Palau High School, after Palau Community College. A year ago I broke up with my boyfriend and decided to leave my city and fortunately I found a job in Makawao which is in Hawaii and went there. For the first time, I was an entry clerk in the Hawaii State Department of Health. After working three months there I decided to change my job as it was far enough from the house I was living in. I found a job in a Hawaiian Bank, I was an entry clerk again. Actually, in one year I changed a lot of jobs, after that, I was a sales assistant in Walmart Downtown Honolulu and still working there, as this is the only job where I enjoy my job and responsibilities. As you can see no success was in my life, you know why? Because I didn't even strive for it, I just want to be full, not thirsty, to have a little home and a strong family. I do not want more from this life, I know some women really have big goals and plans. They want to be independent and confident gait. But this is actually not what I want, I want to reach everything with my future husband, to be a "strong wall" for him.

I am sure many women will be surprised by my words, but this is what I want and what will make me feel comfortable. I don't dream about palaces, Lamborghinis, or tons of money. What I want is more spiritual than material, and I strongly advise all the women in the world to look for a trustworthy man, or if you do not want a relationship, just be spiritually richer and more satisfied, because one day when all the money of the world will be yours, you will feel alone and sad. I really admire rich and independent women, but anyways this is not my type and I want a simple life. The secret of happiness is in simplicity, isn't it?

My Life As A Woman: Palestine Gaza Strip Edition #1

I was born in Saudi Arabia in 1995 and raised there until I became 23 years old. I had a relatively quiet life. I grew up in a loving family in a middle-class environment, I attended public school and university. Getting into a university for non-Saudi people was difficult and very expensive, but I, luckily, had a scholarship since my high-school GPA was very high, but I couldn't choose what to study freely. I had only 3 choices: English language, chemistry, or IS. I chose chemistry, and I graduated with first class honors. I always wanted to be in academic life, I thought it would be the perfect work environment for me because, as girls, we are always intimidated from working in other work environments, thus, I didn't think of anything else.

Living in SA as a woman wasn't very easy or social, I remember my life this way (going to school and then coming back from school, this applies to university as well), and even this simple process was supervised by family and school/university administration. We didn't get to choose, family and schools/universities had chosen for us. One of the difficult situations that confronted me after working very hard in university and getting 4.90/5 GPA, I wasn't accepted to be a teaching assistant because I wasn't considered Saudi. This was unfair.

I wish that I grow up in environment that is freer, more inducive, conducive to engagement and learning, and empowering. We decided to leave SA to Palestine when the Saudi cabinet started charging fees on non-Saudi residents and when they started to layoff non-Saudi employees. I hadn't finish my degree at the time, so my family had to split, my mother and my brother left SA in August 2017, we − my father, sister, and I, couldn't leave with them because of Rafah Border Crossing. If we entered Gaza strip, it would be very hard to get out and finish my bachelor's degree, so we stayed until I finished it in January 2018, we packed our stuff, and we even sold our car and other things, but guess what? We couldn't travel until May 2018, four months of waiting because Rafah crossing border was closed. We left Saudi Arabia eventually (we applied for final exit visa in SA) worrying that Egyptian authorities would send us back to Saudi Arabia, and Saudi Arabia would send us back to Egypt.

In Palestine, the biggest difficulty was that there were no jobs, no way to use my degree, so I took a diploma in web design, I volunteered a lot, and I work as a freelancer in translation and web design now. I did all that to try to make money to get a master's degree, because I think getting a master's degree would be very beneficial for me.

Me studying and looking for other opportunities and not being content are my strengths, and having a supportive family made everything easier. I don't consider myself successful yet, but I can claim that I'm on my way to be one as long as I try every day and don't let anyone frustrate me.

Many women in my family inspired me, especially my mother, she didn't complete her high school education, because she got married and left with my father to SA. In Arab countries, having certificates is very important, even more important than having the right skills, so my mother took many courses in Tajwid (intonation), it's a way to pronounce Arabic letters correctly, she's become number 1 in her field, she was well known back where we lived.

In my culture, I love how close we are to our family and friends; I love how we stick by each other no matter what. I love how Arab people are very generous and bountiful. And of course, I love the food and the music.

The struggles and obstacles that women face in my community are not a result of what society or law imposes, but rather what the family imposes. You may find a father who abuses his daughters or his wife and prevents them from going to school or work, while his brother does not do this to his family. so, they're individual actions, not collective ones. Generally, women here can go to school, work and lead their lives normally and equally.

My advice to women is to create opportunities and not only to wait for them to happen. We are strong enough, and the world tends to be more just for women, so we must stop acting like victims and start benefiting from that.

My Life As A Woman: Palestine Gaza Strip Edition #2

Hi there, I am from Gaza, Palestine. I am 26. I grew up in Gaza since my childhood, where life was difficult because of the Israeli occupation. There was not enough electricity nor water. However, we still have a stable beautiful life and a family bonding that compensates us. I have a lovely family that consist of a mother, father, and six siblings.

My family is my inspiration. The most inspiring is my father, he has always inspired me in this life. He has struggled much at the beginning of his life to get educated, as education was not so common. He therefore worked hard to get work that would save the force of our lives. His common saying was, "God will please us where we do not know."

I completed my education and got a bachelor's degree in English. which I always dreamed of when I was young, I always wanted to be like my father "an English teacher".

For our culture, I love the rich history of art, literature, handicrafts, music, clothing and food. Our Palestinian cuisine is about hummus, falafel, Musakhan and Qidreh. Another favorite is Maqlouba, made from layers of meat, rice, and fried vegetables such as cauliflower, eggplant, potatoes, and carrots. It is cooked in a large pot, then turned over – maqlouba means "upside down" in Arabic – and topped with fried nuts or fresh herbs. We are also known for Embroidery (taṭrīz), which is the art of creating decorative designs on fabric using needle and thread, and occasionally with objects like shells or beads.

According to women, our culture pays a great attention to them, as they are the main foundation of society. Women are protected and treated with respect by all. Our religion requires us to cover the head and the body as it's our own, not see us as others' property, and we appreciate it. Women were also given their rights to study, work and travel.

I work as a freelancer on online platforms, "self-employment business", that involves translation and voice-over. As a woman, I suffer from the lack of jobs and the difficult challenges of life, including the siege imposed on us by the Israeli occupation.

Nevertheless, I'm a financially educated and stable woman, who overcomes the difficulties and constraints of life.

My advice to the Palestinian women:

- Believe in yourself and be strong.

- It's important to be listened to.

- There has to be hope because sometimes that is all you have to hang on to, there has to be a better tomorrow.

- Love yourself.

- Have your own life.

- Don't be needy.

- Take care of yourself.

- Be your own biggest cheerleader.

- Speak your mind.

- Look at all your good qualities and decide to love yourself exactly the way you are right now.

My Life As A Woman: Palestine Gaza Strip Edition #3

Many Palestinian women face cultural, economic, and social barriers that limit their progress and development, which don't consider women as an entity that can carry out their work and self-reliance, but this male society hinders the possibility of women's independence.

I, as a woman who was born and lived in an eastern Palestinian society, in the Gaza Strip, and was born in a conservative family, faced many problems and obstacles that prevented me from succeeding as a woman, but I didn't leave it to chance; I strived to prove myself as an independent entity, just like my father who has always encouraged me to be independent and dependent on myself.

When I was 18 years, I started my undergraduate studies in English literature, my university was not enough to teach me what I expected to be able to master in the art of translation as I had hoped, so I sought, researched and developed myself, intensified my studies on the basics and rules of language, to be able to achieve a record at this field. After many serious attempts, I mastered the art of translation and writing content of all kinds, and I have been working with many local and international companies in this field.

I have now 23 years, I had a great curiosity to enter the field of administration, so I applied for many training courses and volunteered in many organizations, I sought to be the best to reach my goal, so I got a contract to work as an administrative manager for a period of two years, in which I got a lot of experience that enables me to achieve success and progress in any field I may undertake.

As a besieged Palestinian community, I live in the Gaza Strip under the Israeli siege, which hinders my progress in work, and achieving success, as well as obtaining a job opportunity in any field that I may choose. Because of the siege, the number of jobs available in Gaza decreased, the unemployment rates and the number of graduates increased.

Even though the Israeli siege on the Gaza Strip also limited the possibility of traveling abroad due to barriers and closures, as there were many difficulties I faced when I was trying to travel to anywhere in the world to complete my scientific and practical career.

The second obstacle is the Palestinian internal division between the authorities, which is also an impact of the Israeli occupation, which has increased taxes, limited job opportunities, and there are many internal problems, which greatly limit the areas of women's work.

In general, the Palestinian culture is unique. Far from the eastern male society, the Palestinian culture encourages the work of women, calls for adhering to and preserving the stolen Palestinian heritage, and also encourages her children to commit to education and higher education because it is the only way to progress and succeed.

I conclude my story with advice for all Arab and non-Arab girls and women in all governorates of the Arab and western countries, to look forward her education then her work life at the first place, self-reliance and the challenge of force majeure and strict societies, and that women prove themselves with their capabilities and their conviction that they are an independent entity who can perform its functions and face the conditions themselves.

My Life As A Woman: Palestine Gaza Strip Edition #4

"The success of every woman should be the inspiration to another. We should raise each other up. Make sure you're very courageous: be strong, be extremely kind, and above all, be humble." – Serena Williams,

If you told me 6 years ago that I would end up having an MA scholarship and preparing myself to travel to London, I'd have laughed. I live in Palestine, grew up in a very conservative family with seven brothers in tough traditions which prevent a woman from travelling alone or choosing her serious decisions. My story started after graduating from high school and deciding what to study at University. I wanted to be a lawyer like my twin, but my dad refused it. Also, he told me that, "we don't have a woman working with men in the same place." So, I studied for a BA in English without any plan for this job. After graduating with this major, I stayed at home for one year without a job. As a Palestinian woman, my aim was to get married and have a family without building my character like other women in my society. How stupid I was! I think the worst thing in this life as a woman is to live without a professional aim and don't put your job ahead in your life.

My cousin, who is a successful English teacher and cancer fighter, told me that no one in this world will be your safety zone and support you in all your conditions, neither your husband nor your son. She also encouraged me to know my aim and achieve it. Her words inspired me to find out it. So I thought about a goal beyond my skills. I decided to be an eligible translator who transfers the messages between the world. I knew I was late compared to my colleagues but taking the first step as a woman was meaningful to me to prove that I am a powerful person in society, and I am here. One of our shameless things is not fighting your fears to access your dream.

My journey has begun. I faced many struggles; the biggest of them was to convince my dad to let me work and give me freedom in my life. Then I found a small job, an English teacher at kindergarten for 3 years. I depended on myself to save money and took courses without asking anyone for funding. Because of my dream to be a lawyer is kept in my mind, I am taking a legal translation course. During my work, I took translation courses and prepared myself for the IELTS exam, which built my abilities and skills. I worked in the morning, learned in the afternoon, and helped my mum in cleaning at night. Although I did more than 2 things in a day and had a difficult time, I appreciated all minutes on my road to success.

The golden opportunity was when I had a permission to join one of the professional programs in the fantastic organization in Palestine. I participated in the freelance program to be a freelance translator. This opportunity opens the door for my dreams to come true. When I was in Gaza Sky Geeks, I felt confident in myself and my abilities. All of the people there are cooperative, full of power and, give positive energy. One of the key projects I worked on was volunteering with other women translators to translate a booklet from English to Arabic about COVID-19. As women, we feel about responsibilities to bring awareness to our society in this pandemic. All of our society members appreciated ours as women for this successful project.

Now I am working on many translation projects in an international company. Besides, I am preparing myself to travel to London to complete my study. Finally, I feel like a free bird.

If you are a woman who has problems with society or for any other reason about your dreams, you should fight. Don't be silent! Don't be afraid, believe in yourself, and draw obvious lines to access your dream. No matter of failure, when you fail, get up, and you will reach the end.

Every day is a chance to do more and prove that as a woman, nothing can be hard. When you believe in yourself and your way, the world recognizes you. It all starts within the first step to breaking all barriers between you and your fear. This life is a test, and it's not supposed to be easy.

My Life As A Woman: Palestine Gaza Strip Edition #5

My name is Abeer Abdallah. I was born in the outskirts of Gaza under Israeli Occupation in 2001. I grew up with only my mother and two older brothers, as my father was killed in an airstrike before I was born. Growing up as a girl during this time was especially difficult for me because I was never allowed to truly be myself. I saw little Israeli kids playing around, going wherever they wanted without worry of being harmed or imprisoned just because of their nationality. But my brothers and I always played in fear and distrust; constantly looking behind our backs and over our shoulders to see if military officials were coming to get us.

It was June 10th, 2007. I was only six years old, but I remember looking at myself in the mirror one morning in the bathroom next to the kitchen. I recall hearing my mother listening to the news about the latest Israeli government decision; Hamas had taken control of the Gaza strip. This meant that life was about to change for us Palestinians forever. As I looked at myself in the mirror, I gazed deeply into my eyes and asked myself "what did we do to deserve this?" A child should not have these questions. She should be able to live carefree and in whimsical peace and serenity. My mom did not speak to us or anyone else for five days. We barely had food to eat because she was so depressed by the news. So, it was up to me to take care of everyone.

As the years passed, I had to learn to juggle academics with avoiding police interaction; academics with avoiding depression myself. These times were so hard, always hearing gunshots and tear gas canisters outside my window. But it was my trust in Allah, and my undying hope and adoration for what the future could be that saved me. At some point, I did not even feel like I was making the actions in my life, but that Allah was like water in my veins, moving through me and allowing me to control my life's tides.

When I was eleven years old, my older brother Sayeed was imprisoned for speaking out against the government. He had posted a meme on Facebook denouncing Hamas and demanding reparations for the Palestinian people. I have not heard from him since. My mother is doing much better, but there is a silent war in her that even I cannot shield myself from. Most of the days of my life have consisted of struggling to be taken seriously in the academic world, struggling to cope with my war trauma and battle scars, struggling to just be Abeer Abdallah in her truest form. Life in and of itself is a gift. Something to be cherished. But sometimes it is so hard to cherish the chaos that comes with living. Especially the chaos that comes with living as a Palestinian woman.

Speaking of which, I believe that we are the most misunderstood type of woman. The Palestinian woman is born in trauma and sexism and general underestimation. To make matters worse, the outsiders (Americans, Brits, etc.) always try to overanalyze us without even asking us what we think. I am not just some battered woman who is going to do nothing with her life just because I am Palestinian. I am strong. I am beautiful. I have been through war, but the biggest war is the war inside of me, and because of Allah I will win every time. I am me. I am Abeer.

My Life As A Woman: Palestine Gaza Strip Edition #6

Wondering whether or not this is my right place, I realized that I am very different from my fellow citizens.. I have always dreamed of achieving dreams that others consider pure nonsense. This is me, and this is my story.

I am Tasnim Al-Hersh, and I reached the age of twenty-five last February, while I am writing these lines that will inspire one of the bewildered women who are looking for a spot of hope to live happily and achieve psychological satisfaction. We live in quarantine because of the spread of COVID-19.

I was born in the city of Hebron, which is located in the heart of historic Palestine. Palestine, which the occupation turned into shreds and called it the West Bank in the eastern part and the Gaza Strip in the other part. Since Palestine is under occupation and the consequent violation of freedoms, rights, and deprivation of the most basic human rights, as a Palestinian woman who adheres to the culture of her country and civilized history, this has had a significant impact on my life in various fields.

I grew up in a small rural village called Al-Rayyah, located south of the city of Hebron, next to Al-Fawwar camp, which developed in me the meaning of the Palestinian cause. Also, my mother comes from another camp, the Al-Aroub camp, which was established after her family was expelled from their original land, which was Iraq, Al-Manshiya, which the Israelis turned into their own country and called it Quriyat Gat.

As you can see, the geographic location that I grew up in made me historically educated and bear a just cause: the issue of return and return to our original Palestinian land and the dream of national freedom that subsequently entails my personal freedom.

Away from political matters, conflicts and wars. I live in the atmosphere of a conservative family of four brothers and four sisters, fair enough that I came as the fifth sister. She always said joking about my mom to me that she did not want to get me, but in any case, I came to this world to be my mother's favorite and Her father's pampered. My family are simple people with average income, and they provided me all my basic needs, and my father spent a lot on me for my education. I finished high school and then went to university. My entry to the university was a qualitative leap in my life at all levels.

I lived in a complex and militant society, which imposed on me a lack of confidence and fear of everything. But the university turned my life upside down, when I got to know all members of society, and I gained conversation, self-defense, communication, and teamwork skills.

I got to know university lecturers who had the most influence in developing my personality. I learned to speak English brilliantly, and then I started talking to the world from different countries, nationalities, and characters. I got to know new cultures that made strange friendships and learned about the outside world in two years more than I learned during the past twenty years.

Finally, the expected day came, and I graduated from university with a major in English literature, hoping to complete my graduate studies and become influential in society. Professor Raed Al-Jabari told me that I am a distinguished girl with a media voice, and I have a bright future, which has always invaded my confidence and encouraged me to continue and achieve more successes through elaborate advice.

After several years and after trying a lot of work in the field of translation and teaching for children and working as a content writer, I found myself immersed in work experiences that had no effect. I did not achieve what I aspire to, and this feeling that I have always had now and then in every dilemma and every problem I face in life.

The only thing that kept me from surrendering is that I was created with a mind, and it is the treasure of man toward knowledge and truth. I must use this mind correctly and not give in to a society that often prevents a girl from reaching her dreams, which they see as being a danger to her life as a girl.

I have faced the words of my friends who want me to get married and then have children and spend my life between the kitchen and the bedroom. Still, I insist that I was not created to be a mother only, but to achieve myself in order to reach the stage in which I say yes, this is me. This is the Tasneem that I want.

My Life As A Woman: Palestine West Bank Edition #1

"I believe in being strong when everything seems to be going wrong. I believe that happy girls are the prettiest girls. I believe that tomorrow is another day, and I believe in miracles." – Audrey Hepburn

I live in Palestine, precisely in Nablus, a city in the West Bank. I have a simple family consists of 6 members, and I'm the oldest daughter. Appreciatively, I have very supportive parents. My mom, who didn't complete her education, encouraged me to study hard and helped me to be one of the top students in my class. So, my mom makes me believe that the one who loses a thing is the one who can give it the most, and when she supports me, incredible things happen.

When I was at school, I loved the English subject the most because of my teacher. She always encouraged me, so I was on pins and needles to attend her class, waiting for her to know something new. Over time, I felt that I had to study English language and literature at university. At university, I went too deep in the English language, and I knew valuable information about literature, linguistics, grammar, British and American history, and translation, which made lots of ideas and questions come to my mind.

I had two classes in translation, and I started to love this field. My graduation project was translating one of Edward Saed's books "Representations of the Intellectual" and finding the problems I faced during the translation process. It was the first professional project and research I worked on, and all things went great. After graduation, I tried to find a good job. I kept searching for it. I wanted to be a translator. Unfortunately, I couldn't. Hence, I decided to give some English classes for school students at home. Yet, I kept the translation field in my mind, and I was searching for articles and researches to translate for free.

One day, I heard about a translation course, and I told my parents about it. Honestly, it was hard for me because it was in another city, and I needed the course fees and transportation expenses; however, my parents afforded me the required money to register. At the same time, I found a free training course in freelancing; thus, I didn't hesitate and gave it a chance. I had to go to Ramallah to attend the translation course, then get back to my city "Nablus" to attend the freelancing training. If truth be told, the way was too long for me; because we were passing through occupation checks. Moreover, when I was getting home, I was so exhausted; this didn't help me to see my family. Nevertheless, the good thing that happened during the translation course that the trainer was supportive, she opened my eyes to other types of translation and aspects of life and taught me how to use my translation skills to get jobs.

While in the freelancing training, I met lots of great people, and we became friends. The trainers were fantastic; they kept telling us that we can. I could find some suitable projects in translation and other fields like content writing, but I couldn't take them. One of the trainers who is amazing encouraged me to write and write more. She knew that I have the skill, but I haven't ever thought about it because I was afraid to try something new. Yet, my trainers, especially her, helped me to get rid of my stress and fears while writing. I started writing in different subjects as samples, until that day when I got my first project in content writing. The client was so glad about what I wrote. After that, I was able to work on useful projects in the two fields: translation and content writing. Currently, I'm still working as a freelancing content writer and translator.

Now, I'm thankful for having inspirational women like my great mother, my teacher, and trainers, who left sparkles in my heart and life. I want every woman to know how to seize every tiny opportunity, especially if there is a woman by her side. Even if she thinks that she can't or feels afraid to fail, she has to believe in herself and follow her mind and heart. Oprah once said: "Think like a queen. A queen is not afraid to fail. Failure is another stepping stone to greatness," hence stay great, stay happy.

My Life As A Woman: Palestine West Bank Edition #2

Where did you grow up?

I was born in Jerusalem; Palestine, and lived my whole life in Ramallah.

How did you grow up?

I grew up as the first daughter in the family. I attended school, and hung out with my friends. One of my hobbies as a kid was collecting bullets from the streets. Because being born as a Palestinian, we grow up fast, and we learn to be responsible since early age. Growing in the Holy Land was bittersweet, Israeli Occupation made our daily lives difficult. Additionally, growing up in a male dominant conservative society created its own challenges. Nonetheless, my parents instilled the courage in me to not let society define the person I want to be.

Did you have parents or maybe a grandmother who inspired you?

My inspiration was my aunt Rawan, I always looked up to her. Rawan managed two jobs: a journalist by day, and a fitness coach at night. I admired Rawan's work ethic and determination to break our societal barriers, paving the way for Palestinian women like myself to follow our dreams. To this day, Rawan continues to inspire and encourage me to follow my passion, and continue to pave the way for younger generations. In fact, Rawan was the first who encouraged me to create my social media platforms, to serve as an inspiration for others.

What did you study? / What did you want to be growing up? / Why?

Growing up, I always dreamed of working in the fashion industry, particularly fashion design. I always enjoyed creating outfits for my barbie dolls using different materials.

Unfortunately, in Palestine the fashion sector is undeveloped and most people enjoy it as a hobby rather than a profession. The more the idea of becoming a fashion designer seemed far-fetched, the more my focus shifted to my passion in fitness.

I studied Marketing in the Republic of Northern Cyprus. Though the idea of studying abroad was difficult for my family and I, we realized it was best for my future. Living abroad taught me how to become an independent woman, making my own choices and taking full responsibility for my actions. I majored in Marketing because of the job opportunities presented in Palestine.

What do you love about your culture?

They used to say Palestinians fight like Heroes, but now they say heroes fight like Palestinians. While growing, we were always taught to fight for what we believe in, or else we would have lost our land long ago.

One of the interesting things about our culture is hospitality. People tend to help each other everywhere. Furthermore you can never have too many Palestinian dishes. All are delicious! You can have the Palestinian Falafel, Hummus, olives, and olive oil for breakfast. For lunch, Msakhan or Maqloubeh. For dinner, grape leaves stuffed with rice and meat. Last, leave some space for the Palestinian dessert "Knafeh".

Last but not least, being born in the Holy Land, people tend to be more interested in learning about my life, and how blessed I am to be born there. Indeed it is a blessing how we Christians, and Muslims live together as we share all occasions such as Christmas, or Eid el Fitr, without any sort of differentiation between religions.

What are you currently doing for work?

Currently, I am a loans officer by day, and fitness coach at night. In addition, I'm promoting products for Reebok-Adidas Palestine on my social media platform. Besides promoting products on my platforms, I use my platform as a tool to expand my brand and influence my peers, but more importantly to inspire people.

Tell me about your struggles as a woman.

Growing up in a patriarchal society which underestimates the power of women, and undermines our abilities was one of my main struggles. Especially the concept of weight-lifting being linked to males, put pressure on Palestinian women like me who had passion for lifting because many believe lifting gives women a more masculine look. In addition, creating my social media platform and exposing myself to our society made me an outlier, because traditionally many believe that women should be more conservative.

I was blessed with a family that has supported me in every step of my journey. With their support I managed to overcome the obstacles, and managed the courage to believe in myself. I am forever grateful.

Tell me about your successes as a woman.

Balancing two jobs is no easy task, I take pride in my work ethic and setting an example for others. I became a role model for many women in my society, and I began to change the stereotypical image that weight-lifting makes you look masculine. I encouraged many to live a healthier lifestyle, breaking the stereotypical image of the perfect body, and loving our bodies no matter what.

I cooperated and gave many females in my society the courage to break barriers and chase what they believe in. Meanwhile, giving them the confidence boost, and teaching them self-love to prepare them for the dark side of social media. All must learn that queens fix each other's crowns, and they lift each other up. Nonetheless, I bought my own car.

Provide some advice to women from a woman living in Palestine.

I advise all women to believe in themselves, if you believe in an idea, work on it until you make it a reality. And keep in mind that struggles make you stronger, and you should challenge yourself to overcome them, and keep going. At the end of the day, some will tell you, "you can't", you just have to prove them wrong!

Amanda Asbah

My Life As A Woman: Panama Edition

My name is Cecil, I am a Panamanian girl and I am going to tell you a little about my life story. I was born in Panama City, at the Santo Tomas hospital, my mother brought me to the world with 3,700 kilograms and 50 centimeters. From a very young age I was a very smiling and pampered girl, I was lucky to grow up with my parents and grandparents, I consider that as a real blessing.

At 14 years old, I already knew what I wanted to be in life, to be an incredible plastic surgeon, although when I graduated from high school my dream was not fulfilled, since I studied my true passion; journalism. I grew up in Pedregal, a town a bit far from the city, this made it a little difficult to move to study and work, but it never became an impediment.

Despite the constant criticism I received from my family and friends, saying things like "that career will not feed you" or "journalists are very poorly paid", I continued my studies at the university, and then specialized in Digital Marketing, which helped me get very good jobs. I can say that today, I do what I like the most, I write great articles for my clients, I have social media projects and I am continually learning. I have worked with brands like Seiko, Provivienda and Digicel, managing their social media campaigns and attending various events.

My inspiration is the women of my life; my mother and grandmother. They, with great sacrifice managed to carry out my dreams supporting me unconditionally. My father taught me to be strong, not to lose direction and always stay calm, this would take me far.

Also, I have several friends, who I consider as sisters. As children, I remember that we played sleepovers, makeup, cooking and stop counting. Now I see them, and I can see in them, the wonderful women who they have become, and that makes me feel proud.

To be a woman is to know very well the rights that are granted to me, to be a woman is to be sure that I can achieve what I want, since success is in the struggle and perseverance. Being a woman inspires me to think that EVERYONE can achieve anything, and that love is infinite when it comes to family.

In my culture, women are independent; we love to dress up, always keep ourselves beautiful, for OURSELVES, we like to have our own things, travel and love our country, our food and heritage.

For us, our country is like our mother, the homeland that welcomes us and gives us sustenance, it is everything for us. Panamá is synonymous of union and perseverance, because that is how we Panamanians are, tireless workers. Lovers of our beautiful beaches, our forests and rivers. We are a united country; who struggles every day to be better.

What I can really say to any girl who is reading this article, is to fight, not stop, dreams come true, you just have to visualize them, keep them in mind and not lose your way. Life will have many challenges, but at the end of the day, when you see your achievements come true, you will be able to say; I DID IT! And that dear friends, is priceless.

My Life As A Woman: Papua New Guinea Edition

Tuesday, 2 June 2020

I grew up in Port Moresby, capital of Papua New Guinea. Living in this city is very unique. It might not be a fancy place like some other city from overseas, but I love it being simple and unpopulated place. I grew up having my parents always on my side in our village. A simple life from the highlands – with limited access to basic necessities like water and electricity. My parents used to be government employees and struggled their way out to have their own successful business. I am lucky to have them who guided me all the time. Very thankful that they've done their best to push me to finish my studies in the city.

My passion was to follow my parent's footsteps. I was amazed by the way how they balance their lifestyle when I was young considering we were at the highlands with so little access to the city. But when I started my work as an account executive for an ICT Company, my plan got changed. Seems I like what I am doing now, interacting with the customer on a daily basis - ensure their needs are attended in a timely manner and provide customer satisfaction. I enjoy what I am doing right now, and it helps me grow and gain more experience and confidence for myself. I always look forward to stepping up just like others.

Papua New Guinea has about a thousand ethnic groups. Our family coming from a diverse culturally background and blessed to have a cultural group, with a unique language and belief from the highlands of Papua New Guinea. I love the way we celebrate our annual feast as I see the smiles and excitement of each and every one knowing the difficulties they face in their daily life experience.

I am a single mother with two kids. I am working hard to balance my work and the needs of my kids. It is not easy, there are times when you feel like you can't go on anymore, but you have to fight every challenge. Sometimes I feel jealous of other women on what I see on social media or in a movie setting - it seems they have a good environment to give joy for themselves. Anyhow, I am living in a developing country and I want to enjoy the simplicity and fresh air environment that I am experiencing right now. Also, I am a fighter woman and I will consider it as my success.

My advice to my fellow PNG Women is to never stop dreaming – live every day as it is the last day. Take on challenges as you never ever know what the future has in store for you. Live life to the fullest and always enjoy it.

My Life As A Woman: Paraguay Edition #1

Hello, my name is Anna Cantero and I was born in a small city in the department of Alto Paraná, Paraguay, called "Presidente Franco". Currently, I live in a neighboring city to which I was born, its name is "Ciudad del Este", the city where the sun rises, here I was raised all my life, here I grew up to be what I am today.

Since I was little, until today, I grew up in a middle-class family, we were never too poor, or very rich, we never lacked food on the table and my sisters and I were able to complete our school studies thanks to the efforts of our parents without any problem, I appreciate every day for that.

In all my family, the most inspiring woman for me has always been my mom. A great woman, with all the letters, a fighter and a worker, also, the best of friends for her three daughters. Since childhood I have kept this mentality, "when I grow up, I want to be as strong as mom."

Currently, I am studying Business Administration, I am exactly in the middle of the entire career, incredibly, I decided to study this career three months before finishing my studies at school, which seemed to have been a mere impulse, today it is my biggest dream.

When I was little, I never stopped to think about what I wanted to be when I grew up, if they asked me that question, I answered anything random, in order to get out of the situation, I think I had never worried about my future, maybe because it was very immature and innocent back then.

Currently, I only work in a small store that I created myself. Among the things that encouraged me to start my own business, I think, the main ones were, my mother, my university career and my taste for K-pop. Since my store is based on selling products made mostly by myself referring to K-pop, for example photocards, posters, or even personalized t-shirts painted by my own hands, in short, "fan made" products.

Going back to my environment, to the country where I grew up and live, I would like to talk a little about the beautiful things that exist in Paraguay. Paraguay is one of the few countries in the world where people are able to treat a foreigner even better than a countryman. The warmth that exists in the people of Paraguay, with nothing compares, Paraguayans are really very open and friendly people, that's why that is one of the things I love most about this culture, also of course, traditional foods and celebrations typical.

Among my successes as a woman, I want to emphasize again the fact that I managed to start a small business, but my own, it has not been easy and every day is a challenge, but I do what I like, and now my dream is that my small shop will be big someday, and of course, to make a lot of profit.

I think my main struggle as a woman is the mentality of my compatriots still have, that women are "the weaker sex", just because they are women, they think that we are inferior, that we are less strong or less capable and that is very annoying for my I fight against that mentality that the people around me tend to have every day. That mentality has prohibited me from many jobs, I feel that in many job interviews, I have been rejected just for being a woman. Being a woman in Paraguay requires courage to progress, it is a day to day struggle. Almost 2 years have passed, and I am still unemployed, holding onto my K-pop store and studying my college career. I hope that someday it will be worth it.

My advice to women living in Paraguay is that they never think they are inferior to anyone, if you are a woman you are capable, if you are a woman you are a warrior, if you are a woman, you are wonderful, worthy of all the good things in life, please, never believe otherwise.

My Life As A Woman: Paraguay Edition #2

I am Liz Elizabeth, born and brought up in San Lorenzo, a city located in the Central Department in Paraguay. It is the suburb of Asunción, the third most populous city in Paraguay.

As we have a lower-middle-class family entirely dependent on agriculture, most of the family members were not well-educated. Even though both of my parents only knew how to write their names, they solemnly wanted me to be an enlightened human being through proper education.

When I was a little girl, I had to help my parents in the strawberry fields in the morning and after that went to school after coming back home and having a quick breakfast.

After finishing the local high school, when I required quite a sum of money to go on to the university, my parents took a bank loan to afford my tuition and hostel fees. They always inspired me to be a government official and I fulfilled their dream by securing my place in an office under the Ministry of Justice and Labor as an Executive.

Although my parents dreamt me of being a government official, I always wanted to be a wealthy farmer like them who will have lots of lands, farms, and cattle. This is because, I followed my parents, as well as love the countryside we lived in. After finishing high school, I went to Asunción to study at the graduate level. From Universidad Columbia del Paraguay, I completed my bachelor followed by a master's degree in Economics.

Paraguay has a rich culture and is a country full of passion for soccer. Mixed with the Spanish settlers, indigenous Guarani culture has led to a peaceful, warm, and accepting attitude. Like most of the Paraguayans, I am bilingual in Spanish and Guaraní and a big fan of Paraguayan soccer.

Paraguayans are very friendly and have a happy, peaceful, and prosperous life. The community of Paraguay has many festivals celebrating its original skills like craftsmanship, music, instruments, and dance. Paraguayans are known for their joy and flexibility, and the country has always topped the "happiest place in the world."

In Paraguay it is not so easy for a woman to live an average life even. From my childhood to still now, I am facing many struggles to live a better life. Parents of families like ours in Paraguay are reluctant to send their girls to the schools. In my case the scenario was reversed, my parents were my inspiration, however, my uncles were against my going to school. I together with my parents, had to win over this situation.

Despite lots of perils on the way, my life isn't stuck, rather it is going in full swing. Being a successful employee in the office, I was nominated as the best employee twice.

My advice to the girls all over the world is wherever you are and how tough your surroundings may be, stick to your goals and do your daily works on time and you'll reach the harbor of success sooner or later. This is from the lessons that I learned while going my own way.

My Life As A Woman: Peru Edition #1

Just take a moment to think about Peru. What ideas come to your mind?

Maybe you have heard or read something about it. Perhaps you visited Peru and you know a bit more about the country. Well, today I can tell you more about the country where I was born and how my life is as a Peruvian woman. I grew up in Lima, the capital of Peru, the big city with more than 32 million people and for me, the place that I call home.

I grew up with my mother and also lived part of my life with my grandparents. My mother is one of the most inspiring people in my life, she follows her heart and from her example, I learned that everything that happens to us in life teaches us something.

About Peru, many things can be said, but one of my favorites about my country is the cultural diversity. The diversity of the food, the Indigenous languages, the different ways that people speak Spanish, the dances around the coast, the mountains and the jungle, and what I love most, the diversity of musical expressions. Here is where a big part of my life developed.

When music started...

I studied music and my relationship with it was love at first sight, I don't remember when it started but it was when I was a child. I didn't consider it as a viable career choice until I was fifteen, when I started playing drums and percussion. Before that, I wanted to study archeology, but then I realized I was more in love with music. The decision wasn't that hard because I had the support from my mother and I'm always thankful that music found me.

Now, I work as a freelance percussionist, drummer and composer, playing in records, concerts and composing fusion music with my band. I also work as a teacher at a conservatory. I teach popular music in the percussion department, and I enjoy it.

However, being a woman in music is not easy. I have to deal with many issues. For example, there is the fact that I have to constantly prove my value as a musician. People often have the preconceived notion that if you are a woman, you can't play well and when it is your first time playing with a group, they don't trust your skills and you have to prove your value as a musician one more time. Even though this is a hard situation for many women in music, this is changing little by little.

Struggles not only exist in the music field but also in my daily life. As a woman, I have had to deal with other experiences like feeling unsafe when I was traveling alone or when I have to come back late to my house after a music gig. It's not about living with fear but rather taking many more precautions.

But life also has a bright side!

Beyond these obstacles, I have also experienced great moments in my life that I consider my triumphs. One of them is finishing my music career after having tendonitis for two years and not being able to play during that period of time. I went through a hard process of learning everything in a different way but this helped me to live fully in the present and taught me that the most important person in your life is yourself and we should invest time in caring and loving ourselves, thereby freeing ourselves from society's expectations that we are pressured to fulfill.

Another success that I appreciate was being part of a big dance and music production where a friend and I composed the music. It was amazing how music can be translated into movement, how percussion can be felt in the entire body and how people move to express themselves through dance. These performances will always hold a special place in my heart, and this was the beginning of many interdisciplinary collaborations with theater and dance.

Being a woman in this world is not an easy experience, and as a woman living in Peru, I can urge women around the world to support other women any way possible, whether it be through supporting their businesses, sharing their projects, sharing their joy, or supporting them in the hard moments, because it is in these difficult moments that we most need to feel more supported. Also surround yourself with women who inspire you and encourage you to continue fulfilling your dreams. Each woman can contribute in her own way to create a better world to live for all human beings.

My Life As A Woman: Peru Edition #2

My name is Geraldine, I am almost 27 seven years old, I was born on Lima- Peru, in a district named Independencia, since I was a child I lived with my mother, sister and stepfather, he is the most wonderful person in the world, why?, because since he met me, he loved me, cared me, dedicated time to educated me and gave me necessary tools to be the person who I am today. My childhood was a little rough because I had a health problem in my hip, so that I had three surgeries in the hip, it was extremely necessary so I could walk and have a quality life. We had difficult times considering that I was a very young girl of 2 years old, who had to go through complicated surgeries and a long recovery at my young age.

I had a quiet adolescence, I always focus on my studies and on having good grades, my parents always taught me that I must be someone in life, when I finished high school I decided to study engineering but I was a little confused about what type of engineering to study, so I started looking for information about a variety of engineering. While looking for that information will defined my professional life, I met with an academy teacher. I told him about my concerns, and he answered me asking me, "why don't you study transport engineering?" I asked him, "what it is?" I had never heard about this career. After thinking about it and looking for universities, I found one, the only university that taught transport engineering, named Universidad Nacional Federico Villarreal Lima-Peru, it was the beginning of five years of effort, dedication and learnings likewise, it allowed me to meet great friends with whom I have generated strong bonds of friendship that I hope will be forever.

Some years later, I graduated from university and received my college degree. I got experience working at the Lima City Hall, actually, I am working in a public entity named Programa de Gobierno Regional de Lima Metropolitana. Here I work as a transit consultant in the area of studies and projects, we prepare technical files and execute roadworks. For one hand I feel good working here and the salary is good too. Although I have to deal with some foolish bosses and the political bureaucracy of my country, I try to do a good job and do my best to obtain good results.

My fathers and I always live in a rented home, also we have some outstanding debts, but My father's taught me never give up, they were my support in many moments in my life. Nowadays, they can't work, that is to say, they can't bring an income to the house because they don't have a permanent job. For this reason, I have to be responsible of maintaining my house, and I feel happy to contribute with them, although sometimes it's difficult doesn't feel worried about the circumstances that arise in life; despite this I decided to apply for a master's degree, it was the best choice, my teachers are teaching me public management tools, which is what I want to dedicate myself to for many years. I have more projects in mind, I would like to have my own business, I'm working on it and I think I will see results soon.

Let me tell you what it means to be Peruvian. For one hand Living here in Peru, it's wonderful; Machu Pichu situated in Cusco is one of the wonders of the world. Peru has three regions, the Coast, Highlands, and Jungle (Costa, Sierra, Selva) with beautiful landscapes, variety of animals, and exquisite gastronomy. Particularly, I love the food of my country like ceviche, lomo saltado, pachamanca, papa a la huancaína, juane, tacacho con cezina; desserts like mazamorra morada, picarones, suspiro a la limeña and a Peruvian drink named pisco. For the other hand, Lima is a city with a lot of vehicular traffic and pollution, we also have high rates of insecurity and poverty. Like all countries, we have deficiencies, not everything is beautiful, but I think we should see the good side, it is a country with great potential but still developing.

My life was somewhat difficult at my short 27 years, currently I still have complicated situations to attend, but I always keep a positive thought in the face of situations. I recommend to all women who read this story, don't give up due to some problem you have, an illness, the loss of someone, or perhaps a sentimental problem doesn't define your life; I don't have children, perhaps many of you have it, others have parents, siblings or other people who motivate you to continue, do it for they, for those people who love you and for yourselves. Please, always be grateful for everything, even with the fact of waking up one more day, when you begin to thank for every little detail of your day, you will see great things come into your lives, be strong, brave and stay beautiful always, because you deserve the best of life and more!

By: *Geraldine Aguilar Paredes*, Lima-Peru

My Life As A Woman: Peru Edition #3

I grew up in a beautiful district, called Miraflores, in the heart of Lima, Peru. I spent my childhood surrounded by my family, my books, fashion and art. I could say my childhood was quite good and pretty, I remember living near the sea, so I really liked going out and making picnics to witness the sunsets, to this day I remember the afternoons with my family, eating ice cream and my dad playing the guitar.

When I finished the school, I didn't know what I want to study, I had many ideas in my head, but I couldn't catch one, so I ended up choosing my career by affinity: Advertising and Communications. Why not? I always liked to communicate. So, the years passed and with them some of my dreams that I had saved and paused, because I had already decided on something, I couldn't go back. Big mistake.

I've always considered myself a woman passionate and determinate not to settle for something that is not for her, so I left the college and took a plane to Buenos Aires to have time with myself and find out what I really wanted to do, it was difficult to leave at a young age and alone to a city that I did not know, but it was challenging and good for me. This helped me to come back with clearer ideas.

So, I changed my career to Marketing, where I discovered a new world that made me happy. My career took me to places I've never imagined, I opened my first fashion and lifestyle blog, which led me to meet amazing people, I achieved goals on a personal and professional level, I appeared in a TV show for the first time and more. I felt my life, making sense. Also, I started travelling a lot around my country. By the way, Peru is a wonderful country, full of colors and delicious food, definitely one of the most wonderful countries I've ever known, if you ask me, Cusco is my favorite city in the entire world.

Regarding my work, I have more than 3 years working for enterprises in the marketing department. But this year I am dedicating myself to advising small companies and startups as a freelancer. I love what I do more and more, and I do not regret the change I made, because the result was better.

Plus, a have a clothing brand. I always wanted to have something of my own, so a year ago I started doing it, with doubts, but I did it anyway. It is important to believe what we are as women, which will help us stay focused and achieve our goals.

Finding my two passions: fashion and marketing, took me time, one of my biggest struggles was thinking that I couldn't do it. Many times, society pigeonholes us into something that we should be, but we can decide not to believe in it.

I leave you some of my thoughts within my 20s. For me, it was the age when I tried to find what kind of job I liked, to know what I am good at and what makes me feel alive. I think is a perfect age to start the things you love with more maturity and experience. Be patient with yourself and decide to be a person who grows and looks for his own path. Do what you have to do to connect with yourself in a way that feels authentic and real to you, so you can achieve your plans.

Here is the thing, there are people who use those years to learn and grow, to find themselves and go after what they want, who knows what works and what doesn't. And those who continue to be in jobs they hate, maybe good, but not good enough where they can shine. Remember, sometimes we lose ourselves in the things we love, but we find ourselves there, too.

Here is my advice, don't get stuck, move, take risks, try something new, this is a season to become what you have always wanted to be. Make a path and stomp it. Be true to what you believe, find people that match your mind. Don't panic in the mud, get out fast and take advantage of your time, be patient with yourself and keep dreaming. Because those dreams are the ones that will keep you alive forever.

I'm a woman and I'm hungry for whatever comes next.

My Life As A Woman: Philippines Edition #1

I grew up in Rizal, a province a few minutes north of the capital, in a town commonly referred to as the "Bibingka Capital of the Philippines." It may seem like a cliché, but my childhood really did involve a lot of the sweet baked rice cake; it was my mother's favorite dish and I would come home from school every day to find a fresh piece of Bibingka waiting for me on our dining room table. I got home earlier than my brother, so I usually got my hands on the best and biggest piece.

My brother and I were born 11 months apart. I, in January of 1998 and him, in December of that same year. It was a fluke caused by the holiday stress and a family history of diabetes, so I grew up with an automatic playmate and a pest who annoyed me to no end. But I wouldn't have had it any other way. We had each other's backs through the constant pressure that my parents put on us throughout our childhood.

My parents were typical tiger parents, an Asian concept of parenting that demands only the highest levels of achievement and success from children. By the time my seventh birthday rolled around, we had already gone through piano lessons, ballet classes, taekwondo, after-school tutoring programs, Kumon, and more. This may seem rather strict and rigorous for some but looking back at it, I feel nothing but gratitude. I may not have turned out to be a child piano playing prodigy or a prima ballerina, but I did learn discipline and resilience, two traits that helped me traverse my college years.

I also learned resilience from my mother. At 21 and a few months away from taking medical school entrance exams, she found herself pregnant with me. She withdrew her applications, married my father, and started working in the family business a few weeks after graduating. By the time I turned three, my parents were running their own business and had moved out of my grandparents' house. Our first home was small – there was no indoor plumbing and the four of us slept in a single bed – but it was ours and that was what mattered.

I don't think there will ever be enough words to express how grateful I am for my parents whose circumstances forced them to grow up quickly. Right now, I'm a year older than my mother was when her pregnancy test came back positive and I wouldn't have been able to make the same sacrifices that she did.

In university, I took up Legal Management, a management and entrepreneurship course that incorporated business law. I had initially hoped to go into law school after my undergraduate studies but in my third year, I went on a study abroad program and came back home with the realization that I no longer wanted to pursue the law.

Right now, I work in the family business as a Marketing and E-Commerce Manager where my day-to-day tasks mainly consist of running the Instagram store. It's not the most glamorous of jobs and I don't see myself staying here for the rest of my life but for now, it'll have to do.

When it comes to Filipino culture, there are many things to love about it but perhaps what I appreciate the most is the warmth and hospitality that it emphasizes. For instance, we greet guests not with a hello but rather, by saying kumain ka na ba, which translates to "have you eaten yet?"

The Philippines is also a matriarchal society and we value our women, especially in the workplace. There's no shortage of female executives and leaders who have made their marks upon their respective industries. But there's a flip side to this; many women new to the workforce find it hard to admit that there are gaps in their knowledge and refrain from asking their colleagues for help. I've met many female interns and fresh graduates who hated asking their superiors to clarify tasks and responsibilities as they didn't want to be perceived as "weak," "foolish," and "untrustworthy."

However, I believe that being able to admit your shortcomings and limitations is an important trait to have, especially in the Philippines professional world. Women, in particular, shouldn't be afraid to ask questions as doing so allows them to learn from others and become the best that they can be.

My Life As A Woman: Philippines Edition #2

I grew up in a province, northern part of the Philippines where farming and fishing is the main source of income, our location is surrounded by a mountain on the side and a sea on the other side. I was born in a poor family of four siblings and I'm the only girl. I have a loving family. I grew up like one of the boys, I climbed trees, mangoes, tamarind, guavas, and coconut to name a few. Life should be simple for a girl like me. Net fishing is practiced in our province, where people can take part in pulling the net previously thrown by the fisherman over a group of fish in the sea, and I and my siblings often take part so we can bring home fish for dinner, or even money to buy rice if there's a good catch.

My father is a local watch repairer and most honored and trusted in his profession in our province. He is a disciplinarian but loving father, he always makes sure we know our fault before he spanks us and caresses us after spanking. He was a kind and generous man, I remembered him giving money and a piece of pork meat to the thief he caught stealing his chicken. He is respected in our community, people with different problems come to our house for advice, I remember listening from afar. I respected my dad and took most of what he taught me by words and example, in my heart. My father was so kind that he entertained and adopted a stranger with nowhere to go to stay in our house, little did he know that it would affect my life, my growing up years.

I was sexually molested by my father's friend and threatened to kill my family if I told anyone about it, I was 6 years old then, I kept my secret until I was 19 years old. The emotional trauma I had to go through every day for 13 years, in those years I became a self-abuser, I abused myself sexually, but learned to stop it by myself with determination with the help of prayer, yes I have learned to pray and it helped me in my ordeal. But I grew up feeling useless, and worthless because I kept it all to myself and don't know how to deal with my trauma and everything that's happening inside me, I learned to put on a mask and hide what I feel with a fake smile and a jolly personality; I was a clown everywhere I went, but that doesn't change what I think of myself. This ordeal made me escape reality by daydreaming of what I want to be, I never valued myself, I never realized I was worthy and that I can change my life, If only help comes sooner, a person whom I could trust my secrets with and guide me to healing. With all those things going on inside me, I still lived a normal life outside, I remained an obedient and caring daughter. I lived a pretentious life.

Amidst the scarcity of resources and being ridiculed by people around us; neighbors and relatives, because they couldn't take the idea that a poor family like us could think of going to college. My father chose to send us all to college, he never finished college and he wanted to be an engineer, so, he wanted his four children to be engineers as well. I wanted to be a nutritionist but my father didn't accept my wishes, so I studied engineering out of obedience to my father and graduated BS ECE, from a prestigious engineering school in the Philippines. The only regret I had was never practicing it. All three of us are government scholars.

Growing up amidst my gruesome past, it was my father who inspired me to keep on going. I followed what I learned from him in dealing with impossible people around me and used the same discipline I grew up with in dealing with my children. I am currently working as an online English tutor and a wellness coach and worked in a hotel as a pastry chef. Looking back, I am thankful for being raised in a well-disciplined family where children are treated equally. I wouldn't have made it in life without my parents' love and their support. With what I have been through, it could have been better if I had help while growing up, but I know now that those things in the past made me become a stronger person.

I learned to love myself, coming to a point where you really love yourself works wonders, it's the kind of love that affects the people around you, loving yourself means making yourself beautiful inside and out. Realize that no matter what your past is, if you have a goal in your life and strive to do it, you can achieve it. And you shouldn't depend your life on anyone or any circumstances, you decide the stumbling blocks to be your stepping stone, for we have our own race to win, we have our own path to cross. In the end, we owe our success to no one but us. Love yourself and learn to forgive.

My Life As A Woman: Burias Island Edition

Where did you grow up?

Hi! I'm Ara. I was born in Burias, a beautiful island of Masbate City Philippines. However, I did not have the opportunity to experience my birthplace because I grew up in a small city in Bicol Region. In 2018 I went to our place to see my origin. I felt great regret when I realized how beautiful and peaceful our municipality was. Maybe if I grew up there I would be proud that I had a happy life as a child. I also tried to find my mother in that place that I had never met in my whole life. Apparently, I did not get any information about her so it is really hard for me. Maybe I did not really try hard because I feel resentment in my heart. But I hope that one day I will be able to make up for the missing part of my life. I hope I can also be proud that I have a grandmother who inspired me and a mother who raised me full of love but, I don't think human life is really perfect. Sometimes, a whole and happy family can only be found in the book. I knew in myself that it was not for me and that it had stolen a lot of things from my childhood. I do not know what Christmas feels like with the family. I can't celebrate Mother's Day without knowing my real mother. So is Father's Day because I haven't seen them both until now. I also have no idea if they are still alive.

How did you grow up? Did you have parents or maybe a grandmother who inspired you?

I grew up in an orphanage where my mother left me. As far as I know, she was a prostitute when she was young while my father was a tourist. However, I learned to follow orphanage rules. As I grew up, it became increasingly clear to me that I did not have a family of my own. I have never had the experience of having a father, a mother, and a brother. I also have no inspiration but my own situation. One thing I am thankful for is that I grew up close to God. We were trained to wake up early, pray, attend mass, cook and socialize. We were also given our own responsibility and mine was to help wrap the soaps made in the orphanage. There was also a time when it was my responsibility to find the naughty kids who did not come to the dinner table at the right time. But I like to help out at the bakery because I like the smell of the bread being made. Most of all, I can eat hot and freshly made bread when I am there.

What did you study? / What did you want to be growing up? / Why?

Honestly, I grew up not knowing what I wanted. All I know is the importance of education and faith. Because of this, I graduated from high school. But like other province girls, I also wanted to see Manila so when I had the opportunity, I went there with my friend where I worked as a housekeeper.

What do you love about your culture?

Working as a maid is part of the Filipino culture. If you did not graduate from college and went to Manila, the only common reason for that is to be an assistant. I am not ashamed of it but I am proud that we have the ability to serve other people.

What are you currently doing for work?

I work in Saudi as an OFW. I have been here for ten years and I have had many experiences as a helper of a foreign family.

Tell me about your struggles as a woman.

As someone who has not experienced parental love I grew up doubting my own ability to be a parent in the future as well. The fact that I did not study well also made it difficult for me because language hindered my communication with my neighbors. It is difficult to convey how you really feel or think when you do not fully understand the foreign language. It's also a big puzzle to me if my parents think of me as well. I have many questions that I will not be able to answer until I grow old.

Tell me about your successes as a woman.

I can consider working abroad a success because it is something that has given me confidence in my own abilities. It is also a success that I can be considered trusted by my bosses and colleagues. It is also a big thing for me to guide the new OFWs to fight homesickness and make them as happy as I can because in other countries we will support each other.

Provide some advice to women from a woman living in each province.

Our life is like a jeep. We are the drivers and we have passengers on board. Sometimes even when you are hungry or in pain, you have to endure it for a while for the sake of the majority.

Sometimes even if the passenger is heavy, we have to take him to his destination. Like the test of life, it must be solved until it disappears. We cannot stop in the middle of the road just because we can no longer continue the journey. Whatever happens, you need to finish what you started in a good way. Return the car to the garage properly and pick it up again in the morning. Fight!

My Life As A Woman: Catanduanes Island Edition

Where did you grow up?

Hello, I'm Wendy from Valencia, Virac Catanduanes. Eight years ago, we have moved to Antipolo City for good.

How did you grow up? Did you have parents or maybe a grandmother who inspired you?

I grew up with my parents and like most children; I have been inspired to be a good daughter because of their hardships. I have always wanted to deserve all their support until I finished my schooling.

What did you study / What did you want to be growing up / Why?

When I was still in elementary I used to tell my classmates that I wanted to become a teacher; but since I was a government scholar, I had to take up a science-related course. So, I landed up on BS Accountancy and I finished it with flying colors.

What do you love about your culture?

Having close family ties is the best about our culture. Parents allow their children to stay with them despite marrying at a very young age. They support them build their own families and never leave them during tough times. Parents do their best to make these young families grow on their own, be financially and spiritually stable in time.

Filipino generosity is another important aspect of our community. We have this attitude of trying to help somebody else although we don't have much to give. There are times when we also ask for help and receive something in return as a common result of "utang na loob."

What are you currently doing for work?

I am teaching in a Catholic school. This job has taught me a lot of values and strengthens my faith to God because of different religious practices.

Tell me about your struggles as a woman.

I have so much experience with my family especially when my mom was diagnosed with cancer. Since I am the eldest among our siblings, I needed to take care of her. I was beside her during her checkups and operation. I saw her sufferings and felt the pain that she endured in those times; it made me stronger and kept the faith to God until her death I did not leave her side. Although it was very painful, I'm still thankful that she died in a peaceful way because I have offered her life to God and let her go with open arms.

Tell me about your successes as a woman.

As a daughter, being there for my parents when they were dying was an accomplishment for me. I owe it to them for bringing me into this world. As a sister, I have always been there for my siblings no matter what. I help them the best way I can and I continue to be their elder sister who is always available anytime.

As a wife, I have proven my loyalty with my husband. I have assumed the roles of a mother and a father to our children while he was away for many years. As a mother, I have raised good children who will someday give happiness to other people. They will become parents who will also leave behind them good kids. They will contribute something good in the society and spread kindness to other people. This is how we grow love.

Provide some advice to women from a woman living in province.

Trials and failures become synonymous with each other as we grow older. There comes a time when we cannot tell whether a situation is a trial or a failure already. Empower others because you don't know what they're going through.

Life never gets easier as the children grow bigger and parents, older. Love more because at the end of the road, the kids will be left on their own to keep going fueled by our affection. Teach your children to love others because we can never be there for them all the time.

Don't keep something good for yourself. You will never lose a talent by sharing it with others. Make them find their way to earn too. Help them if you can and your name will circulate even if you keep helping others a secret. Be nice to the needy. Give them what you can. It will make them happy, but believe me, it will make you happier.

Prayers are still the best medicine. Leave all your worries behind and everything will be alright.

Just hold on to God's promise; whatever happens He will never forsake us.

My favorite line: LORD THY WILL BE DONE...

My Life As A Woman: Luzon Island Edition

Hey there, I am Aiya from Luzon. Luzon is one of the northern islands in the Philippine. I was raised in my family home with my grandparents, my aunts, and my mother. My father was never in the picture, so I only knew my mother's side of the family. I was told my father was a traveler. Even with that, I had a really fun childhood, I was surrounded by love and affection. To some people my grandparents spoiled me, they gave me everything I could need. I would go everywhere with my grandmother, they used to call me her second. Going to the market and sewing was a favorite of ours. While sewing she would tell me stories about when she was younger. She was my inspiration in life and taught me all the important life lessons a female needs to know.

I attended Luzon Elementary school, then graduated and went to Pampanga High School. After high school, I went to the Central Luzon State University for a few courses. My school tenure was average, I had a few friends, played a lot, and got good grades. Growing up I always wanted to become a farmer. To many, it wasn't the best professional choice. I had my mind set on doing what made me happy, and farming did that for me. My grandfather was a farmer, so he gave me a lot of information as it relates to farming. Going to school was a formality and I just wanted to be better able to market my produce. After high school, I started to work with my grandfather on the farm. we doubled production after a few years of working there, we had to hire people.

My culture is amazing, Luzon is simply a beautiful place to live. I have been to other countries, but none compared to Luzon. Our markets are just very culturally enhanced, you could find everything there. Our people are very welcoming, we are givers. I always remember when people came to our house, and my grandmother ensured they were fed with the best and felt comfortable in our home. It's just in our nature to be like that.

Growing up, even though I had a great relationship with my family I missed out on having a relationship with my father. Due to that I became very guarded and closed to everyone that was outside of my family. I have a few good relationships.

Even though farming is a male-dominated field because it is assumed women aren't strong enough to take on such tasks, I never let that deter me from my goal of becoming a farmer. I had to make myself a stronger to prove everyone that had that mindset wrong. I also worked on how guarded I was, and it improved my communication skills. To all the women of Luzon prove the world wrong. Embrace yourself and do what you love even if it isn't what the world thinks you should be doing. Be happy and be a phenomenal woman.

My Life As A Woman: Bicol Region Edition #1

Where did you grow up?

Hello! I'm Maridel. I came from a family of farmers and fishermen. My mother was a simple housewife who grew up in the province of Rizal; my father was a former soldier from Prieto Diaz, Sorsogon City. Up to these days, I can still remember my happy childhood years in Bicol, but when I was young we moved to Rizal and left my birthplace for good.

How did you grow up? Did you have parents or maybe a grandmother who inspired you?

I grew up with my parents. We are seven siblings in the family. I was the second child but I assumed the role of the eldest because my grandfather raised my sister. My mother was my inspiration. She was hardworking and patient; the life of our family was difficult, but we grew up kind even though we did not graduate from college.

What did you study? / What did you want to be growing up? / Why?

I only finished a vocational course because it was the most practical way to earn during our time. Also, our parents could not afford to support us in our studies for a long time. We have many brothers and sisters and we cannot ignore the others for our own good. There was a time in my life when I felt a strong desire to be a nun. I had this calling when I became part of a humanitarian project and we went to different houses to help people. It was then that I saw how many people were suffering and unable to meet the needs of their families.

What do you love about your culture?

What I like most about our culture is how much we value our family. Whatever resentment we have for our relatives we can set it aside for the sake of the greater good. Second to this is our helpfulness to our neighbors. Even when we have no money, we are able to help others in our own way. Third is our humility in many things and of course I will never forget our example of goodness.

What are you currently doing for work?

I am currently helping my son in growing our business. We have our own restaurant and it also has a grocery store next door. I manage the store especially when it comes to supplies. We have individual responsibilities in our livelihood because it is for our family.

Tell me about your struggles as a woman.

As a mother, I can say that I am truly fulfilled. God has blessed us with nine children. Yes, I had a hard time getting them a good education; but they all studied. At the same time, with all the hardships of life, I have learned to help my husband. I realized that it is not his sole responsibility to provide for the whole family. We need to do this together; and to make the lives of our kids better, I started to work so hard until they all finished their studies.

I also had a problem with my father-in-law and sister-in-law regarding financial matters. That was another struggle for me as a wife. I know that my husband cannot give me his full loyalty since they are his family. I did my best to contain the issue and went out of my way to save my relationship with his family. However, there are times when even if you really want to do something it does not happen immediately because we have our own beliefs and values in life. I prayed that I would be given the courage to cope with the situation and that day came. The intense emotions and resentment towards each other subsided.

Tell me about your successes as a woman.

Having a good relationship with my husband was my first success. Next is being an exemplary mother to my nine children. I can be proud that they all grew up to be kind, respectful, and God-fearing. I am not very educated and also do not have a good job, but my success as a person is visible in my children.

Provide some advice to women from a woman living in each province.

I want to advise all women to be devout so that everything they do, think, and say will be blessed by God.

My Life As A Woman: Bicol Region Edition #2

The author has not been verified, but the story has been proven authentic.

Where did you grow up?

Hello! I'm Leonor. I grew up in Naga City. Our place is the heart of Region 5. It is not so big, but it is the most popular city in Bicol Province.

How did you grow up? Did you have parents or maybe a grandmother who inspired you?

I grew up with my family. My mom was an English professor and my dad was a retired Trial Court judge. When I was only four years old, she used to take me to school, because our relatives took care of my two baby siblings that time. As my mom describes it, I was a shy little girl who used to sit in her class and copy everything on the board. I'm the eldest among the three siblings. When I was in grade school, I was my youngest brother's picker when our mother was still in class.

I didn't like joining school presentations; I used to stay inside the house when I was young. I was always busy reading comics and cartoons. I have a collection of children's books.

I was so quiet and grew up much closer to my father. They used to tell us to study very well so we could become professionals and independent in the future. They didn't have dreams for us to enter into politics. I can say that I have inherited from my parents my diligence in learning. If it weren't for them, I probably wouldn't be as diligent in my studies.

What did you study? / What did you want to be growing up? / Why?

I studied Bachelor of Arts in Economics in University of the Philippines, Diliman, Quezon City. After I graduated, I went back to my province. Inspired by the People Power Revolution, I worked as a researcher and soon I studied Law and became a lawyer. I believe this is what I have always wanted since my father is a retired Judge.

What do you love about your culture?

Since I live in Naga City, I have witnessed the Bicolano devotion to Inang Penafrancia. Filipinos nationwide come to our place to celebrate Penafrancia festival every year. It's like the celebration of the Black Nazarene in Metro Manila. People do all means to touch Virgin Mary because we believe that doing so solves and answers all our prayers. Yes, some locals nowadays are not that devoted but it remains to be part of the Bikolano culture and I love it so much.

Another thing that I am very proud of is the fact that kissing the hands of the elders is widely observed in our place. Elders don't recognize you for your academic achievements nor for your parents. They will remember you for being a very polite individual in the community.

What are you currently doing for work?

I work as a government official.

Tell me about your struggles as a woman.

When I was younger, my struggles were mostly about becoming a good student. I wanted to please my parents and be a role model to my younger siblings.

After graduation, I realized that I wanted to do something else so I applied as a researcher.

I got married and struggled to be a very attentive and supportive wife to my husband who was then a city mayor. We started to raise our kids while I was in Law school.

I tried to balance my life without neglecting any of my roles; I have always wanted to give all the needs of my husband. He was the center of our lives. We're just so lucky because we were blessed with kids who are so loving and wo helped me take good care of their father.

The greatest struggle in our lives was caused by the sudden death of my husband. I had been so comfortable growing old with him; watching our children grow up and giving them what they need from us as parents. After that fateful accident, I found myself continuing his advocacies in life. Everything is new to me since I am not into politics, but because of my love for him, I need to do this and feel his presence in my life every single day.

Tell me about your successes as a woman.

Fulfilling my parents' dreams for me was my first success; as a daughter, I would never want to fail my old parents.

Becoming a good sister to my two siblings is another success; I am the eldest and it is only right for me to guide them by being a good example.

I have given my whole life to my husband and children; I am continuing his role as a father and at the same time, my role as a mother.

I am doing all possible means to not just feed, but empower the poor Filipino families by implementing livelihood programs to help them become productive members of the society.

At present, I am still empowered to do more for my fellow Filipinos. Seeing others follow my path would be the greatest achievement for me; you see, we won't be here forever. We do these things to touch lives and to make the younger generation care for the future of everyone.

Provide some advice to women from a woman living in each province.

Becoming a wife and mother is not the end of self-preservation.

Yes, we please others but we must take care of ourselves too.

We can never tell what the future brings us so it is only right to be prepared and strong for the people that we love.

It is also very important to remember that we are part of a community and the safety of everyone has to be our concern.

Having a sense of duty gives us fulfillment and peace of mind. Sometimes there is a conflict between self-preservation and sense of duty, but we just have to believe that if it's for the betterment of the majority, we need to adjust, we need to fit in and make our lives more meaningful.

My Life As A Woman: Marinduque Island Edition

Where did you grow up?

Hi! I'm Cherry from Gasan, Marinduque. I grew up in Barangay Tapuyan, a peaceful village the said province.

How did you grow up? Did you have parents or maybe a grandmother who inspired you?

I spent most of my childhood years with my grandmother because both of my parents were OFWs. We are three in the family and I am the youngest. I have always been inspired by my mother who works too hard for our family. She has given up many years of our lives together just to provide our needs. She doesn't want us to experience the hardships that she endured when she was a child.

What did you study? / What did you want to be growing up? / Why?

I graduated as Cum laude of BS Computer Science. I have chosen the said course for practical reasons, but I when I took part in a humanitarian mission, I started to have another calling; I joined a Non-Government Organization and started participating in different humanitarian missions.

What do you love about your culture?

Filipinos observe "utang na loob" or debt of gratitude. For me it is the highest form of debt which you cannot repay with money. It has an invisible bond that keeps people closed to one another even when they don't talk for years. It will make you remember someone's kindness even after a decade. The best thing about it is, it stays for a lifetime. Imagine if you do something good to a person each day, in a week, you have seven people who are grateful that you exist. You may not want them to be so vocal about it, but for sure, it makes you feel fulfilled.

What are you currently doing for work?

For 10 years, I worked in an IT company in Makati City. Then, I started to work with a humanitarian group in Asia. We focus on providing food and medicine to poor Asian families including India, Bangladesh, and Philippines.

Tell me about your struggles as a woman.

As a child, it was so hard for me to understand why my parents had to work away from us. Being the youngest, I was so vulnerable during those years. I was so jealous with my classmates who were with their mom and dad. I couldn't explain why I was hurt especially during family days at school when I had to go with my grandma and siblings.

As a teenager, I was confused whether being away from my parents was a blessing or a punishment. There were times when I couldn't relate to my friends who have strict parents because mine were always out of sight. I have thought that this is an abnormal life and that I was deprived with some things as a teenager, but at the end of the day, I have always been so grateful that God has given us kind and affectionate parents who worked so hard for us.

My most serious struggle in life was in 2003 when I was diagnosed with cancer. I couldn't understand my feelings anymore. I was so worried about my family more than my short mission on earth. I couldn't bear the pain of leaving them so hurt that I bravely underwent chemo and other treatments that became very successful.

During my battle, I have realized that the only way for me to accept my fate is to make each minute of my life worthwhile. I have started to take part in different missions and I was so happy and fulfilled as if it was only the beginning.

Tell me about your successes as a woman.

I have lived a happy childhood despite of the fact that I was away from my parents. It was a success because, I can never take it back.

I was a responsible teen; although I could do something freely, I have chosen to be in the bright side of life. It's another success.

Battling cancer is my greatest success in life. There were times when I wanted to give up, but my love for my family made me become a survivor.

Provide some advice to women from a woman living in province.

Always choose to do good even if doing something bad is quite tempting. Life is not about personal satisfaction. The weight of your soul will be measured by the impact that you made in someone's life. Believe me, self-fulfillment is achieved when you put somebody else before you. Let's try to be a blessing to the poor. Giving them a reason to keep holding on is enough to make us happier and inspired. Have you ever asked yourself whether you have touched someone's life? If not, it's about time to consider these things.

My Life As A Woman: Mindora Island Edition

Where did you grow up?

My name is Mika from Roxas, Oriental Mindoro, but I moved to San Pablo City, Laguna in 2010.

How did you grow up? Did you have parents or maybe a grandmother who inspired you?

I grew up with my parents and they have always inspired me to be better than the person I was before; Their dream is to raise children who are morally upright so you can imagine how hard my teenage life was. In addition, we have always been surrounded and closely watched by conservative relatives and grandparents. In a way, life has been a little bit rocky, but since we know what they expect from us, we lived up to their expectations and tried our best not to deviate from what is acceptable for the family.

What did you study? / What did you want to be growing up? / Why?

I am a registered nurse, but I have always wanted to be a fashion designer. While growing up, I have always followed the latest trends and closely studied the evolution of fashion for eight years. I was aware that we were not rich and my parents could let me follow my dream job, so I studied nursing, took the board exam and started working. I don't regret anything; taking care of people who are in pain gives me happiness, but sadness fills my heart when I start to consider my list of "what ifs."

What do you love about your culture?

Filipinos have a very positive perspective in life. There are times when we tend to give up, but because of our family and society, we continue to make things possible. We are also the only race who can smile even in great sadness and that is a sign of humility. We, Filipinos, can never be too proud of ourselves. We always consider the people around us. Most of the time, we put ourselves last to make sure that no one is affected when we do something, when we feel something. We give a reason for everything. We choose to believe and have faith all the time.

What are you currently doing for work?

I am working as a staff nurse in a private hospital in Laguna.

Tell me about your struggles as a woman.

It's a struggle to forget the job you dream of when you know you can excel in that field. You can never be too happy especially when you are very tired and sad. It's hard to go with the flow just because everyone expects you to do so. You have this small voice inside your head that you want something new in your life.

It's a struggle to always say it's okay that when you think that no one actually cares about how you really feel as person. I can imagine women who have embraced the role of being plain housewives despite of the fact that they still want to have a career because they know, they can do both, to be a good mother and a happier career woman.

Tell me about your successes as a woman.

- Being an obedient daughter is a success.
- Setting aside your personal preferences is another one.
- Keeping your own family as solid as possible is the biggest success.

Provide some advice to women from a woman living in province.

Don't forget to PRAY... prayer is the biggest and the most powerful weapon that we have to overcome and surpass our problems in life, spread the positivity always, be optimistic and a risk-taker, always do your very best and always wear your smile. GOD will definitely give the things that you deserve in His perfect time and reason...LIVE LIFE TO THE FULLEST.

My Life As A Woman: Palawan Island Edition

Where did you grow up?

Hello! I'm Abe. I was born in Tinitian, Roxas, Palawan. When I was eight years old, my parents decided to move to Bataraza where my father's farm is located.

How did you grow up? Did you have parents or maybe a grandmother who inspired you?

I grew up with parents who highly value the importance of a family. My father has always been a good provider. He owns a small vegetable farm and sells his harvests to the local store owners. He has only one rule in the house; follow your parents or leave on your own. My mother, the peacemaker, keeps everything accordingly. She always says that clean surroundings show who you are as a person and make you feel good about yourself. She encourages us to be obedient and patiently explains to us things that we sometimes cannot understand. She is indeed the light of the family.

What did you study? / What did you want to be growing up? / Why?

I have graduated as a caregiver and have always wanted to work abroad. My father has been hesitant to permit me, but my mom has been so patient in explaining to him that opportunities knock but once. In 2005, I went to Hong Kong and worked as a nanny. After five years, I was hired as a caregiver in Canada and stayed there up to 2018. I was able to build a bigger house for my parents during my stay in Canada. Looking back, I realized that I never wanted to do another job besides caregiving. Taking care of people makes me fulfilled. I get my strength from them knowing that they need not just my service, but my sincere love and concern for their welfare.

What do you love about your culture?

Working abroad made me realize that we, Filipinos, are very lucky for having great respect to elders; If not, we would need a lot of caregivers to take care of them. It's good that we cannot let them grow old with other people because it's our way of saying that it's about time that we repay them for all the goodness that they have given us. Seeing the smile on their faces drives away all the tiredness that we have in life. If only we could buy them another lifetime, I'm sure that the majority of Filipinos would work too hard to have their parents with them forever.

What are you currently doing for work?

Currently, I am a part time tutor and freelancer. I came back in the Philippines last year and decided to stay for a while. Unfortunately, I cannot leave because of the ongoing lockdown in different parts of the world. In great depression, I started browsing the internet and found out about freelancing. I became so interested about it that I started sending resumes to different companies online. I was hired and from there, sprang other freelancing jobs. Now I realized that I have another love; and that is working from home.

Tell me about your struggles as a woman.

One of my struggles is the misinterpretation of woman's ability compared to man. We are always the inferior ones and I don't know how gender affects that. For several times, I didn't get a job because the employer has preferred a male applicant. Yes, men can do better than women in other aspects, but we have also our own strengths in certain areas so I think it's unfair to be measured just because of gender.

Tell me about your successes as a woman.

I consider myself successful as a good daughter. Everyone can be one, but only a few can do it very well. I have always put their needs before me and it made me very happy. Seeing them comfortable and at peace makes me more fulfilled than ever before.

Being a caregiver with a heart is another success for me. Doing a tough job for the sake of money is not enjoyable at all. I'm just so lucky because this is where my heart is. I don't need to convince myself that I can do it again and again because it is what I want as long as I'm strong and able.

Freelancing is another achievement that I have in life. Just when I thought that there was no hope and I had to start my life from the very beginning, it has opened its door very wide. I am so happy and I consider this as a blessing since I can work with my parents even in times of crises.

Provide some advice to women from a woman living in province.

Believe in your ability. No one else knows you better than you do. Nobody can say that this is your limit. It's not for them to assess you so, have faith in yourself. Develop your potential. You may be very good in your own field of expertise, but time is moving, things change, we must grow with the new generation. Don't limit yourself. We need to face our own fears. We need to try something before we say "No, I can't." Never deprive yourself of something that is within your reach. Enjoy every opportunity to learn. It's an accomplishment and it's beneficial to our health.

My Life As A Woman: Polillo Island Edition

Where did you grow up?

Hello there! I'm Lala. I was born in Poblacion, Polillo, Quezon, but I grew up in Manila area.

How did you grow up? Did you have parents or maybe a grandmother who inspired you?

I grew up inspired by my family members who all worked very hard.

Our family used to own a handicraft business for so long a time. I can say that I was more inspired by my grandfather who had so many incomparable principles and values in life. He was a great man and he had touched more lives by giving them sources of income and teaching them how to survive on their own. He was also known for having the longest term as a government official in our place without claiming any compensation. He was strict and very firm as the head of the family, but he was well-loved by all the people around him.

What did you study? / What did you want to be growing up? / Why?

I studied Journalism and Anthropology in undergraduate and graduate school. Growing up I wanted to work in the media as it seemed exciting.

What do you love about your culture?

I learned about food and practices from our hometown even if I grew up in the city. I love our food and culture of respect for the elders and celebration of festivals.

Until now, I always long for local foods especially when I visit other countries. The memories of my hometown always cheers me up when I experience homesickness. I used to walk in the rain with my cousins and friends. We loved full moons because we used to play "patintero", a traditional Filipino children's game. Along with "tumbang preso", it is one of the most popular outdoor games in our country.

I will never forget how often our parents beat us back then because we played so much under the sun. I will also never forget how strong our chest beats every time we see our parents carrying a stick because we have not come home yet even at dinner time.

Respect for the elderly is very important to us so even though we do not want to stop playing, we immediately follow them so that they allow us to play again the next day.

What are you currently doing for work?

I am a professor.

Tell me about your struggles as a woman.

Being expected by everyone to have children and family is very difficult. I have always valued the important role of the family in our society; I have always been so fond of children, but I have other priorities in life which are equally important for me. I also believe that the essence of being a great woman is not just in giving birth, raising children, and having a family of your own.

Anyone can do something and give back to the society by doing other means such as planting trees, adopting kids, feeding and empowering the poor, and a lot more.

Tell me about your successes as a woman.

I have a Ph.D. and hold a good job as a university professor.

Provide some advice to women from a woman living in each province.

Do what you want to do and don't be limited by other people's expectations. We only live once and we owe it to ourselves to do something that makes us feel better.

It is not for the society to judge you; continue doing what makes you happy; for as long as we're not hurting anyone, there is nothing wrong with living the kind of life that you have always wanted.

Empower others and never forget to be empowered too. Our lives will only become meaningful if it is well-lived and if it has touched somebody else's. The world is too full of negativities, let's try to make a little heaven on earth and be a gift to others. We cannot simply give them what they need today. It would be so much better if we teach them how to have what they need without asking for help from other people.

Love your health. Eat healthy foods that will make you live your life to the fullest. Don't be cruel to animals; eat vegetables and fruits. I have been a vegetarian for more than 10 years and I am so glad to be one.

Above all, I will never forget my favorite line:

Let's have world peace! Mabuhay!

My Life As A Woman: Romblon Island Edition

Where did you grow up?

Hello! I'm Zen and I was born in the beautiful Municipality of Romblon. I grew up in a peaceful community, but I have migrated to Arizona with my husband. It's a totally different place and it takes time for me to adapt myself here for quite some years now.

How did you grow up? Did you have parents or maybe a grandmother who inspired you?

I grew up with my good parents, affectionate brother and sister. I did not grow up surrounded with any grandparents so, I was jealous of my classmates in grade school every time I see them being picked up by their grandparents. I used to have a playmate who was a spoiled brat with his grandmother and it made me feel that something was missing in my life. I can't relate to the stories about no one can beat my grandfather. However, I was very lucky with my parents filling in the gaps in my life. My grandparents' province is far away so we count the years before they can be seen or visited.

In short, it was my mother who inspired me a lot to be a responsible woman.

What did you study? / What did you want to be growing up? / Why?

I studied in a prestigious private school from elementary to college and post graduate, but I did not finish my last two courses. I wanted to have beautiful and adventurous experiences, but if you ask me about my dream job, it's to be a doctor; that is my first choice and my parents dream of me to be a one. It just didn't happen; life and situations have changed it. My siblings and I had to be more realistic so we landed on practical careers.

What do you love about your culture?

With so much culture in the Philippines, what I like most is respect for the elderly. It is sad to think that there are Filipinos today who no longer follow the said culture. Values Education does not disappear at school but there are many aspects that really change the course of society.

The second culture I like is the helpfulness of Filipinos. Often it is not about money but about things we can share with our neighbors such as time, advice, and concern.

The third is having a close family relationship. It is a big thing for Filipinos to be blood relatives and it stays until they grow old. I know some families who are torn apart by money, land and jealousy of one another. Honestly, this is sad for a Filipino like me. That should not be the outcome of a deep relationship.

The fourth is the diligence of the Filipinos. The story of "Lazy Juan "is popular in the Philippines because laziness is a ridiculous habit in our society. But, there are many "Juan Tamad" now.

What are you currently doing for work?

Currently I'm working as educational assistant in one of the middle schools in the United States. It is difficult for me since I am not an American myself and every day is a challenge.

Tell me about your struggles as a woman.

As a woman my personal struggle is how to give a hundred percent of effort in everything I do. I'm a risk taker, passionate and I always try to make a difference in the lives of others. Being the best version of yourself is so challenging especially if you are in another country. Failures become normal as you always have the feeling of being less of a person that you really are. You struggle to be better each day and it's honestly not a joke.

Tell me about your successes as a woman.

Finishing my studies and acquiring a license are my best achievements.

485

Imparting my knowledge to students who are now professionals always makes me feel good and fulfilled.

Provide some advice to women from a woman living in each province.

Always look back where you come from. Your origin and your past have served their purpose in your life and you simply have to look at things from different perspectives for you to truly appreciate your roots.

Always remember the magic of hard work and love. You can reach distant places and work with different people, but for you to fit in, you need to adapt and observe integrity at all times and consider people around you. Life is too short, yet we have a big heart that is capable of sprinkling a little on Earth and it will give a great impact in your life where ever you go.

Education is lifelong learning; do not be afraid to study no matter how old you are because it serves a unique purpose in different stages of life.

Always preserve good culture and values in your own ways. People get to judge us nowadays especially on social media. To do this without offending others and getting bullied, be matured enough to understand that we need not to openly speak about everything all the time.

Be relentless and achieve something not just for yourself, but for others. Remember, victory is way better when you share it with the majority.

Live a life of passion and purpose. The end for each person is yet to come so please, let's all make it worthwhile.

My Life As A Woman: Visayas (Leyte) Islands Edition

Where did you grow up?

Hi! I'm Hazel from Mahaplag, Leyte, Visayas. We live in a remote area where all possible means of transportation are very expensive. To say the least, we have no choice, but to stay in the mountain where life is easier just because it is simple and practical.

How did you grow up? Did you have parents or maybe a grandmother who inspired you?

I'm from a family of farmers. We plant, grow, and harvest crops to live. My parents are my inspiration since I want them to experience something that is extraordinary for us. I want to give them an easier and a better life. Seeing them working under the heat of the sun all day makes me question my self-worth. I am young and strong, but why can't I do something for my family? It hurts to see then grow old tied in the soil. I want to make a difference in their lives while they're still alive.

What did you study? / What did you want to be growing up? / Why?

I studied dressmaking for free, courtesy of the local government of Leyte. I used it to apply in a factory in Cavite. I was hired and worked there for five years. The said factory is owned by a Chinese businessman who introduced me to his Mexican friend in 2009. To make the long story short, the Mexican fell in love with me and now, we have five beautiful children.

I wanted to be a teacher when I was young, but my parents told me that we need to be practical so a vocational course would do. I don't regret being a dressmaker since that's how I met my husband and besides, we have a factory of our own. I can still act as a teacher to my children and it makes me happier and more fulfilled.

What do you love about your culture?

Being a Filipino is an honor due to the unique cultures that we have in the society. I have taught my children to embrace our wonderful culture and so far, I can see them very happy about it and we are proud parents for raising Mexican but very Filipino kids.

I also value strong family ties. My parents are now with me and they don't need to work too hard to earn a living. I am so happy to give them back what I owe them from the very start.

What are you currently doing for work?

I am managing our family business. My husband has been a very good provider, and father to the children. This is the best thing we can do for them, to work hard and prepare their future. We also train them to learn different aspects of the business since the company will also be left for them. As early as now, they have to learn how to run it.

Tell me about your struggles as a woman.

For a Filipina to be married to a foreigner is not that easy. We have different cultures and upbringings. I have to prove my self-worth not just to my husband but to his family. Raising children of mixed races is also a struggle. We do not know how they will react to the culture that we have. Being a good child is also a big struggle when you cannot do something good for your parents. I am just so blessed that God allowed me to be the better version of myself.

Tell me about your successes as a woman.

I have become a good person, daughter, wife, mother, and employer. I keep not just my family but the people in the company who are now part of our bigger family. I keep my parents with me and I am willing to take good care of them 'till the end. I love this country and obeying the rules is another sign of success. We don't get to be a liability of our own society.

Provide some advice to women from a woman living in province.

Don't be comfortable with what you have; things change, people change, time moves, we need to be always on the go and rock n roll with time. May God bless us all!

My Life As A Woman: Poland Edition #1

pl. "Nic nie jest niemożliwe! Tylko twoje pragnienie! Najlepiej silne pragnienie!"

(c. ja)

en. "Nothing is impossible! Only your desire! Preferably strong desire!"

(c. me)

My name is Nataliia (or Natka as people like to call me in Poland). I radically changed my life and I am madly happy with that!

There will be nothing about love and romance, no talk of white and fluffy animals, unicorns, etc. I will share my truth, my life and my success. How I achieved everything by Myself and what I am so glad about, in my 28th. Let's get to know each other. Every girl has her own unique story.

I wasn't a typical little obedient girl. Mom wanted to see bows in my hair and a dress on me, but the reality appeared different. Scraped knees to blood, bike instead of dolls, and from outfits sneakers, jeans and t-shirts not a princess dress. I was not perfect, Mom's barely tolerated me. And of course, the constant tears and hysteria on both sides. I dreamed of freedom and every year I was getting ready for a new phase. The role of a student.

The choice of a university was an important and very turning point for me. My mother's choice was for sure Uniwersytet Jagielloński (the best in Krakow). I saw myself as the manager of the best hotel in Krakow (Sheraton - Love to this day), but my mother had absolutely different views in regard to my future. In her mind, I had to take on a responsible role as a boring economist. BUT, I never liked the economy, the calculations, etc., She already decided instead of me. Of course, it made me crazy!

Many years after, I was furious that my whole world was falling apart. The funny young girl... I realize now that everything that has happened was the best for me. I'm where I should be and I'm doing what I love to do. I had to go through pain and suffering...

I believe that everything in our lives is for a reason, neither situations nor people. The first advice from me, girls, all situations not for nothing, although at first look seems like a complete sh.t. You have to believe, miracles happen. After all, I've had mine, and so you will have as well! But I didn't think so at the time.

Have you lived by the rules of another person? I did. It's been about seven years of my life. Suppression, depression and almost alcoholism at such a young age.

After university, I naturally got into a financial company (my mother did everything for it) and you might think that everything was fine.. for someone, but not for me. A sense of duty. I promised myself to "work off" the university paid for by my parents. That's what I thought then.

I hated everyone, but I hated myself in the first place. That I brought myself to this point. Nothing was happening in my life, nothing changed. I was hiding deeper and deeper into my reports. Constant stress... and like anti-stress every night, a glass of wine, and sometimes two, a bottle. Horrible...

Little by little, my friends started pulling me out from the pit.

They began to enroll me in various courses, meditation, pack me up with books....and hello a psychologist! It didn't work! Why not?! Because somebody wanted it, but not me!

My life was turned upside down by a case, and to be more precise, serial!

After all, I decided to put some romantic lines here...=)

As I remember now, it was a cool, rainy day. I wanted to climb under a fluffy blanket, grab a huge cup of tea with a hare picture and to light a fragrant candle. I wanted to cry. Nothing foretold trouble, only watching a very old TV series that I had not yet seen. That night, I met Carrie Bradshaw. Do you know who she is? Go to Wikipedia.)

This curly girl and her lifestyle! I have fallen in love irrevocably. I wanted something very similar! At that time, I was already writing short reviews of the books I read, and I was always enjoying the process. I realized that I could be a writer. It gave me great pleasure. That night, I decided to change everything. It was 100% my decision! There should be a question: What about parents? I became an adult and finally took control of my life! It was so scary, but the next morning I got fired from a hated job, so I became a freelancer. Now my office is where I decide for myself. Will it be in my home Krakow today or can it go to Poznan or Warsaw?! It's a thrill! I can work with people from all over the world, with people I want, and write what I want. My life has become like a fairy tale. Sometimes I don't even believe that this is my life and that it's so fantastic! I could do it, I took a chance!

You Can Do It, too! You Can Change Your Life! I know it for sure!!

My Life As A Woman: Poland Edition #2

Growing up in a family of artists was an interesting thing. Both my mother and grandmother were theatre actresses while my father was a musician, teaching playing guitar in a local music school. We were living in a house in a suburb of a middle size town in Poland.

As a kid, I used to catch a cold all the time and while not going to school I was spending a lot of time with my nan as my parents were rather busy at that time. I was observing her rehearsals when she was trying different poses and loudly reading a script. Sometimes she wanted me to read a part of an actor, partnering her on a stage. It was nice to see the drama being played in the middle of a main room, and just for me... She was spending hours making faces in front of a mirror, and I was wondering how is it even possible she doesn't get any wrinkles!? My grandma taught me self-confidence and vulnerability, my parents were encouraging me to always follow my dreams.

Having that said the obvious choice for me to become a famous singer or actress, wasn't it? Well, that was my plan for many years but when I was going to school, just before the final exams, I decided to study IT. This decision was partially inspired by my boyfriend, which was a real geek interested in computers and programming, studying Computer Science. I've never regretted this decision although I'm not with this guy anymore because I understood this is something I really like. Currently, I'm working for a software house.

It was a bit tough for my parents to understand why I had chosen this career path instead of following the family tradition. I believe that working in IT is much more stable than being the artist, especially in such unprecedented times we're facing now. Having the full-time job makes me feel safe and I don't have to worry about the future. I can call it a success that I do for a living something that is also my passion.

Since I have kids it's a bit more difficult for me to find a balance between job and private life. I feel guilty when I have to stay longer at the office but at the same time, I don't want to use having kids as an excuse. Luckily, my husband has no regular working hours, and he can look after the kids while I am off. When I was on maternity leave I faced the fear of professional exclusion. There was no chance to attend any work-related conferences and keep up to date with the company's news, and I was worried that the break would affect my career. Luckily nothing like that has happened.

I always encourage women to do what makes them happy and don't look at others' comments. Although the decision about my studies baffled my parents a bit, they were always supporting me on my way, and they're glad that now I live life on my own rules.

My Life As A Woman: Poland Edition #3

When we are growing up we don't yet grasp the idea that our environment – our country, religion, city, and traditions will shape us into the humans and the men or women we later become. That's why, as a young girl, and even up till now, I have given little thought to how my Polish background has shaped me, especially how it affected me as a female. Of course, these are my personal memories and observations rather than a full account of what it's like to be a female in Poland.

Little Polish Girl

I was born in Warsaw in 1988 and back then, (not that I remember) it was a weird post-apocalyptic place. The stores looked and were stocked very poorly. I remember my first trip to France in 1991 to visit family and it was like a different planet. Colorful billboards, people eating and drinking out, different kinds of clothes, and treats in supermarkets. Poland seemed like a utilitarian bunker, in comparison.

I grew up in a typical Warsaw 'blokowisko' (high-rise estate). A 10-story concrete well surrounding you as you enjoy your childhood days in the tiny dirty sandbox and on a few rusty swings. But as you went high, really high and tilted your head back, you saw the end of the well; and you knew there was so much more to Warsaw than this place and so much more to the world than Warsaw.

As a child, I barely noticed the difference between genders - other than 'boys are strong and gross but funny and girls like gossiping and giggling. At school we were probably treated fairly, but in retrospect the boys did get blamed way more often, because if you have muddy, mucky, rough boys or princess-like blonde angels to blame for the broken vase – the conclusion seems but one. Simple sexism - if you ask me now. One of the most important things I got from primary school was the passion for history. My teacher was smart and passionate and her love for teaching to imagine vividly what happened in the past inspired my love of history and helped grow my imagination for years to come. I would say she was my first female role model of 'tough love' and respectful authority.

Teenage life and early adulthood, on the other hand, can be quite challenging for females in Poland as the idea of sexual appropriateness is still evolving there. What in many places seems offensive, some people consider a compliment for a female? When it comes to safety and equality I'd say Poland definitely meets the average score.

Thinking About the Future

Unlike many Polish parents, who decide their kids' careers for them, my mum and dad were supportive of me whatever I chose to do. I spent some time in Scotland where I studied Marketing, I returned to Warsaw to study hairdressing, then became a tour guide, logistic planner and, finally, a personal trainer. The polish education system is known for its high standard and going to university is free. Here, again (if anyone has any doubts), is no gender segregation or discrimination.

The cultural stuff

Having had so many foreign influences, since its establishment in the first century, Poland has a very diverse culture including art and cuisine from Russian, Lithuanian, Hungarian, French and Italian. Polish people are honest, fun and loyal. My hero – my mum taught me that hard work, perseverance and positive thinking go a long way. And even though, unlike the West, Poland will not always welcome you with strangers smiling wide on the street, if you find a polish friend – it's forever.

There is definitely a little more controversy over crazy fashion or flesh revealing clothes, piercing and other unconventional looks than in the UK or United States, for example. But the most disapproval you may get is an odd pensioner mumbling something offensive, and a few head turns. I've always felt that my success as a woman was to be able to be myself and always wear what I like and meet with who I like, and I never got hurt for that. I know, however that (partially to the Catholic Church dominance), many of my religious minority, immigrant or LGBTQ friends can't say that. If only Poland could improve on love and tolerance for others it would be a really fantastic place to grow up and live. They truly have some excellent Universities, and companies from all over the world who lure your graduates to the city as workplaces. There is no shortage of fun bars, street food, and also fine dining. In the summer time, the Vistula (Wisla) shores and their sandy beaches bounce all night with music and laughter with the smell of barbeque enveloping the area… A sight worth seeing: a Warsaw sunrise with your hips swaying to the beat of the music in the background, a hot dog and beer in hand, feet covered in sand.

My Life As A Woman: Portugal Edition

I grew up side to side with technology and the changes in the way people view the markets and the global digital world. I was under the impression I could be facing the biggest possible threat to humankind, or our most revolutionary creation as species. Besides that, I was a woman.

Growing up in Portugal meant we had to face the normality, anti-revolutionist, existence for women: there were no great fights to be fought. And our concerns have always been politics and football and the fair raise of education, health and public institutions salaries. Besides that, women or man, you were growing up facing the reality of having to work too much to gain too little.

As for me, I was born in a family of four: me, my parents and my big sister. My mom was a symbol of a mom: generous, spoiling, preparing food and taking us to school, while handling the assistance task and being a real estate agent in the late 90's and driving a blue Mazda like a real pro – nobody handled the awful reality of Portuguese driving like my mom, and she use to swear a lot towards everyone: "had to be a woman on the wheel, that or an old man!"; "OH! This taxi drivers and their sh***y driving, have you seen this world?. And we simply laugh and made a game of scores per level of "idiocracy" on the road. Although I had a natural conditional love and respect for my mom, she didn't as much appealed to me as a working, professional, revolutionary woman.

My sister was the girl I stood the most for, and the one who most impressed me, nonetheless. She was more than just a woman because she was really strong, fearless and reckless. She unveiled all the lies: Santa Claus, God as a fatherly figure, war, holocaust, the inequality of gender salaries and opportunities. More than a fair judge, she was unforgiving.

I grew up to a be a mix of all the great role models In my life, and to find my own essence also. Although it's true that I found some amazing women along my path, I've always discerned that men could reach places we simply were limited by emotions and social regulations to go to. I followed my dad's steps and brought all the women I've met to my side: to become strong and entrepreneurial, without faith in football or too much about politics, for I saw that was the leverage that really separated men from women: the faith in power systems.

That's how I became an entrepreneur, I started investing in small commerce markets of buying from manufacturers and selling in auction (which was very common at the time), to become a real estate agent myself, until I reached my 25th and shot myself to the position of being my own president, founded an NGO on the objective or shifting the European and global society, founded a gallery for artists and a community for women artists in the genres of visionary, patterns and acrylic art. My NGO is 70% women in power, not because I wanted it to be, simply I found that some of the most hardworking, reliable and mindful towards positive change were the women I had connected to while growing up.

To live and work in Portugal, although with my work I get to travel and live in different countries a lot, is still a challenge for a woman. We concern ourselves very little with this shifts and find that the Portuguese culture is hard to accept change from within. Yet, I can say I've never felt unwanted because I was a woman except in sports (but I also wasn't a good sports person, so I can't blame my colleagues).

It's actually the opposite, the main challenge of being a woman in Portugal, and keep in mind that I'm from the big capital of Lisbon, is facing how wanted we are for the wrong reasons. You can be 10 year old, 20 years old or a 60 years old, and you get the exact same depleting and disgusting treatment when walking on the streets. It happens that cars stopped to whistle when I was a very young teen, and men really don't assist to the consequences of these traumatic events, because they seem honest on an animal, reptilian level of men's brains. Yet, it's a revolving door for fear and gender repression.

I know that if I set a meeting with a man and bring a male partner with me, I lose my personal reach: they want to hear the man. And if I dress professionally, the most taking side of my looks will be my general figure: big boobs or curvy looks; and we can't overcome it by stating the obvious, because the obvious still means to be too emotional, and that's considered professionally unreliable.

Although life has taught me we can't change everything, it also gave me the right tools to work around it when it comes to a professional or a romantic relationship. There's no need to put ourselves in the men's shoes as a mask to survive society, we already made our own, and they're pretty deserving.

As a Portuguese woman, I've seen a lot of hardworking females, working two jobs and Sundays to be mothers and dad's at the same time. I can honestly say that the Portuguese woman tends to put in the hours and to double or triple task everything at once. We're great organizational thinkers and tend to fuel ourselves with the fundamentals for thriving and nurturing our own. Never quitting yet complaining a lot about the things we really can't change.

Maria Rebelo, Portuguese Woman

My Life As A Woman: Qatar Edition #1

In the world where today, gender equality is a priority in almost every society, women can now rise and attain professional goals that were practically impossible sometimes back. My name is Nadia Aljahura, and I'm delighted to share my story.

Family

I am the firstborn and the only lady in a family of six. I was born in Westminster, North London, in 1972. A city where Muslim culture is dominant even to date. Westminster houses at least a million Muslims, according to the 2011 census. Racial discrimination was the order of the day when I was still young, and I remember we never used to play with Briton kids, even in school.

However, things continued to change, thanks to the British government's efforts to fight racism. At the age of 16, just after I had completed my high school education, we went back to our motherland Doha, Qatar. My dad's contract with one of the IT companies in London ended, and unfortunately, there was no extension or renewal offered. Two of my brothers were not yet born then, so they didn't witness the relocation process.

Professional journey

In Doha, my dad, Mr. Arham Zayan, used the little money he had saved to start a small business in the city to keep the family going. My dad always wanted the best for me, but at the time, he could not afford to finance my University Education. Although back in London, I had successfully passed my exams and was qualified to join a higher education institution, relocation to Doha complicated almost all my family plans. I knew that was the end of my dream to become a pilot.

In 1992, a United States of America University scholarship opportunity was announced in our mosque. I applied, and after six months, my application was approved. However, I was a bit nervous; I could not imagine starting a new life in a foreign country at my age without any friends or my parents around. I was almost changing my mind about the offer.

We talked as a family, and I got encouraged to take the opportunity. I spent four years at Florida State University, pursuing a Medical Degree Course.

Career

After graduating, I worked as an assistant Medical doctor in a State healthcare center in Florida for two years. Later, I went back to Doha; I always missed to serve my people back home. I loved being with my community and bringing quality healthcare services close to my people.

Although I wanted to establish my healthcare clinic, sharia laws then, could not allow me to do so. I had to seek employment in the Doha Municipal hospital. Later I got married to Zeeshan Hamdan, a prominent businessman in the city. Together we have two beautiful kids.

In 2016, I managed to establish my Healthcare clinic in Doha, which is so far doing well. Apart from the challenges I faced to attain my dreams, I appreciate my people's culture, love, and support.

For a Qatar woman, it's always a struggle to attain your dreams since our society still believes the male gender is supreme. Sitting down and complaining, it's not a solution either, work, or push towards achieving your life goals. Today, things are better, just focus, work hard, and you will get there.

My Life As A Woman: Qatar Edition #2

Forough Mohammad H. Piroozi

Where did you grow up?

I grew up in Qatar. I was born from a Qatari mother and Iranian father. But I lived my whole life in Qatar.

How did you grow up?

My childhood was not an easy and normal childhood. Growing between an open-minded diplomatic Iranian father and A Qatari mother coming from a conservative community is like having two different sides in life and you have to do your best to go along with both of them.

Did you have parents or maybe a grandmother who inspired you?

I was very inspired by my father's personality, by his way of thinking, his principles, And his self-made that made him stick to all the values he believes in. He was diplomatic and came from a very high culture aristocratic environment. Also, he was a lawyer and he believed strongly in human rights and women's independence.

What did you study? / What did you want to be growing up? / Why?

I did my BA in International Affairs and then I did my MBA in business Administration. While I was doing my BA, I also started my business in fashion designing Since I was obsessed with fashion since childhood. During my BA, I really wanted to work in the field of human rights in Qatar. Unfortunately, when I graduated but I didn't get the chance to work in the field I am dreaming about. And I started working in the media sector in Qatar Media Corporation.

What do you love about your culture?

The big family; my Qatari community is represented by large extended families. You grow up between your family members from your parents side. For my case, I grow up between my mother's family members since my father didn't have any relatives in Qatar. So, my family was my father, mother and my brothers AND my mother's family, my aunts, uncles, grandmother and my cousins.

We grew up feeling responsible to each other, we have to respect each other's and we have to stand for each other's whenever it's needed. A family means sharing everything from the happiness to the sadness.

The strength is in unity;

What are you currently doing for work?

Currently, I am social media specialist for the Qatar media corporation and I have my private business which is my fashion brand FP fashionline. Also, I am an influencer and I have a great passion in social media and because I want to influence people's lives in a positive way.

Tell me about your struggles as a woman.

In a conservative community every new idea created by a woman is a struggle; trying to approve that women are equals in importance to the men is a struggle. Equality means getting our rights with no discrimination. Thank God a lot of things have been changed in Qatar and women were granted various rights. And they got the chance for important positions in the state. Also, they started to represent Qatar In various international forums.

The main struggle we can face continuously is the attempt to change the culture of the people towards women's freedom and the civilized openness that requires women to have the freedom to determine their destiny and their demands.

Tell me about your successes as a woman.

As a woman, I succeeded in building myself strongly, in having the right to express my thoughts and my beliefs.

To combine the study of international affairs and fashion design as a passion that does not stop, and at the same time, I worked in the media field which is completely far from my field of study and passion.

In Qatar, I was the first fashion designer to create fashion collections from recycling clothes and fabrics and till now I am the only fashion designer working in the field of recycling and up- cycling clothes and fabrics. This creativity started with me since I was in my BA study in 2006-2010. In 2016, I launched my first official recycled fashion collection.

Provide some advice to women from a woman living in Qatar ?

- Believe in yourself.
- Don't never ever underestimate your capabilities.
- Fight till you reach your goal, no one will fight for your rights.
- It's only you who can build the personality you are dreaming with.
- It's only you who can create the life you are dreaming about.
- You are very important to yourself and to the world.

My Life As A Woman: Republic Of Congo Edition

My name is Hannah, I'm 28 years old. I was born in the Republic of Congo (Congo Brazzaville) into a Christian family, and since I was very young we went to church. I grew up at my parents' home with my four brothers and life was beautiful, with my friends, we had dreams just like every child and that made me happy, and I even believed that friendship lasts a lifetime.

My mother, one of my biggest fans.

My mother had studied mechanics and what amazed me and that in my country, only men were destined to study mechanics and seeing that my mother had studied mechanics but she was not fortunate enough to have a job in mechanics, and that's when I told myself that I had to study mechanics to fulfill the dream of my beloved mother.

I went to mechanical school, being the only girl in my school who studied mechanics, all attention was focused on me, as if I came straight from planet Mars. I studied in a school with boys as my only classmates.

What I love about my culture

In our country, smoking in public is very frowned upon and people will not have a good image of you, which reduces tobacco consumption in the Congo, and we see less and less people smoking in the street.

My job

I'm currently working in a mechanic's shop. As a woman, that's a big deal. And I'm just clinging to what life has to offer a girl with her head in the stars. I've had some of the most beautiful moments of my life, and since difficulties come after happiness, I haven't escaped difficult moments.

My hard times

In Congo, for the majority of cases, women face many difficulties that prevent them from having a better future. Too many popular and cultural beliefs limit young girls in their schooling in favour of marriage and family life.

Today, everyone is happy to see many girls in primary school. In 2017, nearly half of all primary school students were girls. Unfortunately, at the secondary level, the number of girls is declining significantly because many people still believe that it is from the age of 12, the age at which secondary school begins, that girls must prepare for marriage and running a household. Their numbers are declining because there are many misconceptions about the role of women, as many people think that at this age they should be concerned with preparing for marriage and taking care of the home. At the university level the situation is even more alarming because girls constitute only 30% of the students.

This is inadmissible because in my opinion girls are very resourceful. Without education and professional qualifications, young girls are exposed to early pregnancy and early marriage. They will not be able to access good jobs and, as a result, they will not be able to contribute to the development of the country. Without education, girls are destined to always be left behind boys and men.

Despite all this. Nothing has prevented me from having the success I dreamed of.

My success as a woman

I'm currently the head of a small mechanical engineering company and I'm no longer involved in the technical side of things. I'm happy to be doing a job that I'm passionate about.

I have two girls and a boy who are the center of my world, I travel when I want, I am financially free, I have time to see my family, my friends and I enjoy it very much.

Don't give up

As a woman, I ask everyone to stop being satisfied with the satisfactory results of girls' primary schooling. We must take steps to ensure that all girls can go further and go to university. With educated and sufficiently qualified women, the country will live in peace and harmony.

Continue to hold on

My Life As A Woman: Romania Edition #1

I was born and raised in Bucharest, the capital of Romania, or "Little Paris" as most people call it. I love this city with all my heart, and I will always remember the Sunday walks in colorful parks or on the streets of the old city center. Ever since I can remember, I was always attached to this city, its people, its smell, its rush, and especially, attached to my home.

Living in an apartment, as Bucharest has few neighborhoods with houses, can be crowded sometimes, but full of love. I can proudly say I didn't skip any milestone while growing up: I went to school, made friends, developed hobbies and passions, argued with my parents, had my first boyfriend, graduated high school and went on to dream for a career.

Who am I?

I have my mother's smile and my father's quick temper and my own unique sense of humor. I like to imagine myself like a unique mold gently shaped by all the ones who are or were someday part of my life. I am Dana and I like to always laugh it off, I was depressed, anxious, put down, sad, hopeless and I still laughed it off. My hope is that life will be so gentle to always allow me to laugh it off.

I am passionate about writing since I was a child. I fantasize about stories, adore movies, enjoy every song that touches my soul. It all started with school homework: writing texts, stories, inventing characters, or describing experiences. I have been writing for many years and I am not planning on stopping anytime soon.

How did I become the person I am today?

Today, I can proudly say I have achieved a few of my dreams: graduated from university, discovered new passions, I made new friends and I started my career as a professional in writing. I have worked with people I never would have dreamt of working with, have seen my name on beautiful stories I have written and when I talk about my job, I am always smiling.

In my opinion, it is less about finding your talent and more about accepting your gifts. Growing up I loved writing, but I was always said I was not blessed with "real talent", as I thought back then, like singing, drawing or dancing. I have worked hard to accept myself and be proud of who I am. We are probably meant to work on something that we are passionate about, but sadly, we're quite slow on realizing and accepting that.

When sometimes things get hard

As a teenager, I struggled, as many people nowadays, with depression and anxiety. These have impacted my professional and educational journey. I almost missed a year of high school, I lost job opportunities and sometimes put those around me through hard times. As a woman living in Romania, my daydreaming personality and effervescent attitude don't exactly match the typical process of growing up, studying, getting a 9 to 5 job, marry young, and have children.

I know the sun will shine again

Still, my journey taught me that I can achieve success in my own way. I have found a master's program that has a schedule fit for me, with weeks full of classes followed by some free weeks afterward. I want to study business administration so that one day I can have my own business here in Bucharest. Writing has become my job and I have been for a few years working from home, writing articles for online magazines, blogs, or websites. I discovered there is a road meant for me, even if I don't fit the standard criteria.

I want to travel the whole world, but my heart will be forever missing home

My dream for the future is to have the chance to travel the world and discover as many countries as I can. Still, my heart will forever be close to home, my family, and my country. And if I were to choose the most important element of my culture, that has shaped me, that would be our language. I learned to speak and write in Romanian first, so this language was the one that showed me how beautiful writing and stories are.

My Life As A Woman: Romania Edition #2

In Eastern Europe there is this beautiful country named Romania. I was born in the west of the country, in a big city. Here, in 1989, a revolution took place and it led to the end of the communism in the whole country. I was 3 years old back then and I am proud to have witnessed such an historical and life changing event.

The beginning of my life was quite unusual. I was born before term and my biological family, of which I have no information, had abandoned me. Nevertheless, I was a lucky girl because a loving and caring family found me and despite what the doctors said about me not having any chance of survival, they stood by my side and fought for me. I have been raised in a loving family that has always encouraged and inspired me all along my journey.

I started my career in a call center as an IT Service Desk agent. Being able to speak three foreign languages (English, French, and Spanish) helped me a lot in getting the job. In Romania, there is a big percentage of people who speak one or more foreign languages, as most of the jobs are offered by foreign companies. It's cheaper for them to hire people here rather than in their respective native countries.

After two and a half years I left that company because I knew I wanted more for my career. I took a job in a little enterprise and six months later, I earned a promotion and became a team leader. The client and part of the management of the company were based in a Western European country with a mostly patriarchal society. Therefore, being a Romanian woman in a men's world was not easy. Sometimes I was even asked whether in my country, if there is electricity or if there are supermarkets in my town. The answer is, yes, of course. Romania was and still is seen as the communist country that it was 30+ years ago, full of thieves and poor people. But you know what? I made myself strong and got over all these rude questions and comments.

You might be wondering what my strength was. Well, I had the chance to work with an amazing team. I am people-oriented, emphatic, and a good listener and I would do anything for my team members. All of this has nothing to do with being a woman or being Romanian or any other thing. I put my heart and soul in my work, and I go all out. My whole team has a soul and they are like a family for me. In some cultures, being friends with each other at work is not a thing, but in Romania we do that. We hang out together, do activities not related to the job, attend each other's birthdays or weddings and also we share private life details with our coworkers. As we spend more time at work than at home, I think it's important to have good relationships with the people around us.

At some point, during my journey, I faced failure. I was about to give up. I felt like I was not worth it. I doubted myself. Sometimes, the complex of superiority that my colleagues from abroad had got to me and made me feel little and insignificant. It's sad how people put tags on others based on things that don't depend on us such as our skin color, nationality, gender and so on. It's a pity that we are judged on the brands we wear, on the car we drive or the place we live in. In Romania your value is weighted by this kind of stuff and if you want to fit in, you need to adapt to what society dictates. If you are not beautiful enough or rich enough, your chances to succeed are not very high. Against all odds, because I'm neither rich nor the most beautiful, I managed to achieve my dreams.

Maybe Romania is not a first-hand country. Maybe it wouldn't have been my first choice if I had one when I was born, but I feel lucky and blessed with all the opportunities I've had here.

Romanian women still have to fight with the reminiscent of the communism culture in which the man is the master and the woman has to stay at home, cook, clean and raise kids. Romanian women have to prove themselves that they are equal to women from more developed countries and to men as well. In Romania, there are no fancy schools that assure you a great job right after graduation and a lot of girls don't have access to proper education, especially in the rural areas. In my opinion though, poverty and all the labels we get from others or any kind of obstacle that we might encounter are something we have to use to our advantage in order to strengthen ourselves. All the difficulties and struggles we face should be converted into something useful that prepares us for what's ahead, what we are meant to be and do in this world.

Defy the odds! Believe in yourself! Take the weaknesses others see in you and make them your strengths! Be inspired and be an inspiration! No matter your nationality or your skin color, do not be afraid to raise your voice! If I was able to follow my dreams, you can do it too!

My Life As A Woman: Russia Edition #1

I can definitely say that I grew up in a happy childhood. I was born and raised in the capital of Russia – Moscow. I was raised in a privileged environment, as my parents always had really good jobs, thus we were never short of money. Basically, my parents would get me everything I wanted. We also travelled a lot, so I've got a lot of colorful and enjoyable memories from my childhood.

The one thing that makes me privileged as well is my education. I never went to a public school, never had my education been free. I even went to private kindergarten. So, it definitely wasn't a surprise, when at the age of 16 my parents decided that I should continue my education in the United Kingdom.

Moving abroad wasn't the easiest thing for me at first, as the difference in mentalities hit me like a truck. One – being how much gender equality was an important thing for the girls in my boarding house. Since I was brought up very differently and (by that I don't mean bad, women were never suppressed or underestimated in my family, but sort of patriarchy did exist in our family), I was very much surprised of how much of a role feminism played in the lives of my English girlfriends.

I vividly remember a situation that happened with me in my first year in England, which made me be very careful with my words in the future. We've discussed human rights, and my friend asked me a question that I replied with "because I believe we are a weaker sex", and the whole class went silent. Oh, never would I imagine that my opinion, which in no way I was imposing on anyone, could hurt someone. That girl wouldn't talk to me for a week, and it was hard knowing that some other girls also turned away from me because of that. And the one thing which stroke me the most was, - if you are all offended by that phrase, because you believe women are strong and powerful, then why are you turning away from me? I'm just a girl as well. Shouldn't we support and educate each other?

After a couple of years, I moved back home to Moscow, and I'd had to adapt to Russian culture again. Traditional Russian culture is very specific about gender roles. Obviously it's progressing every day, but also I can speak only for big cities, as small villages in Siberia is a whole other story.

So, in my environment pretty much all girls believed they should know how to cook, clean, please their man, etc. And since I've spent very important ages of becoming an adult in another culture, those "rules" would drive me crazy. Even these days. I honestly hate cooking, and I couldn't give more Fs, what people around think about it. And also, we've got this huge thing that if a woman sleeps with different people she's a whore, if a man does, he's a hero. That's a label we probably will never be able to get rid of.

Comparing to stories we read on the internet, I don't have a right to say that my life as a woman in Russia is hard, However, unfortunately, sometimes I get into situations, which make me want to be a man. I've got a very bad luck for taxi drivers, random guys on the streets, etc. I've been in many situations, when I was scared that a man would hurt me, and I couldn't do anything about it, I had to just pray for myself in my head. Some would say, well you shouldn't walk on the streets at night alone, or you shouldn't get into a cab without providing your ride details with someone. But hey! Shouldn't it be other way round? Why are you accusing me of not defending myself enough, where you should be teaching men that they've got no right over woman, when it's not consensual? That's also another thing, which I don't believe, unfortunately, will be solved in the near future.

On the bright sight me or my friends or people that I know never had to deal with gender inequalities at work. Moreover, I work in a business development department of one of the biggest FMCG-companies, which is run by a woman, and I love my job a lot. Also, almost all of my male friends from university do not have a good stable job, whereas all my female friends are employed and mostly very successfully. And I can definitely say that for now It's a great success of mine that I study at university, work and run my household at the same time, and do it all quiet efficiently.

I don't believe that I've got a right to give an advice for any other Russian woman, as I fully understand, that I already have much more than many women will ever have in their lives. I just believe that if we all could stand up for ourselves and not be scared to be loud, the world would hear us, and we will be able to make changes.

My Life As A Woman: Russia Edition #2

"We need to make sure that we do not take the blame for the violence that is visited upon us. We need to develop a sense of self that cannot be eroded, a sense of self that is rounded and whole. It is what saves a woman in the final analysis." - Rahila Gupta

I was born in a little town in the North side of Russia. I grew up in a conservative society that condemned deviations from the traditional model of women's behavior in society. Despite the fact that I was brought up in a developed society, I did not know my rights as a woman. Since childhood, girls are told change your clothes, this skirt is too short, this makeup is too provocative, this profession is not for women.

In my childhood, I didn't know about the Internet, so I just didn't know that in other societies, there was a completely different life, where women are not told how to live and what to do. My parents tried to make me an obedient girl; they tried to form a patient character in me.

I am fond of social studies, foreign languages, and history. I studied these subjects at school. I made a lot of progress in these subjects. While studying English, I suddenly became interested in world history. It turned out that in other countries, women live very differently. This interested me, and I decided to delve into this topic.

As it turned out, women in a typical economy have only three-quarters of the rights that men have. But only six countries have achieved true gender parity in legislation, the report says. It examines how legislation affects women's economic decisions on eight indicators: the ability to travel, start a job, get married, have children, run a business, earn a salary, manage assets, and receive a pension. Belgium, Denmark, France, Latvia, Luxembourg and Sweden have achieved equal rights for women and men in legislation over the past decade.

I learned about the concepts of sexism, feminism, and fat shaming. This discovery changed my world and shaped my view of my role in society as a woman. Before, guys could laugh and make fun of me, but now I'm not afraid to respond to their insults as before. I won't let them touch my body without my permission, because I'm no longer afraid to say no. Since I was a child, I wanted to stand up for others, because some girls just can't stand up for themselves. I thought it was unfair. The fact that men are stronger than women does not allow them to use this power against us. Unfortunately, many people in my society do not know this.

I wanted to do community service, so I signed up for a UNESCO course that took place at our school. In these courses, we studied the structures of society in different countries and their interaction to solve global problems. In these courses, we studied the interaction of countries to solve global problems, and we also studied the national cultures of different countries.

I like the culture of Russia because it has very kind, hardworking and generous people who are always ready to help you. My country has a rich history. However, our society needs to make a lot of efforts in the fight against the Patriarchal foundations of our country, so that women have equal rights with men. And I, as a woman, make a certain contribution to this struggle.

Currently, I write reports on women's rights in the modern world and win prizes at competitions. I want to leave my mark on history so that I know that my fight against prejudice against women's abilities in science, politics, and sports was not in vain.

I want to instill confidence in Russian women in their importance, because when I was little, no one told me that I had the whole world in my hands, and I had no idea that I could do everything. I was made to be ashamed of being a girl, but now that I'm older, I realize that it's not a disadvantage, but an advantage to be a woman.

Our generation is very lucky to have a critical mindset that allows us to unite in the fight for the rights and freedoms of our women and to assert our importance in the international community. We will do this for future generations of women who will not be told how to look or behave.

My dear, Listen, if you are reading this, know that you are significant, you are beautiful in your body, and don't let anyone make you doubt it. If someone tells you that you will not achieve your goals, that your dreams are meaningless, don't listen to these losers. They just underestimate you. You will be successful and show them all how wrong they were about you.

Don't let anyone laugh at you. Don't be afraid to say no and fight back. You're strong; you're not a commodity, your feelings matter. If you don't want to do something, then don't do it and don't let someone force you to do it. Just please never forget it.

Develop your critical thinking, educate others, and speak openly about the problems of your society, because we will never be able to solve them by hiding these problems. Don't be afraid of being judged and don't judge anyone back. You are wise, you are Mature, and you know what to do with your body and your life.

You can do absolutely anything, because the whole world is in your hands, and only you can decide how to manage your life. Fight for your rights and freedoms, because you deserve to live in a just world. Support other girls in their endeavors. Finally, never give up! You know that I believe in you, my dear.

Let's bring peace to the minds of men and women together!

My Life As A Woman: Russia Edition #3

Hello there! My name is Nadi. Well, actually my full name is Nadezhda and it's so weirdly unfamiliar to you because it's Russian. As well as me, I was born and raised in a small town called Oryol, just a five-hour ride away from the capital.

Even though my town is a place where a lot of famous Russian writers were born, I'm not really fond of it. I can't tell you that there is something wrong in particular, but I always felt the lack of life in this city. You always go to the same places and see the same people you don't want to see. We even only have one shopping mall where you can meet all your ex-friends, ex-boyfriends and some family friends you don't even remember. Small towns are always the place for the juiciest gossip, so there is a lot of that.

I grew up in a big Russian family which includes parents, siblings, grandparents, and a ton of cousins, uncles, aunts and who knows who else. All of the above involves lots of family dinners and a bunch of random people asking you weird stuff about your life at every gathering. A traditional set of questions covers such topics as your studies, your looks, your personal life, and dating in particular. So, that's fun, right?

On the other hand, a big family gives you a variety of role models to follow. I didn't search long for mine; I was living with them since I was born. My elder sisters are my biggest role models and these two are the people who influenced me the most apart from my parents. I'm the youngest of three daughters which can be tricky sometimes. You are treated differently as you are the smallest and in my case I had at least four people taking care of me. I always felt lucky thinking about that. However, it easy for me to be grateful now. Growing up, we went through some ups and downs in our relationships as most people do.

Let me tell you a couple more things about myself. I was a dreamer from the start. I always wanted something artsy for myself. At first, I dreamt about becoming a ballerina (so Russian), I was obsessed with that idea when I was around five years old. I would spend hours practicing my imaginary ballerina moves. Over the years I switched over to becoming a singer. The only problem I had was the lack of singing talent. In between my dancing, singing, and art sessions, I used to imagine myself as a teacher. I always liked to be organized and to explain things to others. All of these dreams faded with the time right until I found my true passion – foreign languages.

I love everything connected to my language obsession: starting from learning the basics and finishing by being able to speak to people in their native language and being able to express myself in every language I've learned. This hobby has transformed into something bigger as it grew into my studies and career choice. I studied linguistics at University and made languages my source of income as I do translations and writing online. I've learned English, Spanish, French, Italian, and Portuguese but it's not the end. This is unbelievable how languages have changed my life and how I've become a role model of hard work and devotion to my own family.

I guess my story leads me to the things I love the most about my culture. Russian people are really hard-working and ambitious. We like to finish what we have started even if it's hard. We are not afraid of challenges because after all, we've been through as a nation, we understand that even the hardest thing can be done. Another thing that I like about my people is hospitality. It's weird to foreigners that we can be so hospitable when we seem so cold and so serious. I can tell for sure that all this coldness is just a protective layer that hides the true colors of a Russian soul.

My advice to all the women out there is not to be afraid to show your true colors. The world is a scary place, but we have the power to make it kinder, better, and safer for all of us and for future generations. Every little step we take, makes a difference in the end. Believe in yourselves and don't be afraid to show your true you!

My Life As A Woman: Russia Edition #4

The best thing that was ever created by the world is a woman. Woman is like a bottle of wine that is becoming more amazing with age. Unfortunately, some of us do not realize the beauty of being a lady, but I hope that once you have read my story, you will absorb all energy and power that I put onto it.

I am an Armenian girl and this fact makes me so proud, and I was born in Russia and this point also makes me proud because I ended up with two different cultures inside of me. I did not grow up into a wealthy family, but I always knew that my mother and I were the ones who would make the world a better place for us all by making our inner world a better place for ourselves. My mom is the greatest person that I have ever met in my whole life; she is a wonderful lady with so much spirit, she is a fighter with a big heart. The way she helps people, the way she tries to bring peace into the world encourages me every single day. Indeed, it is thanks to the efforts of my mother that I have become the person I always wanted to be.

Back in 2015, I was full of thoughts such as «Where should I go to continue my study?», «Do I really want this?», «What is my true calling?». I thought that as a woman I would not have enough power, experience, leadership qualities to achieve what I want. Little did I know that I would be so close to my dream. My mom told me then: «Look, I know that it scares you, I have been there, really, but you are a woman. Can you imagine how lucky you are?»; that phrase was the beginning of my adventure. Of course, I went through a lot of difficulties because of perspectives, because of my nature but the fact that «I am a woman» did not let me give up. I studied management, but I always wanted to create a system which will be a confluence of intercultural communication and management at the same time. I love it when people from different walks of life become closer. So, I started to plunge myself into a bunch of events, forums, conferences; started to meet people and broaden my circle of acquaintants.

I always knew that working and doing my best as men do would pay off. After some time, our student manager suggested that I be a chairperson of the student council, given the fact that I was the only woman in council, I was over the moon. I took advantage from the fact that I entail two diverse cultures and started to organize multicultural events. I could not imagine that I would be able to run the part of my university, but I did it. Eventually, during the graduation ceremony the director of University rewarded me with a certificate of appreciation for outstanding contribution to the institute. My mother also was rewarded with a certificate of appreciation for contribution to my formation. Being rewarded feels so nice especially when you realize that you struggled a lot to govern a team of men, to be a lady-leader. I was not taken very seriously, I had troubles when I tried to reason with sponsors for our events, I got weird looks at the meetings of leaders of associations, etc.

Now I am working in a well-known hotel and I could actualize my dream of being a manager among intercultural communication. It feels so good when you can feel your inner beauty and what is more, your strength and use it as a secret weapon. We, women, are flowers and people (men) should have a desire for taking care of us, but they won't do it if you do not love and appreciate yourself first. Love is contagious, self-confidence is contagious, so you should have those things to encourage others to have that towards you as well. In Russia, it is not always easy to be accepted immediately, especially if you are a woman, but it is all in your head. Indeed, everything depends on you and only you can decide whether to be loved or hated. You are a woman, you are the only one who can bring a new life to the world, see that big advantage? Be proud to be a woman and remember, you are wonderful!

My Life As A Woman: Rwanda Edition

Where did you grow up? How did you grow up?

Hi, I'm Paula Annette Jabiro, 22; this is my story. I grew up in the beautiful small city of Kigali, Rwanda. In a Rwandan middle-income family of 7, with four siblings who are all boys. YES, am the only girl in the House. Growing up in Rwanda as a girl is both complicated and exciting. But let's start with the exciting part.

My family treated me like a princess, as the only girl and the last child, I must confess I did enjoy certain privileges that my friends didn't. I had most things my way, which was exciting to me. However, not everything went my way, after all, I was still a "Girl" My society had this expectation from a girl child. I was expected to do all house chores, why the boys sit around and watch TV. If I complained, my mom always had a line for me. "is this how you will complain in your husband's house"? I was not too fond of this, because it made me feel like there is a future master I was preparing to serve. But, hey, this isn't just exclusive to Rwanda, it is an African thing.

Did you have parents or maybe a grandmother who inspired you?

I have been inspired the most by my mom. I admire her strong mentality, hard work, and a positive outlook on life. My mom lived through the Rwandan 1994 genocide, but despite all she went through with her family, she still built a successful life.

She always reminds me of her remarkable story, and that has been a great source of inspiration to me.

What did you study? / What did you want to be growing up? / Why?

As a kid growing up in Rwanda, I wanted to be everything, doctor, engineer, lawyer and all things that sounded cool. My parent and relatives mostly fueled this. In Rwanda, four or five career choices make people take you seriously. Anything outside of those, everyone thinks you aren't smart enough, which can be a source of shame to your family. People can even see you as a disappointment.

Meanwhile, in high school, I took a combination of electronics and telecommunication, which was strange, because this wasn't typical for a girl. In fact, in a class of 27, only three girls offered this combination.

Fast forward to college, and I decided to pursue Leadership and Entrepreneurship. I chose this because I love the idea of owning my own business someday.

What do you love about your culture?

The first thing that I like about my culture is the traditional dance since it is the first thing that foreigners notice, and it is what represents us as Rwandese. The dancing represents how we practiced cattle farming. Dancers' arms typically represent the cow horns.

I was privileged to go to Egypt for a conference, and the first thing Egyptians asked me to do was our traditional dance.

Secondly, I love the Rwandan spirit of hard work and solidarity, as Rwandese, we believe in honesty, hospitality and being true to oneself.

What are you currently doing for work?

Currently, I work for a company that is producing facial masks to help in the fight against the COVID-19 pandemic. I should be in college right now, but the school is suspended in Rwanda until September 2020.

I also volunteer for a charity that helps teach street kids how to read and help promote a reading culture in my city.

Tell me about your struggles as a woman.

One of my biggest struggles as a woman is anxiety. I'm a sensitive person, I have anxiety, especially when I have an essential task to complete or when I am expecting something to happen.

Also, I struggle with giving my time and attention to building relationships with men. Sexual harassment is also a big problem in my community; men are always giving me unwanted attention, and sometimes pushing too hard makes me very uncomfortable.

Tell me about your success as a woman.

My most significant success so far came in 2018, when I was selected to attend a conference in Egypt on global peace, this was the first time I ever left the shores of my country.

I was selected to become a Global Peace Ambassador out of thousands of other applicants.

I gained a lot of experience and met people from other countries; this was one of the high points of my life.

Provide some advice to women from a woman living in Rwanda.

1.   Believe in yourself, and don't let anyone tell you otherwise.

2.   Whatever situation you find yourself in life, remember there is someone out there going through the worst situation.

3.   Never forget you are the acolyte in the altar of your destiny.

My Life As A Woman: Saint Kitts And Nevis Edition

When I close my eyes and concentrate, I can feel the icy-cold sea water gently lapping my ankles. In my mind I'm transported back to Frigate Bay Beach. I'm standing on the scalding hot, yellow sand and staring out at the sparkling, aquamarine water of the sea.

I am Janelle Mills and I live in St. Kitts and Nevis, a tiny island-state in the English-speaking Caribbean. It is a beautiful tropical country with the major towns hugging the coast and villages scattered around lush, green rainforests in the mountainous interior. Unsurprisingly, its natural beauty makes the country a popular tourist destination.

You may think that living on an island is an exciting, exotic experience. In some ways it is! I have fond memories of beach excursions every weekend with my siblings, and hikes in the nearby rainforest where we lived. Sounds idyllic, doesn't it? But I imagine that, in other ways, my childhood was quite typical. I shared a modest home with my mother, father, an elder brother and sister. Sibling rivalry was no stranger to our home. I could fill a book to chronicle our epic arguments and the occasional tears. Thankfully, my mother always ensured that we made up in the end.

Looking back on my childhood, I realize that my mother sheltered my siblings and I from the many ugly realities of life. From her 20s, my mother was forced to provide for her children with determination and optimism. She rose to the challenge remarkably, working long hours to ensure that we were always fed and well taken care of. She never showed us any resentment, despite the undeniable difficulty of catering to our numerous needs. From her modest salary she even managed to take us on holidays that opened our minds to the outside world. From these experiences she sought to teach us how to relate to people from different cultures. I am amazed when I reflect on how she, like so many Caribbean mothers, gave us everything she had so that we could be suitably prepared to enter our global village. Needless to say, my mother is my greatest inspiration, and growing up I often prayed that I would inherit even half of her strength and courage.

Despite my upbringing, as a young woman I felt insecure: I was very shy and more introverted than my siblings and peers. This made me quite self-conscious, yet I longed to connect meaningfully with others and understand them. During my university studies I met people from around the world and my insecurities increased. Was I smart enough? Articulate enough? Or was I small-minded and ignorant since I had been incubated on a "small island"? I struggled with comparison and it was a difficult journey to overcome those insecurities and appreciate my individuality and cultural background.

Studying Psychology at the tertiary level seemed to be the perfect way to understand myself and others and increase my social competence. Indeed, learning about human nature and our common insecurities helped me to become more self-compassionate. Ironically though, I learned that counselling was not the path for me! Instead, I chose to become a freelance research assistant working with scholars and students internationally.

Growing up in a Caribbean island greatly influenced my achievements. Since educational opportunities were more limited than in larger countries, the fierce competition propelled me to be an excellent student. Imagine vying for only one national scholarship offered to a pool of over 300 other students! Needless to say, my mother's support also inspired me to be a high achiever, and at the age of 23 I successfully completed my master's degree.

Upon returning to St. Kitts after university, I felt renewed pride in my small island nation. Despite its small size, Kittitians are bold and confident with great loyalty to their culture and country. In fact, it is the strong spirit of the people that resonates the most when I reflect on our culture. The shining beaches, rich eco-diversity, historical landmarks, festivals and hospitality of locals are other sources of my pride.

So, what have I learned thus far from my Kittitian life? It doesn't matter whether you're from a tiny town or a metropolitan city, everyone has unique characteristics and strengths. Even your perceived "weaknesses" can be used to your advantage on the global platform. Use them to distinguish yourself! Take it from a successful small-island girl with big dreams and big goals. Even woman should acknowledge her own worth, regardless of her origins. And guess what? We are all worth quite a lot!

My Life As A Woman: Saint Lucia Edition #1

"She's a bright child"; they'd almost sing in harmonious chorus.

I can vividly recall my family, teachers and peers sharing this and similar sentiments when they spoke of me. Everyone seemed to have expectations of what this "bright child" should become – a doctor; a teacher; an architect, even. They "just [knew] it!"

I was never certain, myself; but, as clear as day, I was set on being a "somebody". Clarity would come much later – after I'd taught grades five and six for close to four years at one of my island's private elementary schools and still later after venturing into Media/Broadcasting/Communication.

Growing up in rural Saint Lucia was much like the hills that swelled verdantly along the fertile landscape and the valleys which plunged with majestic beauty in my backyard on the north-eastern end of the island. Ups included the strong support of my predominantly matriarchal extended family, where I was inspired to NEVER treat hardships as stumbling-blocks; but to convert them into stepping stones.

My mother, a single parent of six, with modest means, ensured that my siblings and I were fed on a diet of values; "hard work brings great rewards" exemplified by several hours spent on the floor of our two – room house, completing homework assignments, under the dim flicker of candlelight were more than fair exchange for a coveted place at one of the island's leading educational institutions. Or, perhaps; "actions have resulting consequences", so that when my sister and I decided that our trip from the standpipe, nearly a quarter mile away to fetch water, would be much more fun if we raced each other home but then discovered that we had almost empty containers mere feet away from the house where my mother stood waiting with her hands propped on her waist.

As a single mother myself, who is currently a freelance media consultant and student at university, the challenges of being ever-present for my pre-teen daughter while at the same time excelling at courses in Early Childhood Education and Family Studies can be daunting, at times. Being outspoken and willing to stand up to authority, on occasion present as challenges; however, any intimidation brought on by associated circumstances are quickly quelled with reminders that I owe it to myself to stand up for what I believe in, adhere to my value system, my personal code and guiding principles.

Having seen firsthand the impact of mass media, I have become convinced that my opportunity to be that "somebody" I'd always wanted to be will materialize in service to the young and vulnerable. My goal, therefore, is to seek out and develop strategies which would aid in my quest towards helping other "somebodies" to be the best they can be.

Prior to the birth of my daughter in 2009, my perspective of success was that if I could reproduce what I had been taught, have read or seen, then I would have attained the heights of achievement. In the most candid ways, my daughter has shown me that while it is very important to have expectations for children, it is also necessary to allow them the freedom to create their own independent thoughts. This underscores what I most appreciate about my culture as a Saint Lucian – the richness that is diversity.

I live by a few principles which have sustained me as a woman:

✓   Strive always towards achieving excellence.

✓   Work ceaselessly towards becoming and remaining self-reliant.

✓   Be guided by the maxim that 'in every adversity there is opportunity'.

✓   Note that respect is commanded, not demanded.

✓   Build relationships on trust, mutual respect, honesty, sincerity and integrity.

My Life As A Woman: Saint Lucia Edition #2

My name is Stacy Duncan and I grew up in the lovely community of Desrameaux, Monchy. I grew up with my cousins, siblings, grandparents, aunties and uncles as well as my parents. So basically, I was brought up by my immediate family or should I say the community. I grew up with food always being on the table, and not with the golden spoon.

Well my inspiration came from my parents. I never once got up and never had anything to eat despite them not being rich or fortunate to give us the bogie meals. They always got up every morning with the motive of heading to work, saying their little prayers, wishing us to have a bless and safe day whether at school or at home, staying positive and keeping our heads on. These two still continuously inspire me on a day like today. They never once gave up in my eyes.

My last school attended was the Sir Arthur Lewis Community College, where I studied Secretarial Studies – Office Administration. I always wanted to become an accountant, but I never pursued it. It's just amazing, the fact that you can do anything with numbers, even being able to calculate anything without a calculator.

Our culture is a beautiful one, I really love the food, the people are exceptional, the music, the different cultural activities and practices. Currently, I work at the Gros Islet polyclinic as a Medical Receptionist, on Fiverr and I also do my coconut oil and ice lollies for sale.

My struggles as a woman is getting the support needed from different Ministries or Authorities to push yourself further to really be what you want to be. It's difficult to get a job, you have the qualifications and the experiences and yet still you can't get a job. Number one that recruiter will hire his or her friend as well as if you're willing to sell you're yourself. Sis aren't about that life. I graduated from high school in 2014 and I only got a chance to secure a proper job only in 2018. Just because of determination, persistence and much more. I'd be dropping applications day after day after day, calling those business places to follow up and showing my face frequently.

My successes as a woman is that I never really gave up. I don't settle for nothing less; I engage myself in all free or affordable courses I see that is fit for me. Today I can stand here and say I am proud of where I came from and I'm proud of where I'm heading. I graduated from college with some awesome grades, now I work permanently with the government of Saint Lucia and I haven't stopped. I always prayed for a part time job and here I am on Fiverr. There's much more coming soon.

I want to encourage each and every female to stay strong and be independent. Motivate yourself, empower yourself, don't settle for mediocre. Stand up for what you believe is right! Get up and do something for yourself and always remember people's opinion doesn't matter. Be Bold! Be brave!

My Life As A Woman: Saint Maarten Edition

Yet small but so beautiful I must tell you about my love for Country Sint Maarten. It is peaceful and quiet in almost every neighborhood with the friendliest neighbors. Living in Sint Maarten you get to meet with people from all over the world. Sint Maarten is a melting pot mixed with all different kinds of people sharing their culture, background and knowledge.

I grew up in a small area called Cul-de-sac where I had the best neighbors, we would go on date nights by dining at different restaurants, attending the movie theatre and going on boat cruises around the island. Growing up was only myself and my mother in the household but I was surrounded by awesome neighbors who would have given full support if my mom was not there.

When it comes to inspiration my mother is the perfect person as she is kind, caring, hard-working, reliable, confident, trustworthy, adventurous, and a highly motivated person. She will push you at your lowest and comforts you during your darkest moment. She has the drive that will keep you going, and this allows me to try harder.

Attending school on Sint Maarten was a wonderful experience starting from high school to college. Sitting in classes listening to students' presentations, working as a team on projects, and going on field trips made up the entire school semesters. Growing up I always dreamt of being an architect, but I took less art class even though I have a love for art. That's something I teach myself by watching YouTube tutorials and step-by-step drawings in my spare time. I always think of doing something fun, something that I would not lose interest in and it would be a necessity in today's environment. I studied Business Administration and yes, I know this has nothing close to do with my dream job, but it works, and I love and enjoy doing it.

Culture in St. Maarten is not so easy to tell apart because of the mixture of Dutch, French, British and African heritage. However, if you want to get a taste of Sint Maarten and what we have to offer it is best to visit around Carnival time. This celebration starts in March and lasts for approximately 33 days and it is held every year except during a pandemic. So, if you missed it this year there is a greater opportunity that you will be able to experience it in the following years to come. Get booking if you ask me. Around this time of the year, you will see thousands of people coming out to get a taste of the food, feting and the costume parades. Taking it to the streets you will experience the high energy of the people whether they are wearing a vibrant costume or a DIY J'ouvert outfit you should just expect a colorful celebration in this tropical paradise. In the Sint Maarten Festival Village is where most people will hang out during this time, here you will be able to get a taste of the island through the mouthwatering foods that are sold at different booths. Each booth has something special to offer whether it is through tasty food or a mixed drink you would want to try. Make sure to get a Johnny Cake as you go, and Chicken sautéed with peanut sauce.

I encountered a few struggles along the way as Sint Maarten is a small island that is frequently visited by tourists and everywhere is closed by dust. Not having a car can be a bit frustrating at times as you must stand for a while to catch a bus to get from Point A to Point B. Even though there is an active bus system in place it is not done in a timely manner. Late nights would catch me on the street after attending classes, therefore; I had to catch a bus or rely on classmates, friends, and/or family to pick me up and drop me home.

One of my biggest successes was being able to partner with my friend to start an online clothing store called Ker'Ti Kloset. This boutique is geared towards women. Currently, we are providing clothes and accessories for women ranging from small to plus sizes. In the future, I would love to include children's clothing and men as well.

A piece of advice to women living in Sint Maarten would be to get out there if it's not here, it can be found elsewhere. Do not be stuck in the mind thinking that it can't be done.

My Life As A Woman: Saint Vincent And The Grenadines

My name is Izzy John. I grew up, born and bred in Saint Vincent, which is the mainland of Saint Vincent and the Grenadines, an archipelagic state in the Eastern Caribbean. Growing up on this small island drives home the meaning of "it takes a village to raise a child". Although my mother was a single mother, I grew up in an extended family and had the presence and influence of my grandmother, cousins, aunts, and uncles in my life. My father was influential in many ways, but his constant presence was still left to be desired. Therefore, it was my mother who inspired me. Despite not being able to attain education beyond the primary level, she did her best to provide more than just my needs and inspired me to achieve, attain and maximise my fullest potentials in ways she was unable to.

Resultantly, through her encouragement, and financing from my Dad, I was able to obtain a Bachelor of Science in Geosciences from the University of the West Indies, Mona Campus in November of 2019. As a woman in STEM, this is just a steppingstone towards working in the natural hazards and disaster risk and vulnerability field in the future. This has been my goal since childhood because growing up with hazards incited this fear in me which made the science behind them interesting, and the subsequent importance of safeguarding against them clearer to me. Currently, I am an intern Energy Officer at the Energy Unit, working to promote and encourage sustainable energy uses and practices alongside increased integration of renewable energy technologies in energy generation in Saint Vincent and the Grenadines. This work contributes to the efforts to combat the issues of climate change here.

While Saint Vincent and the Grenadines is unique in many ways, the culture is like that of other Caribbean islands. However, the most impactful thing about our culture is the obvious creativity and diversity of the Vincentian people exemplified in different artforms.

Being born female, the odds are generally stacked against you, but this does not have to define your trajectory. The struggles I have faced include being judged as too "blunt" or "hostile" instead of being classed as assertive in standing up for myself or my views, and lack of opportunity and respect in different environments. These struggles are multifaceted and real. However, they give me more incentive to persevere and rise above them.

Conversely, the successes I have realised include attending the St. Vincent Girls' High School – the top female high school on the island, becoming a prefect, and young leader at that prestigious institution, and becoming a Chief Commissioner Guide while at Community College here. Also, I graduated from University with honours after overcoming many challenges during that time and was selected by a regional organisation to become a part of their annual internship programme shortly thereafter. I am also recognised as a positive role model for girls and young women, and confidently represent myself in the face of opposition.

What I would emphasize to other women is the importance of obtaining a quality education and achieving financial independence so that there is lesser likelihood of being taken advantage of and disrespected by men. Furthermore, I would encourage women to become self-motivated – not only to improve their present circumstances but to incite positive change for generations.

My Life As A Woman: Samoa Edition

Hey everyone, I am Mali from Samoa. I lived in a small village with my family. The village had a close-knitted relationship, we were one. My father was one of the best builders in the village, and he also had a farm that my mother assisted with. He grew banana, coconut, and other fruits, depending on the season. My parents had six of us; four girls and two boys. We all had our roles, my brothers had to help on the farm in the early morning. While my sisters and I, were to assist my mother in the house. Growing up there was no one that I admired; we were all in the same condition. The village was stagnant for a good while.

There weren't any official schools in my village during my time, so I attended a school started by a village Elder. We would go from Monday to Thursday in the morning to midday. After that, we would have to go and work on the farm with our parents. We were taught the basics: how to read, write, and simple calculations. As a child, I did not aspire to be much. I just wanted to be successful in life and have a life better than my parents. I got married to a nice man when I was eighteen years old. My job was to be a good wife, take care of the children, maintain our space, and weave baskets when I had the time.

I love my Samoan dance culture. Our dancing is so different; it captures every different emotion. It's like communicating using your body to make rhythmic movements. Also, I admired how close we were as a village, we would help each other and make sure everyone was okay.

In my country women are treated as equals, there's inequality in the job opportunities and wages received. We were left at a disadvantage. We were taught how to be a wife, not how to be independent or ambitious. Our only goal was to find a good man and get married. Also, living in a poor village with very little resources set us back in life. We didn't get the best quality education, so the types of jobs we could do were limited mostly to agriculture.

To the people of my village, I was rather successful. My husband and I had two homes, we always received a high yield from our farm, and my husband took very good care of me and our children. But for me that wasn't my success, that was his. The only thing I could claim as mine was my weaving skills. Later in life, after moving from that village I decided to do better for myself and went to school. I only did up to high school, but I am still proud of myself. So now my success is being able to get an education, despite my struggles and cultural background.

To all the females of Samoa, your only goal in life shouldn't be to be a wife. You can do far more than that, you can accomplish things for yourself without the help of a man. You need to believe in yourself.

My Life As A Woman: Sao Tome and Principe Edition

I was born at a remote area near Jou in a family of ten siblings and I was the first born. My parents were not educated and as a result they never valued education. My mother was the bread winner in my family since my father had indulged in such heavy drinking that he never provided for us.

Despite our poverty, I was enrolled into primary school at about age eight. I could occasionally miss out on classes to help my mother in working in the cocoa farms to provide food for my siblings. When dad came home he used to be so violent that the home was inhabitable. This went on for some period and before long I was married off at an early age to a man thrice my age.

My father never valued education, especially of a girl child. During his drinking spree, he arranged for my marriage to one of his friends who was thrice my age. I was married off to that man at such an early age, curtailing my education. This event was like coming out of the frying pan to the fire. Economically, the situation was not any better as I continued working in the cocoa farms to supplement what my husband could earn. Before long I became a mother of six children whom I got at short intervals.

One day, while my husband was returning from work as usual was attacked by thugs who seriously injured him. He was rushed to the nearby dispensary for first aid before being referred to a better facility. Unfortunately, he never made it; he passed away before getting to the hospital. This made life so difficult for me and the six children.

My fortunes started changing when I started visiting a nearby catholic church for Sunday masses. With time, one catholic sister by the name Wilmah got interest in knowing me better. After listening to my story, she was touched and introduced me to a programme ran by the Catholic Church for empowering young mothers. It was designed to equip young mothers with skills that would help alleviate the poverty levels in the community. I was trained as a Kindergarten teacher, a skill that enabled me to be employed as a teacher and left the menial jobs I was earlier engaged in.

The number of girls who drop out of school in Sao Tome and Principe is so high that very few make it through secondary school and university. This has directly affected the quality of education in the country. I am grateful to the Catholic Church and other organizations like the Red Cross for their interventions that has continued alleviate the plight of women in this country.

I am now leading a better life courtesy of sister Wilmah and the church for their intervention that gave me a new lease of life. My children are all enrolled in school and my family is happy.

My advice to the women of Sao Tome and Principe is that we should value education and be supportive to one another. Was it not for a fellow woman coming through for me, my life wouldn't have changed for the better.

My Life As A Woman: Saudi Arabia Edition #1

I have been reading many blogs regarding life for women in Saudi Arabia; the life for women is really hard and restricted in Saudi Arabia so I just wanted to share my thoughts for future readers. I am a Pakistani woman living in Riyadh, Saudi Arabia for 3 years after being married. My husband works here, so I got a chance to come to my dream country. I always wanted to live in Saudi Arabia since my childhood because of religious beliefs as it is a country where every Muslim wants to come at least once in a lifetime, so my destiny brought me here.

If you ask me one word about KSA that would be: "Luxurious". Life here is extremely peaceful and private. No one interferes with whatever you do, we are free to go anywhere we want but carrying a passport or resident ID is as important as breathing. There are huge malls, hyperstores, shopping centers, parks having every facility where I can freely go whenever I want leaving behind all previous cultural taboos, which were famous about Saudi previously, and I enjoy every bit of that as women loves shopping more than anything,

Here in Saudi Arabia, I got a chance to experience world cuisines which is my favorite part of being a food lover, it is a community of diverse identities, so the food also is diverse. I found Yemeni, Turkish, and Indian food as the best one so far. Not to forget the special "Arabic Gehwa", which is Arab's special black tea which I found phenomenal.

I am so happy I am living here, a life many of us only wish for, life here is extremely comfortable, a little expensive but jobs are also high paying so one can afford it if having a good job. Days here are quiet and nights are lush. When I talk about whether, well it is really hot out there as we keep on listening about KSA commonly, but the availability of air conditioners has made our lives as easy as possible, so I don't mind if it's hot outside, as my room is chilled whether its summer or winter.

I would share one problem which I mostly face while living here in my dream place, that is as I am not a native, and beside living here for so long, I have not learned Arabic, which many of times create difficulty while shopping, as many of the sales personals in shops are Arabic and they don't know English, so the communication gets hard. Once I got up in this situation, I wanted to know about a price of an article and I was unable to understand what sales girl is trying to tell, well she ended up by writing the price on calculator and I ended up leaving empty handed because of the failed communication. If you want to live here, it is important to learn some basic Arabic which will make your life easiest

ABAYA, a long cloak - black robe, which is a compulsory dress code for woman here is something which people think is a restriction for woman but actually is a religious act according to them, I have no issue with that actually I love to wear that, it is so comfortable I can go to any mall in my night suit even, just by putting abaya on. And if you live here you will get that it is has become kind of a fashion thing to have a few and fun ones.

Give it a try; I think you will be surprised how nice it can be living here in KSA!

My Life As A Woman: Saudi Arabia Edition #2

When I was growing up, it was not a very ideal environment. Girls would play inside the homes only. And if we go out, we have to go with parents/elders of the house. I was always fascinated and curious about the outside world. Oh! I forgot to introduce myself, I am Tayyaba Ali, a Pakistani-Muslim girl, born and raised in the Kingdom of Saudi Arabia.

When I was around 5-6 years old, I used to watch people walking outside from under the main gate of the house. I remember watching it for hours every evening. All I could see was feet moving. Being a Pakistani raised in KSA it was a norm for us to go out with family only. But on the other hand, I always wanted to move freely and alone. It is not like going out alone was not safe for women, but it was just not normal in society. I did my high school from Pakistan Int'l School Jeddah. And went to Pakistan to pursue further studies. Those four years that I spent in Pakistan really broadened my view over life and it also help me build confidence. In Pakistan, even though it's not very safe and secure for women to roam around freely but women are very independent, doing their own chores and earning for themselves and their families. I lived in a hostel for four years and it made me and trained me well to depend on myself and be self- sufficient. I got courage to fulfill my own basic necessities. I travelled alone in public transport between the cities. That was really empowering for me. I felt freedom. I never had to ask anyone to take me somewhere because I could go on my own. I could do everything by myself.

After I graduated, I came back to Jeddah and started living with the family again. It was really hard to depend on others once again. I cried days and nights because I felt suffocated, felt like I am caged, so I started looking for a job so I can at least go to work by my own. I started working as a teacher. Job opportunities for women here are less, especially for expat women. So, most of us end up being teachers. It was of course not what I wanted but it's definitely better than staying home. Now that I am working, I get to go buy things myself, I go out with friends, I take cabs and roam around the city alone and most importantly, I can fix my own problems. I believe being self-sufficient is the kind of empowerment we all should strive for. There should not be any gender roles or tags. We human beings should be self-sufficient while being kind and caring for fellow human beings. I think we need more to emphasize on women getting equal rights in every field of society. Women driving, women working as civil engineers on sites or women flying airplanes should be considered normal. Women are made to make this world a better and peaceful place. I now aim to travel around the globe alone and free. To all the beautiful women out there, all I want to say is please be you. Please be whoever you are. Don't feel bad or guilty about how you truly feel and how you want things to be. Aim for it and fight for it.

My Life As A Woman: Saudi Arabia Edition #3

Saudi Arabia, a battleground for the oppressing males and the suppressed females, this is the general stereotype that revolves around the name of the Royal Kingdom. However, having spent more than 21 years of my life in that realm, my recollections of it are much different. I was born in the metropolitan city of Dammam which is known for its administrative importance for the country. Even though my memories of that place are quite vague, my mind still drags me back to the spacious roads my family and I would drive through and the broad, blue beaches that spread an earthy aroma all around.

After a few years my family and I moved to Jeddah which is around 85 kilometres away from the Holy city of Mecca. Growing up, I became very fond of a few spots. Mainly, the Jeddah Corniche which runs along the Red Sea, which was the go-to weekend getaway for most Saudi families. The chaotic buzzing of people having BBQ parties, boys and girls kiting and cycling on the pavements and mothers running after their toddlers to make sure they weren't too close to the coast all had a sense of serenity to it.

I was privileged enough to attend an International school where I had the opportunity to interact with people from all around the world. The teaching staff there was mainly female dominant and that is where I met some of the most inspiring women. All through middle school and high school I was surrounded with women that carried themselves with utmost dignity and grace. They had their ways with the children and could manage to instill respectability, integrity and righteousness even in the naughtiest of students. The poise I noticed in those women was what I aspired to be when I grew up thus teaching became a profession I wanted to pursue in the future.

The main pillar of the Saudi culture is honour. This is applicable on both genders however women enjoy the fruit of it more than men. I have personally travelled to many different countries, but I have noticed that the amount of respect that a woman receives out on the streets in Saudi Arabia is unmatched. Majority of men tend to lower their gaze when a group of girls pass by while other men open doors for ladies that walks in and out of stores. In addition, another act of chivalry that I observed in some Saudi men is that if they noticed a woman waiting in a long que, they allow her to cut the line, make her purchase, and leave the crowded area as soon as possible.

Times in the kingdom have changed quiet drastically over the past few years and the lifestyle that people followed has revolutionized to a surprising extent. I have been fortunate enough to experience the pre- and post-revolution customs. Previously women weren't allowed to drive which increased their dependency on the men in the house. This proved to particularly difficult for women who didn't necessarily have a male figure who could provide transport. I personally had to wait on my father to drop me to the gym or take me to the mall. The situation has taken a 180 degree turn now and women have been given the liberty to drive which lifts the burden off of men.

My advice to other women, especially those who see KSA as the land of female oppression, is that you make of what you have regardless of what gender you are. If people believe we are the birth-givers of leaders, why can't we be chiefs ourselves? Patriarchy should not be an excuse in order to hold ourselves back from our true potential. We can make our own opportunities why lifting each other up. Saudi Arabia itself has prominent names of women like Bayan Al-Zahran (first Saudi female attorney) and Hayat Sindi (first women to be appointed as a member of Saudi Arabia's Shoura council, the Kingdom's legislature) who have made their mark in the world by having a stead-fast attitude and working hard towards their goals. Being a woman is beautiful in its own way and we must celebrate that!

My Life As A Woman: Saudi Arabia Edition #4

As-salamu alaykum (Peace be upon you). My name is Malaika. I am born and raised in Kingdom of Saudi Arabia. I'm settled in Jeddah with my family. Just a small little family: my mama, baba and two younger brothers.

My father before his marriage came to KSA from Pakistan looking for a better job and luckily he found one Ma'sha'Allah. Then he got married to my mother which was an arrange marriage like most of the Pakistani households. Love marriage today is acceptable in most of the families but a few years back it was just considered a symbol of vulgarity. My mom and dad traveled to Saudi Arabia, and I was born later after their marriage. At first my father was not financially stable, and we had a small apartment. It was more like a joint apartment with many other rooms in a corridor. It was a company's residence, for which my baba is employed. It wasn't big at all. I remember it having an entrance where we had a sofa placed and a small TV. Then going in it had a small bedroom, a kitchen and a bathroom. That was enough for my mama, baba and me. There was a small playground outside with a merry-go-round in it.

After some years, my father got promoted and we were given a bigger apartment. That was the time when my brother was born. Being little, I used to watch my parents talking to each other nicely and lovingly which is one of the things I love about my family.

We as a family used to visit Pakistan once in a year. My grandparents live there, and they are literally THE best people I've ever met. While in Pakistan I used to notice the difference in traditions and cultures. Giving an example of Ramadan in Saudi Arabia is so full of love and light and blessings. In the month of Ramadan there are plenty of discounts, promotions and most of the things are free. People are giving out free dates for Iftar. It's so beautiful. While in Pakistan all the fun and joy happen around Eid. Ramadan is mostly like normal days there. Eid in Saudi Arabia is mostly like giving sweets other families and greet with 'Eid Mubarak". We cook delicious meals. A sweet dish on Eid is mandatory. All the kids get ready. Boys usually wear the colorful Pakistani shalwar kameez while girls have different styles to suit themselves. Girls apply henna on their hands and wear bangles and jewellery. After getting ready we go to our elders asking for Eidi. Eidi is basically money given to children from their elders in the family as an Eid gift.

From a young age I wanted to become a doctor. I wanted to help people and see them happy. But as I grew up my interests changed but I still had a great love for Biology. So later I went to Pakistan for my higher education. I did MS English literature from a university in Islamabad. Also, I took some side classes for Biology.

There was an excessive difference between the culture and people of Pakistan and Saudi Arabia; I just couldn't adjust myself in the start. But later with the passage of time it all became just fine.

Well, the traditions and culture of Saudi Arabia has improved over the time a lot. We, women, in Saudi Arabia didn't have the permission to drive earlier. But now we are allowed to drive but it's just for the working women and I think that is really disappointing. Most of the departments, factories, offices have men in them. You can barely see a woman working between men and she also will be of Saudi nationality. They do not allow foreign women to work. So basically, here women are just depending on their men of the family. Now that I am a working woman I got the permit to drive and it felt like I reunited with my soul, lol. At first I couldn't find a job anywhere because of the male female discrimination. But after I tried like a 100 times I got the job. I was so thankful.

But the thing I like the most about this country is that WOMEN FEEL PROTECTED. You can see so many rape cases happening around the globe. But you'll barely hear a single case related to KSA. That is because of the extremely strict rules of the kingdom. But the fact that when I visited Pakistan, I saw families there and it was so disappointing to me that if a girl got raped her parents didn't allow her to raise her voice or go to the cops or anything just because it'll cause a shame to their family. People will look at them as if their daughter has committed a huge sin, so girls are suppressed there. They aren't allowed to raise their voice. If anyone steals, they cut hands. And if anyone rapes, they hang him to death. That's how this nation is still protected and growing. But let me just share a short story. I was around 10 years old when my father hired a Qari (the one who teaches the Holy Quran). He used to come to our house to teach me and my brothers. He touched me inappropriately several times and told me not to tell anyone as he was my teacher and he always thought good of me. I was small and had no sense of the things, so I didn't tell this to anyone. I am 23 years old today and can never forget what happened with me. But at least today I can tell this to you all reading this. Never stay quiet girls. Never! Let them know who you are.

But the good thing is whenever I go out I don't have to worry about getting pickpocket; and I can say this because I lived in Pakistan as well and there I couldn't even get out at night or near night because of the fear that a person is sitting waiting for a girl to come out. In Saudi Arabia all the women wear abaya (a long dress worn over clothes) whether you're an American or a Philippine, a Muslim or a non-Muslim, it's compulsory to wear. Head scarf is not forced on everyone. Those who want to wear it, can.

Our society is greatly influenced by Arab and Islamic culture, and it's deeply religious, traditional and family-oriented. Women are given a lot of respect here in every case. But there were a few things I faced most of the problems in. Because I personally am brought up in a pretty open-minded family, so I always wanted to be free and go out etc. I wanted to have the kind of freedom given to guys like as little as going out at night. I wanted to enjoy. But that couldn't be possible sitting inside a house where I had to wait for my dad to come home and give me a lift. Because most of the Muslim families don't allow their daughters to go out on an Uber or something. That's basically because the drivers are male (as women are not allowed to drive) and the male drivers are "na-mehram" and a young girl sitting alone with a stranger is thought to be completely un-trustworthy.

Well at last I'd just say that no matter how strict this country is for girls, it groomed me in a better way. And everyone loves their country, so long live Saudi Arabia.

My Life As A Woman: Saudi Arabia Edition #5

I am from a conservative family who come originally from Makkah, my ancestors have served as prayer callers in the Grand Mosque. My family has moved to Jeddah where I have been raised. Just like any Saudi girl, I went to girls-only school and university. I have always been considered different in my family in my interests and thoughts.

Since a young age I loved to draw and paint. I am passionate about art and therefore I have participated in several art exhibitions and workshops and I have tried my hand on Abaya design and event design. Because I love art I have chosen to complete my bachelor's degree in advertising (graphic design) I went in a challenging journey to Makkah where I had to travel between Jeddah and Makkah every day to complete my degree.

Although I liked working in my major, however, I still believed there is more to explore in this world other than just sitting for hours in front of a screen to do some designs. Hence, I could not work in a typical office atmosphere and thus I quit my job just to try different things including traveling and enjoying new experiences like exploring nature, hiking, yoga, and running. I have always loved to travel but because of family restrictions this dream has always been postponed.

I have been brave enough to confront my family to allow me to follow my passion in exploring the world, however my family support in previous jobs and art works have turned mimetically to disagreement, however, as I insist on my dream they finally allowed me to travel to Nepal. Although many might consider Saudi women as financially dependent on their families, this however is not the case with everyone. Personally I have self-financed my own trips and I have worked in several jobs and done freelance tasks just to remain fully independent.

I have chosen Nepal because I wanted to try an extremely different lifestyle, having lived in luxurious life compared to any young woman of my age in any other country, Nepal trip was an extreme experience for me. This trip to far Asia has in fact been a turning point in my life, it is my all-time inspiration. I leaned in Nepal that travel can be affordable and enjoyable including the challenges faced.

I have learned in this trip to break my fear to be open to new cultures and people and to help others. I learned to try new things like supporting local people and starting a new lifestyle in which I become environment-friendly, and most importantly I learned that satisfaction is a key to happiness. This lifetime experience has inspired me to come back to Saudi with a totally different mindset and to start applying what I have learned in Saudi Arabia.

My Life As A Woman: Saudi Arabia Edition #6

Khadija Ashraf

Where did you grow up?

I was born and raised in Jeddah Saudi Arabia and have lived my whole life here.

How did you grow up?

I grew up with 4 siblings, we are 4 sisters and one baby brother, for me my childhood was crazy adventures , because we used to travel between cities in our mini car with no air conditioner in it. the whole family in the hot desert sunny weather of Saudi Arabia . Yes back than it wasn't that fun but now when I look back at it, it's like we created our own little adventure stories Some happy and some sad.

I used to go to school and then just come back home like everyone else. And then I was the only one that used to go outside and play with kids and neighbors on the street. I was a bit tomboyish back then.

Did you have parents or maybe a grandmother who inspired you?

I grew up with the sweetest father and mother, my father is an accountant and my mother is the most hardworking house wife I have ever seen, they have always thought us why and how we should be kind to everyone, and how we should never lie to someone who loves us and cares about us, why we should never judge anyone. they taught us how to be strong no matter what situations we are in, how not to give up ever in our life no matter how hard it is to get what u want! They taught us how to take care of a family.

My father and mother always cheered us for studying and getting a degree so we can one day have a better bright future and won't be needing to depend on a man!

My grandfather passed away way before I was even born. My grandmother was very strict about girls, but she also taught us all to be independent but somewhere she didn't like the culture of now days she likes girls to stay inside all the time and she used to tell us a girl should be very gentle and not to ever raise her voice in public, and all those kinds of grandmother's talk which we usually get to hear.

What did you study? / What did you want to be growing up? / Why?

I studied in an Arabic government school in Jeddah Saudi Arabia . I completed my high school there, but I was interested in studying more, sure I wanted to get a degree, but because somewhere I really wanted to make a good fun friend circle , a good social life , and wanted to travel a lot . And studying was quite boring for me.

What are you currently doing for work?

I work as a content creator, I started as a music creator and I worked as a freelance model and after all these years and hard work, my family and fans support who I am. I am writing all this for you to share my success story with everyone. I love what I do and inshallah will work harder to achieve more success.

What do you love about your culture?

Since I was born in 2000 s in the City Of Jeddah KSA, My eyes see everything so beautiful in this city. May it be the people or the Mixed Culture here. From the Childhood trips to the beaches, to the Tallest Fountain, to the Old Markets Of Balad and to many more. I has a very special place in my heart.

It is part of our culture here to be with each other in one's happiness and in hard times, despite of their nationalities. For me, it's growing up and making friends from different cultures is the amount of knowledge you gather. You learn about their world, beliefs, practices and more. The whole neighborhood knows when someone dies or gets married and we all celebrate and share gifts. That's what I love about our culture.

Tell me about your struggles as a woman?

To reach the lifestyle I have now I had to face my own family first. I didn't get any support I should normally get not just but because I was a woman in in Saudi Arabia. But also because my father is a very religious man and he never approved for all this. Yes he wanted us to achieve success but not on social media and on camera, and because here in our society they don't approve any of the things I wanted, I wanted to travel the world, and be independent. I wanted to be a free woman seeking her dreams. But No one gave me permission or support to do so because "women are not created for this" everyone says. , I had to fight my way through it.

Tell me about your successes as a woman?

Making my dream come true wasn't easy! But my sisters they played a huge role in it, since m the youngest sister of them all, they all loved me and took care of me a little more, and somewhere they wanted me to achieve my dreams because they couldn't achieve theirs.

My elder sister (Mona), she was the first one to always support me and encourage me and told me to never give up on my dreams! and she was the one who sneaked me out to give my first audition on (Arab's Got Talent!) where I performed something in public for the first time.

My parents played a huge role in it . Yes they didn't support the idea of being famous in my first year on social media, but gradually they did understand in what my happiness really is .

Yes I faced a lot of criticism and faced a lot of mocking and racism but got loved a lot more and got support from all my fans whom I'm really thankful to after Allah, Alhumdulillah for everything, and inshallah for the what I want next to achieve.

My advice: if you want to do something or if you don't want to live the same lifestyle you are living now, or if you have dreams, then work hard for it and never give up because success will not come overnight! And most importantly, believe in it!

As Saudi women, we had struggled for long to get a chance to even travel or move around or freely explore our own country. We had to always be accompanied by a male guardian and we could not drive. Things have changed now and as young females we can drive and travel on our own even in remote places. After being allowed to drive and having built relations with other female travelers in my country we now do what we love together and we help others explore our country in an affordable and wise method in which they learn to be environment-friendly and adventurous.

Along with my friends we toured around different Saudi regions. I can say with confidence that Saudi Arabia is as diverse as the entire world is! Each region has its own culture, heritage and tradition. I loved the varied topography including sea, desert, valleys and mountains. The welcoming nature of our culture is yet another factor that makes me enjoy traveling around our small towns and villages. After seeing all the potentials in Saudi tourism I have started along with my friends Qairawan, non-profit travel community to help others explore our beautiful country.

We arrange for trips to explore different Saudi regions, we try new experiences such as camping, hiking, climbing, swimming in valleys, exploring caves. mingling with locals and we enjoy the mouthwatering local food. Through my experience in travel I have succeeded in convincing my family and the community as a whole that a person can be different and yet successful. I have managed to let everyone know that it is doable for a Saudi woman to go in adventures in my country. I am still starting my new path in showing the beauty of my country to the world through a female lens. I opt to have a special TV program devoted to tourism. I also hope to start a project to document female traditional outfits in each Saudi region.

I get many comments from young women on my Instagram who want to be as courageous as I am. Hence, I believe that the first thing a woman should do is to break her fear of being different. Stand for her dream and believe in herself. I urge all women to never give up and always take the challenges as factors that make them much stronger in achieving their goals.

My Life As A Woman: Senegal Edition

"Sally, we are not going back", those are the words my Moroccan mum said when I asked when will we go back to Senegal ,although I was five I was aware enough to be pained, what about dad and my older sister? They were still there, would they come too? We have been in Morocco for enough time why won't we go back?

Now that I'm 25 I came to the realization that as a woman; making tough decisions to save yourself and your kids from messy family situations is a must. My parent's relationship was not the most perfect but they still had a lot of respect and love for each other, their main goal was make it work no matter what but my dad's family was not on the same page. They kept putting her in very difficult situations so she would feel fed up ,we later discovered that they had another woman in mind to be my dad's wife. Typical Senegalese move, as always according to the common mindset the woman is the weakest link so attacking her was supposedly easier therefore her only solution was to leave. The next step was convincing my dad to follow, meanwhile she was the only one struggling, leaving me with my grandmother and being out looking for a job, by herself she managed to get me in private school because language barrier, her pay would usually be poured into my education while my dad was still trying to make a decision whether to come or not, she knew she was on her own, she had to take matters with her own hands and raise me properly for the time being.

On the bright side I had the chance to spend a lot of time with my grandmother, she was the book I loved to read her life was so inspiring, listening to the times she had to be the handyman with her husband carrying bricks, building their home, when done she would go to the villages near by picking apples and being paid the lowest wage just to help her husband financially .Being surrounded by these two strong women I had no excuse not to make it, my dream was to be a doctor ;not to sound dreamy or to give the proper response when asked ,I had it all planned out since I was twelve, I already knew whether it be Senegal or Morocco they needed more doctors, but obstacles were lurking. Now that my dad was with us, me going back to Senegal to finish my studies was a big no, He left everything to follow us, but I had better chances to get in a Senegalese medical school with a scholarship "you are a woman long studies will only come in your way of getting married and having kids its either you choose a career or the stability of a home you cannot do both" is what I've been told but my eagerness pushed me even further, I did not want to give up I missed Senegal the warm sun, the beaches, people hide their stress behind jokes so I was always laughing and women here are so inspiring, hardworking. Coming on vacation here once in a blue moon was not enough, my heart wanted more.

After being accepted in medical school things were still not easy, my day would resume in carrying documents from a place to another. I started noticing a pattern all girls were treated the same in the hospital, even examining the patients was hard to do because according to them we wouldn't be able to handle seeing certain things; assumptions, women and ambition didn't make sense, their way of thinking would have affected my learning If I hadn't been speaking up, asking questions, be more involved and prove my presence. Being oppressed is not the way to thrive, we have a lot of struggles and mine bounced between never being taken seriously in my field, always being seen as a piece of meat or some insignificant being whose only desire is to be a mom and a wife, yes It's an honor carrying a child and being someone's life partner but it's not all there is about me, some women don't want to have kids some women don't want to be married. Why is there a double standard if it's a man it's okay but if it's a woman must be a glitch in the matrix it should be fixed because it's abnormal.

Speaking up is now being a bitter feminist, that will probably end up alone because men prefer them soft and tender mute and blind ,well I believe in mutual respect ,equal rights and opportunities and no its not bitterness it's just common sense, which is not as common apparently. Be yourself, chase your dreams and don't let any Person stand in your way unless they want to hold your hand and walk that path with you, because we all want to be loved but we don't have to pay the price of leaving behind who we want to be.

My Life As A Woman: Serbia Edition

I was born in a small town in the south of Serbia. A town where everyone knows everyone. Where information is always spreading like a wildfire. Where no one minds their own business, but on the contrary, they like minding yours. A town where you were always supposed to be aware of what other people might say.

But despite that, growing up in such a town wasn't so bad as you may expect. My family didn't force me to conform in any way, so I always tried to keep an open mind. I was fortunate enough to have a happy childhood, without any major traumatic experience. Primary school bullying was the only bad memory for me. Since I was little I was taught to always stand up for myself, and I found motivation in it really. I kept telling myself that if I keep learning and working on myself, I would be successful, and that would be the last thing that my bullies wanted. And now, many years later, I can confirm that I was right!

My parents weren't merely people that gave me life, they were my role models. My source of strength for overcoming any obstacles that life threw my way. They instilled moral values in me, that I should always love and respect other people, they gave me unconditional love. I was fortunate to have both parents by my side, if you are too, always remember how valuable they are to you.

While I was in kindergarten I wanted to be a policewoman. I often pictured myself as a superhero, catching bad guys, being a protector of people. I wanted peace and harmony, without bad things happening in the world. Boy, was I naive? After reality hit me while I was getting older, the decision about my future profession didn't come easy to me. I was an excellent student, I pondered about being a lawyer, pharmacist, architect, journalist, and ended up studying IT. I was good at programming while I was in high school, so I decided that was the career that I wanted to pursue. My teacher was very encouraging towards me, and I realized it was a lucrative career, so that pushed me to make such a decision and never regret it.

The thing that I love the most about our culture is that women weren't held down in any way. If you had the capacity to achieve something, nobody would push you down. Women were also working beside men for a long time and contributed in the same way as men did. This thing is often overlooked, but it was something that crossed my mind when some of my international friends talked about their cultures. I don't know exactly where this stems from, but I am proud of it!

I was always imagining myself as a young businesswoman. Although I am still a student, I was always able to find some side jobs for myself. This is not like in some western countries where studying and working is normal. It is not normal in Serbia, and it is very hard to balance work and studying if you want to go down that road. The majority of students focus on their studies, and when they graduate, they find their first job. When I was a freshman in college, I decided to apply the knowledge that I got in the first semester and I started my own little business. I made jewellery and sold it online. It was my first step towards learning marketing skills, customer relations, negotiation skills, photo design, and website development. As it is the case in all STEM fields, women aren't represented enough in the IT domain as well, so I guess we have to work a bit harder to prove ourselves.

So, ladies my advice to you is to be ambitious, educate yourselves, read as much as you can, and don't be afraid to take a leap for the things you are passionate about. Even if you fail, you learned something new. FAIL is just First Attempt In Learning. Never stop learning. Be positive, be successful, not just for your own sake but so you could help others. Trust yourselves and never lose faith!

Esraa Rayes

My Life As A Woman: Seychelles Edition

The condition of the environment, view of the islands, the trees, the whispering wind, beach and the way people dance and plays. Also, when they sing using the traditional strings and many festivals, the dressing style, the people's generosity etc. are the things that I love about my culture. those all make my city to be loved and missed by foreigners and even by us. I was born and grew up in the beautiful city of Mahe, Seychelles. I have one sister who is five years older than me. My father died when I was a little girl. My mother became the bread winner of the family since then. She worked really hard to raise us, send us to school. when I grew up I wanted to be a manager. Because I want to help people manage, evolve and grow but things began to drastically take a turn for the worse When my mother passed away.me and my sister cried until our eyes out for months. I lost hope in everything. I even lost the meaning of life and the purpose of living. God was being unfair. Life became hard and harder.

Thanks to the strongest person in the world, my sister, Fmia. I survived. My sister was a child raising a child. At a time of sorrow, my sister grew wiser. During a time where we two felt weak, my sister grew stronger. Such strength and faith at her age still leaves me speechless. My sister is my hero. She is a teacher for all my life lessons. She gave up so much of her life so that I could have a better one. She has been there for me, my biggest cheerleader, a shoulder to cry on, inspiration for life and she gave me the biggest gift that is to believe in myself and the belief that it is okay to try and fail because it is the trying that counts.

Now that I am all grown up I did not want to be a burden to my sister. In order to save some money for college and to make a living I got a job as a waitress in Lazare Picault hotel. It is a well-known hotel in Baie Lazare Mahe. The hotel is located (set) on a hilltop offering amazing views of the ocean. At first, learning how to multi task and how to read customers body language which is crucial for being a good waitress were a great challenge for me. But later I was a pro at multitasking and reading customers mind. I make my money mostly on tips, so I love great tippers. And always happy guests are great tippers. I always do everything I can to satisfy guests' interest. There are some lot customers who tips you very generously. I get frustrated when I serve the guests well and then receive poor tips. That is just like a slap in the face. For most people being seated and served have no way of knowing what it feels like to be a waitress. Working as a waitress is so stressful it could leave you with problem of your feet, knee as well as back and shoulder problems'. I got blamed for the food I did not even cook. I was the person the customer complains to and punishes with puny tips. And I had to work there for long hours, it was hard to get time off to relax. I was constantly in a stressful state of mind. Since the hotel is always full of guests I had no time to eat, and on top of that I had to deal with the rude customers that treat me like crap or a slave that they can buy me with a money. Most of the customers in the bar abused me, slapped me on my buttocks. I did not complain about any of this to the owner or manager. Actually, they encouraged us to flirt with male customers to get drink sales up. There were also customers that leave a nasty note on back of their receipt that attack me personally. But I have to shake my anger off then smile for the next customer. I really wanted to quit but then I realized I had to help my sister. I wanted to make my dreams come true. So, I told to myself that I have to face these obstacles and in no time, I would get used to it. And some day, I would show all the men and customers who looked down on me or did not respect me what I am worth for. I never showed any sign of weakness or tiredness at home.

Now I am a college student. I am studying management and also I am taking short language courses. Due to the fact that I can translate languages, the hotel is also paying me well. I don't have to deal with the rude customers anymore. I also sent my sister to school. She continued from where she left off. We women have to believe in ourselves. We should show the world how hard working we are; we should never give up on our dreams. What is meant for you will never pass by you. Just Look forward, think positive and face the challenges and you will find yourself on the top.

My Life As A Woman: Sierra Leone Edition

Ann Marie Bangura contributes to the project by talking about her life growing up as a woman in the tropical country of West Africa called Sierra Leone.

"I was born in 1993 in Makeni, the Northern Province of Sierra Leone. I grew up in a military family and my father was in the police force. Due to his job, he was always on the move and he took us with him everywhere he went. As far as I remember correctly, he was last transferred to the very large and beautiful city of Freetown, also our capital, and that is where I grew up. I remember most of my childhood on the Lumley beach in Freetown, fantastic place. Growing up was all right. Being in a military family, we had our privileges."

As Ann Marie goes on to talk about her inspiration, she says, "My father was the one behind the inspiration for my career by showing me how important it is to pursue passion when I barely had any. Not only he but my mother, an amazing woman raising six children while running several businesses demonstrated to me as well how one can be a good parent and be a successful entrepreneur side by side. Also, her support and motivation led me to form a publication career."

Bangura says that growing up, she wanted to be an accountant. She wanted to build a career in this field mainly because of monetary benefits. According to her, accountants are respected a lot in Sierra Leone. However, this dream of hers only lasted up until now as she says, "I don't know why but now I want to become an actress. Something changed inside me, not because I didn't want to do it anymore, but because of my financial status which worsened as time passed."

Next, Ann Marie talks about her culture. She says, "In my culture, I love how close we are to our family and friends. Their support matters a lot and is super important. Aside from that, I really love the food. Especially my mother's homemade dishes. The music, I cherish the music. Our music is like meditation. You listen to it at home and you'll feel the beauty of Sierra Leone."

Unfortunately, when she sat in her examinations in 2014, her parents couldn't afford to send her for higher studies then. "Things can get very bad in Sierra Leone. Sometimes, you really have nothing. Despite that, I'm running small businesses for a living now."

When asked about her successes as a woman, she replied, "I just really thank God for my life, nothing else in particular. I'm happy that despite being a woman, I was able to start multiple businesses, small though, and run them. The business life is hard but it's worth having, and I'm grateful for that. I'm also a really good hairstylist and I'm fond of that. Many of my customers are male and I receive their appreciation on the daily."

Addressing the women of Sierra Leone, she says, "My message to other women is that, the woman who can create her own job and struggle to make her own money, that's a real woman. I'd love it if women here had a one-track and goal-oriented mind to achieve success. The world is changing at a fast-paced rate and we have to keep up with it."

Ann Marie is now starting an acting business where she's going to make a drama series called 4Her.

This concludes My Life As A Woman: Sierra Leone Edition.

My Life As A Woman: Singapore Edition

I was born as Maria Slamat, the eldest daughter to my mum. And the only daughter of my dad. Because my parents were divorced when I was about 3 to 4 years old, my mum remarried when I was six. My dad did not. At that time, I was too young to know why my parents were divorced, why my mum decided to remarry and not my dad. I was living with my maternal grandparents – my mum's parents. They took care of me very well. I was even schooled somewhere nearby where my grandparents were staying. My mum, my step-dad and step-siblings would pay us a visit every weekend.

My life in school was not a good one. I was known to be ugly. I was socially inept, and I did not have many friends and I was always withdrawn and by myself most of the time. I would normally go into a quiet corner and read my story book. Not many talked to me in school. Boys from my class and other classes did not even smile at me. They conversed with me only when necessary. The other girls got their attention, instead. Not a single boy in my school found me attractive. My self-image was totally destroyed, and I lost my self-esteem. I went to absorb all the negative labels and nicknames given to me. I was a total social outcast, a nervous wreck. Almost every other girl from my school, be it the seniors or juniors had boyfriends. I was only having unreciprocated crushes.

To mask my low self-image and act as if everything was okay when I was burnt and devastated inside, I decided to join a singing contest, held in my school. Words spread like wildfire among my peers that I had joined in the school's singing contest. One by one, criticism and sarcasm were thrown at me by my peers. They had never heard me sing before, so they were amused to know that I was one of the participants in the singing contest. I was the only bold one among the lower secondary classes to join the singing contest under the solo singing category.

When my name was announced as the winner for the Solo Category, the whole school hall vibrated with applauses. Even days after trying to prove that I was good enough, the name calling and bullying continued. Though I won the Solo Category, no one seemed to care and let alone congratulate me on my winning. I soon started wearing an iron mask and became very thick skinned. I could not care less. I had achieved something, which was to sing in front of a big audience. What have they achieved so far? For a short while, I felt very proud of myself.

One fateful day, I was hit by a taxi. The next few days were a nightmare. News about me getting into the accident spread fast. I got condescending stares, chuckles and a nasty remark thrown right at my face. I wanted to go out from the school and get hit by a car again, upon hearing all those nasty remarks and hoped this time that I would not survive! But I just could not do it. I value my life. I want to live. I want to do my O Levels, get into a Polytechnic, then University.

When I got my O Level examination results, a couple of months later, I was disappointed. I could not be enrolled into either a Pre-University or a Polytechnic but that did not deter me. I retook my O Levels as a private candidate while working as an Assistant teacher. As I was doing that, I had to decide for the next step in my tertiary education.

After my private O level results, I was disappointed yet again because I still could not enter into local institutions. Hence I began my quest for an alternative route. I did research on all private institutions in Singapore. There was another stigma attached to those who could not make it to the Junior College/Polytechnic/Pre-University - from rich family backgrounds. I came from a not-so-rich family. This worried my family members as I chose to proceed with this idea of a road less travelled by others, pursuing for my private Diploma course in Computer Studies, followed by a Degree in Business Administration.

My family was initially against with me pursuing further studies because of the fees, but I was very determined to be a graduate. I could not explain it to them, but I had my own reasons for why I wanted this degree so much. Perhaps, because of this low self-esteem I projected during school days, I just wanted to show them (should I be seeing them again in future) that I was better than them. I knew it was hard. I knew I could just have a diploma, but I wanted something more! I wanted people to look up to me with, "Woah, didn't expect Maria to be a graduate! So successful."

Still, my family gave reasons for why they were unable to assist financially with my degree. I assured them it was alright. I had enquired earlier at the same private institution I studied for my diploma, if I could pursue my degree as a part-time student. That would mean that I worked in the day and went to school in the evening.

Life as a working adult is not that easy. I had to finish my work on time and leave the office by 6 pm. It was quite bad initially when I just started my module. But after a while, I got used to it. Routinely, I would take a light dinner, as I could not attend class with an empty stomach, not be able to concentrate well.

I was working in an intellectual property law firm, while studying for my part-time degree. Three years later, the day I was waiting for. My graduation. Graduating from university was a huge accomplishment and I should be proud of myself! To be honest, some things were tougher than expected along the way and I had experienced moments of self-doubt. Now that I had graduated, I got to look back on those tough times and say to myself, "I did it!" And that was certainly something to be proud of.

Months after, I resigned and worked at a call centre. That was when I got to know him, my husband. He was one of the Team Leaders for the section I was in. From colleagues, we became friends. Our other colleagues tried to bring the two of us together as they said we were compatible, and both were single.

He proposed after 13 months of knowing each other. I was rather surprised. Yet, he sincerely wanted me to be a part of him. We got married a day after my birthday, the following year. The marriage made me reflect upon my journey thus far. I admit, the first couple of years of marriage were tough. I was trying to adjust myself. Despite it being the most natural thing for an adult man and woman to live together as a married husband and wife, the first few weeks, months, and years of this cohabitation were a crucial time of adjustment.

My husband and I had no plans for children for the first two years of marriage because we both believed that we should settle down, adjusting to our new life and focus on fulfilling each other's happiness. However, the people around us just could not understand our decision. For that couple of years' period, I struggled to make myself happy and ignored those sarcasms and harsh remarks. I was often asked intrusive questions by well-meaning people. Some that breaks me. These innocent comments might seem to be over the edge.

It was like scratching a deep wound in my soul that was on its way to healing slowly, cell by cell, and such heart breaking questions just made the wound rise back again. At times, I could not take it and I cried.

"When are you two going to have a baby?" This question was repeatedly asked to me, mostly from my husband's relatives on every family occasion. I had been made to feel guilty, ashamed and less worthy of a woman because of not having kids, and this had greatly affected me for a long while.

It was a depressing moment for me. Why was I to be blame for not having children? Why not my husband? Was it because he was not the one giving birth? Initially, I felt like a failure as a woman who could not give kids to my husband. They did not know how many times I fraught with guilt and fought my desire for a child.

One day, it hit me hard. So hard that I cried myself to sleep. I wanted to get out of all this. I condemned and hated myself. I wanted to give my husband children. I numbed myself and wanted an escape from all this ridicule and guilt. I looked for validation from my near and dear ones that I am a capable women and not a failure.

In my quest for love and acceptance, I had the blessed opportunity to meet up with a mentor and coaches, a learning and earning platform. Through the self-development courses, I learnt that an attitude of gratitude towards what you are blessed with and loving oneself is the route to manage our emotions and progress in all aspects of life. It is loving myself first that is the key to loving all the relationships in my life. I learnt and practiced concepts such as the 'Art Of Letting Go', 'The Art Of

Forgiving Oneself And All Others', and 'Emotional Freedom Technique Of Tapping Away For Immediate Emotional Relief From Hurt And Anxiety'. The biggest lesson I learnt was that despite the many flaws I had and the mistakes I made, I had to first be compassionate and loving to myself and accept myself fully without any judgements.

Slowly loving myself, and I had accept my past, my flaws and every wrong turn I take. If I love myself, I would be able to forgive myself. I would mute that nasty voice inside my head that can be eviler than anything ever thrown at me. I would start to treat myself kind and gentle while learning to take really good care of my body, my mind and heart. To stop comparing myself to others and instead focus on my life, my development, my own progress.

"All things happen FOR You and not TO You." I realized that I had allowed those who hurt me to give the permission to hurt me. I had let them define me with all those negative and degrading words when I should be the one knowing myself better than them. I have learnt to mute my own nasty Mickey Mouse voice inside my head that can be crueler than anything ever thrown at me. I started to treat myself with kindness and gentleness while learning to take the utmost care of my body, my mind and heart. I stopped comparing myself to others and started focusing on my life, my development and my own progress. I stopped being a complain Queen and moved away from self-blame and blaming others for my problems. I have taken 100 percent responsibility of my life and happiness.

I started to love myself slowly, I started to control my emotions. I started to do inner work and reflect. Thank you God, I see changes in me, a life work so to speak. My relationship with money, my family, friends is improving.

This view is succinctly expressed in the following quote of self-help Guru, Marianne Williamson:

When our minds move in harmony with love –

Through forgiveness or prayer or the simplest

Tender thought – then

Mountains move and the universe shifts.

My Life As A Woman: Slovakia Edition

I grew up in a little town in Slovakia. As a little child, I moved several times and had chance to experience both city and village life. My parents got divorced when I was five and my mother married another man when I was ten. Growing up with him was quite painful. He changed my mother to totally different person and was emotionally abusing us, especially her for few years. I don't know exactly when it started but I can tell for sure that my teenage years were pretty much ruined by this man. He changed my view of men but thanks to him I learned a lot.

I learned how to recognize toxic man from mile away, how to power myself with negative experiences and that if someone is like him, you have every right to leave. We left him seven months ago, but I feel that I became distanced from my mother. Sometimes it happens when you don't talk with your child a lot or when someone else wants attention away from the whole family. In my childhood, I created hate towards myself and in my teenage years, I didn't know how to cope with it. Right now, I'm finally working on myself and learning to love myself the way I deserve.

My dream career was changing all the time ever since I was little. I wanted to be dancer or actor but after we moved to the village, I had to give up my acting and dancing lessons and I lost confidence in performing in front of crowd of people. Then I wanted to be teacher, pharmacologist, therapist, and environmentalist. You can see that my view of world and future changed a lot. In the past two years, I became interested in environmental field and topics like climate change, melting permafrost or rainforest fires was slowly becoming more important to me than my studies.

At age eighteen, I'm still searching for my purpose in this world and choosing a university is a big step for me. Recently, I discovered a college in Denmark that fits the model of my dream school. If someone asked me to lightly describe this school, I would call it "school of life". They are training teachers of the modern world and preparing them for life. Students are going on humanitarian trips to Western Africa by bus, trips all over Europe to spread awareness about environmental problems and problems of third world countries like poverty, corruption, wars, etc. They also get chance to go on their own humanitarian trips with their teams. This represents everything I want to do right now and in my future.

There are not many things I'm proud of in my culture. Slovak people can be bitter, disrespectful and cynical. But many of us are friendly, caring and proud of our origin. Slovakia has beautiful nature and that's why so many Slovak people who live abroad still like to come back.

Currently, I'm not working because of the COVID-19 pandemic, but I always have some kind of part-time job as a student. My latest job was a waiter in a coffee shop. I have to work because of our financial situation as a family. I have three younger siblings, so my mum can't give me a lot of money and I have to earn some by myself.

My advice for all women is simple: "Don't ever let anyone make you feel like you're worthless. You're strong enough by yourself and you don't need anyone to make you whole or to help you to be unique. You already are unique, and nobody should tell you otherwise."

My Life As A Woman: Slovenia Edition

I cried into the world 31 years ago, more precisely in 1988, just a few years before the war of independence, when in 1991 Slovenia seceded from Yugoslavia and became an independent republic. I don't remember that period as well my parents and grandparents do. It was a period of great optimism and hope for the future, marked by socioeconomic changes.

Childhood on the Slovenian coast

I'm Tjaša. I grew up by the sea, in a small town on the Slovenian coast, which lies on the upper part of the Adriatic Sea, between Croatia and Italy. Her life was moving slowly, we were used to tourists and the lively promenades by the sea. On the weekends, my mother drove me to my grandparents, who still live in the hinterland. Here I was discovering the nearby forests and nature with my cousins.

Elementary school - entering the world of literature

In the mid-1990s, I started attending elementary school, which was only a few hundred meters away from home. In the first grade, I was reading books for children, and later I became more interested in novels and literature for adults. My aunt soon noticed my interest in reading, so she encouraged me to take part in various children's literary competitions. She also gave me books for my birthday.

Growing up with entrepreneurial parents

My parents were entrepreneurs and spent a lot of time at work. They were engaged in the wholesale of cosmetic products. At that time, there were no big shopping centers in Slovenia, but only smaller and privately owned drugstores and cosmetic shops. I spent the afternoons on business premises, where my friends and I played hide and seek in a big warehouse.

The teenage years in high school

I later entered in high school since I wanted to go to university afterward. The high school years were a typical teenage period when my classmates and I explored the boundaries of the environment we knew so far. The enthusiasm for literature did not pass, but it had transformed a bit. In high school, I also discovered psychology, sociology, and philosophy. I also won state recognition in writing a philosophical essay.

Choosing the study course

Before graduating from high school, I attended college programs at several faculties to get detailed information. My decision was also influenced by my parents' opinion, who suggested that the social sciences are not promising as a career choice and that I might experience difficulties when searching for a job. Therefore, I enrolled in a University of economics. After two years of study, I couldn't find myself in the field of numbers, financial calculations, and statistics. Despite that, I completed my diploma and entered the job market at the age of 23 as a young Bachelor.

Different work fields

After graduation, I started to work in accounting, and later I worked in a family trade. During this period, I attended lectures and completed training in Neurolinguistic Programming, which gave me insight into interpersonal communication. Now I dedicate a lot of time writing. I write PR and sales content for various Slovenian marketing agencies.

Social health and education system

I am proud that in Slovenia we are still trying to maintain the social system, as health care is relatively affordable in comparison to other countries. Also, studying in universities is free, so that even those who do not have finances can get a degree. In the business world, I have no experience of employers making differences between men and women. Work environments are safe and assure that you can get promoted as a woman.

Good conditions for moms

Parental care in Slovenia is very well regulated, which means that women can take paid maternity leave for one year. Mothers can be employed part-time when they return to work, while the difference to a full-time payroll is paid by the state. Mothers can get the help they need. Also, the price for daycare is determined according to wages, so all families can afford child care in this form.

Women in my life

Slovenia certainly has its shortcomings, so we must help each other, considering that only two million people live in the country. Regardless of the overall picture, the most important is family. I am grateful that I grew up with my grandmother and mother, who taught me a lot and prepared me for an independent life. I am also grateful for my female friends, with whom I have been hanging out since we were kids, my classmates at college, and later my female co-workers, who introduced me to the world of entrepreneurship.

My Life As A Woman: Somalia Edition

I am Sadia, born and raised in Somalia, especially in Hargeisa. I was born when the central government of Somalia collapsed. At that time civil war and conflicts began at the Somali territories. That left me with a lot of pain because two of my family members died. After refugee and displacement, normal life in Hargeisa resumed after 1994. We returned to Hargeisa where my family and I lived. From there we started life again. My mother and father were the reason for my upbringing and care when I was younger. Four years later, I have started my education trip here my city. Although the situation in the country was difficult, we were provided with free education from humanitarian agencies and the government.

I grew up, completed elementary and secondary learning, and finally joined to the university in 2012. I studied social work faculty. And finally, I graduated. The most important person I received financial support and advice from was my older brother and uncle, who was educated during Siad Barre Rule. My brother was the one who advised me to study and be knowledgeable. And my Uncle used to pay me for college because my parents were ignorant.

The opportunities that the girls have here in Somalia are limited. There are traditions and customs preventing girls to learn like boys and because of this, girls experience severe setbacks. Currently, there are civil wars and conflicts in some parts of the country, so the girl who learns is a girl who always faces challenges. Nowadays, girls are heavily supported by government and civil society organizations like Nagad Network.

When I was young I always wanted to be a doctor, but as I grew up I realized that I am good at social studies. When I graduated high school, I started college in social work. I was a part-time worker in an organization that specializes in social issues, especially non-formal education. I was a teacher in the afternoon shift, and I am glad to have participated in educating a lot of people who are now able to write and read. I am still working at the Mangalool Academy, an academy that works in community awareness on Khat, tribalism, reading and writing. I am director of finance. One of the people I taught to read and write was my mother who was an illiterate, but today she can write her name.

During my long educational journey, I faced many difficulties. I remember that many times I decided to quit school, because I didn't have anyone to support me and my family didn't have the money to pay for it. I'm talking about high school. Being a female student has many challenges including; shyness because you're studying with boys numerous than girls in the same class, so you can't participate actively on what's going on in the class. On the other hand, it is often preferred for men to study.

Part of my family has often pressured me to give up education and only boys are good at learning. They often discouraged me by saying, "The girl is good at house chores, only men can learn." Because here, Somali culture is harsh and cruel to women. Imagine we only had 9 girls to 35 boys in one class. It's really a tough situation. Things like menstruation causes girls to drop out of school since they don't have or cannot afford the proper hygienic tools to use in order for them to stay in school to keep learning. Parents often send boys to school while girls are to remain home for house chores. Later, I also faced employment challenges, because men still dominate the labor market. Currently only five women work at Mangalool Academy with twelve males.

I believe I have succeeded in the long process of my studies. And so far I am ready to achieve much more. Next year I want to start a Master of Social Science. I also took many career skills, including party decorations. I feel like I am in a better situation.

In Somalia, a woman's rights activist is harassed and accused said to be driving western ideology. Many women have been forced to quit their jobs for insulting them so becoming an active member of Somali society is also a challenge. My advice to women in Somalia is to trust themselves first, to learn and support one another, because men don't give them a chance. In 2020 there are many girls attending schools and universities. A brighter future for Somali girls is ahead. There are advocacy organizations that support the rights of women and children. Everyday life changes. Knowing that Somali women are living in difficult situations, I would say that women are better educated than men in many places.

My Life As A Woman: South Africa Edition #1

Salutations Queen. Today I greet you from sunny South Africa. My name is Zoe, and I was raised in a city named Eldorado Park. It sounds like the name of a funfair, right? In an ideal world. The city I speak of has become known as a gangster's paradise as the level of crime is rife and the community is notorious for being a playground to many a drug lord. I, unfortunately, lost my mother to a long battle with cancer, and my father soon moved on and remarried. Be that as it may, I was raised by my grandmother, a staunch Catholic God-fearing woman, who made me the independent, strong lady that I have become today. She instilled strong moral values in me, and she taught me, above all else, the importance of being a good person, a woman of integrity.

At the tender age of four, I decided that I wanted to a gymnast. I loved the poise and confidence that they exuded. This quickly changed, and I was convinced that I would be the next Martina Hingis. I was impressed with her skill and how agile she was on the tennis court. Fast forward to a few years later and I changed my mind, yet again. I set my sights on becoming a "Legal-Eagle" and was convinced that that would be the profession for me. In my view, lawyers were people who "had it together", acted with precision and were respected by the community at large. It is a good two decades later, and I am not pursuing either of the careers. Do I feel like a failure? Absolutely not. I am a seasoned short-term insurance specialist, the proprietor of a company that supplies goods and a successful online freelance business owner. I believe that this would not have been possible had it not been for my phenomenal grandmother's teachings coupled with the democratic multi-racial society that I was raised in.

The thing that I love about my country is the fact that there are so many diverse cultures, twelve official languages to be exact, and a multitude of colors. Each language represents a different ethnic origin and has a rich history, all of which is reflected by the official coat of arms, captioned "!ke e: /xarra //ke" which is the Khoisan language, and means diverse people unite. This to me encapsulates the objective of our nation. There is so much power in numbers, and so much can be achieved when co-operative strategies are developed.

I moved away from home after completing my tertiary studies and I must say, those were among the greatest years of my life. I was a liberated woman, living in modern society, and I was ready to take on the world. I learned a great deal of responsibility during that time and this transition prepared me for the world. The challenges which I encountered, include the fact that there had always been stereotypes that dictated that women were not as good as men in the corporate world, and because of this I had to work extra hard to earn my place at the table. Also, living in a post-apartheid country, I had to prove my worth as an individual of non-European descent, and it was through those actions that I managed to build a name for myself.

Before that, I had always had this supposition that once I had qualified as an attorney, I would travel across the globe with my fox terrier named Gigi, and we would take over the world. Today, I have a beautiful daughter and a loving husband. I am neither an attorney nor have I adopted my beloved Gigi yet, who knew? Life sure has its way of unfolding, all whilst you are busy formulating your plans. My plans for my life have done a complete 360-degree turn and yet, I am so proud of myself because above all else, my grandmother succeeded in her quest: I have turned out to be a good person. The fact that I have not followed through with any of my career goals does not make me any less of an individual. A degree can never overpower your innate abilities. It is through my life path, that I have come to know peace.

A word of advice, repurposing and a redirection is sometimes needed for you to reach true potential. Never sell yourself short; Never undermine your capabilities and always remember that you are a worthy Queen. You owe it to yourself.

My Life As A Woman: South Africa Edition #2

The life of a South African woman

While I, as a white woman born in RSA, could in no way possibly comprehend the struggle women of color have been through, I have learnt a fair share from the country that has raised me which I would like to share with you.

I was born in Durban, a city center of RSA, where I would spend half my childhood. I was lucky enough to have parents who earned a decent salary as my mother was in banking and my father in construction, this gave me the ability to attend a partially private school in Durban. My classes were diverse, as I tried to make friends with as many people as possible having started school a year early. We learned Zulu and Afrikaans as second languages, although I was far more fascinated with Zulu and all the different clicks the language used. While my family was well off, the economy did not express the same sentiment. The countries impeding junk status, brought on by a corrupt government, pushed my parents to start planning to move away. Although New Zealand was the plan, certain circumstances kept us on South African soil.

We planned to move south, within the border, away from the city and all its crime. I found myself in the quaint little town of Plettenberg Bay, in the Garden Route. It was a small town, with not many jobs available, just like the rest of South Africa. My mother started waitressing until she could find a job, which she got and left. Waitressing in a tourist town proved to be far more beneficial and profitable in comparison to a 9 to 5. We moved in 2010, the year of the FIFA world cup, held in South Africa.

My first memory of Plettenberg Bay was the South African soccer team beating Mexico, as I watched at a local golf club in the outskirts of town, this was the only game RSA would win while hosting. The raw passion and excitement are something that so greatly inspired me, seeing a group of people from different backgrounds, races, and ages enjoying the spirit of the game. It reminded me of the person who inspired me most, my great grandmother. A 99-year-old woman who we called chicken gran because she owned an insane amount of chickens for no other reason than to love them. My great grandmother had infinite amounts of love and passion to share, something South African people are so well known for. Her love for God was so pure, and at her age, you would expect different norms, but she accepted everyone as if they were her own. She was the embodiment of Ubuntu.

Growing up in RSA

Africa is known as the motherland and heart of the world for so many reasons, the evergreen natural scenery being one, but the community is the main for me. Apartheid was a terrible era of segregation, which many South African people are still feeling the burden of, it is something that will forever haunt our people, our land, and our economy. Despite the dreadful actions taken by my forefathers, South Africans want nothing more than to be the rainbow nation. Any time there is a rugby, cricket, or soccer match, South Africans have their flags, beers, and voices ready to chant with joy and unity. Ubuntu is a Zulu word or saying that sits very close to my heart ever since I found out what it meant. Roughly translated it means "I am because we are". To put it into action can be explained as a whole street of people standing in solidarity and silence as a single household mourns the loss of a loved one, as to not 'party' in the face of others' sadness. There is so much more to it, obviously, but to put it simply it's beautiful. It is this wholehearted love for our country which has made me want to pursue psychology, even since I was a child.

While being a woman certainly isn't easy, being a woman of color or a child of color is so much harder. All I have ever wanted to do is break that barrier of race and pain and help people grow from it. Being a woman, and knowing the additional struggles that come with it, has only made me want to fight harder for the things I and other women deserve. People of color deserve to know their worth, and while our corrupt government keeps free education and other amenities away from them, they deserve to know that they do deserve it. Our government has been stealing taxpayers' money for years now, money that could easily go towards helping fund underprivileged peoples' education so they can break the bonds of apartheid.

There's a lot they can't or don't have, at the end of the day, I at least wanted to give them a person who wants to listen and help. As a writer, I have made it my goal to bring attention to South African businesses and women, running a website that I hope will grow and give me the ability to sponsor full school years for underprivileged children. Any woman living in RSA not only has to struggle with the burden of the wage gap, domestic violence, and everything in between, we are also fighting a broken government and economy.

The future of RSA and South African women

Although the crime and government have made it harder for our economy and women to grow, the country has so much to offer. I hope that moving forward, we take all that love and passion trapped inside our people and we transfer it into the power of change. With an endless array of wildlife, vegetation, cultures, and people, South African people are beyond blessed to live in the heart of the world. If I could give any advice to a woman still growing up in RSA, it would have to be the cliché saying of "be the change you want to see".

We all have the power within us, some people see their powers less than others, so be that person to use it and share. We are the rainbow nation, but we wouldn't be so without our diversity, diversity that was once segregated. We need to take what little time we have on this earth to make it better so our children's children can live in a world without racism and sexism, but rather in a world of growing love for one another. It's best expressed by "I am because we are". Never give up hope, especially if you like me are living in the most beautiful country in the world. Appreciate your land and use the endless resources it has to do more. Do more so the country can do more, our strength is in our unity.

My Life As A Woman: South Africa Edition #3

I grew up in KwaZulu-Natal, and in my Zulu culture, we know that the toughest of all warriors in our history, King Shaka Zulu, was made so by his mother, Queen Nandi. She adored her son and made history by raising him into the man he became. She advised his war strategies, and each of his successes expanded the Zulu people's territory and influence across the land. In our history, women were regarded as strategic masterminds, and men executed their strategies down to the letter, from the family to the political level. In many traditional households, women still have the last say, although this has been diluted over time, as men used to believe that women were more closely connected to nature and the spirits, and therefore our counsel was sought and seen as the counsel of the spirits themselves.

Today, many homes are held together by grandmothers, aunties and older sisters, as they have the wisdom and foresight to guide those around them in accordance to what should be done to retain balance and harmony in the family. And we all hold these matriarchs in a very special place in our lives as we know we would not be where we are without their wise counsel. My mother's eldest sister, my MamKhulu (Big Mama), was that figure in our family. All of my cousins and I loved spending time around her because she understood each one of us and related to us individually, while taking up the responsibility of the traditional rituals and ceremonies that had to take place within the family. She was very strict about chores and respect when things had to get done, and when there were family gatherings in her home, she made sure we were well fed and taken care of, even letting us sneak into the cooler boxes to pour ourselves drinks in coffee mugs without our parents' knowing.

Growing up as my mother's only child, we developed an almost sisterly relationship with each other. She would take me on her shopping trips and thought it was the most fun activity, but I didn't like shopping for anything that wasn't for me. My main issue was how particular Mama was about what she bought: a bra had to come in a matching set or else she wouldn't buy it, even if we had spent close to thirty minutes looking through the intimate section for an exact match. Even though these shopping experiences were like pulling teeth, they apparently made a good impression on me, as I now design intimate sets and loungewear as a hobby in my spare time. By embracing my femininity, I help myself and many others to find joy and beauty in themselves.

When I grew up, I was overwhelmed by the options available in terms of vocation and career, it was almost impossible to choose. At one point I was determined to be a doctor, then a teacher, and even an accountant. I remember career day at my all girls high school, the buzz it created amongst us as the possibilities were almost endless. Most career options lured us in by emphasising how much money we would make, but I soon discovered that some of my strengths and affinities did not match up with conventional jobs that we available then.

After much research and help from my step-dad, I discovered a degree called Human Movement Science, which was a delicious mix between psychology, fitness and wellness. I studied that after high school, and because of the nature of the degree, it became apparent that I was going to have to build my own business with it. I have spent the past few years collecting experience through various work environments, from being a Ballroom and Latin-American dance instructor, to working in a private gym and even starting a massage business. I have accepted that it may take some time to build my business up to the level I desire, so I'm happy to grow at my own pace while I administrate for more established businesses to learn their systems and groom my customer service skills through interactions with their clients.

As a young woman, my biggest struggle yet has to be recognising that loving myself sometimes means saying 'no' to people and circumstances that undermine my potential and inner peace. While saying no often pushes away some friends, lovers and even relatives, it creates a breathing space where we learn to love ourselves correctly, and subsequently attract new people who will do the same. And my country is so full of beautiful women on the journey of self-love, we often inspire each other and build each other up, and form loving bonds with each other everywhere we go.

My Life As A Woman: South Africa Edition #4

As a 30-year white woman from South Africa, I would be considered privileged to have grown up with both my parents and grandmother, all under one roof. On the surface, we were a middle income, average family who were often disconnected, but ultimately, you knew you were loved. My mother was overprotective and perhaps this was because I was an only child. She always wanted the best for me, but this was often at the sacrifice of allowing me to learn what they don't teach you about life in school. She fought most of my battles and would come to my defense when I was shy; however, her strict standards that demanded the utmost academic performance, often created a cold, conditional relationship. My grandmother was softer and kind, although she could be pretty stern too! She passed to Alzheimer's Disease in 2015, which left an incredible hole in my heart, but her gentle and accepting smile remains one of my most comforting memories.

Women all over the world struggle with confidence and as a Southern African woman, I shared in that struggle. From primary school through high school I was bullied, even by my closest friends. I simply didn't know how to stand up for myself, and every insecurity from my weight to my academics, was under scrutiny.

Upon my admission to university, I was forced to think independently. I had to learn how to use public transport (which is not always reliable here in South Africa) and never being on my own, it was incredibly intimidating. My choice of major was psychology (no surprises there), and I went on to complete my post-graduate study. It was during my years of study that I began to consider my worth, what I could contribute and how I could take responsibility for my future without holding onto my past. One of the best lessons I learned was embracing those who had my best interests at heart and believing in my achievements no matter the challenges that came my way.

As a woman, you constantly compare yourself to others. Am I good enough, am I smart enough, am I pretty enough? I consider myself fortunate to have experienced a rich cultural diversity through high school and university, but the comparisons tend to intensify among women, no matter your background or race. Whether at a club waiting for you to trip in your newly acquired heels or the satisfaction of a "one up" when beating your score on a test, women tend to thrive on an unhealthy competitiveness rather than embrace one another. Today, I understand that confidence and self-love all depend on believing in yourself and knowing you are worth it, no matter your past, no matter your race or even the country you live in!

In South Africa, I have experienced crime. I have also experienced social prejudice based on economic standing, by white South African men and women. I live behind high fences and tend to look over my shoulder when out on my own, but I have also had the incredible opportunity to embrace and learn from so many different people with unique perspectives and life experiences. Each one, whether good or bad, has contributed to building my inner strength and helped me discover that I have a voice too.

I currently work as a counsellor for seniors, providing others the support they deserve while expressing my creativity and passion for language as a professional content creator.

From one South African woman to another, I want you to know that you are valued, you are strong, and you have the confidence to dream big. We share in the same struggles no matter our history, our financial status, or where we come from.

My Life As A Woman: South Africa Edition #5

Talking about life, Annika Jabulani has given her two cents growing up.

"Quite amusingly, my childhood was spent in quite a few places. Most of my early years were on a farm, in and around Pretoria, Guateng. When I was 11, we moved to a town called Richards Bay. I'm not afraid to put it out here that I grew up very poor. We barely had anything to eat at times and I certainly didn't have the best life growing up. My parents were always fighting with each other and me being the oldest, I had to take care of my two younger brothers, one of which was three and the other, eleven years younger than me."

Talking about inspiration, she says, "In my life, no one in particular inspired me. I always worked hard myself for what I wanted to achieve and accomplish. I guess you could say my motivation comes from within me."

Moving on to education and what Annika aspires to be, she says, "Currently, I'm about to get my degree in education at the National University of Tainan. As long as I remember, I've always wanted to be a teacher. I want to be a teacher to inspire children to be better and help those in need."

Annika goes on to say that, "What I love most about my South African culture is the social gathering. We love to get together and have what we call a Braai and have some beer. We as a group are friendly and love to socialize and just talk to each other."

Currently, Annika is a part-time teacher at a cram school in Tainan and she says that she absolutely loves her job.

She says, "As a woman, it is very difficult to get, especially the male students, to respect you. It is also hard to get things done because people think that I'm unable to do anything or decide by myself. In South Africa, it's dangerous for you to go somewhere alone and as a woman, it's even more challenging. This is because some men in South Africa see women as objects, use and abuse them. Men are also held in higher regard than women in my country."

No matter the odds, Annika says that nothing has let her stop as she's going to get her bachelor's degree soon. She says that this was made possible due to a substantial amount of financial aid from her family. She says, "I have succeeded in making a good life for myself in a foreign country and this is what I can call a personal achievement, or in other words, success. Where I come from, this is really something out of the question but here I am, I think I made it."

Annika has a bit of advice for the women of South Africa. She says, "My advice to women living in South Africa would be to take the bull by the horns and don't let a man walk all over you. If I can do it, you can too. Always go out with a friend and take care of each other. Try to learn smart ways to do everything and do your best to enjoy life."

This concludes My Life As A Woman: South Africa Edition.

My Life As A Woman: South Africa Edition #6

I grew up in a small town, about two and a half hours away from Cape Town, South Africa. I was fortunate enough to be raised in a loving stable home by both my mother and father, unlike many others around here. We lived with my grandmother, before moving into our own place when I was seven years old. Growing up I dreamt about becoming a Nurse, I always said, "because I sleep better during the day" and it was either going to be that or a police officer, I had no idea they work during the day too until I was much older. And unfortunately, I didn't get a chance to further my studies or even finish high school for that matter. I guess life just happened and threw me under a bus. We didn't have the money,'

I suffered from extreme anxiety and shyness, I fell pregnant when I was 19. The list goes on and on, on why I didn't complete all those things that I needed to, but I had a backup plan though, I couldn't do my two most loved careers, but I wasn't going to call anyone boss either! Throughout the years I've always looked for ways to be my own boss. I played the lottery, I've done sports betting, I made stuff, I sold stuff, I don't think there's anything I didn't do, I even started selling Avon at one point! I made money but not the kind of money that I wanted to be making. I'm still doing some of these projects because, hey it definitely pays my bills, but I discovered that I'm really good at baking and decorating "theme cakes & cupcakes". I started a business out of that and recently, before the COVID-19 pandemic, I celebrated making and selling my 100th custom ordered cake. I'm comfortable where I'm at in my life right now because I have everything I want and need, I can even provide for my son on my own, and this is something that I never thought I could do.

Here in South Africa, I identify as being "Coloured", and what I love most about my culture is the food! What I love most about South Africa is the diversity and warmth in everything. I wouldn't want to be anywhere else than right here at home.

The struggles I have/ had as a woman is probably, at one point feeling like a failure because I couldn't make my horrible relationship with my son's dad work and that I won't be able to survive being a single mother but I did and I became very successful at it, but that's a story for another day. My advice to other women is ladies please stop thinking the world owes you something, you'll find out the hard way that it really doesn't owe you anything. You have to make things work with what you have right in front of you. Don't expect anything from anybody, because in the end, all you really have is yourself.

My Life As A Woman: South Korea Edition #1

Hi, I am here to share how my life as a woman in Korea is to you out there. Let me briefly introduce myself first. I am an 18-year-old Korean girl, living in a small city near the capital city of South Korea, Seoul. I went to a Women's high school and now I go to one of the most famous universities in my country, majoring in engineering. Regarding my personality, I am very outgoing and extroverted, so I enjoy hanging out with my friends a lot. Lastly, I have a boyfriend, with whom I have been together for a little bit less than a year. Ok, so I guess that was enough for a brief explanation about myself.

In my city, where I've grown up and still live, the average wealth of citizens is higher than that of the nation, which, in turn, means that people are usually more conservative than radical. Actually, this is one reason I could possibly think of while trying to understand why one of four high schools in my city has to be only for women. It was in the freshman year, when almost all the girls in my school, obviously including me hated the fact that there's no single boy in high school so much that we were trying to convince ourselves of the existence of our own school. (lol) But, surprisingly, throughout the 3 years of high school, we happened to find out we were kind of lucky to be assigned to a women's school. Personally, I think it was one of the main reasons why I was able to enter my current university, because I could fully concentrate on my study without any need to care about my appearance or having a crush on anyone. Also looking back from now, I think it was when my high self-esteem formed, since I am one of those people who easily get hurt by boys.

After graduation, the environment around me had changed a lot since I had majored in engineering, where boys are the majority. So currently I not only hang out with boys a lot, but also there are many occasions where I need to cooperate or compete with them. Although they usually try to help me out and care about me, I often find being the only girl in a group uncomfortable. But it's usually about small facts like me not enjoying video games as much as they do, and I think that kind of feeling arises from the fact that I'm the minority there.

Since I always try to think positive and am still young, I don't really confront struggles as a woman in my daily life. However, I do see many people who have struggled, and they sometimes really impress me. For example, I want to be a CEO in the future, and one day I was doing some research about it, which led to finding out only less than 10 people from the list of CEOs of 100 major companies in Korea are women. Shocked, I seriously started to question the possibility of becoming a decent CEO as a woman, not to mention a successful one. At the same time, I could feel the pain that many potent female entrepreneurs should have gone through when they confronted those glass ceilings.

Though, what I love about my culture is that people are willing to make changes to those extreme outcomes. As a young Korean, I see many girls taking up important positions in many different groups whether they are academic or business, and also boys don't think they should be on a higher status than women, which is quite different from the expectations of prior generations. Therefore, if I am to give advice to those girls who are growing up in Korea, I would tell them just not to even think about those barriers between sex, and only focus on becoming a better person. Then, they will naturally end up being beloved and respected by people around them.

My Life As A Woman: South Korea Edition #2

Let's start here: I was born in Seoul. My parents are well-educated, and I was afforded every opportunity I wanted as a child. Back then, blissfully unaware of my relative position in society, I never thought about my privilege; I just asked for what I wanted. Piano lessons? Sure. Taekwondo? Why not. And finally, when I discovered my passion for books, a private writing tutor. My mother was stingy about spending on my entertainment—I grew up staring longingly at my friends' toys and gadgets—but she never turned me down when I asked for money to buy books or lessons. I owe everything I am now to this.

Seoul is an incredible backdrop for a childhood. A mountain standing in the center of a sprawling metropolis, galleries and museums at every corner, an intense nationwide passion for education, and most of all, the glittering lights of the Han river at night. And the people! Young professionals in crisp suits, old women selling yoghurt drinks at the street corner, and people from all over the world gathering in Itaewon bars to unwind after a long day in a foreign country. I grew up in this beautiful chaos, and I grew to love it. But not since the beginning.

I had trouble dreaming big, because on a certain level, women are not taught to dream big in Korea. This has been changing rapidly, but nevertheless, it is a culture that persists, and it was certainly present in my childhood. During our annual New Year's family gatherings, all the women were called to help out in the kitchen and carry the food to the big table set up for our ancestors. They were undoubtedly the ones cleaning up afterwards, too. My family is fairly progressive, and the men always gave a hand, clearing the table and bringing the plates back and forth, but most families just a couple of decades ago had all men sitting in the living room watching television and talking politics while the women toiled away. And besides, perhaps the most dangerous group in any unequal system of power is the "fairly progressive"—those who believe they are doing enough, and therefore that they are absolved of guilt, while still perpetuating the power they hold over others while maintaining a facade of empathy.

At one particular New Year's gathering, a distant relative asked me what I wanted to be when I grew up. I hesitated before answering, "I think I'd like to be an author." He instantly laughed and replied, "an author? Why would you want to be something like that?" To this day, I wonder if he would have said the same thing had I been a boy and not a girl.

Thankfully, my own mother had long since been fed up by Korea's misogyny and was determined to raise me differently. She never told me I had to do something or couldn't do something because I was a girl; in fact, I grew up seeing her wearing "girl power" t-shirts. I was in high school and my passion for feminism was just beginning to intensify when the Me Too movement broke out across the world. My mother was the first to sign and circulate a statement on behalf of female professors standing in support for the movement and calling for Korean universities to support women. It was at that time that she first opened up to me about how she had faced workplace discrimination all her life. She had been turned down for countless jobs when she moved back to Korea from the U.S. and told employers she was raising a small toddler. She had been passed up for promotions despite having done more work and written more papers than the men. Even now, in her position of success at the best university in Korea, she is often the only woman in the room.

And as disheartening as those stories were for a young teenage girl to hear, my mother thought it was important for me to know that I was swimming against the current. But the current was growing weaker, thanks to the powerful women that have come before me. Women like her. I am now working towards my degree in creative writing at Stanford University, and when I start doubting my work, I remind myself that I have a duty to dream big; to continue fighting against the current, to show those women that their fight has been worth it, and to create a better world for my future daughter. Korea has a long way to go, but I, like my mother, will help its journey.

My Life As A Woman: Spain Edition

I grew up in a condo in the outskirts of Madrid, in a fairly average family for the time. My father worked in construction while my mother was a homemaker. I am an only child, so as you can probably imagine, I was brought up in quite a coddled way. We used to spend the weekend camping in nearby towns with our caravan, sometimes on our own, sometimes with friends and other campers. That was a big part of my childhood and one that I really enjoyed! My parents taught me the love for travelling and discovering new things and that has stuck with me throughout my life.

I used to talk a lot to my father, I remember him reading books with me sitting by his side and reading the same page. I thought he didn't notice that I was reading back then, though in hindsight I can tell, because he turned the page when he noticed that I was getting anxious and not a moment before! I talked to him about all the things that I wanted to be when I grew up. I had an architect phase, followed by a time where I wanted to be an archaeologist and then a cook. Thankfully for the gastronomy world, I didn't choose the latter!

I went to school in my neighbourhood where I met friends that have stayed by my side until this day! Not to brag, but I was a fairly decent student! Then came the time to switch to high school, where I discovered a passion for history and philosophy and in the end, I enrolled in college to get a History degree, which I must admit I never finished.

I got caught into travelling! In the space of a couple of years, I got to know England, France, Italy and Perú. I was so captivated by the lifestyle in France that my trips there started to become recurrent, specially to the south of France and Paris. France is a very special country that keeps some of the Mediterranean warmth while incorporating a heavy influence of Northern European countries that create what to me is a perfect hybrid of both places!

My many travels started to make me feel more and more detached from my country at first, but eventually, the more I travelled, the more I learnt to appreciate my own country and its way of life! We Spaniards have a quite particular character, an absolute lack of respect for personal space, a tendency to speak louder than necessary, and a kind of addiction for being on the streets! However, we have a natural warmth, great social skills, and a predisposition to see strangers as friends to be that I haven't found anywhere else.

Living as a woman in Spain doesn't come without challenges. While we are a fairly open country and we are working towards becoming more and more egalitarian and inclusive, there is still a bit to be done in matters of gender equality when compared to other European countries. It is incredibly challenging to be successful in your career at the same time that you have a family, and there are still many companies who find it appropriate to ask whether you're single or married or if you're planning on having children during an interview.

Fortunately, I've managed to have a successful career of my own as a writer and translator that works in my own terms, so I feel fairly lucky! My life is nothing like what I pictured, but I wouldn't change a bit of it!

Nowadays I work in the comfort of my home office, surrounded by my four cats and my husband, in a house that means a lot to me for its history! It is my advice to women from my country to learn to stand up for yourself and lose the fear to say no, especially in career-related affairs! Know your worth and don't be afraid to negotiate, there are many opportunities out there for you if you are patient enough!

My Life As A Woman: Canary Islands Edition

"A woman should be two things: who and what she wants." -Coco Chanel-

I was a child, but I perfectly remember that hot August afternoon, when my grandmother, in a vain attempt to fix my rebel curls, said to me: "My little girl, hope that your today's dreams come true tomorrow, and that you could turn every challenge of life into a possibility."

Many years have passed since that afternoon, and today, when I look in the mirror, I'm proud of the woman I have become: an independent woman who chose her own way. My name is Manola M. I grew up in a small town in the north of Italy, Zingona.

As everybody knows, "THE FAMILY" is the most important aspect of the Italian's culture and mine, was very traditional; there was my father, the worker and head of the family, who dreamed of me as a teacher, and then there was my mother, the perfect housewife, who had given up her career to take care of the family and saw me as a future wife and loving mother. My younger brother? Well, he could be simply who he wanted to be.

Fortunately, there was my grandmother, who the only thing she repeated to me, was to choose my own path and grow up as a "free" woman. I studied Languages at high school and Communication at university. I wanted to travel, discover the world and translate it into words. But I wanted to escape from a future that others wanted for me, too. While around me my friends got engaged, formed a family and planned how to furnish their houses, I saved all the money I could to travel and enrich my thirst for knowledge.

When I finished the University, I decided to study Journalism, between the mumbles of my mother, more and more upset by my choices and the reticence of my father, who already imagined me as a globetrotter with a notebook and an uncertain future.

I let them talk, and I thought angrily about the typical stereotypes that wanted women responsible for taking care of her husband, children and house; as if a woman's life was enclosed in a series of "roles". Wake up girls! There are no duties to follow! every woman is first to fall a free individual, with her own life and her way to go! With these beliefs I did not think twice when I received an e-mail from Rome for an institutional collaboration as a journalist. Years went by, I earned good money but the frenetic rhythms of the city, mixed with those of work, were turning me off; I had no more time for myself and my passions. I felt like I was in a cage, in a big and chaotic metropolis.

I decided that it was probably time to make new choices, take on new challenges, so in 2014 I bought a one-way ticket to Fuerteventura of Canary Island. I needed to experience new opportunities in a different and more relaxed setting. The beginnings were not easy at all. A new country, a language to learn, and no one to count on, but I was determined not to give up.

I started making friends and I soon realized that here too, stereotypes about women were strongly rooted. Traditional culture was quite patriarchal, and it was not so strange to see young mothers of 15 or 16 years. Later, I found out that the school dropout rate was very high especially among girls, and for many of them the process of empowerment was seen with diffidence.

I was so angry! I had flown 4000 km away, and here too, the process of female emancipation was far from being fully accomplished. For my part I reinvented myself a thousand times and in a thousand jobs: I did online translations, gave private English lessons, worked in an excursion agency and as a tour guide. Every challenge is for me a new opportunity. I don't have children, I am a mediocre housewife, I can barely take care of succulents, I don't wash any husband's socks and I love to travel alone.

No pre-established role to be respected, only my life to live. Girls, break down barriers, escape from roles. Be free to be who you want to be and live the life you chose without regrets. Then, look in the mirror and be proud of the woman you are.

My Life As A Woman: Solomon Islands Edition

I am Rose, I am currently living in Honiara, Guadalcanal. That's a part of the Solomon Islands. I was born in Santa Isabel, which is also in the Solomon Islands. That's where my parents met and planned to live until my mother died from the flu. After my mother's death, my father moved to Honiara to raise me and become a teacher. My father and I have a very close bond, he's the only family I had. We did everything together and ensured each other was okay. My father is my inspiration, he was one of the very few male teachers, and even though he faced challenges, he still loved his job. He always said teaching was one of the best ways to change the future of society. He said if you change the mindset of the children, you can change the outcome of future society.

The school system in Solomon isn't as important as they should be, school isn't compulsory. Half the students don't even finish primary school. The literacy rate is around 76% and there is more attention placed on learning a vocational skill. My father made sure I knew the importance of education. I attended the Burns Creek Primary School and then went to the King George VI National High School. I always wanted to be a ballerina, but I realized that wasn't a practical career choice for my current situation. I decided to attend teachers college after finishing high school. I became a mathematics teacher and started teaching at a local primary school.

I love our strong Christian faith. I was raised in the church, and my father took his faith very seriously. He made sure I understood how faith works and its importance. I love how crafty we are; we can create beautiful pieces from any random material. We have some of the best wooden craft and weave crafts. Creativity and quality of our items are the best.

Growing up, I was always jealous of the relationship other girls had with their mother. Even with my father playing an active role in my life and always being there for me, I still missed having my mother there. They are things only a mother can understand and teach you. Also going to school made me feel like a misfit, because education wasn't important. It felt like I was odd. More than half the children my age were not going to school.

With all of that, I realized I wasn't the odd one. They were, getting an education is the most important thing. Becoming a teacher, I am now able to inspire children to stay in school. Inspiring them brings joy to me, it makes me feel like I am doing my part to change Solomon Island. To all the women of Solomon Island, your education is very important. Education is the only way you can get out of poverty. Being out of the situation will make your life better. You are not restricted to poverty, you can get out of that situation. Also, not because everyone is ignoring school you should too. You have two choices, one following the norm, or two creating your part.

My Life As A Woman: Sri Lanka Edition

Sri Lanka is a highly tourist attracted country that is popular for the amazing history it carries and of course the tea! You can visit Sri Lanka as much as you want but the beauty is hearing the story of someone who already lives there. My name is Sarah, and this is my story as a woman living in Sri Lanka.

The first memory I have of myself is staring out of a window in a small town called Kandana. The house I lived in back then was averagely small yet very comfortable. And my two elder sisters and I would play all day long. Sometimes I would just watch them play through that window and that memory stuck with me all these years and I still have no explanation as to why I still remember it but here I am now at the age of 20 telling you all about it.

The preschool I went to was in that same town. And secondary school was a 20min drive. When I was in 2nd grade I would point at this particular class and I would tell my mom "mama I will be a teacher in that class someday". I loved to teach when I was young especially because I was a very weak student in class. Both my parents and teachers were worried for me as I was a slow learner. I couldn't read or write until 5th grade and I used to score pretty bad marks and I was always positioned among the last five students in class. I had very few friends who would support me with studies and when it was time to read aloud, I would stand up for my turn and just silently stare at my book until the teacher would ask me to just sit down.

However, when I was in 5th grade I tried to read books and I began to write small stories on a tiny book such as "myself". And I would draw something next to that story to dictate what I've written. Soon enough I was able to read and write. And here I am today a professional writer, artist, and a college going student who is always among the top scorers and for my friends, I am the go to person for help with assignments. And of course, reading became my favorite hobby. Whilst working in my dad's company and handling college education, I also do freelance writing.

As a woman in Sri Lanka one of the biggest struggles is the misogyny. I grew up hearing stories about women who were forced to marry at a young age and how people believed a 'housewife' is what a woman should be. In the 1940s, women in Sri Lanka were not believed to have big goals and ambitions. And my mom would say about a common phrase people used those days "a woman's brain is not more than the size of a wooden spoon". I would be so disturbed hearing this.

Yet my parents always made sure me and my sisters would have big goals and ambitions. My dad would always tell us that we could even be President if we worked hard for it and my mom would say, "it's important that a woman is independent and has her own job because being dependent narrows down your decisions". Because of this I decided never to settle for an average life. This became more realistic to me in hearing the story of the world's first non-hereditary woman head of government Sirimavo Bandaranaike, when she became the prime minister of Sri Lanka. These situations have led me to realize what a woman is capable of. And that a woman is more than just a "housewife".

A woman is not made just to cook and clean. You are much more. You are talented, you are ambitious, and YOU are capable. Don't ever give up searching for the purpose in your life. That curiosity might just about lead you to your destiny. But if you don't try you'd never know.

If you are a wife or a mother and you feel this void deep down your heart that says "you are much more than this" then I must say you are able to do much more. I'm not saying that you should file a divorce and leave your kids. Definitely not! What I'm saying is go and search for who you are really meant to be. It can be a writer, influencer, and banker or if you never got to go to college then go ahead and do that too! You will never know what it might lead to. Who knows, you are probably a hidden bud waiting to blossom?

When I was young, struggling to read, write and draw, I never thought I would be a writer someday nor an artist. And I never expected reading to be my hobby either. And of course, never did I think that I would even be a top scoring student in college. I thought I'd hardly pass secondary school.

Just think, what if YOU were supposed to be the first woman to ever discover a new planet or what if you were supposed to be the first female Prime Minister or President in your country? But you never got to do that because of the misogyny in your country. Don't let circumstances or who you were when you were young define who you will be someday. No matter what, you are capable!

My Life As A Woman: Sudan Edition #1

I am Alia Ansari from Port Sudan city of Sudan. I was born in Khartoum, but I grew up in Port Sudan. We live in a city where you can enjoy different things, at least the sea view makes it one of the best cities of Sudan.

My family is a very modern family. My father has a big supermarket in Khartoum. Unlike the majority of women in Sudan who work in agriculture, my mother works in an office in Khartoum. I am, however, a little far from them. My brothers are still studying.

The way I grew up was very different. My father is a man of principles. He has many principles that how to live or how to respect others. Even when we sit in a table to eat, we have to remember the etiquette of eating. We grew up in a very modern way.

When I was 14, my family moved to Khartoum, just because of some financial problems. But when I got my bachelor's degree, soon I came to port Sudan. I studied law in university of Khartoum. I work at the office of ministry of finance. But the reason why I moved to Port Sudan was something completely different. I moved to Port Sudan because I wanted to work at the city where I grew up.

I want to have an online business to use my time to help others from different parts of the world. I have already started my own business online, but I want to make it bigger.

Islam has influenced everything in my country, including our culture. But at some points, people abused the name of Islam to do many bad things. For example, music is very popular and also a traditional thing in our country, but some of the most popular singers have been arrested. This is a very old idea that music is prohibited in Islam. This is a completely personal thing of how someone receives something.

The thing that I love a lot about our culture is that our people are very kind and also very sweet. Respect to elders is very important for us. For example, when we sit around a table to eat, we don't start eating until the eldest member starts eating. I think that this is unique.

In Sudan, women live very poorly. About 70 percent of them work in agriculture. But only 10 percent of them work in offices. Girls only study the basics of writing and reading. But boys study university and go further. For me, studying at university was very hard. You can rarely see a girl studying at university.

My biggest success as a woman is that I started maintaining my own needs when I was in high school. I was working as a freelancer and had the job of editing and writing articles.

My message to all women in the world is very short. I say to all of them to think differently. Thinking positive makes everything different.

My Life As A Woman: Sudan Edition #2

I was born in El-Obeid a town in Northern Kordofan but was raised and continue to live in the capital Khartoum. I am the youngest of six siblings and I come from a middle class, Muslim, lenient and an educated family. I have amazing parents who raised and treated us well.

My siblings and aunt were my inspiration when it comes to how they perceived life and their achievements. Although each were having their own struggles they were the people I looked up to.

Ever since I was little, I dreamt of travelling to other places, therefore I used to draw different sceneries than the ones in my environment and always replied 'Ambassador' when asked, "What you want to be when you grow up?" But my life took a more creative turn.

'Reality Check'

As an introvert Sudanese woman, everything changed for me once I got into college socially and mentally. I was hit by reality. It felt like I was living in a bubble maybe because my parents were trying to keep me safe. The outside world was cruel. People think differently, people were shallow. People were racist.

As being a woman in a country that has an identity crises with many layers to it, just like a babushka as it's not enough that I am a woman, there's more discrimination to the word on the basis of race, ethnicity, religion and gender.

So, as long as you are a Northern Sudanese woman with Arabic facial features, lighter skin tone and good financial status, you are privileged and consider yourself on the top. Other than that, your life will differ as you are a minority. It affects all aspects of your life.

Who you'll marry due to different tribes refusal to marry from each other and of course when it comes to the north, they see themselves as pure Arabs and they don't want to ruin their race. Moreover, how others treat you, job positions, etc. Needless to say, that this leads women of darker tones to bleach their skin to feel beautiful and be accepted in such a society. It makes both genders from the minority question themselves worth. I blame mothers, as they make societies and racism, which is surely taught, as nobody is born with it.

'Women are women's worst enemies'

As a result, you find yourself longing to run away to a healthier environment where you don't struggle to be yourself. However, what happens when you make the wrong decisions or for other women in Sudan who are helpless and have no support or haven't completed their education; traditional marriages happen.

My sisters, for example, suffered from society's pressure to get married no matter what they achieve in their professional life, they get reminded of what they are missing.

But there are women who find it easier to adjust with the society and its customs, traditions, and terms. They somewhat looked content to me, much happier. So I told myself, why not try this way as my goals from marriage was to settle down, focus on my studies, try intimacy for the first time and lastly make a warm home, but 2 years later, I returned to my parent's house with a 16 month old boy and more determination to chase off my dreams.

As the mindset of a typical Sudanese man refuses to accept a rebellious woman no matter how open-minded he claims he is, a smart Sudanese woman has to cramp her intelligence in order for the boat to keep floating. Consequently, my experience has taught me that there's a solution for every problem and to never take a shortcut or settle down for something lesser than you deserve, to fix myself first and to believe in it. Work and education can be like oxygen, and when you love yourself and accept it no matter what external factors you encounter, they will not affect you.

My Life As A Woman: Sudan Edition #3

Hello, universe. I am writing this article on behalf of all women in Sudan. I was raised and born in Sudan and I live in a small city called Port Sudan. Life in Sudan is very difficult and complicated for a woman because you cannot fulfill all your dreams because your name is only a woman. I grew up in a community where almost anything that women do, is shame on them! As for my family, their thoughts are not as complicated as most of the Sudanese. They didn't cut my wings, but at the same time, they did not give me absolute freedom because I am a woman.

For me, I am a very curious person and I love studying and I don't like anyone to tell me that I can't do this and that I love to try everything by myself. I found that I took my personality from my grandfather and my father, because they love studying and sanctifying work, and they inspire me to move forward and fulfill my dreams. I have completed my basic and secondary education and enrolled in the university that I want red sea university, and I am now studying English and media.

As for my talents and dreams since I was little girl, I loved fashion designing. I always drew designs for dresses and costumes. I am grateful that finally one year ago, at the age of 17, I achieved one of a thousand of my dreams in Sudan, and I am now designing the most beautiful outfits. What I love about Sudanese culture is our constant generosity and sympathy for others, and we do not have racism and we are very social, we cannot sit one day at home without visiting our neighbors and chatting with them. If one of our neighbors or our family has a marriage, we complete all the marriage. We do not let them pay anything. The neighbors do not let you bring a chef, they cook for you all the food, they don't let you clean the house, they clean for you and everyone supplies food products and drinks they do the same at funerals. As for marriage, the family of the groom and bride they don't let you leave without putting henna on your hands for both men and women and they make sure that you are well and filled with hospitality. The groom's friends bring him the sheep and cows and give him money to complete his marriage, and they always volunteer. The groom honeymoon trip all pays out.

In Ramadan, fasting men break their fast on the street, every man brings his food and drinks and they invite all the strangers and homeless people who fast on the street to break their fast with them. Our Sudanese culture is endless, I can't talk about it in one night, this was just a simple example from our culture. Currently, I am studying but I work from home because I cannot work outside the home until I complete my university. We have no such thing called equality between men and women.

In Sudan, men can achieve anything they want, even if what they do is wrong, nobody tells them they are wrong, why?! The answer is simple just because they are men. But woman, huh!!! If she breathes, shame on her. Anything we want to achieve, we just can't, our simple, shattered dreams, our pent-up feelings, the struggle inside us, that nobody hears. We just want our most basic rights, we want equality, we want to live as you live, men.

Most Sudanese women success and work from home, they can't achieve their success outside the home because their men will not allow them to, and I am one of them. Sudanese women work from home as chefs, or tailors, or painters, and the list is still ongoing, all of them are creative, but no one appreciates their creativity. Not only Sudanese women, there are many women around the world who have not attained their most basic rights and they will not if they are silent and allowing this to happen.

Last word from one woman to another. Never allow anyone to shatter your dreams and tell you that you can't do it, you will never know unless you try it by yourself and make mistakes once or twice. Nobody birthed success. There is no difference between us and them, the difference is that they fought for their dreams. Show them that the impossible is possible. Fight for the things you love and do all what you want to do. Don't let anyone stop you. Don't wait for tomorrow. Do it now. Don't be afraid. Put all the confidence in yourself and you will do it.

written by: *Shima Osman*

My Life As A Woman: Suriname Edition

Growing up I was the quiet child in the house, an introvert, the one that did not care for mindless chatter and family get-togethers. My mother did not mind my reclusive nature as she also had introverted tendencies. Family members, on the other hand, could not stomach my inherent nature as in the Surinamese culture it is frowned upon to be a hermit.

I was born and raised in Suriname, a small tropical country situated on the northeastern Atlantic coast of South America. Suriname is known for its rich cultural diversity and history. Suriname is a melting pot of different races and cultures. The country has a population of approximately 500,000 inhabitants. But what I like most about my culture is first and foremost the good food and the tolerance we exhibit for each other's race and religious preferences. I mean only in Suriname will you find people from all backgrounds, races, and religions come together to celebrate Holi Phagwa as one big party.

I grew up in a single-parent home where my mom was the matriarch, queen of the castle. To say that I inherited a lot of her mannerism is an understatement. My mother was a hard worker and so am I. Even though I had a great relationship with my father while growing up, his mannerism did not rub off on me as strong as my mom's did.

I remember my school years as being fun. From elementary to high school, it was really fun I should say. While growing up entrepreneurship always appealed to me, so I wanted to be an entrepreneur. Even though my mom encouraged every last one of my decisions, the thought of being an entrepreneur was not entertaining to most people and I did not receive the support that I needed to get started.

After graduating from high school, I entered college and studied tourism management. I graduated in 2014 with a degree in Hospitality and Tourism Management. That year I also started a blog to jot down my thoughts and feelings. For me writing was liberating, a tool I could express myself with, something I could use to reach out to the world and connect with the world.

After I had graduated college, I entered the job market and that's where my struggles as a young woman looking for a job in a male-dominated workforce, where friends are preferred and diplomas and qualifications are repelled, started. Even though I was college-educated with a degree, finding work was a struggle. It was exhausting! I ended up working a couple of dead-end jobs until I got fired in the fall of 2017. That's it, I said, I'm going to focus on my writing and transform it into a business I can earn a decent income from.

I ended up taking a couple of courses to learn how to monetize my writing. And because I already knew a couple of influential people online, this really wasn't a problem for me. I blogged rigorously on my own website, guest posted on several influential websites such as addicted2success.com, and started to sell my writing services on fiverr.com and other platforms.

Today, I am a successful freelance writer and blogger. Apart from writing articles, I also create case studies, news releases, email marketing newsletters, and more. My specialty is writing about finance and financial related topics, but I have written about literally every topic imaginable. You see, in my country, most people are still stuck in the old way of thinking. They still believe that the only way to gain financial security is through a job especially a government job. The old adage of school, then working for a boss for years, and finally retire is still deeply ingrained in their psyche. Especially, young women who just graduated high-school or university, they all seek government employment.

As a woman living in the smallest country on the continent of South America, I want to let young women know that it is OK to strive for more than just government employment. It's O.K. to believe in yourself and what you have to offer this world and go for it. Finally, thank you for reading my story, if we never meet in real life, through this story, we have met.

My Life As A Woman: Sweden Edition #1

I grew up in Gothenburg Sweden, the second biggest city in Sweden. My country is known to be one of the most equal countries in the world and on some levels, I believe that's true. Personally, I've never really faced discrimination because of my gender, which I'm very grateful for. however, I've felt unsafe during night time and I've heard others express stereotypical opinions on women.

I grew up in a very hard working and supportive family, they've always supported me and wanted me to be the best I can be. I've wanted to be plenty of things during my short lifetime, when I was younger, I wanted to be a dentist for some odd reason. As I grew older, I wanted to be an actress and then a heart surgeon to help those like me with heart issues. But my goal was always changing and I'm still not sure what I want to be. During my life, I've never really had anyone who inspired me except for myself. I am my own inspiration and I believe that I'm the only one who can help myself succeed. However, I still look up to the woman in my family. All of them have always been very hard working and determined, my great grandma started working at 13 years old in a perfume store during the 1940's. My grandma was a nurse before she retired, and my mom is currently studying to pursue her dream. They all seem to have known what they want and went for it.

A year ago, I graduated from high school. I studied the technology program with focus on design and production. Therefore, my class was mostly filled with guys. We were around 4 girls and 26 guys in my class which for me was a huge change from compulsory school where the majority of my class was girls. When I met my new class for the first time, I was very nervous, I had never really talked to guys before and now I kind of had to. But most of them were very kind and didn't look down on me for being a woman studying a game development focused program. Even though I was never really treated differently at my school because of my gender I still believe that studying this program made me realize how big of a problem stereotype still are. It seems as if things such as technology and gaming are interpreted as a "guy" thing and something most girls don't engage in even though that isn't true. In one of our courses we had to write a paper on technology and gender where we wrote about why there's such a small number of girls attending these kinds of programs. I believe it's because gaming and technology is mostly marketed towards boys which makes girls believe that it isn't something for them and that is a stereotype we need to break.

I haven't lived a very long life so far; I've only been on this earth for 19 years and therefore, I haven't been able to experience a lot of career successes yet. For me it's the small things that I'm proud of such as graduating from the technology program after 3 years of studying. And getting into vocational university to study to become a Public Bid Manager. I'm proud of getting a good grade on a test, managing to start writing on a book and to finally find the courage to stand up for myself when I have to.

My advice for women in Sweden is to fight for what you want and don't let anyone get in your way. You are your own inspiration and only you can help yourself so do just that. And don't be afraid to stand up for yourself and what you believe in.

My Life As A Woman: Sweden Edition #2

Dear sisters, today is a great day in my life. I am humbled that the Stockholm women's group has selected me to speak today on behalf of women not only here but all over the world.

Ella Andersson was born on 12 June 1995, Stockholm slum in Sweden. I grew up with my father, who was a gateman in our school, and he did everything as a father to support us. We were born only two girls in a family of three boys. Life was tough, but our father tried the best for his family.

I would like to thank my father for not clipping my wings and for letting me fly. My dad, he inspires me to be patient in life and always speak the truth. Those words are still a strong message to any woman out there, always focus, and be patient as I learn that from my father.

Dear sisters, when I was young, my dream was to be a doctor and help as many in the world, including my people from Sweden. I did my best in school to achieve my goal. Since I was not born from a rich family, that did not stop my dream. My father always used to tell us, "education is one of the blessings in the life of a girl." That has been my experience during the 24 years of my life. I tried my best when I was in college, studying what I wanted to do. There were challenges, but I always believe in God that one day I will defeat poverty in our society.

Sweden culture

Over my life, I have always been proud of my Swedish culture. One thing we grow up knowing is that you need to respect someone and listen to others whatever he or she is saying. We are proud to be born in a Nation where people speak softly and calmly. Because of the egalitarianism in Sweden, every child including girls, are encouraged to raised and believe that they are all equal. We thank our government for always being there to support kids, especially the effort they put on our girls.

My work

Right now, as I am speaking to you, I am working as a doctor in Karolinska Universitetssjukhuset Solna. I am now able to save my people from Sweden, and I travel to different parts of the world. Despite all the struggles, I have gone through, I never give up and always believe the key to success is patience. I am working in a different institution not only to speak as a woman but also to strengthen all women.

Challenges in life can also give you hope and hard work in whatever you are doing in your days as a woman. My advice to a woman, we need to raise our voice in our society and educate our girls. Do not allow challenges you are facing today to overcome you. Remember, today may be hard, tomorrow will be much better. Work hard and stay focused in your life.

Lessons

Always remember as a woman, you have to stand firm and other people will follow your path. I was born in a low-income family, grew up in a slum that did not stop me from where I am today. Dear sisters in our nation and the rest of the world, we must work, but not wait. Let us all, women and girls, decide to be the last and become the first generation that decides all girls must give equal education like a girl and start working in big factories. Let us stop forcing a girl into early child marriage. Let us all act right here, right now, and support our girls to study hard in schools. Thank you so much.

My Life As A Woman: Switzerland Edition

I live in Switzerland, a country known to be well organized, clean, and rich. It's viewed as the land of banks, money, wealth, and punctuality. Here is a take on how I grew up and how that probably gives me a bit of a different view on Swiss life and especially Swiss life as a woman.

Me, myself & I - in Switzerland

I was born in the Italian part of Switzerland but spent the first 5 years of my life in Zurich in the German part of the country. Then my mother re-married and we moved to Crete, the Greek island. I spent the rest of my childhood in Greece and went to school there until I returned to Zurich as a teen for attending a professional ballet school, while my family stayed in Greece.

I was a determined kid and quickly learned to be independent. This might partially be owed to the fact, that I initially found myself in an unknown environment when we first moved to Greece, that I did not speak the language and my mother had to work long hours. But I am also simply quite an introvert, very much love my personal freedom, and often not patient enough to wait for others to get things done.

By the age of 13, I decided to move back to Switzerland, because I got accepted by the Swiss Professional Ballet School, which at that time was a dream come true. I lived with my grandmother for the first 3 years, who was originally Italian and then moved into a residential group home for young people. Most of my flat mates came from difficult circumstances, so I once more was somehow a "unicorn".

During that time, I began a commercial apprenticeship and had to give up ballet due to a boost of polyarthritis. Admittedly the prospect of becoming a professional ballet dancer also decreased because of my body going through quite a change, becoming more feminine to say so. It was a time of change in general and I also decided to move into my own apartment shortly before becoming 18. I just felt I needed my own space.

Although I had times where I seriously considered moving back to Greece, it somehow never happened. After the apprenticeship, I worked for a while and then started studying communication and journalism. During that time, I also started working for the executive department of gender and diversity at the university I studied at and with that finally found a field I really liked and was interested in. By 22, I got together with my now-husband and after 5 years, during the last year of my studies, I got pregnant with my first child. By now I am a proud mother of three kids and still work in the field of communication.

Same, but different - women in Switzerland

Obviously living in Switzerland, I got the chance to do all that. Studying, working, being a mother, and living an independent life, even if married. And although that is for sure also due to the good system in Switzerland, I believe it's also strongly due to my personal views. For the views regarding women are often old school here. Yes, women are a part of the working force, but they very often work part-time. And yes, they have a good salary, but it is still 20 percent lower on average. And yes, men are also involved in childcare, but it's still by far not 50/50.

I remember people, especially other women, giving me "the look" because I worked full-time from the beginning although having kids. I still get "the look" when I bring up gender-related issues and for involving my husband in housekeeping and childcare on a higher scale than the usual one. And people still think I should be utterly thankful, that he is doing so willingly.

So yes, my life here is good. But at the same time, there is still a long way to go from the perspective of a woman. And for all you women out there, considering moving here: Make sure to find yourself some strong and joyful women with humour that you can share with and process whatever old school struggles might come up.

My Life As A Woman: Syria Edition #1

I am Fatima from Damascus city of Syria. I am a poet and at the same time a good writer. I grew up in Aleppo city which is always in the headlines of newspapers. As a woman with strong emotions, I have always been looking to help others.

My family is a very small family with a very sad and emotional background. My mother and my father died in a bomb blast when I was just 3 months old. After the death of my parents, my uncle who is a great man, took on the responsibility of the upbringing of me and my twin sister. In fact, I don't know how it feels to be with your parents. My uncle lost his brother, but we didn't lose our father. My uncle is so loving, so caring. He never lets us feel like an orphan. He is like my father.

I graduated from school when I was 16 years old. But soon after that, all the universities and schools closed because of war. My uncle decided to leave Syria and migrate to Turkey. I studied Arabic literature at the University of Istanbul. Soon after I graduated from university, I decided to find a job. I was working in reception of a hospital in Istanbul. But that was a very big headache for me because my field of study was very different.

I wrote my first book in 2010. Its title was, "Spirit of poem". It had a very motivational message to all people who fight against innocent people. Now, I own a small cafe near the parliament state. My daily routine widely depends on my mood. If I feel that I am tired, I don't go to work, and because of that I had so many problems with my boss in the past. At least now, I am a little bit free to do what I want, because I am my own boss.

From a very early age, I was interested in writing poems. There is nothing else that can relieve my pain but writing poems. I always say that the best thing you can do to express your opinion is writing.

Our culture has been very widely affected by unstoppable war in our country. For example, the freedom of women to act effectively has been affected by war. In the past, women had a very active role in society, but now it has been shrunk. But the thing that I like the most is the role of Islamic sharia in tradition and culture which hasn't been changed over centuries. When Syrians accepted Islam, Islam changed everything and accommodated them with sharia.

Being and living in Syria is not a very easy thing. This is a big struggle for a female in a country where there is no sufficient room to grow. When I was a little child, I lost my parents and after that, I migrated to Turkey. Imagine how hard it is to grow up as an orphan and leave your country just because of war.

Success is a very nice word for me. I didn't work hard to achieve it, it came to me by itself. While I was writing my first book, I tried hard not to be very personal, but because I was a little bit personal, my book became popular among book lovers.

I want to say to all women in the world that it is not important how hard you work, you should work smartly. Forget your past and use your time constructively. Don't say, "I will do it tomorrow, I am bored today." Maybe tomorrow will be late too to act.

My Life As A Woman: Syria Edition #2

I am a makeup artist Abeer style From a Syrian father and a Turkish mother And the eldest among my brothers I grew up in a good. and conservative family My father was working in the auto parts business and my mother is a high-class housewife. We used to live next to my grandfather's house, my father's family. May God have mercy on him (a sheik of the noble Qur'an). I learned from him the origins of the letters to read and write and memorize some parts of the Noble Qur'an and learned tajwid (God have mercy on him).

I was beloved and spoiled by my father and mother, and that was because of my being sweet and kind and a rational little granddaughter. I entered the elementary school, and after two years my grandfather made me continue my education in the Islamic Sharia school. Although it was tiring, when I grew up I understood my religion and my life, and I knew very well the difference between good and evil, halal and haram.

And at the end of middle school, everyone began to notice my tendency to make hairdos for me and my sister, and supported me and rejoiced at my touches. Although it was simple, praise be to God, day after day my talent grew and entered the world of makeup and I began to experiment on the girls of the neighborhood and spent my spare time and vacation with this talent.

My sister and my father decided to open a special salon in the garden extension of our house, and his name was (Neighbor of the Moon), and we became famous and my sister and I worked for a sweet period. After two years I got married, had a son and a daughter, and I moved with my father to reside in UAE because his trade work between Syria and UAE. I entered the world of beauty in the UAE and began to discover the differences and gained new experiences and worked with the most important artists in the country. I developed myself more and more and my husband helped to establish a women's salon project (Abeer Alward Salon).

At the beginning over 15 years ago, it was a strong competition because there were famous makeup artists, and I was an outsider, even though I was so patient and honest. I used to buy the best types of masks, and even the best products for hair. I was working from my heart for my work and my clients, and year after year, I became famous and I had clients who loved me and I had a famous name. But unfortunately, my husband passed away and I was very sad and felt broken due to his sudden separation and my exile, and I was at a crossroad.

After the death of my husband, I thought of returning to Syria to be with my family and complete my life there for me and my children. But, unfortunately, there was no country to return to, as it became a country torn by war, a war city, distorted by the smell of gunpowder, blood, destroyed houses, and broken streets. My beautiful and beloved country wasn't the same as had I known from when I left in 2005. I retreated from this idea for the safety of my children and because I felt that my residence and work in UAE and my financial support to the family and people (those who lost their homes and their limbs) was one million times better than staying among them. My future is unknown, or perhaps at a moment of treachery, I was a project of a martyr who wasn't guilty of the war that took many poor people, who were before the war, businessmen, doctors, and engineers at the head of their work.

Syria was once a paradise on earth and a good, civilized country. All people visited Syria and had a wonderful impression and would visit over and over again. The beauty of Syria's nature is known for everyone, from a plain, a mountain, a sea, springs, rivers, fruits, ancient structures, modernity, covenant, and civilizations from thousands of years old and in many of them, Aleppo, my dear city. It was necessary to wash my face and stand again and please myself and know that God is with me means I'm fine and I took care of my work. I took courses for self-development and strengthening myself, and every period I did something new and better than before, I traveled to other countries. I became a trainer and gave courses to the makeup and poetry, and my name grew bigger and our Lord gave me strength and I completed my work.

And I thank my Lord that he was a God of wisdom, that He developed the talent of a child and that it became the source of my livelihood and compensated me. I can rely on myself, thanks to God, and thanks to my work in poetry and writing.

My first supporter was my grandmother, who is also a famous seamstress and knows the value of art and beauty, and my mother and all of my relatives trusted me in my beginning, as if in my beginning, the makeup was a self-education and inspiration, a gift from my Lord, and I always developed it.

I remained living in UAE, as I gained renewal of my experience from the experienced makeup artists, and new skills befitting an open country with different nationalities, and I learned a lot with my creativity, skill, and taste, and the most important thing I learned is the kindness of every girl, especially the brides. I treat them as my sisters. By absorbing her tensions and giving the sweetest spirits so that she can relax and make a sweet memory of her beautiful day. I opened a beauty center and proved myself among all, thank God, and my dealings with the most beautiful personalities, including artists, actresses, and media figures, and my title became the beloved makeup artist of the famous characters.

I loved the good for all people and praised the work of every makeup artist, I was busy developing myself and defeating abeer style a year ago, and I didn't waste my time in conflicts because the door to livelihood is open to all.

I advise every woman who would like to live in UAE to be tactful, gourmet has a high degree of culture and awareness, loves good for everyone, cooperates with everyone, and always links her name to something special so that she will stay in the first grade.

The UAE is an elegant, beautiful, safe country, and life in it is a dream for every ambitious and hardworking person. I wish to complete my life in this good country and give all my love, energy, and talents, and always remain renewed and hands outstretched for the good to happen all around me.

Don't hesitate to reach me and make your presence known through social media!

My Life As A Woman: Taiwan Edition #1

Here's what Chia-Ling has to say about her life as a Taiwanese woman.

"I grew up in Tainan and ever since the beginning, I was taught that girls have to be independent. Almost all the people close to me in my family are women. What men can do, women can do as well. In Taiwan, we take pride in being a woman. Women don't have to depend on anyone if you ask me. We can do anything if we set our mind to it."

She goes on to say that she took a life-long lesson from her grandmother and was taught the importance of feminism during her growth. "My grandmother had a hard time growing up due to patriarchy in our society. Thus, I realized the importance of feminism from her. Women aren't items, they need to be treated equally and with respect.", she says.

"Not only men can contribute to society, women can also do that", she says as she designates herself as a software engineer. She studied Computer Science in school and later opted for Software Engineering.

When asked about her struggles, she replied, "I've always promoted gender equality, but still there are many people out there who sexually objectify women. This is something I despise from the core of my heart. Growing up, I realized that the older generation has still clung on to patriarchy. Not many women are in my line of work as I'm told by all those who ask me about my job."

Our woman from Taiwan really likes the current culture. Unlike the mainstream way, she's spoken in a different manner and shed light on the fact that everyone has now started to promote gender equality in Taiwan. "It makes everyone to be treated equally.", she says.

"My successes?", she asks, "I haven't been able to achieve a lot yet, nor can I call myself successful but, I feel successful knowing that I'm a woman and women can take care of everything by themselves. I believe, women in the society are an absolute necessity. A misogynist is only a misogynist until he hasn't met a great woman. Similarly, I really think that we don't know the importance of something till it's gone. People respect women here now in Taiwan and I call this success."

Her Advice to the Women of Taiwan

Chia-Ling really believes that as the passage of time leaves us contemplating and becoming a better person than yesterday, the future regarding women is not so bad. She thinks that the overall concept is shifting to being broader and more sensible. She says, "I think living in Taiwan now is utterly happiness because of the gender equality that's starting to make a mark. The younger generation with all the technology that's coming out every day, is starting to change the patriarchal mindset. This is really something to look forward to. I'd advise the women of Taiwan to take advantage of this golden opportunity to make a name for themselves. Put up such a relentless fight that could make every man admire you and think beyond. Not losing confidence is the key, I believe, and that is what I would like to say to our women. We should be more confident in anything we do. Lastly, my life revolves around feminism but in an extremely positive and goal-oriented way. It would be in my interest to advise Taiwanese women such as myself, to promote feminism and show men what we are capable of." This concludes My Life As A Woman: Taiwan Edition.

My Life As A Woman: Taiwan Edition #2

While I'll talk about my life as a woman, I'd like to introduce myself first! My name is Mei-Shu. I grew up in Taipei, the capital city in Taiwan. Both my parents inspired me a lot. As the only child at home, I own lots of freedom, but also lots of attention, from my parents. My mother wanted me to study hard so that I could get more and earn more in the future, however, my dad hoped that I would be responsible for myself, and by the way, treat every daily problems as funny challenges. They held for me a kind of philosophy of life, and an attitude toward changes.

I studied occupational therapy, part of science of rehabilitation. But, don't ask me why this particular choice because I had just a few ideas about what to do in my passing future. However so far, I also worked as an occupational therapist. And I found that I love to interact with people in need. I love to listen to and somehow take part in different life stories, though some were sad, but some were touched. It's my pleasure to be a listener and helper in their tiny part of life. Whenever I help them get through physical or psychological problems, they also help me accumulate my eyesight of people and their unique life. "Occupation" is not only a profession, but a viewpoint and solution of society.

Taiwan is a democratic country; therefore, we have high degree of freedom. In the same time, we are learning to respect each other here. Taiwan is one of few countries that agree with same-sex marriage. As a woman in Taiwan, I feel there's lots of comfort zones. On one hand, helping me feeling safe, and so that, I don't need to bear and fit in that much social framework and expectations of economic status and unequal criteria. But on the other hand, comfort zones are also forming part of constraints, our rights and recognizable abilities. Although women have a lot of freedoms in Taiwan, many of them are still restricted by old Chinese culture, such as women should give up promotions in jobs and take care of their families more. We are expected to devote to housework, everything related to child, and so on, but rather than achievements of careers. Therefore, women in their 30s mostly will struggle with choices between family and work, following others or having self-actualization.

Fortunately, I am still leading my life directions so far. What I've done is all about my own choice, not a compromise toward any factors. I also hope I can continue to be a master of myself, continue to lead my life choices. I believe all women in Taiwan are able to pursue the lives they want. The world is changing; women have the same education as men that help us to know what we want. We should be more confident to realize our dreams and believe we have powers to do that.

My Life As A Woman: Taiwan Edition #3

My name is Zenobia Chen, a Taiwanese literature master student from Taiwan.

As a woman, I am very lucky to have been born in an environment like Taiwan — a country with more sex-equality than the surrounding places. I feel proud and confident to say that because I was safe in my childhood, and happily grow up to be an energetic person.

I won't say Taiwan is a utopia that didn't have any sex discrimination. I often hear some ridiculous news about unfair treatment of women or see awful hate speeches against women in online forums. There are some annoying things that happened to me too. When my hairdresser, nurse of the clinic or neighbor knew my major, they always said, "It's okay to study liberal arts. You can live a happy life as long as you marry a rich husband." Just like, I have to become a successful doctor or engineer to prove myself, or marry a millionaire, otherwise, I will be a loser. To most of the people, the liberal arts major in an unpopular department isn't a wise choice in Taiwan, not to mention as a woman.

However, I said no to the outdated concepts. The colorful childhood inspired me to study literature. With the support of my parents, I stepped on the road to explore the literary world of Taiwan. During the research, I found female writers didn't take many places in the history of Taiwanese literature. Although many male writers write for women's rights, I barely hear women's voices. Looking at these clever and brave female writers who try the whole bag of tricks to grab the opportunity to write, I deeply understood how lucky I am — living in a relatively freedom era. Freedom isn't our right at birth. Without those people's blood and tears, Taiwanese women wouldn't have a chance to do so many things.

If I only can choose one woman who inspired me the most, I would choose our President Tsai. It's nothing to do with my political affiliation, just because the words she said in a talk show: "In Taiwan, women can do anything, even to be president and supreme commander." So, I believe now is definitely the best time. I can do anything as a Taiwanese woman. That is why I devote myself to this beautiful land to discover more encouraging stories about women in Taiwanese literature. If there is a chance that comes to you, just grab it and try your best. Sometimes Your effort may be useless sadly, but if those women live in the old era were not willing to bet on it, it's impossible for Taiwan to become the most sex equality country in Asia.

To sum up, the advice I want to give Taiwan women is to be yourself. Be any person you want to be, don't let them stop you. You will never be wrong but brave. After all, the country we love and live in is getting better and better.

My Life As A Woman: Tajikistan Edition

This is the story of my life, a woman living in Tajikistan. I was born in Tajikistan (back then, Soviet Union) and spent most of my childhood in Tajikistan. I was born in a middle-class family. I was the 3rd child of my parents following two brothers and followed by a sister. My father used to work in Moscow as a laborer while my mother was, by profession, a nurse, and a housewife. While my mother was at her job, my grandmother used to look after us.

Most of my childhood was spent in the part of Soviet Union which came to be known as Tajikistan today. The culture is the same as our neighboring countries such as Uzbekistan, Turkmenistan, etc. We really enjoy music, family gatherings, weddings, etc. One of the best parts of our culture, in my opinion, is the bright and colorful embroideries which we sew into carpets, cushions and my favorite, our cultural dresses. We find happiness in the smallest things in life and live life to its fullest. We have festivals we celebrate as a community and enjoy these moments throughout the year.

I was brought up in a patriarchic society where a woman's education was frowned upon and women were viewed as housewives and servants to men. It was tough being a woman in that society and there but luckily my mother was there to help me out. She was an educated woman and knew the value of education, being a nurse herself. She insisted on my higher education when my paternal family was strictly against it. It was due to her perseverance, steadfastness and endless efforts that I was able to complete my further education as a nurse which was my dream. I always looked to my mother as a role model and wanted to be a nurse like her. My mother made sure that all her children are educated and that my sister and I receive the same education and status as of our brothers.

After my marriage, we had to go through some rough times after Tajikistan got its independence from the Soviet Union and the civil war erupted. Times were tough and we were not the most economically stable. My husband couldn't get a job due to economic crisis. I was the sole breadwinner of my family and used to work as a nurse at a local hospital. I was soon blessed with a boy and a girl. As times got better, my husband, like most other men in Tajikistan left for Russia to earn a living and I was left with my son and daughter. Although, my husband used to support us financially, it was tough taking care of two children as a working mother in a society which was male-dominant.

Today, I still work as a nurse, but life is better. Our economy has gotten better, and I have also found a permanent job as a head nurse in the local hospital. I still live with my children, who have now grown up. Following the footsteps of my mother, I made sure my children got proper education. My son studied to become a dentist and started his residency period at a local hospital recently. My daughter is in her final year of nursing school and will soon become a nurse just like me and her grandmother. I have had many ups and downs in my life, but I consider bringing up my children and educating them the biggest challenge and success of my life.

My advice to women in Tajikistan would be to get educated. It is one of the best things to have happened to me. By the efforts of my mother and myself, I have been able to get proper education. Due to this, I can happily claim that I am an independent woman. In Tajikistan, most women have minimal education and get married at a very young age. Their focus should be on educating themselves rather than marriage, but unfortunately, that is something they cannot control due to the arrange marriage culture. Most men in Tajikistan leave for Russia in search of a living and some even divorce their wives when they find someone they can marry in Russia for permanent residence. This is when women find themselves with no support. With proper education, women can fight with any situation in life.

So, my advice to Tajik women would be to focus on their education, and if they are beyond that point in their lives, to ensure their children, specially their daughters, get educated.

My Life As A Woman: Tanzania Edition

Women play a vital role in the society and have an essential place in the society too. They're never left out in critical decision making. They help in their children's upbringing and ensure their morals are intact. In the corporate world, women are making it big. The phrase, "Their place is found in the kitchen" no longer applies. Let's look at the little bio of My Life As A Woman.

I grew up in the Mbeya Region, a thriving town in Southwest Tanzania that lies at the foothills of the towering Loleza park. Mbeya is one of Tanzania's 31 administrative regions which the regional capital is the city of Mbeya. Tanzania is known as the 'Soul of Africa' because of its diverse culture and beauty. It boasts of having over 120 tribes and has the most varied cultures in the world. All the ethnic groups found in Tanzania speak their local language, but the most exciting thing is that most Tanzanian's are fluent in the national language Swahili.

Swahili is a coastal Bantu language that was influenced by Arabic.

The other thing that amazes people is how friendly and polite Tanzanians can be to visitors. It is a national pride and reflects throughout the country. Tanzanian's love for people is out of this world. They offer to love freely without a struggle.

The other thing that stands out is how they bring up their children in a disciplined manner.

My growing up was just like other kids in a family set up though, after the age of seven years, I moved into my grandmother's place because my mom had to get outside country because of work-related matters.

I never got to enjoy the bond/ love that children experience with their parents. My grandmother was a woman after God's own heart and a hard worker. I learned a lot from her since we spent most of the time together. She was working hard to support her husband and ensured that the family was well taken care of, and their children got a good education.

I admired her effort, and her inspiration played a big part in my growing up.

Like any other kid that has a future just figured out on their mind, which most of the time gets inspired by people they interact with each day, I was not an exception. I wanted to do nursing. It was brought about by seeing how people struggled with their health at home. Back on my mind, I knew that if I did nursing, I was to be of great help to the people of Mbeya or rather anyone that I encountered and needed help, because of lack of finances.

While in high school, my focus had shifted from nursing to teaching. The urge to do teaching was so strong, and I bowed to the pressure.

After going to college for two years to do teaching to complement the love I have for children, I only taught for three years where after that, I felt like I wasn't doing my best or rather doing what my heart wanted.

Since my days in primary school, I loved writing. I was the best in grammar, and my mastery in poetry was admired by many. A friend from my home village and school mate reached out to me and opened my eyes and told me more about online writing. I had no idea that people earn in the comfort of their homes.

It came in handy because, being a mother; I can work from home as I bring up my children. I now work as a freelancer in the comfort of my house, which is the best decision I ever made. Passion matters in everything.

From the world outlook, being a woman, you may seem like you have it all together, but I got my share of ups and downs. Having children and earning can make society raise the bar of expectations higher. Juggling between work and raising children is not a walk in the park. Raising my kids sometimes wears me out, especially when, at the same time, I'm fighting against anxiety and depression.

As I mentioned earlier, spending my early years with my grandmother made me have lose close contact with my parents. The fear that I harbor most is not having a bond between me and my children.

Success is multi-faced and can be interpreted differently by different individuals. My success is executing projects, improving myself, and developing myself as a brand each day. Being in a position to do what I love most and bringing ideas to life and change someone out there, I count it as success. Being in a position to influence the community and encourage women to get out of their comfort zones and put their best foot forward is also my success.

As a woman, don't ever reach a point where you feel that you've accomplished much. Get out there, do what you love and give it your all, not forgetting to reach out to other women who may only need some motivation to get things going.

We all have that thing that pushes us to wake up each morning. Evaluate yourself first. What do you love doing most, and it brings out satisfaction to you? Don't let fear be a barrier. Put your best foot forward and face your fears. You never know what you're capable of doing or achieving unless you get out of the comfort zone. Don't let anything deter you.

If you love writing, get out there, dig information that is all over the internet, and earn a living through different freelance works. Whenever you may feel like you don't have what it takes to stand out among the rest, encourage yourself that you can do it. Don't you ever let that draw you away from achieving the best things in life. Wear your crown and fix it perfectly well.

My Life As A Woman: Thailand Edition #1

I was never fluent in Thai since I was a kid, but my parents used to always say my English wasn't that great either. I was a typical Thai kid who went to an all-girl school in Bangkok until I was 10, when the folks had a brilliant idea to send me abroad to Singapore to further my education. Back in those days, it was a pretty big deal and privileged to be moving into a developed country while my mom and dad stay to do their business and support the family.

Don't get me wrong, we didn't come from a wealthy family background but fortunately, we were comfortable. I studied in Singapore for eight years where I did my Primary and Secondary School. Picked up Mandarin and made loads of friends from different races and religions. Singapore made me a tougher person than I could ever imagine I would have been if I have stayed in Thailand. The small little red dot (Singapore), has no natural resources, not even clean water. Yet, the country still rises to the top and is one of the most developed countries in the world. The key to that success is its people. Competitions to outdo your classmates were necessary, whether in school or the extracurricular activities. I can't say I hate it, but those pressures sure shaped me into a person I am today. Looking back at it, I think my parents sure made the right decision in investing in my education.

Then, I moved back to Bangkok. It took me a while to adapt to the slow-life culture and an easy laid back environment as compared to Singapore. Yet, it was what I needed after so many years away from my country. The Land of Smile's environment made me a little more compassionate and less aggressive.

My mom and I were never really closed since we never really spend much time together until I came back to do my bachelor's in business in Bangkok. She was always very strict when I was younger, but I knew she wanted the best for her only daughter. As a businesswoman, Mom wanted me to follow her footpath in taking over the family business. She wanted me to take good care of the people and the business she and her husband had built. It sure was a lot of pressure taking care of the plastic manufacturing company, but I got used to it now. Perhaps because I think I'm good at what I do although I don't particularly enjoy it.

I supposed my biggest difficulty is my struggle with my own pressure to achieve greater than my Mom ever did. Sometimes these pressures are a really good pushing force but a lot of times it could be really toxic when I beat myself up. I'm still learning to be easier on myself.

My success story would be that I have made my mom proud of whom I am today. I'm imperfect but she still puts up with all of my nonsense and how I'm married to my job rather than finding the right man to put her mind at ease. My advice to the other ladies would be to go out there and achieve great things in life as your heart desires but never to forget the old folks at home waiting to have dinner with you at the end of the day because they are the ones who love you best, not your job.

My Life As A Woman: Thailand Edition #2

Know your worth

"Before…people around my boyfriend always treat me so badly because I'm ugly, so that's why I am always jealous and over thinking" my friend told me while we had talked about the trust issue. My perspective is that he is a good looking man. He is helpful, talkative and cheerful. Let's say he is a really nice one. I don't think that the other people will treat him badly just because he thinks he is ugly. "My boyfriend always supports me, he told me I should be more confident and try to improve myself to be the best version of me. Everyone has weak points, and no one is perfect" I totally agree. "Now I have more confidence in myself and I changed my mindset to be more kind to myself" He keeps saying "Not just the confident but you should be proud more about yourself" This is one of my friend's stories but how do you know your own worth? I kept asking myself as well.

I was born in a moderate family in Chiang Mai which is one of the beautiful cities in the north of Thailand. I studied in the private school which is a popular school in Chiang Mai. I am in a lovely family. I have a lot of lovely friends in a great school. I'm good at Thai dance, show, art, sports and music. Everything seems like a happy life but… When I was young, I didn't want to go to school not because I am lazy or because I wanted to stay at home, but I got bullied every single day. I am 100% Thai with freckles on my face. Absolutely! It is weird for the other girls and most of my friends are always curious why I have them on my face. I don't know why they are on my face, but I think I just had bad luck from God. Some boys always use bad words to call me just because I am different from them. They said freckles are ugly. That is my weak point because I'm ugly, I thought. Day by day and year by year since then, I used to hear bad words and I can handle my thoughts. My mom always supports me and tells me every day about the real beautiful. "The way that I am different from them is a lovely present and not bad luck. People will love you because you are beautiful from your inner and remember that no one can judge you as long as you don't judge yourself" she said. Then, I changed my mind and I could smile for any bad words about my freckles and have more confidence with myself. "No one is perfect, and no one can judge you as long as you don't judge yourself" I shouted out loud to give myself the motto of the new starting day.

Finally, I know the meaning of these words "Know your worth" That's an inspirational word to make you have a better day and a positive mindset. As long as you value yourself, you have a high self-esteem and the other can't judge you. Believe in yourself to do the things whatever you want and make it happen. Proud about you, respect yourself and others. Accepted that everyone has a different character which makes the world evaluation. "Imperfection is beauty" you probably heard this idiom before but who knows the real meaning until you will figure it out by yourself.

Don't let anyone kill your happiness. Just know your worth.

My Life As A Woman: Timor-Leste Edition

Hi, my name is Ana. I grew up in Baucau but later moved on to Canada for a better life. Ana was born on an isolated farm in Baucau on January 29, 1954. My name was supposed to be Orpah, but because of the difficulty of spelling and pronunciation, she was known as Ana. My unmarried parents separated soon after I was born. As a child, my family was super poor, with my mother only working. I barely ate, and the only thing to keep me entertained was the outside. Since I only lived with my mother, she inspired me a lot. My mother is super hardworking, with her jobs and at home. She takes care of us, as I have two other brothers. I grew, up barely paying enough for high school. I wanted to be a lawyer, so I went to law school for 4 years. I wanted to be a lawyer, to make enough money for my family, and also, I hated crime, and killers.

Lawyer is a great job, and my grandfather was a lawyer, so I wanted to continue the trend. Since I came from Timor-Leste, our culture was the finest. Timor-Leste culture is strong, unique and reflects many different influences: traditional animist beliefs; a former Portuguese colony; the impact of WWII; the more recent Indonesian invasion and spirited Timorese resistance; the role of the Catholic Church and the effects of other minority groups such as Chinese traders. I liked our culture because it's different, you reflect on what happened in WWII, and how it changed us. Saying, that I wanted to be a lawyer, it, unfortunately, didn't work out. I got kicked out, and it was hard to find a job. No one wanted to accept a dropout.

A few years later, I applied for a job. The job was PS Senior Consultant. This job is the natural developer that will be responsible for developing natural-based software solutions to implement client system enhancements and changes associated. The job was fine, although there wasn't a high pay rate. Some struggles I have are money-wise. "Not making as much money as someone equally as qualified as them who just happens to have different genitalia" things. Not only do I have to worry about this, but a lot of my friends have even convinced themselves that this isn't a real thing. I also have to worry about my period being late, but even then it's only on a need to know basis. However, there are some good things about being a woman. Some are having a nice husband, good friends, and I have a nice child. Those are the happiest and most successful things I have, and the most grateful things ever.

Before this ends, I want to give some tips to Timor-Leste women. There's never going to be a precisely right moment to speak, share an idea, or take a chance. Just take the moment—don't let thoughts like 'I don't feel like I'm ready' get in the way. Look to see if you have the main things or the opportunity will pass you by. Don't let perfect get in the way of really, really good. Remember to be yourself, and always be happy.

My Life As A Woman: Togo Edition #1

My name is Justine Segla. I grew up in the north of Togo, in a town 400 km from Lomé, the capital of Togo, whose name is Kara. I grew up close to my parents, my father is a school teacher and my mother is a housewife, she also trades charcoal when she is not doing housework, charcoal being the main source of energy for cooking or heating water in harmattan time which is similar to winter time in Europe or the United States. She gets up early in the morning to prepare everything she needs for her children, i.e. cooking and cleaning for the family, and then she goes to the market and sells charcoal from which she returns in the evening. I often help her with the kitchen when she is busy and when I have finished my homework. Thanks to her worries, she has been able to raise us her three children of which I am the eldest in my second year of law school.

My father is a very generous man who helps my mother to take care of us with his meager income and my mother is the one who has inspired me the most, she has fought for us and continues to fight to see us succeed and my only motivation is to become an important person and relieve my mother who since our youngest age, wakes up early for her company and for all of us by giving the best of herself for our development.

Currently, I am studying law at the university, the university is called University of Kara, one of the two great universities of Togo which brings together students from all over the country. One of my victories is to have managed to obtain a very good average for my first year of law which did not fail to delight my parents. My two little brothers are in high school and know the sacrifices that our parents made for our success so they also study seriously to give pleasure to our parents and I help them as much as possible.

I would like to become a lawyer to defend the rights of women and the poor, although it is a discipline that requires a lot of concentration and seriousness. I take myself very seriously while studying every day and not looking for any excuse not to regret tomorrow. I want to make my life an example and a model for all the young girls in my neighbourhood who are respectful and who want to become like me when they grow up. I want to be the pride of my parents and help the poor and women to be heard and have their rights respected nationally and internationally. My struggle as a woman is to succeed in imposing myself as a woman of law in an environment dominated by men where women are less privileged.

I give my all in my studies to succeed in the legal career and my advice to women all over the world is to always fight in their environment to bring out the best in themselves because the inferiority complex is mental. Every woman is well capable of doing as much as a man and the prejudices and conceptual causes that want a woman to be just at home or just a mother must not in any way influence us women.

I advocate gender equality and with my student discipline, I only want an emancipation, integration and equitable sharing of resources between men and women. The global struggle for the emancipation of women and gender equality must be the ownership of each government because the time when women should be subject to men staying at home to raise their children is over and globalization must be that fuel that ends ignorance and allows a broad education of women so that our ideals, our contributions, and our inventions are widely cited in the scientific or medical fields.

My Life As A Woman: Togo Edition #2

West Africa, Where I was born

I was born in a village call Atakpame, in Togo West Africa, before my parents move to the capital city of Togo where I grew up in Lomé, the capital of Togo. I was raised in a middle class family with my five siblings; my father was a farmer and mother was a trader at a market called Assieye, located in the city of Lomé. Life is not easy as an African. It is a hard life but with determination, vision, and courage, I scale through and became who I am today.

My Education Life

I attended the British Model School of Lomé Togo Latter. I was admitted to the Federal University of Lomé Togo where I had my Higher National degree in Mass communication.

My Grandma's Place Changed My Vision

Having spent time with Grandma during summer, I was inspired by grandma's sister, my grandaunt, who was a news caster, she spent the summer with Grandma. I had wanted to read law while growing up but seeing this aunt in Grandma's place, I changed my mind and wanted to do what she did.

What I Love About My Culture

I'm the type of person who has right to make my own choices and do whatever I feel like which makes me happy and everyone around me will be happy also. I do feel as if my culture allows for a certain amount of freedom for women to be who they are. I love that we respect our elders and know that whatever they say is important. We listen to them and often do as they suggest because it is believed they have the highest sense of wisdom, hence why I so fascinated and enjoyed being with my grandmother and grandaunt. Although I have lots of siblings, I enjoy the fact that we are still close and help each other out whenever in need, even as we grew to be older adults, we still have a very strong bond.

My Current Job

I am presently working as a customer care representative, a freelancer, and I also carry out survey work for some companies, usually online, but sometimes I do go door-to-door depending on the type of survey.

My struggles as a woman

Presently, I am struggling to make sure Togolese girls will have a job and a say especially in politics and in all ramifications, because women are not always recognized here in Africa and overlooked, especially in my country, Togo.

My success as a woman

Apart from working, I won the best staff of the year 2018 and was used as the face of the company. I'm a proud feminist who embraces her femininity. I feel sometimes we are made to feel self-conscious and ashamed of our accomplishments, but I owned this one. I did it. I worked hard for many years, even when I watched others achieve what I only dreamed, and I finally accomplished it. And I am proud just to be recognized for it!

My advice to all women

Strive to be the best you can be. If you participate in a charity, then don't just donate. Get involved and spend time with those who need it most. Internal motivation is key, because if you're not pushing yourself, who will? Also, embrace change. Most fear it, but it's a beautiful thing. When I was working at LTK in my early 2015, I was making great money and exceeding all my sales goals, but I had a gut feeling that I could do so much more and provide a service to change women's lives in Togo. With big risks come greater rewards and the chance to make a difference.

My Life As A Woman: Togo Edition #3

The place where I grew up.

I was born 30 km from the capital Lomé, in the small town of Agbodrafo named by the Portuguese navigators Porto Seguro. I spent part of my childhood there before moving 15 km further to Aného where I currently live.

How did I grow up?

To paraphrase Charles Baudelaire, the author of the Flowers of Evil, I would say that my childhood was only a dark storm. I suffered an abusive and irresponsible father who was never present for his children. It made me the eldest who sacrificed herself for my little brothers. I had to go from house to house to do laundry for people or to get water to earn a few coins.

RECKYA MADOUGOU, a Battle Woman of Beninese origin living in TOGO: my source of inspiration.

I am very inspired by this woman through her career, her professional success and her fight for African women. She makes me want to succeed every day so that I do not have to undergo the same treatment as my mother in the future.

My field of study and what I wanted to be when I was a child.

I stopped school in the third year, but a few years ago, I started school again in the evening. Today, I am preparing for the Baccalaureate with the hope of obtaining a diploma later in the health field. This is my greatest dream now. I wish I could take care of the sick.

When I was a kid, I had a lot of dreams. I wanted to become a surgeon and also an air hostess, then a fireman. I found it rare to see women in this occupation. I believe that my most crazy dream was to want to be the first lady of my country, like the German woman of state, Angela Merkel.

What I love about my culture?

I love everything in Guin culture. I love our way of being, I love our ways, our traditions, the richness and quality of our culinary art. I like the importance we place on the family hierarchy, the respect of our community leader. Culture occupies an important place in our country.

What I'm doing now for a job?

While waiting for my baccalaureate in the evening, I am babysitting and cleaning of the houses of my neighbors and surrounding areas in my spare time. I am doing all this to make ends meet in order to deal with the financial difficulties that are prevalent in my country. I've never really had a fixed job, I've always been doing everything that falls into my hands and that can generate income.

My struggles as a woman.

They are both ideological and moral.

I fight a daily battle to earn my place in society with dignity. I struggle to channel my inner desires and demons. The fear of losing my dignity because of the conditions of my life.

My successes as a woman.

First of all, my school reintegration.

I took the courses and I will study well again to succeed in my baccalaureate and to take professional training in medical assistance. But before I graduated, I managed to achieve a stable standard of living while I was away to stay at the bottom of the social ladder.

Advice for my sisters.

Failure is also part of the future success, because without my failures, I will never have reached where I am now.

AYELEVI

My Life As A Woman: Tokelau Edition

I grew up in Tokelau, a small island that can be accessed by sea from Samoa. Living on this island has always been exciting, and this is because people are so friendly. Growing up in Tokelau, I would watch as my father and brothers went fishing as it was a man's job to do so. My mother taught me how to cook and to take care of my future family. This was a time when public service jobs were yet to displace the gender roles in society. Thus, I grew up knowing that I, as a woman, was limited to certain activities. My thinking was altered when my father converted to Christian, and this meant that the whole family had to follow his lead. In this local parish, I met a young, friendly nun who became my role model. She would tell me stories about Europe and other far places that I knew by name. From her stories, I wanted to travel the world, and I studied hard with the sole purpose of getting a good job and traveling to see the world. I would later go to mainland New Zealand where I pursued a post-graduate in Business and Commerce.

After getting a job at a large organization, I was excited to find out that the head of my department was a woman. I saw this as a huge opportunity to advance my career because my boss understood what it was to be a woman in a man's world. However, I would realize that the case was different than I had interpreted. I was handed low-level tasks, and during meetings, my opinion mattered less. This treatment was impactful on my self-confidence, and I almost accepted that my mom was right, and there are roles for women and men. I even felt that I deserved to carry out the low-level tasks despite my educational attainments. Every single day, my self-doubts increased and also started to see a psychiatrist about my situation.

By seeking help from a professional, I was able to build up myself again, which contributed significantly to regaining my confidence. I did challenge my boss about why she was not giving me opportunities, but I was shut down. I decided to file a legal case against the department head for sex discrimination, and I won. I had gone through a lot, which was a great victory for me and one of my success stories. It was unfortunate that I had to bring down another woman even though she should have supported my career or given me equal opportunities. In the present, I have enjoyed success in my career and can take business trips to different countries.

My advice to women in Tokelau is that the times are changing where women can achieve as much as men. No longer are women constrained by gender roles. However, women face plenty of challenges, which means that we should support each other as women. If one is successful, the least you can do is eliminate barriers for other women instead of enabling these barriers.

My Life As A Woman: Tonga Edition

Written by Ashley Paquette

I braced myself to see the devastation. I secretly knew all along that while our family was safely riding out the category 4 cyclone, our family built hut was being ravaged by the monstrous winds and debris. Our roughly cemented sticks and chicken wire walls had survived the brunt of the storm, but the entire bamboo and plastic roof had collapsed in from a neighbors roof that had taken flight and smashed into ours. We pulled aside vines and branches to see that the inside of the house was covered in water and a layer of cyclone muck. My husband and I walked around assessing the damage in a numb haze as the hot tropical sun started to emerge from the remaining clouds.

I was tired. This was the third hut we had to rebuild in the past 6 years and by far it won worst if there was a contest. We had weeks ahead of work to do with no electricity or comfort from the extreme heat that followed the storm. We focused on the positive: we had a comfortable house to stay in while we rebuilt, a few years back, we wouldn't have had that. We had amazing friends who rallied around us and helped with the rebuilding. We had neighbors who joined us in cleaning up the mess. We had friends and families overseas sending funds for screws, nails, timber, and more plastic for the roof.

I listened to my Tongan neighbors laughing and joking even as their huts suffered similar damage. Admittedly, there are a lot of unique cultural oddities that I struggle with in Tonga, but this isn't one of them. This is the way of life here. The resilience of the Tongan spirit, especially in the women, is one of the things I admire the most. After a storm you wake up the next morning, thank God for what you have and start cleaning and rebuilding from whatever crude materials litter the landscape. Neighbors are quick to help and kids and teens (yes teens!) offer to help in whatever way they can. I knew we would be fine; storms come and go, and this hadn't been the first or the last. I was surprised to notice how I was slowly assimilating to the simpler Tongan way of life even as I had been so opposed to its hardships.

Born and raised on a cold corner of the east coast of the US, Tonga wasn't even a thought in my mind growing up. I was raised in the church by Christian parents who did more than look the part but also made every attempt to live what they believed. My life was easier than most and although we never had excess, my parents made sure my siblings and I never went without basic needs. I dreamt of traveling and writing for magazines when I graduated high school. But these plans got delayed when I married right out of high school and became a mom. So, when my husband of 5 years heard the call to go to Tonga, I agreed. I was ready for an adventure, I imagined I would adapt easily and find my faith was solid.

We left with $1700 USD in our bank account, a one way ticket, three small children, and a quest to see if the faith we believed was real. The life I had romanticized crashed and burned around me. Within a few short months reality settled in. Yes, it was a beautiful island, but far removed from the resort I had stayed in on our honeymoon in Bora Bora. My eyes were opened to how the majority of the world survived. An entire day was spent washing clothes by hand. Kids were sick off and on adjusting to our new environment. Lice was accepted as normal. Boils and skin infections were common in the humidity and they were a constant battle for us. Bugs literally rained from our coconut leaf roof while huge (thankfully nonpoisonous) spiders teased me from the walls. At night during storms, I would lie in bed trying to sleep while the bamboo rafters and plastic flexed and hammered in the wind. Everything and everyone, including myself, was muddy and smelled during the hottest months. My faith was crumbling as I slipped into self-pity. I was miserable, depressed and angry. I was cruel with my words and refused to see the good in anything. I just wanted to go home.

Although homesick and missing my suburban American lifestyle, I learned the fascinating and also confusing Tongan family structure. The nuclear and extended family worked as a single unit with layers of hierarchy that protect and maintain the Tongan way of life. Members know their role and accept it. The auntie, who is the Fahu, the eldest sister and brother, the grandparents and father and mother all have separate roles, and each have the power to make the final call depending on the family issue. Even naming children is left to the father's sisters. I observed how some family members abused their position of power for self-gain while others used their position to make sure every family member succeeded and thrived. Times are changing and so are the family dynamics. Even in the 8 years I've lived in Tonga, some of the culture's structure is breaking down and respect and honor are not as prevalent with the advancement of Western philosophy. But change is inevitable, and I learned it sometimes can bring good things too.

Two years have passed since the cyclone destroyed our home. May 2020 we celebrated eight years of being in Tonga and coincidentally, I started the process of becoming a Tongan citizen. As the years have progressed, so have we along with most of the residents of Tonga. We live in a treehouse my husband built alongside the Tongan boys who have become like family to us. We wash our clothes in an automatic washing machine, enjoy indoor plumbing, even hot water! Our roof is solid metal and we have a car instead of the old three wheeler bicycles we used to get around on. I spend my time homeschooling my kids along with bookkeeping and freelancing jobs on the internet. We plan on opening a campground for backpackers and community events and hope to rebuild our skatepark for the local youth.

I have found that success is not measured in what I have or my position in the world or how comfortable I am. A change of heart and mind is far more valuable. I'm thankful for everything I have now, and I've developed a love for the Tongan people in my life. I've shared some of the same struggles and I have a better understanding of what life is really like as a Tongan. My heart's desire is to help their children succeed as if they were my own. Life in Tonga can be hard, but we have so much to be thankful for. The cyclone was proof I had changed. My view of God changed as I stopped dictating who God should be or what God should do. I no longer blamed God for struggles but instead accepted hardships as my teacher. The journey is far from over, but I look forward to what lies ahead for my family in the Kingdom of Tonga.

My Life As A Woman: Trinidad and Tobago Edition

I grew up on the twin isle republic of Trinidad and Tobago, a land most celebrated for its rich and diverse culture. My upbringing however was not as typical compared to many of my peers. I never participated in Carnival or had any desire to do so, I'm not a frequent beach goer and my playlist consists of a variety of genres but not soca or calypso. It doesn't take away the fact that I am indeed a "trini" because I was born and raised here, and I have no issues with the land or its people and especially not with its delectable local dishes which I grew to love because my mother was an excellent chef. The culture of liming never bothered me either and despite being something of a loner I enjoy the occasional party.

With the topic of family at hand, mine was pretty normal in the beginning. I'm the last child of four, and both my parents worked for many years in the photography industry. My father apprenticed with the Chungs who the pioneers of photography on the island were and worked with them for many years from a young age until he opened his own branch. For this reason, he was a workaholic, so most of my parenting came from my mother. She was the glue that held the family together.

It was my mother who let me be my own person, she never forced ideals on me, or pushed me to pursue a particular career path. She let me stay indoors and read all day when all the neighborhood kids were outside playing. She was a fan of oldies, country and contemporary music and played her radio all day long, from the Beatles to Bon Jovi, she loved it all. She saw that I was different and didn't force me to change. I stayed out of trouble and I did well at school. We weren't wealthy but we weren't poor either, there wasn't much for me to complain or rebel about.

When I was 10 years old, my parents divorced, and I moved with my mother and sister to my grandmother's house shortly after she succumbed to cancer. I wasn't very close to my grandmother, I suppose it was because I was so little and I didn't really keep close to anyone in general, except my mother. I adjusted to the new setting quickly and my mother became an entrepreneur herself and founded her own photo studio and retail store which my sister helped her with. She also even travelled abroad to work as a caregiver on short term posts. She was always very resourceful, knew a lot of people and great at giving advice. I would always admire the way she never brushed anyone off but always had a subtle way to exit a conversation she did not care to be part of.

She passed away when I was in my late teens. I had just started university to pursue a degree in Linguistics and her death made it all lose its appeal. I struggled for a few years with grief and bad coping mechanisms. My life became a rollercoaster of ups and mostly downs. Eventually, I got married and became a mother myself. The marriage didn't last long, and I endured a lot of abuse before leaving. So, I became a divorced single mother. I found myself in a pickle, a child to raise, an unsupportive ex-husband, no career, no family to assist and not a clue as to what I really wanted to do in life. I worked part-time jobs, I attempted a small tutoring business with a school friend which was deeply affected by economic downturns in the country and things just couldn't seem to stabilize.

Because of these daily challenges I looked for work online. I was always fond of writing, so I decided to promote myself as a freelance writer while looking for other part time opportunities. I'm not close to a steady or stable income as yet but because I often think of my mother, I feel inspired by the way she was. She never gave up, and she always found a way to accomplish goals. She had more resources than I did to start over a new life after divorce but her drive and her ability to see the good in every bad situation and be grateful for the simple things in life is truly motivational.

My Life As A Woman: Tunisia Edition #1

I grew up in a small town named 'Hencha' which belongs to 'Sfax-Tunisia'.

What I really like about my culture is:

- People should be addressed respectfully

- Our food is so delicious

- The government and some wealthy benefactors support the arts

But in my town, people do need permission for art and difference, we suffered a lot and when I say we I mean 'GIRLS'. We are supposed to be NICE as they said and SUPER QUIET.

People had to treat me as if they know the way and I have to follow them blindly, for some of them being smart and having an ambition can cause a danger.

Girls in my town are not allowed to wear the type of clothes they want, no shorts no dresses and no make-up (this may look sarcastic, but it's reality).

One day, I was watching a TV program with my older sister and there was a talent competition, a boy was singing and the judges were wowed by his voice, at that time, my sister looked at me and she said, "this boy is your age, he is a singer and he showed himself, what about you?"

I felt ashamed, I felt like I got to do something. I learnt the same song the boy was singing, and suddenly I sang it! And that was amazing I discovered that I'm talented! I was a very good pupil, always the first on my class, I am good at Science and literature, but what I really want to do? Art. I adore painting and singing, but I couldn't follow what fulfilled my soul because of my fear!

Yes, I was afraid of being judged: Art won't bring you money! Artists are less valuable than anybody else. So, I followed math again, I am an engineering student and a singer! I discovered that nothing in this world can take me away from loving and continuing my art and improving my talent!

My father always had to tell me, "your life is your responsibility, if you don't chase what you want, it's all my fault."

Today as a Tunisian woman, I'm really grateful and happy with what I got and what I achieved: Waking up early every day, hustling to get more knowledge, following my dreams, brave enough to talk about my needs and what I really want, cultivated, I knew my worth and how free I am.

That's what every single woman deserves and even more. You lady, you deserve to feel free, fantastic, and worthy. I really advise every single Tunisian woman to feel proud because of being a woman, to glow, to follow her dreams no matter what comes your way, be brave and dare to say NO to the struggles. It's during the tough times that YOU have an opportunity to elevate yourself to your greatest of possibilities. The way we make it through hard times is by making our decision out of love and not allowing ourselves to fall into the clutches of fear.

My Life As A Woman: Tunisia Edition #2

Ever heard of Elyssar? The beautiful princess who fled her empire then found a land where she then built Carthage. I happened to live where that woman landed. Tunisia. Being a Tunisian woman has been everything but a walk in the park and I would more than love to dissect it. I grew up on the biggest island in north Africa named Djerba. The island is diverse in races as there are Amazighs, Arabs and Jews. My family is a mix of Arab and Amazigh heritage. The island is a mix of religions and my family happens to be Muslim which is the majority of people here. The island has stunning beaches and a heritage that it boasts.

My parents are quite nice. They are strict and made sure I had good grades. If I did, I was allowed to be whoever I wanted. I was taught that excellence is a must but being decent is more valuable. I grew up around boys and had very few women my age around and only contacted girls at school. Growing up, I spent most of my time reading and it was my hobby.

Both of my parents inspire me. My dad is very pragmatic and detail-oriented and I probably got that from him along with his knowledge in literature. My mother is very smart and capable of calculating things and is empathetic. They impacted me heavily but often allowed me to roam on my own and learn. We finish high school at 18 and have to choose majors even then. Mine was mathematics. Then I chose to go to university which is free. I went through two years of preparatory education. Then I made it to engineering in industrial IT and automation. I also took one year of exchange studies in psychology on the US. When I was a kid, I wanted to be an astronaut or an aerospace engineer. I am definitely not any of those, but I am close enough.

I love the fact that my culture assimilates a continental breakfast. We are very religious and yet we are not and are considered liberal Muslims. We are a mix of races. We are into drinking but drink in hiding, we are into singing and sing loud and dance during Ramadan. We are as diverse as Africa can get.

We were Carthage, we were roman, we were nomads, we were Arab Muslims, we were Ottomans, we were French and now here we are. I am still an engineering student and I am now discovering internships. My current internship is in diplomacy however and I am working for the U.S embassy. My next internship will be at the airport and I cannot wait for that.

My struggle is that I am not seen as a good enough engineer at work or clubs and I am sometimes viewed as someone who will never make good robots. On the other hand, I am also expected to be married by age 30 if I don't, people from my family will push me to meet random dudes.

As a woman I succeeded in breaking stereotypes and was the first female engineer in the family. I also succeeded in being the one with the highest SAT score in the family. As a woman I made sure I supported females around me. As a woman I felt a connection with people from my gender that I would never feel with a man despite the fact that I am heterosexual.

What I want you to retain: as a Tunisian woman, I think you should all learn to overlook nationalities. External aspects of womanhood differ but I believe we are exactly the same at heart. Some things are not relevant to geography.

My Life As A Woman: Turkey Edition #1

I grew up in Turkey and my life from the beginning has been very good because there are too many women that inspired me. This is one of the best parts that I love about my country. My country cares about women. There are a lot of opportunities for women to improve themselves. My university department is English Language and Literature and I had to go far from where I lived to study at the university. Luckily, I had no difficulty there. I had a lot of friends and they did not exclude me because I am a woman.

If you are thinking to visit Turkey I strongly recommend, not because it is my country but because I believe you are welcomed here. For example; Let's say you get on public transport and there is no place to sit, If you are a woman, I am sure someone of the opposite sex will definitely give you a seat. In my country, there is respect for the women. We all know that. The other example is, If you are a working woman and if you are pregnant, the company you work allows you to rest, even when you have the baby. As I said before, there are too many women that inspired me and inspiring me. Actually, I am interested in aviation. Sometimes I do research about female pilots. They are really good on their job. I adore them.

Turkey is a country that is socio-economically very advanced. Every year the numbers of the female pilots are increasing and in my opinion, this is a really good point. In some countries, women are not given the right to speak. They think that the opinions of male managers are taken more seriously. This kind of problems used to happen more often in my country, but now we are a developing country. The job of pilot has no gender. And this step really helps women to have success in something. There are some studies about "Women's Power in Culture" in Turkey.

The result of those researches shows us that Turkey is developing itself in this regard. There are also disadvantages as well as advantages of being a woman in Turkey. But as I said, Turkey is developing itself because the social perspective has changed in a positive way. If I talk about myself, I am very happy to live in my country. Some problems we have as women are the same all over the world. But the important thing is how to overcome these problems and as a country, we have come a long way. I can't live anywhere else. I graduated from university five months ago. I do translations online and I work from my house. It helps me to improve myself and as a woman, I am improving myself day by day. I do not need anybody. More precisely, I do not need anyone to improve myself. The day will come where I will serve my country and I will be a useful woman for my country.

My Life As A Woman: Turkey Edition #2

My name is Bilge. I am a computer engineer from Turkey. However, I currently live in the U.S. I am working for a tech company and I am also a freelance writer. I am here to tell my story and hopefully inspire you. I grew up in Ankara/Turkey, in a small family. I had a happy childhood and I was raised in a very friendly and a welcoming culture. I still think, being hospitable and welcoming to everyone is the best feature of Turkish culture.

I was a very curious kid who was questioning everything. Then, I grew up, but this habit never disappeared. When I started middle school, I noticed my passion for computers, and I wanted to learn how they function. So, I decided to become a computer engineer. However, when I started high school this, habit was not appreciated by most of my classmates an even by some of my teachers. Therefore, I felt very discouraged and started to plan on being a typical teenager. At that time of my life, my father made a very empowering speech to me. I still remember his speech very clearly. Amongst all the things he told me, this part always stayed with me: "Time changes but the people and their obsolete mindset will never change. Because you are different, you can be excluded sometimes but never forget that there are people like you in the world. Some of them are even better, more curious, more intellectual than you. Do not change your dreams because the people around you say so. Go, explore the world and find those people who are like you." After that speech, I started to ignore people who would demoralize me. And guess what, I became much happier than I had been before.

At high school, I discovered a new passion: WRITING. I did not plan to make a career out of it, but I knew I wanted to maintain this passion as far as it goes. In my sophomore year, I thought the best decision for me would be to study abroad. So, I did my research and planned to go to the USA for a bachelor's degree. That is still one of the boldest decisions that I have made in my life. Because, before college, I had never been out of Turkey and I wanted to go to America. Also, even my father supported me from the beginning, my mother was very skeptical. She had concerns about how I could afford the school and how I could thrive in a community, where I've never been before; especially as a young lady. But at the end, even she was convinced because she saw the dedication that I had for it. Then, I went to Ohio State university and graduated as the best student in my class. As I was studying, I also worked at my school for four years and managed to pay for my tuition.

After college, I decided to stay in the US. I applied to several tech companies and got into one of them. Till then, I thought I had been through the hardest obstacles that I could have ever encountered, but I was wrong. Surviving in a company that was male-dominated was a very compelling job to accomplish at the beginning. As I was gaining more experience in the field, I realized that in terms of gender inequality; no company is different than the other. I have encountered many silly questions as a female engineer who wanted to venture and become a member of the company's board of management. However, I believe the silliest one was this: "Do you have children or are you planning to have in the near future?" But, this really should not scare you. Because, once you can attain to show off your skills, they stop asking these silly questions.

Finally, what I can advise to Turkish woman is that; if you believe you have the ambition for the career you want to pursue, nothing and no one should stop you. Sometimes, you can even be in a position that you have to confront with your own parents. But remember, this is your life and therefore those are your decisions. Be aware of the fact that, at the end of the day you will be on your own and have the full responsibility for everything you have and haven't done. To me, one of the most intimidating things about life is to feel remorse on your deathbed for the things that I didn't attempt. Because, you can learn a lesson even from your worst mistake, but you can never know what you are missing when you don't attempt to do something. Always keep that in mind and show off what you are capable of to everyone.

My Life As A Woman: Turkmenistan Edition #1

As a living woman in Turkmenistan, (Central Asia) a little story from my life. I grew up in Ashgabat capital city of Turkmenistan which is known with its marble buildings around the world. I was born in middle class family and my family is nuclear family, including my brother and I, and our parents. It is really interesting to be women in here. From childhood your parents or elders teach you how to behave like Turkmen girl, girl's behavior in family is vital. Typical Turkmen girl is with long hairs, long dress, master of sewing and cooking, loyal to family and children, prioritizes ethics, morals and father's pride, respecting elders. Boy is the someone who should protect and continue family generation, in other hand girl is considered to be the honor of father and if you have brother you are like your brother's angel.

I remember when my brother told me, "I am your guardian angel, and I will do anything to help you have a better future". Girls are considered as their brother's face. While I grew up my mother taught me how to sew and cook and she learnt from her mother, it's early tradition in Turkmen culture that every girl should learn sewing. There is saying that "girls every finger should be master at something". I finished my secondary school in one of the specialized schools of Ashgabat for languages. Our ancestors were patriarchal society, women were only to sit in their home and take care of the children and do the house works and sewing. But with the globalizing world it changed time by time. So, I didn't want to sit at home, I wanted to be teacher. Why, because I like teaching children's and students and engage with them it's what I am good at, I think.

What I adore about my culture is that children are supposed to take care of their parent's when they get older especially boys, it's every child's dream to look after their parents. Your parents look after you until you get married and leave the home, even they bear every financial problem you may have. And as a girl I am the angel of my father, it's every parent's dream to see their girls in bride's white dress in our culture. Another thing is that here most of the population is Muslim so, mothers are considered as an entrance to heaven in our culture, there is a saying that, "key of the heaven is lies under the foot of your mother" it means you should respect your parents.

I work as a teacher in school, I teach student's and prepare them for life and University entrance exams. Actually, I don't have any struggles as a woman in my field, here more than half of the teachers are female ones. Only struggle could be if you are a new and young teacher, it's challenging to teach teenagers for starters. My success as a woman is that I can continue my career wherever I want. Now I am planning to be the director of a school in the future. Turkmenistan is known with its high gender equality, if you want to work or study, you can do it freely, even government pays for your secondary education it's free and compulsory and another good thing for women is that they can retire earlier than men and we have maternity leave for mothers.

To conclude from my personal experience, it's free to have your own career, no matter your gender is. So, my advice to women in my culture is: if you have your dreams, chase it, use the opportunities that's being provided and respect your culture since it's something unique and heritage meantime be open to new ideas.

My Life As A Woman: Turkmenistan Edition #2

Where did you grow up?

My mum gave birth to me in the heart of Turkmenistan in the capital of Ashgabat. This is one of the historical and modern parts of today's Turkmenistan. I completed my school and college here, unfortunately for most of the women, getting a degree in University is restricted or have strict regulations where they are only able to acquire a degree in religion.

How did you grow up?

Fortunately, my father nowadays is working in the U.S., therefore the payment he has been sending us for about 15 years has been more than enough live on for good conditions. But the cost of it was high, as almost my entire childhood was provided in my grandmother's home and mummy's kind-hearted relation to me, however, I was without my father's lessons about life and how to succeed in it.

Did you have parents or maybe a grandmother who inspired you?

My father is an outstanding IT programmer, he graduated Stanford university in Palo-Alto. Nowadays, he is making applications for dealing with the coronavirus. He was born without parents, he didn't even live in children's community houses, where someone could take care of him. Due to his eagerness to study and making business he succeeded. This is the reason of achieving goals such as migrating to US, getting a degree, and taking his life expenses by himself which made him strong individual that seeks new trends and fields to thrive.

What did you study / What you want to be growing up / Why?

I have completed my professional college in business administration. This field always drives me, getting familiar with new formats of business and being able to manage huge a company with thousands of workers is great responsibility that I want to take. I think only three people in businesses bring it to breakthrough:

1. Idea holder
2. Investors
3. Managers and businesses administrators.

Even though, contribution to society is huge, therefore the strong intentions make bring it to highly competitive environment.

What do you love about your culture?

Probably the sense of patriotism. Nowadays, here in Turkmenistan economic situation is under UN official aid and many organisations, yet almost all compatriots living in developed countries make contributions to government and society at whole.

What are you currently doing for work?

Neither studying nor working. I am in my gap year, trying all of the fields at minimum to understand which one will suit me most. Hope after passing all of the exams like TOEFL and SAT is would be admitted by top universities in US.

Tell me about your struggles as a woman.

It is an unpleasant topic for all women in Turkmenistan, girls were born to be a slave for their husbands, they are exploiting them and taking advantage of them by sexual harassments on daily basis. If someone wants to get a particular girl to be beloved and make a family, they don't ask their permission for this, it is like a tradition to kidnap beautiful girls to make them slaves for the rest of their life. Sometimes mutual agreements occur to build a family but if you had sexual contact with someone else,

584

a high school nurses will check your virginity, and if you are not a virgin, you are blamed, shamed, disgraced, and you are no longer considered suitable for marriage.

Tell me about your successes as a woman.

Learning languages and taking the SAT was an extremely challenging period in my life. I am crisscrossing my fingers, hoping to get a high result, which will allow me to realize my potential in other developed countries.

Provide some advice to women from a woman living in Turkmenistan.

Never stay calm and live in a situation where you do not want to be. Consider your life as a game starting from level 0 you have to get to 99. I know being financially successful in Turkmenistan is not possible, because more of the 70% of population live in poor conditions. Try to go overseas to show your performance and where you can be famous and adorable. Even though, don't forget about your homeland, always help people from there and devote something to elaborate the political and economic situation.

My Life As A Woman: Tuvalu Edition

Another small but full of interesting things, a country called Tuvalu is situated in Polynesia, Pacific Ocean. Yes, it is a poor and really small country, but people here are very trustworthy and kind, and here is the explanation why in Tuvalu the level of crime is zero. Our cuisine is different from other popular world foods, and the one I like most is our traditional food called 'pulaka', it is swamp culture. As we are a sea country, our fishing is very developed, even a big part of our government revenues comes from fishing, so it is the other factor to be proud of my country.

I am a young woman, my name is Alesi and I am from Funafuti, but I grew up and still live in the capital of Tuvalu, Fongafale. I was born in a full family, with parents, grandparents, brothers, sisters, and even with uncles and aunts. All my life I was taught to respect others, their rights, and their thoughts and in general everyone. My parents showed me and my siblings how to do that, and they were good teachers for us. With their strong support, I entered the University of the South Pacific, the faculty of business, and economics. The university is located in Fiji, so I temporarily live in Suva, Fiji waiting for my graduation. After that, I am planning to go back to my lovely family and look for a job there. I do have a lot of plans concerning my career, as the faculty I am studying in is really serious and I have to approve myself that all the effort worth my time, that I passed there.

At the moment I do not have any job, but I hope on the best and really dream about being rich and every day makes my parents' and relatives' life enjoyable and full of presents. At this time, I'm not even thinking about marriage to someone or making a family, my first and the most important goal is to buy a big house for my family, to give them all they need and make a lot of surprises for them.

I don't even have a rich life experience or haven't gone through difficult situations so it is a really challenging and responsible thing to come up with a piece of advice for all the women in the world. Anyways I will tell you some things, which come from my heart and I would love to see in our women. I want them to be respectful to others, to be kind, and to help others with anything they can. I want women to love themselves, to be confident, and never be shy of their look or face or other parts of their bodies. Go ahead and find the things that inspire you, that make you happy and satisfied. Never strive to be like others, and remember you are unique as you are, you are beautiful and amazing.

My Life As A Woman: Uganda Edition #1

Hello, my name is Annet. I grew up in Kampala, Nakawa, Kataza. Kampala is the only city in my country Uganda and it's also the capital city. Nakawa is a crowded place, therefore had a large number of neighbors.

I still remember my childhood days when I usually woke up at 5 am daily, I freshened up, had breakfast and then went to school. I walked to my school which was approximately 2 kilometers away. I returned back to my home at around 4 pm. Then I freshened up right before having my supper which was normally some porridge. I later did my school homework. Then I helped my mom in doing some house chores like washing, cleaning, cooking etc. My family always had dinner together and immediately we all went to bed at approximately 9 pm.

Every year, our government organizes the Kampala City Festival, where Kampala becomes animated with flamboyant sights, vibrant sounds & lively rhythms in concert with an array of floats winding through the streets with dancers on show as they spin, whirl & twirl to mesmeric beats of celebration along the festival route revealing all facets that uniquely depict our profusion of brilliant culture and social life. When I was 17 years old, I and my friends decided to participate in the festival and so, we created a small dance group. When the day came, we dressed up in our cultural clothes and performed the Acholi traditional dance in front of a roaring crowd. This is one of the most memorable and amazing times of my life.

We lived in a fairly small house with only two bedrooms and one sitting room in it, I had to share my bedroom with my siblings, I have three brothers and two sisters. My mother was an inspirational figure to me. She was a hardworking, committed, loving and caring woman. This set an example for me to look up to and fueled me to work hard in life myself.

My school was named Uphill School located in Mbuya. It was a fairly large school with approximately 685 students and 5 teachers per class. We had extra-curriculum activities like sports (netball, basketball, football etc.) science club, arts and crafts classes. We studied geography, chemistry, math, English etc. in school. I wanted to be an Artist when I grew up. I was really good at art, I thought it was fun and relaxing.

I belong to the Acholi culture of western Uganda, we speak the Luo language. I love my cultural food which is Millet Posho with sauce or as called in our local language, Malakwang. This is really tasty and healthy. I and my family go to church on every Sunday to do our weekly prayers.

When I grew up, I had to support my big family, therefore I had to leave my studies and start doing a job. Due to high unemployment rate in our country, it was getting hard to get a good job, so I ended up working as a housemaid. I am currently working as a maid at Namuwongo Area, Kampala.

I got married and I have three girls, my husband wasn't able to support our family and one day he left me. Now, I have to support my whole family on my own. This includes sending my children to school, paying rent, plus a lot of other expenses along with working a fulltime job. I also had to send two of my daughters to boarding school as I couldn't afford to keep them home with me.

During this pandemic period, I have to deal with a lot more challenges, for example, I have to walk a long distance of 10km everyday just to get to my workplace due to shutdown of public transport services. Even though I have to go through all these struggles, I still manage to live a happy life.

I advise all other Ugandan ladies to be hardworking and patient no matter the hardship. You should never give up and always trust in God. And also, always listen to your elders.

This is from an interview with a female staff member of mine, Ms. Annet.

My Life As A Woman: Uganda Edition #2

Uganda is a beautiful country with good weather and fresh food. It also has its challenges as a developing country. It is home to over 40 million people, speaking over 40 different languages. That should give you an idea of the diverse culture.

I was born and raised in Kampala, the capital city of Uganda. Both my parents come from the Eastern part of the country, although they speak different languages. Growing up, I was influenced more by my mother's language and culture since she was the stay-at-home parent. Unfortunately, this seems to be the case in most households in the country, whether the woman is working or not. The children tend to favor her culture or language unless the man takes it upon himself to educate his children on his language and culture.

My family comes from a very humble beginning, my father grew up in serious poverty, with a father that had over 10 wives, and yes, you guessed it, very MANY children. My mother came from a reasonably well-to-do family although her father also came from serious poverty.

When my parents got married, they used to stay in a single room, with barely any coins to rub between their fingers. By the time I was born, they had moved into a two-room house in a community housing (funded by the government). I am the last of three children.

With hard work and perseverance, they have managed to bring their family into the beginnings of middle-class living. All children managed to be taken to schools that provide good education. I never really thought about what I wanted to become when I grew up. I always thought I would follow what my parents wished-which was to join the medical field. I, however, have always been creative, something which has helped me as I grow up.

I love traditional dance, but unfortunately, hate the one from my mother's side. It doesn't have as much flavor as the one on my father's. All the waist-twisting vigorous dancing and smiles plus profuse sweating can be enjoyed on my father's side of the family.

My father greatly influenced me growing up. I wanted to be as successful as he was. I also vowed to get as good and caring a man as him for my husband. I remember getting very poor grades in Mathematics, something he was good at and something that would help in my Medical course and he tirelessly worked to ensure I passed it. I am proud to say that I took up mathematics up to my university where I studied Software Engineering. Unfortunately, he died when I was still a teenager.

I used to fear my mother A LOT! African mothers tend to discipline their kids a lot. Just to give you an idea, an old-school African mother can beat you for doing something bad then beat you for crying. If you are unlucky, you can also find one who will beat you for not crying, then, you guessed it, proceed to beat you for crying!

I used to think she wasn't my mother. She was a true militia when it came to discipline! I was a timid little mouse when around her then I would beam from ear to ear when dad was around. When my dad died, I thought I was finished!

We had to struggle through uncles looking to snatch the deceased's property thus leaving us with nothing. I started to see my mother with different eyes. She is one phenomenal woman and she is still my inspiration! She managed to out-smart the greedy uncles, retain the family property, and as if that was not enough, she managed to multiply it while raising and educating us! She is still militia but underneath it all, I call her my little pussy cat. She will roar like a lion but is the sweetest, caring being you will ever find! She has turned into my confidant and best friend over the years.

As a woman living in Uganda, I have had my share of struggles. But, I am blessed I didn't get the wrong end of the stick like some women I know. Think things like being harassed for sexual favors at the workplace or having to live with an abusive spouse and equally abusive in-laws. My struggles have majorly been in expressing myself in the local setting. Unfortunately, most women are harassed by hooligans in downtown market areas, from the market vendors to the boda-boda(motorcycle riders) and taxi drivers. You just need to develop a thick skin to push through.

I was lucky enough to get my first job in a prominent telecom company just as I was about to finish university. I loved working there for about two and a half years till envious workmates reared their ugly heads. I left work and pounded the streets for new work. I ended up working in an Indian's shop for exactly 9 days until I asked myself what I was doing! I earned a measly 5,000/USh (approximately $1.2 USD) a day, working from 7 am to 6 pm-6 days a week!

As mentioned before, I have a very creative streak and tend to self-teach myself A LOT! I wondered what was stopping me from working for myself. I started with online research for online work. I landed on good contracts at the first try and that gave me hope. I left the corporate world in 2013 and I have never looked back!

To supplement my online work, I also taught myself baking, décor, and wig-making and these have helped me survive with no regrets.

What advice would I give a woman living in Uganda? I would advise her to never stop learning. Soak up as much knowledge as you can and utilize it to better yourself-whether financially, spiritually, or mentally.

My Life As A Woman: Ukraine Edition

My name is Tetiana, I'm 26 and I am from Ukraine. Despite the fact that I was born in Kazakhstan, my father in Ukraine, and my mother in Belarus, I still feel being Ukrainian. I don't know what made my parents, maternal aunt, paternal uncle and dad's parents rage quit and sell in total three houses, all livestock, leave their jobs and move to Ukraine, where only one house for everyone was bought in a small village and initially no one had any potential job. (Nope, it seems that I lied, we didn't sell all the cattle, I remember how huge freight containers came with our stuff and our cow arrived in one of them.) I asked my relatives about the reason for our 'expatriation', but no one really was able to answer. Some only suggested: "In search of better fortune." And it worked out very well.

The first two grades I studied at a rural school, then on the recommendation of my godmother who has been living in Ukraine all his life my parents with a heavy heart sent me to a private school for girls only. It was a fee-paying school with a schedule from 8 am to 8 pm and those who lived far away could stay for a whole week, only leaving for the weekend. This was my case. And from now on I visited my parents only on the weekends.

In addition to general subjects, we were taught music, dancing (classical, ballroom and folk), horseback riding, sports training, ethics and etiquette, valeology and culinary. Each year, we held winter and spring balls with cadets invited from the military lyceum located in the same city where our school was, went camping with them, visited philharmonic, theaters and opera. It was the most eventful and one of the happiest periods in my life. Such schools are a rarity, probably not only for Ukraine.

Recently I realized that it was the headmaster of this school who was my mentor, whom I still strive to be compliant with. Finding time for each class, and if necessary, for each schoolgirl, she explained that we need to achieve everything ourselves, we always need to strive for excellence, be human, be able to prioritize our life, understand what we want and, choosing one path, be aware what the cost might be and risks might occur, eventually not to be disappointed. This slightly contradicts the initial Ukrainian sentiment and understanding when Ukrainian woman should be exclusively the guardian of the hearth, a good mother and wife, a real mistress. We were taught to listen to ourselves, to hear others and respect their opinions, we were taught to think independently, soberly and uncommon.

I graduated from one of the country's most prestigious universities and dreamed of becoming a diplomat or any other representative of my country in order to protect and promote its interests, achieve success at the state level. I still want to support my country in any possible way. At the moment, I work in engineering and consulting company, which helps the relevant ministries to implement transport and infrastructure projects in different Ukrainian cities. It is very inspiring when you can see any positive result (new comfortable buses and trams, new stations, rest areas and new bicycle lanes etc.), in which there is your contribution. At times like this you feel significant. You want to create more and more.

When I was asked at the job interviews who I see myself in 5-10 years, I have to come up with an answer that would suit this vacancy or my interviewer. Because the answer "I just want to be happy with my life and not regret the past" or "have a job that inspires me" is not suitable for the employer. Maybe it's not good that I don't imagine myself being a big boss or business woman that I don't dream of leaving my country, as most of my peers do, whatever, to be honest, like most of my fellow citizens do.

All I want is to be happy, but many of my entourage either do not believe me or consider me undecided. No doubt, I want more than I have now, in all perspectives, moral, intellectual and material. Currently I am a project assistant and my manager is younger than me, but I really don't fret at all about it or about level of my position or prestige. I can even be a maid or work three jobs, but if this job is not stressful and doesn't get on my nerves (after 5-10 years I would like to be a healthy person on top of all), an income is satisfactory and allows me to live as I want, whatever someone would say, I'd be delighted.

The end.

There is an important and deep-rooted aspect of the Ukrainian habitude (maybe not only Ukrainian): "what will people think" or "it's not right". At the moment, I have been living in a civil marriage for almost

7 years and I am happy with everything. Except for one - my relatives and my common-law husband's relatives who constantly insist on our marriage because "it is not good to live like that so many years, and grandparents are already waiting impatiently, and all the other relatives want to go your wedding, etc. It even seems to me that if we finally get married, we will soon divorce, like Angelina Jolie and Brad Pitt or a bunch of other similar examples. Everyone starts to scare me with alimony or a division of property, but it doesn't work on me. And not because I love my husband and trust him completely, but because I don't care what happens afterwards, for some reason I'm sure that I can handle it anyway. This is desperate, but it's so for the moment. Therefore, I feel how important it is to respect someone's opinion, not to interfere in someone's life with your thoughts and stereotypes when you are not asked for and just enjoy your life.

My Life As A Woman: UAE Edition #1

My name is Saeeda Ashraf, a well-educated woman who has been living in the U.A.E for a decade as of today. I have chosen this area because it is one of the most civilized, respectful, and safest regions in the Gulf. To have the lowest crime rate in the world that crime is not an issue for travelers. The quality of life and overall living standards in Dubai are exceptional. Notably, there are no restrictions for women on where they can go or what they can do. However, men and women are both required to respectfully attend certain events separately, including schools and prayer. Also, locals are friendly and well known to have a reputation for offering travelers and immigrants with hospitality.

Although this may be true, I found it difficult to follow and deal with the luxurious lifestyle that includes private accommodation, personal transport, and most importantly, the struggles of facing racial discrimination, where a standard educated white man is given more priority by locals than on a master's degree holder of a brown man. I have felt the most racism and partiality here, but you must ignore the bitter injustice when you have several other possibilities. As a woman, I have suffered similar harassment where I am treated as if I am their private property. I had to quit my job one time because I believe that losing a job is better than losing respect. In this society, you can easily be fooled by men, specifically when you are alone then you are their primary target. I've fought tremendously in my life's battles, but I've won plenty.

In my childhood, I was raised in Qatar. I once belonged to a conservative and close-minded community where education was impossible for a girl, but now it's allowed with the passage of time. As a Muslim woman, I love my culture and my religion Islam, which allows women to inherit property, divorce, and make her husband responsible for her expenses. I have the right to get an education, vote, marry a man of my choice, and get a divorce where I can marry again.

My father is my role model, who went against the system and enrolled me in a school where he told me, "Don't let anyone prove me wrong by getting you an education". I will cherish those words in my heart forever. Therefore, I had the purpose to prove my father and myself right. My first milestone in life was succeeded in getting my master's degree in business administration. I remember on the day of my convocation when my name had been announced, I can vividly see my father's bright smile become a frown when my name was mispronounced as Saeeda Akhtar instead of Saeeda Ashraf, named after the female, doctor whose hand I was born into. He was upset and I told him, "Dad, you've written on my birth certificate Saeeda Akhtar instead of Ashraf Do'h," He then smiled at me. It was my dad's joy to be the first girl to not only open doors of education for many other girls but also be the first to drive a car in my village by not being involved in love scandals, drugs, and harmful addictions. My father's word of advice for life was to choose a respectful field, pursue it, and make a difference in a conservative society through positivity.

I had two dreams, one to go to the USA for certifications today, I am a USA certified HRM and Reiki Master. Western culture taught me a great deal about women's freedom, discipline, and confidence. My second dream was to be a professional female golf player and win several championships. It was my dad's love for golf that he played in our vast backyard. However, it took a lot of money and determination that I lacked both in. After my father left this world, I have more responsibility to support my family with a smile. Today, I am a successful Human Resources Expert with well-deserving earnings, a vehicle, and a flat in Dubai. During this global pandemic, I have rediscovered myself to begin playing golf once again and seek to get interested in the upcoming Fatima Bint Mubarak Ladies Open in UAE. This is an opportunity given by UAE to follow your dreams, and now it is only up to you to take this into account and to progress forward because we must try even if the possible outcome is a failure.

My Life As A Woman: UAE Edition #2

Where did you grow up?

I was born and raised in the old Dubai mid-town, when all the flavors of traditions, economic growth and temp of daily modernization was exciting and yet relaxing.

How did you grow up? Who inspired you?

I was raised by a very educated father and an extremely dedicated mother to be as productive and useful in the society as possible, this process was not without stress because the correctness, integrity and humbleness together With an absolute perfection were the only measurement criteria for my father. This was always eased off by the kind and comforting hands of my mother.

The combination of both fatherly guidance and the love of family with an open eyes for the present and future was presented to me in the fern of my brother, he showed me ways and methods and told me when what and how, he surely had the biggest influence in farming my character and in my development to whom I am today.

What did you study? What did you want to be growing up? Why?

I was blessed enough to have both the family support and the helping circumstances to study what I always wanted and dreamt of as a child, becoming a TV presenter and a media personality was calling and this fortunately for me was realized.

What do you love about your culture?

The UAE culture is beautiful, it is a mixture of old and new it is a mixture of Arabic/ Islamic and international. But the most interesting for me and what is in my opinion not very common is the culture of change and development which is, of course, based on the culture of tolerance and the desire for perfection.

What are you currently doing for work?

I'm diverse in my activities, but of course within my own main line (media), amongst which is media consultant and certified media and self-development trainer nevertheless, my current main occupation is senior news reporter for Emirates news, which is part of Dubai Media Incorporated.

Tell me about your struggles as a woman.

UAE is an extremely unique place when it comes to gender related equality, we have never felt any difference at work or educational institutions, having said that, I have to say that I was one of the very first woman in UAE to choose This line and proving myself required a bit of time and effort, but due to the amazing culture of equality reaching to goals and to people's ears and eyes has always been possible nevertheless this doesn't mean that I have not had everyday usual life difficulties, such as being a loving mother a dedicated wife and a reporter at the same time such as working and studying for further development at the same time, and such as facing challenges of dangerous work environments as we lately had due to the COVID-19 pandemic and its impact on our daily life because obviously there can't be a choice between safety of family members and reporting extremely important news that will uplift the spirits of the society, both are crucial for life continuity both have to be taken care of.

Tell me about your successes?

Thanks to God Almighty, I have had many successes, but what I consider as my biggest success is being able to stay at an age between 8 to 9 years old and have continued up till now, even during my studies, I had the pleasure of presenting and conducting programs.

Provide some advice from to women from a woman living in UAE.

As woman we should not consider ourselves different in every aspect, we are all human and we all (man and woman) have the same desires, hopes and wishes the difference is in the way we preserve and react, but not necessarily in the way we wish and we perform. Forget your fears, overcome them, they are nothing but a creation of your own imagination and unnecessary insecurities, so be yourself, give generously, do not get tired and continue In your path till you succeed, because you diffidently will inshallah.

My Life As A Woman: United Kingdom Edition

UK To New Zealand: Life As A Woman Navigating The World

As I approach a half century (which I can't quite believe) it seems like a good time to reflect; where I am now, how I got here and what I have learnt from my experiences.

Huge caveat here: this is just based on my experiences and my personal views. There is no scientific background to any of these statements!

I was lucky to grow up in a strong family and a nice area of the UK. My parents are still together and worked hard to give my siblings and I a balanced upbringing and a good education. This is despite the fact that, as a girl, my paternal grandparents would have taken me out of school at 16 to learn to sew and cook. Did anything have a massive impact on my future? It probably all did, but there are only a couple of things that really stand out to me now. My maternal grandmother, who loved us dearly was a massive constant in our lives, albeit a little annoying to the teenage me sometimes. My sports. I loved, and still do love, sports. I was lucky to be given the opportunity to try a number of different sports including sailing, which still plays a huge part in my life; it is how I met my husband, my children sail, it offered me a co-ed environment (despite my all girl education), gave me the opportunity to compete as an equal, helped me develop a number of useful business skills (resilience, strategy, tactical moves and more) and perhaps provided me with one of the biggest influences in my young life; Maiden.

I was 17 when the very first all-female crew started the Whitbread Round the World Race aboard Maiden. The story of how they got to the start line is an inspiration in itself, but I was interested in the race. Tipped to fail at every hurdle and probably not get back alive the crew not only finished the race, they won two legs (of six), finished second overall and still hold the best result for a British boat in this race. For a 17-year-old girl the message was clear — women can do anything they choose.

My late teens and early adult life were fairly ordinary. University (Business Information Systems), a job (Marketing), marriage and first child. Then my husband was offered the chance of a job in France. Eleven years, three countries and two more children later we finally arrived in New Zealand. It all sounds, and was, a truly amazing experience and I will be eternally grateful to my husband's career for these opportunities. Expat life does present its challenges. Pack up your lives, leave friends; build a new life, make new friends, have new incredible experiences; and repeat!

So, what have I learnt from all this:

Be open-minded: Growing up in the UK, I somehow learnt that my friends should be people like me. Those with the same upbringing, social class, values. If I had stuck to this I would have been very lonely and missed out on some of the most amazing life experiences. I now have friends all around the world, from many cultures, who have taught me so much about myself.

Don't judge others: A little like the above, but seriously, everyone has a story. From the helpers in Singapore who work to pay for education for their children that they see once a year, to my friend from Venezuela, who left 5 home helps to move to Switzerland and always had a smile on her face (the cleaning must have been a shock!).

Be who you want to be I loved architecture and teaching growing up. I was put off architecture by a professional, who said it was too male dominated a profession for girls, and put off teaching, as society gave the impression this career was for those not clever enough for a real job. By the way, we change as we experience life so it's ok to change your mind too!

Step out of your comfort zone: That's where the magic happens. Moving around the world was something I never thought I would do but has provided me with the best years of my life (so far!).

Get support when you need: And don't be afraid to ask (the hardest part!). There were plenty of times when I needed practical help or emotional support and I would not be where I am today without it. As a mother this is particularly true and as a mother trying to balance a work too even more so.

Have fun: The UK culture is often about glass half empty, or stiff upper lip. Ride the emotions and don't be afraid to express them – the good and the bad. They are all part of the journey. Most of all have fun.

Take up sailing: Well, do what you love. Actually, scratch that, take up sailing!

The next adventure: My boys are growing up and it's time to get back into the business world. I've re-studied and am slowly working my way through a massive to do list to start my new career.

If you'd like to know more about Maiden check out www.themaidenfactor.org.

My Life As A Woman: Akrotiri and Dhekelia Edition #1

My life has been part of a fairy tale, I have been living in Akrotiri with my family all my childhood. As a woman or a girl that has been living in the British Overseas territory part of the British army, I have to be very strict and organized. In the base, we had everything from schools, shops, library and also markets with music and entertainment two times per year.

We have been living in a very closed society of soldiers and the military. My mother always said to me that I am a small princess which had a very difficult mission to be learning and keeping the tradition of England in our small village. We had a security entrance and we have been living all together, only military families. I should always stay ready for changing our house because of my father service at The British Army.

As a woman in our small village, I have been reading fairy tales about queens and kingdoms. And my mother had made our small fairy tale with special tea ceremonies every day with an interesting book and beautiful clothes for princesses. She made my life very easy and amazing with a lot of reading but with a positive environment. I was sure that we were part of the British Queen family because we were closed from the other world and we needed to learn more than two languages. Our schools were very strict and difficult, we were studying almost all day long. The training of our body and health was second priority to our education but a very big part of our life. But why I am saying all this, nowadays, I am a military doctor. As a woman in a world full of men, especially living a military life, I feel like a princess still because I am living in a society which has huge respect for women.

My family taught me to believe that there are no impossible things in the world. They always respect every woman and man, they always keep the British tradition and they always describe beautiful places from the world. I was dreaming of being part of the army but with responsible tasks. And when I was a teenager I fell in love with biology and chemistry, I found the amazing life of the animals and how they take care of their health. My mother taught me to think positive to concentrate and she was a very open-minded person. I start yoga with her and sometimes I help my patients with methods of birthing from the yoga study.

What do you have to know about me?

I am a mother with a very important "life work". Lifework means I am always ready to save lives and to help people in danger. I am a soldier and I am proud of my life as a woman. I never felt different as a soldier woman and I have always respect because of my job. But the most important in my life was my family positive and healthy life even in one very small and closed society where all women have great respect. And nowadays I see many articles about successful women, and I believe that if you do not a separate woman from a man you can have success stories. And my society teach me to be grateful for what I have and how to respect all people and the rank of all them that means difficult and hard work. Believe in you and do not forget we are women with beautiful clothes and strong willpower.

My Life As A Woman: Akrotiri and Dhekelia Edition #2

I am a Cypriot woman from the military family that it had lived in Dhekelia. This base in Cyprus is very small and it is a British territory with Sovereign Base Areas of Dhekelia. The areas, which include British military bases and installations, as well as another land, were retained by the British under the 1960 Treaty of Independence, signed by the United Kingdom, Greece, Turkey and representatives from the Greek and Turkish Cypriot communities, which granted independence to the Crown colony of Cyprus.

My father is Turkish-Cypriot who was living in one small village in the Paphos area before the Cyprus Turkey war in 1974. In 1975, he went with his family in England and later on he got part of the English army.

He was telling me stories of his life before the war and how they lived in harmony Greeks and Turkish Cypriots. He went with my mother to Cyprus in Dhekelia because both of them are in love with Cyprus and they would like to keep the peace in the area.

I am a Catholic woman with Turkish roots. All my life I learned how to respect others and their beliefs. My grandmother wasn't living with us, but the little time with her was the best moments of my childhood. She always described to me how she met my grandfather and how they fell in love. He was a soldier in the Turkey army and she was a beautiful Turkey girl living in Cyprus. The magnificent story of how they were struggling to get married. I was so excited to find the love of my life and to fight for it that years later I fell in love with an English soldier. And the story of endless love becomes a true story.

My family is very polite and respectful to other nations but in the beginning, they weren't very happy. He was ten years older than me and he was subordinate of my father. He was a big friend with my family and he was coming to my house every Sunday lunch to have souvlaki and baklavas. He was so grateful to come and be part of our family which were side by side. And I think he was dreaming to have a wife to cook tasty food and keep clean his beautiful house.

I am a housewife even if I was taught by my family that the woman can be a very big rank in the army and that men respect women in the army. I wasn't thinking about a career in the army. My family was so focused on my education and knowledge that sometimes I think they forgot my will. But I told you my father and my mother was open to new life and safe relations between all people. One year later, after several speeches of my father, they said "Yes" for our wedding.

And now I am living with my amazing husband John and our three kids back in Cyprus in Dhekelia for the past five years. Time has taught me that the main idea of a happy life is not who you are, what nation you are from, or what your job is, it is all about love and respect. I believe in karma and how the positive emotion brings positive coincidence. I am a happy woman living my dream life with a big amazing family.

My Life As A Woman: Anglesey Island Edition

Where did you grow up?

My name is Sharon Hughes. I was born on in Holyhead on the island of Anglesey in 1970. Anglesey is an island but is connected to the mainland by a bridge, so it doesn't feel too remote.

How did you grow up?

I lived in a council house with my parents. My dad worked on the ferries that go over to Dublin, so that kept him busy and he always seemed to be away from home. My mum had jobs on and off – her health was never too good, so I spent a lot of my time looking after her. I didn't have any brothers or sisters, but I had a pet cat – Charlie. It was a happy childhood – we weren't rich or anything, but always had enough to get by.

Did you have a parent or grandparent that inspired you?

My grandmother used to come around sometimes to help out when my mum got too ill. She was so caring for us and never seemed to think about herself. She helped me look after my mum even when her own health was not too good. I liked her caring attitude and hope that I have that too.

What did you study and what did you want to be when growing up?

I worked hard at school and always wanted to be a doctor, but I knew even back then I was not quite that clever. I still worked hard though, as I wanted to get good grades and make my family proud of me.

What do you love about your culture?

On Anglesey most of us still speak Welsh every day. I use it at home with my family and you can still hear people speaking it on the street, not just in the small villages, but also here in a larger town like Holyhead. I like that – it makes me feel part of my culture. Anglesey is an island, but as we have a bridge to the mainland we can easily leave the island if we want to, so it's good that we can still enjoy the island culture and at the same time be part of mainland Welsh culture.

What are you currently doing for work?

I didn't manage to become a doctor, but I did become a nurse. I've been doing that most of my life – I used to work in Ysbyty Gwynedd which is the largest hospital in the area, but nowadays I work in Cefni Hospital which provides care to elderly patients. I love my job and wouldn't change it for anything in the world.

Tell me about your successes as a woman?

Being able to forge a career that I love, that is my greatest success I suppose. I now live in a nice house in a nice part of town and when I compare that to how and where I grew up then guess that gives me an idea of how to measure how successful I've been. I'm good at my job too and have had promotions.

Provide some advice to a woman living on Anglesey?

Never think that you're living on an island, as if you do that then you will just become isolated. Rather think of yourself as living in an interesting part of the world and then you might get to see the wider picture. Work hard, both in your studies as well as in your career, and you can achieve anything.

My Life As A Woman: Anguilla Island Edition

My name is Samara Jones, born and raised national of Anguilla. Growing up in the Valley, which is the capital, was one of the best things that ever happened to me. The largest town in the center of the island, which is The Valley is flat, quiet and peaceful. It was a heaven-sent gift raising up in that area because, the environment booming. Everything you needed was within your reach. Amongst three children, I was the last and believe I was spoilt rotten. I really couldn't help it but to keep myself together and do what was best for me.

I lived with my Grandparents and siblings. They all would be together in the kitchen making all the delicious cuisine's you can think of. So, I always admired how everyone would come together and cook almost all the time. I then developed a love for cooking because I was greatly inspired by them all.

I studied Culinary Arts in school just because of the love I had for cooking and was always willing to create something new, so everyone at home could sample. However, growing up, nursing was at heart. I enjoyed caring for persons whether they were well or not especially the elderly. I have always been motivated by helping others to achieve anything they would like. Really and truly, nursing offers a unique opportunity to help people work towards achieving a healthy state of being which is one of the most important aspects of life.

The culture up here is something to experience for one's self. As for me, I really enjoy the traditional holidays as well as the annual Anguilla Summer Festival. We also use the United States currency. I am proud of our peaceful and unique culture, which places a strong emphasis on faith, family and friendliness. Not forgetting our lovely sandy beaches, the coral reef and the delicious food. Our culture is one of a kind, there's no other like this.

Due to COVID-19, I am now a Housekeeper, before I was a Chef, and I also did all types of pastries as well especially custom baked cakes. My struggle as a woman was finding a job. Yes, I grew up without having to struggle so much but I was always determined to get my own financial rewards. In my opinion, there isn't sufficient jobs for ladies so it's a little void. I still do pastries once in a while but only through orders and we know how the ongoing pandemic has slowed down everything.

My greatest success is being a Chef as well as getting an opportunity to go and do nursing which is one of the many things I always dreamt of. So, I try my best to balance it and it has been working out well so far. Soon I will be a certified graduate, with my Culinary Arts qualifications on the other hand.

My advice to the women living in Anguilla is; No matter what your background is or was, never give up and keep on pressing on even though the jobs are limited but the more we educate ourselves the better for us. Continue to be the good ladies we are! Follow your dream, and always surround yourself with persons that will empower you to do better or to move forward. Don't forget to always stay happy, support one another!

My Life As A Woman: Bermuda Edition

Bermuda is actually one of the most unique and mysterious places in the world. Actually, it seems that many people do not know about such a formidable place like Bermuda, which is a real pity. Bermudians are really nice people, and this kindness is in everyone's genetics as we are really kind polite and honest people. Briefly, Bermuda is a heaven on Earth, it is unique with its rich and interesting history, its kindest habitants and breathtaking places where you can definitely forget about your problems and enjoy a simple view. What I like more is that people are full of love and her life seems easier.

I am Karen from Hamilton, Bermuda and I am a psychotherapist. I was born in Hamilton and grew up with my grandmother, who was like a mother for me. She gave me everything I have now, education, motivation and strength. Actually my education history is really rich, I was always striving to be the best and this led me to Florida where I did my masters. After my granny died I moved to the US to continue my education and find a job. As I graduated the faculty of psychology I wanted to study another branch which is called transpersonal psychotherapy. To be simpler it is a spiritual therapy, I mean it is a study of mind-body relations, consciousness and human transformation. It is a form to encourage and help a person to get acquainted with his/her potentials, to see their inner capabilities and to help grow and develop.

I wanted to help people who are in depression or who cannot properly evaluate themselves, their capabilities and potentials. I want everyone in this world to be inspired and psychologically stable, strong and durable. I work with many people, who see a real change in their spiritual field. Here is what inspires me and motivates to continue living and working. Helping people is my mission which I am ready to do in every moment of my life.

As I am a psychologist, my advice will be a bit psychological. Dear women, never let anything or anyone make you psychologically depressed, broken or under a strong pressure. Remember, we are the most beautiful creations of the world, never deprive you of the simplest but most important, try to combine everything at the same time work, do household chores, and always remain feminine. During my life I have worked with many women who were suffering from totally different things, but all the things led them to a depression, some women didn't even knew about their capabilities and only passing some séances with me they found out more about themselves. So this is really important for not only women but men to know what they are worth, know their potentials and get busy with their self-development. I am happy that I went to Florida and studied this profession, which only helps me to earn but also to always stay strong and be able to help people.

My Life As A Woman: British Virgin Islands Edition #1

The beautiful British Virgin Islands are territories owned by the British but lies in the Caribbean seas. It is made up of four large islands – Tortola, Virgin Gorda, Anegada, and Jost Van Dyke – and fifty smaller islands and cays. I grew up in Sandy Bottom, Virgin Gorda. My siblings and I went to school at Bregado Flax Educational Center near the mail office. We had to walk to school four times a day because there was no type of transportation when we were growing up. We woke up extra early with enough time to stop at the bakery on the way to school and grab some food. Our island was late on getting electricity, so our power isn't very strong especially when the storms come. When we are home from learning, we go crabbing. We mainly dip for lobster, fish, and conch. My family would also plant most of our meals, such as potatoes, peas, and many more. Some people might think that the way we grew up was bad, but I loved my family.

My name is Ashleey Gardener, and I am 28 years old. My grandmother helped my mother raise my siblings and me, and there are three of us. We have a piece of property up the hill, and we would tend to the sheep and goats. The good old days were when my mom and grandmother would strip us naked, and we would go into the ocean and play all day. They also taught all of us how to cook and fend for ourselves. This club teaches young people about the small necessities that are important in life, such as learning how to sew, make quilts, and do embroidery. The club was called the Virgin Gorda Welfare Club, we would have fun and improvise on little concerts and plays the kids would put on.

I currently have two boys and one girl. Both boys are very active and enjoy playing with their friends, and my baby girl is very hands-on and loves to learn new stuff just like her mother. Growing up with my mother and grandmother raising me, I have always been taught to be independent and not depend on anyone else. I can take care of myself and my family without any help from others. Like the Caribbean, we have our pride to hold against our names, and we would always try to find a different way to accomplish what we need instead of asking someone for help.

As life goes on, we will all have to face some challenges that come along with it. My mother has always been a strong advocate for equality, and she is still fighting for what she believes in. Any advice I would give to this generation of young girls would to be more confident in your work, don't let the negative energies influence your outcome. Also, never stop learning, knowledge is money.

My Life As A Woman: British Virgin Islands Edition #2

Hey everyone, I am Maria from Road Town, Tortola. Tortola is one of the islands that makes up the British Virgin Islands while Road town is a small place nestled in the middle of the Tortola island, My life didn't have the best start, my mother had me at a young age. She never told me about my father, but after a while, I realized why she never spoke about him. I had a good relationship with my mother; it was always just the two of us. Even though she was a young mother she showed me all I needed. She ensured I never lacked anything. My mother was my inspiration, she did it when everyone said she couldn't. She had me at 15 years, finished high school, and went to university. While everyone said she couldn't make it and that she's just a static "teen mother". She ensured I didn't make the same mistake she did.

I attended St. George's Primary then attended St. George's Secondary school. I took life very seriously because of all the things my mother told me. In school I had a few friends and kept my contact neutral, I wasn't going to let what happened to my mom happen to me. So it was just going to school and back. Growing up I wanted to be a social worker, so I worked hard. I got accepted to the top university in the Caribbean and left to study at the University of the West Indies, Cave Hill in Trinidad. I am currently in my second year and I work part-time as a makeup artist. I think after university I'll still continue part-time with the makeup business, but social work will definitely be my full-time job.

My British Virgin Island culture is the best. Like all the other Caribbean islands our people are warm, welcoming, and always looking to assist. We have some of the best-tasting food known to man, I can imagine having some kallaloo and steamed fish with johnnycakes right now. I have visited a few other islands and no other beach compared to our beaches. Our sand is white and powdery. The air has a fresh scent and with the palm trees overhead and the sun barely caressing your skin, is an amazing feeling.

Growing up the only struggle I had was people constantly judging me because of what happened to my mother. There was a level of pity that constantly overshadowed my life while growing up. Everyone assumed I would be just like my mother; having a child at a young age with no father. That I would come out to no good, but I made sure to prove them wrong. As I grew, I used their pity motivation to push me further.

To all the women in the British virgin islands, especially Tortola uses your struggle as a motivation. It won't be easy but it's possible if they say you can't do it just to prove them wrong. Success is the best revenge.

My Life As A Woman: British Virgin Islands Edition #3

by Erin Lotz

"What am I doing here?" I wonder to myself as I work away at a pile of halved onions, slicing them thinly with my diligently sharpened knife, pressing against an ever guiding hand that keeps the cuts even. "I should definitely start writing some more of my thoughts and ideas down," my stream of thought continues, a silent monologue keeping me company as I work. "It's so simple to do but I'm so tired when I get back to my room. Sometimes, I miss the simplicity of a tiny cabin, rocking gently in the forward hull of a yacht in the Caribbean seas. Sure, it didn't have a desk, but I feel like my thoughts were more ordered then, but then again, maybe it's just the haze of hindsight that has me thinking this way." I sigh, loosen my tightly wound shoulders that ache more and more each day, and continue my looping reverie as I slide the glistening slices of onions into a rectangular container, scraping them along to the edge of my chopping board and over with the back of my knife.

The idea that ignorance is bliss is something that cannot be overstated enough, in my opinion. For sure, I'd had my struggles working on a heavily chartered catamaran that sailed around the British Virgin Islands. It was always bustling with wealthy guests, eager to maximize their enjoyment of this paradise that I called home, not to mention the living situation where I couldn't fart without my crewmates overhearing and having a giggle at my expense. No, life hadn't been the idyllic picture that others seemed to paint but I had the job satisfaction of being paid to travel and spend my days preparing meal after glorious meal with a song in my heart for the joy that working with food brought to my soul.

My life began in the middle of a stormy May afternoon in Cape Town. I was birthed into the world by my exhausted mother who had suffered through induced labour for something close to 30 hours. My arrival was punctuated by a much larger change that was arriving in South Africa at the time – the oppressive Apartheid regime that had reigned in the country for the previous two generations was finally seeing it's downfall. I was born amongst a set of peers who would pave the path of a new way of life for many who had suffered the horrors of the brutal system.

My family is white, and so, in many ways, my predecessors principally benefitted from the cruel laws that the South African government introduced between the 1950s and my birth. The white privilege that we were furnished with was and still continues to be unfair to the people of my country, and moreover, to people of colour around the world. As a child, I grew up naïve to the divides that had so recently separated my fellow citizens, but as I grew older, I learnt more about the country's sordid past. This knowledge weighs heavily on my heart, since it imparts an ancestral guilt that I can only try and hope to make amends for. There are so many beautiful, interesting and diverse people that decorate the lands of my home and who have influenced me as I have grown into an adult. I am aware of the incurable pain that so many South Africans bear, yet I can never understand how deep it runs, how debilitating it may be, and many other aspects that it may embody in their lives. Nonetheless, I am intensely grateful to be a member of a generation that has experienced a mixing of culture, language, ethnicity and ideas. My life is much richer because of the amazing diversity of my peers and I am in debt to those who paid with their lives to achieve this reality for my country.

On a practical level, my upbringing was relatively comfortable, compared to many other children growing up in the world. My parents created a beautiful sister for me when I was three years old, and we lived in a big house with a swimming pool and green grass to play on. By the time I was 9, they made the decision to separate, and were divorced the following year. The legal termination was officiated on Valentine's Day, which certainly added insult to injury.

In the years that followed, my sister and I lived with our mother, who worked tirelessly to afford some version of the lifestyle we had grown accustomed to. It was a difficult and sometimes, impossible task for her to fulfil, yet she was relentless in her efforts to give us a good life. We attended decent schools, enjoyed a variety of extramural activities and were always fed and safe from danger. Our dad was also present in our lives, and we spent every other weekend with him, as well as Wednesday nights, where we'd either stay over at our grandparents who lived by the seaside, or at his home which was at least an hour's drive out of the city. I always longed for a more 'complete' family when I was growing up. All my aunts and uncles had moved far away, most of them to England, and I had this idea that my life was lacking because I didn't have my whole family nearby. In hindsight, my sister and I were the lucky ones, because we grew up with both sets of our grandparents, whereas our cousins did not.

South African culture is built around eating, as most cultures of the world are, so good food and cooking have always been a part of my life. Family gatherings, although small though, always involved food and braais (known as barbeques, in most parts of the world. Preparing and consuming food is a trait shared by humans across the globe. Moreover, we can travel around the world in a single bite, directed by the ingredients, flavours and dishes from different cultures. I am amazed by the interesting, unusual and adventurous tastes that are readily available for all to enjoy. My mother, who is also a food product development manager, and my grandmother, who has run her own businesses in the past, both inspired me from a young age with their delicious, healthy food.

Throughout my childhood, I'd always shown promise at achieving greatness, with top marks throughout school, a healthy social life and a talent for art and modern dancing. I was seldom the best at anything, but I was consistently good at all the things I put my mind to, and it spurred the hope that if I was going on this track in my younger years, success in my future would be a done deal. But, disappointingly, my skills at being an all-rounder didn't set me up to select a career that I could focus on and rise through the ranks straight out of school. No, it took me about 5 years of university and gap years to realize my passion and hunger for working with food.

Initially, food preparation had been a fulfilling and meaningful distraction to keep me from fully focusing on my thesis. I was due to complete a bachelor's degree of Science, specializing in Genetics and Archaeology. The thesis was a study on the recent findings on ancient DNA and its usefulness in the scientific world. A fascinating subject, with monumental depth and room for expansion, too, but not quite the connection that I thought I would have to my life's calling. Nonetheless, I enjoyed my time as a university student, particularly the practical aspects of the courses I took, which afforded me the opportunity to apply my knowledge through experiments. I am a hands-on person, so I thrive on producing finite products. My degree taught me many valuable skills, however I did not have the zeal or funding to continue my studies to postgraduate level. I believe that only if you love something with your whole heart, will you be the right person to do the job properly.

The main reason I'd chosen to pursue the degree was because it was based in the field of biology, my favorite subject in high school. It wasn't a very well planned choice in terms of the career I would have like to see myself in, but that was a big part of the problem; the fact that I didn't actually know what career I wanted for myself…

The food industry and I were first acquainted when I started waitressing at a bakery and coffee shop to earn some extra pocket money as a teenager. It was located in Muizenberg, a seaside town that attracts hordes of surfers to its shores for the never-ending waves that roll in from the edge of the Indian Ocean on the African continent. My time waitressing there was memorable – particularly my shift breaks, where I would receive a cheese and tomato sandwich on freshly baked bread of my choice, and I'd walk along the shore, enjoying the sunshine. Usually, I'd be whirled by the wind, too, causing my hair to frizz out of it's neat and tidy plait, and bristle at the edges of my face like the leaves of a tree.

My experience with waitressing expanded as I held positions at various Cape Town restaurants in the years that followed, and my passion for the industry kept growing. I felt alive when observing chefs creating their masterpieces. I loved how each element of what they did fed into the next, and while creating one component, the next ten were prepped in their head!

The cooking thing seems obvious when I look back at my life. As a child, I'd loved getting the opportunity to help my mom prepare food, especially when it came to anything sweet, really. I recall hovering in the kitchen as a young girl, desperate to help my mom bake cakes, and to lick the spoon at the end, of course! Yummy treats were certainly a big part of the pull factor, but the process in and of itself was always fun. The thing I recall disliking the most about spending time in the kitchen in those days was washing up. Adulthood and a more developed sense of responsibility have lessened that dislike, thankfully. I can't truthfully say I look forward to washing up, but I do have nostalgia towards mornings, mid charter, hands deep in soapy water and getting into the flow of quickly cleaning the breakfast dishes before we set off to our next stop off for the day. The exhilaration of going somewhere new, as well as the satisfaction of when everything was cleaned and back in its place, were more than reward for the time I cleaned all of those plates, cups, teaspoons, serving bowls, platters, chopping boards, frying pans and more.

Life handed me the golden ticket the year after I graduated from university. It did not come without considerable effort - I had dedicated most of the preceding year to aligning myself with this reality. One competition entry after another, I poured my heart into the passion for attaining a career working with food. I defined my dream: to produce food that is naturally and ethically sourced, that feeds the body and the soul while minimizing wastage and having a sustainable impact on the environment. I identified my role models. The main person in the industry who motivated me, and still does, was Chef Luke Dale Roberts. His multiple award winning menus elevated the names of the various restaurants he headed in Cape Town, which further boosted the city as one of the top food capitals in the world. I admired his worldly experience; he worked in many countries, thus gaining knowledge about a variety of cuisines. His creativity and drive to produce outstanding and unique dishes inspired me to do the same. I was further inspired by his success and passion in an industry that is critiqued by many people, including food critics and everyday customers. Yet, his restaurants were always fully booked, and I was fortunate enough to dine at one of them: The Pot Luck Club.

The experience from the moment I stepped foot onto the premise was unforgettable. I was blown away by the menu, the food pairings, the plating, the venue, the service – everything! I gushed to my waiter, saying that it must be like a dream to work there, and his response was something that changed my life: they were looking for more waiters, and I should come in and apply! Needless to say, the next day I arrived with a freshly updated and printed CV. The manager spoke to me for a few minutes and we arranged a trial shift for the following week. The rest, as they say, was history.

The year and a half that I spent working at The Pot Luck Club was life changing. I learnt so much about food, and it further confirmed my resolve to become a chef. The golden ticket I mentioned earlier appeared in the form of a Mystery Basket Cook-off Challenge that I was invited to participate in as a result of one of the numerous competition entries I had made. The prize: a bursary to attend The Sense Of Taste Chef School and complete a City and Guild's Certificate in Food Preparation and Cooking. That day, I arrived as an unstoppable force. Every part of my being was set on winning that competition, and in the end, I did! The year of learning to prepare food as a professional seemed to fly by in no time. I had so much fun and lapped up the knowledge like a thirsty animal.

My step brother had been captaining charter yachts in the British Virgin Islands for a few years and while I was doing my chef training, he mentioned that he needed a chef aboard the yacht he was working on. A good friend of mine had worked aboard super yachts, and the stories of her experiences were certainly captivating. The vessel I would work on was much smaller than the ones she had told me about, but nonetheless, I knew that seizing this opportunity was the right thing to do. This is how I found myself in the Caribbean, and more specifically, the British Virgin Islands.

What I loved so much about my job on the yacht was spending my time preparing food that appealed to my taste, having a nibble and then serving the spread to hungry guests. Every so often, they'd come in and thank me for the tasty meal, complimenting my dishes and expressing their enjoyment of the past few moments. It was such a pleasure to go beyond just meeting people's needs and actually giving them an experience that brought joy to their day, and to the holiday that they planned to have onboard our vessel. I wasn't too interested in the personal praise, but more the knowledge that behind that came a being who was genuinely fulfilled in that moment.

Leaving my post as chef aboard the yacht came down to a number of reasons, but if I am truly honest with myself, the primary reason I left was for love. Rowan and I first crossed paths one evening in May, just days before I was about the celebrate my 25th birthday. The timing could not have been better, and the encounter and what developed from it were a major source of joy and encouragement in my final months of the charter season. Rowan was unlike anyone I'd ever met before. Genuine as they come, funny, knowledgeable and gosh darn sexy. We would spend hours on the phone, night after night, talking ourselves into the brink of sleep and then picking right back up on the conversation the next day. We texted messages of appreciation throughout the day, motivating each other by sharing the different activities we were doing in our separate kitchens and sending photos of the dishes, ingredients, equipment or scenes that caused our hearts to beat faster. Over this time, our connection grew and our feelings for one another became progressively deeper.

I found myself feeling quite unhappy and isolated on the boat. The perks of the job that I mentioned before were all still valid, but I had a growing appetite to explore the connection with the human who seemed to be my soul mate, and for a bigger team to share the experience of working side by side with, together striving for excellence. Rowan put forward the suggestion that I could come and work as a chef at the resort he was based at. They had a fully equipped, newly fitted kitchen, chefs with skills that I could learn from and a more regular schedule to their weekly lives, with two days off a week and a living area outside of the work zone. The salary was a step down from what I was making, but part of the contract covered accommodation, meals and amenities. To be fair, so did the contract I had with the boat, but I still see these things as non-monetized benefits that appealed to me.

The trauma of making the decision to leave actually landed me in hospital, mid charter. My throat swelled shut overnight, a physical response to the fact that I was unable to comprehend how I was going to break the news that I would not be part of the new endeavor we were planning. It began as a prickle in my throat that evening. I was ravaged by a sleepless night fueled by mounting fears and a tightening vice, gripping the lining of my throat into a fury of swollen tissue that refused to yield each time I tried to breathe or swallow.

That morning, I literally could not utter a sound more than a gasping croak. It was alarming for everyone in the room and my crew immediately told me to go and lie down while they figured out what to do. A tap on my cabin hatch sounded sometime later, and the captain explained he was taking me to the hospital. Within no time at all, we had arrived at the dingy dock on Tortola and were soon making our way through the uneven streets of the main island center. A steep and narrow hill lead us to the door of the purple clad building that housed the emergency center. My captain explained to the receptionist what was happening and after filling in some paperwork and waiting for it to be sorted out behind the glass of the reception desk, a door opened and one of the nurses beckoned for us to make our way into the treatment area.

First, a male nurse performed the standard admittance procedure by measuring my height and weight and asking a few questions about my current condition, to which I could only reply with painfully formed gargles, strange versions of simple words that I had never realized could be so hard to speak. He disappeared for a few minutes to consult with the doctor on call and when he returned, a robust female nurse entered the area just behind him. She had an air of authority, with a commanding presence that made me feel safe and secure. Without hesitation or fluster, she gestured for us to follow her and we made our way through the inner workings of the emergency facility. Everything around me seemed clean, simple and there for a purpose. The odd touch of personality came from posters giving information on different health conditions, but for the most part, the areas we walked through were purely functional. The nurse led us to a well sized room with an adjustable navy blue treatment chair at the center. The walls around it were dressed in glass cabinets, displaying white boxes with black writing that was too small to make out from where I was standing. The finishing's of the cabinets were painted in a pastel shade of lime green. Practical, efficient and sterile, this room seemed to give the impression that any malady could be conquered within its wall and this calmed my nerves as I settled into the chair.

The nurse explained their prescribed course of treatment, while we waited for the doctor to make his appearance. It's a funny reality, the working practices of nurses and their overseeing doctors. I always get the impression that the nurse's actions are responsible for healing the patient, but it is the doctor who gets all the credit. Eventually, the physician arrived, dispatching directions to the nurse while pacing the wall bordering the entrance, glancing over at me as an afterthought in the whole situation. The doctor was so absent during this consultation that I can't even remember whether they were male or female. In any case, the nurse handled all the interactions with me, aside from the doctor giving me a once over, tilting my head from left to right while examining my neck and the swelling around it. Moments later, the doctor was gone again, departing swiftly after issuing hushed instructions to the nurse about what dosages to administer the drugs that would alleviate my suffering.

Once the fluid entered my bloodstream, it took no more than two minutes for the swelling and pain in my throat to abate entirely. Shocked at the speed of my recovery and giddy with strength that was not my own, I babbled out a string of sentences to the people around me, expressing my surprise and gratitude for this welcome relief to my suffering. I broke the news to my crew a few days later, and they were far more accepting that I had imagined. We finished off the season in style, chartering our own family around the Caribbean as we slowly made our way south to deliver the boat to Trinidad for hurricane season. Learning to speak my truth had proven to be a much more dramatic lesson than I would have anticipated, but all the more reason to leave the situation with sound knowledge of my education in that regard.

A few months later, I returned to the British Virgin Islands as a temporary resident, and I have been working here since. Life in the BVI is different to what I grew up with. People here are far more friendly than what I've experienced elsewhere. They greet one another in the street, or when entering a building. Casual conversation is not a cause for suspicion, but a source of unexpected entertainment and simple joy. Life is not rushed. Island time is a reality, and for good reason. The climate is hot, hotter than an average day in Cape Town, and the heat barely subsides at night. When it does cool down, the temperature doesn't dip below 23°C and it seldom lasts long. Women that are from here are strong and unapologetic about their nature. They're sassy, confident, kind and honest. They are examples of independence, beauty and poise. Although it is not easy to know what they are thinking, when one does open up, you are rewarded with a meaningful, thought-provoking interaction that will leave an impression long after it is over.

Following me heart has led me to this wonderful part of the world, often referred to the "jewels" of the Caribbean. It's true, I do feel as if I have found treasure here, in the form of life experiences. What I've learnt from my time here and from the people of the British Virgin Islands is how to live by the concept that honesty is the best policy. The BVI is richly populated by people from all over the planet. Citizens from islands all over the Caribbean live here, as do citizens from countries further afield. People here come from places such as my home, South Africa, as well as from many regions of the United Kingdom, the USA, the Philippines and more. The diversity reminds me of the beautiful cultural heritage of my homeland, and I feel blessed to contribute my story as part of the BVI's narrative. My voice is but one of many women who have a story to tell in this small piece of paradise.

My Life As A Woman: Cayman Islands Edition

Hey There, I am Gloria from Bodden Town, Grand Cayman. Growing up I lived with my mother and grandparents. My father was an expat from the United Kingdom, who died while I was younger. My grandparents own a jewellery store, which my mother now manages. My family was very religious so every Sunday we would attend the Webster Memorial United Church Hall. I had a very special connection with my grandmother; she understood me when no one else did. She played a vital role in me being the woman I am today. When I was younger, she ensured I had a true understanding of the world I would be facing when I got older, she spoke with me about investments, education, people's behavior and how to stay a level-headed independent woman. I remember her always saying, 'A regular 9 am-5 pm won't cut it, baby.' My mother also motivated me, but she was barely there. She was always busy with work; she also worked as a writer.

I first attended the Theoline McCoy Primary school which was formerly known as the Bodden Town Primary School, then I matriculated to the John Gray High School, In my last 2 years of secondary school I did 10 CXC subjects. I later went to University College of the Cayman Islands to do my A-level in 2 years, followed by my tenure at the International College of the Cayman Islands studying chartered accounting. As a child I always wanted to become an oncologist, but overtime I realized I had a fear of blood and that being a doctor wouldn't be a suitable job for me.

After completing years of studies, I took one of my grandmother's advice and went to find myself. I took a month traveling Europe alone, from one place to the next. I saw how different the world was, especially for people like me. After my trip, I came back and worked at the family store to gather some more experience. After a year I started applying for some positions and got a job a few weeks after. I have worked as a chartered accountant at a prominent resort in the Grand Cayman for the last 6 years, while doing a few other short-term jobs and assisting with my grandparents' store.

After traveling, I had a greater love for my Caymanian culture. Caymanians compassion is compared to none, we just have a love for helping and ensuring everyone is okay. Like most Caribbean people were also very intuitive, we can just tell. I am a big foodie, so our food is one aspect of our culture that I love. We make a nice spicy conch stew, johnny cake, and cassava cake.

As a female living in today's society, we are told gender inequality is no more. It is assumed that we are long past those times, but as a woman, I have first-hand experience of those inequalities. I wasn't given the same opportunity as my male counterpart; when it came to vocational skills. Even though they wouldn't outright say 'no you can't take this course', it would be looked down on. A woman is expected to learn skills related to beauty, secretarial training, hospitality, culinary, or massage therapy, while men were expected to learn plumbing, electrical, mechanic, etc. We as women also have to deal with the constant catcalling, if you refused to answer you would be faced with disrespectful outbursts.

Even when faced with inequality, I was successful. I attended university and have a career I am very proud of. I am sure my grandmother would be proud too, I am living the free independent life she has always wanted for me. To all the women of today's society, just know you can do this. You are strong, beautiful, and intelligent. You need to fight for what you want, don't let anything or anyone deter you from achieving your goals.

My Life As A Woman: Falkland Islands Edition

Hello, my name is Ellen, I was born in Falkland Island, in Stanley, I grew up with my family in this small town. My mother was diplomatic and came single to the islands and met my father in one of the bars of the island, which is one of the few attractions in town, and then I was born in the only hospital on the island. Then my mother fell in love with life on the island.

I went to the Infant and Junior School (IJS), which is for students aged three to 11, and the Falkland Islands Community School (FICS), which is for student ages 12 to 16 and then, I receive funding from the Falkland Islands government to attend college in Peter Symonds College in Winchester, but during this period, I missed my family and my small town, and as soon as I finished, I returned to the island declining further funding to attend University. 70% of the people that go to the college return back to the island.

You wonder why I did this? Because I love my small town in the end of the world, with no rush, no worries, and a simple life with everything a woman needs. Nowadays, no regrets and I'm happy with the decision taken. I started a new life as an adult woman; I got a job as a cashier in one of the two local supermarkets, I met my husband and then we faced the war in 1982. It was a hard time with hearing bombs and guns throughout the day and night, in a place that is usually calm and quiet. The conflict was because Falklands belong to the UK but is located in the south Atlantic Ocean 300 miles away from Argentina that historically claim sovereignty over the territory. Fortunately, there were only three civil casualties. I don't want to talk about foreign policy, but we are so close to Argentina and so far from the UK.

Now, I'm working in the same market in the administrative section, there is not much that changes with the job because we are only 3,000 people in the town and my husband works in one bar. We have two children and a lovely wood house. I followed the path of my mother and continue to love this land. Later, she decided to change a successful career in diplomacy to a calmer life and I feel that she inspired me to have my actual life.

It's not easy to live here because of the cold weather, wind, and lots of snow during the hard winter. During the summer, the days are windy but warm. We feel far away of the civilized world because we only have two weekly flights to the continent, one primarily for military purposes, from RAF Brize Norton, near Oxford via Cabo Verde, however, a number of seats are allocated to civilians and the second one provided by LATAM airlines to Santiago in Chile via Punta Arenas in the south of Chile.

Overall, I feel happy with my life and the place I live, and I encourage other woman to be like my mother that preferred a quiet place with no stress. I follow your advice and now I can proudly say that I'm a happy woman. I believe that this hard life in this hard environment makes me stronger than the standard woman, but I chase my dram every day. Follow your woman dreams!

Ellen

My Life As A Woman: Gibraltar Edition

Hi, I am Roxanna Duarte. I am from Gibraltar. I grew up in Gibraltar it's a British overseas territory located on the southern tip of the Iberian peninsula. I grew up the youngest of three sisters and two brothers, I had a happy childhood. Gibraltar has many beaches and it's always good weather, so I always remember being at the beach or going to the park with my siblings. Being the youngest daughter, both my grandparents passed away before I was born, so I only had the influence of my parents and my siblings growing up, my mother passed on all her cooking skills as she is a chef and my father with his DIY skills.

I studied child development in the Gibraltar college of further education after passing my exams at high school, well, like every little child I wanted to be a doctor or a vet for animals, I loved the idea to help animals or people. Everyone loves his or her country's culture. I also like my culture. Gibraltar is very unique, its multicultural and cosmopolitan. In Gibraltar, you have various religions living in peace and security and everyone gets along. I love the vibe and warm Mediterranean sun.

I am currently an enrolled nurse in St. Bernards Hospital in Gibraltar, the government paid for my teaching and now after four years of studying and practical work, I will be a nurse this year working for the Gibraltar government. Gibraltar's people are very warm, but the problem is its who you know in Gibraltar. As it's a small community where everyone knows everyone, I have no doubt whoever you meet they will take you under their wing and help you any way they can. Thanks to this generosity, I have had no struggles like in other countries and I am very grateful for this. In Gibraltar, we are all equal and you can count on friends and loved ones to help you all they can.

It's the culture here in Gibraltar, finding work in Gibraltar is easy also as it only has a one percent unemployment rate. The only downside are the housing prices, that's why most children in Gibraltar stay with their parents until they are 23 or 27 so they can afford a house, this is what I did. All in all, Gibraltar is a great place and I would love to bring up my children here in the future as I was, as it is a safe loving community. So my advice would be to come to Gibraltar and see how it goes for you, you have sun, sea, well-paid jobs, great health service, and government that will help you out all that it can. To date, Gibraltar currently has a population of 34,000 and a high growth rate of GDP so Gibraltar is only getting bigger and better every year that goes by. Since I was a child, it has changed a lot but still holds a unique style, customs, and culture to this day.

My Life As A Woman: Guernsey Island Edition

Where did you grow up?

My name is Lawrie Thomson. I was born in 1969 and grew up in the parish of Saint Martin, on the island of Guernsey. It's the second largest of the Channel Islands.

How did you grow up?

Fairly middle class I suppose. My father worked as an insurance broker and my mother used to work for Guernsey Telecom, so both my parents had pretty well paid jobs. We lived in a good-sized house which had a large garden, and I would spend all my time out there playing. I have an elder sister and she became a teacher in France, in St. Malo and we would visit her often as it's not too far from here.

Did you have a parent or grandparent that inspired you?

I never really knew my grandparents as they died before I was born, but my parents have both inspired me very much. We had a nice house and a comfortable lifestyle and that was because my parents both worked hard their whole lives to achieve that, so I have always been inspired by their hard work.

What did you study and what did you want to be when growing up?

At school I got a broad general education, but I wasn't academically gifted. I never knew what I wanted to be, and still don't to be honest, so when I left school I started working in a local hotel. After a few years I ended up working at various hotels in the UK, working myself up and getting the occasional promotion. It's not a life I had planned, but one that I fell into more or less.

What do you love about your culture?

Guernsey has a culture all of its own, and still keeps its old institutions and bureaucracy. It might seem a little bit stuffy or old-fashioned to outsiders, but I love that. We used to have our own language, Guernesiais, which is kind of like French, but we don't use it so much these days although I do understand it, and that's a part of our culture which I hope we can keep alive.

What are you currently doing for work?

I spent so many years working in hotels and ended up as a hotel manager in Edinburgh. That hotel closed a few years back, so I returned to Guernsey. Now I work as a gardener – I said that I loved our house's big garden when I was growing up and that had never left me. I've always enjoyed growing plants and tending for them, so I became self-employed doing something I love doing.

Tell me about your successes as a woman?

In my hotel work I did quite well – my first hotel job was as a chamber maid and eventually I got so many promotions that I became hotel manager. That was probably due to me realizing that my parents were successful because they worked hard, so I took that sentiment into my hotel career.

Provide some advice to a woman living on Guernsey?

It's a small place, but the opportunities to do well in life are limitless. You can be whatever you want to be despite living on a small island.

My Life As A Woman: Isle of Man – Edition #1

Gaelg as Mish/Manx and Me: Sarah Gell her story…

Being brought up on the Isle of Man has been a special experience, as the Island has exceptionally beautiful surroundings and the "Manx Nation" are a proud people. They value their heritage, language and more. Although it only has a population of around 80,000 people, it has all the independence you would expect to see in any European nation.

We have our own parliament and it is in fact, the longest continuously running parliament on the planet, as it has been in existence for over one thousand years. In addition, the Isle of Man has its own language called Manx, which is a Celtic language not dissimilar to Irish or Welsh Gaelic.

I began learning Manx as a child at primary school in the capital city "Douglas". I have always been fascinated by language; words like chocolate and hockey are just nice words to say and hear.

I can remember sitting in our garden with a song book which my aunty Maire gave from her travels in Spain. I would leaf through it meticulously, studying the words to the same song written in Spanish and English trying to match words and compare phrases. She was like me…a lover of sounds, whether it was the spoken word or music, it really did not matter. Although she is no longer with us, she inspired me to follow my love of language.

I wore out that book thumbing through it pages for answers as I wanted to understand the song with the message as it was originally intended to be expressed. Although I could understand the story by listening to the English version, the original Spanish was always more beautiful to listen to, the rhyme and rhythm were natural and the sentiment somehow more genuine. As much as it was important to me to understand those songs exactly as they were written, I have always enjoyed being lost in language.

Foreign languages have always intrigued me and the way in which the language that you speak influences the person that you are. I have met such a diversity of fascinating people from the island and around the world.

Whenever I was about to travel to a new country, I would buy CDs, etc., and try to learn some of the language of that country ahead of me being there, but this was expensive to do. However, by accident I discovered that I could spend a long time sitting outside a cafe in a foreign country listening to life around me and watching the everyday interactions of people happening as they would in English but with a slightly different emphasis. The small variation put there by the cultural but also the linguistic differences.

Although our initial reasons for learning Manx may be different, we very quickly become united when we are bitten by the same bug. The joy of learning Manx is that the discoveries I make about the nuances of the language are discoveries about my heritage, my culture, and my people and not somebody else's.

The songs I enjoy translating now are Manx songs that are not only beautiful to listen to but mean so much more to me as they describe contemporary and traditional aspects of my own country and its values.

Gaining the ability to communicate in a second tongue has a certain exhilaration anyway but combine that with all the little 'eureka' moments when words, phrases and place names that you have used (or misused) for years suddenly hold meaning and gravity, add in a cup of coffee and slice of cake at 9 o'clock on a weekday morning and you have a recipe for addiction!

Unfortunately, this addiction is further fueled by the fact that Manx is a language that can actually be used on a daily basis and I do use it in my daily work life as a freelance language tutor and musician.

Other languages that I have learned, even to quite competent levels, have regrettably been forgotten as their use is limited to sporadic trips to the relevant country.

I use my Manx every day at home, at the school gates, music performances, playgroups, cafes, shops, and countless social events.

I wonder now how I ever managed as one of the minority of the world's population who can only use one language, as with the Spanish songs I used to listen to, sometimes there just isn't a good enough translation and I find myself using Manx to communicate my true feelings. The way we use language influences our lifestyle but equally the way we live shapes our language. I am proud to be regarded as "Manx as the hills, yessir" and we locals say…lol.

The phrase "Learning Manx" translates as **yindyssagh erskyn towse!**

Interview by Rob Edmanson-Harrison

My Life As A Woman: Isle of Man – Edition #2

Creativity & Me: Jane Slattery her story…

I was born in the Northern part of the Island a number of years ago and "NO" I will not say how many years, how very rude of you to ask a Lady her age…lol.

Andreas is a village in the north of the island, it has been good to me and my family all this time. I believe that it is different to other areas of the Island because the people up north are, in my opinion, more accepting and open to new ideas.

From an early age I have always been interested I how things looked and more importantly for me how to achieve a result, whether it was a texture, lighting effect or something else to bring out the best version of painting or design.

When I was at school however, I had a brief period where I took part in some plays and this made me want to be an actor, especially as my Art & Drama teacher Mrs. Andrews was so inspiring and enthusiastic about both elements. I was equally as enthusiastic as her in my efforts to be an actor, but after several attempts both she and I knew I was a much better Artist than I was an actor. So, she encouraged me to follow a more Visually creative pathway.

After leaving school my first job was as an assistant in a public library, which was "Boring as hell" for most of the time, but I was always an avid reader and used to immerse myself in the Art section of the Library as often and for as long as I could get away with it.

During this time, I taught myself the theory of many forms of art and design, but I was particularly drawn to abstract, fabrics and textile designs. After this I fell pregnant with my Daughter Eve or Eve' i.e. as we call her…so cute, but perhaps I am a bit biased.

I did not actually go back to work till she was older, and I decided I wanted to pursue a career in the Arts, but was not fully sure how, where or which type of the arts I wanted to do.

Today, both as an Artist and mother, I hope to be an inspiration to my little girl and often help her with her creative projects.

I offer to help her as much as possible, but much to my dismay, I find that, even at the tender age of 6 years old, she already has developed her own style and her own ideas of what creativity means to her. In truth I am proud of how independent she is and actually a little jealous, as this means she is already smarter than I was at her age, ha, ha.

You ask what Qualifications/Training do you need for my job?

Well, for painting, you need a natural ability and an eye for a pleasing composition. For the type of paintings, I do at the moment, you'll need a keen eye for detail. I really only began painting properly in 2015 and I now have my own studio and business because people want to buy my work! In respect to qualifications for Art and Interior design business, for my upholstery work, I trained across.

{Our readers will want to know, what you mean by "ACROSS"?}

(Oh yeah, sorry here on the Island, we refer to everyone/everything form the UK mainland as …coming from "Across" … just a local expression ha, ha)

So, I have no formal qualifications but spent time with a professional Upholsterer on workshops which I found to be invaluable. For my sewing projects, I'm self-taught. I owned a Singer sewing machine and began when I was 18 years old, I simply have never looked back.

You ask what do I regard as the best and worse things about my job?

Best things are - Being my own boss. Being creative - I love starting with a blank canvas or with beautiful material and producing a piece with which my client is delighted. Being able to plan my week so I can rest on the sunny days and work on the not-so-sunny days. Seeing the 'fruits of my labours' i.e. I am not some small cog in a big wheel where my contribution gets lost. I see directly what I make and the impact it has. Therefore, job satisfaction is high.

The most difficult thing is that, being a Sole Trader, there's only me, so I have to wear several different hats. It can be daunting, but I use my transferable skills from my previous roles to help me, and I have had help and advice while attending the DfE's Business Grant Course and courses held at The Engine House.

You ask what are the most important qualities I need in my role?

You need to be able to self-motivate. You need to be organised. You need to be good at work/life balance. You need to be able to work on your own - for quite long periods. You need to be a good observer. You need to put the effort into self-training. You need to not see failure as a blockage, more like a wake-up call.

And if you had to give someone advice about getting into the same industry, what would that advice be?

I would say, go for it! Look at me! I wasn't really sure I could even paint until I was 25 years old. Let alone how to earn a living at it. I took advantage of the training and help available on the Island, and still am (I have a consultant helping me as part of the DfE's Grant initiative).

The Island is alive with creativity - so much going on now. I think it is impossible to actually flood the market because your art or crafts because they will not be exactly the same as someone else's, and this means of course that...There's always room for you and what you have to offer!

Interview by Rob Edmanson-Harrison

Public Service & Me: Barbara Williamson her story…

Although I am originally come from Wigan in the United Kingdom, I have lived in Ramsey since I was a kid. My Grandparents originally came from the south of the Island a place called Port Erin, which is the largest town in the south of the Island. My father went over to the UK after he finished school here and that is where he met my mum, his wife Michelle. After my mum had me, my dad got a job offer to come back to the island to work in the Finance Industry, which is big business over here now, back then not so much.

My mum was always public spirited and joined the organisation called the W.I. or (Women's Institute) who have a branch here on the island. In addition, she was at the forefront of many charities from Animals to Children and everything in between ha, ha.

In hindsight, I guess she in the person who most inspired me to follow in her footsteps and do the same, as I have leading roles in several local boards and charities, but my main job now is as a Service Manager for the local Authority.

As a child in school, I once was asked what I wanted to be when I grew up…at that time I could see myself working as a Nursery Nurse. Little did I think my life and people I met would influence me to such a degree that, my thinking would be altered, and I would follow a totally different career choice today.

You ask can I remember what my first job was…ha, ha, "Cheeky boy" …I'm not that old you know…lol

Yes, it was working as a shop assistant in a shop on the corner of my road.

You ask what it is I do for work now and to tell you about it!

Ok, so I work as a Technical Services Manager for the local authority and I am training hard to get my qualifications with Higher National Certificate in Construction and the Built Environment, NEBOSH Health and Safety certificates and some leadership training to name but a few. I love my job, mostly. The best thing about it is the diversity of the work that we do to serve the Town and the staff. However, like all jobs, there can be difficult times too and for me… the most difficult part is managing the public's expectations as to what we can deliver.

I think the most important qualities I need to successfully do my role are patience, quick thinking, and sense of humour…Boyyyyy, do I need my sense of humour sometimes…Ha, ha, ha...

What advice would you give to someone who wants to get into the same industry?

Wow, that's not an easy question…hmm... I suppose just "study hard" and don't be afraid to have a go at everything so you can have a better understanding of what people need to do to achieve the desired outcome. Most important of all, keep learning and don't stop!!

Interview by Rob Edmanson-Harrison

My Life As A Woman: Isle of Man – Edition #4

Sustainable Development & Me: Maarit Bbjornstrand her story...

As you have may already guessed from my name, I am not originally a "Manxie"

I was born in Växjö which is a city in the heart of Småland, an area located in southern Sweden, close to Kronoberg County. I now live in Peel, which is a lovely fishing town on the west coast of the Isle of Man and although the island for me has my links to Norse culture due to the Vikings having invaded your island back in the past, for me, I still miss my homeland at times. Perhaps more now than ever, as f this virus.

My earliest memories there are of visiting my grandparents who lived near the newly built airport or at least it was, back in 2010.

My grandfather was a strong silent man who worked as a caretaker in the <u>Småland's Museum</u> which is Sweden's oldest provincial museum and opened as early as in 1885. My Grandmother Karin was a high school teacher of science before she became a guest lecturer in the new Linnaeus University and in truth, she developed in me a love of science and engineering which I have used in my everyday life.

You tell me to say to you about my school and what it was I wanted to be after...hmm...

During my first years in school I wanted to become a police officer. Later through high school I was very interested in Chemistry and Math and this I think comes back to my Gran' Karin, who was I would say, a definite inspiration to me and helped me to be the type of person who was inquisitive and innovative in the way I thought about the world.

You ask me to tell you about my job or work...

OK, well it is now today, I am in the Interior designer / Project Manager role. My first summer job if we go way back in time was on the goods receipt at SAAB Automobile in Trollhättan, Sweden, where I lived with my cousin Helge. However, my first full time job was as an Economic assistant for a sports betting company in Malta, this was both scary and exciting for me working away from my beloved home for the first time...wow, so many firsts when I bring this to my mind. I now think how I ever did it, I was so brave.

Now you say, tell me of my Qualifications/Training...OK then I will!

I have a Master's in Chemistry Engineering & Sustainable Development. I have also completed plenty of courses in Project and Construction Management. Learning the Project Management and the building process first before going into interior design was extremely helpful and a strength for me, I believe.

The Interior design projects I started off with when working as a Project Owner at a real estate department for a Swedish bank, SEB. I got the opportunity to be responsible for part of the design projects in the bank and there was where I started doing Interior design professionally.

In my opinion when it comes to interior design the fact is that, either you have it or do not. For me, interior design is more of a feeling and a vision, that you can see and feel how a room can change. I don't think you can become a talented interior designer if you don't have the talent naturally, just taking courses.

Now I tell you about my job and the things linked to it!

The best thing for me is that, I'm working with my biggest passion in life! However, the most difficult thing about it is that, you can't force creativity and some days you don't feel creative at all. I learn more and more now, how to plan my work so that days like that I can do admin and sort more practical things.

What advice would you give to someone who wants to get into the same industry?

I see, well my advice I would give to someone who wants to get into the same industry would be to have qualities like… structural, informative, creative, sociable, being bold.

I would also recommend any person going into the Interior Design business in some way and learn the building process or do a degree in Interior Architect, so the technical background is there. In addition, they should be practical, it's easy to create nice good-looking spaces but, when it comes to how we live our life's… it has to be a combination and the result will turn into a functional beautiful environment.

Interview by Rob Edmanson-Harrison

My Life As A Woman: Isle of Wight Edition

Good morning...my name is Louise and I grew up on the Isle of Wight. I was born there in 1977 and grew up on Newport which is the largest town on the island. Newport was a great place to grow up as it's a fairly large town with everything you would find in a large town on the mainland. Also, the Isle of Wight is fairly close to the mainland, so it is only a short ferry trip to get to Portsmouth or Southampton, and I can get to London in about two hours, so it's not an isolated place at all.

I grew up in a council house in Newport – my dad worked in a betting shop, and my mum worked for the council. They divorced when I was 12, and I lived with my mum. I respected her so much being a single parent – it must have been so hard for her juggling her work and family life around, and I'm a single parent myself so I now see a lot of her in the way I am. I went to a fairly typical comprehensive school in Newport and worked well enough at school to get decent grades. Back then I wanted to work for the council, like my mum, so I was hoping to get some sort of admin job.

I love living on the Isle of Wight, despite being a small island, there is a large population and there is always a lot to do, so I never get bored. I've already said it is so close to the mainland, so that you never feel cut off or isolated, and I like that about this place – I really can't imagine living anywhere else. We also have lots of nice small villages to visit, and the coastline is amazing – we have some really nice seaside places to visit. I now live in Ryde, which is on the north coast, and it's popular with sailors, so I like to see all the boats coming in. That's what I find special about this place.

Nowadays I work on the mainland, in a call centre in Portsmouth. I get the ferry over every day and I really enjoy that part of my commute. I suppose it is pretty much the admin job I dreamt of when I was back at school. I'm a supervisor in the call centre, so I don't make many calls myself, but I help out when a call needs to be escalated for whatever reason. I've been working here for seven years now, and I love my job.

My struggles growing up as a woman was mainly that I became a single mother, and things were hard to start with, but I wanted to work hard to provide a good life for my daughter, and I think I've done well at that.

Maybe I could turn that around and say that is also my success in life? – to do well and provide well for my family. Also, I have my own house in a nice part of Ryde, and when I look around me I see that this has been because of my determination to do well.

If I could give advice to a woman growing up on the Isle of Wight, it would be that you are fortunate you live on an island so close to the mainland so try and take advantage of that and get a good job on the mainland while keeping your own link to the island by staying there – then you can have the best of both worlds.

My Life As A Woman: Jersey Island Edition

Where did you grow up?

Hi I am Anne Le Sueur. I grew up in Saint Aubin, in the parish of Saint Brelade. It's a small town in the southwest of the island.

How did you grow up?

I was born in the latter years of World War II, and at that time we were under German occupation. I am too young to remember those times, but my parents said they were always fearful, and they never spoke about it much. My father was a fisherman, and my mother worked from home looking after us and our house.

Did you have a parent or grandparent that inspired you?

My grandfather lived near us, and when I was a child I always thought he seemed so old and wise. He had been a fisherman when younger and I loved listening to his sea tales. I don't think he could speak any English – back then we all still spoke French, or rather Jerriais as we call it.

What did you study and what did you want to be when growing up?

I went to my local school, but the education for a young girl was not so good then – it was more practical and taught us to be housewives. We learnt how to read and write, and sew, and had some dancing lessons too. I didn't want to be a housewife, but the options on Jersey were limited then. I wanted to own my own shop, but after school, I ended up working as a hotel maid in St. Helier.

What do you love about your culture?

Although people tend to think of us as 'British', we are really French. Until my youth, most people still spoke French at home, and even my name is French. I can go to France and everyone thinks I'm French because of my name and my accent. Jersey is a small island and very beautiful and I love the way that our culture is a clash of Britain and France.

What are you currently doing for work?

Well, now I'm retired, but I did eventually get my shop. My husband's family ran a small grocery store in St. Helier, and I worked there most of my life. I wouldn't have changed that job for anything in the world. My daughter works in the same shop now, so it is a real family business.

Tell me about your successes as a woman?

Getting to run my own shop made me feel successful, as I never wanted to only be a housewife – I wanted my own purpose and running the shop made me achieve that ambition. I got to know all my customers really well and felt immense pride that they would choose my shop to come to. Seeing my daughter grow up and have amazing children makes me proud too – I feel that my own success is contributing to their future success.

Provide some advice to a woman living on Jersey?

Jersey is a small island, but our culture and our heritage is so rich, and you should never forget that. No matter, where you go in the world, always remember where you came from and that you're a Jersey girl at heart.

My Life As A Woman: Montserrat Edition #1

I grew up in Haiti in a place called Gonaives. Things were not going well with my family. My mother was the only person in the family working and struggled to take care of the family. We left Haiti and moved to Montserrat because life continued to get more difficult. We are a big family, so for us to get to Montserrat my mother had to go first.

When my mother arrived in Montserrat, she found out she was pregnant. My mother had to work in Montserrat while she was pregnant to make money and sent for my dad. It was exceedingly difficult for her. Being apart from my parents was not an easy thing. I could only talk to my parents once or twice a month. Then, both my mom and dad worked together and sent for my two other sisters and me. Despite all of what my mother was going through, she did not dare to give up because she believed in the almighty God. Our greatest weakness lies in giving up.

I felt a bit sad leaving Haiti. I knew I will no longer get see nor talk to my friends. It is hard to make other friends in a foreign country especially when you do not speak their language. I was not mad at neither one of my parents because I knew they wanted the best for me. What I was sad about is that when the first of January comes every year, I will not be sitting with friends and other family members to eat soup and drink ginger tea. This is a cultural tradition we practice in Haiti; it symbolizes the Independence Day in Haiti.

When I moved to Montserrat, I celebrated my 12th birthday here. My mother went through a lot of difficult times, but she stayed strong knowing that she was not going through it by herself and God was her refuge and strength, present help in trouble. With her sacrifices and hard work, she showed me how to be strong and courageous. That makes me love her even more. I am currently going to school and now I am in fourth form getting ready for Caribbean Examination Council (CXC) exams next year. My dream is to become a pediatrician and make my mother proud and let her know that whatever she had done is worth it in the end. I made up my mind about my career choice after seeing my godmother's child die.

Thanks to my mother, she laid the foundation so that I can live a better life and pursue my dreams. There are no shortcuts to any place worth going. We as women should not let our struggles discourage us. We got to be the change we want to see. If you want to go ahead you must start working towards it. I cannot pray to God to pass my CXC's and I am not studying. God is not the one who is going to sit the exam. Faith and hard work lead to achievement my mother is proof of this and I hope to one day become as strong and resilient as she is.

My Life As A Woman: Montserrat Edition #2

Hey everyone, I am Kaley from the beautiful island of Montserrat. I grew up in a small city on the coast, everyone knew everybody. I lived with my mother and five siblings, my father died when I was younger. I was always told that he was a great man, my siblings got a chance to interact with him when they were younger. I heard all the good stories about him and ended up forming a connection with him even though he wasn't here. My mom did her best to take care of us and I appreciated what she did. She is one of the strongest women I know, she was always there for the six of us, worked full time, and helped elderly people in the community. I always wanted to be as strong as her.

I attended the Brades Primary School, during my primary years and then advanced to the Montserrat Secondary School. I did nine CXC subjects, only the ones important for my career choice. So I did sciences, information technology, English, and mathematics. I had the average school life as a child, which included a lot of friends, playing and exploring new things. After graduating high school I applied for the University of the West Indies, Mona campus. I got into the nursing program and moved to Jamaica. I am currently part-time as a brand ambassador. I love my job, but I can't wait to become a nurse especially with the current COVID-19 pandemic. I wish there was a way I could help those people, but for now, I just have to wait. I'll get my chance soon enough.

I love my Montserratian culture because we fit in everywhere, we are just a blend of varying cultures such as African, English, and Irish culture. Due to this variety, we celebrate a mixture of holidays, we celebrate St. Patrick's day, Jump Up day, and Boxing day just to name a few. When we party, we party big, so these celebrations are massive with great meaning to our people. Our music is sensational, it's very upbeat and lively. It has one of those beats that forces you to dance.

Growing up I didn't have any problems, I felt comfortable with everything I had and got all the love I needed as a child. I started to have problems when I moved and started university. Initially, I felt like an outcast in a completely new environment. Over time I started to feel more accepted and started to embrace my culture. The next problem I had was the constant catcalling from men, it was never-ending. A negative response always followed when I did not respond to their liking or not respond at all. I don't know why men feel that's okay, I felt so violated when they did it because they made the most derogatory remarks. Sadly, this is something I had to get used to, there was no changing it, just to accept it and keep it moving.

I am so proud to be a woman and I am truly grateful for the wonderful women that came before me and fought for the privileges we have now. Because of their actions, I can attend school now and even attend university. To all the women of Montserrat, we as women have come very far, so make use of all the privileges you have, because a lot of women before you didn't have such privileges. You can be more than a homemaker, you can be anything you desire to be. You just need to put in the works. Nothing comes easy but you have the opportunity, so make use of it.

My Life As A Woman: Scotland Edition #1

Growing up in a little town in the Italian Alps may sound like a dream for many, but it has certainly been more like a nightmare for me. Since a very early age, in fact, I dreamt about a different life, made of travels, new people and, especially, freedom. Most of my relatives could not be more intellectually distant from me, prisoners of their simple origins and ignorance.

My parents were quite "progressive" for that time (a divorced man from the South, an older woman from the North, having a child outside of marriage) and they loved me very much, but that life for me still wasn't enough. My grandmothers were the furthest thing I wanted to aspire to, and also my mother was very different from me, with interests that I considered trivial and boring, such as cleaning or knitting. Despite being a woman, I always wanted more from life than a clean apartment and a quiet day. I was always having arguments with the rest of my family because I was the only one that had opinions and was not willing to stay silent.

My mum's mum was very strict, she often judged my clothes, my way of seating, my loud voice and always tried to shut me up when I was whistling. "It is not feminine, shush", she used to tell me. And I rolled my eyes, thinking "Why? Why is whistling not feminine? What is feminine?". Then, as a young teenager, during my summers in Sicily, I got to experience the "strùscio". In the evenings, girls dress up and walk up and down the main street, while boys sit along the promenade and catcall the most beautiful ones by whistling at them. Maybe that's why whistling is a "man's job"?

My dad's mum lived far away from me (in Sicily) for most of my life, so we never had the chance to bond. Although I don't think we would have bonded anyway. As it was customary in the 50s, she got married very young to a man that she loved, but who never treated her kindly nor with respect. Her example to me as a granddaughter was of a submissive woman, victim of a husband-owner who dictated the yeses and noes for her entire life.

I chose to study foreign languages in high school because I hoped it would open the doors of the world to me, allow me to spread my wings, and leave behind the hypocrisy of the little town. I didn't have big career dreams when I graduated, so I chose a Uni that was in a faraway big city! Few years later, that same city and then the whole country became "not enough" for me anymore, but I was extremely lucky to find a man I loved, and we started traveling and moving abroad.

During the six years I lived here, I rarely heard of dangerous situations for women in Edinburgh and Scotland. I feel that living here, as a woman, is not particularly dangerous: we go out and we come home late at night usually without fear.

I used to live in Brazil and the situation was completely different. Being safe in my home, in the car, on the street is a feeling that cannot be traded with any amount of sunshine, beach or caipirinha!

From a career point of view, I saw a lot of managerial and high-level roles held by women, so I think we are definitely moving towards a gender equality workplace in Scotland. My being a woman, immigrant and not particularly beautiful never penalized me in my social or working life in Scotland. There is a culture of respect of the rules, people and equality (unlike Italy or Brazil).

Having seen other realities such as the Scandinavian countries, I believe that British women try too hard to change their appearance and to be provocative. They wear make-up, do their hair and get dressed up in such an exaggerated way that they almost lose their individuality. Women in Scotland can't resist going around in sandals and miniskirts in winter and, like men, drink far too much.

All the women in my life, despite their flaws to my eyes, were good people and each of them has certainly helped shaping my personality in a way or another. As a 37 years old woman, I am proud of having retained the smile, warmth and happiness of my Italian origins, mixed with the respect, openness and forward-thinking typical of the Northern Countries that I so love much.

My Life As A Woman: Scotland Edition #2

Where did you grow up?

Hi, this is Elizabeth McCaffery. I was born in Dundee in 1935 and grew up in a tenement flat in the Polepark part of town.

How did you grow up?

I lived in the flat with my parents, and my younger brother Joseph. It was a very small flat – just a living room and one bedroom which we all shared. There was no kitchen – we used the range, or the fireplace to do all our cooking and washing. We didn't have a bathroom or toilet, all the people in the buildings, fourteen families I think, all shared an outside toilet cubicle. Both my parents worked in the local jute factory, which was the main industry in Dundee back then.

Did you have a parent or grandparent that inspired you?

I didn't get to meet my grandparents, but I always admired my mother. She worked long hours at the jute mill, and then came home and worked hard keeping our flat nice and clean and making sure we had food, and that we were clean. She must have had a difficult life, but she always looked so happy and I wanted to grow up to be just like her.

What did you study and what did you want to be when growing up?

I had a primary education, but that was about as far as my education went. I learnt to read and write, and I was taught to type and that was what I enjoyed most, so I thought that if I worked hard at that then I might become a secretary one day. My mum died unexpectedly when I was 14, she had breathing problems (maybe due to her work at the mill), and then my dad died when I was 16. Both of my parents died before they reached 40, so after my dad died, I had to become independent and help provide for my younger brother. I started work at the same mill my mum worked at, first shifting bobbins in the factory, and eventually I became a secretary there.

What do you love about your culture?

Dundee is maybe not the richest place in Scotland, or even the nicest, but the people here are so friendly and have their own sense of humour and I would never like to live anywhere else. The town has changed so much from when I was growing up, and we now have museums and tourists are coming from all over the world to see this town and that makes me proud.

What are you currently doing for work?

I retired almost 30 years ago, and I'm enjoying my free time. I spent all my life working as a secretary, and after working in the jute mill I started work in the Timex factory, which was a huge employer in Dundee and the salary was much better. After that I was a secretary in a school until I retired.

Tell me about your successes as a woman?

I became independent at 16 as I had to start work and look after my little brother Joseph. Growing up we were so poor, but through my education I was able to escape from that. It was difficult but I got there in the end. I now live in a nice house with a nice garden, and I'm quite well off, and so is my brother Joseph. I think my biggest success is to see us as successful pensioners considering we were left orphans at an early age.

Provide some advice to a woman living in Dundee?

Dundee is maybe not the best place in the world, but it is home. Work hard and you can achieve whatever you want.

My Life As A Woman: Barra Island Edition

Hello to you. My name is Helen, and I am from Barra in the Outer Hebrides. I was born there in 1940 and have lived there all of my life. In my life Barra hasn't changed all that much – sure it has been modernised, but the spirit and the feeling of the island is something that has never changed.

My parents were crofters, we had a plot of land not far from Castlebay and we spent all our time working on the croft. We grew some crops, mainly for us to eat, and also had sheep and chickens. When I was a child, Gaelic was the only language that we ever spoke on the island. Growing up I always admired my great grandmother – she seemed so ancient to me and as if she came from a different time, and I suppose she really did. She had no English that I know of, and she would always tell me old stories about life on Barra and who lived there. I went to the community school in Castlebay – it was small and only had a few teachers. I learnt to read and write there, and also learnt to speak English – Gaelic is my first language, and the one I use most, but from time to time I meet people that only speak English.

As a child I never really had any ambitions about what I was wanting to do after school – I was from a crofting family and knew that I would grow up to live on a croft of my own one day. I love my island, and I really do believe that it is a special place – we have an airport in which the plane lands on the beach. That is a good sight to watch and I could watch it all the time. Also, we have an old castle in the harbour – Kisimul, and it's a beautiful old building. Until recently most of us spoke Gaelic, and the language is a very big part of our culture.

I always wanted to have a croft of my own, and I married a crofter and ended up living and working on a small croft not too far from the one I grew up on. I raised my family there and still live there, although it is my son and grandchildren who look after the croft these days – such is the way of life.

My struggles as a woman are that there is not much work for a woman on Barra, unless you stay here and work the land, and I know that is not for everyone.

But my success in life is that I am still here – I believe that happiness means everything and you should be wherever you are at your happiest, and for me that is on Barra – I wouldn't live anywhere else. I have lots of good friends here and my family is here, and people seem to respect me as a wise old woman for some reason.

If I were to give any advice to a young woman growing up on Barra, it is simple – be yourself and find yourself.

My Life As A Woman: Greater Cumbrae Edition

Interview with Louise Beattie (Greater Cumbrae)

Hi there…I'm Louise and I come from Millport, on the island of Cumbrae. Millport is the only town on the island – it's a very small place. I was born there in 1960 and grew up on the island with my parents. My dad was a postman on the island, and my mum worked in a shop on Largs on the mainland. I didn't have any brothers or sisters, but I always wished that I did.

Millport was a great place to grow up – people would come from Glasgow to have their holidays there, so I felt like I was always living in a holiday resort. I was always close to my mum, she was the one person that I knew would be there for me no matter what. She died when I was quite young, but she was an amazing mother and I wanted to grow up to be as good a mother to my children as she was to me.

I went to school on the mainland, in Largs. It is not far away so all the pupils from Cumbrae would get the ferry over in the morning and walk up the hill to the academy. I loved that school- it was really big and I made lots of friends there, but unfortunately I didn't do too well in my grades.

I never really knew what I wanted to be when growing up, I'd be happy with anything that made me money to be honest. After school I went over to Largs, and spent time working in shops and bars and stuff and that got me by. I loved growing up in Millport- I have already said that it is a holiday resort, but there is so much more to the place. We have some unbelievable views right down the Clyde and over to Arran and Bute too, and as a child I used to love the dragon rock – that's what everyone knows about Millport. I also like that we are so close to the mainland – most of my jobs and social life has been spent over in Largs, and I can get to Glasgow quite easily too. At the moment I work in a shop in Largs, but I still live in Millport, so I get the ferry over every day.

My struggles growing up as a woman was mainly when my mum died- my dad was working and I used to do all the housework and make meals and things, so that was hard for me and might be why my education suffered.

As for my successes, I have a nice family and I'm now a grandmother and love to see my grandchildren growing up and although I'm still a bit too young to retire, I look back on my life as being a happy one and I don't think I would change a thing, so I suppose that is how I can measure my success.

If I were to give any advice to a young woman growing up on Cumbrae, it would be to never forget the place you grew up no matter.

My Life As A Woman: Islay Island Edition

Hi, my name is Alison, and I come from Port Charlotte, on the island of Islay, in the Inner Hebrides of Scotland. I was born on Islay, in Bowmore, in 1960, and I have lived there most of my life. I grew up in Bowmore and Port Charlotte with my parents, and I was an only child. Both of my parents worked in the local whisky distillery – that is the main industry on the island and most families have at least one member who works in a distillery.

My father used to make the barrels used for the whisky, and my mother worked in the office as a secretary. I had a happy childhood – Islay is a great place to grow up, it's so quiet here and life moves at a slow place. One family member that inspired me when growing up was my uncle – he always wanted to leave Islay when he was younger, so he went to live and work in Australia, but came back after about 10 years. He used to tell me tales of Australia, and it always sounded so exotic and I wanted to visit there – I finally got to visit there a few years ago and it was amazing, even better than my uncle had described it to me. I went to school in Bowmore, and never really liked my time there. I guess education works for some people, but it was never really for me.

I liked all my friends there, though, and despite not liking school I managed to leave with good marks. All I ever really wanted to do was to own my own shop, but that never happened. I love living on Islay, many of us still speak Gaelic and we have a very rich Gaelic culture and history, so the island has its own distinct feel to it. Also, Islay is famous for its malt whisky, and as my parents both worked in the whisky industry, I feel that it is part of my heritage although to be honest I don't really like whisky that much. After school I worked in a gift shop in Bowmore for a while, I never did get to own my own shop, but I enjoyed working there, nevertheless. I then worked in a hotel for a while, then got married and didn't really work again until my children grew up – and now I'm back working in a different shop this time.

I think my struggles as a woman have been that on Islay the job prospects for a woman are quite limited, and that has been something I have experienced, but I would never want to live anywhere else.

My successes as a woman – raising an amazing family and seeing them grow up to have families of their own – my grandchildren mean so much to me and I spent all the time that I can with them.

If I could give any advice to a woman growing up on Islay, it would be that you should always keep your friends close to you – they grew up the same as you and had the same life experiences at the same time as you, so you should never feel alone and always have someone to talk to – that is important when you have grown up on a small island.

My Life As A Woman: Isle of Arran Edition

Hello. I'm Anna and I come from Brodick, on Arran. Brodick is the main town on Arran, but saying that, it's not very large – only a few hundred people live there. We always get lots of visitors and day trippers though, so the place always feels busy and it never gets boring. I was born there in 1967, and grew up in the guesthouse that my parents ran, along with my younger brother Ian.

I had a great childhood, as we ran a guesthouse I was always meeting new people, so at least I was never lonely. My parents worked hard to make the guesthouse convenable – my dad was good at fixing things, so he was almost like a handyman, and my mum was good at running the place and keeping the guests entertained. They worked hard to give us a good life, I suppose. I never knew my grandparents, they were gone before I was born, but they all grew up on the island too and came from farming backgrounds, but tourism is the main industry on Arran so that's where my parents decided to make their money.

I went to my local school in Brodick, then to the academy in Lamlash. It was a small school, only about 200 pupils but we had an amazing education, probably better than in a lot of places on the mainland. Our classes were small, so the teachers had a lot of time to spend with each pupil.

I loved my time at school, and made lots of friends there – lots of good friends that I still have. While at school I didn't really know what I wanted to be, but I always good at cooking at school, so when I left I went to Ayr and studied catering and hospitality – I hoped that would give me a good job on Arran, given that there is so much tourism.

What I love about my culture, is that Arran is a small island, but very beautiful. They say it is Scotland in miniature, as it has all the good things about Scotland but concentrated on one small island. Also, it's an island but is still close to the mainland so I can easily get to Glasgow if I want to. And that's handy, because after I left college, I stayed on the mainland and worked as a cook in various restaurants and hotels, but I could easily get back to Arran to visit my family and friends when I needed to, and that means a lot to me.

As a woman, I think that my main success has been in being able to forge a career as a chef – it's a good skill and I can use that to work anywhere in the world, but importantly it allows me to have a job I adore.

As for struggles as a woman, I feel that I have given up a lot of my personal and social life to pursue my dream as a chef, but at the end of the day that was my choice.

If I could give advice to a woman growing up on Arran, it would be to remember the place if ever you leave it behind and to be creative about finding ways to stay on the island if you want to.

My Life As A Woman: Isle Of Bute Edition

Where did you grow up?

Hi, my name is Louise Campbell. I was born in 1958, in Port Bannatyne on the Isle Of Bute. It's not far from Rothesay, the main town. In fact, the island is so small that it is almost one town in itself.

How did you grow up?

My parents ran a bed and breakfast in Port Bannatyne, and it was always really busy. People would come on trips from Glasgow and other big towns on the west coast – they'd call it "going doon the watter", a dialect term used to describe taking a boat trip down the Clyde to visit places like Bute or Arran. It was a good childhood, and as we ran a bed and breakfast there were always interesting people turning up to stay with us.

Did you have a parent or grandparent that inspired you?

My grandmother stayed with us in the bed and breakfast, and she always made breakfast for our guests, and even would make them cakes and things if she liked them. She always seemed to have so much energy and was always working hard to please the guests. I hope her hard work ethos has worn off on me.

What did you study and what did you want to be when growing up?

School was OK, but I always knew that I wanted to follow my parents into running a bed and breakfast. Bute is an island that relies on tourists, so it would only make sense. After school, I went to college on the mainland and got an HNC in hospitality and came back to Bute to help out in my parents bed and breakfast.

What do you love about your culture?

Bute is a small island but is so close to the mainland that it does not feel remote – I can be in Glasgow in about an hour if I wanted to. We get so many tourists that it feels like the island is changing every day. I enjoy seeing the tourists come here and enjoy the place I grew up in, and that they want to keep coming back. It is a welcoming place, and recently many Syrian refugees have settled here. They have opened up businesses such as restaurants and hairdressers and I love seeing how that is helping to change the cultural life of the island.

What are you currently doing for work?

I now run a bed and breakfast – it's the same one my parents ran and so I'm proud that I have been able to keep the business within my family. It keeps me busy and I enjoy meeting all my guests.

Tell me about your successes as a woman?

Running my own business makes me proud and makes me feel successful. I know I wouldn't be doing it if it hadn't been for my parents hard work, but I've been able to add to the business and add more rooms and the like.

Provide some advice to a woman living on Bute?

Never give up.

My Life As A Woman: Isle of Coll Edition

Hello....my name is Margaret, I come from the island of Coll, in the Inner Hebrides. I was born and grew up in a town called Arinagour, which is the large town on the island. When I say it is a large town, it isn't really as there are less than 200 people on the island, but it is the largest town we have.

I grew up on a croft with my parents, who were both crofters, and Coll was a nice place to grow up, although I must admit that it got a little boring sometimes as there was not much for us to do, especially when I was a teenager. I was born there in 1969, but left the island after I left school. Lots of people inspired me when I was growing up, but probably the most important one to me was my mother. It was a hard life working on the croft, but she always seemed so bright and cheerful and I could talk to her about anything.

I went to the local primary school on Coll, but there were only a couple of pupils and one teacher. There wasn't a secondary school on Coll, so I went to secondary in Oban. Lots of pupils from the islands go there and stay in the boarding school – that was fun, and it was good to meet people from other islands too, it made Coll somehow feel less remote. I would get on the ferry and go back to Coll at weekends, as it wasn't too far from Oban. Back then I didn't quite know what I wanted to do after school, but one thing that I did realise was that my future would not be on Coll, much as I loved the place, there were no real prospects and so I always knew that my life was to be on the mainland.

Coll is a beautiful place, but lonely and remote. Whenever I tell people that I come from Coll, most people don't really know where it is, but I suppose to them the thought of growing up on an island sounds exotic, and I like that. I also like that we still have a bit of a Gaelic culture and all the rich traditions that go with it, although I must admit that I don't really speak the language myself – only a few words. Nowadays I live on the mainland, in Oban, where I work in a hotel – tourism is the main industry here and I enjoy meeting people from all around the world. However, Coll is not too far away, so I try and get back over whenever I can to visit family and friends.

My main struggles growing up as a woman were the lack of jobs on my island, unless I wanted to be a crofter like parents, something that never really appealed to me.

As for successes, I live every day one day at a time and I'm proud of some things I have done although I do believe the best is yet to come.

If I could give advice to a young woman growing up on Coll, it would be that I know there is nothing to do and no work prospects on the island, so don't be ashamed to leave it. The harsh reality is that we must leave it to succeed.

My Life As A Woman: Isle of Colonsay Edition

Hello. My name is Catherine Keith, and I was born in 1946 on the Scottish island of Colonsay. My parents were both crofters and we lived in a small croft near Scalasaig. It was a difficult life for us, and we didn't have any electricity in the croft when I was a young girl. Also, we had no water supply and had to fetch out our own water. People nowadays don't know how simple their lives are compared with when I was growing up. We had little entertainment back then, but I was inspired by a local seannachaidh (story-teller), and his tales would keep us all entertained for hours on end.

I went to my local school, but there were only a handful of pupils there. I learnt to read and write, but not much more, and I had no ambitions to do anything after I left school – to leave the island you would need a far better education than what I had. Also at school I started learning English – most people on the island still spoke Gaelic back then.

I love Colonsay, but it is very small and very remote. We have excellent views of some of the other islands – Islay, Jura and so on, but it takes a long time if ever we need to get to the mainland. A trip to Oban feels like a trip around the world to me, but Colonsay is my home and where I feel at my happiest. After I left school I worked on my parent's croft until I got married, and my husband was lucky to have a larger croft – more of a smallholding really. I have lived there and worked on that croft the whole of my life, and I raised my family there too. My son Iain works on the Cal Mac ferries, but he helps out on the croft when needed and he will one day inherit it.

My struggles as a woman have been many – if I was a man I would probably have had more chance for a better education and maybe even become rich, but my destiny was shaped by where I was born and by my gender – saying that, I have had a happy life, but I often wonder how it would be if I was to have been born somewhere else.

My successes as a woman is mainly that I have raised a very nice family and my children now have their own families. When I look at them that reminds me how fortunate and successful I have been in life, as not everybody has that. I live in a nice home too, and I'm reasonably well off, so that gives me some feeling of success.

If I were to give a piece of advice to a young woman growing up on Colonsay, it would be to work hard at school and then go to the mainland and get a good education at college or university, or maybe learn a trade. Doing that will help you in your life and you can go and live anywhere.

My Life As A Woman: Isle of Eigg Edition

Hello…my name is Alison and I was born and grew up on the island of Eigg, which is quite near Skye. I was born there in 1971.

When I was growing up, Eigg was a very lonely place, and had a tiny population – only about 50 people I think. My parents were tenant farmers, as were most people on the island that time. The island was owned by a landlord, a German man named Schellenberg and we had to pay our rents to him and suchlike.

My parents never complained but I don't think they liked that situation. When growing up, there were few people outside of my island to inspire me, although I do believe that the island itself has been my biggest inspiration – I love its scenery and its colours, the place is very special that way. I had a basic education on Eigg, but after I left school I went to the art school in Glasgow.

I always wanted to be an artist, it was growing up in a beautiful place that allowed me to first appreciate form and start making my own drawings, and so that is what I chose to do. Eigg is an interesting place – when I was living in Glasgow, the islanders got together and with the help of the Scottish government they bought the island from its owner, so that we all now technically 'own' the island. We run it as a collective, or an organisation, and it has been a difficult but rewarding process. We generate our own power and electricity, and we encourage people to come to the island to start up a business and encourage growth – the population is now larger than when I was growing up.

I will always be proud of the day that the islanders bought the island, and that has enabled me to be able to return here and set up my own business. I mainly work as an artist, from my home, and although people do sometimes come to the island and buy my work, most of my work is commissioned online, so that allows me to live and work here without leaving my own home.

My struggles in life were that Eigg is such a small place, and growing up I really didn't think I'd have a future here, so I had to leave the island to find my own way in life.

My successes in life, the main one is that I was part of the community buyout of the island, and I am proud of that. It was a big step and change for us, and now I am able to work and live here in an amazing little community, which has a positive outlook for the future. I'm now living here, and have a moderately successful business, and I don't think that would be the case had it not been for the community buy out back in 97.

If I could give a piece of advice to a young woman growing up on Eigg, it would be to encourage your hobbies and skills and find a way to develop them into a business, or rather a cottage industry. I used my art to be able to continuing living here, and so you could try something similar as the community would encourage you to develop a business and stay on the island.

My Life As A Woman: Isle Of Jura Edition

Hello...my name is Lesley, and I come from Jura, in the Inner Hebrides of Scotland. I was born there in 1978, and grew up in Craighouse which is the main settlement on the island. Both of my parents were council workers and spent a lot of time travelling backwards and forwards to Islay with their jobs, but we always stayed on Jura.

This is a large island, but has a small population, so that everyone knows each other, more or less. I can't really think of one particular person who inspired me when I was growing up, but I always had a soft spot for Miss Grey, who was my schoolteacher once. We all loved her at school and she was an amazing teacher that I will never forget – as a child I wanted to grow up to be just like her. As for that, I enjoyed my time at school – the primary here is tiny, with only a few pupils, but I went to high school on Islay, and I liked my time there as it was good to meet people of my own age who didn't live in my island- I made lots of good friends there and we still keep in touch. At school I was good at science and I loved gardening so I always wanted to work in horticulture or gardening, and after school I went to the Oatridge Agricultural College, near Edinburgh and studied land management.

I love the culture of Jura – the island is very large, but it is dominated by mountains which take up most of the land, so not many people live here. I love the mountains on Jura – The Papps, and just at the top of the island there is a large whirlpool and people come from all around the world to see that, and it makes Jura a special place. It is very remote, but I like living far away from the rest of society and it helps me feel less stressed living here. After college I got a job in the Forestry Commission in Edinburgh, and I still work for them, although my work has now brought me back to Jura and this is where I live and work now.

My career in forestry management is important in the upkeep of the island, so I feel very privileged in what I do as it helps maintain and protect the island's beauty and resources for future generations.

I have had many challenges as a woman – although I now have a promoted management position, in the early days of my career it was difficult for a woman to get promoted in this job, and we got paid less than our male counterparts.

But at the same time, that led me to my greatest success – gaining promotion to what I do now, in what is still largely a male-dominated profession.

If I was to give a piece of advice to a young woman growing up on Jura, it would be that life on Jura will always be tough but to get good skills and stay here to help the island society to grow and prosper.

My Life As A Woman: Isle Of Lewis And Harris Edition

Where did you grow up?

Hi. My name is Rona Macrae. I was born in 1961 and grew up on a small croft near Gress, a small village on Lewis. It's about 10 miles north of Stornoway, the main town on the island

How did you grow up?

My parents were crofters, and our croft was not very big – just a smallholding really. We had a good number of sheep, so we sold the wool and sometimes we sold the sheep for meat too, but we would always get more money for the wool. I worked on the croft too, my parents would always give me chores to keep me busy. At home we spoke Gaelic, most people around here rarely use English, or at least back then they didn't

Did you have a parent or grandparent that inspired you?

At the time I was a child, my grandmother was still living in a croft with no electricity and no running water. It was the same croft she was born in and she had lived there most of her life I think. Looking back on it I can't believe there were still people here living the old life in the 1960s, but she was always so happy and content and I loved her more than anything in the world. She was always singing old Gaelic working songs too.

What did you study and what did you want to be when growing up?

My school education was pretty typical for someone in Scotland at that time, although we were encouraged to speak in English rather than the Gaelic. My main memories of school are the friends that I met there – when you grow up on a croft sometimes you feel you're the only child in the world as it's so remote, so it was good to meet people my own age. To be honest, I learnt more working on the croft than I ever did at school. Here in Lewis there is not much to do job wise, just farming, fishing and maybe some shop or admin work, so I always thought I would grow up to be a crofter like my parents.

What do you love about your culture?

Everything is so relaxed here – life moves at a slow pace. Whenever I go the mainland everything seems so chaotic and rushed, so I enjoy the peace and quiet. I also love that we have Gaelic as our first language.

What are you currently doing for work?

At the moment I'm working as an administration officer with Comhairle nan EileanSiar (the local council). It's based in an office in Stornoway. I started working there as a way to bring in a steady income. I married a crofter, and although he works hard, it is never always guaranteed that there is money coming in, so my job helps to make sure that all the bills are paid on time. I still help out on the croft too.

Tell me about your successes as a woman?

I don't know...maybe raising a family, and still living in the area I grew up in. Most people move away from the island as there are so little opportunities here, but I've managed to remain here and have a good comfortable life.

Provide some advice to a woman living on Lewis and Harris?

Have a good system of friends – island life can be lonely so make sure that you have plenty good friends that you can rely on.

My Life As A Woman: Isle Of Mull Edition

Interview with Elizabeth Watson (Mull)

Hello, my name is Elizabeth and I come from the isle of Mull. I come from a town called Tobermory, which is where I was born and grew up. I was born there in 1971 and have lived on Mull most of my life. I grew up with my dad, Tommy, and my mum Sarah.

My dad used to work for Caledonian Macbrayne on the ferries over to Mull, and mum was a housewife. I had an elder sister, and a younger brother too. Growing up we never had too much money, but we had a happy life and we were well cared for. I knew my grandparents quite well when growing up, and I loved going to my granddad's garden. They lived in Tobermory, which is not too far away, and what I liked about visiting my granddad was his big garden – we didn't have one in our garden and he used to tell me how to grow things best, and that gave me a really useful skill.

I still love growing things. I went to school on the mainland, in Oban, and I really enjoyed my time there. Pupils used to stay at the school if they came from some of the nearby islands, so I got to make friends from quite a large area. I had a good education and I was able to go to university in Glasgow. I studied education there, and left with a postgraduate certificate in education, so that allowed me to work as a teacher. What I love about my culture is that we still use the Gaelic language on our island and that is a huge part of who I am. I'm fortunate to have grown up on such a beautiful island, and Mull is still close to the mainland so it is not completely isolated.

My struggles as a woman, were probably a lack of prospects, but I was fortunate in that I became a teacher, but had I not done that than things might have been different for me. Some of my female friends struggled to forge their own careers, so I guess I was lucky in that respect.

My successes as a woman was getting to find my own way and life and get a career in which I am financially independent – that means so much to me, that I could never take that away. At the moment I am still working as a school teacher, here on Mull. I teach in a primary school, and I'm fortunate to still have a well-paid job and be able to live on this island that means so much to me – I wouldn't want to live anywhere else.

If I could give any advice to a young woman living on Mull, it would have to be to work hard at school and get the best education you could possibly get. That way your future prospects will be limitless, and maybe one day you could even return to the island with your skills and inspire the future generations.

My Life As A Woman: Isle Of Skye Edition

Where did you grow up?

My name is Seonaid Morrison, and I was born in Uig of Skye in 1971. I grew up in a larger town on Skye called Broadford. I moved there with my family when I was very little.

How did you grow up?

My father was an electrician and had his own business and my mother was a teacher, so we were quite well off. I had a good childhood, quite a typical one for someone of my age. Living on Skye meant that I missed out on a lot of the cultural stuff that mainland children of my age were doing, but I still have fond memories of growing up there.

Did you have a parent or grandparent that inspired you?

My grandfather was a ferry man. He would steer the ferry over to the neighbouring island of Raasay. As a child I thought that was so clever, and I thought it seemed like good fun going backwards and forwards over the water all day, but I suppose the reality was different for him. It was a dangerous job and he wasn't well paid for it, but in my eyes he always seemed like a great adventurer.

What did you study and what did you want to be when growing up?

I enjoyed my time at school and I worked hard there. Growing up I wanted to be a teacher like my mother, so after school I went to Glasgow University. I missed Skye – Glasgow was way too big for a girls from a small place like Skye.

What do you love about your culture?

When I was growing up on Skye everything seemed so innocent. It was a small place and we all knew each other, and living in Glasgow made me miss that innocence. We still spoke Gaelic at home, and that's a big part of me. Skye is a beautiful island and people come from all over the world to see the scenery of the place I grew up in, and I love that.

What are you currently doing for work?

I'm now still living on Skye, and I work at Sabhal MorOstaig, which is a Gaelic college. After tourism that is probably the biggest employer on Skye. I give lessons part time, so I suppose I ended up a teacher after all. I also run a small guesthouse – I live alone and my house is quite big, so I rent out the spare rooms as bed and breakfast. Skye has a lot of tourists so I always have many visitors staying.

Tell me about your successes as a woman?

Finding myself. I think my time in Glasgow made me realise that there is more to the world than just Skye, but that Skye was a place that would always define me, so I've never forgotten my roots.

Provide some advice to a woman living on Skye?

Skye is only a small island, but we have visitors from all around the world and there is so much we can learn from them. If ever you have to leave the island, then always remember the place and never forget where you come from.

My Life As A Woman: Isle Of Tiree

Hello, my name is Anne and I come from the small island of Tiree, off the west coast of Scotland. It's a tiny island and only has a population of about 700, but I was born there in 1963 and that is where I grew up. I grew up at home in the town of Scarinish with my parents – my mother was a housewife and my father was a fisherman. I had a younger sister too. I had a happy childhood, and have lots of good memories of growing up on Tiree, although it was a small island, and there was lots of space and clean air and I enjoyed playing with my friends. We were not a rich family, but we had a happy life and I loved both of my parents dearly, and growing up I was inspired very much by my aunt – she was deaf and I learnt sign language to communicate with her.

Tiree is a Gaelic speaking island, so the mixture of her deafness and that she could only understand Gaelic and some English must have made communication difficult for her at times. I went to my local school, and loved my time there, but at school I didn't have any idea what I wanted to do when I was an adult – I had absolutely no idea what I wanted to do, but I did want to see some of the world and travel a bit.

Tiree is a beautiful island to grow up on, but it is rather flat and there are not many trees, so it is a different kind of beauty, it is the island life that I particularly love, it is as if the island has its own soul and that what is so special about the place to me. I also love the fact that we are so remote, it is difficult to get here and people really do have to make a special effort to come here, but once they do they are rewarded with a very rich culture indeed. I travelled the world and taught English in different countries – Turkey, Taiwan, and Slovakia, but I came back to Tiree as an adult, and got married and now live here. At the moment I am working in a whisky distillery on the island – it's quite small but I really enjoy my job, although I really don't like whisky all that much.

My struggles growing up as a woman on Tiree there is not many job prospects, typically you grow up to be a housewife and I wanted more in life than that – I wanted to be my own person, and that's why I left the island to travel the world.

As for my successes, that was being able to travel and experience lots of different cultures, so that when I came back to Tiree I was able to bring back a new found sense of wisdom with me and hopefully that has developed me as a person.

If I were to give some advice to a young woman growing up on Tiree, it would be that Tiree is a special place and the world is so much bigger. Take time to do things off of the island, and when you return you will be a much wiser and far more experienced person.

My Life As A Woman: Orkney Islands Edition

Hello to you. My name is Ann and I come from Kirkwall on Orkney. That is where I was born, way back in 1966, and I have lived there most of my life on and off. I had a really happy childhood and have lots of good memories about growing up on Orkney.

My dad was a school teacher and my mum was an office secretary. As such it was a fairly middle class upbringing, but I didn't have any brothers and sisters, and I desperately wanted to have a little sister, but sadly that wasn't to be. I did have a dog though and he was my best friend. When I was growing up, the one person that I admired most was my grandfather – he loved music and could play the fiddle. He taught me to play it, in the distinctive Orkney style, and when he died, he left me his fiddle and I still treasure it so much. He instilled a passion for music within me and I only have to listen to certain old tunes to be reminded of him. I went to school in Kirkwall, and I was always a bit of a geek, and worked hard at school. I loved my English teacher, Mrs. Peterson and she really inspired me to read, and reading is still my favourite hobby. After school I went to university in Edinburgh, and got a BA (Hons) in English Literature and History, and I loved that course.

I really enjoyed my time in Edinburgh and made lots of good friends there, most of whom I still keep in touch with. Orkney is a place that means a lot to me – my family have lived here for generations, so we are true Orcadians.

We have a very Viking and Scandinavian history, despite being part of Scotland, and that gives us a very distinct culture. Also, the music in the Orkneys is beautiful, especially when played on the fiddle, so I like playing the old tunes on my fiddle whenever I feel homesick when I'm away from Orkney. After university I returned to Orkney as I couldn't ever fully leave the place behind. I used my university degree by getting a job as a librarian here in Kirkwall. That's the perfect career for me because I have a real passion for literature and I enjoy sharing that passion with the people that visit the library- I'm very lucky.

My struggles as a woman have been many, and sometimes I feel that the lack of equality when I started working was a huge challenge – I wasn't getting the same pay as a man doing the same job as me for example, but things are fairer nowadays.

My main success has been that I left Orkney and got a degree, and came back and was able to find a decent paid job that used my degree skills – I was very fortunate in that.

If I was to give a piece of advice to someone coming from Orkney, it would be to think outside of the box as to ways that you can forge a career on the island using the skills that you have.

My Life As A Woman: Shetland Islands Edition

Hello…my name is Andrea and I come from Shetland. I was born in Lerwick in 1978, and I was raised in Scalloway on the west of the island, and it was in Scalloway that I spent most of my time. It was a great place to grow up, but very cold and windy. Scalloway is on the coast and the sea around us was wild, always with big waves, and growing up next to the sea is one of my happiest childhood memories.

At home I lived with my father, who was a fisherman, and my mother who was a housewife. I had no brothers or children. I always admired my father – he was always away at sea, or especially in the cold seas with his job. It must have been difficult for him, but he worked hard to make sure we were not poor and that means a lot to me. I went to primary school in Scalloway and the classes were very small, and then went to high school in Lerwick – most children on the island went there and it seemed very large, although looking back on it, it was tiny. I did well enough at school, and left with a few Highers, and was able to go to college, but that meant going to the mainland to study in Aberdeen for a few years. At school I wasn't sure what I wanted to do, but I studied tourism and hospitality at college.

I loved growing up on Shetland, and we have a very distinct culture – although in Scotland we have a strong Viking heritage and we are proud of our history. We speak a dialect that people in Scotland find hard to understand and sounds like Norwegian. We have a very rich culture and traditions, and one of my favourites is Up Helly Aa – most people know that about our island – the men all dress up as Vikings and set fire to some boats. There's lots of fun – it's an event that all of the islanders look forward to and rather than just make a night of it, we make a week of it.

Nowadays I work on the island as a tour guide, I do organised trips and bus tours, and in recent years we get a lot of cruise ships coming in – it's mainly American tourists, but I enjoy showing them around my island as it is such a special place.

My main struggles growing up as a woman was that there no job prospects on Shetland, so to get a better education I had to go to Aberdeen then come back here.

And my main successes were being able to get a good education and use those skills that I learnt to become self-employed and have my own small business – that is what is important to me and what I am most proud of.

If I was to give any advice to a woman growing up on Shetland, it would be that if you want to stay here you have to find your way on the mainland first and then come back here with whatever life skills that you have.

My Life As A Woman: South Uist Edition

Interview with Rosina Macdonald (South Uist)

Hello, my name is Rosina and I come from near Lochboisdale on the island of South Uist. I was born here in 1946 and have lived on the island most of my life, and it is a place which is dear to my heart. I grew up there on a croft with my parents and two elder sisters. The croft had been in our family for generations and my grandparents used to croft there too.

It was a difficult life, the weather here is not usually good and we have so much wind and rain, that to work outside all day gives us a hard life. At home we spoke Gaelic all the time, and that is the language that I am more comfortable using to this day. I was deeply inspired by my parents for all of their hard work. Crofting is a subsistence living, so we just ate what we grew, little else, and there was never any money for us. I went to school in Lochboisdale and learnt to read and write, and how to speak English as well. I liked school, but the most useful things in life I learnt from helping out my parents work on the croft – that's a thing you don't learn at school, but it is the most important for someone from around here.

I had no ambitions at school, I knew that it was all very likely that I would marry and stay on the island, and that's what I did. I'm happy here and wouldn't want to leave all this behind. What I love about my culture is our Gaelic language – most people speak it around here before English. Also, we are a very remote island and our community means everything to us. We still work the land that our forefathers from generations ago used to work, so we still have a link to the land that is important to us. I ended up marrying a man from the island, and he was a crofter too, so my whole working life has been spent working on the crofts.

I said earlier that it is a very difficult life, and it is so, but it is a life that I have always known and comes natural to me. I like working the land and feeling the connection with those who have come before me, and working that land keeps them in respect to us.

My struggles as a woman have been that South Uist can be a difficult place to survive – you have to work hard to provide for your family, and if you want an easy life you will not find it here.

As for my success that would be that I am able to live and work in the same place that I grew up and holds such a special place in my heart- if I was to move away from the island I would not be so happy, that would be impossible.

If I was to give advice to a young woman growing up on South Uist, it would be to persevere – life may be hard, but the rewards are great.

My Life As A Woman: South Wales Edition

I grew up on a small farm in the 1970's about 2 miles outside the village of Solva. Solva is a small village and harbor 20 minutes to the west of Haverfordwest and not too far from St. David's. My parents were part time farmers, Dad also worked for the Co-Op in Fishguard 30 minutes to the North. The farm was only around 40 acres with sheep and some cattle and not big enough to generate sufficient income on its own. It had originally belonged to my Mum's side of the family. She had grown up there and worked on it all her life. She was an only child whose father died when she was 12. Dad came from outside St. Davids a few miles away.

My abiding memory of growing up is of doing so with a feeling of security. We didn't have a lot, but we never lacked for anything, never went to bed hungry and if Mum and Dad had worries and issues, they kept them from us. I had lots of cousins and uncles and aunts from Dad's side and as a family we are very clannish, mess with one and you messed with all. I tend only to see most of them now at weddings and funerals but we're still close.

I have fond memories of working on the farm, feeding lambs, bringing in the hay and digging potatoes. Hard work but out in the open air. Life had a great since of freedom that isn't always there now. Life also resolved around the village, the church and school and the rugby club in St. David.

My parents were incredibly hardworking people and that has always inspired me. A few years ago I made a mistake of telling my Dad I was tired, he looked at me and said, "how can you be tired, you only go to meetings?". The concept of being tired from non-physical work astonished him. He was a big strong man whose strength came from physical work.

Despite holding a full-time job and being a part time farmer, Dad was also heavily involved in local activity. He and Mum never saw this as volunteerism or anything like that, it was simply things you did when you lived in a country area.

I don't recall ever having a plan about what I wanted to be when I grew up. I had the usual dreams about being a pop singer or actress but aside from that I don't recall anything specific. However, more importantly I knew what I didn't want to do, namely I did not want to become a scientist or an accountant as science and business were two subjects that bored me to death in school. I ended up doing a BA in English and History in Swansea. I've since done an MA in English from Bristol where I lived for a few years in the late 90s.

I'm very conscious that there is in effect, two cultures in Wales. One is British and the other one is Welsh. I feel more Welsh at times then British and living in England for 5 years in a funny way reinforced my Welsh culture. I love the sense of community in Wales that I don't find elsewhere, I love the pride in language and music and of course I love the rugby. Rugby provides a focal point for many communities that I often see lacking in other places outside of Wales.

I am currently teaching English in a secondary school outside Swansea. I know I am fortunate in that I haven't endured the same issues that many women elsewhere have had to. I grew up in a close and loving and protective family and I always knew I had somewhere to turn to if I needed help. My parents valued education, perhaps knowing that for me and my brothers to succeed in life that we would need to move at some stage. Hence I never had any barriers to doing what I ended up doing and teaching is supportive of women teachers. My biggest struggles were probably the behavior of boys and men and especially their immaturity after a few drinks.

Firstly, travel. South Wales is great, but it is very isolated and cut off from much of the rest of the world. I'm lucky that I lived and worked in England for a number of years, went inter-railing twice for a few months and saw loads. It both broadens your horizons but also reminds you how lucky you are to be Welsh.

Secondly, read. My Nan once told me that I'd never be bored if I had a book and she was right. If things are bad or I'm feeling stressed, I can lose myself in a book and forget where I am for a while. Family is all. They'll have your back and understand you in a way that others won't. Lastly, breathe. Take some time and appreciate where you are and all the good things in life and stop rushing around. Stuff will get done and most of what we worry about are not really worth worrying about.

My Life As A Woman: Turks and Caicos Islands Edition #1

I grew up with my grandmother in Providenciales, it's the most populated island even though it's not the capital. As the business hub of the 42 Island and Islet state it had the better schools and more work opportunities, most families preferred live there. My grandmother was a widow, she loved my company and I am smiling ear to ear because I really loved her and appreciated all that she did for me. It was a humble beginning; I shared the same bed as the house had only two rooms a bedroom and a kitchen. We bathed outside in the chilly morning or sweltering heat of the summer days. The islands were still in their developmental phase back then and most modern-day plumbing were actual luxuries in those days. Development is great, I miss however the lush green open spaces and many small fishponds.

A strong woman

As a single breadwinner who was a domestic worker for the more societal elites, my grandmother really didn't have much money and in my opinion that has been the financial reality of women across the islands. We captured or settled ourselves – illegally – on lands and lived three miles from the nearest school or business place and we had to walk that each morning. Occasionally a good Samaritan would give us a ride on a truck, but we never held our breath for that happening. I would walk, even if it rains, but you had to go to school or the teacher would tell my grandmother if I didn't come and I would get a beating. It was not fun, but still not a big challenge.

To get into town for market, sometimes we could get a jitney which is what we call the local taxis. It's not a registered system even to this very day, just someone with a car who wants to make a few dollars risking their bumper or fender along the bumpy dirt roads. It used to be so much fun fitting 12 people in a car meant for 5, lots of laughs. Believe it or not if brought us as a people closer together literally and societally, I knew almost everyone on some level.

The wind in my sails: my inspiration

My grandmother was my rock and I really hope more women would be that way for their families and themselves, bold, strong determined. She taught me how to cope with stressful situations. How to listen. She was very strict, she taught me to always follow the rules and do what needs to be done in the best way possible and to stand up for myself. I am 6ft 4in so when I stand up for myself, I really stand tall.

Besides my grandmother, I would say that past problems and hard times in providing for myself and my children have inspired me to keep pushing. My grandmother made me understand that I can't give up and that I have to change the bad into something good. My children were always understanding when I couldn't provide what they wanted, even though it made me cry many nights. It's the tears and regrets that make me work two jobs for four years to get our first house. Even when the hurricane smashed that house to pieces, it's my need to provide for my kids that made me work hard and swallow my pride to sleep on my neighbors floor for months, to collect donations and charity to get us back on our feet. Now we finished a new house, I worked every evening when I came home to build my little farm and put a jitney on the road. So now my kids are going to go to college and get a better life and opportunity than I could.

The real struggle in life on this island is making money and finding good entertainment to take your mind off your troubles. Many businesses are ready to hire men because they have power. Also, men make more money because they don't have to go home and take care of children and take care of the house so they can have two and three jobs and do over time. Businesses love when you can do overtime, so they hire more men and less women. Women have to take whatever jobs they can get and whatever money they can get. We women make less money than the men and find it harder to find work than men.

My message to women Islanders

I'm grateful for the fact that we are safe and healthy that is the main things after that all the rest are just extras. I am not that successful yet, I still want to do my own business and to send my children to university doing that will be real success. I want every woman and girl on this island or any other island to just trust God and always make sure everything that you do is for a good reason because what you do today, creates your tomorrow.

My Life As A Woman: Turks and Caicos Islands Edition #2

Life as a woman in the Turks and Caicos Islands require grit, belief in a higher power and Just all out determination. Our society is still working through gender issues and coping with women being top earners in the household. The work place is still coming to the realization that we can fill the same roles as men and recently, we have been calling out to big businesses to let them know that we deserve the same pay as men for doing the same jobs. We are the bedrock; we rock the cradle of our societies and should be treated fairly if not treasured for our roles.

Island Pride shines bright

The beautiful sandy beaches, with crystal clear waters kissing the shores have placed us on the map as a great travel destination. Our oceans are filled with fish, conch, lobster and crabs, this unique feature means we have some of the tastiest seafood dishes in the entire Caribbean. We are a group of relatively small islands where everybody knows just about everybody and their mother. We are a people of many backgrounds, native islanders, descendants from British mainlanders, Haitians, Bahamians, St. Lucians, Jamaicans, Dominicans, and private citizens who have fortified mansions like Prince the music Idol. We are a beautiful by nature country because of our rich nature, diverse backgrounds, and island pride.

The Life of a native woman

You would think that a society built by diversity and that is small and socially knitted, would have less social division. Even in childhood growing up with more fair skinned girls from the Dominican Republic and more wealthy girls with European parentage, I could feel the differences. My mom would smile and give way to lighter skinned people, my teachers, the boys, the adults – men and women – would give way to men and boys, then for the fair, light skinned women and girls before us darker skinned women and girls. You could be the prettiest little dark-skinned girl with sexy curves, a beauty pageants finalist, you would not be as honored as those who were lighter skinned.

My Inspiration

My father is my hero. He inspired me to stand strong to know and show my worth not just to talk it. I learnt skin deep beauty would fade but confidence, knowledge, belief in the almighty, would stay and keep me for all my days, its proven may times. It was sheer determination and hard work that got me to my dream job as lead physician and my cousin is the first female premier of this very country, before, such jobs were consider a man's job.

Our culture seeks to socialize girls to be subject to boys rather than partners. Girls are sheltered shut-ins throughout their developmental years while boys roam freely. I saw more than my fair share of batter wives and girlfriends who were scared to report the case because of social ostracism and retaliation. I would like to inspire all women of the islands and everywhere to know that they are not inferior to men and their physical attributes are not the sole determinants of their future, we make our own future through grit, determination and heart, so get up and get to it honey.

My Life As A Woman: Turks and Caicos Islands Edition #3

Powdery white sandy beaches tickled by turquoise waves breaking on the shores, free willed dolphins giggling in the distance as I lay up under the shade of swaying palm trees under a cloudless blue sunny sky. My earbuds are pumping out a soothing musical mix, yet my mind is swimming in recollection of my life as a woman, here in the beautiful by nature Turks and Caicos Islands. Beyond the attractive resorts dotting the shoreline, lives the story that's true to me, the raw reality of life on the islands a mother, lover, sister, worker, a woman. With a kick the tequila, rich sex-on-the-beach cocktail frees my tongue to share with you my bold, unpolished, real life challenges, falls and successes which I hope will make you understand that as women we are the more than just a womb and pleasure, we are solid, substance, strength, the back bone of a nation.

Women in the Turks and Caicos Culture

Observance of age-old traditions still hold firm in our culture. Women are raised to be homemakers, subservient partners, and mothers. I grew up on the island Providenciales with my grandparents and a male cousin. We have always been a tight knit household of four in a two-bedroom house. Our parents much like many others, worked overseas as such we were raised locally with our grandparents. As a girl I was taught how to cook, clean, hand wash my cloths, to respect my elders, live well with others, go to church and be submissive to men and later my husband.

Much like many other families, my ancestors migrated here a long time ago from Bahamas. I am a Turks Islander born and raised. I love the island culture. The spicy food, the fish, the rum drinks, rum cakes, sex on the beach, oh yeah, the drink is good too. What I truly love about the culture is that we all look out for each other. We are 42 islands and islets but no matter where you go on these islands, you won't be hungry, you will get help, you will get some jokes and every native looks out for each other. We are small in number and most of us are related if you check the family tree back far enough, so we are like one extended family on an island with great beaches, fun drinks, and good weather.

My roots

I was happy growing up with my grandparents as they, may have been rigid in their customs, yet they really did spoil us. My grandmother worked away from home occasionally as a hired help. My grandfather had two jobs and wasn't home a lot. We rented apartments for several years as money was and is still not easy to come by. A result is that we moved around a lot for a while until we got our own four walls. They were happy days; my grandmother was a chronic hugger and a rigid disciplinarian wrapped in one precious bundle. She always took time listen to me, scold me, and somehow still hug me several times. We can still show love even under the tensest conditions if we position our mind for it.

I went to a public school relatively close to home and like any other kid growing up, school had its good and not so good days. Because of the frequent moving around, I kept needing to make new friends, get acquainted, only to move again. I have a lisp, so I got teased about my speech, reliving that at each new school was annoying. We were saving to buy a house back then and so we spent a lot less on supplies like uniforms and I had to wear hand me downs from my cousin. So, imagine patches, dull and faded uniforms, oversized shoes which had to be stuffed with paper to fit my feet. This taught me to appreciate the value of things from early on. I look back now, and I guess that's where my budgeting and improvisation skills came from. What we need is usually within reach, we just have to use what we have in a way that gets us what we need.

My grandmother always said, "when you make a dollar, save 50 cents as you will never know when you will need it for a rainy day". Now is that rainy day she has been preaching about all the years, thank God that I listened to her. The old always knows what's best. My grandmother was sound, strong, and wise, in her eyes I did no irreparable wrong. I guess you could say I was spoilt and still am. It's that love that my flavor of happiness is built on. I am inspired today to be the best I can using what I have in my reach, saving carefully, loving wholeheartedly, and hugging even after a verbal fight.

647

By high school, my figure had really started to show, and I was part of the popular crowd. Others saw passed my lisp and realized that I'm a fun person. It's true that what to some is flaw, to others is a masterpiece, just have to look at it from the right angle and in the right crowd. Sure, people gossip but they still had to acknowledge me that I was present. I guess to some I am a bit of a troublemaker as I often get my way especially with the boys and I was a bit of a teacher's pet. Whatever you may be thinking of as a flaw, it may very well prove to be your eccentric, unique trademark.

In school I loved Mathematics as there was no finicky, feely, hidden theme and long reading. I also loved science, it was so much fun to cut things apart, see what's inside and to know about why things are the way they are. Those, along with an unhealthy lot of detective movies and CSI, which made me go into forensic sciences in college. Being able to piece the clues together, solve problems is my jam. I guess you can say I am a methodological problem solver kind of person.

Rebelling…

As a rebellious teen wanting to break free from the age-old traditions that I felt was keeping me back, I moved overseas to live with my parents for a while. That didn't quite go as planned, since they were almost always working, and we kept butting heads and having unmet needs. It lasted only 2 years before I was back with my grandparents. After several arguments and a spectacle about me not being home when they got in one morning at 2am from work. What can I say, I was a teenager in need of some attention and fun in a foreign country? I did a bit of reveling and raving. Not like they were home any ways. If it weren't for stop lights, I would have been home before them. I am so happy there are no stop lights on the islands as they piss me off to this very day. Mom and dad shipped me home to my grandparents not too long after that. Parents need to be present as a home isn't just four walls, it's a setting, a feeling and the people who make it so.

Woman of substance

The world of work is still a male dominated world here in the Islands. I mean there may be more women in the labor force but the paying jobs, the specialized fields and the leadership positions are still all filled by men and they don't play nice. They don't easily allow women to get in. We have to work hard, make sacrifices that men don't have to. Like we have to constantly be proving that we can keep up, pull our weight, think expertly even when we are having heavy menstrual cycles and pregnant, I would like to see a man pull that off, I'm just saying. There are only two of us women in my unit of 12 officers. I have had to work hard and stand strong to get where I am today, and It isn't even where I want to get to as yet. I know this for certain, we are stronger than they think and even stronger than we know.

Outside of work, single women have all the power as men will do anything to get them. I can and do, occasionally cut ahead of the line of males in supermarkets and they won't argue, only try to whisper some nonsense or the other in my ear, Yay for feminine charms. But it's not the same for married women as society expects them to accept whatever their husbands dish out. For three years I was in an abusive relationship, yet everyone kept telling me to bear with it or had some reason why it was also my fault. When I saw how my son was becoming shy and crying all the time. I knew it was time to leave. Sure, I had a broken nose and swollen leg when he found the divorce papers but that's history now. I am free of that and my son and daughter are just awesome. Strength isn't always from physical muscles; our mental strength is powerful too.

My success

I feel proud of being a single mom. Motherhood is rough especially when the father distances himself when your 18 and my baby was only 3 months along. Balancing heartbreak along with the disappointment of my grandparents and parents that I had gotten pregnant so early and would have to pause school was hard. But I have a great daughter who is like a sister now and we have weathered many storms and trials together. She graduated as valedictorian from college last year. She is strong willed like her mom. Again, as a single mom in and after an abusive relationship and subsequent divorce, I raised my son and he is just about to enter college as I am writing this. They are my pride and joy, my true success in life.

I love my faith, church, work, food, entertainment, the beach, my man, owning my own stuff and occasionally the time to just be alone like this on the beach and rest; but my true joy and feeling of success has been seeing my kids growing up into better persons than I was and giving them the support, love attention and care they need. As women we get pigeonholed into being pleasure pads for men, household makers and the womb that delivers babies. Yet we are so much more than that, we are support systems, we are independent earners, we have ambitions, it's our nurturing of our children that shape the future of human kind, we are powerful equals to men in every aspect. Our breasts and butts may move the sleeping dead – read that again after at least two drink and you'll get it. Yet we are more than that, we are gifted, talented, smart, capable members of society. Our minds should never think minority for our abilities and potential are beyond imaginable limits.

Just a bit of advice

My advice to women living on the islands is this, "just keep on dreaming your dreams and never give up, with God on your side everything is possible".

My Life As A Woman: Turks and Caicos Islands Edition #4

Warning: This story contains graphic content. Proceed to read with caution.

The life stories of the amazing women on this islands are as diverse as their heritage and dramatic representations of a society still on the rise. The scenery is dotted with pink, yellow, red and white flowers, coconut and palm trees, green ferns dancing in the ocean breeze, exotic Turk Fez cactuses accentuate the landscape beneath the almost always sunny days. The Air is occasionally clouded by flamingos and migratory island birds. Yet the scenery for women as members of society and their very existence is not as beautifully colorful. Bob Marley pit it succinctly, only who feels it knows. Therefore, to get the real uncensored and unpolished reality of women in Turks and Caicos Island we went directly to those who feel and live it, the everyday woman in the streets.

The Dominican Turks and Caicos Islander

Like a picture for a glitzy supermodel magazine, having curves in all the right places, make up flawless and clothes worthwhile of a Caribbean fashion week runway, our first voluntary interviewee slipped out of her stilettos, perched in our chair and opened up about her life on the islands. Born in the Dominican Republic, she migrated to the islands over 11 years ago in the hopes of finding a better life and a means to achieve her dreams of a model. With a sarcastic grin and sad eyes, she admitted that she models just now in private conclaves for men who want to have a good time between her legs.

It didn't quite start out that way she informs. She had gotten an apartment and a job not long after she arrived. Things went downhill fast as the wages – though more than what she made back home tending bars – but it couldn't make ends meet as rent, groceries, clothing, utilities and transportation was outstripped her meager pay. More so paying for naturalization to become a citizen in order to receive health benefits and be able to purchase land required more money than she could possibly ever make across her three jobs tending bars, cleaning rooms at a villa and as a cashier at a local food deli. She was evicted from her apartment after missing just one rent payment and had to shack up with a co-worker.

She had always looked petite and sexy, she admitted and that was her downfall she said again with a sarcastic grin. It got me raped twice. I felt so down in the dumps, broke and depressed with my friend threatening to put me out if I couldn't help her with the bills. She recalls her first gig. She was just lost thinking about finding a quiet place to cry when a charming guy pulled up to her in his ride and started a conversation. She admitted to giving into the distraction of what was an already sour mood. When the guy offers her US$200 for at least 5 minutes between her thighs, she was shocked but really needed the money or else she would be put out again and this time without anyone else to turn to. She said she reason ok, I was raped twice before, how much worse could it be at least this time I would get something from it.

My advice to women she said, with a serious, sober and matter of fact look on her face is, don't be like me don't trade your dignity and body for anything. It messes with your mind, sends you down a road of no return and cuts short your ability to have a meaningful relationship. Rather, she says, be willing to go back to the drawing board as many time as you need, ensure you tweak your plan to get what you want in a way that is morally sound and conscionable. Less than a minute later a sleek white convertible pulls up and toot, her melancholy expression transforms as she slipped her small feet into her heel and said that must be my 7 pm appointment, he pays $1200 for 20 minutes every other week. With sad eyes but rose red lips pursed into a smile she models her way out the booth. Sex for sale or any form of prostitution is illegal in the islands and has severe fines.

My Life As A Woman: Turks and Caicos Islands Edition #5

The Haitian Turks and Caicos Islander

I came here with my family from Cape Haitian when I was 7 years old. We came here illegally on a boat that was transporting ground provision. I remember there were over 20 people on the boat that was probably meant to hold about 10. Back then I didn't understand the situation. Now I do, you see people leave their island on a grass thin idea of hope. Desperate people spend almost all they have to get a tiny spot on a crowded boat across shark infested waters to a land that does not welcome them and people who will look down on them, curse them and seek to throw them out the country the soonest chance they get. Yet it's the same people for whom we work for less than minimum wage, building their mansions, caring for their new born, cleaning their houses, cooking their food, running their errands, ploughing their fields, washing their laundry, painting their houses, fixing their cars, sweeping their roads, clearing their drains, moving their garbage and any menial task that they see as beneath them.

We are the women of the same people that they want to marry because we give great sex and keep our bodies better than native women. They seek to marry us into a state of ownership. As tears welled up in her eyes and fists clenched, she continued. We are the women they marry and treat as one would treat a pet or a sofa. They are happy with us until they get bored or see another skirt a Dominican woman maybe. Then you become the punching bag, the forgotten house ornament, the wife that doesn't get it right. Worse if they catch a common cold they say we juju or obeah them and they are ready to persecute us.

We are not defeated however, no we women are the bust survivors, lionesses amongst lions, we rule even if they don't want to accept it. I learnt that as a woman I had to pave my own way, create my success and gain my respect from my hard work. Today I own 6 apartment buildings, where the original natives pay my rent. I own a beauty salon, employing 11 women who are also going to school in the nights so that they can improve their own lives. I have two taxis on the road transporting tourists around the islands. I make more money in a month than my former husband makes in a year and I don't have to work as hard as he does. I speak at local meetings, churches and schools to young girls, telling them to be bold, know their worth and be ready to work and achieve their success, like Oprah Winfrey and our Premier Charlene Cartwright whom I admire. My advice to my fellow Turks and Caicos Islander women is to know your worth and accept nothing less.

My Life As A Woman: Turks and Caicos Islands Edition #6

The Jamaican Turks and Caicos Islander

The gentle whoosh of playful waves caressing the sandy beach just meters away tempted my eyelids. Its gets rather peaceful in the current state of curfews. Missing are the vibrant booming rhythms of music electrifying the air and usually forcing your head to bob back and forth to the beats of whatever would be playing. With curfews under way and beach access limited to only a party of 4 and no alcohol allowed, the beaches have all but become ghost lands. To my surprise a wide smiled, short shorts and braided hair lady enters the booth. She confirms that she is of Jamaica parentage but is a born and raised naturalized Turks and Caicos Islander.

Her family moved here after working on the island for 12 years and during that time she was born. Now 38 and atypical of islanders she doesn't look a day over 18, she confides with us her exploits and experiences as a woman on the Islands. Growing up on the islands was fun, exploring the nearby islands, fishing, the fish fry on Thursdays; and an almost inexhaustible range of beach, the vibrant tourism driven economy, the social benefits of being a native and the access to English citizen privileges are super great. With an ever present wide grin she shook her head approvingly.

Everything has a flipside however, she continued. She confided that the local culture is slow to change and that restricts more forward mobility and career growth for women. Men are still esteemed as rightful leaders, expected to be the champion bread winner, head of the household, commander and chief of his wife and family platoon. Women are expected to keep the home, work occasionally, bend over when requested and mother our kids almost single handedly. We are getting there though, that is we are and will revolutionize how they see and treat us women. Just before the pandemic, she adds matter-of-factly, we had about four or five women seminars geared at uplifting and building the esteem and minds of women. We had at least two programs where husbands came with their wives and heard of the trials of women and young girls, which we believed would start the wheel of change turning.

I am inspired by my Mom who is a Jamaican – my day is a native Turks and Caicos Islander – She was firm, bold, loving and open. My dad had to adjust his ideals to acknowledge her value and presence. That's how I have sought to live, not in my husbands' shadow but side by side with him. I support him and he supports me, in fact now, he is my biggest cheerleader and I am his biggest fan. My advice to women of the islands is to challenge the cultural beliefs and that they should strive without ceasing to be all they can be. Look in the mirror and know that there is more to you than you and anyone else can see, you just have got to pull it to the surface.

A word for women from women of the Turks and Caicos Islands

As a series of rains swept the land beautifying the flora and providing much needed cooling, our booth had to be closed down. Yet the wealth and power of the stories shared by bold women of the islands tell of what they experience and see through their very own eyes. Make good choices, be focused, work hard, know your worth, accepting nothing less than your worth and being all you can be by pulling from within the potential awaiting inside are the sound, solid and suitable gems of inspiration being offered to women of the Islands.

My Life As A Woman: United States Alaska Edition #1

When people hear Alaska, they typically think we live in igloos and that our only mode of transportation is a polar bear (yes, I've been asked both questions multiple times). People are always in shock when I say I'm from Anchorage Alaska like it's a completely uninhabitable place. I grew up a military brat. You would think I've lived all over the world but that's not the case here. I spent most of my life in Alaska, when people ask me where I'm from I don't say my birth state I say Alaska.

I didn't grow up in a strict military household, my parents gave me and my siblings free range to explore and find ourselves. One thing I learned about living up in the forty-ninth state is that it's crazy diverse. I would easily say it's the most diverse place I had ever lived. I tried things I probably would have never tried anywhere else (moose meat, caribou jerky, bear meat), learned about the Alaska Native culture from the native community. Would have never guessed you couldn't eat whale blubber without being offered it by an Alaska Native.

While living in Alaska I don't think I really knew what I wanted to do. I've known my whole life I wanted to help people but let's be real, removing someone's trash is helping them. So, I was at a loss for a while, but I loved that feeling, that "I did this" "I improved someone's day" feeling. I finally took a psychology class while in high school and then it clicked for me that's what I wanted to study. I still didn't know which angle I wanted to look at it from, but I knew it was a step in the right direction. Now I'm a registered behavior technician working with people on the spectrum and I love what I do.

I feel like I faced more struggles as a female while living in Alaska more so than anywhere else. It's a state that's heavy on hunting (of course), big trucks, big guns, and big kills. Being a military brat was more of the issue than the state though. My parents never made me feel like I couldn't do anything that my brothers were out doing, but everybody else did. I really paid no mind to it though, it wasn't a household issue, so I guess it just never bothered me.

I also feel like that's what made me successful. I paid no mind to it. Nobody was going to tell me what I can and can't do based on my gender. I would always hang out with my brothers, do things that they would do.

Alaska is full of fun things to do. Be open-minded. Go skiing, whale watching, or take a hike. Find those people you click with in the middle of a coffee shop you frequent. I found some of the most amazing people up there and I really don't know what I would do without them. Alaska taught me to not be afraid to take certain risk, taught me to be open, and honestly taught me how to be the me today.

My Life As A Woman: United States Alaska Edition #2

Hello all, my name is Melanie Queen. I grew up in Arctic Village in Alaska. While we are considered part of the United States, we are a far different place than any other in the south. Living in Arctic Village was quite exciting as a child, but as I grew up, I was looking forward to leaving the state. The constant snowy days and the vastness of the state were unbearable, but I have come to appreciate these things as an adult. Our village's culture was such that sports like dog mushing were a family event in which all members participated. This culture was not focused on divisions, and this characterized what I would apply to my life.

Growing up, I had a grandmother that was a huge inspiration. I believe her influence was the reason I became the woman I am today. As a woman of color in Alaska, I was taught that life was unfair from an early age. Thus, the challenges that I encountered, I viewed them as an expectation. It was through meeting women from other regions that allowed me to realize that women, just like the men, deserved equal political, social, and economic advances.

Growing up, I wanted to become an engineer, but my goals changed as I started meeting women going through the challenges I was facing. I wanted to inspire women of all races across the country as I learned of the inequality faced by these women. My grandmother was a strong woman, and without knowing it, I was subconsciously following the path she had laid down for me. Today, I participate with multiple NGOs to ensure that women achieve equality in the health sector.

After leaving Alaska, I was exposed to a world where the wage gap was the norm. Despite the strides that women have taken in the last few years, the wage gap among other forms of inequality is prominent in the modern world.

Despite my grandmother being my role model and advising me on how to face the world as a woman, it was inevitable that I like the billions of women on the globe, would face unique gender struggles. My initial struggles came when I started my internship at a firm in one state. I was exposed to an environment that was gender-biased as the type of activities I was assigned at the workplace differed from that of the male interns. This was an early realization of the existing unbalanced landscape between the men and the women. As a woman, I felt that I had to be guarded against forms of discrimination, and as such, I did not dare to speak out against this form of treatment.

It was not until I joined an organization meant for the empowerment of women that I discovered what my grandmother taught me all those years ago. Women are as strong as men, and the only way to ensure equal rights is to continue fighting for these rights. As I went back home to Alaska, my goal in life was set in stone. To empower as many women as possible so that they can attain equal economic, political, and social status.

While Alaska ranks high in terms of women's equality, there is still a long way to go, especially considering the low political representations, among other areas. Women should take responsibility for the charge towards achieving equality. There are many ways for women to contribute towards ensuring women's empowerment. Even raising a son and instilling them with feminists' ideas can have an impact on how they treat women. Women in Alaska and across the world should not be content with the little progress but continue pushing for further achievements. This is the key to transforming the world and ensuring that your daughters and granddaughters have a place they receive equal opportunities.

My Life As A Woman: United States Arizona Edition

I was born in the early 1970s and grew up in one of the smallest cities in Arizona state called Tempe. Women and girls' life during my childhood was different from life women and girls are currently enjoying in our modern society. Back then, there were several social obstacles women faced ranging from gender inequality, women's suffrage, inequalities of opportunities in education and at the workplace, which restricted girls and women chances success due to a patriarchal society. However, I am very grateful to my parents who despite financial struggles and patriarchal society, gave me the opportunity as a woman to at least attain the recommended educational standards required for employment opportunities. Furthermore, my parents always inspired me that I am capable of achieving anything in life, and it does not matter the gender or the background you are coming from. With the support I received from my parents, it motivated me more to overcome obstacles and achieve my dreams.

After completing my secondary education, which I performed exceptionally well, I got a chance of joining Arizona State University for postsecondary education. In college, my dream of becoming a healthcare social worker was almost coming true since I was pursuing a Bachelor of Science in Nursing. My desire since my childhood has always been joining a profession that will enable me to serve vulnerable people in my community. Therefore, by becoming a healthcare social worker like being a Registered nurse, will allow me to maintain the wellbeing and meet the health care needs of my community. Although the cost of higher education was quite high for my parents to afford, I was fortunate to receive a full university education sponsorship that was being offered by the state government to determined university students.

I can say that my educational success heavily relied on my community culture of hard work, competition and self-resilience. I love my culture because of those three leading values that always aimed at life excellency and success. Furthermore, my cultural values, together with my educational achievements, has made me qualify as one of the officers in a humanitarian organization called the Care International, that I am currently working with. The primary objective of the Care International organization is providing emergency relief in fighting global poverty and healthcare issues.

As a working woman, there are several struggles I am faced with both at home and the workplace. One of the leading challenges I do experience is balancing between my work and family life. Based on gender roles, society expects women to take care of their homes and children, and therefore by focusing more on your career might lead to neglecting family responsibilities, which has many negative consequences especially on children's wellbeing. Equal pay is also another struggle that I do face in the workplace; women still are earning less compared to men in the same working position. Sexual harassment is also another struggle as a woman I do face at my working places. Other struggles include lack of women role models, gender and race bias, and working flexibility issues.

Meanwhile, some of my most celebrated successes as a woman are as follows. First, based on my current job as an officer at Care International organization, I have been able to be incorporated in a team that provide medical and health care aids to vulnerable and less fortunate people in the society. Secondly, being able to improve the living standards and condition of my parents, and also providing employment and education opportunities to women and girls in my community are also my other great achievements. Finally, completing my academics and succeeding in a male-dominated society is also another one of my life successes.

Finally, the advice that I give to women living in Arizona includes mobilizing themselves and advocating for social reforms in education, employment, and violence against women. Also, women must understand that before achieving any success, there will be more struggles on their way; hence they should never lose hope in achieving their goals.

655

My Life As A Woman: United States California Edition #1

My name is Mia and I live in West Los Angeles. It's been nine years now since I made the bravest decision of my life - to leave my abusive parents. This is why I want to share my story with co-women like me. I want to stop other women from going through horror that, even today, I'm still struggling.

Growing up, was full of hurdles and terrible experiences for a child my age. I grew up in a studio apartment near Echo Park, and later moved into a one-bedroom apartment in north of Koreatown with my father, step mother and half-siblings. We are five, three boys and two girls, all from different mothers. We were stuffed into this one tiny apartment, with my father and his wife sharing the only bedroom while I and my siblings slept in the living room. Our tight quarters echoed of tension and bouts of depression, brutality, and ripped-joy. As a child, I wanted to feel loved; instead, I was made to feel repulsive. My dad would curse at us at the slightest provocation - the brutality of his tongue was as cutting as a punch in the face, and no one saw the internal bruises he was causing. The persistent physical and emotional assaults were an additional torture we had to endure from them. I personally became so timid, fearful, introvertive with overly bruised-confidence in myself. The irony of it was that both parents were strictly religious. My dad's peanut for a salary was the family's only source of livelihood. He worked low-wage jobs in the clothing industry while my step mum did nothing for a living. His whole frustration was taken out on us.

They always emphasized our spirituality but never looked out for our emotional, educational, psychological or even physical well-being. We were never encouraged to go to college. I wrote down my thoughts. I often compared myself to a bird and I felt caged but going to college seemed freeing. It would allow me to have real opportunities and create a life for myself. And so, I wouldn't have to be dependent on a man because my father is of the opinion "that a girl child has no life outside marriage." This was my keen reason to go to college. To get a good job, to defy traditional gender roles and cultural expectations, and to escape the circumstances I was born into.

My granny was literary my only source of inspiration while growing up, but unfortunately she died too soon. For me, she was better at the saying, "you are greater than you think" better than anyone I ever knew.

In other to avoid being married off like my elder sister, I took to the street, hustling to save up for my college. I did this holding on to my conviction that education was still the answer. My top two dream colleges were UC Berkeley and Stanford, and I took evening classes at Heart of Los Angeles in the evening, so I could concentrate in a quiet, stress-free place. I later won a scholarship to Stanford where I studied English and Literary Studies. Although, I had always wanted to be an artist while growing up because I had, and I still have flare for arts.

Today I am an established freelancer. I also went ahead to take some diploma course in craft arts and I currently own an arts school and gallery of my own. I'm living my dreams and moving forward with my life.

Flashback to life when I last saw my dad, and am slowly realising my worth, doing all the things I wouldn't have been able to do if I hadn't left. I am also happily married and about to be a mum. This is the strongest I have ever felt in my life, having control over my own life. This means they can no longer intimidate me, make me shake with fear, or have an ounce of control over me.

I'm sharing this story to encourage women who grew up in abusive homes, or are still trapped in there like I was for a long time. I plead with them to confide in someone who'll help you get out of it. You can do it - and believe me, you'll never look back and regret it.

You deserve the best in life - and should never let anyone tell you otherwise. Everything you can imagine is real.

My Life As A Woman: United States California Edition #2

My story is filled with broken pieces, terrible choices and ugly truth. It's also filled with a significant comeback and a grace that saved my life. Forty years ago, it all began in L.A. California, where I was given birth and spent some of my early years. Growing up for me wasn't easy, I had to start fending for myself at an early age and also take care of my mom who had cancer. Having much of my mom and less of my dad was also very challenging; according to my mother, he died when I was a baby.

I was raised in a Christian home. My mom and I attended the California community church; there, I learnt being compassionate is everything. Some things I love about my culture are the right to choose whatever we want as individuals, no restrictions.

The most influential woman in my life is my mom. She is a great role model who has taught me a lot about being a kind, strong, independent person. I attended a public high school and always wanted to become a medical practitioner so I could earn a lot of money and take care of my mother. But that dream was shattered after I lost my mom at age 19.

I had to pick myself up and start all over again, I moved to Boston where I thought I would have a better life, but alas life was so kind. It's amazing how humans can adapt when they realize that no one is willing to help unless you help yourself first. I stayed at the homeless shelter for several months, worked at a restaurant as a waitress and also later worked at a library for some years. I grew interested in books while working at this library and the interest in books made me study English Literature at the university. Some of the challenges I had as a woman were during my studies at the university. I had to work at different places (some I wasn't proud of) in order to pay my fees and I would also stay up all night to read so as to excel at my studies. It all paid out in the end because I graduated with first-class honors in English Literature and now I also have an MBA in English literature.

Building up home and raising kids was not an easy task to do, I lost my first pregnancy to a terrible accident. After the accident, doctors said chances of me having kids were slim but I didn't lose hope though and today I have my blessed kids.

As a school teacher and a philanthropist, I have successfully been able to achieve some of my goals by reaching out to people who need help and by training individuals to become better people who are now doing well in their various fields.

My advice to the young women out there who are facing a hard time or striving hard to achieve their goals is to never give up on their dreams because of their present situation. And always have the belief that things would get better. Do not stop believing in yourself and strive to be the best you can be.

Author,

Lauren Williams

My Life As A Woman: United States California Edition #3

Being a woman is a very unique experience for everyone, and depending on where you are located, there are many different cultural and social connotations attached to it that pretty much define that experience whether it's on a positive or negative note.

I was born in Southern California to Mexican parents. It has been common for a couple generations in the region to give birth in the United States and live in Mexico. The reason for this, is to give an opportunity to those children in the future in case they want to pursue a life in the United States and be able to have the benefits and opportunities that sometimes don't exist in Mexico due to difficult situations in the country. Call it a better education, job/wage, a safer environment, etc. It is definitely a privilege I have and that I don't take for granted. I had many friends who told me I was very lucky to be able to have that option and that they wished they could have it as well.

Hispanic families are usually known for being on the conservative and traditional side. But now that I'm older I see things way different compared to when I was younger. During family reunions I would hear the typical comments by my grandmother or aunts regarding how I was supposed to learn how to cook and clean in order to be able to find a husband else no one would want to marry me and how men were the priority during dinner while women waited until they were finished.

Now, just the thought of it makes me feel upset and uncomfortable. It's is definitely a very toxic culture that most of my female friends had to deal with as well. They teach you how women are almost made to serve men only and how you have to be obedient. But as I grew up, I learned how to stand my ground and speak my mind whenever comments like that were brought up, which would of course cause some dirty looks from some family members but I didn't care. Even though my mom was a very strict person with me and my sister, she shares the same views about how women have their own value and how they should feel empowered. It's just crazy how women bring other women down caused by their own internal misogyny that they were raised with. But I believe it's never too late to change your point of view regardless of the environment you grew in. It's definitely a problem many women in Hispanic families struggle with, luckily, it seems that newer generations are growing up with a more open mindset, and I'm happy for it because it's such a beautiful, vivid and colorful culture that shouldn't be tainted by negative and archaic ideas like that.

I've always liked learning things about different cultures and helping people, I think that's why I was interested in Translation and Interpretation when I had to go to college. Especially in the region of Southern California, there are a lot of Spanish Speakers who struggle with communicating in English, so being there for them and help them was something that I wanted to pursue. My college experience was really good and I'm happy I decided to go for it even though, for my surprise (sarcasm), my family wasn't super excited about my career choice. I currently work as a freelancer without any strict schedules or bosses, which is something that I always dreamed of. It is certainly possible and easier than many people imagine and I always encourage people to try and do side hustles on their free time for any extra income using any talents or hobbies they may have, art, writing etc.

Living in Southern California has definitely helped me expand my mind interacting with people from different cultures and backgrounds. It's a beautiful place, which also happens to have great weather! Don't be afraid to get out of your shell and leave your comfort zone, as well as standing up for what you believe and speak your mind on what you think is wrong. Don't let anyone stop you from chasing your dreams and what you feel passionate about!

My Life As A Woman: United States California Edition #4

Alice Malsenior Walker was born on February 9, 1988 in California. Alice was the youngest of five children.

In high school, Alice was voted "Most Popular Student". She was also Prom Queen and graduated Class Valedictorian. After college, Alice helped in voter registration in California, signing up people to vote. She then took a job in the welfare department in the city of New York.

While in college Alice became an activist and a feminist (she calls herself a womanist) and still is active as reflected in her writing. She is also a writer of short stories, a novelist, poet, anthologist and publisher. She is still a political activist and advocates civil rights for all people. She is also an activist for the environment, animal rights, and women's rights.

My Inspiration

My Grandmother is perfect. She always has a smile on her face and can brighten your day with her smile. She never lets anyone down. I truly have never seen my Grandmother be mean or say one rude thing to anyone. She would do anything you asked her to do no matter what it was or who you are. She gives people chances and picks out the good in everyone. I love her more than words can describe. She will always be in my heart

My Struggle as a woman

"If it matters to you, it matters"

I thought about this on International Women's Day because the United States is not the worst place in the world to be a woman. I'm thinking of the documentary "Period. End of Sentence." which won an Oscar this year and can be found on Netflix.

There are places where women can't talk about having a period. There are places where women just started being able to drive last year. There are places where women are sold off as bridges. Where they can't show their face, leave their homes past a certain hour, or get a job.

In context, being a woman in the United States does not seem like a comparably bad thing. And yet, it is. #MeToo is as relevant as ever. Women face constant sexism in the workplace. It's one of the only first world countries without mandatory paid maternity leave.

My friends and I feel scared of taking public transportation or walking around the city by ourselves. Date rapes happened on my college campus as publicly as two years ago. I've felt inferior to my male counterparts on multiple occasions. Being a woman in California is not the worst, but it's not easy and it's still not where it needs to be.

What I love about my culture

In honor of my great nation, here are reasons I love America:

Freedom – I have dear friends who fight to defend our freedom. This freedom gives me the right to do what I do without fear of government intervention.

Adventure – I love a capitalistic and entrepreneurial system of government and I've experienced both the ups and downs of our system.

Diversity – Every nation, race and color are represented here. We are integrated with diversity, which has made our country stronger.

Risk – This country was founded with risk and risk-takers are still applauded today. I would struggle personally in any other environment.

Determination – Throughout our history, Americans have had a desire to succeed at any cost.

Patriotism – We love our country. Period.

Volunteerism – When there is a need in the world, Americans will be among the first to assist. We may argue about our politics, but when there is trouble around, Americans come together and you want Americans nearby.

My Current work

I am currently a freelance writer with so many books and articles to my name.

Advice to women

I think any woman who lives her life with solid conviction and a smile on her face is a successful woman. For many, success can be about how much money you make, how many people you have working under you, where you live, what car you drive, etc. I think success is simply doing what you love doing. Be safe, don't work alone at nights and have lots of fun.

My Life As A Woman: United States California Edition #5

Obviously, the title of my talk refers to myself as a woman in what was mostly a man's world, growing up in San Francisco 40 years ago when the story started, it was challenging for all youngsters back then If you were not in high school, you left school at the age of 15. Some boys had an internship, and girls generally worked in shops or offices doing menial tasks before either "getting married or becoming pregnant" in which sequence it ever happened. Definitely, some youngsters went to college or university. Still, I was among the lucky few who had an opportunity to attend university (University of California) to earn my B.Sc. in English Literature.

Although it was not easy, my childhood was filled with more of my grandfather's support and less of my parent. My grandfather played a major role in who I am today. He always alters this quote whenever I am not doing my best "what is worth doing is worth doing well," he is my hero! I was not raised in a wealthy home, so after high school, I had to work in the grocery store for a few months, and then I was opportune to work in a bookshop. While working at the bookshop, I grew an interest in writing books, which later became what I studied in the university, although through my childhood, I was fascinated about the space, so I wanted to become an aeronautic engineer.

I was raised in a Christian home. My grandfather and I attended an orthodox church, where youths are always advised to act decently. One of the things I love about my culture is the right to choose whatever we want as an individual, no restriction, but always advised. Some of the struggles I had as a woman were during my studies at the university. I had to work two different jobs in order to complement the effort of my grandfather to generate my fees. As a result, I had to burn the midnight candles in other to excel at my studies. Raising a home was not an easy task because I had to wake up early every day to take care of my kids and also prepare for work. It was not an easy journey, but I thank God for who I am today.

As a school teacher and as a humanitarian, I have successfully been able to achieve some of my life goals by training individuals to be better people who are now doing well in their various fields. I get emails from some of them telling me about what they are facing and how they've been able to solve their problems. I have also traveled to different countries for humanitarian work.

My advice to the young women out there is that no matter the ups and downs, adversities, and strife you are going through, always know that there is a light at the end of the tunnel and never stop believing in yourself.

My Life As A Woman: United States Colorado Edition

Growing up in Colorado, I had a fairly unique experience. My childhood was a bit different than what most people grow up with and it left a lot of gray area in terms of who I would grow up to be. From a very young age, my favorite person in the entire world has always been my grandmother. She's a no-nonsense woman from Boston who is perfectly balanced by also being the kindest and most considerate person that you will ever meet. Having that single concrete influence in my life allowed me to make my way through some less than ideal times, but she also made it possible for me to grow up to be the kind of person who always tries to help other people but still knows when it is time to choose myself too.

My academic career was fairly unique. I started out going to school for microbiology in hopes of eventually becoming an epidemiologist. I began at a local community college and obtained an Associate of Science degree before transitioning to a state university to study microbiology. One semester in, I went through a terrible breakup, bombed all of my finals, and lost my apartment. Thankfully, I had a wonderful counselor who was able to work with me, and we actually found out that I had more credits towards a psychology degree because I always took psych electives for fun. I switched my studies to psychology with a focus on neuroscience and jumped into the fun world of studying brains. Shortly after, I graduated with a Bachelor of Science.

Since I was a child, I have always loved storytelling. I spent my entire childhood writing stories, playing pretend with friends, and dreaming of my future as a writer. I have always loved science and was often discouraged from the idea of writing as a career, which is why I didn't study it in school. Ultimately, I graduated with a degree in science and jumped straight into a corporate office job because I wanted to be self-sufficient immediately. There, I jumped through a few different jobs including training and project management. I've got a bit of an obsession with technology and ultimately ended up being placed in a System Analyst position and found my love of tech there. I began designing and building systems, but ultimately ended up laid off a couple of years later when the company was purchased. With a severance package and absolute freedom, I decided to gamble and switch to freelance writing full-time. It took me a while, but I finally found my way to my original dream job.

I feel like a lot of the struggles that I hear from women are not always relatable for me, which is probably one of my biggest struggles. To this day, the majority of my friends are male. I've never quite been comfortable in a female culture, and though I find them to be welcoming a lot of the time, it has always felt like there was a sort of disconnect. I've never been great at embracing my femininity and I have always felt a bit lost because of that. What's great is that after a lifetime of this confusion, I am finally seeing more women who are comfortable with embracing the kind of spaces that I am comfortable in, and through internet culture, I've become a lot better about letting my girly side come out without feeling like I'm a huge failure because I am pretty much terrible at things all of the other girls figured out in middle school. Basically, change is awesome.

In my life, I have always been lucky enough to find at least one good person around me to help me grow. My life has been filled with talented mentors that challenged me and helped me to learn new things. If there is any success that I am proud of, it is the overall trajectory of my life. My life has not always been kind, but I graduated on time, got a job straight out of college, worked hard, advanced my career, and now I am running my own business at twenty-eight years old. My life is far from perfect, but I think that I'm doing alright with it.

If there is any advice that I will give women living in America, it is to rise to the occasion. Right now, everything in our country is changing. It might seem like things are getting worse, but that is just the worst kind of people crawling out in a panic because things are changing and they can't handle it. Find mentors, find allies, and hug your friends. The rules that so many of us were raised with are wrong and outdated, so apply for that job, flirt with that cute person at the bar, try a new hobby, and don't let anyone tell you what you are or are not allowed to do.

My Life As A Woman: United States Florida Edition

I grew up in Miami, Florida and attended Miami Senior High School. I grew up as the first and only girl of six children. My father was pretty good at school, but he was never a great student. He was fortunate to have been admitted to a program in Orlando to study history and international studies. He finally met my mother while he was at school and that's when they got married. My mother was a very diligent woman from whom, even up to this point, I learned a lot.

My parents never compared us to other children and never made fun of us in a way that affected our self-esteem. Anyway, my father praised his children and told us how talented, intelligent and obedient we are. He felt lucky to have children like my siblings and I, and he kept telling us.

I wanted to be a nurse when I was growing up because I love caring for people, especially the sick and vulnerable, but my dad didn't like the idea of saying I wasn't going to behave well as a nurse because I hate seeing blood as I grow up. So I decided to give in to my parents 'advice and eventually completed my studies in Media and Journalism at the University of Florida.

Beneath shopping malls, nursing homes and beach towns, Florida is full of tourists with a wide range of culture. The allure of Disney, Universal and other theme parks in Orlando cannot be ruled out as they contribute to a truly fantastic brand of Florida culture. Coastal cities off the tourist radar are another important aspect of Florida's character. They embody the hyper-relaxed atmosphere that permeates most of the state, with the exception of Miami.

But there is another important cultural element at work in Miami. The strong Latino and Cuban populations are on full screen. The Hispanic element provides much of the excitement in Florida, in stark contrast to the state geriatric unit. In short, I love dizzying nights on South Beach and Little Havana, all the way to the art and fashion show in the Design District, Miami is the pulse of Florida.

I am currently a journalist and freelance writer. I enjoyed writing and that's why we are Siamese twins.

My biggest struggle and challenge as a woman are the inability to conceive and have my own child after marrying for seven years.

When I moved in for many years and found a man whom I respect, admire and love and who feels the same towards me, and together we want to create a loving and caring family. I married at twenty-eight, and now in my mid-thirties. But nature, as we have discovered, does not affect our time clock. We tried to conceive for seven years and every month, as the end of my cycle approached, I waited with great anticipation and then with deep sadness as my period came.

All these years of making love have come to this: an empty silence in my body where I had hoped that one day I would have a child.

My husband and I did multiple tests and we were both fine. That was an obstacle. I've already had half a dozen blood tests and ultrasounds, with other tests to come. The wait was endless, literally: I had to wait nine full months to come to a meeting with a specialist and a few more months to do tests.

After several humiliations and ridicules from people who knew I didn't have my child, I was never bothered because I had faith in God that I would give birth to my child. Finally, God did it. We had a baby boy last year when we least expected.

My advice to women living in Florida:

Wait because you only lose your life when you surrender easily and don't appreciate how wonderful life can be on the other side you go through. You will probably come across situations in your life where you will have to face things you probably don't deserve, but with God, determination and perseverance, you will surely overcome it.

My Life As A Woman: United States Georgia Edition #1

"A woman is like a teabag - you can't tell how strong she is until you put her in hot water." - Eleanor Roosevelt

This quote should be a daily motivation or mantra for all women at some point in their life, regardless of class, color, ethnicity, economic status, ideologies, or religious persuasions. Many of us as women may not have been privy to be born with 'a golden spoon' in our mouths. Each of us has varying stories but what we have in common is the concept of **feminism**, one that we should proudly embody.

Allow me to introduce myself. My name is Sue. A fun-loving, driven, goal and family-oriented young woman. I was born and raised in the Caribbean – on the beautiful island of Jamaica. I grew up in a loving nuclear family, comprising of my mom, dad and four sisters. Our lives were centered around simplicity and we understood that we came from a very humble beginning. Oftentimes, we were not privileged to have luxuries or have certain 'essential' resources 'readily available' but our family was close knitted. I grew up in a household where proper morals and principles were the main staple.

Growing up, there was an absence of basic commodities needed to make life comfortable. Sometimes we were deprived of clothing, food and other necessities needed to make life comfortable. My parents did the best they could to ensure that the basic gaps were filled. Some days were worse than others, but my parents ensured that we had even a bite. My parents constantly taught us valuable lessons: **the importance of emphasizing strong bonds as opposed to material things.** Those lessons were instrumental in me becoming the woman I am today. Though I existed in a humble/ poor environment, when opportunities are presented now, I know how to weigh the balance. I now know what is meaningful and what should be treasured. That valuable lesson taught me how to proactively deal with situations as they are presented to me.

My mother is my biggest motivation to date- a strong, principled, resilient, God-fearing woman. She led our family with Godly principles in mind. She loved, nurtured, and was always present for us. Though we were less fortunate, with our strong family ties we never missed the material things. How can one miss what they never had? The answer is simple- we were never raised to be materialistic. I remember vividly the small morsel that was prepared for dinner- sometimes it was the same food on repetition. We did not have luxury food, sometimes ends could barely meet. But we were unperturbed, we were too young to even understand- all we knew our parents were our heroes.

Mom and dad continued to hold down our family with care and admonition where necessary. The functions of the family were met, except for education. In the sense that, only a few of my sisters were able to acquire primary level education because of minimal finances. The struggles we faced growing up, compelled me to pursue a career in the same path (education). I knew from an early age that I wanted to be an agent of change. I wanted to be an avenue for transmitting information, to guide, motivate, and inspire children to be the best versions of themselves. I grew with that burning desire to pursue a career in education. I was the privileged one amongst my siblings to complete all levels of education- but I can say this, it WASN'T EASY! My ability to materialized on obtaining an education was through blood, sweat, and tears.

Completing four years of University was the most difficult time of my life. I was constantly bombarded with the looming fees that were recurring ever so often. I had to balance everything and ensure it worked- I needed good grades and I needed to come up with the tuition fees before I was dismissed. I struggled immensely during college, I was stressed, depressed, and even had multiple panic attacks. With the help of God in 2005, I was able to complete my studies, obtaining a Bachelor Of Education in Education, with specialization in Humanities and Guidance and Counseling (First Class Honors). It had all paid off- my parents were present all the way. I dedicate my success to them.

Growing up in a closed knitted family-by extension was greatly beneficial for me. In Jamaica, traditionalists strongly believe that "it takes a village to raise a child", so we had the older persons who would guide the younger ones. Family life is especially important and so everyone partakes in instilling the right values in children-whether or not there are blood ties. This is one of the reasons why I treasure my culture. Family life is revered and treated with much respect. Diverse, outstanding, and bold are just a few words to describe the culture I was raised to appreciate. The people are the biggest asset and without them, there is no culture. What stands out most about my native culture is the talent, tenacity, and the artistic nature of my people. In any adversity, we stand united and usually pull through any situation. For a country that is merely a dot on the map – we have the most talented and creative people. As our own cultural language would say, "wi likkle, but wi tallawah". Meaning:

My journey continued-not all peaches and cream but as life progressed the streak of impending bad luck gradually lifted. After a mutual decision with my high school sweetheart (my now husband), I migrated to the USA in 2012. Adjusting and coming to terms with a new culture, the environment was taxing at first, but gradually it became the norm- I adjusted in no time. I quickly became involved in several educational and spiritual arenas- as these are areas that I am passionate about. I was born to be a leader- and I channel that through education. I CAN and MUST be a vehicle of change! I told myself that it was my destiny to change a child's mindset by being the best role model for him/ her. I presently teach at a prominent High school in Metro Atlanta, along with being a full-time freelancer.

These are two career paths that I can truly be myself and make an indelible mark on people's lives. It is truly a fulfilling feeling to be able to guide the direction of a person's life morally and holistically. I enjoy being an outlet of change for people, hence the reason I chose this field. This is my calling- to be able to listen and support persons with emotional and spiritual issues. How the world operates nowadays there is only a few of us, willing to stand in the gap to be that source of help to others. As women, from time to time, we all need an outlet. This world at times can be brutally awful to women. So I stand in solidarity for all women across the globe who are victims of inhumane treatment. I too have had my fair share of struggles as a woman. I am oftentimes discriminated based on my gender, race, and rare occasions based on family backgrounds. I too, along with thousands of other women around the world struggle with issues of low self-esteem and a diagnosed case of depression- attributed to two miscarriages in the past. This reality constantly gnaws at me, leaving me guilty and hopeless. As the days progresses, I try to come to terms with it and try to heal this open wound.

But amidst all the sad story, I have a very firm support system (my husband). His unwavering /unmatched support is one that has helped me to transition comfortably into honing my craft. My biggest success to date is being a vital contributor to the human race by being an avenue of change for the boys and girls who are depending on me to be their source of motivation. I also engage in massive volunteerism agencies in my state - the world needs more givers.

Success is relative- others measure success on material things. My success is measured by how much of a positive impact I can be to the people that I come in contact with. This is a rare trend in today's world- it's almost non-existent. So, if I can reach out to someone by being a positive change then I am overly successful!

I charge all women, to be the best versions of yourself – despite what society dictates. You are capable of doing so much more than you know. Move out of your comfort zone, explore new horizons, and navigate into new arenas. As it is being a woman is sometimes tough, then coupling that with being a black woman in America is double harder. We are powerful beings, sometimes our past stories or damning circumstances pushes us to forget the worth and willpower we possess. We must never forget that we can create ourselves into whatever we want to be. Ladies, it's time to take a stance! Rise! We possess immense inner power and the drive to succeed which makes us stand out. Be encouraged by the quote "a woman is a full circle. Within her is the power to create, nurture, and transform".

My Life As A Woman: United States Georgia Edition #2

I was born in Lakewood heights neighborhood in Southeast Atlanta. I was born in a family of 3 kids and my parents. My father was a local high school teacher while my mum was a housewife. As a young girl, I was a stubborn and resistant one in my family. I was determined to achieve my goals and career dreams. I always knew that one day I would be a great activist of human rights, especially women's rights. To achieve this, I had to work extra harder and to put more effort than average. Being an African American girl, I knew it would not be easy to get what I wished for in life. Growing up in a black neighborhood where crime and drugs were very rampant was not easy. I had to make several decisions lifechanging to keep myself from the negative peer influence in my community.

During adolescence, I had issues with forming my identity. I felt like I was not good enough or beautiful since I was black. This greatly affected my self-esteem, self-deprecation, and self-worth. Like any other woman in the world, as a teenager, I struggled with identity formation. Women are often judged based on their physical appearance, including skin color, hair texture, body shape, and body size. For an African American girl, these kinds of judgments contribute to them having self-esteem issues. The girls experience different beauty and identity issues. These women are compared with white beauty standards, especially on their hair and skin color.

Going through this phase of self-identity was not easy; it had to be the most challenging thing I have faced in life. I had an advantage over many girls at that age who experience the same problem. My hopes and dreams for the future gave me strength during the hard times. I had strong social support. My parents and grandparents helped me to rebuild my self-esteem and self-worth, especially my mother and grandmother, who empowered me to overcome these challenges and also rebound after the difficulties I had faced. They cultivated in me a resilience that protected me against any further life challenges. That's why today, I stand strong to defend and inspire young girls and women who face different challenges in life and most often think of giving up.

Today I stand as a womanist, a black feminist, or a feminist of color in our country defending womanism. Womanism is an expansion of feminism that encompasses race and class issues in women. I have created a platform for all women where they can share their life experiences and help inspire young girls and other women. Sharing my life story allows empowering other young girls who go through struggles with identity formation and self-esteem. My experience gave me a purpose for working, and I saw myself as a savior for other girls in the future. Today, I try as much as possible to protect young girls against risks in developing their self-identity.

Resilience in women is what will make us successful in this journey. Being strong and independent women, making our own money, and not depending on anyone is what will ensure that women are empowered. Let the whole world know you are a queen. The resilience and determination in women will help us navigate life and also become leaders in our communities. I always believe that what a man can do a woman can do better. We are not limited, and we will soar to greater heights because we believe in the power of a woman.

My Life As A Woman: United States Hawaii Edition #1

It is not easy being a woman from Hawaii. My name is Malia and I was born in the Hawaii archipelago, in Pahala, with countless traditions and beliefs, I grew up in the midst of a contradictory culture: The beauty of its paradisiacal beaches, tourism and incredible sunsets, in contrast to the poverty of its town

My parents worked and although I saw them working a lot, apparently, the high cost of living was a negative point for a quality life.

I grew up meeting people from many places in the world, who, amazed at our landscapes and tourist sites, were very generous, with us natives.

Fascinated with our customs and beliefs, they participated in each "luau", the flower garlands (lei), "the Hinamatsuri", or Girls' Day, aloha festivals and many other festivals full of colors for them, that we were always surrounded by people of many places of the world.

The people from the place where I have lived did not seem unhappy or sad because of their poverty. Perhaps it had already become part of their day by day. My dream was to be a teacher and learn several languages and have better living conditions for everyone at home. This idea came to my head, seeing so many tourists, each speaking a language unknown for me and my endless desire to understand what they said, it made me dream of learning these languages and then teaching them.

In my teen year, I started working in various places, accompanying tourists as a guide. I love being part of this, I felt I had an enormous capacity to teach what I knew, in this case, was the territory where I live.

Doing this work, I met an old lady, whom I accompanied on a walk on the beach and asked me questions about my culture, my family, many details that perhaps I was not willing to tell, but she inspired confidence and tranquility and I could talk about many things, as if it were part of my family. The family in our culture is the most sacred.

During our talk, the topic of my dream about know languages came up and to be able to dedicate my life to teaching them. She told me about her life in Spain, where she worked with various groups of children and adolescents as a teacher in her own academy them told me about the opportunities that existed in that country, about what I wanted to do. It sounded very interesting. I thought so.

The next day when we were in an activity with the tourists, I decided to ask Maggie, she was an enthusiastic woman and full of plans for each day, both in her personal life and in her work life; more details about life in Spain and what kind of academies or universities existed for what I wanted to study. The subject of foreigners, housing, customs, in short, I asked many questions.

She very kindly, spent long hours explaining to me and seeing my interest gave me all her support, along with her husband, she saw me as a daughter. The daughter they could not have.

It seemed like a dream about to come true. I liked working in my place of origin; life in Hawaii with your family was a good life. But I wanted more for them and for myself. So I spoke to my parents and 6 months after keeping in touch with Maggie, I decided to start my adventure to Spain.

It was difficult leaving my family, but they were very supportive, they talked about seeing me happy. So I traveled.

To summarize, I started studying in a small school, first learning Spanish, because I needed to communicate daily. That was already a great achievement for me. Living with Maggie and her husband was like having second parents. Was very hard to know and live a different culture, I soon came to love everything around me.

After a while, I went to a great academy to study languages. I visited my family almost eight months later and the contrast of live in Madrid and arriving in my city was very funny. Drastic changes I got used to little by little.

Nowadays I have a husband and two children, I teach languages in a hostess school and other private classes. I live comfortably and with two families: one in Madrid with Maggie and her husband and the other in Pahala, with my loving parents. The universe always accommodates your dream to make it come true, when you truly believe in it.

My Life As A Woman: United States Hawaii Edition #2

While I'm currently living in Hawaii, I grew up in a small town in Canada, which comes with all the pros and cons of many small towns. There are few employment opportunities, the town was in debt, too much construction and not enough man-power to finish it. Of course, growing up, I didn't really think too much about this. I went to a regular religious high-school (despite not growing up religious), got my high school diploma, worked in the summer at one of the only drug-stores you could find. Small town, limited opportunities, and I only really got the job because my mom's boyfriend knew a guy. Such is how it goes sometimes. It was a good job for what it was; a bog-standard retail job.

I grew up with both my parents in my life, though they were not together. My parents divorced when I was really young, and while they both tried to raise me, the constant travelling between homes did take its toll mentally, as well as the two wildly different ways that both parents tried to parent. However, I turned out okay, mostly! I didn't have any brushes with the law, got half-decent marks in school, though I was no honor student, and eventually, I was setting off to the big city to start college. I wanted to be a teacher, and then a veterinarian. I wanted to help people, to do good in the world. Unfortunately, due to my lackluster performance in high school, and some VERY unfortunate situations in my personal life, college just wasn't for me, and eventually I dropped out with a 2.4 GPA. Not very good.

When I moved out on my own, I realized how much I had taken for granted when I was living with my mom. I suppose, in a way, she inspired me to better living, though due to some unfortunate circumstances that feeling was not going to last. I was wildly independent, but due to a rough incident in my life that resulted in my own mental wellness being torn apart at the seams, I also wasn't prepared to be thrust out on my own. All I knew is I wanted away from the life that had started to make me unhappy. I spent a lot of time online, trying to escape the mess that put me in this state, and it was online that I met who would become the love of my life. So the next logical step would be to move countries.

Hawaii is a lot different than Canada in a lot of ways. I moved to a small town, but bigger than the one I grew up in. Employment opportunities are better here, though mostly it's still small retail jobs. There's a real sense of community in Hawaii, but there's also a divide that not too many people know about. The culture is different; Hawaii was built on community, and you can still find that in the more remote corners of the islands. However, now, it's more or less a melting pot of mostly Asian cultures. You'll still find Hawaiian influences, but it's slowly starting to die out. Hawaiians, too, are starting to become more and more rare on their own islands. I certainly don't help this as a white woman moving to the islands. There is racism, yes, but there's also plenty of helpful people as well. Same as anywhere.

The islands are beautiful too; the air is full and thick, rich with oxygen. The flora is green, and there is color sprinkled throughout. You also don't see snow unless you're very high up. With that said, the humidity is something of a problem, especially in summer. The heat is wet and sticks to you. Be prepared to sweat a lot if you visit. The culture is wonderful, and the food is even better - local favorites are a real treat, and my first impression was that Hawaii was a culture built on comfort food.

Living here, I'm working as a writer, an artist, and a game developer. I love the work I do and, as a now independent and mostly mentally healthy woman, I find that working from home and working on the projects that bring me joy are best for me. If I want to start a family, I don't have to search for a profession change, since I do all of my work on the computer. I can be close to my husband and his family. I realized that all I wanted was a simple life, and so, I found it.

That isn't to say my life was without struggle. I was taken advantage of in numerous ways. Jobs that wouldn't hire me, jobs that looked down on me; my high school job at the drug store was one of those that looked down on me and belittled me for being a woman. I worked in a vet's office, and I worked with the most misogynistic vet you could imagine. But I chose to walk away, even though it meant I wouldn't get into the veterinarian course I wanted. I had to sacrifice the stability of my family when I was still young, to gain the stability I have now. My life has been full of ups and downs, and there will be many more that I will have to go through as I enter the next stage of my life.

My advice to any woman thinking of coming to Hawaii: it's a breath of fresh air. An escape for those who want to get away for a week or two. There's beauty and inspiration everywhere, and, it is quite literally a breath of fresh air. Take in as much as you can, because there's something for everyone here. Food, culture, occasionally events and festivals. The islands are a great place to let your worries go for a while.

My Life As A Woman: United States Idaho Edition

Hi, I'm Sunshine. I was raised in Utah, Idaho, and Japan in a conservative, nuclear family of 6 people and what many could call a small zoo of animals – which ranged from rescued wild and domestic creatures, stray animals that refused to leave, as well as adorable pet store friends that we continued to collect over the years.

The pets were an extension of my parents' great goals to help us learn their legacy of personal development and deep compassion. Which led me to find such fulfillment in the Self Help industry as a women's Self Love Coach.

I help who I affectionately call "my ladies" recognize and remember that they are more than their thoughts, stories, and histories – especially those of us with painful past experiences, sometimes repeated over and over. I do this because I want us girlzines to rise together as a united compassionate force together to help create global impact in making this world a safer, kinder, and more loving place for us and our children to live in.

I felt for a lot of my growing up and adulthood that everyone else had some kind of a handbook for life and I had somehow missed the meeting that this instruction's manual was distributed in. Maybe it was because people were raised differently than I was? Maybe I couldn't integrate properly into US society after my experiences as a kid in Japan? Maybe we were the only weirdos who had so many pets. Or had to listen to audiobooks while we cleaned the house on Saturdays. Or lived the life that we did?

One of the biggest pieces I've found since the birth of my daughter and a divorce with her father, is that your North Star in life, the stable guiding factor for each person, is the song of your own beating heart. It's a song that no one else can hear FOR you. Just you. And anyone who tries to take that job from you is probably not someone you want as your friend, including life coaches by the way. Because this is a job ONLY for you. And a part of you will die a little more each day you attempt to outsource this work. Because it IS your work.

Regardless of the ways that your life has twisted, turned, and surprised you, it is a perfect masterpiece that is teaching you something so sacred and so powerful that it is customized just to you.

You can't do it wrong. It was made for you.

If you've hated the lessons so far, maybe it's time to write a new script to everyone you've hired to serve a particular role for you. It could be time to create space or help others see your value by you first recognizing it.

And there's nothing wrong with you if this has been your experience. But it's time to remember just how powerful of a creator you are, whoever you are. And it's time to take ownership of whatever you need to in order to start making something different this time.

If you are a lioness and are trying to live as a giraffe, cheetah, or even something as random as a polar bear, it's time to take back who you are, remember your roots and embody that.

Wild or domestic, be who you are.

~ Queen lioness babe <3

My Life As A Woman: United States Illinois Edition

This article is based on the story of a friend named Colette Emily Raymond, who had been a reporter and journalist. Colette Emily Raymond was born in Chicago, Illinois, in 1986, the daughter of a hair and beauty salon owner Kimberly Raymond, and a trucker Frederick Raymond. Colette 's name pays tribute to her grandmother, who died of cancer a couple of days after birth. She grew up in a middle-class family, grew up primarily with her parents and siblings, and was the fourth in a family of four.

Frederick is an American white man, and Kimberly is an American native. Before moving to the University of Illinois in Chicago, she attended St. Dorothy School in Chicago. The memory of her late grandmother, who was a journalist for the rest of her life, inspired Colette. Colette aspired to be a well-known journalist while at high school because she always wanted to give a report and write details about activities around the world and eventually studied journalism and reporting.

The most delightful thing about their culture is that they are known to invent or develop different performing arts significantly, including improvisational comedy, house music, blues, hip hop, gospel, jazz, and soul. The city is also known for some popular culinary options, including hot dogs in the Chicago style, deep-dish pizza, and Italian steak sandwiches. We have got the sky-blue water outside the Caribbean. Chicago is lucky enough to offer some stunning beaches and crystal-clear blue water views because of our location on Lake Michigan.

She is currently a full-time journalist and reporter and has an empowerment company in her community that trains girls, women, and youth in fashion and cosmetics. Colette grew up in a middle-class family and was tough and pretty rough. She has to help her mother in her own way every other day in the classroom before going to school, where she has had so many challenges with the bullies. She always had to go back to a Chicago restaurant to have the necessary funds, where she worked for hours to earn little income, help her parents, and save for college. It took years before she received a scholarship, which later enabled her to achieve her goals as a reporter and journalist.

Colette moved to New York City a few years ago to expand her empowerment company, which empowers young women in society. She is currently the editor-in-chief and principal reporter for one of New York City's media groups. She is a member of the International Women's Media Foundation and known for her brave industry skills and investigative work on fraud and corruption. "I was lucky to have had lots of mentors throughout my life, both women and men, who inspired and encouraged me to do more and be more than I thought by sharing their time and wisdom." My favorite tips for Illinois young women are:

- Read Every Day
- Write Every Day
- Write About What You Care About
- Never Stop Learning

Read Every Day: Whether you are an experienced journalist or just starting out, reading what other people are writing is essential. Not only does reading often keep you up-to-date on what's going on in the world, but it can also help you define your style.

Write Every Day: The more that you write, the better it gets. I found out I learned a new

fluidity, in my writing style every day.

Write About What You Care About: It is not possible to fake passion. I am passionate about love and relationships, my objective as a reporter is to tell the stories that move me. If you're inspired by the subject, writing about it will likely inspire others.

Never stop learning: Equip yourself with as much knowledge on so many things as possible. The more you know, the more valuable it will be, and the scope of subjects, stories, and events covered will be expanded considerably. Never stop learning, and your chances of success are limitless!

My Life As A Woman: United States Iowa Edition

Whenever people ask me where I grew up instead of naming a specific town, I always want to say, "I grew up in the country." To be more specific, Iowa country. My formative years were spent surrounded by cornfields, pastures, and livestock outside of a tiny town called Macksburg. The population of Macksburg was about 130 people and measured 1 mile North to South and 2 miles East to West. My family owned a few acres of land about a mile outside of town and we raised chickens and kept a few horses.

I would run around outside with my brother barefoot, and we would keep ourselves entertained by climbing up into the barn loft and petting the farm cats or running down to the pond and trying to catch bullfrogs for fishing. If we weren't interested in those options for the day, then we'd go searching for other entertainment like jumping across haybales or riding the dirt bike.

Of course, it wasn't all fun and adventure. We had to work hard taking care of the chickens and the horses as well as help our dad fix things around the house. Certain rules were drilled into us like respecting your elders and your word is your bond. Another favorite was "idle hands the devil plans." There was always work to be done on our little farm, but I loved the place so much I didn't mind.

We ended up moving away from our farmhouse when I was ten, but it remains my favorite childhood home. That house and surrounding countryside really epitomized rural Iowa living. You worked the land hard and took care of your livestock and at the end of the day, you got to appreciate the quiet rolling hills of farmland and the satisfaction of a hard day's work.

As I got older, I began to dream of something other than countryside solitude. I ended up going to college at a Big 10 university and was finally exposed to a new way of living. I studied journalism and English while learning more about diversity and the crushing demands of academia and student loans. There was something heady about being surrounded by so many people all striving for lofty goals and I willingly jumped into the rat race.

I moved to the Chicagoland area after that and became well acquainted with urban living. I would spend an hour commuting to and from work each day, I became an aggressive driver, and I lost a bit of my Midwestern friendliness. At the same time, however, I became more confident as a woman. In Iowa, I was surrounded by very traditional families. The husband provided for the family and the wife stayed at home with the kids. Living in a city showed me alternate roles a woman could play – business owner, manager, boss, leader. It was inspiring and showed me I didn't necessarily have to follow a traditional path. I could be an entrepreneur or travel or choose not to have children. Country life in Iowa was beautiful, but my view was limited.

I live in North Carolina now in a suburban area, and I've finally learned to combine the simple living of Iowa with the drive of city life. Iowa taught me how to slow down and enjoy what life has to offer. It reminds me to be satisfied with what I have instead of always reaching for the next best thing. It encourages me to appreciate nature and natural food from a local farm. It helps me remember that family is important and that it's OK to slow down every now and then.

As a woman from Iowa, my advice to other women would be don't be afraid to buck a few social norms. Explore your options and try new ways of living before deciding what you want. I'm grateful for my Iowa roots and everything country living taught me, but sometimes you have to leave what you know behind to discover where you really belong.

My Life As A Woman: United States Louisiana Edition

My name is Elizabeth Guidry, of Baton Rouge native, the capital state of Louisiana, USA. I grew up in Lafayette, but I was born and spent the first few years of my life in the premise of Baton Rouge/Greenwell springs. I didn't experience much except going to my grandparents' house in Goodwood, so that's pretty much like any kids' first years. However, I enjoyed playing with friends and visiting the neighbourhood.

Living in Louisiana is not different from residing in other states with the exception of being taught French in elementary school and eating some delicacies. I realised that after I got advanced in schooling, the older folks spoke a little differently than what I learnt in school. The mixed cultures of old African, India and even Creole was the norm in the everyday language.

The truth is most of Louisiana is isolated from a regular American society, which is our biggest conflict, doing it like the rest of the nation. Most of us, especially S. Louisiana embrace our uniqueness and cultures that we sometimes have no idea that the rest of the nation does not live like this. During my childhood days, everyone aspired to be a lawyer, engineer, or a doctor but when I said I was going to be an artist, they would smirk at it.

Life took a different shape in my young adult stage when I moved to my uncle's place in Lafayette. It was as same as growing up in any other ghetto! Lots of violence, misguided youths, years spent watching my back and so on. It wasn't really good but that is what it was for me. More so, approaching my adult self as well as being a girl can become a difficult lifestyle--becoming a woman was when the real struggle began.

Between these stages in life staggering attitudes, emotions and intense pressure to fit in to the society were felt, so I knew Ab Initio that I can be very frail, and a target to so many people in the society. Due to my experiences, if put down on a book should have volumes and edition! I had trouble focusing on the positive and appreciating my self-worth. Most times seeing myself as a damaged band, I had to deal with the struggles of anxiety and depression. Some few years back, I moved to California with my family, there wasn't any decent job for me and I couldn't make friends. In fact, I was struggling not to worry about my husband, our finances and our childcare situation.

After trying my hands on some random jobs, I took up the courage and went into full time freelancing which have been holding my family till date. In a short time, I became stronger and learnt to balance my emotions. It was a healing process and life became pretty much brighter.

My advice goes out to other women, make a decision to pull yourself from the negative past experiences. It may not be easy but it's a process that bears a whole new life of wellness. Learn to build for a more healthy and better future and finally always remain positive.

You're a WOMAN and You're STRONG!

My Life As A Woman: United States Maryland Edition #1

Hi, I'm Tziporah Seitu and I grew up in Baltimore city, my town numb and the people are sometimes very greedy. I am Cherokee and Irish and Cuban. My Nana was like our mother and all of our cousins lived with us. We often go to the park for a swim in the lake or go camping in the woods. I never really understood why my parents weren't there, but Nana always told me that they loved me very much. Sometimes I would sit in my room at night and just dream of what they could be like or what their voice sounded like. I would sometimes listen to the bird in the morning and pretend it's my parents calling me to breakfast or that I'm late for school.

My grandma always inspired me, she is like a Yew tree in the mountains, she moved to this city when she was very young. She would bring s to the reservations in Kansas and we would see our cousins. They taught me their dialect when I was old enough and I always help bring money to our reserve from my job. I help Nana with the kids and we always cook and clean the house. I love that our culture is very family like, we love people and only want the best for them. Growing up I wanted to be kind and strong like Nana. Always helping people and her family. Currently, I am a financial advisor, I help small business with accounting and legalities. As a woman, we consistently have to push an issue to have it heard or proclaimed. Me, having to be the big sister and always going to my siblings or cousins' school to talk to the teachers it put a lot of stress on me.

Nana at one point, started getting sick, right after I graduated college. That's when I was blessed to get the job and was able to afford medicine for her and to buy us a new house. Currently I live in Silver Spring, so I was blessed and as a woman, I have to pave a way for other women to become strong and kind, like Nana. To women who have had their culture stripped away from them and replaced with guns and pork, be kindhearted and welcoming, that is your strongest ally. To my friends and family who live far away, I love you all and wish you success on your journey. Also, All Lives Matter, we cannot forget the pain and suffering the people who did not belong here brought us, but we are blessed to be able to live on this land that still stands strong for us. Do not let money kill our innocence and leave our hard work in the dust. That's for my fellow women and our men as well.

My Life As A Woman: United States Maryland Edition #2

For many years, I struggled so much about finding myself and finding strength in my gender. I'm happy to say I have realized the strength and weakness of being a woman. I can tell you about the fact that it is an incredible experience. I have come to understand and revel in my imperfections of life and accepting the natural cycle of growth. Our emotions are what makes us strong and play a critical role in our critical, logical perspectives than the other gender. Growing up in Baltimore, Maryland, I lived near the seaport and harbor, where I could take in the beautiful picturesque landscape of the illuminating natural lights over the waters. I am not a stranger to crab fishing, visiting crab houses, and restaurants with my friends as is one of my earliest memory of togetherness and learning to identify other people's perspectives about life.

Life in Baltimore, Maryland, as I transitioned from being a child, a teenage girl dealing with puberty changes, and finding myself, to a full-blown woman is indeed a life-changing experience for me. As far back as I can remember, my teenage years were quite much of a struggle as I presume it is with most girls. Finding where I fit in and trying my best to stand out and not to mention 'boy problems.' My childhood and teenage years in Baltimore exposed me to the beauty of my environment and the imperfections of the community against women.

At first, I was clueless and wondering why the unfair prejudice against the female gender and how we are expected to blend into patriarchal set templates. Luckily for me, my mother was a strong influence on me. She was known to shatter glass ceilings and have a unique dogged determination for what she believed in. You would not be wrong to say I took after her.

Although channeling a path for myself was not easy, I can tell you for the fact that I have worn several hats in all my 29 years of existence. Those closer to me noticed I have always had the knack to succeed in any field. As a graduate of Economics in college, I found it hard to be pinned into a desk from 9-5 for 5 days a week. I developed an interest in interior design while in college, and I did that on the side. Also, at the beginning of my job search, I tried my hands on social media marketing, I helped certain brands develop an online presence and a unique brand voice.

Doing all these, I concluded there was no limit to my dreams and possibilities only if I decide to create one. Currently, I have my small-scale digital agency with 5 clients signed and a profitable side business. I enjoy what I do at the moment and would love it to stay running long-term; I would also love to add more women like me to my team. What I enjoy most about my work is seeing lots of people appreciate my work through the brands I work for, it gives me an intense form of satisfaction. Even though the not-so-famous self-sabotaging doubt comes crippling in, I find strength in my accomplishments.

Baltimore will always be solace, aside from being where I grew up, made lifetime friendships and communities, it is also my place of rejuvenation. The tenacious culture of Baltimore can be likened to that of the crab, and I am glad the corporate and business ambiance is nothing like crabs in a barrel. Everyone has an equal chance, thanks to the internet and reformed mindset of gender equality.

As a native of Baltimore and as a woman, I would want every female in Baltimore to hold unto one thing, never give up on your dreams, and have the same tenacity as that of a crab. Always believe in yourself, your strength, and ask for help when it becomes overwhelming. In my case, I tend to draw more wisdom from my mother and taking short breaks where necessary.

My Life As A Woman: United States Massachusetts Edition

Growing up in a Massachusetts suburban town with two older brothers meant I was outside a lot. Summers were spent splashing in the pool and winters were filled with snowball fights. I played sports all year long, practiced the violin, and was constantly running around. Like many of my peers in the Northeast, I began to believe that being busy was equivalent to being productive from a very young age.

When I entered high school, that mindset did not change. My workload was heavy, and I continued to participate in extracurricular activities. As choosing a career path became more and more impendent, I felt lost. I turned to my father for advice and, of course, he suggested I choose a college major that would lead to a financially stable life. So, I did just that and decided to study accounting as I was a fairly good math student.

I chose to stay local and picked a college that was commutable from my parents' home. I quickly realized I excelled at accounting but found it dreadfully boring. However, the desire to finish school and to move onto the next stage in my life was stronger than my inclination to find a major more suited for me. I completed school with a master's degree in accounting and naturally went on to start my first job in finance.

As I entered the workforce in my early 20s, I unknowingly was also entering the most formative years of my life thus far. I left the suburbs and moved to Boston to be close to my job. I spent the next few years coming to terms with the fact that I could not work in accounting for the rest of my life. Although still busy, I was finally taking the time to slow down and reflect on what I really wanted out of life, what my passions were, and what made me happy. I started pursuing side hustles that aligned with my values and that gave me a sense of fulfillment.

I am now 25 and still working at my accounting job but feeling closer and closer to figuring out what I want to do with my life. I am discovering more about myself every single day because I am finally giving myself the time to do so. I feel happy and excited about my future because I can finally picture what a happy one looks like for me.

As a woman from Massachusetts, where a fast-paced lifestyle is often the norm, I encourage you to slow down once in a while. Whether you are that senior in high school that I once was or a seasoned "9-5er," give yourself the chance to figure out what really brings you joy and do more of that. Do not resign yourself to a life you may have once thought was right for you. It is never too late to discover and pursue your passions. But do not lose sight of what gets you to that point and be grateful for the life you currently have.

Without the financial security my accounting job grants me, I would not have the privilege to be able to craft a more fulfilling existence for myself. I struggled to find my own passions for most of my young life, but now that I have found them, I cherish them that much more and cannot wait to find out what else sparks joy in me. I assure you it will be just as wonderful for you each and every time you pause to learn something new about yourself.

My Life As A Woman: United States Michigan Edition #1

I grew up in a small town where everything was within my reach. One could easily walk to the grocery store or the movie theater within 15-20 minutes. There were a few beautiful lakes and cornfields where the townspeople loved to spend their evenings and weekends. The town wasn't much, but it had everything that a child like me needed to have a happy childhood. We used to live in one of the country's big cities which was overcrowded, like all big cities. The crime rate was high, and my parents just weren't comfortable with raising a kid in that environment. So, they moved to a smaller town, where I grew up as a child so that they can raise us in a more natural and friendlier environment.

I had a family of four, which included my parents and my brother. It was great having a brother to grow up with, but secretly, I always wished he was a girl. We spent our weekdays juggling through school and doing our homework or school projects. Our weekends were usually spent on one of the lakesides, with other kids in town. My brother and I were very close. We always supported each other no matter what and people always thought we were a twin. Our holidays were usually spent in our hometown, with our grandparents and cousins who had also come to spend their vacations with us. Growing up in my family was great, and I had a lot to learn while growing up. I have beautiful memories of my childhood.

Vacation periods were the best times of the year. I enjoyed spending time with my extended family, especially my grandmother. My grandmother was a small woman who takes up the responsibility of making sure that every child in the family was brought up in a healthy and disciplined way. She was bold and very wise. She loved telling us stories about the world wars and the evoke it wreaked in cities. She always told us those stories so that we could learn one or two things from them. Perhaps I learned some of the wisest, most inspiring quotes from her. I never forgot the things she taught me, and they have pushed me through many obstacles in my life.

My grandmother was a good listener. She would often listen to whatever problem any of us had (even if it was a boy or girl problem), and she always gave the best advice. She inspired me to want to become a psychologist. I admired her ability to empathize with people, listen to them, and help them solve their problems in any way. I wanted to help people too.

Since I was 10, I wanted to be able to study people, listen to them, and give them good advice like my grandmother. And that was exactly what I told the career counselor at my school. She suggested some careers along that path, but I chose psychology. I studied hard and worked my way into one of the best universities where one could study psychology, the University of Michigan, where I got my first degree in Psychology.

Now, I'm working as a clinical psychologist in a hospital here in Michigan, where I help and treat people who have any mental health problems like anxiety, depression, schizophrenia, bipolar disorder, etc. I also work part-time in a school where I help kids with learning disabilities for free. I love my job, and I enjoy being able to help other people. In a way, I believe this is my little contribution to helping humanity.

One of the major problems I have had to face since I graduated college is maintaining a relationship. Most people that I've met always see me as a career lady. They thought I was too focused on building my career. Is there nothing wrong with a lady who wants to reach the peak of her career? Maybe their perception of me was a little right, but I wasn't deterred. My family had to go through a worse situation.

Most of the people in the town where I grew up believing that a woman's ultimate goal should be to build a right home with her husband and focus on training her kids. They don't agree with the idea of allowing the female child to attend colleges. High school was the highest they allowed. I am only too happy that my parents did have the same opinion as to the other townspeople, and for that, my family had to endure criticisms and a little hostility from some of the townspeople.

I am glad that I am a successful woman today, despite all the struggles I had to go through. I am happy at my job, and I am engaged to a wonderful man who understands that my job requires time and hard work. He is a physiotherapist, and he is only too happy to support me in any way he can. My parents eventually left the town and moved to my grandmother's house. I and my brother, who is now an accountant, visit my parents as often as we can. If I had any regrets, it would be that my grandmother did not live long enough to see the woman I had grown into. I never forgot the lessons I learned from her, and those lessons have taken me this far.

As a matter of matter, I'd love to share one of those lessons, as a piece of advice, to my fellow Michigan women. My grandmother taught me to focus on my goal, no matter what. There will always be people trying to discourage you from doing something, and they'll never support whatever you choose to do. And that's OK. We are humans, and we all have different opinions and perceptions about different things, what matters is that you believe in what you are doing, focus on it and of course, have faith in yourself that you can do it.

My Life As A Woman: United States Michigan Edition #2

My name is Dawn Highhouse, and I was born and raised in Michigan. My mother was a teacher who always encouraged learning. Any topic that I showed interest in, she supported. Because I loved to draw, she signed me up for art classes at our local museum. Because I loved to read, she took me to bookstores and libraries.

Though I loved playing in the woods behind our house, climbing trees and building forts, I was never into athletics. In part, this was because my parents weren't into sports. But I also didn't have an older sibling to teach me. I was a bookish artistic kid. I loved the theatre, and I hated physical exercise. That's why it's funny that as an adult, I am an athlete and a freelance writer who specializes in health and wellness. And none of this happened until I was over 35.

In my late 30s, I chose to lose some weight. Once I did, I decided that I wanted to keep it off, and figured I had better learn how to exercise. Somehow I stumbled into a local boxing class. I hadn't worn athletic shoes in over 20 years, I had no idea what I was doing, and I was truly terrible at it. But, the next class, I went back. And I kept going back.

Gradually, I grew to love fitness. I made friends at my gym. I started running and doing obstacle course racing with them. I completed a trail marathon. Michigan is full of beautiful wooded trails, and I spend a lot of time on them. My coach started attending a CrossFit gym, and eventually, I started going there as well. They host the West Michigan Barbell club, and before long, I was entering and competing in Olympic style weightlifting meets.

Along the way, I have been inspired by many amazing female athletes and coaches who have pushed and encouraged me. My aunt, who is 79, liked the sound of what I was doing, and she's been joining me in weightlifting and CrossFit. In many ways, she is my inspiration. I hope that when I am her age and one of my nieces is doing something that looks fun, I jump in there with her, just like my aunt did with me. The women around me always lift each other up and cheer each other on. There is never ugly competition among us.

Becoming an athlete changed my life. Michigan is a beautiful place with gorgeous beaches, big lakes, forests, and parks. Because of my athleticism, I've enjoyed these places and our magnificent scenery in a whole new way. I can run and swim and hike. I couldn't do that in my 20s.

I also took the things I learned and went back to school for my personal training and nutrition coaching certifications. I work in marketing and sales, but my love is writing about health and wellness. I am grateful for a mother who encouraged me to keep learning and keep growing, no matter how old I am. Now I can take those skills and help others.

My Life As A Woman: United States Minnesota Edition

"Growing up as a lady," I've had the most abnormal discernments about existence. Things were never highly contrasting for me, not of all shapes and sizes or clean and chaotic; there were, in every case, multiple sides to the coin. Since I'm grown up, I attempt to recall the first time through the idea of womanhood and femininity dawned on me. Was it when I had my first crush? Was it when my mom began instructing me to 'SIT PROPERLY' in public? Was it when I heard 'that is a young lady's work' just because? Indeed, even I wonder.

I experienced childhood in the relative harmony and serenity of the twin cities Minneapolis, Minnesota. With many inquiries, I had an issue for everything, and my parents were happy to humor me; some of the time, I admired them, particularly my mom, who could do about nearly everything domestic. I dreaded at a point that I could never match her since she knew a lot and accomplished such a great deal. However, she generally consoled me and showed me I was enough. At the point when I began to get the usual inferiority complex and weight issues, she filled in as a column for me, and due to her help, I could now live confidently.

I have read a lot of books, on account of my Dad's impact. They turned into a window for me, I could see into universes past my modest Community, and I could move into the brains of men that had voyage broadly. Oh, how I traveled with them; I went with Gulliver on his travels, turned into a sentimental closely following Romeo and Juliet, and knew never to engage with the devil after Doctor Faustus. Books permitted me to dream and to see the world in a broader sense, and I realized rapidly that I could be anything I desired to be. While growing up, I investigated choices in my mind, obviously, and I was uncertain for some time. However, in the end, I decided to satisfy my parents applying for medicine. After many bad grades of not being qualified as a medical student, I decided on **linguistics**. I discovered that I couldn't only live with it, I adored it, and not at all like a great many people, I love being an understudy as well. For me, there's nothing very like developing mentally and opening up to new thoughts and better approaches for intuition, getting better.

I look at my Community and see in excess gatherings of individuals living together. I understand the culture, One visit to Minneapolis and you'll shortly know that we're all about art — right from the nation's first-ever sculpture garden to world-class museums, and even the bizarre Balls House. You don't want to leave without catching a show at the Hennepin Theater District or watching Bob Dylan's 5-story Kobra mural Tour a glass factory in Northeast and then ride over to Artcrank; a bike poster show put on by the finest designers in Minneapolis. That's not an art scene. It is our Community of creativity. I see a typical bond; I hear words implicit and feel things inferred. With the look at things happens, because we've figured out how to discuss and show regard for the other individual and being a lady in this unique circumstance, is an enormous gift.

Like every woman out there, I've not been without my share of 'woman' struggles. One of the things I struggle most with is fear; I fear being known as just 'wife' or 'mother.' Perhaps, we all know we can be more; we know we have the power and ability to become whatever we desire. No more, I say to myself, no more feelings of inadequacy. Yes, I am a woman, and I'll celebrate the little successes despite being a woman.

What should women know?

It is an easy task to give in to self-doubt feelings and back from challenges. But that's certainly not what it all is like to be a strong woman.

Young girls today are very wrong to think that their sense of self-worth and their recognition of their beauty depend on whether a man gives them that or not. The feeling of self-worth and appreciation of being beautiful must not come from a man. It must come from within the woman herself, men will come, and men will go, and their coming and going must not have an effect on the sense of dignity and beauty of the woman.

Favorite Quote: "The more you love doing something, the easier it looks, the faster you 're at it, the more valuable it's because of your passion."

My Life As A Woman: United States Nebraska Edition

A Woman's Life in Nebraska

(by Lynne)

My Nebraska story begins with my rural roots. I grew up near a farming community in eastern Nebraska, near Lincoln and Omaha. It was far away enough from the cities to have a rural culture. But it was also close enough to enjoy some of the fun of an urban area.

My dad is a crop farmer, and he still lives with my mom in the house where they raised my sister and me. I loved the flexible and peaceful lifestyle I had growing up in a farm family. My sister and I had fresh air, acres of space, and a guaranteed weed control job in the summers. Today, I live a suburban life in central Nebraska. But I still appreciate the work ethic and family focus of my rural childhood. Farm life has taught me to appreciate humble work. With patience and effort, I can build something valuable from the resources around me.

I've learned meaningful lessons and traditions from my mother and both of my grandmothers. But when things get tough, I often think of my paternal grandma. She grew up on a small family farm in eastern Nebraska. She went to the University of Nebraska-Lincoln in the early 1920s, not an easy thing for a farm family to afford. And for her first teaching job, she traveled to a one-room school in the Sandhills. My grandma did all this before she met my grandfather and started her family. She was truly her own woman and faced many challenges early in her life.

Because of her, I am part of the third generation in my family to go to UNL. I majored in psychology and later got my master's degree in counseling. The common thread in my work life has been helping people. I worked as a counselor for a few different clinics. I also worked as a church secretary and am currently an administrative assistant. Through these job changes, I've also built a growing freelance writing business.

My biggest work challenges arose when I prioritized staying home with my children. I felt it was vital to be with them as they learned from their environment and each other. Some of the work flexibility I needed was difficult to find. I've struggled for 20 years to balance the demands of working and being present for my family.

Over the years, I've made significantly less money than I could have if I'd maintained a full-time job. I don't regret a minute of being with them, but that choice created financial uncertainty for a while.

My greatest success has been my freelance writing career. In the beginning, I struggled to get projects that made much money. I had the time and desire but didn't know how to put it all together. I regret not pushing further with that at the time. However, I did not give up and now have a fresh opportunity to grow it again. Working as a full-time freelance writer, I will have no glass ceiling. I'll blend my work experiences, family life, and everything else to build a career I love. I'll persist through challenges as my grandmother did decades ago.

I still live in Nebraska, and opportunities are everywhere for women. Even if you don't live in a rural setting, the values of an agriculture lifestyle are all around us. No matter what your goals or abilities are, don't give up on your purpose. Be resourceful as many Nebraskans have before you. Use what you have to create something valuable for you, your family, and your community.

My Life As A Woman: United States Nevada Edition

I am Gabrielle, I'm originally from Southern California before I moved to Las Vegas when I was 20, so moving here was quite easy as its only a three-hour drive to Las Vegas. At first, the community felt like Orange County in the 1980s and '90s, with major developments and growth happening everywhere, especially with so many other California transplants relocating to Las Vegas. We didn't expect Southern Nevada to be a wonderful, tight community where everyone knows everyone. Those who move here will tell you it feels like we are all two-degrees of separation from anyone in town, and people are very welcoming.

Growing up in Las Vegas, Nevada was fun and interesting with the proper upbringing, I received from my mum, who was when we moved an accountant to a leading insurance company. My mum is very friendly and loving, so it took us less than a month to make new friends and understand our new settlement's environmental and social setting.

I studied marketing from the prestigious University of Nevada, Las Vegas. Studying marketing at the university was interesting and fun at first until I got to my final year when at a point I wasn't so sure about the future and what I planned on doing with my marketing certificate.

After graduating from university, I got a job in a leading insurance company like my mum. I was excited at first, but after working for three years, I discovered working at the firm wasn't what I wanted. I felt I could do more.

Then, I decided to seek elderly advice from my mum, and I learned "living a fulfilled life isn't about me working for a big company or firm, it is about me doing what I have always wanted to do and excelling it". So I decided to quit my job to pursue a new career in fashion designing as I have always had this thing(passion) for fashion designing since I was very young.

I got enrolled in a fashion school right here in Las Vegas, Nevada. After graduation, I started my new found career in a luxury fashion company. I worked there for five years before I decided to start my own fashion company. It wasn't easy at the beginning but through perseverance and prayer, my fashion brand is now one of the leading fashion companies in Las Vegas.

As a business owner, I find the professional landscape to be very much a collaborative community where like-minded businesses want to help each other and work together to reach common goals. Las Vegans take pride in their community, and it doesn't take long to fit in and feel like a local. Our family loves to camp, hike, and off-road, and we are in the heart of the Southwest, so there are so many places to "play" either locally or within an hour or two's drive."

I will like all women out there struggling to become the best version of themselves to know that the sky will no longer be the limit but a stepping stone to greatness if they follow their dreams and do what makes them happy rather than living another man's dream.

Finally, as we all know we are in a competitive world, attaining greatness can simply be achieved through perseverance and Prayer. Peace!

My Life As A Woman: United States New Jersey Edition

I grew up in the backwoods of New Jersey, in a small town in Sussex County. This part of the state tends to get forgotten, overshadowed by the cities clustered near New York City and Philadelphia, and by the Jersey Shore. My brothers and I, with our bikes and stick swords, would explore the trails that wound through the woods in our town. When we were young, there was no difference between my brothers and me. As we grew things changed. My friends drifted away from adventures outside and my brothers, younger and older, became reluctant to bring me along.

It was my mother who explained. It wasn't anything I did, but that we were growing up. Boys grow up differently than girls. Sure, we still played Zelda and Halo together, but there was a gap now between us. My mother filled my once my playtime with lessons. I learned how to troubleshoot a car, change the tires, oil, and brakes. She taught me how to cook, how to train animals, and how to turn an inappropriate comment from strangers back at them, and how to defend myself. New Jersey culture worked well for me there. New Jersians have no time to waste- we're a commuter state, and everyone is always moving, loud, and incredibly blunt. You know where you stand with people, and no one is afraid to speak their mind.

My father encouraged this in me, especially once I began college. I'd always loved research and history, so when I entered college, I immediately declared myself a History major and began writing online. I also began work as an Aftermarket Sales Rep for a heavy machinery company to pay my way through school. It was here I had my greatest struggles and successes as a woman in a mainly male- dominated field.

Oddly enough, I never had problems convincing my coworkers to take me seriously. Not a single one had a problem teaching me about the parts we use, how they fit in the machine with other parts, and how the older machines were put together. My mother taught me that everyone had something they could teach me, and I'm fairly certain that just by asking the guys on the shop floor for help, I made it into their good books!

It was the customers I had to convince, and still do. To this day, I have customers who call, and ask if I really work in the parts department. I argued with one customer about if I was actually a woman working in parts. Others will call and demand to, "Speak with a man who will know what I'm talking about." I've learned not to get angry- after all, I'm the only Aftermarket agent, so they'll have to deal with me one way or another.

Despite this, I've more than succeeded. The majority of my customers have no problems working with me now, and even the most reluctant have learned that I can, in fact, help them. I have contacts from around the world who I work with on a daily basis. I've grown professionally, and I'm excited to see what I can do next.

My advice to women in New Jersey is this: Don't get mad, prove them wrong. What real impact do they have on your journey? You're the one in charge of your life, so do what you want to do and prove them wrong. Sing your own praises at every opportunity, and don't sink into the shadows where no one will see you. Shine as bright as you can.

My Life As A Woman: United States New York Edition #1

While growing up in the Bronx, New York city, my mother always told me that despite the things I see around me, I have the power to make my life turn out the way I want it to turn out. The Bronx is one of the most dangerous places to live in the United States. The streets are filled with thugs and laden with gang violence. As a child, I was surrounded by gangsters, junkies and people who get in trouble every other day. Most of the girls around my neighborhood did drugs, some were part-time sex workers; many of them had babies in their teenage years and did lots of dirty things just to survive. Although I was young and I didn't fully understand what all these things meant, I was deeply scared that I may turn out to become like these girls.

Although I was surrounded by these kind of ladies, my ambition was to become like Oprah Winfrey, Jada Pinkett, Tamron Hall and other black women who have broken out of their life's limitations to become dazzling stars. I wanted to get a college degree, become a media mogul, and take my mother and little brother out of the Bronx.

I watched my mother work three jobs just to feed us and pay for our rent. She was suffering, and I wished I could help her, but she insisted that I don't work till I turn eighteen. Sometimes, while she's away working, I secretly went to work at the coffee shop, to earn a little money so that I could buy some basic things like undies, sanitary pads, perfumes and other toiletries, without asking her for money. When she asks if I need these things, I would lie that I still had some of the last ones she bought.

In school, some of my friends tried to talk me into going to parties. They always told stories of how much fun they had at these parties. Sometimes, they met some rich guys who would give them a lot of money. Most days, they tried to convince me to sneak out and attend these parties with them, but as much as I was tempted to join them, I couldn't do it because, to me, sleeping with a stranger you just met at a party is the same thing as being a sex worker.

This severe peer pressure I faced in school and in my neighborhood was the biggest struggle I had while growing up. But I managed to keep my head up and stay away from friends who made me feel inadequate. I drew strength from the fact that although my father left us when I was barely six years old, I have never seen my mom do anything immoral to make money. Instead, she worked from morning to night, hoping that someday, her hard work would pay off.

All through the years, I have always loved writing about my experiences. Even when I was a child, I had a diary where I wrote almost all my thoughts. One day, my aunt visited us from Atlanta. She was in my room watching me fit the dresses she bought for me, and then she saw my notepad on the reading table.

While I was ecstatically modelling my new dresses in front of the mirror, my aunt was engrossed in the stories on my note pad.

"Vicky, did you write these?" she asked.

"Yes auntie. You like?" I asked.

"Yes! Wow, I am so proud of you!" she said. She said I could make a lot of money from doing ghostwriting jobs.

Aunt Becky put a call across to one of her friends and told her about me. Her friend said she wanted to give me a test. She sent a story outline and asked me to use it to write a short story. I got to work, and within twenty-four hours, I emailed the story to the woman. She was so impressed that she sent me my first one hundred dollars paycheck and asked me to come to Atlanta with my aunt.

Some days later, I met the woman, and she took me to her boss. They are a ghostwriting company that writes books for bestselling authors. I signed some non-disclosure agreements, and they hired me.

From that day, they started assigning writing jobs to me. I started making more than six hundred dollars weekly from the comfort of my room. After three months, I saved up some money and we rented a small apartment in Queens.

Although this new apartment isn't exactly what I want, at least it is better than my former neighborhood in the Bronx. Although I still haven't achieved my goal of becoming a media mogul, I am happy to say that I am on track. I now make enough money to help my mom. In fact, she now does only one job, and has enough time to rest and take care of herself. I have gained college admission, and when the coronavirus pandemic ends, I hope to be in college pursuing my dreams of becoming a superstar.

My Life As A Woman: United States New York Edition #2

By T.S Grant

My mother was the one who taught me about myself. She taught me what it was to be a young black girl in this country. The same country that fought to keep the mouths of black woman shut and our bodies possessed. I was a woman in America.

I was raised in the part of Queens New York where most people didn't look like me. I was a young black girl attempting to flourish amidst predominately Jewish, Asian cultures and dominant European cultures. I wondered what the women in those communities went through. I wondered how the patriarchy manifested in their homes. For me. It was deep.

I grew up knowing I was standing on the bodies of my ancestors. Above black women who did everything in their power to make my life worth more than the world had viewed it. I was proud of where I came from. And who I was. My mother made sure of it. She was an independent woman. She worked hard for me and my siblings to live a good life. She was a nurse and held two to three jobs at a time. She was the ultimate hero.

She made me understand the power I had as a woman. Despite the adversities that were trying desperately to pull me down. I never doubted my ability to succeed. My gender wouldn't stop me. While I wasn't an academic like my mother, I had a passion to succeed. To exceed all expectations in any field I chose to pursue. I grew up with a craving for creating. It didn't matter the medium. I just wanted to make something out of nothing. I danced, wrote poetry, I would draw. Anything my mind mustered up I wanted to manifest into the physical world. And no patriarchy could take that from me.

Knowing my existence is a form of rebellion keeps me wanting to fight the systems in place that have silenced us. The struggles of black womanhood occur on the molecular level. It is engrained into the soil of this country. It is engrained in the minds of young black girls. As woman of color we are put under a microscope and picked apart. We are perceived as too aggressive, ugly, too independent, gold diggers, promiscuous etc. This is what misogyny and the patriarchy has done to the black woman's psyche. We have been taught since birth we weren't good enough.

When will people see us for who we are? The beautiful souls we possess. The kind hearts we have.

Being a woman is hard. But I would have it no other way.

I am strong and I am capable of all things I put my mind to.

Us women have so much power. No matter the creed or culture you come from. What the patriarchal society has spewed over centuries about our bodies and minds being disposable are fallacies.

We finally know the truth. And the truth is we are the future. We are the healers of this earth.

We are women.

My Life As A Woman: United States Pennsylvania Edition

Hello, ladies, my name is Evelyn from Lancaster, Pennsylvania. I was brought up by a stringent and religious family that lived the Amish life. There were substantial restrictions concerning the use of telephones, clothes, cars, and electricity in my community. Every woman in my town would wear long dresses that reached down to our ankles. Each morning, I would wake up and feed the cattle before going to school. After school, there was no time for playing. I would be churning butter, pitching hay, cleaning, and cooking for my family.

I loved my community because of the various activities done to generate money. During holidays, I would spend most of the time doing farming and sewing. I would sew clothes for my siblings, for sale, and charity. Being a Christian, every Sunday I would join my parents and siblings to church. Since my community did not have a church building, we would hold church services in our homes. We had a list of church members where the services would be held each Sunday till the year ends. Various functions were held in different rooms because our houses, being constructed by hand, were large enough to contain several rooms.

Since electronics were not allowed in my community, I had a radio hidden in my bedroom, which I would listen to at night. My elder cousins, who once visited us, were the ones who gave me the radio. Since I did not know the variety of music, I listened to older music like Eminem each night.

When I reached eighteen years, traditionally, this is the age that the community allows one to go and experience the world of technology without any judgments, known as Rumspringa, which is like a rite of passage, lasting about a year or two, depending on the community one lives in, and after returning back to the community, a choice must be made to stay or leave. Those who choose to stay now know what the outside world is like and have the freedom of choice to know what they are doing and what they are giving up. Those who decide to leave and are gone only a short time usually do not have any issues returning, but those who are gone for long periods of time, and then want to return, are usually no longer ever allowed back into the community. Once one chooses to leave, all ties with the family are broken and communication with all family members ceases.

I went to New York City. In the city, I was surprised to see how people lived. The clothes they wore, the cars they drove, and their houses were different from those in my community. Each time I went shopping in the supermarket, I would see different people dressed differently and driving different kinds of cars. Since I was from a community bounded by cultures, I viewed those people as living a lifestyle that was not good. I never knew that there was nothing wrong with listening to the radio or driving a car.

As I interacted with people in the city, I was inspired to be a model. My idea of becoming a model was because of my passion for sewing clothes when I was ten years old. When one year ended, the one year authorized by the community, I decided not to go back to my community but stayed in the city to pursue my modeling career. Currently, I am a model and a fashion designer who graduated from the best school in the city.

My advice to Amish women is that our community and parents restrict us from participating in some activities because they may cause us troubles. They should remain obedient, and when their time to explore the world of technology reaches, they should be wise to accomplish their dreams.

My Life As A Woman: United States Rhode Island Edition #1

Rhode Island was a beautiful place to grow up. My childhood memories are full of days at the beach, swimming with horseshoe crabs and other captivating creatures. I was amazed by animals at a very young age and my parents happily fostered this fascination with books, summer camps, trips to zoos and days at aquariums. They are animal lovers too and as long as we were around no animal would go homeless or without help. The result of this was a house full of every animal you could imagine. Over the years I lived with adopted critters that ranged from scaly to furry and everything in between.

By the time I was 15 we had moved to Connecticut and I made the decision to attend a magnet school. Highschool is a time when you want to fit in, find yourself, and make friends. When I made the choice to attend a magnet school I gave that up for lab coats and science fairs. It was a daunting decision at first, but I could not pass up the opportunity to combine my love of science and animals in their aquaculture department. During my years there I helped raise baby lobster and jellyfish while expanding my understanding of ecosystems. In case you are wondering, jellyfish are extraordinarily difficult to raise, but they are a living example of the value and beauty in hard work.

I graduated with a sense of confidence and adventure which fueled my search around New England for the perfect university to study veterinary medicine. Since I was a child on the beaches of Rhode Island I had played with the idea of becoming a veterinarian and as I grew it became my life goal. This goal guided me far from Connecticut and my family. Over the course of those four years I worked hard so I could one day better the lives of animals and educate the public about their beauty, like my idols Jane Goodall and Steve Irwin had done.

As my experiences expanded my view of the world began to change. A summer working as a trainer at a zoo brought out my love of rehabilitation and responsible conservation. However, these feelings were muddied by my concern over the ethics of keeping wild animals. How happy could an animal be if it has never known more than the four walls that make up its enclosure? Can animals even feel "happy" the same way humans do? Suddenly the ethics of animals was a deep interest to me. An internship at an aquarium had me marveling at the ability of sharks to recognize certain people. A summer as a barn hand taught me great respect for the animals that live by our rules for our desires. I left all of these experiences having learned so much about the animals I loved and yet, I had more questions than answers.

By my college graduation date I had decided to put my dreams of attending a veterinary university to earn my Doctorate on hold. Of course I still want to learn how to heal the creatures I love but, medicine and the human animal relationships that exist on this earth are much too complex for any text book to explain. After making this decision, a job application at a veterinary clinic that I took on a whim, brought me back to Rhode Island, where I currently reside. I still work with animals every day, I still look at them with a sense of compassion and awe, and I still have more questions than answers. I work alongside a team of strong women who show compassion and strength to animals of all species and sizes. It is a blessing to work alongside people that share my values and childhood memories of beautiful Rhode Island beaches teaming with life. My desire to travel and continue learning will inevitably lead to another move far from my roots, but I'm sure something will always bring me back for a visit at the very least.

My advice is to lean into the discomfort of change as you pursue your passion. The place you call home may change and your views may change, but true passion will guide you to the answers you seek and the people who understand you. So pursue your passion, whatever it may be.

My Life As A Woman: United States Rhode Island Edition #2

If you asked me two years ago where I'd be living, I would have answered in New York City; probably going to school in NYU and studying literature. However, my life has indeed taken a different but sweet turn and I ended up finding solace in a smaller but creative and vibrant town in Providence, Rhode Island.

Let me tell you my story. I grew up in a big country in West Africa called Nigeria. My family was blessed enough to send me to high school in a prestigious academy and I did eventually move to New York City for college. I attended Pace University for one year and, I got to experience the little charms and electric vibes that New York City had to offer. I got to shop in Time's Square, see a play on Broadway and ride the subway throughout the boroughs. At first, I thought I was living the dream life.

Although I was in a fantastic city that never slept, I often found myself getting lost in between the hustle and bustle of the big apple. I hit rock bottom when I began to notice the environment that was living in. My room was a mess of clothes and papers all over. I was constantly tired and, overwhelmed because I was busy running around in circles all day in New York. The city swallowed the whole of my dream.

A year later after a couple of bad decisions, I decided to go and live with my sister in Providence, Rhode Island. I transferred to Johnson and Wales University and changed my major from Journalism to Entrepreneurship.

Ever since I moved to Providence, Rhode Island the essential thing on my mind is finding my purpose— and how to carry it out in everyday life. When I lived in New York it was easy for me to chase one hundred dreams at a time and not catch any of them but in Rhode Island, it was different because I could finally begin to make a name for myself in a city filled with so much creative energy.

I found my faith again and joined the Christian fellowship on campus where I met lifelong friends who inspire me to be my best self every day. I began to do extremely well in my classes and my life became more organized and satisfying. Providence became the perfect city for me to thrive because it is small enough for me to grow and vibrant enough for me to experience new things.

In one year, I managed to dive headfirst into entrepreneurship and I founded my own successful small jewellery business while working as a freelance writer and going to school. I am making progress as an entrepreneur and learning every day how to perfect my craft. However, I wouldn't have been able to achieve this if I didn't join the Small Business Association in Providence, Rhode Island. This phenomenal association that is filled with great minds has helped me develop my business idea, and they also gave me a loan to secure it.

During this entire process of growing my entrepreneurial spirit also while attending college, I met my soul mate who is now my fiancée. We met at a party that I was hosting on campus to promote my jewellery business and we clicked almost instantly. He is tall, handsome, and a fellow business owner. He is thoughtful and kind which in my opinion is rare. I opened up to him and showed him my culture by taking him on a visit to Nigeria earlier this year in February. He immediately fell in love with the food, music, and people in Nigeria and he was sad to go back to the US- shortly after we left Nigeria; he proposed.

My advice to women who are pursuing a dream as a woman from Africa who is an entrepreneur living in providence, Rhode Island is to remain focused and consistent. Please, do stay away from situations that can distract you from your goals even if that distraction is your current living situation. If your environment is toxic for you then for your sake you have to leave, to grow and thrive. An old African proverb says you cannot grow an apple tree on infertile soil; you must go to a fertile land to thrive.

Living in New York City was toxic to my growth and well – being. I have since discovered that my fertile land is in Providence, Rhode Island where my Jewellery business and husband- to- be is with me. Where ever your place may be, quit wondering and take that chance!

My Life As A Woman: United States South Carolina Edition

I grew up in Columbia, SC during the 1960s and 70s, a time of great turmoil in the US. This means that I grew-up seeing anti-war protesters on the evening news and hearing my adult relatives holding the same arguments. Mine was the first generation to attend integrated schools. We were taught that one of the best things about the US was our democratic system of government. If something is wrong, we citizens have the right to change it. Activist women like Shirley Chisholm, Jane Goodall, and Margaret Mead were my idols. Sadly, my mother and her husband bought into the "if it feels good, do it!" ideology of that era. They were much more interested in being party animals than in being responsible adults. As a result, my brother and I pretty much raised ourselves.

More than anything else, I wanted to be an astronaut when I was growing-up. This was as much due to the influence of Star Trek as NASA. In high school I was most interested in my science classes, especially Biology. However, after changing majors several times, I finally picked History and Anthropology. At my university I had outstanding professors such as Dr. Kathy Reichs as my teachers. Some people told me that I was silly for choosing these subjects. One friend even told me that I had a "useless major!" But I have never regretted my choice. It has given me a far greater appreciation for my own culture as well as helping me understand others as well. I love my Southern food culture where food from 3 continents has combined to make a new cuisine. And I love the stories behind the foods and how they have spread across the world. But most of all I love our history of resistance to injustice.

At this time I am a multimedia artist and a content creator. In addition I volunteer with youth and try to give them some of the support and inspiration I received when young. I have not only successfully integrated into a new society, I am thriving. My advice to women is "never give up." When someone puts you down, get up and keep going. When I was in high school a teacher told me that I wouldn't get accepted to college. I didn't listen and not only was accepted but also received a scholarship. Then my mother told me that I would probably just flunk-out. Instead I made the President's List whereupon my Granddaddy laughed that none of his children (including my mom) did that in their first year of college. Educate yourself! A good education trains the mind as well as providing job skills. But the most important role model in my life is someone I didn't meet until I was 19 years old.

Dr. Mollie Camp Davis was a professor in History and Women's Studies. She was in her mid-fifties at the time. Like so many of her generation she fought so that future generations of women would have better lives without getting to enjoy the benefits themselves. They demonstrated for daycare but by the time it arrived, their own children were too old to need it. They fought for women's right to choose even though they were too old to become pregnant by Roe v Wade. Her encouragement and emotional support have been crucial during the past 30 years.

My Life As A Woman: United States Texas Edition #1

I grew up in suburban Texas surrounded by strong ladies. My mother's mother was a math professor at a local college. Whip-smart and dry-humored, she bought me puzzles and science kits for Christmas. My father's mother was doting and kind, the sort of grandma that played dolls for hours and always stocked up on my favorite foods before I came (strawberries, eggs, cookie dough ice cream).

My own mother took me longer to appreciate. She didn't have the luxury of novelty and occasional visits, but instead trudged (usually) patiently through my (frequently) difficult teenager-hood. We butted heads near daily as high school drew itself out, and she was the recipient of many cutting words and not-so-nice surprises, like the night the police brought me home from a house party that got too rowdy. When it came time for me to leave the nest for university, I couldn't be so predictable as to attend a state school, and instead wanted to get far away, even if it meant leaving all those strong women behind. I ended up at New York University, but on their Shanghai campus.

China was the gateway to so many things--most importantly my ability to see the world and write about it--but came with, at the risk of understating it, some real adjustments. It was my mother who taught me the power of "Mind over matter," and that you are a product of your choices and attitude. Even though I didn't get it in my younger and more stubborn years, perhaps nothing else has had such a fundamental impact on my character. This idea is now one at the core of my beliefs and the way I approach the world.

It is what let me take all those leaps that led me to where I am now, finishing up an undergraduate degree in journalism and preparing to plunge into my next adventure. I always wanted to be a writer, from when I was toddling around at two or three, making up stories out loud to anyone that would listen, to nine or ten, when I would steal my dad's work notebooks and pen long, winding fairy tales in the margins.

My mother and I may split on our ideas about religion, politics, and traditional paths of career or family building. She pushed me to take a few dreaded courses in high school—honors physics, AP computer science—that still haunt me, because those are industries women make good money in, she said. But from China to the Czech Republic, Argentina to Indonesia, my mother supported every one of my crazy moves. She didn't flinch when I spent my summers globe-trotting financed by freelance writing instead of applying for serious internships. Now, whether I'm working on a political think piece or an entire novel, my mother will be my first reader and dutiful editor. Everywhere I travel, I make notes of the places I want to show her someday.

I've watched her suffer in workplaces where men occupied higher positions and received higher pay, while it was her ideas that drove the company forward. She told me to always fight for what I deserved, even if as a woman that will label you as aggressive or overbearing.

I love the United States for exactly this reason--that these are things we recognize women can and should be taught. I love it for the opportunities it offers to both genders, something I am reminded of again and again as I travel through countries where this is not the case. I love it for the strong women it gave me--family and teachers and mentors--without whom I would not be where I am. Sometimes it takes leaving a place or a person to really appreciate everything they gave to you, and that makes it all the more wonderful to return.

My Life As A Woman: United States Texas Edition #2

My name is Barituka Loomma and I am Nigerian. I was born in Lagos, Nigeria and in 1998 my family joined the refugee camps in Benin and received the opportunity to fly to America. In 1999, my family landed in Houston, Texas and began their establishment in America. We were foreigners growing accustomed to the American culture day by day. I grew up in an African culture household with the influences of the American culture on my shoulder.

Watching my parents break through the barriers of cultural differences taught me to never forget where I come from because that is the foundation of true success. What I love most about my Nigerian culture is the richness of our language and history, I was taught to never forget my history and I am proud of who I am. I am currently working as a behavioral therapist for children with autism. In fall 2018 I graduated from Lamar University with a bachelor's degree in psychology with a minor in chemistry.

I am currently working on my master's degree in clinical mental health counseling and plan to open my own practice and clinics in low income environments. I want to educate minorities in mental health in hopes to increase success in the minority communities. As an African American woman, I face the challenges against my self-identity every day. Am I good enough? Am I pretty enough? Are my standards too high? I realize that no matter what situation I am placed in, all eyes are on me because of my skin tone and my gender. People sexualize me, belittle me, and place my character in a box to be controlled but I do not let that intimidate me. Instead I use it as fuel and channel the questions and attention into the answers they seek.

My success as a woman living in America is due to my determination to keep my head high and to always seek knowledge. For all the young woman that face these challenges everyday know that you are perfect. Who you are is exactly what you should be confident in because it will never fail you?

Being a woman is a blessing, it is the construct of society that makes us feel like we're not. We are more than what society defines us, so do not expect less from other, keep your head up high and if the barriers in your life seem too high just remember that together, as women helping one another, we can go far.

My Life As A Woman: United States Virginia Edition

I grew up on the East Coast in a small town in Virginia. Being raised by a single mother and my father who was out of state due to their divorce was not the easiest. My culture stems from being Korean, African American, and English. My culture has strong roots with family being important and amazing tasting food. Developing a palate for spicy to tangy and just having a strong respect for people of other cultures as well is a big take away from being a Mixed American. My parents are people I look up to for their hard work. While, at the same time I was always alone because of their long work schedules and taking overtime if necessary. Their work ethic will always be something inspiring to me. They made sure I was cared for with food on the table, clothes, and a place to live no matter where I was.

Currently, I am a stay at home mother, home school teacher, freelance writer, and an avid lover of volunteer work with my church. I studied biology, business, and some other things while in school. My goal was to be a pediatrician and retire as a school teacher. I have a real love for wanting to help shape and spend time with children. They're cute little sponges who need nurturing and care to be our strong leaders into the future.

A struggle I have had as a woman would have to be with my appearance. It sounds silly but, I have never felt like I was that great looking regardless of what others may say. I have had a lack of self-confidence my entire life and never felt that my life was worth living. Only until now have there been so many movements to care about people's mental health or to give some type of awareness to it. It has taken time to heal and grow from the many different afflictions I have faced.

Finding God was the biggest and best thing I could have done. To break the cycle, I was living of wrong men and they were in a different "looking" package. My greatest success would have to be my children. They came from many different means and have suffered their own growth pains and learning curves already at their young ages. Being able to be with them and help them grow is the biggest blessing and privilege I have ever been given.

My advice to another woman would always be to remember, "We are not to compare one another. You are doing a great job and you can do it even when it feels hard." There is going to be lots of times in our lives that we will have to struggle and get through things whether it feels like we are alone or in a sea of people and still are alone. Also, your five closest associations reflect you. If you are holding tightly to people who are negative and don't have your best interest at heart you won't have any way to grow. Learning to let people go who are toxic is not an easy feat for anyone. That is the human condition where we are becoming more complacent with what is easy and comfortable. Most people have judgments and can say, "Why didn't you leave? Why are you still in this _____?" It is easier for people to go back to what they know than making a change. So, again remember you are doing your best and every inch towards the right direction is better than nothing. Never let anyone tell you, you're not doing enough because your milestones will be different than someone else's milestones and same with your struggles.

--- Mixed American Woman

694

My Life As A Woman: United States Utah Edition

I spent my childhood years in rural Mississippi but moved to Utah when I was a teenager. My family was extremely conservative, but I knew their precautions were only because they wanted to keep me out of trouble. Now as an adult, I'm grateful for their strict attitude—but I can't say the same for when I was 15! My mom was my hero growing up, as she was the most attentive mother on the planet. I always knew my wellbeing was her first priority, and not one day went by that I didn't feel her massive love for me and my siblings. However, my mother wasn't the biggest proponent of my choice of career.

I aspired to be a lawyer, but the culture in Mississippi and Utah is that homemaking should be a woman's main focus in life. This is an aspect of my culture I'm torn about, because I do believe that family comes first, no matter the career! However, I also think it's important for women to chase after their own dreams, or they'll spend their life with regret and resentment. This is why, despite some slight pushback from my family and culture, I'm proud to say I'm graduating college this year and will go on to pursue the career of my dreams. I'm currently a full-time student while working in a law office as a paralegal to gain experience in my field.

I struggle often with feeling judgement from my friends who already have children and expect me to jump on the bandwagon. Many conversations turn from lighthearted to "when-are-you-getting-pregnant?" in a matter of minutes. I know they have my best interest at heart, and they truly believe that I won't reach my full potential of happiness if I only focus on my career. Honestly, I believe that too! But I have my whole life to make my own family, and this is the only point in my life where the only person I have to worry about is myself! I know it might sound selfish, but in order to be the best wife and mother I can be, I first have to be the best individual I can be, which includes pursuing my dream career. For any woman in Utah struggling with the same dilemma, I want you to know you're not alone!

Your friends and family might have opinions on what you do with your life, but you're the one who actually has to live with those choices! I have too many friends who have pushed their dreams aside to comply with the desires of others. Don't be one of those women! Even if there's a taboo behind you wanting to pursue a career, don't be afraid to step out on faith and go for it. I want my children to see that their mother had the determination and willpower to reach her goals. How can I inspire my children to run after theirs if I never did? Everything we do to better ourselves will work out in the long run, especially for generations to come.

My Life As A Woman: United States Wisconsin Edition

I grew up in a family of three children in Wisconsin. I could remember that at age eight, I woke up every day to discover my father was not home. I only learned that he had checked into a Tuberculosis sanatorium. I can recall any reaction than confusion. That would change to something darker.

I was born as early as 1990, at a depth of the depression. I was unaware of the world around me because my father was suffering from tuberculosis and knowing that he is a handsome, athletic, talented, and smart, self-educated engineer. We had an apartment on the edge of the best neighborhood in the city, Green Bay, and even a piano.

My mother was a beautiful woman, clever and smart, in her late 30s. She had come from a family of seven children. I only realized that those families each had been - and produced - smart, handsome, successful, and emotional people who never in all my memories, once said aloud to each other, "I love you." Knowing all this, I wondered what type of family I was born into where everyone had to do things on their own. Growing up, I missed the father aspect. You know your dad lives with you and seeing him everyday kind of makes you happy as a kid. But for me, my mother has been the one representing the Father and Mother aspect of my life; I get to see my dad once in a while.

Academically, my mother had been the only person I could rely on when it comes to choosing a career and a part that fits every aspect of my life. I have always wanted to work in the medical line due to my father's health status; I feel like knowing more. After in-depth research on my strength and weakness, I decided that to Study Medicine at the University of Wisconsin. However, I had to obtain a degree in a medical course before I can further for Medicine, and after doing that, I applied for Medicine. Luckily, I gained admission to study Medicine. I can now say that I am a medical doctor that specializes in infectious diseases or lung diseases, also known as a Pulmonologist, and I work at the University of Wisconsin Hospitals.

The thing I love about Wisconsin and its culture are listed below:

Spending summer at Festivals

During the summer, I could remember that we used to spend every summer weekend at a different festival in Wisconsin.

Develop a cheese addiction

Living in a dairy state, we have access to fresh cheese, and I can proudly say that there is no place in the United States that you can get a much fresher cheese than in Wisconsin. If you live here, you will easily have access to fresh cheese.

Reserve Fridays for fish fries

This abundance of fresh fish helped create the Friday night fish fry tradition. In Wisconsin, fish fries aren't reserved exclusively for the Lenten season but enjoyed every Friday of the year. Despite many places serving them as all you can eat, Wisconsinites can't seem to get enough.

Struggles as a woman

The only thing that has been a struggle is balancing my marriage with my family.

Advice to women from a woman living in Wisconsin

Learn things without stopping because it leads to continuous improvement. Commit yourself to advance your skills, knowledge, and expertise. The business environment is changing, and your understanding of the leading practices, thinking, and emerging tools will help you manage for better results. Be a lifelong student.

Use your stumbling block as your stepping stone. Take your most challenging task by the balls and control it.

Find your passion and believe in it. When you feel you are making a difference in people's lives, it becomes so much more than a job.

Use every opportunity around you to get out of your comfort zone.

Balance your work and family and focus on what is in front of you-be it a conversation with your husband or kids or working on a business case. Please don't feel guilty about enjoying your work-your kids are getting a great role model in shaping their future happiness.

Success in business is passion combined with fearless execution. The most successful people I know focus on the things they can control and perfect the details.

My Life As A Woman: American Samoa Edition

I am Talia, from the sunshine island of Tutuila. Tutuila is a part of American Samoa. I grew up with both my parents playing an active role in my life. My father was a retired businessman from America, and my mother was the typical housewife. My parents and I had a very close relationship, especially with being an only child. We would do everything together and I could tell them anything. Even with the closeness to both, my dad inspired me the most, we had a special connection. He was my hero and I was his princess. There would be days that he just sits and talks with me about the most random things. He taught me how to be independent, how to fish, and business knowledge.

I attended the Manulele Tausala Elementary School, where I did exceptionally well. I then attended the Tafuna High School; my time there was a little difficult. I wasn't understanding the teachers and students were constantly bullying me. My parents decided it was best to homeschool me after my first year. I had difficulty grasping the lessons my mother was trying to teach. After a while the lessons became easier to understand. I did my GED at seventeen years old, and I got a successful grade. I then attended the Samoa Community College, intending to study liberal arts. While growing I always wanted to become an actress. I always loved Angelina Jolie; she was just so confident and strong. I had withdrawn from the university and went to try acting, but it didn't work out. So I tried modeling, which was very successful.

My American Samoan culture is known for our strong family relationship. I wasn't fully accepted by my people, they would still try to involve my family in some of the events. I always loved going to the early Sunday service and later going to watch the preparation of the food. After all the cooking was done, they would all sit and enjoy each other's company. the place would be filled with laughter and joy.

Growing up, I was judged for my mother's action because she married a very older ex-pat man. It wasn't normal to have such an age gap between a couple, especially with an international man, but they still went ahead and got married. Due to that, I wasn't fully accepted by my people, and I didn't have many friends. My only true friends were my parents. At school, I was forced to go through the constant taunting, and it started to affect my learning. My parents decided to home school me. I was grateful for the change, but I started to feel closed off from the world in a sense.

Going through all of this, especially at a young age, taught me a lot of things. The first thing learned was not to care about how others viewed me. They will always have something to say. I just need to do what makes me happy. Just like my parents did. It made me stronger and more confident. I only have one advice to females of American Samoa is to 'be you'. This means even if it doesn't make the world happy and it makes you happy, do it. If you want to be single and enjoy your youth, do it, don't feel pressured by society.

I grew up in a military family.

Didn't have anyone that inspired me.

I went to school for psychology and going back to be a nurse.

I love him respectful and kind everyone else to each other.

I am a daycare provider.

Men look down on us and assume we are weak.

I got my own car and I am supporting myself.

Keep working hard and show kindness to everyone.

My Life As A Woman: Guam Edition #2

I was born on Guam but I spent most of my childhood in the Philippines. I didn't come from a very fortunate family, but I enjoyed the simple life I was given. Since both of my parents were busy, I grew up admiring my hardworking grandmother. I'll be attending college soon now, and I am interested in becoming a Registered Nurse due to the influence of my mother and my older sister who are both nurses.

My Life As A Woman: Guam Edition #3

I grew up on Guam. I was always around family. My parents got divorced when I was ten so I grew up with a mom that played both roles. Both my grandma and my mom inspire me. They both sacrifice so much to provide for our family. My mom has taught me love through sacrifice and support. I aspire to give that same love to everyone around me.

Growing up, I knew that the one thing I wanted to do was change the world, to help the people around me. At first I wanted to be a nurse because of my mom but as I'm about to transition into college, I am going into pre-law. Difficult experiences in my life have sparked my interest in the legal field, allowing me to personally help individuals.

One thing I love about my culture (PH) is how much I was taught the value of hard work. A good future does not come easy and we must work for the best things in life. From living on Guam all my life, my favorite thing about the culture is the importance of respect. Being taught respect when I was younger has brought me to be an understanding and accepting individual. It has allowed me to treat everyone around me with kindness.

I don't work. I did not grow up with the easiest experiences. I've been sexually assaulted by multiple men in my life, when I was 6, and again from 8 to 16 years old. I experienced victim blaming and my vulnerability was taken advantage of.

One of my biggest successes definitely has to be breaking my silence and sharing the story of my abuse. Other than that, I do really well in school despite my experiences. I've stood as a leader in my school (SGA president for 2 years). I'm in honor societies and various organizations. I volunteer in my community. I received a student excellence award my junior year from the rear admiral of the join region Marianas. I am graduating in the top ten of my class.

Some advice I could give to women as a woman from Guam is to stand tall. Stand your ground. Advocate for what you believe in and chase your dreams. Do what's best for you despite what anyone may think. Do not allow anyone to hold you back from your success. Love yourself as you love everyone around you. Do not allow your gender to define what you are capable of achieving.

My Life As A Woman: Guam Edition #4

I grew up basically everywhere, but what I consider growing up is at Guam.

Growing up was difficult due to me being a military-brat. It was always different homes for six months then move to another home within the month. I was exposed to many cultures and beliefs growing up from different states to countries. It was always difficult because I couldn't be too attached. Due to this, I became distant from my family, making, me detached from my own emotions.

It all change when writing became my safe place, it inspired me to have comfort in the life that I grew to hate. The person who inspired me was my father and grandmother—they were always the one who made me feel as if I belonged somewhere even though I didn't have a physical place to call home. They were my home in the comfort of a physical being.

With that being a reason, I wanted to become a writer. Someone who can touch heart and relate to people who can't express their emotions and feelings into words. It always inspired me because I had no voice growing up. I was always frowned upon by my mother who did not support the dreams and ambitions I've had.

What I love about my culture is the diversity of what it's made of. I'm mixed: American, Chinese, Hispanic, and Filipino. A blend of infusion from different parts of the world. It makes me truly appreciate how in touch I am with my culture, able to communicate with my elders and understand the struggle of what being free from the oppression of what they went through.

I'm currently self-employed, I run a business that recycles old clothing. Basically, a thrift shop to reduce fast fashion since it harms the environment in so many ways. I do sustainable clothing ranging from vintage to in-trend styles.

My struggles being a woman are the expectations from society. The fact that we are looked down upon because we're incapable of doing what men are supposed to do. Because to their eyes, we're just weak and fragile—if we surpass a man's expectation we're always considered a bitch or stuck up. When it took the same hardship as a man, getting, to the goal. Growing up as a child, I was always taught that I should be the one staying home and taking care of the children because I'm a woman. It's the sexiest comments coming from my family damaged me. Especially, when I saw my mother and father being unhappy in their relationship—to the point my mother changed her whole physical appearance to satisfy my father's needs. It hurt me because it brought me to the mindset that a man will never love me for me, but for the body that I carry.

For me, I'm still finding my success. I still haven't achieved what I wanted for myself and not for other people. I'm still in the process of building my own empire and understanding the hardships I will go through without anyone, tearing, me down.

Growing up in an island with limited resources in living the life you want compared to Guam. I would like to say, never give up. Cliché, how it sounds to give that advice; but it's something that's true. Always work hard for the things you want in life despite people trying to break you down in the process of it. Despite the limited resources that we have here on the island, it shouldn't stop you from achieving your dreams no matter how hard it is. Just because we have less does not make us unfortunate.

My Life As A Woman: Puerto Rico Edition

I am from the northeast coastal regions of Puerto Rico. Growing in separate parents' homes, I grew amidst different environments throughout this metropolitan area. My mother tended to live in the suburbs "so to speak" of Bayamón-Guaynabo municipalities and my father tended to live in more urbanite regions of the capital city, San Juan. I oscillated between a quiet, reserved residential area and a neighborhood full of expressive public life in Viejo San Juan (Old San Juan), the historical, district of the capital.

A Saturday in Guaynabo consisted of driving through errands nearby while in Old San Juan plans unfolded organically through encounters and gatherings in the street. A common element found in both of these environments was the connection to the humid air, a binding substance between one's body and the environment, and to a sense that wild natural forces live just at one's reach.

San Juan is embraced by the Atlantic Ocean, and Old San Juan is specifically surrounded by the military fortress of El Morro. I tend to orient myself in relationship to the ocean, a habit that follows me when having lived in other places. Similarly even in the closed residential neighborhood my mother lived, one could imagine how the streets could easily become incorporated into the rainforest habitat that makes up the north of island, known as the Carso Tropical. With friends growing up I enjoyed seeking spots where the neighborhood fence was damaged in one way or another, allowing one traverse into the forest to find little creeks and streams of water.

I feel to follow ways from my family like for example my father's humble and generous, benevolence to others and my maternal grandmother's desire to eat the world whole. I studied at a Liberal Arts College in New York that encouraged curricular freedom. This led me to compose my studies around dance, literature, painting and drawing, psychology and sociology.

At the end of all of these seemingly scattered studies, I was left in some sort of open space where I did not feel like assimilating or inventing quite yet a professional identity. I managed to find light teaching jobs in the education department of a children's museum in New York City, while the rest of the time, I made mixed media paintings in my shared apartment. These paintings developed around my family history and identity and were sourced from collages I made combining family albums and more current photos taken on trips to the island.

While making these works, I grew to realize that I wanted, or almost needed to return to Puerto Rico at some point. Living in New York felt like racing blindly. I felt constrained and isolated making paintings in a room. The city felt way too huge to connect with, thus I ended up applying for the city college's graduate art program. While being there the past year and a half, I have meet amazing creators from different backgrounds and have felt the powerful capacities of allowing artistic practice to take different forms, in and out of making objects that are "art."

Before the pandemic situation and in the middle of this program, I moved back to Puerto Rico. At first I thought it was going to be for a few months, but then the situation deepened and as we know everything has seemingly frozen while our heads continue ideating and projecting towards a future whose nature unfolds day by day. I am currently as open as ever for different creating new lines of work as I know that me and the world will both be changed after this period dissolves. I am currently working on online art teaching jobs, learning digital programs, still taking graduate classes, while maintaining a painting and dance practice.

I now find myself in another open, uncertain space that inevitably mirrors the global state, yet I am grateful I am in Puerto Rico. Grateful for the persistent blue skies, blazing sun, and oceanic air. I love waking up here and knowing that when I leave the house, even if wearing a mask due to the COVID-19 pandemic, strangers and acquaintances will greet me by smiling with their eyes. I love the community oriented, effervescently buoyant nature amidst people found even in difficult times such as these. My advice is not really specifically for women, but for all, and it is to follow the pursuits that make sense to you from the skin to the bone. It is after all, only your journey.

My Life As A Woman: Federated States of Micronesia Edition

Hey everyone, I am Athena from The Federation of Micronesia. I live with my extended family and my father. My mother died of sickness. My family had a love for plants, and everyone works in the plants' field, my father was a herbalist, my uncles are farmers, and my aunts worked as cooks. Growing up, even though we had very little material things, we had a strong bond and love. I remember spending a lot of my time just walking around looking for new things and running odd to various rivers nearby. I had a fun childhood. I grew up with all my cousins and siblings around me. I don't remember having any role model or inspiration, I just wanted to be me and create my path. There were a few individuals that I liked and respected, but I didn't want to be like them.

My school journey started at the Nett Elementary School, I graduated then moved to the Bailey Olter High School, where I obtained my secondary education. I was one of the mischievous children in school, if something went wrong in class it was mostly because of me. I gave most of my teachers a hard time, I only liked my science teacher. After graduating from high school I left for America, to find a better life. I have been working as a housekeeper for the last 4 years. While attending school part-time so I can get a better job, I am now studying to become a registered nurse.

I love that our culture is so rich. During my year parading through the island, I realized how beautiful the island was. Even to this day, you can still find the federation of Micronesia people wearing a grass skirt and having a village feast. Although I no longer reside in The Federation of Micronesia, it will always have a special place in my heart.

Leaving my island was the biggest test of my strength. I had a major culture shock, everything was different, especially my status. I didn't know what to eat or how to approach the people. I didn't feel safe being a woman on a strange land, especially with the constant stares. I had to be extra aware of my surroundings. Finding a job wasn't as easy as I thought it would be.

After being there a while I got accustomed to the stares and learned how to defend myself. My biggest success to date is studying nursing, even though I just started I am motivated to finish and be something I can be proud of and help people at the same time. For all the women of the Federation of Micronesia, everyone's journey to success if different. You can't judge your level of success to someone else, you both took two different paths. Measure your success based on where you're coming from. As Micronesians, you are strong, smart, and wise, so I believe in you and know you can do this. Just keep your eyes on the prize.

My Life As A Woman: Northern Mariana Islands Edition

Hey everyone, My name is Tania Tan. I was born and raised on Saipan Island. Saipan Island is the second-largest island in the Mariana Islands archipelago, after Guam. the Northern Mariana Islands is a commonwealth of the United States of America. I was pretty active growing up and spent a lot of my time outdoors exploring. I played soccer for a while even though I wasn't the best at it. Also, I played tennis and went to the beach a lot. My dad inspires me the most, he has a love for service and helping others. He is always trying to find a way to help people in need, and he also does a lot of volunteer work for the community.

I attended the Saipan International School., from pre-K to high school, I later graduated high school. I did well throughout my years in school, I was active. I played sports, I was a part of clubs/societies and I got really good grades. Growing up I always wanted to study the ocean and be able to travel around the world. Living in Saipan only increased my love for the ocean. I am still on route to achieve my goals, I am now a sophomore at Fordham University in New York City.

Living in Saipan is so different from living in other places. I love how connected we are and how tight-knit everyone is. There was always a warm and welcoming greeting awaiting you. We were very united, whether it was chilling on the beach or hiking a trail. the weather in Saipan is great, I love soaking up the sun on the beach and having wind caress my skin. Visiting the beaches on those days is very relaxing.

As a woman in today's society, I tend to fear going out at night alone in dark places. I have to be very conscious of what to wear. I have to ensure my clothes are not too showy or short. It's unfair that we as women have to think like this because you would never hear of a man worry about if his clothes are showy, or fear going out at a certain hour. If something happens, we are the ones that are blamed, we are told our clothes were too revealing or we should have protected yourself. Why not teach men to better control themselves.

My journey has just started, but I have already started to see my success. It first starts with me being the valedictorian for my high school graduating class. That was a major accomplishment because the majority of my class were males. Next, I was accepted to university, it may not seem like much but this is just the start. I am on a path to be a change factor in society. To all the women of the Northern Mariana Islands, especially Saipan, be yourself, have confidence, speak from your heart, and don't let others pull you down. With that, you'll be a powerful woman, on your way to make changes.

My Life As A Woman: United States Virgin Islands Edition

I'm Kiki. Growing up on the Island of St. Croix, in the Virgin Islands of the United States, I was raised primarily by my mother. She worked very hard to take care of me and our household. My parents had a verbal shared custody agreement, which meant I would spend weekdays with my mother and weekends with my father.

My mother will always be my greatest inspiration. With a very ill mother, she made many sacrifices including not finishing school to take care me and my nine younger siblings. Deriving from an underprivileged upbringing, she taught my nine siblings and I to take our education and success seriously. She strongly believes education opens up limitless opportunities to create a better life. Through her, I knew from a very young age that I wanted to become an educator. I am currently in my final year of studies at my local college, the only HBCU in the Caribbean, studying Elementary Education.

My culture is something that's near and dear to my heart. Reason being, it has an unbelievable level of vibrancy and expressiveness to it. I would describe our culture as a "madras tapestry" ; where each color strand represents the tastefulness of our cuisine, the natural sunshine in our smiles, our community's connectivity, our innate resiliency, zeal for life, the freedom and liberation of "playing mas", the hypnotism of our music, and a way of life that has found a way to manifest despite an oppressive past.

We are a people, proud of every aspect of who we are. So much, that anytime you see someone from the USVI, our natural charm and charisma means to announce, with co-existing humility and boldness, precisely where we are from.

Currently, I work for the 33rd Legislature of the Virgin Islands, within the office of one of our island's Senators. I also double as an on-air personality for one of the territory's most notable radio stations.

As a woman, some of my greatest struggles have been managing both the support and backlash stemming from me exerting my own independence and establishing a name for myself professionally, at a very young age. I have been blessed to have successfully achieved and accomplished many things in my short time here on Earth, and it's baffling to many, with how I managed to do so, only recently turning twenty-three.

With regards to success, I have been able to brand myself as local household name, promote change though student leadership, positively impact our local youth and enjoy the fruit of my various God-given talents, all while maintaining my humility and the desire to become my best self.

I would encourage women from the USVI to walk in the likeness of our local heroines and "Fiyah Bun Queens". We came from a long line of female freedom fighters. The ability to withstand and survive through adversity courses through our veins, and as women, we must all live our lives as such.

My Life As A Woman: Uruguay Edition #1

Women have been struggling with society's stereotypes since a very long time now. From the beginning there was this rule where you couldn't do anything else than staying at home and look after the kids if you were a woman. And we are all aware that this situation is worse in some countries. But now, people's mind is changing for good in some places, and I am glad to recognize Uruguay is at least trying.

I have lived all my life in the city of Uruguay: the big old Montevideo, where people are supposed to be more open-minded than in the rest of the country. However, during my childhood the concept of the father as the head of the family was still there. And I must admit my grandfather still manages it. This didn't mean my mother or anybody at my house forced me to stay at home and learn how to cook like they used to do, but the exact opposite of that. I remember that as a child I wanted to be a writer and even though in my country it is very difficult to be recognized, my mother always encouraged me to write by contacting radios to read my stories on-air and gifting me an old typing machine. She was there even when I was a 7 year-old writing about a mouse named Roberto traveling around a world I clearly didn't even know. But I loved it and my mom knew it so she supported me.

Of course Roberto didn't work out in time and I discovered my interest in sciences as I was growing up so I applied to medical school (I have to mention that I was 18 years-old and didn't know what I wanted to do with my life at the time). This cost me four years that were, not to say the least, painful. None of the members of my family had a degree and my mother motivated me to get one or to do something else than what was normal in my family.

So to say, part of me getting into medical school was to fulfill my mother's dream. After all that time I became a very frustrated woman in her twenties until I found the job that led me to know what I really wanted to study. This place was an Intellectual Property Law firm where I work as a Patent administrator and, off the record, as a technical adviser (which I'm not being paid for). I had my first encounter with biotechnology in this job and the next second I was applying to the career. My parents weren't happy and didn't help me this time, but it didn't stop me.

At my job, I have to recognize the amount of work is massive and I enjoy it because I like to stay close to what I study, but at the same time I just want to quit like the rest of the other women working there. I bet you can imagine why: they pay us cents compared to the stress we have to manage sometimes. However, it isn't a place where women get paid less to do the same as a man, like others are. But being paid less is the least of your problems as a woman in a society corrupted by sexism.

I must admit that I struggle with walking the streets at night because I'm afraid of being assaulted. I'm terrified to fall in a toxic relationship that gets me killed before I can get out of it or if I can even get out (and this happens a lot). Not less stressful, I'm also afraid of "compliments" men yell at you just for walking down the street doesn't matter the hour. Nowadays things are getting more awful because the amount of femicides is increasing and the media is trying to make it a common thing through the news. However, and this is something I like about our society or at least here around people in Montevideo, is that women are standing up doing mass people manifestations and remembering those who we lost due to sexism. We are starting to help each other breaking up the silence and even the government is helping with a lot of campaigns.

As women we are starting to succeed at being heard, people is starting to notice what we have to live day by day. And this is just the beginning of something bigger.

My advice to all women out there is to never live hiding behind the shadow of a man because you can shine bright enough to create your own. Stand up and be that change you want to see in the world doing what you love the most. The majority of us have to start with tiny baby steps and probably have no idea where to go first, but don't give up. It will sound like a cliche, but you only live once and you only have one opportunity to lead us out of the darkness this society is trying to pull us into. Be brave and don't stop doing things you love because you are afraid.

My Life As A Woman: Uruguay Edition #2

Montevideo, 23 de mayo de 2020

I start with my blank sheet.

PART 1

I will start at the end my struggle as a woman and my success as a woman and I will provide advice from woman to woman in Uruguay. I consider that the emotional and the spiritual wealth is of greater value, something that we form in the family nucleus. I start like this… because it is the most interesting part at 53 years old. I can make a balance of my current life, something that the woman or man usually does every ten years of life completed.

STAGES OF MY LIFE BY WAY OF SUMMARY

Stage 1.

DECADE OF THE 20 years. I can say that until the 32 years I studied basically. Between languages of institutes, the UDELAR public university, Faculty of Architecture, international conferences, I have also worked 1 year all by competition, a 9-month student trip around the world from the East, North America, Europe and the Nordics. My advice is that they study more and more and prepare for small Uruguay and for the whole world, since our education is free and secular and there they have the tools of freedom and independent and innovative thought. We are in a world that every time women fulfill a fundamental role in peace and taking care of our rights, our children, our land. At this stage it is not ideal to have children, we live life and nature with friends, the beaches Uruguayans, barbecue, travel. Let's be nature consumerists, in my time there were no shopping malls until I was 24 years old, we were not consumerists and I always did outdoor sports such as tennis, hiking or running because I valued food and healthy living.

WE ARE MIND; BODY AND SOUL; REMEMBER THIS

Stage 2

DECADE OF THE 30 YEARS I got already received from Architect at 32, I had my home 6 years and I had two children one year apart, the only husband I support and forget to think about myself. My advice is to have a home or family, it is the natural law of love, living together and knowing it but that of a good man, having family nights and peace in front of the fire and having the courage to know that the role of families is shared today between men and women, that is, between both genders within the respect, today and always for the WOMAN, THE LOVE OF A COUPLE is a great support whenever it adds up. The WOMAN is the nucleus of the FAMILY AND OF THE SOCIETY, this still remains in Uruguay with some problems, it continues to be our VALUED VALUE center both in the country and in the city. OUR CHILDREN, my children were born in my womb and in an extended family, surrounded by cousins, uncles,   grandparents,   there   are   born   human   and   social   values.

Stage 3

DECADE OF 40 YEARS. I divorced and raised my children alone dedicating myself to them. I worked as an independent architect always liberal, I was growing exponentially every year, having the fortune of a country that was in positive economic escalation. Here in 2004, with my first cell phone, I was unaware of social networks and had my first computer at home with little Wi-Fi connectivity and very little   global   connection   to   the   world.
Year 2013 although I am hired by competition in investment projects, not in accordance with the state I go to a contest for female entrepreneurs in 2013 called 8 M Women of MIEM, I do entrepreneurship

courses, I go to an Endevor seminar, then we win together with an Engineer in systems and other women in Ingenio Latu, the 2nd prize in technology. From here I begin to value in Udelar my own entrepreneurship before Emprenur Udelar School of Economics, even today without concluding due to lack of money and investment, as there has been a change of government this year 2020 the ANNI has been complicated, not ruling out anything and still thinking.

Stage 4.

DECADE OF THE 50 YEARS TODAY, having had a stable partner for 4 years and formed a real estate business which I closed at the end of 2019, I am still an enterprising and liberal woman and I love what I do, Architecture and everything related to Art, with creativity and honesty. I work and keep my original clients who see my value. I have planned since I am a professional what I will do later in my retirement, I will even dedicate myself to pictorial art and travel more. I continue with my independent liberal work and every increasingly connected in networks to the world. My advice as a professional is the exchange in local incubators of ideas, to follow with tenacity the passions that are born from the soul, to use technology as a means of work and thus capital will come, it comes through our CAPACITY AND VALUE of person. Man needs women, to support each other and I see that for 21 centuries they only had the means of work, we have a great fight for women today, they are great conquests and it is for each woman.

My struggle today is to remain honest, it is to remain in a less and less macho society, it is to be a delicate woman among so many men, it is to go to my architectural works and value the WORK that my grandparents and parents taught me as the only way to live alongside the challenge of INNOVATION AND TECHNOLOGY today. Prepare in technology and apps, applicable to everything, is the future in Uruguay since today we export to the world, and to compete EXCELLENCE from the value of being human, it is the way that the world opens up to us and thus accepts our KNOWLEDGE. PERSIST on what we love, tenacity, innovation for later if that good job or big capital arrives. Show yourself in the networks, globalize since this communication did not exist before.

Let us remember that we are MIND, BODY AND SOUL and at the same time a woman guides of our children and MODEL for them of struggle and here I could extend myself and say that I see today that my children have learned from my STRUGGLE. Think about our retirement and more at this age think that we will do for our autonomy in old age and to leave our children. Our well-being is not being in health homes, my grandparents died at home even with very serious illnesses. LET'S NOT let a nursing home take us. Let us take care of the elderly since Uruguay has an aging population, but it was born from the love of family and children, disengaging from the material and trying to lead an autonomous old age. My parents are still 89 years old and both have lived with their love since they were 16 years old. The one who succeeds is the one who has a clear conscience because he has lived in love and his passions and has his home or nest to be in until he dies.

PART 2

I will now write what was requested at the beginning.

Summary

WHERE I GREW UP AND HOW, INSPIRATIONAL PARENTS AND GRANDPARENTS, WHAT I STUDYED AND WHY AND WHAT I DO FOR WORK TODAY

I was born and raised in a working middle-class family, an Italian tradition of great-great-grandparents, an engineer father and a music teacher mother, grandparents one a Bayer salesman and another an entrepreneurial builder, bank aunts. The women in my family as aunts worked for a time before getting married and a divorce in between. I already talk about the year 1965, but then my mother did not work.

I had a father model that supported women to be independent because sister is a doctor and brother engineer, I am an architect. Small families but my family nucleus of love. Grandparents with great talks from man to teenage woman, my father works even on Sundays, matriarchal and patriarchal family model. I live in a coastal area facing the middle class and I attend public education always, except in private English studies in England. I study architecture because I draw very well and I love pictorial art and the reason is to be self-sufficient in the future and to work in a world profession that I love. Currently I keep my clients and work for Uruguay and abroad, this has been a path of my own struggle, even today, since I work from Monday to Sunday without time restrictions, this is being an entrepreneur. My debt is my own house and the couple, that home of two in which I was born.

YOU LOVE YOUR URUGUAYAN CULTURE

I love this village with red roofs, which I see when I get off the plane, surrounded by that line of white beaches, where I can be free and run on this boulevard and my friends that I see and don't see. Time does not pass here.
I love this Uruguayan social culture of the entire FAMILY gathered together, of the value and basic values of a society, which where that value has been lacking leaves room for the violence seen in the streets. We have little work here and that increases the violence, the not having the basic solved. I love that Uruguayan music by Zitarrosa, Rada, the public Symphony, You are not going to like it, Museums, neighborhoods, pictorial, Uruguayan architects like Ott, Vignoli I love varied beaches, soccer, Benedetti, Onetti, Galeano, Majfud writers, equality with values in all, public education that teaches us to think and to be equal and to be useful human beings and not to compete, respect.

Thank you for being able to count and I hope this talk will be of wealth and love… well, I consider it a talk.

Sandra

710

My Life As A Woman: Uzbekistan Edition

Where did you grow up?

From hindsight my ancestors were born in Djizak, this is the region between two capitals Tashkent (modern city) and Samarkand (cultural ex-capital). But after my first year my father got a job proposal in Tashkent, therefore we moved.

How did you grow up?

My life wasn't as similar as other normal teenagers, my family coming from the verge of financial bankruptcy, not being able to purchase necessities for normal daily life was depressed and dismal. I was an only child in my family, thereby bullying at school worsened my life even deeper. However, at that time we were not in a good social position I always had been working and studying hard to help my family to meet the ends. Perseverance and determination in being first at school and in languages helped me a lot to achieve my goals and beloved once.

Did you have parents or maybe a grandmother who inspired you?

Grandmother was my role model her skills up to 4 language by self-studying and more than seven unwritten novels that created without writing them on the paper, just editing and remembering by her brain was really astonishing. By far, she didn't even graduated from school and didn't have a job to grow such skills. Nowadays, we have all of the materials and guides at a push of button by googling, but most of us cannot even master one foreign language. This made me ponder over and was an internal turbine to understand how people without any technologies and guides could make a breakthrough.

What did you study? / What did you want to be growing up / Why?

THE challenges endured in prime of my life – poverty, discrimination of thoughts and ideas restrained from official statements, bribery – all of these malfunctions arose retaliation in myself towards illegal system thriving amidst government elite. Therefore, I decided that I wanted to be an actor of this complex environment of social change that we live in and help to implement the process of social stabilization by proceeding justice happen again. Picking up all basements from Romanian law in order to be a judge in UN as a prime goal, would be a great opportunity to realize my potential and gain a greater understanding between law systems in CIS and EU as to be citizens of the world, consolidate relationships and build strong citizenship on international level.

What do you love about your culture?

There are a lot of outstanding acts of humanity that are traditional in my culture, hence giving priority to them is really hard and incorrect, however aspects such as helping in trouble is the most appreciated one. Uzbeks from their childhood fostered to help to relatives, friends, guests and to everyone in difficulty of unpredictable life challenges.

I presume a nation does not live longer without their local cousin, because it gives flavour to understand the culture. Uzbekistan is not an exception. World renowned pilav or pilaf it has a lot of pseudonyms in today's world but all of them originated from Palov. It is Uzbek traditional meal came from historical ancestors Ibn Sina and Amir Temur. Rice, carrots and meat are amazing consistency in this meal, that everyone tries to sink their tooth into by first possible opportunity.

What are you currently doing for work?

Nowadays, I am a head teacher in English language centre helping others to learn English and to implement it on their daily life. Moreover, I am learning society as a whole democratic institute with decisive power to rule the country.

Tell me about your struggles as a woman.

To say the truth women in Uzbekistan encounter the biggest issue in their way to success as an individual. Witnessing gender inequality in all steps of life is disgusting and devastating. I have send my CV to apply for work, especially in government positions. I have got more than hundred rejection letters even from starting positions in executive authority. This is unwritten rule to hire mostly men to work, they imply it by showing higher results achieved by male rather than female group. Even though, new government tries to supply big gap between genders by making strong designations to leading levels. One particularly salient example of this is Chairwoman of Parliament.

Tell me about your successes as a woman.

Endless efforts to make my country great again, particularly, gathering compatriots from all walks of life in order to make contribution to our country by building new version of Silicon valley in Uzbekistan. Additionally, involving more business ladies to this project and bearing young girls with their plan to find investors that were born in Uzbekistan.

Provide some advice to women from a woman living in Uzbekistan.

Work hard and fight against antifeminism, try all of your best to show your great performance in any area, mostly stay financially freedom from your parents and husband to keep desire to create new things. Never go married in early ages, this is golden time, no one can bring it back. Stay patient and show that men not better than women and propagandize ideas of feminism.

My Life As A Woman: Vanuatu Edition

Not so famous but a really interesting and unique country-island called Vanuatu is a safe home for many people. Breathtaking coral reefs and canyons can make you fall in love with this spectacular island. What I really like about my hometown is that it is not that expensive for tourists, as many islands are, it is very safe and full of attractions and new emotions for a visitor. This island is a Pacific adventure that offers flashy resorts and luxurious holidays, ancient culture, and high-level diving opportunities.

I am Mariana from Santo, Sanma which is in Vanuatu, where I was born and passed all my childhood after my parents got divorced we moved to Honiara, Solomon Islands where I entered Solomon Islands National University and studied in the faculty of Education and Humanities. I graduated in 2019 and started to look for a job, and my brother helped me with this. He showed me freelance online platforms through what I started to earn money and helping my mother with some money. I want to give everything she wants, my mother is the strongest woman I know and she is really a good example for me. I was always being shy of my appearance as it is enough different from today's standards and this made me really depressive. After a person appeared in my life and helped me to change my mind and think differently, he inspired me so much that now I am ready to face any difficulty.

Nowadays a lot of women make different surgeries to become perfect, trendy, and stunning, and Instagram really makes people jealous and depressive as you follow and see many girls being really beautiful than you look in the mirror, and your self-esteem decreases. So this was my biggest complex, but one day I realized something that every woman is incredible as she is, every woman should accept her as she is. It is really difficult but you have to. Yes, you have to take care of yourself, smell good, and look good. But young women today are very mistaken to be thinking that their sense of self-worth and their acknowledgment of their beauty depends on whether a man will give that to them or not. And so what will happen when the man changes his mind about her? Tells her she's not beautiful enough. That she's not good enough? Cheats on her? Leaves her? Then what happens? She will lose all her self-worth, she will think she is not good enough, she is not beautiful enough, because all of those sense of self-worth and acknowledgment of being beautiful must not come from a man, it must come from inside the woman herself. I want women to love themselves, as all of us are incredibly unique, our face, forms, eyes, nose, and everything is absolutely unique. Do not try to be the same as you see on Instagram. Be real, be natural, and love yourself, after you'll see how people start to love you more and admire you.

My Life As A Woman: Venezuela Edition #1

I was born and raised in Caracas the capital of Venezuela, an amazingly beautiful country in South America. I grew up in a multi-cultural family, my father being from Caracas, and my mother from the island of Aruba. So, ever since I was a little girl, I have been surrounded with people from different cultures, especially since I've moved a few times over the last years. Although I have been blessed to have the experience to live abroad, I would say there's nothing like the Venezuelan culture! What I like the most about people from my country is that they are pretty positive, always looking for the funny side of everything. It is super easy to make friends, everyone is super outgoing, and the best part: we love reunions! No matter if there is a celebration or not, we love to get together to eat and catch up, especially in our homes.

As much as I love my country, the tough political and economic situation we were going through back when I graduated from high school made it hard for me to stay. So, I decided to move to the United States to pursue a career in Advertising and Public Relations when I was 18. Studying advertising was my dream, I wanted to be a successful woman working at a top ad agency just like in the movies. I had an excellent education in high school but my English wasn't that good, however, that didn't stop me. Of course, I was scared to move to a country where I didn't know anyone but at the same time I had the support of my family and that was more than enough to take the courage to leave and start a new life.

The hardest decision of my life ended up being the best one. I not only graduated Cum Laude thanks to my effort and dedication but I also made the most amazing friends from all over the world. I was extremely grateful to be surrounded by different cultures at all times. This cultural experience contributed to my education, helped me enhance my communication skills and it also opened my mind to new ideas. Three years later, I still haven't gotten a job in a successful ad agency like in the movies, but I have done things more interesting than that have also made me a successful person. I have worked for big companies, small boutique agencies and multicultural startups with great ideas and amazing people. Eventually, I would like to start my own business in my country, but I know I am not ready yet, there is still so much I need to learn. In the meantime, I am finishing my master's in digital marketing, doing freelance to get more experience, and keeping up with growing my connections.

My advice to other women living in my country would be dare to try new things! Sometimes we get scared when we think about moving away from our families or from our culture even if it's just for a few months. Truth is, there are tons of opportunities out there. Don't let your fears stop you from doing what you love, pursue your dreams and most importantly: never give up on your ideas. Becoming successful is not something that happens from one day to another, you need to work hard and show people how good you are!

My Life As A Woman: Venezuela Edition #2

Hi! My name is Betzaida Ruiz, I am 27 years old and currently living in my hometown, Los Teques. Today I'll tell you a little about my history and what my life has been like living in Venezuela.

Of course, I must start by telling you that my childhood was very happy since I had my parents, my sister and a beautiful family who were looking for excuses to meet every weekend and spend quality time at my grandparents' farm, schedule a trip to the beach or to any magical place in Venezuela.

From a very young age, I had my mother as a source of inspiration. A working woman with a teaching profession and who looked for the time between her two jobs to spend time with her daughters, educate them and help them carry out their tasks in the best way. And, although she is already retired from her job, she started one of the most important projects of her life and our family: The History of the Oropeza Avilán Family, fulfilling the wish of my grandfather Marcelo Oropeza.

As a second part, my musical life. Said love for music began when I was 6 years old and became part of Los Niños Cantores de los Teques. A group that made my afternoons filled with children's melodies and songs, in addition, allowing me to make my first international tour to Peru, where we were able to perform concerts in Lima and Because and visit the wonderful lost city of Machu Pichu.

We can't help but grow, so we turned 12 years old and we had to bet on a bigger project, we planned trips to the capital and became part of the Coro Metropolitano de Caracas. Which, with time and hundreds of concerts, became the Coral Juvenil Simón Bolívar. While being in this group I had the privilege me to visit few cities in the USA, Germany, Colombia, Wales, Portugal, Italy, London, France and meet the love of my life, my husband.

But what about my academic career? Well, I can tell you that my entire school and high school life is very quiet. My grades were good and I only had one thing in my mind: studying something for the future that would allow me to work in a lab. So I applied for a Bachelor of Chemistry at the Universidad Central de Venezuela.

Over time, I became discouraged with the career since I had some problems at the Chemistry Faculty, and also my musical life was progressing in a better way, not only fulfilling my academic needs but also financially, so I decided to change my bet on a similar field in 2017. So, currently I am studying the second year of Pharmacy at the UCV.

On the other hand, there's no secret about the huge problems Venezuela has being going through the past few years. The reason that led me on the path I am currently on is that in 2014 - after being very depressed by the news and events that were taking place in Venezuela - to make a decision that would make my life happier: opening my blog of fashion and beauty **Mi Burbuja**.

Over the years, the blog has become a job that I enjoy a lot and my escape site since, in addition to talking about the latest fashion trends and working with other brands, I can capture my experiences and curiosities about different natural products, makeup and cosmetics. And also, my blog became the reason that made me want to study and specialize in cosmetology in the future.

What else can I tell you? Well, now I am studying something that I really like, working with something that gives fulfills me and living my third year of marriage in a home that I love. Did you leave things on the way? Of course, since I had to leave my musical life to nurture and focus on the career that I like. In addition, I have had to say goodbye to friends and family who left looking for a better fortune in other corners of the world.

Some advice? I think I am not the best for it, but in my life path it has helped me a lot to lean on my loved ones, trust my instinct, fight for what I love and always remember why I never quit along the way.

I hope you liked my little anecdote of life. Greetings and a huge hug from a Venezuelan woman.

My Life As A Woman: Vietnam Edition

It was the crackling fireworks celebrating New Year's Eve that made my heart pound every time I rushed to the rooftop with my little brother and my father. My mother and grandmother would be downstairs decorating the house with cherry blossoms and preparing Vietnamese traditional rice cake and steamed chicken for the big gathering in a few hours. I remember watching the fireworks with marvel and admiration until the last shot. Every building around us seemed so small and every noise faded into the background as we stood on the roof. This was our tradition every year during my childhood - gatherings and homemade food.

Back then I was a curious child with a knack for making things with my hands and a thirst for discovering new things. I spent hours drawing, writing short stories and comic strips, and composing songs. My brother and I would bring a dim lit lantern and explored the dark winding narrow alleys in those winter days. My summer days revolved around building sand houses, planting banana leaves and chasing dragonflies in our big garden. And in the evenings, my extended family gathered together around the old TV with an antenna to watch our favorite show.

My childhood wasn't all glory though. Summer came with its unbearable scorching heat that we had no means to cool ourselves other than an electric fan and a bamboo mat on the floor. We were "blessed" with massive floods that soaked our house for a few days, so we had to wait upstairs for the water to recede before coming back down to wash down the house.

In spite of the challenges, we laughed and cried through the brightest and gloomiest days. We were always there for each other. My mom and dad worked full time at the same job for most of their life to ensure us food on the table and a good education.

As time slowly went by, I watched in pain and regret houses after houses smashed down and erected into taller buildings. The big sky view I used to enjoy in my childhood no longer existed. All I saw was a narrow corner of the sky, overlaid with entangled electric wires. There was no more nervous anticipation for fireworks every Lunar New Year. Less time and gatherings outdoors and more time indoors. Living up to my parents' increasingly high expectations to mold me into a "good girl" started to suffocate me and mute my identity. I became disenchanted and melancholic. Something gnawed at me, urging me to run away.

I think we all try to run away from something. For me, I decided to leave Vietnam for America, with the hope to reinvent myself, or so I thought. I went to college and studied economics. Life was unpredictable as it could be. I ended up taking on various jobs during the summers and even after college. I met people from all walks of life; talking to them helped me see myself for who I am. As a result, I gradually became more open-minded, less judgmental, less distressed, and more empathetic.

If someone asked me what I have learned throughout my short existence, I would say, just be yourself and let it shine through. It's alright to be confused and frustrated when you are out there by yourself and start making adult choices. Hop on a train and see where it takes you. Try as many jobs or hobbies as possible before deciding to settle because you'd better off being a late bloomer than settle for a job that drains your soul. Your wealth is defined by your experience and memories, not by material assets. And finally, don't ever forget your roots, for it will come back to serve you.

My Life As A Woman: Western Sahara Edition #1

My name is Sultana El Ghalia, I'm 37 years old married and I have three kids, two girls and one boy I'm from the Occupied territory of Western Sahara, as they call it Africa's last colony it's called this way because we are still in ownership dispute with morocco. When Spain lifted the colonization morocco and Mauritania claimed that Western Sahara was part of their lands before Spain took control of it, some people in Western Sahara consider themselves as Moroccan but it is not the case the land was no longer theirs once Spain colonized it

While Mauritania gave up Morocco didn't; they invaded the majority of the Sahara in 1976 during the green march which was a mass demonstration lead by Moroccan troops and citizens against the Sahrawi Polisario front, many people ran away to the borders between Morocco and Algeria as refugees to protect themselves from the war which separated many families and I'm one the victims as my two brothers are refugees in Dakhla. After few years Morocco allowed a referendum on independence that was never ever materialized which left the region in diplomatic stalemate ever since, the only thing that was signed is a ceasefire agreement, right now they are using up the natural resources we own like phosphate selling them to western countries as if it was their own.

Many journalists and news channel from all over the world do not cover this issue because they are not even allowed to step on our territory unless they have an approval from Morocco, those are usually either clueless or bribed not to reveal the truth, that's why I decided to become a journalist, a dream of mine since I was a little girl seeing all the injustice that my people lived without it being covered by the media. My mum passed from serious injuries she had during a very bloody altercation, my people's suffering will not go in vain therefore I took classes in journalism and photography to broadcast to the world what we live and how we are treated when we march to get back our rights.

Women have a strong place in Sahara, they are fearless and resilient as many protests are led by us, we are as important as men; when most men left for war against Moroccan as the Polisario front, only women stayed leading the remaining people; those were the ones who filled the jobs of police, doctors and head of districts, now men are used to having women on their sides we do the same jobs and we are equal, we fight for our freedom and we even lead protests they need us as much as we need them, but sadly at every protest we get bruised hit and assaulted our cameras get confiscated and our footage destroyed, many women were brutalized and tortured and sisters are still kidnapped by the Moroccan kingdom with no records of their arrests.

What we want is a war because the referendum was not respected and now only violence will help us get back our lands and have our families come back from the Dakhla refugee camps, indeed we would much rather not have a bloody altercation with Morocco, but if it's the only solution we have, we are ready to fight back, and as Sahrawi women we are not backing off unless we get the final victory and liberate our homeland. The beatings will not stop us from continuing the fight even if we have to die trying; it will be a sacrifice so that our sons and daughters and future generations can live in the freedom that we have been denied.

All women should have this kind of engagement, it's our duty to gain back our freedom so it's your duty to always fight for your rights and raise your voice against injustice.

Where were you born?

I was born and raised in a fabric tent in the Sahrawi refugee camp southern Algeria.

How did you grow up?

Life of refugees in general and refugee girls in particular is different from the life of any other person born with rights, an identity and belong somewhere. I lived my life with steadfastness, struggle and patience, in simple and peaceful ways. I am dependent on the provision of the food aid to refugees; my body did not grow in the right way; it always lacked something. I did not know about what television or entertainment games are until after the age of 9 when I went to Spain within the Vacations of Peace program for Sahrawi children. There I saw another world, other people, another language, and a totally different way of living.

I was studying a lot because my mother told me that studying is what will save us all from this. It was enough for me to play with mud and stones, and here comes the role of books to save what is left of my life as a child. They were not even available that much so I had to re-read any piece of magazine or a book brought by the wind and stuck in the ropes of our tent. I then moved to study my intermediate school and then my high school and the university thousands of miles away from the camps and my family. There I had to completely rely on myself from the age of 14. I began to discover who I am and my ability to persist, all by myself.

Did you have parents or perhaps a grandmother who inspired you?

My mother did not receive sufficient education; she got married at an early age. My father died suddenly, she did not live with others; she just lived with her children. She insisted that everyone in in the family should finish their study and get the best certificates even if it'll end up somewhere stored in our mud house, even If it is at the expense of what she wanted. She faced society with an iron shield, my mother is my model and she is the iron woman for me.

What did you study? / What did you want to be growing up? / Why?

My mother was like any other hard working mother, she suffered from joint diseases and back pain for a long time, and because I am the youngest in the family, she attached great hopes on me to become a doctor. I loved that profession ever since. I wanted to see my mom get some comfortable sleep without being overwhelmed by pain. I wanted to help the other mothers as well, I wanted so badly to become a neuroscientist, but I was not lucky enough so I studied biochemistry and I am satisfied with it now.

What do you love about your culture?

When I was young and in the midst of all of this struggle we are going through, I saw women giving clothes to each other, I see men helping each other, you would think they are brothers. I like the simplicity of the Sahrawi, their solidarity, harmony and generosity, I like how women choose what they want to become according to their will, they cling desperately to their dreams.

I also like that they did not give up on their traditional costumes even in the furthest of places and the most sophisticated. I like that we stick to our goals and dreams, to our solidarity as a community, a community that is going through the ordeal of occupation.

What you are currently doing for work?

Currently, I am still trying to finish the study I started, I am active in different civil society associations, NOVA; nonviolence association, and how to spread the culture of nonviolence in our Sahrawi community and in the Arab world in general, I volunteer to work for some periods in the hospital.

Tell me about your struggles as a woman.

For a woman to be born and lives all her life as a refugee is the biggest challenge I believe. I wake up every day just to remind myself that I almost don't exist. I work tirelessly. Everyone wants to be independent, to make something that would make them feel like they contributed to changing or adding something worth mentioning in their life, I don't get feel this as long as I live in a refugee camp, I almost don't exist, I repeat my home routine every day.

I find it difficult to just organize my time. When will I finish this book? When will I listen to this podcast? When will I meet my friends? My mind is always full of unfinished tasks and many questions without answers. I want to travel but the word "travel" can only be seen as a tool for migrating or to collect money, nothing else, or to buy a new tent that is not worn out. Everything here needs to be mended. I don't have time to think about what I really want. My life as a refugee stands in the way of my ambitions and what I want. What could be an ordinary life of someone could be the dream I always wanted to have, and the sad part is that this situation will not change for a long time.

Tell me about your successes as a woman.

I lived on with all my power in the midst of a place that doesn't have anything. I try to make a change in my community. I faced some extreme challenges, such as study abroad and at the age of 12, and when the community says, "Women were created to be at home, not to study", "Marriage is what will make a woman settle down", I throw the community's words across the wall, I demonstrated to the community that a woman was created to study, was created for creativity, was created in order to do things far greater than to be limited just for a home and a wife.

Give some advice to women from a woman who lives in Western Sahara.

The woman has an innate power inside her, if she knows how to use it well, she will surpass the. Do not stop smashing obstacles and achieving your dreams because of society or because of your situation. Live according to what you see, and not what others see for you. Do what you find meaningful for you, do not forget that a woman cannot be simply understood from her looks or by material standards, but through her strength and will. The conditions, society, torture, war, displacement, exile and all these bad and difficult things, you are stronger than them, and always able to overcome them.

Sígueme en Instagram! Nombre de usuario: mimi_hamma

My Life As A Woman: Yemen Edition #1

Somaya G

Where did you grow up?

I was born and raised in Sana'a, Yemen. I lived my whole life there until I became 19.

How did you grow up?

My childhood was just the typical childhood of a Yemeni girl; from home, to school, to Quran lessons. Playing on the street with my neighbors and cousins ended at puberty, and so began the life of responsibilities and wearing the hijab. Perhaps the only difference I had from the average Yemeni child is that I used to read a lot and watch a lot of movies. I grew up in an intellectual home, full of books that exceed a thousand.

My father taught my sisters and I the Sharia (Islamic) studies in episodes between Maghrib prayers and Isha prayers. And so this was my life with my family until I decided to fly away from the nest and make a life for myself. I remember everything was prohibited for a girl. I can't do this or that because I am a girl and this was difficult for me. It raised questions and led me to more research and readings trying to understand my society, myself and what I want in life.

Did you have parents or maybe a grandmother who inspired you?

My family members were all doctors and one engineer uncle. So we as kids were always pushed to excel in school and become either doctors or engineers. My uncle used to create everything at home from scratch, it was so cool and I loved engineering because of him. Being an engineer felt like having superpowers as you can create machines that can make your life easier, I wanted to be an engineer like him, an engineer who is an astronaut that was my dream.

My grandmother is a strong Russian lady and I was always inspired by her strong personality, she was able to build the house we grew in and send all of her children to school and higher education. My dad respected her so much as I did. I wanted to be strong like my grandmother as well.

What did you study? / What did you want to be growing up? / Why?

I studied Industrial Engineering but I wanted to be an astronaut when I was a child. Space was exciting for me, and I was curious about exploring the outside whether it was space or planet earth. But that dream didn't come True yet.

What you love about your culture?

I love my Yemeni collective culture, as we care for the neighbors and the people surrounding us. When Mom cooks she makes the portion big and then asks me to go give our neighbours some of what we cooked. The neighbors in return never turn the given dish or container empty, they would return it full of something they cooked. It was part of the culture. We share our happy days and sad ones. The whole neighborhood knows when someone dies or gets married and we all celebrate and share gifts. We visit the sick and care for them and care so much for our elderly as we consider them the luck charm of the whole family. We never give them up to elderly house care.

That's what I love about our culture. I also like the art we have, manifested in clothes, songs, traditions, etc.. that are unique and not like any other nation which adds color and a different taste of life.

What are you currently doing for work?

I work as a content creator, I used to work as a freelance export/import specialist and I did websites in my spare time for clients, I also worked as a teacher to sustain myself when I was a student.

Now I am a digital nomad working online, and not bond to any location, I like this lifestyle more and I see that it fits my personality very well

Tell me about your struggles as a woman.

To reach the lifestyle I have now I had to give up almost everything, I lost the love of all my relatives and I was deprived of any support I should normally get because I was a woman in Yemen. Let me explain.

My society didn't approve of any of the things I wanted, I wanted to travel the world, study abroad and be independent. I wanted to be a free woman seeking her dreams. But no one gave me permission or support to do so because "women are not created for this" everyone says. Hence, I had to do it my own, I worked for two years in Yemen after high school to get the money I needed to travel. I also organized my escape out by myself which is very difficult in Yemen. Because women usually depend on men to do most of the work outside of their home. I traveled and had to take whole responsibility for myself not being able to seek help from anyone I know because none approved my decision. It Was tough to live alone in a strange country especially when I was a girl who only knew home and school. But this made me stronger.

Another difficulty was the reaction of the people when I started my social media, I got so much hatred and bullying, I was considered a shame for the society and I had to have a very strong well to continue what I do and ignore the hatred and threats I received. Yes, I got many death threats from so many telling me they would hurt me if I don't delete my videos. All because I didn't wear headscarf, they were also against a woman from Yemen traveling alone.

Tell me about your successes as a woman.

To a privileged woman who lived in a free society, I am not considered an achiever. But for Yemeni women I am a success story. Because, I fought so hard for the life I want for myself, not the life the society wanted or anyone else. For that, the price was high, but freedom is always expensive. I am considered the first female Yemeni traveler and one of the first female YouTubers in Yemen. I gave hope to many Yemeni girls that they can do whatever they want, because I am like all of them with no special circumstances. Yet, I did it.

My Life As A Woman: Yemen Edition #2

Warning: This story contains graphic content. Proceed to read with caution.

I am Nada Al-Ahdal from Yemen, from "Al-Hodeidah", a city known for its high temperature throughout the year.

I am one of my nine siblings, I used to spend my day serving the house to buy home needs from the market, which is 2 kilometers from my house in a very high temperature, I was trying to reduce the temperature of the earth by hiding under whatever shade I could find, I was barefoot.

My morning starts with going to school 4 km away from my house until 9 am, I get back home to have breakfast and then return at 10 o'clock to complete my lessons, when I return I put my bag and then go to buy vegetables under very high temperatures.

In the evening I used to spend my time with my aunt who is 4 years older than me and my sister who is 3 years older than me, we used to play and have fun.

A few months later, I was prevented from playing with my aunt on the pretext that she became married and it's shameful to play with her, I was very sad because she was my dearest friend, my aunt gave birth to a girl and she was suffering from violence by her husband, who is 40 years older than her, and he justified his violence to her as a child who did not understand responsibilities And take care of her child, My aunt thought that to end the pain, she must end her life. She committed suicide by burning herself out and died, and I couldn't sleep from crying, and from the pictures that I saw when she was disfigured with burns and her body was covered by a shroud.

A few months later, I moved with my uncle to Sana'a to learn in the capital. My uncle received a call from my family telling him that I would get married, and I was 9 years old at the time. My uncle ended that marriage.

After a while, my family asked me to go home, and my uncle was leaving for outside Yemen. I was surprised that my marriage ceremony after a week was to be his wife instead of my 13-year-old sister She Committed Suicide by burning herself as my aunt did before for refusing marriage, but we managed to save her from death.

I was shocked and escaped and recorded a video explaining the reason for my escape, the latest video had a global impact and caused the issuance of law to try underage marriage in Yemen. I was imprisoned for 10 days to prevent the effect of my story in the media. My family pledged not to marry until I reach the legal age.

On the other hand, I was banned from traveling outside Yemen.

Three years later, she tried to travel through "Aden" airport and was kidnapped by Al-Qaeda for 14 days.

After being released, I left Yemen for the Kingdom of Saudi Arabia, and there I met some Yemeni government officials and established the Nada Foundation for Girls Protection, which implemented many projects.

The foundation won the With and for Girls Award 2019 in London as one of the best organizations concerned with defending girls' rights in the Middle East and North Africa.

The Foundation has established several humanitarian programs with high impact to promote education and protect girls from child marriage and domestic violence.

One of the programs

1- "Our dreams flourish" for teaching girls the English language. The girls who benefited from the programs were 600 girls in six cities in Yemen.

2- A "safe haven" to protect girls who are victims of child marriage and domestic violence.

Many girls have been affected by these programs, one of them is the child Shaima, who was violated by her parents when she was 6 years old, but the Public Prosecution didn't accept Shaima's case and refused to protect her. She went on a hunger strike in a live broadcast on Facebook for 3 days, in protest to the public prosecution's ruling for not protecting the girl and punishing her father, And the Public Prosecution was pressured and we contacted the Public Prosecutor, and her responsibility was transferred from the father to her grandmother, and her father was imprisoned, and now Shaima lives with her grandmother and she receives an educational grant in private schools annually from the Foundation, and she dazzles us with obtaining the first rank annually in all results, and is now in her third year of benefiting from the education.

We believe girls are part of building and developing society, to develop society, we must give girls an opportunity to be leaders and give them all their rights and develop their ability to influence society.

For every girl, rights are not given but taken. Don't wait for society to grant you your rights on a plate of gold. Fight and fight for your rights and don't allow anyone to violate your life for any reason. Don't give up and acquiesce in any form of violence.

My Life As A Woman: Zambia Edition

My name is Tiku Phiri. I was born in 1990 in a town called Samfya in the Luapula Province of Zambia. I lived with my father, mother and brother for the first eight years of my life. However, my father passed away before I turned nine years old and I was raised by my mother thereafter.

The death of my father caused great hardship for my family. This is because all my father's assets were taken away by his relatives as property grabbing was very rampant at the time. Due to the property grabbing, my family remained with no assets or belongings because everything had been taken away.

My mother was unemployed when my father died so life became very difficult for us. We had to move from Samfya to a town called Mpika where we lived with my grandmother for about five years. We then moved to Kitwe where we stayed with my aunt for another 8 years. Living in very large families forced me to learn how to bake, farm, hunt, and gather fruits from nearby hills because food was quite scarce.

Growing up the way I did made me strong and self-reliant at a young age. It made me focus on my education to escape the hardships I had encountered. In eleventh grade, I had to teach myself the subjects on my own because my mother had no money to pay my school fees and none of my relatives were willing to pay. However, I was determined to become a lawyer to improve the quality of my life and get justice for the property grabbing that my family had experienced. I also wanted to protect people from similar injustices. I eventually went on to study law and graduate from a university in Lusaka, Zambia's capital city.

I am currently working as a lawyer at one of the law firms in Lusaka. I am also doing agriculture as a side business. Farming is my way of trying to ensure that no one goes hungry because I know how painful hunger is.

Throughout my life my mother and grandmother have been the sources of my inspiration. They always encouraged me to fight through all the challenges in my life. They also taught me our Zambian traditions. I am consequently appreciative of my culture because of the simplicity and respect it teaches. From an early age, Zambians are taught to be respectful and kind to everyone regardless of their status or background. I additionally love the rich variety of food which is an essential part of my culture.

My biggest challenge as a woman is not being taken seriously by men in business and in my profession just because I am woman. On the other hand, my greatest success is that I have managed to be creative and self-reliant through hard work without depending on men or losing my dignity.

My advice to women as a woman living in Zambia is to remember that as women we are smarter than we realised. We should be objective and decisive. We must also aspire for leadership and set a good example once we acquire it. Most importantly, we must never be ashamed to embrace our femininity. We must be kind and motherly while standing strong and firm.

My Life As A Woman: Zimbabwe Edition

I am a woman born and breed in Zimbabwe. I have recently turned 35 and I feel I have barely begun my life. Other people would think otherwise but now I can see that only when you reach a certain age and are a lot wiser do you really know what you want out of life.

I grew up in Harare, the capital city of Zimbabwe. I always liked to call myself a city girl. I come from what they called back in the day a middle class family. My family is all girls and I am the last one, so I had a very big female influence growing up. We were always a very close family. My father was a headmaster and my mother is a nurse. So education was always priority and in his way our inheritance.

My father was always very conscious of the fact that he had only girls and he was determined to make sure we were empowered. Sadly he passed away when I was 13 years old from cancer. It was a difficult time but my mother really stepped up and there became my hero.

Despite having lost her soulmate she did not let grief take over and bury her. She instead went back to school to work on her degree so she can get a better job. She wanted to provide and fill the gap that my father had left. I could see it was tough and becoming a single income home it had its stresses but she never gave up and made sacrifices. She did well in her career and it opened doors for her. Unfortunately many women who I had seen lose their husbands tended to give up, they would give up on life and just be swept away in the grief. My mother was judged by many for going back to school and for working hard. Widows in our culture are meant to be sad and struggling and she refused this stereotype. This is one of the lessons I learnt from her. Despite adversity you pick yourself up and you carry on.

I always had a love for people, helping them, being there to listen. So I wanted to study psychology. However being in an African society, psychology was not seen as anything that leads to a good job. So instead I studied organisational psychology and industrial sociology at a university in South Africa. This would then lead me to work in Human Resources.

I returned back home to live with my mother and to be her support just as she had been mine. But finding work in Zimbabwe was not easy. I ended up in different fields. This is not entirely a bad thing because it opens you up to learning new skills. I have worked in roles that involved marketing and advertising, administration and managing teams. All these roles I felt gave me the skills I needed to start my own business. This is the one thing I find very admirable about Zimbabwean women. They are very enterprising.

I am married now with two children and I enjoy taking on challenges, setting goals and achieving them. I am running an online gift shop, putting together gift deliveries and making people happy. I am also an online freelance writer. I discovered from all the reading I had done, I enjoy writing too and can make a decent living out of it. Because of the environment we are living in, one needs to have several sources of income so ideas are always rolling in on what to do next. I am thinking of growing vegetables and selling because I have discovered a gap in the market. Also gardening is very therapeutic.

The struggles I find that have affected me and a lot of women out there is trying to balance family and still being an individual following you own dream. Usually the individual tends to suffer as you sacrifice who you are to become a wife and a mother. Society feels that if you marry and have children then you are successful. Anything beyond that is not really regarded as a win. Because of this you don't always find the right support to follow your dreams. You still encounter judgement and ridicule when you attempt to have it all.

I enjoy the work that I do and I have found that sometimes we are caught up in titles to define us. Because of my business I have had the opportunity to meet other women who are starting and running their own out of the box businesses and it is working very well for them. They are happy and also find it easy to balance work and their social life. The way the world was twenty years ago is not how it is now and it needs for us to think beyond what we are told in school. Women need to keep their minds open to the possibility of trying something new and not sticking to the social construct of the old.

My Life As A Woman Project: Conversation Insights

Easily my favorite part of the project was talking to so many women, convincing them that they should join this project, mostly on Fiverr and Facebook Groups. A team member of mine that I hired went further than that and recruited women from Instagram. Women were all chosen at random on Fiverr, where the vast majority of countries and islands were found. On Facebook Groups, I posted about a project and if any women were interested, they could message me, and this is where I obtained several of the islands, such as Niue Island and Christmas Island. On Instagram, however, the majority were from the Middle East and shed a whole different light on the fact that "modern views" of the Middle East are far more modern than what is often portrayed in the minds of people from around the world. Instagram and Snapchat are a daily in the lives of many Middle Eastern women who are quite photogenic.

Talking to women from all over the world was exciting, but talking to the Middle Eastern women changed my perspective of how the media portrays them. They were fun, intelligent, and really had a lot of insight to share. Some even had a great sense of humor. To get a chance to speak with so many women who I would never really have any context to speak with was quite interesting. The Palestinian women, whom I had thought would never ever want to talk to me, were actually forthcoming and happy to share their stories.

While most women were all about business, there were some who would joke with me, check up on me, and just wanted to share more about their lives then what they actually put in their stories. For the most part, the project sold itself and many women were on board right from the start.

The hardest part was convincing some women that a project like this actually existed. In the beginning, there was no website and there was nothing to go on but my word. I had to convince the women to trust me and believe I was doing what I said I was going to do. While many hadn't known I was going to turn it into a book, as this started out as a blog project that was going to be published on my website, I realized the significance of it, and decided it would be better to turn it into an eBook and a book. The point was proven when my entire server crashed and my website was lost for a time. To have this important history of women needs to be solidified in a book, not contained to just a website. Despite all my efforts, there were women who did not believe me, did not trust me, or just did not feel comfortable giving over such personal information, even with the promise of being allowed anonymity, but since no woman was forced or even bribed to be a part of this project, there were no hard feelings about any woman not wanting to be a part of such a massive project.

From May 5, 2020 until July 1st, 2020, just before Fiverr banned me, I spent months talking to women on the chat, navigating through each country and asking women if they were interested, trying to sell them on the idea of a project like this. Since the women were in quarantine lockdown, most of them answered within 24 hours. Considering that I am based out of New Mexico and was contacting women throughout the world, it did not take many too long to respond, as I was working and talking to women in 24-hour time blocks. I would walk away from my computer for a few minutes and have a dozen women who responded to my messages. It was, at times, overwhelming even for me. I tried to have some templates ready, but for the most part, networking with many women did require some deeper conversations to let these women know what the project was about and why they should join it. For the most part, many were right on board. Each woman was given a week to return her assignment to me, with week extensions granted upon request. All assignments had to be returned in English.

As a programmer, web developer, and technical writer, I also specialize in documentation, so I did manage to keep up with the records and experiences I had during this project, with no specific order. I experienced good and bad, but mostly good, and this is a mixture of all the conversations I had during the project:

My Life As A Woman Project: Budget and Challenges

Having the privilege of speaking to so many women was nothing short of a miracle. Taking the risk of starting this project, not knowing if I could or would finish it was a gamble I had to take. Upon the moment I started to have doubts, a feeling in me, a voice within stated, "just keep going, don't worry about the money." And so, not questioning it or even doubting it, I kept pushing forward with this project. There was no doubt that I faced many obstacles and challenges along the way. From the platform to the women themselves to everyday life, I pushed on through to ensure this project was going to happen, especially after making a promise to so many women that it definitely was.

While I cannot fully disclose what a project like this cost, I will say that the budget was in the five-digit mark. The project was started on May 5, 2020 and officially ended on August 28th, 2020, for a total of 115 days. This project was mainly funded by my savings. When I was around 25 or 26 years old, I co-founded an organization, called Yahel Israel, which was supposed to have a reunion in 2020. Unfortunately, due to COVID-19, this was cancelled, and so, I had the partial funds to begin this project that I had saved up. After the funds ran out, I started using my PayPal credit card, PayPal credit account, and a VISA credit card, all of which were eventually maxed out.

Personally, I tried to ensure all women were paid between $10 - $20 USD for the project, with some women in more rarer countries being offered slightly more. No woman was paid into the 3-digits for her story, as I could not have ever afforded to do a project like this if that were the case, so all payments among all the women were kept fair. This project took a special type of woman to join. While I would have loved to pay the women a lot more for their participation, having to hire the women, the assistants who helped obtain women's stories where I did not directly have access to any women, the interviewers, and the translators, it would not have been possible to obtain all countries.

While Facebook Groups is a point-and-click to join, many did not even allow me to enter into their groups. If I did get in, they were monitoring the messages, and many did not approve of my message trying to recruit women for the project. If I did get through and the message was approved, then I had to hope women were willing to participate in the project. Niue Island, Christmas Island, the Aboriginals of Australia, and Kiribati were the only ones that were interested out of dozens of islands, though a team member was able to obtain the islands on various other platforms.

During the project while on Fiverr, I had to contact PayPal twice, who froze my account. The credit card company froze my account at least four times, though Fiverr and the credit card company seemed to blame each other along the way, so I had to keep trying to find or swap my methods of payment until one or the other worked. After all was said and done, it was a total of about eight times that access to my money had been frozen for whatever reason. Though looking at it from a computer's perspective, paying out to various countries, though most of it was through Fiverr, might have thrown up a red flag or two. Fortunately, all payment companies involved were able to get it all resolved.

Having spoken to over 1,000 women on Fiverr came with its risks, especially in the era of "everyone is offended by everything" and Fiverr is a platform that will ban both seller and buyer if there is any complaint that is found to violate the Terms of Services. There is this stigma that Fiverr favors buyers over sellers, and for the most part, it's true, but Fiverr will also ban buyers without hesitation or question with absolutely ZERO appeal process. Once you are banned, according to Fiverr, you can never be unbanned. While I had been warned just once overall, I was not banned for the incident. It was not until I had gone around the world and returned back to the United States that I was banned. There was no second warning for me. Fiverr is quite interesting because, despite being a publicly-traded company, it seems to be one of the only platforms who will ban its users that bring in or spend tens of thousands of dollars, and they don't seem to care one way or another. Just google horror stories about Fiverr banning its users for no real reason and you'll see what I am talking about. Looking up Fiverr on the BBB will confirm any suspicions as well.

While it might seem like a good idea for investors to think that Fiverr is a money-making platform, it is probably the worst company in regards to how it treats both its sellers and buyers. Sellers think Fiverr favors its buyers, yet I spent thousands of dollars and had planned to spend thousands more on their platform and got banned for "violating multiple Terms of Service" is all they would reveal to me. I can only imagine what investors would think if they knew that the practices of Fiverr involved banning people who were spending thousands of dollars on their platform were losing them. I, personally, as a stock market investor, knowing what I know, would never ever risk my money investing in the Fiverr corporation because of the amount of money Fiverr is actually costing themselves and their investors. Fortunately for Fiverr, they are now technically too big to fail and used by too many people with a constant flow of new sellers and buyers. It's still a great platform, the best of them all, and while I do harbour some negative feelings towards Fiverr, I know Fiverr is still a great tool for freelancers.

To make the long story short, I went through several scenarios of what could have happened, as Fiverr was not forthcoming with the reason and would only state that I "violated multiples Terms of Service". Further inquiries showed that Fiverr is unwilling to forgive, prevent you from knowing who your accuser is, and not tell you exactly what you've done. For the first scenario, while the person did not seem like a scammer, she had promised to help me, like so many others had done previously, but returned to me stories that all seemed to follow similar structures, as if she had written them. The point of having people help me, and it was made clear: a unique woman must write them, and she must be from that specific country or area that I asked. While it was never proven whether this person got me banned or not, there were certain things she did afterwards that raised serious red flags.

There were also other reasons I thought I was banned, but Fiverr would not fully confirm or deny any accusations. I had mentioned the word, "f*ck" to a man I was having a conversation with. It was not offensive towards him, but rather, an expression of distaste and resentment for a certain government. We had been talking about how governments tend to favor big corporations and will let small businesses and startups suffer. Nothing wrong with this type of conversation, at least to my knowledge.

At the time of my ban, I was speaking with a Chinese woman about COVID-19 and the Chinese government, obtaining stories that no media would ever report, and she happened to provide insight into more about the virus and China's involvement than anyone else I had hired for their COVID-19 story, so I thought this could be a possible reason for my ban. Again, Fiverr would not confirm or deny this.

Finally, at the same time, with all of this happening, as I did have a lot going on, I was also talking to multiple Palestinian women, obtaining their stories, which was an interesting time to get banned. A platform built by Israelis banning a Jewish man trying to obtain stories from Palestinian women looked highly suspicious. Go figure that one out. Again, the Israel company, Fiverr, would not confirm or deny these allegations.

Unfortunately, it was determined that I was a grave threat to the Fiverr platform and they permanently banned me, and I was not able to finish receiving all of the stories, or if I received the stories, Fiverr prevented me from paying the women, so I do apologize to any woman who did not get paid for this project. I am happy to compensate you if you do see your story within the project and were not paid for it.

In my attempts to get unbanned, Fiverr would not budge at all and came to the conclusion that they do not and never will unban any accounts. What could I do? While I still needed to get some women, I hired someone to help by using their Fiverr account. But ultimately, I decided I would not try to create or create any fake accounts using any other names after those transactions. Why give a platform that banned me anymore money? Thus, Fiverr lost out on a lot of money, but it did prevent me from doing anymore for this project on Fiverr. I had never thought in a million years, after being a buyer and seller on Fiverr's platform for over 6 years, that they would ban me, but they proved me wrong. Loyalty does not matter to Fiverr at all. Nor do their sellers and nor do their buyers. Yet the irony is that Fiverr always needs sellers and buyers to keep their platform going, and fortunately, sellers need money and have a service to offer, while buyers need that service.

So while I must be grateful to Fiverr for being the primary driver in making this project happen, I must acknowledge my love-hate relationship with Fiverr for also banning my account. Unfortunately, I had to accept that despite spending thousands of dollars on their platform and being the best possible buyer I could be, they decided I was a threat to their platform and permanently banned me.

An appeal to my "VID-Concierge" team, who proved mostly useless, as I never even got to utilize them, yielded absolutely no help at all. Apparently, my "Very Important Doer" status which I had literally just achieved just a week earlier actually meant "jackshit" on Fiverr.

Fiverr even had the decency to screw over the remaining women who delivered their orders to me, by refunding me, as I was unable to complete their orders. I do apologize for this very much, ladies, and I hope you can find it in your hearts to forgive me.

No amount of pleading or show of good faith was going to make this Israel company unban me. If you do want to check out some interesting points about the Fiverr company, while I do praise the freelancers on the platform, especially when you can find great ones, as I found many of these women, you need look no further than its Wikipedia page and the BBB website. The actual organization itself had an F rating before deciding to finally respond to its users, bringing its rating up to a B on the BBB (Better Business Bureau), but only maintains a 1-star rating, with a slew of over 50 negative comments and over 200 complaints. While this book is not about bashing or taking down the Fiverr corporation, as I can only continue to praise the company for making this project possible, they ought to have better business practices that are fair to both the buyer and sellers.

"In 2017, Fiverr was criticized for portraying unhealthy living and excesses in work behaviours as ideals to live up to. Fiverr also gives 100% privileges to buyers thereby neglecting seller rights. After a job has been completed, a buyer has the full rights to request for a refund.[24] Critics argue that Fiverr needs a balance in their equal-rights policy for both sellers as well as buyers.[25]" – Wikipedia's Fiverr page

"In 2018, Fiverr received an "F" rating from the Better Business Bureau, which is the lowest grade that can be given. In 2019, Fiverr received a "B" rating after responding to customer complaints." – Wikipedia's Fiverr page

Just a few weeks later, I sent an email just to try one last time to see if they would show any good faith towards a loyal Fiverr user of 6 years, but unfortunately, the typical response was expected, and I knew I would no longer be using Fiverr ever again. Thank you for your service Fiverr. It was a pleasure that you made this project possible, but since you banned me, I will not be able to do anymore future projects like this with your platform again.

I am sure whatever I did deserved to get me a ban and I cannot do anything about it but accept the judgement against me. Fiverr made their final decision and put an end to my activities on their platform. I wish no ill-will towards Fiverr and only hope that the women I hired on Fiverr continue to find success and receive buyers as considerate and friendly as I was. I appreciate your business with me and for helping me to make this project possible through Fiverr. Good luck to all of you and may you find success in your lives, no matter what you do!

My Life As A Woman Project: Epilogue

As I was finishing up this project, I did have a few women ask me, "What did you learn in speaking to so many women?", "What did all the women have in common?", "Are you changed after reading all these women's stories?" I ask you, as well, are you now changed from reading the stories of all these women? As I said in the Prologue, you cannot read these stories and not be forever inspired, influenced, and changed. Whether you are going through hard or rough times in your own life, picking up this book and reading a few pages is motivational.

I expected nothing less from very strong-minded women. I cannot fully say whether this was the intention or not, but honestly, the women who participated in this project wrote from their heart with you in mind. They wanted you to not lose hope, not feel lost, and not give up. They wanted you to be like them: the changers of the world, the inspirers, the influencers, the rebels, the achievers, and the doers. Regardless of their situation, these women never seemed to give up, no matter how much they were told no, that they couldn't do it, that they should just be silent, "act womanly", "act feminine", "act like a girl", or told where her place is and should be, and accept life how it is. They couldn't and they know you shouldn't either. At least not until you discover what you want and hopefully find happiness in all that you do.

As for what I expected to hear from all the women, it was as expected. Within every story was the personality of each woman, some were more serious than others, and some instantly could not help themselves but write with both a seriousness and managed to keep a sense of humor while writing. It was nice to see humor in their stories, because despite what women have been through, in their own way, women all have their own sense of humor, and they do find things that still make them laugh. For me personally, a laughing woman, especially being able to make a woman laugh, is one of the greatest pleasures in life. Behind the scenes, I got to talk to many who clearly knew what humor and sarcasm were and we usually hit it off instantly, as I thrive on humor and dark sarcasm.

The good is that women have a great desire for more, to be educated, with many who are interested in becoming or already are doctors, lawyers, politicians, scientists, mathematicians, fashion designers, teachers, etc. Women want to get involved and they want to be involved in matters that change the world. While I was never raised to believe women as inferior or men as superior, it is clear, after reading all of these stories, that women are far from any gender that could be inferior. They do not complain about the responsibilities placed upon them, but step up, to become the best version of themselves. They all go through phases of the unknown, being scared, but they rise up. And I must say, I think great opportunities would be lost if all women were only expected to be in the kitchen. Both men and women have their place in the kitchen and that is to make food and clean up afterwards, but certainly not stay there all day and let other opportunities pass them by, save for those men and women who actually have a passion and desire to be chefs and make their careers in the kitchen!

With the good also comes the bad and with many stories, I did see mentions of gender discrimination, sexual objectification, sexual harassment, sexual assault, being taken advantage of, and even rape, for which women who were part of this project did not even fully express in detail such a horrifying event, which yields a lifetime of trauma. They have also largely been overlooked in the workplace. Favoritism of the male child does occur, which did surprise me somewhat. Women are still being sold as property to be someone's wife which had me taken aback. Child brides, unfortunately, is still a thing! Any reasonable woman who has or has not been married is probably cringing at that very line, as they were when they read the stories in previous chapters. I had obtained stories from women around the world at random, so it was even horrifying for me to read about a little girl being sold off to be married for money. These problems are not country-specific, they are global problems, and they need to be solved immediately.

I do not believe, as a man, I've ever felt unsafe walking anywhere, though I am a big guy and although I can be nice most of the time, life has certainly delivered its fair share of situations to ensure I would be tough as well. Even when I worked in downtown Chicago and used to ride my bicycle through the alleyways at night, I really had no fear of anything. After all, I was working in a liquor store in downtown Chicago until 3 AM every night, so nothing phased me. Fortunately, I never had to deal with any burglaries, as I don't think anyone would've been happy with a liquor store closing early, so whether citizen, police, or petty thief, everyone was happy to pay for their medicine. Then again, I was in my 20s. I did have a few female friends who had been mugged and even a male friend who fell asleep on the train, woke up, to realize his jeans' pocket had been cut open to find his wallet missing. While there are plenty of countries where women feel safe at night walking or even just walking alone in general, there are too many countries in the world still, where women live in constant fear. Whether it is harassment from ordinary citizens or the police themselves. Immediate thoughts might be that these women are making it up, they are just too soft and sensitive, or they are just "being girls" and are "afraid of men and everything else", but it is not that simple. Due to past traumas, cat-callings, and even hints of harassment, sexual or otherwise, it can be very overwhelming and fearful for any woman, no matter what age she is, no matter her background. The cover of darkness can bring out the worst in people.

There is still a lot of work to be done to protect women and children from abusive people in this world, particularly from abusive men, from abusive systems, from abusive outdated customs and traditions, from abusive twisted belief systems, from abusive policies, and from abusive governments. With social media, you might be unlucky enough to come across or see videos of child abuse happening in your own country or countries around the world; social media is a damned if you do, damned if you don't. Because with or without social media: it is happening.

I have only made you aware of these issues by starting this project initiative. These brave women spoke out to make you aware as well, of their own issues, and how they are fighting their own fights.

There is still much work to be done in this world to protect women and children from being abused and sold into the sex trade and the slave trade, which still exists in many parts of the world! There is still work to be done to prevent child marriages from happening. What is tolerated will be tolerated! What is allowed will be allowed! There is absolutely no excuse, no reason that any grown man should be marrying a child! Nor does it even seem sane for any parent to offer their child's hand in marriage, thus technically sealing and throwing away any hope for their future. Whether it is in a 1,000 plus year old religious book or not, it should be forbidden by anyone!

There is still work to be done on educating men that just because a man marries a woman, he has any right to raise his hand to her, he does not! She is his wife, the love of his life, and he is her protector. He is to take care of her, try to make sure she is living a good and decent life, even if she may not always be happy, he should always try to ensure her needs are met. He may argue with her and disagree with her, but marrying her did not give him any additional rights to abuse her or any children within the family that they share together. If a man cannot handle this responsibility, then he ought to divorce her and accept responsibility for whatever they both decide to do, as well as the court's decision placed upon him, in order to get him to understand that just because he and his wife will not be together anymore does not exonerate him from the responsibilities of raising his children.

There is still work to be done to educate societies, political systems, government systems, and justice systems on belittling rape culture and sexual violence to ensure that it is taken more seriously, as rape and sexual violence is a very serious traumatic experience that no woman or child or man should ever have to live with for the rest of their lives.

There is still work to be done on educating women and providing services, government or otherwise, to ensure that they know that no man has the right to raise his hand towards her or her children, and if he does so, this is no man at all, and does not deserve her. There is ZERO excuse for any man to beat a woman and his or her children. Disciplining children in a manner so they understand right from wrong? Sure. But outright beating children with a fist and a belt for no real wrongdoing other than the fact that he may have become agitated or irritated? Absolutely not. These women must be given the proper tools and knowledge to know that they are not stuck and they do have a way out of an abusive relationship.

There is still work to be done to get more women into politics and government, business ownership, mathematics, the sciences and education overall, and overseeing welfare services and healthcare systems. In 2020, it was never more apparent, and the stories of these women confirm that there are many issues still facing our world today. Ladies, if you do not take these issues seriously, no man will take them serious for you. The desire to change what has been tolerated, accepted, and allowed before you, must come from you. Nothing that advocates for the suffering, torture, or pain of any living being is nor should it ever have been part of the norm. Absolutely none of you, not a single one of you, would even exercise the idea of your child or children being abused, and especially once you are empowered, choose to acknowledge your empowerment, you would never accept being abused yourselves. Where any man, woman, or child is being abused, there is still and always will be work to be done. These are just the stories I was able to obtain. There are millions of women whose stories have yet to still be told.

I also noticed a very common theme for many women and this seems to be throughout the world. Many women face issues of body image, self-esteem, and self-confidence issues that affect their lives, and oftentimes, it is issues that stem directly from family, society, and men's expectations of how women should think, act, behave, and look a certain way. This affects their mental and physical health and well-being. While the pressure isn't on so much for men, a specific way of dress, makeup, and how women present themselves is something on the minds of women as they wake up each day and go out in public. There is no doubt that within each of these stories, every woman can safely admit that she has faced some form of depression or anxiety in her life due to everything that is expected of her.

What is most surprising, however, and very unfortunate, in 2020, is the lack of education worldwide, particularly in Africa. The fact that families, rather than governments, must be personally responsible for educating their children shows a serious problem with the entire world. Education should be a government-sponsored effort, no matter what country, no matter how poor the country, children should be receiving at least a basic form of education of grades K-12, regardless of status or income. Keeping the world illiterate and uneducated can lead to nothing good, especially when it comes to women, who grow up without education and are not only susceptible to abuse to any males who come into their lives, but they are kept with the mentality of, "it is the way it is", and they are likely to bring up future generations of children, daughters, who follow the same traditions and lifestyle, thus never really providing any hope or understanding of any possible way out of this life they were born into, other than the obvious, and not-recommended path.

On a positive note, what I did learn was that women are doing a lot more than I ever thought they were doing. Women are inspiring change. Women are making change. Women are demanding change. Women are teaching change. Women are not settling for anything less than what makes them happy in their own countries. These women are the reason the world is changing. They are taking on roles and challenging the status quo, the workplace, and the expectations of their parents, specifically their fathers. They look at their mothers and while they seem to adore their mothers and absolutely love their mothers, they are the women who cannot just accept that this is all there is to life. They all know there has to be more. Although truth be told, it is really all just taxes and death, but joking aside, everything in between and what you do with this life does matter.

As most of these women already knew, I was a man who already got it, inspired by my first strong role model of a woman, my mother. I attended a feminist class in college called, "Psychology of Women", and although it didn't give me any life-changing experience or make me feel any different, as it went through modern feminist to extreme and radical feminism, I purposely didn't mention feminism too much at all.

Most would consider me a "male feminist". I watched dual-working parents where my mother and father seemed to find their ways to make money and contributed to the general household just the same, no more, no less. There wasn't much discussion about who made more or who did the most work and contributed the most, though I do know my dad had the mentality that a man should be taking care of his family. My mother, whether she accepted this notion or not, had always been a strong and independent working woman. Rather than follow the rules in place for typical stereotype gender roles, she preferred to be the one who wrote new ones to best suit her, especially when it came to defining her femininity. She certainly took on the duties of cooking and cleaning and making sure her children were taken care of, but she did far more than that. Had it not been for her stroke, she would have never slowed down, settled for less than working multiple jobs, or even retired. By any categorical standards, this book is classified as a feminist book, but not in a million years, did I ever think I would be co-writing a book like this.

Set forth by the example of my parents, I'm an equal opportunist, as I am an egalitarian. If your mothers, grandmothers, and great-grandmothers fought for your right to leave the household and contribute more in the world, then they have done that for a reason, though not all women agree to such a standard. There are still plenty of women who believe their place is in the home, taking care of their families, and raising their children. There is absolutely nothing wrong with a woman who chooses this life. For some women who choose such a life, their success is their children. After all, mending such a bond between mother and child is what makes for a more kind and loving future generation. However, a working mother who must leave her child each day for a time can still exhibit and give her child the same amount of love. Fortunately, the majority of women, once they do have children, realize their lives are forever changed, and will seemingly do just about anything for their children. This seems to be the same across all women.

I have seen many strong women, but I've also seen many vulnerable women, who had potential, but may have also thrown their futures away due to drugs or crime or just being too dependent on their abusive relationships. Life is not easy for anyone, especially not women. I will say that men also do struggle in this world too and we face our own gender discrimination and reverse discrimination as well, as I have experienced multiple times in my life. Both the patriarchy and the matriarchy must be updated to understand that men do not always have to take the dominating role, while women do not have to be a submissive gender in order for things to work.

There are also certain things that both men and women must accept, such as regardless of how much we try, men will never be able to biologically have children, just as women cannot help but have the feelings and desires of wanting to be mothers or even caregivers. And there are even women who never feel this way and that is okay, too! But once they feel that spark of life within them, they are usually always forever changed. Women still must realize the power they are capable of no matter where they are in their lives.

Women have come a long way since the beginning of time, sometimes standing behind man, but also standing next to man as well. Women are capable of many great things, with or without man standing next to them. While it is acceptance or approval that sometimes holds women back, there isn't always a need for it. No one gave me permission to do this project. I didn't ask anyone nor did I seek approval. Not a single one of the women who contributed a story to this project asked anyone if it would be okay to participate. They just did it like they do many other things. Some women chose to participate, while other women did not want to take part. Either way, they made a choice and the rest is now history. They wanted education, so they found a way, and they did it. They wanted to vote, so they found a way, and they did it. They wanted to start businesses, so they found a way, and they did it. It might not be an overnight change, but with enough persistence and perseverance, women are able to make change happen, so long as they have the desire and are willing to fight for it. Whether a mother, a housewife, married woman, or a single woman, women can contribute to the world in their own special way.

I had already seen what women were capable of first through my own mother, then my sister, and then the many women who happened upon my life at one time or another. I have seen strong women shed tears. I have seen strong women break down. I have seen strong women challenge the norm. I have seen strong women break records. The one thing I have never seen a strong woman do is give up. No matter what, all strong women, no matter how much life has beat them up, torn them down, took things away from them, they stand back up on their feet, and they fight, and they keep fighting. They never stop fighting. Strong women have dreams. Strong women have goals. Strong women have ambitions. Strong women have confidence in themselves. And strong women know that without them, the world would be worse off. So no matter who you are or what your situation is, you are a woman. You have every ability to be a strong woman. You command the respect you deserve. You demand people to value you. You ensure that no one ever treats you less than how you know you should be treated, like a princess or a Queen, but even more so, like a warrior.

Many of my words may be taken from the women in all these stories, but as I write this final epilogue, I am only referring back to what is in my memory of reading these stories, of feeling connected to and speaking with these strong and brave women, and I know you too, just by reading this book, just by being curious in what these women had to say, you already knew you were different than many of those around you.

You have the power to change the world. You have the power to do anything you want to do. So what is it, exactly, that you are waiting for? Go and be the woman you were meant to be. Go and be the woman you wish to be. Go and be the woman you want to be. Do not let anyone, man or woman, ever stand in your way of achieving what you truly want in your life. You may not know exactly what you want just yet, and that is okay, go explore and experience the world before you settle on what you think you want. Go and change the world. And as a woman, make sure no one ever forgets who you are or what you did for the betterment of our world. You deserve to be empowered. You must be empowered. Make the world a better place on your own terms. There is a power within you that you do not even recognize. There is a power within you that is stronger than you can ever imagine. There is a power in you that you must realize. There is a power in you that you can use to create and build up entire worlds. There is also a voice within you that knows exactly what to do in this world. You are the mother goddess. You are a woman.

Do what you will with the inspiration from this project and the women who have spoken to you and given you their voice. If you don't change the world for yourself and for others around you, who will do it? You can sit idly and silently, as many women before you did, though perhaps wishing they just did something, anything. And still, many others did. But the fact that you even picked up this book and came this far, to the end, reading this epilogue shows that you already know exactly what I am talking about. You were meant to do more in this world than anyone ever told you. Once you understand, you will know exactly your purpose.

As many women were asked to provide advice to women around the world, I will also provide the final piece of advice to you. There are three ways you can look at your life: from the past, from the present, and from the future. All are just as equally important, because all of them involve you, three amazing women who are you, able to see each other.

Imagine the young girl that is you is looking ahead, is able to see her entire life, as it were to become. She must do everything she needs to do in order to make all those dreams come true, but first: she must have those dreams and aspirations. What does she see of her accomplishments? What does she dream? What does she want to do? Who does she want to be? Is she proud of the woman she is going to become?

For the present you, you are currently living your life and you are always you, the one who is in the driver's seat, controlling every aspect of your life. The decisions you must make, the people you listen to, the books you read that will influence your life, the men and women you meet and allow to be an integral part of your life, what you choose to study, and what your aim to do in your life is, including the choices that are specifically geared toward women: mother, career, or both?

And finally, you are the older woman, looking back at her life, able to talk to the young child that was you, and the younger you that is the now-you, are you happy with your life and all that you accomplished? If your older self could give advice to your younger self, the self of the now, what does she say to herself? Does she need to change anything? Is she on the right path? Did she live a satisfying and fulfilling life? Did she do everything she wanted to do? Is this older woman version of you happy?

Religious or not, spiritual or not, atheist or not, we can talk and dream about an afterlife, and I don't dispute any of your beliefs at all, you are free to believe what makes you happy. I once asked a Rabbi – Rabbi Zev Kahn – "What makes you think God exists?" His reply forever changed my thoughts and he responded. "I'd rather exist in a world knowing that God exists than exist in a world knowing that God doesn't exist." A beautiful answer, as most answers from Rabbis always are.

And many women might ask of their situation, "if God does exist, than why does God allow this to happen to me?" The answer comes in two parts: God gives you the opportunity to be born into a family and exist for a time. God must provide free will to everything that exists, thus God cannot control the situation around you or the family you were born into, but you can always find a way and take control of your own situation.

In a way, you chose your family before you were born. You chose where you would be born. You were born there for a reason: because the place you were born into required your presence to improve the surrounding situation. The second part is that a tree without the elements cannot grow to be strong without those elements, such as the rain, the wind, the snow, and the air, but each day, the sun comes up, and provides the tree with all the love and warmth it will ever need to live its life.

For the conclusion of this book, however, we won't fully get into any metaphysical and philosophical discussions, because what is really important is always in the present, the now, the current you, who makes all things possible, and is living in a reality that may or may not always be good, but a reality that is your life. What you choose to do in this world, what gifts you choose to share with this world, are completely yours, and it is always up to you in how you will share them.

If you choose to remain silent and never reveal those powerful and magical gifts within you, then that was always your choice, and no one ever knows about it. But, if somehow, you did something different: you shared yourself with the world, made yourself just a little vulnerable, only to step outside of your comfort zone, and revealed your true power to the world, what might you be able to accomplish in your life? More importantly, just how will you change not only your world, but the world around you? Let that passion out. You now have the tools to show the world who you truly are and the mighty power within you to change whatever you want in your life.

I could tell you things are going to be easy. They aren't always going to be that way. I am going to tell you something that you hardly ever hear, but that in almost all of your life situations, you are going to be okay, and you are going to make it. As a male writing this part of the book, I'm not going to tell you that men have been perfect and you shouldn't blame men for the way certain things are. I am also not going to apologize on behalf of all men for their treatment of women since our time together on this Earth, because I am just one man, and that would do nothing for anyone. I am certainly not the man to blame. Men have been running things for a very long time and have kept things in place for whatever reasons. I am not here to apologize for men or on behalf of men at all. I am not here to tell you that things are going to change overnight nor are they going to favor women in an instant. What I am going to tell you is that blaming the patriarchal society for all of your problems is not going to get you anywhere. Blaming men for the way your life is, is not going to make your life any better. Blaming your parents for not giving you a more proper education or for not raising you the way you ideally hoped or not doing certain things for you is not going to make your life any better. What is going to help you is the recognition that blaming the world isn't going to do anything for you.

The reality is that the world actually owes you nothing. NOTHING. It never will owe you anything. In fact, you are the one who is taking up space in it and using its resources. So, you owe the world more than it will ever have to owe you. The world sometimes is the way it is and it does have you in it to try and improve it. Instead of blaming others, you too, must realize that you have your responsibilities within your family and your world to start making the difference with your very presence. There's no reason to be mad at men or the world for the problems you have faced or the problems you are facing.

Women are working on changing this and you are going to be one of them as well. Many women have held grudges for their entire lives and the irony is, they never really get to live the life they wanted, because they may have been so bitter, and so focused on what was done to them, they could focus on nothing else. Never forget, but don't let whatever happened to you control your life to the point where you forget to actually live life. Use it as your power to change what you need to change. Acknowledge it, accept it, own it, and let the bitterness go, to rise above and be the woman you are supposed to be.

A lot of this may read or sound as cliché to you, or maybe you've never heard any of it, or you don't believe it, or maybe you think I am just full of it. Sure, I like to give solicited or unsolicited advice sometimes and provide motivational speaking once in a while. Just remember, I am only one man and yet from May 5th, 2020 to September 1st, 2020, the official publication of this book, I had a vision, a dream, and a desire to make something come true. I managed to get in touch with a woman from every country on the planet Earth while in quarantine lockdown during the COVID-19 pandemic. I can sometimes perform miracles and make things happen, at least, according to some people.

Everything I did still required me to put forth the effort and use my power, to use the magic within me, and share it with the world. I didn't know any of the men or women I contacted beforehand, I only knew that this project was important and I had to find men and women who shared my vision. For every woman who said yes, she had at least two to three counterparts who said no. Fortunately for me, the experience of being rejected by women is not new, and the realization is that, despite the many "no's", life must go on, and things still need to get done. And as a result, we have this completed project. I put myself out there, I took a risk, I took a chance, and I made something happen. *Thy will be done.*

I did not have unlimited resources or time, especially not money. I was not born into a rich family. I don't have a lot of friends nor do I really know a lot of people. But I had a dream of making this all come true. If I could do this, I know you can do anything you set your mind to do. No one told me to do this, and maybe I had no reason to do it, but I don't even know you and I believe in you. All these women who are part of this story believe in you. I know you will bring great change to this world. Maybe while I am still alive or maybe long after I am gone. This is but a glimpse of just some women in the world in the 21st century.

Even in your century, you will need to continue doing good and bringing change, as these women did. They are the brave and courageous women, just like you, who took a chance on a project that was meant to change the world. The world needed to change and they started to make the difference. **Are you ready to continue their mission and start your own?**

Thank you so much for taking an interest in this project and thank you for reading this book. May you inspire others and change the world.

This is the *My Life As A Woman* Project Initiative.

My Life As A Woman Project: Special Thanks

As I am someone who wants to be and strives to be largely independent, something I've always struggled to do in my life is ask for help. Asking for help causes me anxiety and is not something I like to do often, but after I accomplished my first set of goals for this project of obtaining stories from women of the countries I could obtain them from, there were several countries on Fiverr that only had men representing them. I made the instant decision to start asking not only men, but women for help after they had completed their own writings.

There were countries where it was going to be impossible for me to reach because of limited Internet or no Internet at all. What I ended up doing was informing these men and women that I could not reach these countries, and to reach out to their friends, families, and networks to see if they knew anyone from those countries. The pay was slightly more to compensate them for their time, but 34 men and 10 women ended up being interested in helping me accomplish my mission of having a woman from every country in the world as part of this project. Without them, I would have only had about half of what I have.

These amazing people pulled off miracles beyond explanation, reached out to parts of the world that were so remote and isolated, and managed to find someone who was interested. Not only did they obtain the story, but they also helped me with the translations back into English. Without them, the stories of the Inuit, the Indigenous of Australia and New Zealand, the Native American, the women of the Western Sahara, women of the communist countries, the Amish, and the many women of very remote islands and villages would have not been obtained, yet by some miracle and luck, my team managed to pull it off.

It is amazing what I was able to accomplish as much as I did with just a small team of men and women who believed in this project as much as I did, and they did whatever they needed to do to help me finish. I cannot thank any of them enough, even when I went through my own challenges of having my payment accounts frozen, they were more than willing to still do work for me on commission until I was able to get things resolved.

Although this team and I only knew each other and spoke over the course of about two months, they were as dedicated as I've ever seen a group of people, they were the angels who truly helped me connect the world together and bring all of these women's stories into this project.

A special thanks to the 34 men and 10 women who went above and beyond to help pull this project together!

My Life As A Woman Project: The Collaborator

If you were wondering where my introduction was in the beginning and why I waited until the close of the book to introduce myself, the reason for this was because, as I said in the Prologue, I am just the messenger who obtained these stories and was passing on the message of these women, who remained silent for so long, or who had no platform to tell their stories. I collected these stories from women all over the world with a mission: get that message out into the world for current and future generations. Whether it was for the records of the history of the world or just to tell their stories, or show what women were going through, it is something I had to do. Who I am was never the most important part of this book which is why I didn't include it in as one of the first chapters. Besides, as a gentleman, raised by a loving mother who taught me manners, I gave the women the opportunity to introduce themselves and take their turn in speaking about themselves before I did. Who I am is hardly relevant to the importance of the overall project, however, it is only right of me to also introduce myself.

Hello, I am Matthew Gates. I was born and raised in New Jersey and lived my young life in a town called Linden where I attended elementary school and middle school. The remainder of my childhood, my teenage years, was spent at the Jersey Shore, more specifically, Toms River. I was raised by middle-class very hardworking parents, mother and father, as I can remember, both of them always held at least two jobs each, giving my siblings and I, for which there are three of us, and I am the oldest with a brother and sister, a great life, but always with chores to do. We were all, boys and girls, for the most part, raised with gender-equality and other than liking "boy things" while my sister liked "girl things", we were all treated fairly, although I must admit, I think my younger brother was the most spoiled of us all. I remember earning $1 a week and then somehow negotiating my pay raise up to $5 at one time or another to wash dishes, vacuum, and do other household chores. My sister is just about a year younger than me, so we have a close relationship, and even closer after she almost lost her life in a hit-and-run accident by a drunk driver. Fortunately, she survived, but lives with occasional epileptic seizures and while I live across the country from my family, it doesn't mean that I still don't somehow manage to involve myself in their lives in some way. My brother, on the other hand, is the youngest, and I admire him so much, as he was the one who had to grow up the fastest. I served as a father to him for some years, even teaching him how to raise himself in a way that would allow him to make good decisions for his entire life. Simply put, "What would Matthew do? Do the opposite." It's funny because it's true: my brother would constantly ask me about what he should do about situations, and he would always do the opposite. So one day, I told him to have a conversation with himself and use the other voice in his head as my own. To this day, he still has conversations and arguments with himself with me as the voice of somewhat reasoning. And still to this day, he usually does the opposite. I am a very proud brother to both my siblings.

I would have to say that everyone in my life is some sort of influence and inspiration. Starting with my maternal grandfather, a World War II veteran, who was very particular and used to make me count my pennies he gave me in order to keep them, then he would manipulate the count, and make me count again. To tell the short version of the story, one day, the ice cream truck was passing by, and I grabbed 5 cents, thinking this was enough for an ice cream. My grandfather said 5 cents could buy nothing, but that I would need at least $1.25 to get an ice cream, so I counted it, 125 pennies. We went and got the ice cream. Once we got back home, he made me recount my pennies. Less than 50 pennies. He asked me, "Was the ice cream worth it?" Honestly? To this day, ice cream is always worth it. This made me think about how money is spent on everything you want: do you want it or do you need it, thus teaching me about the true value of money. He passed away when I was 10. My paternal grandmother, who was very loving and kind, and made the best chocolate pie, and a recipe I finally learned how to make a few years ago: her chicken and rice dish, she passed away when I was 20. My mother, and I could be considered as a "momma's boy" for a time, though not much anymore, she raised me and protected me and saw me through my younger life. My father, who used to always have conversations with me about life, and while I can't say I fully understood everything he was saying at the time, I came to appreciate those conversations when I would lie in bed and he would come talk to me, just before he left for work. Now our conversations often have me providing him with some wisdom. My sister, who grew up with me and fought with me but always loved me. My brother, who is more than just my brother, but my soul brother. My uncle, aunt, and cousin, who saw me through a big part of my life, especially my university years and beyond. My paternal cousins, whose North Carolina summer visits always made life worth living. My maternal cousins who were always fun and loving and made Jewish holidays enjoyable. My wife, Josie, who showed me what real lovingkindness can be, who is always there when I am feeling down and pushes me to keep going, even when I feel like giving up. My stepsons, who, despite our awkward relationship at times, have shown me time again the meaning of friendship and family. To my professors and everyone along the way who had something to teach and even if I don't remember your names, I do have some part of your lesson within me that has made me who I am today. To my best friends, although two of you are no longer alive, you saw something in me that made us closer than friends, closer than family, a special bond. DJ (1986-2015). Wayne (1985-2012). Yacov, my dear Israeli friend who helped me rediscover my Jewish roots. And finally, to my friends, if we've met at one time or another, known me for a time, and then that time was gone, but still kept in touch, only to stay friends with me, despite how awkward I can be, but I always seem to bring humor to your life, as well as, at times, serious philosophical discussion. Thank you everyone for being my inspiration.

While both my parents were always loving and caring and mostly in the picture, my parents divorced when I was 15 years old and I was your typical high school student who was a loner, but mostly a gamer and programmer, that stayed in his room. My grade average in high school was average, B's and C's were common. After high school, I worked a menial security job that let me know I was going nowhere and I can even remember asking my boss once for a raise after 3 years of working for the company, and he jokingly gave me an extra penny raise in my next paycheck. When I inquired about it, he said it must've been a mistake and laughed about it. It was at that moment I knew I had to start making something more of myself. While I waited a few more weeks, realizing it really was just a joke and I was not getting a raise, this escalated my decision to go to college and use the company time to not only continue making a paycheck, but to pay for college and to study, which I did for many years.

Sometime before I entered college, my mother had a stroke, causing me to have a wakeup call and realize the reality of my life. Later on, my father had a heart attack, and somehow, with his strength, he managed to drive himself to the hospital, 45 minutes away. Luckily, both survived their ordeals. This forced me to look into my own life and health. I expressed interest to my Uncle – my mother's brother – who has since become more than just my Uncle, but my friend, that I really desired to go to college after those traumatic events. While he was visiting and helping the family, we drove to the college campus and the rest was history. I started out at Ocean County College in Toms River and received my Associates degree in Social Sciences, always interested in Psychology.

During my time at OCC, I came across the Educational Opportunity Fund (EOF) program, which helped the less fortunate with funds to pay for college. Considering I was only about 22 at the time, with a disabled parent, and one who was living in another part of the state, and working a minimum wage job, I was lucky enough that this organization helped me ease into college life. During my time at college, I joined several organizations, but one that particularly stands out was something another student told me about, called the Ocean County College Student Leadership Development Program.

Yes, it is a mouthful, but it is a program that changed my life. It is for very select students who have to go through a process and some are not even selected. It was here that I noticed two very strong women leaders, Jen and Alison. Fortunately, for this opportunity, I was selected three times, three years in a row, which was very rare for any student. So I received over 100 hours of leadership training from this program that focused on Emotional Intelligence. To give you the very summed up and dictionary definition of what that is: **Emotional intelligence (otherwise known as emotional quotient or EQ) is the ability to understand, use, and manage your own emotions in positive ways to relieve stress, communicate effectively, empathize with others, overcome challenges and defuse conflict.** What I learned from this leadership training is how I still continue to live and lead my life. The important questions that were asked and the takeaway from even mentioning this program was from the organizer himself, Don Duran, who asked three questions:

- Who Am I?
- Where Am I Going?
- How Am I Going To Get There?

He said to me before I graduated, "No matter what you do in your life, make sure you at least get your bachelor's degree." I am so glad I listened to that advice. Another statement he made that always pops into my mind every time I drive past a McDonalds. Don said to a room full of students, "You could easily skip making yourself a healthy breakfast in the morning and instead, make the turn and go straight to McDonalds, and get yourself whatever you want. You could do that every day. And after a time, you will start to notice the results: either you ate McDonalds every day or you opted for a healthier breakfast option." Why this statement was so important and still sticks with me to this day is because every day, we all make choices, and there is no right or wrong in many of those choices. Some of these choices are miniscule with minor consequences, though sometimes they do add up, but there are many choices that we must make each day of our lives that have major consequences. I graduated from Ocean County College with a 3.5 GPA.

After I graduated with my Associates degree, I would make a hard decision that led me away from my family. I moved to Chicago to attend Loyola University Chicago to major in Psychology. I loved living in the city of Chicago and explored so much. It was here, at a Catholic University, that I got to rediscover and interact with Judaism and Jews my age. The Hillel Director, Patti, was a very bubbly woman and inspired me and gave me hope in the many times I thought about quitting and going home. I also came across a very lovely lady, Amy, who always inspired me. She inspired and drove such ambition into me with her love and passion that she put forth with everything she did. To this day, she still continues to inspire me, and always has her place in my heart. I met many strong women throughout my college years who showed me strength, intelligence, and courage, no matter what they were interested in. I graduated with a 3.0 GPA.

After graduation, I had an opportunity to go to Israel, with the sponsorship of another wonderful woman who oversaw my time at Ocean County College for the Educational Opportunity Fund, Catherine Dixon-Merker. With Cathie sponsoring me, I was able to pay the fees of the Israel program. I got a flight for free to Israel via Shorashim Israel which is an Israel Birthright, foregoing my return flight, selected a program through MASA Israel which helps young adults navigate an organization that best suits their interests in Israel, and co-found Yahel Israel, which was a brand new organization at the time, founded by a very strong and focused woman, Dana, who saw a struggling people within her country, the Ethiopian-Israelis, and decided to make her own change for the better in this world, a social change that is still progressing a decade later. I am very blessed to have helped her be the change she wanted to see, as well as working with some of the best men and women leaders I've ever known. The mission was to help Ethiopian-Israelis live and learn in Israel and teach English to Israelis, while also exploring many other aspects of Israel, such as the Israeli-Palestinian conflict, women's issues, political issues, etc., and experience life in Israel. Being the first among five other young adults there, we established its official foundations which has allowed it to grow and prosper to this day. While it was only established in the city of Gedera at the time, the organization is currently thriving in multiple cities in Israel.

After living in Israel for a year, I decided to return back to New Jersey, as my student loans were calling me home because they were due, and while I had thought about faking my death or making Aliyah, I decided to be an adult and accept my responsibilities and I returned home to pay them off, with a plan to eventually return back to Israel at some point in my life.

As life would have it, it had other plans for me. I got a job as a programmer, my first real job out of college, utilizing that skill I taught myself when I was just 12 years old, working for a tyrant boss, learned all I could, taught myself web design and web development, worked for another company or two, until I found the right fit, where I am currently working now for my day job, as a web designer, for a company called CISION – MultiVu/PR Newswire, which specializes in multimedia news distribution, where I have been for nearly a decade. While it was a remote job at first, at some point, the company decided everyone, dozens of people should move to New Mexico to work in an office or get laid off. Out of those people, only two of us braved the transition. The other person who came with me is someone I met while working at that first job out of college, who is now my wife. We have been working together for nearly a decade. And that is how I ended up here, in Albuquerque, and now you are all mostly caught up with my life.

Eventually, with the start of the COVID-19 pandemic, it ended up returning back to a remote job. For my night job, I'm working as a technical writer and product ambassador for a Malaysian company called RunCloud, which specializes in cloud computing management technology. It was this job that really exposed me to Muslims first-hand. Before working with this company, I had a stereotype within my mind that was not a great one, as I was exposed to too much American media, and it was only after working with them for just a few weeks that I realized that they were family, and in October 2019, just before the COVID-19 pandemic hit, I flew to Malaysia to meet them.

Aside from that, I began my website, about 7 years ago, in 2013, called **Confessions of the Professions**, a site dedicated to understanding jobs, careers, and the workplace. This website has to do with my love for psychology, social psychology, and industrial-organizational psychology, which ties them all in together and keeps me connected with my passion, since I was not able to do it professionally, as my profession required that I needed more education. Looking at the wage difference between what I am doing now, and the profession of the area I studied, I actually make more money doing what I'm doing now then if I were to go invest myself back into higher education. As you enter the workforce and are out of college for some time, you tend to measure everything by the ROI (return on investment). **Confessions of the Professions** is a website that started out as a hobby but has since turned into a professional website used by businesses, freelancers, and marketing agencies to share public information with the world. Every year, I often try to come up with some random project for my website, and this year, **My Life As A Woman** is the project that was long overdue.

Finally, in November 2015, I also started a side business called **NoteToServices,** which is a web development company that specializes in creating SaaS (software-as-a-service) web applications and WordPress plugins that help developers and users advance their products and lifestyle through the Internet. Between my day job, night job, and side business, I'm often working and kept busy for 12-16 hour days. I also enjoy trolling Facebook, looking up random facts on Google, binging Netflix, and finding funny memes.

As for what I enjoy doing outside of the Internet and work, I love riding my bicycle, swimming, hiking, reading, dreaming, and traveling. While I've traveled multiple times across the United States, lived in Israel, been to the United Kingdom, I still have a whole world left to explore. I'd love to backpack across Europe, visit China and parts of Asia, and hopefully explore the Middle East someday. After this project, of getting to know so many people, I cannot wait to visit all of their countries, and hopefully meet these lovely women personally. Being exposed to so many people and the world as I was while engaging in this project and writing this book, I cannot help but realize just how small our world is. Although it did take three planes to get to Malaysia! It is quite sad to note that all things come to an end, but while they were happening, despite the COVID-19 pandemic and lockdowns around us, doing this project, talking to over 1,000 women and just over 30 men was probably one of the most exciting times of my life. Although most of the project took place in my backyard, it was hardly uneventful.

If any of you are reading this who got to speak with me or participate in this project, please do not hesitate to visit my websites, or in particular, www.mylifeasawomanproject.com, and use the contact form to send me a message. I'd love to get in touch with you again! I loved working on this project with you and making it happen and I am glad you finally got to read my story, as I got to read all of yours! In the eyes of the universe, you have but a moment to do something in this life and in this world, so make your moment matter.

Made in the USA
Monee, IL
02 November 2020